Style manual

For authors, editors and printers

Sixth edition

Revised by Snooks & Co.

John Wiley & Sons Australia, Ltd

First published 1966	Reprinted with corrections 1968
Second edition 1972	Reprinted with corrections 1974 Reprinted 1974, 1976
Third edition 1978	Reprinted with corrections 1979, 1981 Reprinted 1986, 1987
Fourth edition 1988	Reprinted with corrections 1990, 1992
Fifth edition 1994	Reprinted with corrections 1995, 1996, 1998
Sixth edition 2002	Published by John Wiley & Sons Australia, Ltd Reprinted with corrections 2003 Reprinted 2005 (twice) Reprinted 2006, 2007

National Library of Australia Cataloguing-in-Publication data:

Style manual for authors, editors and printers

      6th edn.

      Bibliography.

      Includes index.

      ISBN 0 7016 3648 3 (pbk.).

      ISBN 0 7016 3647 5.

      1. Authorship—Style manuals 2. Printing—Style manuals.

      3. Word processing—Style manuals. I. Snooks & Co.

808.027

Client agency: Department of Finance and Administration

Design: David Whitbread, Julie Hamilton

Copy editing and proofreading: Chris Pirie, John Greig, Loma Snooks

Index: Michael Harrington

Printed in Singapore by
Craft Print International Ltd

Contents

How to use this book   iv

Contributors   vii

Acknowledgments   ix

Introduction   1

Part 1 **Planning the communication**   **2**

1   The publication plan   4

2   The publishing team   18

Further reading and resources   33

Part 2 **Writing and editing**   **34**

3   Structuring documents for readers   36

4   Effective and inclusive language   48

5   Grammar   63

6   Spelling and word punctuation   78

7   Sentence punctuation   95

8   Capital letters   118

9   Textual contrast   136

10   Shortened forms   150

11   Numbers and measurement   162

12   Methods of citation   187

13   The components of a publication   233

14   Editing and proofreading   252

15   Indexing   270

Further reading and resources   285

Part 3 **Designing and illustrating**   **288**

16   Visual identifiers   290

17   Design and layout   302

18   Typography   322

19   Tables   346

20   Forms   359

21   Illustrating   374

Further reading and resources   404

Part 4 **Legal and compliance aspects of publishing**   **406**

22   Restrictions on publishing   408

23   Identification and access   422

Further reading and resources   435

Part 5 **Producing and evaluating the product**   **438**

24   On-screen production   440

25   Paper-based reproduction   462

26   Monitoring, testing and evaluating   492

Further reading and resources   502

Appendixes   **503**

A   Titles, honours and forms of address   504

B   Metric conversion table   519

C   Standard proofreading marks and how to use them   521

Index   **528**

How to use this book

The design of this manual is aimed at presenting a vast array of detailed advice within a useful, interesting framework that will help you discover what you need easily.

Part titles
act as dividers to help you find your way around the book. They introduce the themes that are covered in each part, with the introductory text providing an overview, and the main topics being listed under the relevant chapter titles.

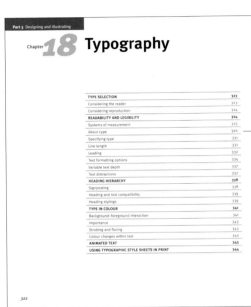

Chapter openings
offer a detailed contents list for the chapter, with page references to help you find information quickly.

'About' pages
are shaded in pale grey and are interspersed through the chapters. They introduce fundamental concepts or provide background material, sometimes supported by explanatory diagrams. You can read these 'About' pages separately from the surrounding text to gain a quick grasp of a topic.

Text pages

comprise one main text column, with a side column for comments, additional information, cross-references and illustrations.

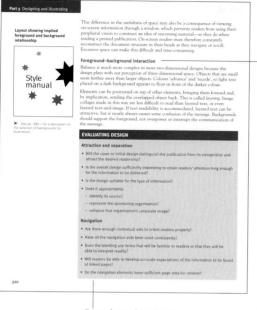

Frequent headings act as signposts throughout the text.

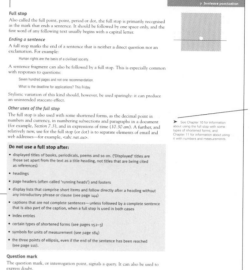

Arrow icons distinguish cross-references in the side column.

Boxed text highlights checklists (often found at the ends of chapters) or draws attention to other important points or reminders.

Further reading and resources are listed at the end of each of the five parts. They direct you to other useful publications, organisations and web sites.

Contributors

This revision was prepared for the Commonwealth Department of Finance and Administration by Snooks & Co.

Members of the Snooks & Co. team:

Loma Snooks

David Whitbread

Pam Peters

Chris Pirie

Michael Harrington

Victoria Richardson

Graham O'Loghlin

Julie Hamilton

Shirley Purchase

Lindsay Mackerras

ROLES OF CONTRIBUTORS

The preparation of this sixth edition of the *Style manual* represents a true team effort. Individual authors were allocated specific chapters, for which they undertook the research, drafting and final overview. Other contributors reviewed the successive drafts—sometimes providing additional material as well—with the result that each chapter reflects the substantial input of several team members. The designers' ideas also influenced the manual's structure as well as its style of presentation.

The following notes summarise the contributors' primary responsibilities on the project, and the expertise they brought to the team.

Loma Snooks

Responsibilities: Team leadership and project management; integration of content; Chapters 1, 2, 3 and 14; revision and substantive editing of all chapters.

Background: Twenty years' experience in leading editing and design teams on publishing projects around Australia and in the USA and Asia. ACT representative on National Editing Standards Working Group; Inaugural President of Canberra Society of Editors; Honorary Life Member of South Australian and Canberra societies of editors.

David Whitbread

Responsibilities: Chapters 16–21 and 25; art direction and design overview; some chapter revisions; illustration sourcing.

Background: Previous positions include Head of Graphic Design at University of Canberra and AGPS Design Director. Author of *The design manual* and numerous articles; Secretary of Australian Graphic Design Association, ACT; National Secretary of Design in Education Council Australia.

Associate Professor Pam Peters

Responsibilities: Research on trends in language usage; Chapters 4–6, 8, 10 and 11.

Background: Associate Professor of Linguistics, Macquarie University, and Head of Graduate Program in Editing and Publishing. Author of *The Cambridge Australian English style guide*; member of Editorial Committee of Macquarie Dictionary; Director of Australian Style Council Centre (responsible for usage research in Australian and international English, Style Council conferences and *Australian Style* bulletin).

Chris Pirie

Responsibilities: Chapters 7, 9, 12 and 13; some chapter revisions; majority of copy editing and proofreading.

Background: Twenty years' freelance editing experience, including more than eighty volumes of reports to government. Wrote referencing chapter for fourth edition of this manual.

Michael Harrington

Responsibilities: Chapters 15, 22 and 23; indexing of the manual.

Background: Author of three books on Australian government publishing, and previously responsible for copyright administration at AGPS. Wrote indexing chapter for fifth edition of this manual and indexed past editions. Chairman of Australian Society of Indexers Registration Panel.

Victoria Richardson

Responsibilities: Electronic publishing input; Chapter 24.

Background: Director of Netimpact Online Publishing. This Canberra-based company has won international awards for information design and a travel award to research emerging trends and standards for digital document design.

Graham O'Loghlin

Responsibilities: Chapter 26; some chapter revisions; contract management advice.

Background: Management consultant. Previously Director of Coopers & Lybrand Consultants. Past Councillor of the Institute of Public Administration; member of assessment team for annual report awards for Commonwealth statutory bodies.

Julie Hamilton

Responsibilities: Design and page layout; some chapter reviews; illustration preparation.

Background: Director of Mirrabooka Marketing & Design. Twenty years' experience in designing printed and digital documents for government and commercial clients. Councillor of Australian Graphic Design Association, ACT.

Shirley Purchase

Responsibilities: Various chapter reviews; editorial advice.

Background: Author of *The little book of style* and *The Australian writers' dictionary*. Editing career includes positions with Melbourne and ANU university presses, and as freelancer for AGPS, National Gallery of Australia, Australian War Memorial, ATSIC, and Oxford and Cambridge university presses.

Lindsay Mackerras

Responsibilities: Specialist advice.

Background: Previous positions at AGPS included Head of Editorial Unit, Style Manual Editor (1995–97) and Manager of Standards and Style. Introduced *Stylewise* magazine and *The little book of style*. Currently Managing Editor of *Air Force News*.

Acknowledgments

In preparing this edition, the Snooks & Co. team has been fortunate in having valuable support and advice from many people.

An external review panel was appointed for the project, and its members spent considerable time reviewing the document at second draft stage. Thanks are due particularly to plain English consultant Dr Robert Eagleson, who commented in depth on every chapter and to whom the team is indebted for his wise counsel. Further valuable suggestions on specific chapters were made by other members of the panel, which comprised Stephen Hall (Stephen Hall Associates), Susan McKerihan (PricewaterhouseCoopers), Judy Hutchinson (Commonwealth Parliamentary Library), Noel Crichton (printing industry representative) and Lexia Bain (Joint Committee on Publications, Commonwealth Parliament).

Information and comments were also received from specialist areas within government. Thanks are offered to the following officers for their assistance: Peter Hamburger (Parliamentary and Government Branch, Department of the Prime Minister and Cabinet) for his advice about compliance requirements for publications to be submitted to parliament; Kerry Morcombe (Awards and National Symbols Branch, Department of the Prime Minister and Cabinet) for his review comments on the sections on national identifiers and Australia's honours and awards; Sue Hayes and Paul Robertson (Office of Disability, Department of Family and Community Services) for information about accessibility strategies and for reviewing relevant sections; Andrew Wilson (National Archives of Australia) for advice on the government's metadata and record-keeping requirements; and Paul Bambury (Office of the Federal Privacy Commissioner), who commented on privacy aspects dealt with in Chapter 22.

Other help from government sources, which is gratefully acknowledged, was provided by Helen Wortham (National Standards Commission), who assisted the team in refining the measurements section of Chapter 11 and Appendix B; and by officers of the Intellectual Property Branch and Information Law Branch (Attorney-General's Department), who commented on copyright and privacy aspects in an early draft of Chapter 22.

In addition, Peter Haddad (National Library of Australia) reviewed the section on international numbering systems and library services; advice relating to aspects of inclusive language and the use of the Aboriginal flag was provided by Wendy Neil and Michelle Paterson of the Aboriginal and Torres Strait Islander Commission; and Brendan O'Connor of the Torres Strait Regional Authority checked the information about the Torres Strait Islander flag. Thanks are also due to Rob Burnside (Australian Bureau of Statistics) for information on the bureau's approach to table design and layout.

Significant contributions to the work of the team were also made by a number of experts outside government. Extensive research assistance and other input to Chapters 4–6, 8, 10 and 11 were provided by Adam Smith of Macquarie University's Style Council Centre. Chris Toogood (Netimpact Online Publishing) supported the team throughout the project with technical advice on electronic publishing trends. The detailed comments on Chapter 11 made by measurements expert Pat Naughtin (Patsey Pacific Publications) helped to ensure that the information in this chapter reflected current national and international standards. Robert Hyslop, ISO, rendered valuable assistance by revising the appendix on honours and forms of address that he had prepared for the previous edition. Professor David Sless (Communication Research Institute of Australia) supplied information relating to forms design, and reviewed a draft of Chapter 20. Useful suggestions were also made on Chapter 25 by David Pritchard (Graphics Arts, Canberra Institute of Technology).

Members of the National Editing Standards Working Group offered helpful advice as well as specific comments on early drafts of several chapters. For this support, thanks go to Rhana Pike, Amanda Curtin, Janet Mackenzie, Jan Whelan, Catherine Gray, Kathie Stove and Catherine Bruce. Some information on publishing practices was kindly provided by Maggy Saldais of John Wiley & Sons Australia, Ltd, while Richard Rudzki of the Bindery offered details on new binding techniques. The team also benefited from the advice of Nigel Harding, Dr Janet Salisbury, Dr Gregg Berry and Jennifer Prosser.

John Greig's editing and proofreading services, which were of a very high calibre, were greatly appreciated, as was his sense of humour. John Rankin, aided by Peter Rankin, provided additional support through a careful copyholder proof. Racheal Brühn's help in preparing some of the illustrations is acknowledged with thanks, as is Debbie Phillips's assistance with word processing.

Thanks are also offered to the following organisations for permission to use images from their collections: the National Library of Australia, AusPic, the National Archives of Australia, ATSIC, the Torres Strait Regional Authority, Oxford University Press and the Macquarie Library. The landscape portrait on page 381 is a detail from *The landing of Captain Cook at Botany Bay 1770* by E Phillips Fox.

The team's greatest debt of gratitude, however, is to the numerous contributors to earlier editions of this manual. The quality of their work is reflected in the esteem in which the manual is held by those involved in professional communication and publishing activities throughout the country. While many of the chapters in this sixth edition are new, much of this earlier advice remains perennially valuable and has been retained or updated.

The team also wishes to thank the many people who took the time and trouble to submit comments on the fifth edition. All these suggestions were considered, and helped the team to refine the scope of this sixth edition.

Introduction

This sixth edition of the *Style manual* provides guidance for anyone faced with the task of preparing material for publication: from publication managers and authors to designers, editors, screen-based publishers, indexers and printers. This edition represents a major revision, in response to the rapid changes that have been occurring in publishing since the fifth edition was produced in 1994.

Access to the Internet is revolutionising communications. Technological developments in word processing and design software and in digital printing are also changing the way in which traditional printed publications are being produced. This manual provides advice on how to go about preparing publications for both screen-based and print-based delivery in this evolving environment.

Readers today are confronted with a plethora of information from which they must sort out what they want and need to know. This edition therefore emphasises the importance of focusing on the audience's needs when planning, structuring, writing, designing and editing a publication. Drawing on extensive research, it takes account of the changing trends in language evident in the Australian community. It also reflects a more multicultural and global outlook that recognises the influence of the Internet on publishing.

A further important change from the fifth edition is the emphasis on 'information documents' of the type produced by government and many private sector organisations. With ready access now available in most offices to desktop publishing tools and the Internet, it is tempting to produce publications quickly, bypassing the quality checks that traditional publishing processes provided. But this is usually not the way to achieve authoritative and cost-effective publications. There is also a trend towards outsourcing much of the specialised work in publishing, which can mean that in-house staff with little knowledge of publishing may be called upon to manage a publication project.

With these needs in mind, this edition has been structured around the procedural steps in publishing. It describes what is involved in the separate publishing activities; it explains how to plan, undertake and evaluate a publishing project; and it suggests how to find and apply the specialist help required.

And of course this edition continues to provide the detailed advice on best practices in writing, editing, design and production—updated where necessary—that has made the *Style manual* a standard reference work for all those who understand the value of effective communication.

Planning the communication

When preparing a publication, many authors might be tempted to think primarily of the content—of what they want to say. But there is more than that to communication.

Potential readers' needs and expectations must be considered if they are to read, understand and use the information in the way the author and publisher intend. An assessment of the readership will help in choosing the most suitable scope and structure for the document, its language and tone, and the design style and format. It will also help in deciding whether to publish in printed or electronic form, or both.

P L A N N I N G   T H E   C O M M U N I C A T I O

1 The publication plan   **4**

Publication goals and audience needs

Managing time, cost and quality

Guidelines for writing, editing, design and on-screen usability

2 The publishing team   **18**

What publishing professionals do

Deciding what publishing help is needed

Assembling and managing the team

These considerations are all part of the preliminary planning that underlies successful publications. Other vital planning decisions relate to:

- the balance between the often competing factors of quality, time and cost
- the publishing expertise needed to achieve a professional result
- the management processes to be followed to ensure that the publication fulfils its purpose.

Chapters 1 and 2 discuss the various aspects of publication planning. Poor planning can result in a publication costing far more than envisaged, in terms both of rework and of damage to the reputation of those involved. So avoid the possibility of embarrassment by planning carefully.

PLANNING THE COMMUNICATION

Further reading and resources

Some recommended references and organisations   33

Chapter

The publication plan

COMMUNICATION STRATEGY	**5**
Purpose of the publication	6
Assessing the needs of potential readers	6
Print and electronic delivery modes	7
About electronic publications	8
Identity	10
Compliance with legislation and standards	10
Budget and timetable	11
Criteria of effectiveness	12
MANAGEMENT PLAN FOR THE PUBLICATION	**13**
Confirming the resources	13
Drawing up the management plan	13
Managing variations	13
Monitoring and reporting	14
GUIDELINES FOR DOCUMENT DEVELOPMENT	**14**
Writing and editing guidelines	14
Design guidelines	15
Guidelines for screen-based publications	16
Amalgamation of guidelines	17

Successful publications are usually founded on a carefully considered publication plan. The basic elements of publication planning described in this chapter are relevant to the production of any publication, no matter how large or small it is. Naturally, though, the scope of each plan should reflect the importance, scale and complexity of the particular publishing project.

There are three main elements of a publication plan:

- a communication strategy
- a management plan for the publication
- guidelines for document development, aimed at creating an effective, integrated and consistent publication.

The processes involved in developing the plan are discussed in the following sections.

Developing a publication plan

STEP 1	STEP 2	STEP 3
DETERMINE THE COMMUNICATION STRATEGY	**DEVELOP THE MANAGEMENT PLAN**	**DRAW UP THE DOCUMENT GUIDELINES**
Purpose of publication	Confirmation of resources	Contents and structure
Audience assessment	Team assembly and briefing	Style sheet for editing
Delivery mode (print, screen)	Integrated schedule	Design guidelines
Identity and compliance aspects	Monitoring procedures	Layout template
Indicative budget and timetable	Document management system	Screen-based guidelines
Effectiveness criteria		

COMMUNICATION STRATEGY

The communication strategy should be tackled first because decisions taken at this stage will affect all other project choices. Before the strategy is developed, the following questions must be answered:

- What is the purpose of the publication?
- Who are the potential readers and what information do they need?
- How will the publication be used?

- Should it be designed for print or as a screen-based publication, or both?
- What factors relating to the image of the sponsoring organisation need to be taken into account?
- What legal and other standards should the publication comply with?
- How are considerations of quality, time and cost to be balanced?
- What criteria should be used to judge the publication's effectiveness in achieving its purpose?

Purpose of the publication

It is a good idea at the outset to define and record the reasons for publishing the document. This statement of purpose will then serve as the focus for decisions about the document's format, structure, writing style, design and production.

Although a document's goals are generally well understood by those initiating it, this understanding is often implicit. If the goals are listed in order of importance and then checked against each phase of the work as it progresses, these primary interests can be better protected against other pressures that might arise during the publication process.

Assessing the needs of potential readers

A careful assessment of the potential readership of the publication is vital for clear and effective communication. In addition to the readership at which the publication is primarily directed, there may be other groups whose needs should also be considered.

What information do readers require?

When deciding on the scope of information readers will need, consider the likely extent of their knowledge of the subject and their interest in it. Also, what sort of attitudes or misconceptions might they have about it, and what aspects are likely to be of most interest or use to them?

➤ See Chapters 3 and 4 for advice on tailoring the text of a publication for its readership. See Part 3 for a full discussion of designing and illustrating text to meet readers' needs.

These considerations will help in matching the size, organisation and emphasis of the document to readers' interests. They will suggest the amount of background material that should be included and whether extensive explanations and a glossary might be necessary. The design style and the number and type of illustrations used will also be influenced by this assessment.

What style of language will be suitable?

Will a relatively formal or a more relaxed language style suit the topic and the desired relationship with readers? Decisions about vocabulary (which could range from the colloquial to specialist terminology) should also be aligned with the perceived educational and cultural backgrounds of readers and their familiarity with the subject. These findings should influence the development of the writing and editing guidelines.

How will readers want to use the publication?

Some readers might want to read the document from beginning to end; some might merely scan it to gain a general impression; others might be interested only in searching for specific information. How should the document be structured to accommodate these different approaches? Will it be used as a frequent reference, or is it likely to be read only once? Will readers expect to have access to it online? Are formal responses required from readers?

The answers to these questions will be additional influences on the choice of the document's content, structure, design style and mode of publication (paper-based, screen-based, or both). They will also suggest the type of access aids readers might find most useful for gaining an overview of the content and finding specific information.

Print and electronic delivery modes

The rapid technological advances in printing and electronic communications mean that authors and publishers need to assess which form of publishing will best suit their purposes and the needs of their readers. Depending on the type of publication, a combination of print and electronic modes may be ideal.

The Commonwealth Government has adopted this combined approach. To make government information more accessible and to encourage interaction between the public and government, the Commonwealth requires that all new (non-commercial) publications released by its agencies be made available both in printed form and online.

Benefits of electronic publications

Electronic publication greatly expands the opportunities for people with computers and Internet access to obtain information. It can also benefit readers with various disabilities by allowing them to access material presented in different forms.

Depending on the type of electronic publication chosen, other potential benefits include the ability to:

- integrate text, sound and images
- update and correct information as required
- encourage interactivity and reader responses
- provide direct links to associated material outside the publication
- provide more detailed information than might be economically viable in a printed document
- customise information to suit the different interests or needs of readers
- avoid the time and costs associated with printing, distribution and storage.

Benefits of printed publications

Traditional printed publications—which are the only option for people without Internet access—also have their advantages. Readers generally find it faster and easier to read a long document on a printed page than on a screen; and the binding, double-sided printing and page design of book formats have reached great sophistication in terms of user-friendliness. Digital printing and print-on-demand may also make printing an increasingly economical option.

Government online: The Commonwealth's commitment to joint publication in print and online is detailed in *GovernmentOnline* <http://www.agimo.gov.au>.

➤ Chapter 23 discusses publishing obligations under anti-discrimination legislation and the standards to be followed in producing widely accessible electronic publications. For further advice, consult *Guidelines for Commonwealth information published in electronic formats* and information provided by the Department of Family and Community Services and the Human Rights and Equal Opportunity Commission (see p. 33).

(continued on p. 10)

ABOUT
Electronic publications

Electronic publishing is evolving rapidly. This manual attempts to cover the basics, but even these are likely to be overtaken sooner or later by new approaches. For greater detail and updated advice on electronic publishing, consult the manual's complementary online publication, *Guidelines for Commonwealth information published in electronic formats* (see page 33).

Types of electronic publications

Portable formats: Disks, CD-ROMs, videos and other portable forms of electronic publications need to be distributed physically but are designed to be viewed on screen.

Electronically delivered publications: Accessed via the Internet or an intranet, publications of this kind can be designed either:

- for viewing on screen and printing out if the user wishes

  or

- specifically for use on screen rather than for reading on paper.

In this manual, *screen-based publication* means material that is designed primarily for use on screen (whether delivered electronically or in a portable format) and that exploits the distinguishing characteristics of the medium. Material designed for print and merely digitised for electronic delivery does not come within this definition.

Preparing electronic publications

Readers' expectations: Readers expect that on-screen publications will use the medium's capabilities wherever relevant—which may include, for example, interactivity, electronic links and animation (Chapters 17 to 21). They also expect material on a web site to be kept up to date.

Screen characteristics: The size, shape and other characteristics of screens must be considered. For instance, the horizontal configuration of most current desktop screens does not suit the vertical design of most printed material, and most users will not be able to see all of a traditional A4 page on screen without scrolling. Reading on screen can also be more tiring than reading printed text because of the screen's emitted light, flickering and pixelation (Chapter 3).

Structuring, writing and designing electronic publications: These activities require an understanding of the differences in reading patterns for printed and on-screen material. For example, users of on-screen material tend to skim rather than to read closely; because of electronic links, they may not read the material sequentially; and their eye movement patterns differ from those employed for reading paper-based publications, with a greater focus on the central part of the screen (Chapters 3 and 17). Screen-based material is also best divided into small, independent units linked logically to associated material (Chapter 3). The conceptual design, organisation and linking of screen-based material—often referred to as 'information architecture'—thus needs to be undertaken in an integrated manner (Chapter 2).

Navigation and labelling systems: It is vital to have navigation and labelling systems that help readers find the publication, move around it easily, and understand the context of each screen. Successful systems are based on knowledge of the ways readers use on-screen material (Chapter 17) and of the increasingly standardised elements expected for web sites and online documents (Chapter 13). Careful indexing (including the use of metatags to alert search engines), clear and consistent labelling for hyperlinks and headings, helpful contents and menu structures, and logical links all play their part (Chapters 17, 18, 23 and 24).

Conversion for the web: This often involves translating the text into a mark-up language such as HTML (Hypertext Mark-up Language) and using suitable file formats for graphics so that the document can be accessed by a web browser. Alternatively, it may be appropriate to use a file format such as PDF (Portable Document Format), which can provide an exact replica of the pages of the original document (Chapter 24).

Capabilities and configuration of readers' computers: If the intended readers are to access and use the material easily, technical aspects such as bandwidth, access speeds, file sizes and browser compatibility must be taken into account (Chapter 24).

Testing: While the document is being developed and again before its release, it should be tested to make sure that all electronic elements work properly, that it will operate efficiently on users' computers, and that it will meet users' needs (Chapter 24).

Maintenance provisions: These are necessary to keep the publication's design and information current, respond to feedback where required, and ensure that all elements continue to function as intended (Chapters 24 and 26).

Legal compliance and standards

Relevant legislation and industry standards, as well as aspects of the Commonwealth's requirements for online publishing, are discussed in Chapters 22 to 24. Among the matters that need to be taken into account are copyright; equity of access; metadata standards; international identification and cataloguing systems; publication lodgment; and legislative provisions relating to privacy, defamation, contempt, trademarks and trade practices. Details of compliance requirements for Commonwealth online publications can be found in *Guide to minimum website standards* <http://ww.agimo.gov.au>.

Exploiting the potential of each publication mode

If the benefits to be gained from both print and electronic publishing options are to be maximised, the distinguishing characteristics of each option need to be exploited. In the case of screen-based publications, this means structuring, writing, designing and producing documents to match readers' expectations when working with on-screen material. If readers still prefer to print out the publication rather than to use it on screen, the benefits have probably not been optimised.

Identity

Any publication produced by a government agency, an institution or a commercial concern affects that group's public image. The publication's quality and style send a message about who the authoring body is, what it does, and how it does it. For this reason, most public and private sector organisations are keen to ensure that their publications are of a high standard and present a cohesive image.

The Commonwealth Government has additional obligations to consider in this regard, since its publications are a reflection of the credibility, expectations and aspirations of the Australian people. Any material it publishes therefore has to be accurate, timely, and of a quality suited to its purpose. It should be clear and readily accessible to its intended readership. It should also represent value for money.

In addition, all publications produced by the Commonwealth Parliament and by Commonwealth agencies must be readily identifiable as such. There are rigorous controls on the manner in which national symbols such as the Commonwealth Coat of Arms are used. The aim is to establish and maintain a consistent image and quality in all government publications; so there are also standards relating to paper sizes and qualities, a common approach to editorial style is recommended, and Australian spellings are preferred. Government agencies often apply a further level of publishing specifications to reinforce their particular identity. Such cohesiveness in presentation is very important in gaining and maintaining public acceptance of government services.

➤ Chapter 16 provides guidance on matters associated with Commonwealth identity and the use of national symbols in publications.

➤ Chapter 2 describes the range of expertise that may be needed for a publishing project and suggests how to go about finding people with these skills. Preparation of document guidelines and style sheets is discussed on pp. 14–17.

Given these considerations, in-house or external assistance with editing, design and on-screen publishing is usually required for any significant publication, especially government documents intended for public distribution. Clear document development guidelines and style sheets are also essential for achieving a uniform publication style.

Compliance with legislation and standards

Legal requirements relating to copyright, defamation, contempt, indecency, trade practices and legal deposit affect all publications. Other legal provisions—such as those dealing with social justice, access and equity, freedom of information, privacy, and management of official records—are also important, particularly for government publishing. In addition to this, there are evolving standards aimed at increasing compatibility between electronic systems. Standards issued by organisations such as Standards Australia, the International Organization for Standardization, and the World Wide Web Consortium should also be supported in government publishing.

The implications of the legislation and standards need to be understood when planning a publication, and provision should be made for achieving compliance. The legal requirement for government information to be made available in a non-discriminatory manner may necessitate, for example, the conversion of some material to braille or voice systems. Then there are design and content stipulations for certain types of Commonwealth publications, such as those to be tabled in parliament.

➤ Chapters 22 and 23 provide advice on compliance requirements; Chapters 24 and 25 describe production standards relating, respectively, to screen-based and paper-based publications.

Budget and timetable

The next major influences on the communication strategy are the budget and timetable, and these inevitably affect the quality of the publication.

Striking a balance

For every publication, a realistic balance has to be struck between three competing goals:

- high quality
- timeliness
- minimum cost.

Varying the importance attached to each of these goals produces different results. It will cost more, for example, to produce a high-quality publication within a tight schedule. This is because there will probably be additional costs arising from the need for more staff or overtime, queue-jumping at the production stage, and compressed delivery time. On the other hand, to produce a publication within a compressed time frame and at minimum cost will generally mean some sacrifice of quality. And if the aim is to achieve a high-quality publication for a low cost, it will take longer, because the project schedule will need to coincide with periods of low demand at each stage of the publishing process.

The publishing challenge: The main concern will always be to balance quality, time and cost to achieve the best result for a project.

A sound communication strategy will determine an acceptable balance between these factors by assessing at the outset:

- the imperatives of the project—those goals that must be met to satisfy the publication's purpose
- the options (in terms of format, delivery mode, scope, level of quality and timing) for meeting those imperatives, and the costs associated with each option
- the financial and staffing resources potentially available for the project, and the estimated returns from sales if the publication is to be available commercially
- realistic schedules for carrying out the work—including research, writing, reviews, editing, design, screen-based publishing inputs, approvals, proofreading and indexing (and repetition of some of these tasks at various stages)
- potential problems and ways of avoiding or responding to them.

➤ Chapter 2 recommends early consultation with experienced professionals to help determine realistic schedules and costs for a publishing project.

The results of this analysis then need to be supported by a carefully monitored and controlled management plan for the publication (see page 13).

Life-cycle costs

In addition to the immediate production costs, the full cost over the life of a publication needs to be considered. Documents that are well planned and executed tend to satisfy their users better, and for longer. They therefore have a lower life-cycle cost because the need for revision or replacement is deferred.

Most publishing projects can be undertaken in different ways: with in-house resources or by contract; with one technology or another; and swiftly or in a more measured fashion. All practical alternatives should be considered in order to determine the full life-cycle cost of each approach. Straightforward costs such as those for salaries and printing can readily be determined, but many other costs are often hidden. For example:

- if contractors are used, in-house resources are needed to manage and administer the contracts
- in-house staff attract overheads and other non-cash costs that should be included.

The costs involved in keeping a publication up to date or in responding to feedback also need to be taken into account. Balanced against these costs, of course, will be the benefits of having current information available to readers, a consideration that is more relevant for some types of publications than for others.

Criteria of effectiveness

The communication strategy needs to include some criteria against which to evaluate the effectiveness of the planned publication. These criteria will be derived from the publication's purpose and the other goals already established during the planning process.

'Usability testing' of the writing process has traditionally been done by an editor (as the 'advocate for readers'), to ensure that the concepts, structure, language and presentation will match readers' expectations. In addition, the document might be evaluated by an independent assessor with a special understanding of the audience's needs, or a review by a relevant panel or focus group could be arranged.

For an electronic publication, testing for accessibility and navigability must be built into the publication schedule. Before release, the document should also be rigorously tested, to check that it functions effectively in a variety of possible user environments.

➤ Chapter 24 discusses pre-release testing, while Chapter 26 deals with post-release assessment of success.

Following publication, responses received from readers can help in gauging the publication's success and may suggest improvements that can be incorporated in future publication programs. Provision should be made for monitoring and assessing these responses and for documenting them for review when updating the information, planning the next edition, or planning a similar publication.

MANAGEMENT PLAN FOR THE PUBLICATION

The aim of publication management is to ensure that the project is completed on time, within the budget, and to the specified level of quality. This is a discipline that requires careful planning, and a commitment to the management plan by all contributors to the project. Good communications and regular monitoring and reporting of progress are essential.

Confirming the resources

A central management task should be to confirm that the indicative budget and timetable established as part of the communication strategy will be adequate for the project. If they are found not to be, renegotiation of the balance between time, cost and quality will be necessary. (If the budget or time frame is inflexible, for example, the publishing client may have to accept a less ambitious publication in terms of size or presentation.) Beginning the work with insufficient funding or time will inevitably bring problems later, resulting in a degradation of quality that satisfies nobody.

Drawing up the management plan

A draft of the management plan should be drawn up as soon as the communication strategy has been developed and the adequacy of the allocated resources has been confirmed. This draft plan should include:

- an assessment of the expertise required in terms of in-house staff and contractors, and of any specialised equipment deemed necessary
- definition of the proposed scope of work for each team member, and the intended allocation of responsibilities, authority and accountability
- procedures for selecting team members who are not already available and for ensuring that all participants receive a comprehensive briefing on the project requirements
- a schedule for each phase of the work, aimed at integrating all team members' inputs and including reviews and approvals where necessary
- a planned expenditure budget, with a procedure for managing any variations
- an effective system of document management that identifies each draft version and the sources of all changes and comments, and ensures that the team and any reviewers are always working on the current version.

The draft plan will need to be adjusted and confirmed after the team has been appointed and final agreements reached on costs, schedules and responsibilities. Once the publication management role has been allocated, this person should take responsibility for finalising and implementing the management plan.

Managing variations

Many publishing projects are subject to change while they are being planned or implemented. For example, there may be changes in the commissioning organisation's requirements, in users' needs, in the legislative environment, or in the focus of the content. The later in the production process that changes occur,

The publishing 'client': In this manual, *client* refers to the entity with overall responsibility for a publication, or to the entity's representative or delegated subcontractor. The client may, for example, be a government agency, an institution, a company, a committee, a publishing house, or an independent author.

➤ See Chapter 2 for advice on appointing a publication manager, selecting and briefing the members of the publishing team, and integrating the work.

the more disruptive and costly they generally become. If non-essential or frivolous changes are discouraged, the publication management task will be made easier and a better final product will be achieved.

However, eliminating all changes is not realistic, and processes for approving and incorporating changes must be established. The two keys to effective change management are:

- to assess all proposed changes carefully, advising the publishing client of the time and cost consequences and any risks to production quality that they may represent
- to have well-established protocols for recording proposed changes and their acceptance or rejection, as well as for recording the steps taken to incorporate approved changes and to check for ramifications throughout the publication.

Monitoring and reporting

The management plan is the basis for control over the publishing project. The plan should be reviewed regularly to determine whether progress, costs and quality are in line with expectations. Early detection of variations from the plan allows time for corrective action to be taken and for realistic progress reports to be prepared.

Team meetings are a useful device for reviewing progress. Each aspect of the project can be reported on, and an approach agreed for dealing with any emerging problems.

➤ For further discussion of monitoring and quality assurance, see Chapter 26.

GUIDELINES FOR DOCUMENT DEVELOPMENT

Before publishing work starts in earnest, preliminary guidelines should be drawn up to cover the writing, editing, design and screen-based publishing tasks. Although the guidelines will have to be expanded and adjusted as the work progresses, establishing an integrated approach at the beginning saves time and expense.

Writing and editing guidelines

If an editor has not been selected before writing starts, the publishing client or author may need to start compiling the writing and editing guidelines. Editing input at this stage can, however, prove very useful if it can be arranged.

There are two main elements of the writing and editing guidelines:

- an outline of contents
- an editorial style sheet.

Outline of contents

The contents outline should show all the elements planned for the publication. For the print-based version of a government report, for example, this would include the proposed chapter and section headings as well as a list of any planned illustrations, tables and subsidiary material (such as a foreword, preface, acknowledgments and appendixes). For the complementary screen-based version, the various structural units and their relationships would need to be identified, along with the general access and navigation tools to be used. These embryonic contents lists can subsequently be updated and used as a checklist as work proceeds.

Editorial style sheet

The next step is the creation of a style sheet detailing points of editing style relevant to the document. This calls for close consultation between author and editor. Although the editor will need to expand the style sheet continually as editing progresses, many decisions can be made at the outset. Consultation with the design and on-screen publishing contributors is also necessary, since style decisions in each of these areas must be in harmony.

The scope of the style sheet depends on whether the publishing client follows a particular style manual or guide. If so, the style sheet will complement the general approach described there; if not, it will need to cover a much greater range of topics. All document-specific editorial style sheets should include, as a minimum, directions for the heading hierarchy; the choices for capitalisation, spelling and hyphenation; and a list of any shortened forms and specialist terms used.

Design guidelines

Customised design specifications play a vital role in almost every publishing project. Even if a document consists entirely of text, and even if it must comply with predetermined client guidelines, professional design input can improve the document's readability and readers' comprehension of the information presented.

If a screen-based publication is envisaged, the design guidelines for screen display should be developed in parallel with the other screen-based publishing guidelines. If a document is to be designed for both print-based and screen-based delivery, the design specifications should complement each other. Similarly, attention should be paid to ensuring that there are design links between different documents on the same web site.

Detailed design and production specifications

The project designer should draw up the design specifications in close consultation with the client and other members of the publishing team. Incorporated in the design specifications (where relevant) will be page and screen layout instructions for margins, indents, fonts and line spacing; specifications for the heading hierarchy; details for headers and footers and any footnotes; and instructions for the design and placement of identification information, navigation icons and menus. Specifications for illustrations and tables should take account of the need for visual consistency and information comparisons, as well as defining the style for titles, legends, labels, internal table headings and so on. Instructions relating to any relevant client identity schemes and colours should also be included.

Production specifications for print publications should be drawn up at this stage too, since they will have budget and scheduling implications. Materials such as text and cover stocks, the binding style, the finishing processes, and the print run will need to be decided upon—usually jointly by the publishing client, the designer and the printer.

➤ See Chapter 13 for detailed discussion of the standard components of a publication, and Chapter 17 for guidance on creating effective screen-based navigation systems.

➤ The development of an editorial style sheet is discussed further in Chapter 14.

➤ These design and production aspects are discussed in detail in Chapters 16, 17 and 25.

Electronic tools

Many of the design specifications can be applied through electronic tools such as typographic style sheets, master pages and layout templates that can be used to achieve consistency during the writing and editing processes. The final document will usually be prepared using specialist publishing software, and some of the typefaces specified may not be available on the word processing software used to compile the drafts. When this is the case, fonts of similar size should be used for the drafts, to give an idea of the lengths and layouts of the various elements of the document.

Guidelines for screen-based publications

Although many editing and design principles apply to both printed and screen-based publications, particular structural and design factors associated with access, on-screen reading and navigability must be taken into account when developing the guidelines for a screen-based publication. The time spent by authors and information designers in assessing and tailoring the communication to the medium and its intended uses translates into time saved for readers. Look-up time is a crucial factor when structuring information for retrieval and usability.

Access

The technical capabilities of readers' computers must be carefully considered when designing an electronic document. Bandwidth, access speeds, file sizes and browser compatibility are all crucial factors affecting the ability of readers to view the material and access the content efficiently. If electronic files are constructed with care, equity of access can also be improved for people with disabilities—for example, in enabling visually impaired users with text recognition software to access the content. Accessibility standards are dynamic and change as technology evolves; they should be monitored regularly.

In addition, attaching metadata to electronic publications and web sites helps readers find information. Metadata describes the content of a publication in a structured and consistent way in accordance with accepted classification standards, and is used by search engines to find and classify material. This information is contained in the 'head' section of web publications and sites, and is seen by users only if they choose to look at the mark-up code underlying the document.

On-screen reading

Generally, considerably less material at a readable size will be visible in a screen window than on most traditionally sized printed pages. Readers of on-screen documents must scroll through material; and this means they must remember information they can no longer see.

To avoid hampering reading efficiency by too much scrolling back and forth, documents intended for on-screen use are often divided into 'chunks' that can be viewed independently. Other aids for screen readers include the use of frequent headings and the placement of important material at the top of each section (where it will be visible without scrolling).

➤ Design and production of screen-based publications are discussed in Chapters 17 and 24.

➤ Chapters 23 and 24 discuss access standards.

Metadata requirements: All Commonwealth publications are required to be 'tagged' with metadata—see Chapter 23. The metadata guidelines are contained in the Australian Government Locator Service Metadata Standard, which is maintained by the National Archives of Australia <http://www.naa.gov.au>.

Navigability

Unlike readers of printed documents for whom the author defines the access path, users of screen-based documents can chart their own path through a document by following cues from hyperlinks, headings and menu buttons. As a consequence, they can access information without the relevant preamble. Their understanding of the context of any screen therefore becomes important if they are to locate and comprehend the information contained in the full document.

Effective, consistent navigation systems are essential in maintaining readers' awareness of where they are in an electronic document and where they might best go next. Problems with navigation are the most common cause of readers abandoning a search—either because the navigation structure did not meet their expectations or because they had insufficient knowledge to find their way around the document.

When developing navigation systems, an information designer must look at a document from the viewpoints of the various users and prefigure the access routes that people are likely to follow intuitively, whether they are scanning the material, reading it in depth, or searching for specific information. Generally, a minimum number of steps should be required to find the information, while keeping the navigation path transparently logical. Also, icons must be clear and consistent, and the range and structure of the information must be obvious and logically accessible through straightforward heading and overview systems.

Specifications for screen-based documents

The specifications for a screen-based document will relate to the labelling, navigation and indexing systems; the average size of the text files; and the frequency of sound, animation or graphic files. The design of graphical interface elements such as icons, banners and corporate style elements should be developed in conjunction with the graphic designer and incorporated in the design specifications. A template for text mark-up should also be produced where relevant.

Amalgamation of guidelines

The aim in developing the various guidelines is to produce a cohesive, amalgamated set of specifications and templates for all aspects of the document. This comprehensive (and continually updated) resource provides all members of the publishing team with a detailed understanding of the overall approach and is an essential tool for achieving consistency throughout a publication.

Chapter **2**

The publishing team

WHAT PUBLISHING SKILLS ARE NEEDED?	**19**
The spectrum of skills	19
What publishing professionals do	20
MANAGING THE TEAM	**21**
The publication management role	21
Flexibility and integration	22
Scheduling	22
FINDING THE SKILLS	**25**
SEEKING QUOTES	**25**
Project description	26
Task-specific briefings	27
ASSESSING CANDIDATES	**29**
Knowledge, skills, equipment and approach	29
Quality of services	30
Fees and prices	30
CONTRACTING THE TEAM MEMBERS	**31**
ACKNOWLEDGMENTS	**32**

Producing any publication to a professional standard calls for some specialist knowledge, skills and equipment. The earlier this input is available, the better. Editing, design and publishing advice is valuable during the planning stage—for example, in drawing up the guidelines for the document. This advice also helps in establishing a realistic time frame and the likely costs involved in preparing the document for printing or screen-based delivery, or both.

Specialist publishing services represent a substantial portion of the overall investment needed to produce a successful publication—one that fulfils its purpose and meets its readers' expectations. Some organisations have all the necessary publishing skills in-house; more often, though, at least some of the work will need to be done by contractors. This chapter offers guidance on identifying, assembling and integrating the skills needed to take a document from concept to publication.

WHAT PUBLISHING SKILLS ARE NEEDED?

The spectrum of skills

Depending on the type of document and the delivery mode, people with skills in the following areas may be needed:

- research and writing
- editing and structuring for accessibility
- graphic design, illustration, photography and animation
- navigation systems
- production formatting
- proofreading
- indexing
- usability testing
- prepress work and printing
- replication
- distribution.

Not all of these skills are needed for every project, and some individuals or organisations might be able to offer expertise in more than one area. A large publication produced in both print and screen-based formats might require one or more individuals for each area of skill, whereas a more modest publication can generally be prepared by a much smaller number of people with skills in more than one area.

Publishing teams should be assembled to match the needs of the publication. They will therefore vary in size and structure, and in the extent of each participant's involvement.

What publishing professionals do

Authors

Publications begin with an author or group of authors producing a draft manuscript. Their primary concern is to produce information that is accurate, relevant and comprehensible. Authors may be either generalists (as many professional writers and journalists are) or experts in the subject. They might do the necessary research as well, or they might need researchers to help locate reference material and to check references and data.

Editors

> Chapter 14 details the tasks involved in a comprehensive editing service.

Editors work with the publishing client and the authors to ensure that a publication's focus, structure, expression, style and format support its purpose and will suit its probable range of readers. They work with the rest of the publishing team to promote consistency in the document's style and approach, and to ensure its overall integrity. Finally, they prepare the approved content to a standard suitable for publication. Good editors can greatly improve the quality of a publication and increase its chances of success.

Designers

Designers concentrate on creating a visual experience appropriate to the intended readership, understanding what will attract and hold readers' attention and help to communicate the information. They design each part of a publication for its purpose. For example, covers and home pages should attract attention; illustrations should clarify the text and encourage continued reading; type selection and page layout should improve readability and emphasise the hierarchy of information; and icons, menus and labels should be clear and consistent, so that readers can find their way through the publication with ease.

> Part 3 discusses the many factors to be considered in relation to visual identification, typographic and page design, effective use of tables and graphs, and illustration.

Graphic designers consider how to achieve these goals through a cohesive design approach that will tie the publication together visually and reflect the client organisation's visual identity. They brief illustrators and photographers to ensure that these contributions complement the publication's overall design. They also check the final material to ensure that it is complete and suitable for reproduction and they may supervise the production process as well.

On-screen publishing professionals

The on-screen publishing team develops the access schemes and the organisational, navigation and labelling systems that bind on-screen information together and make it easy for people to use. They work with graphic designers in creating graphics, icons, backgrounds, animations, video inserts and the screen layouts for the publication.

They also prepare the programmable functions (such as search and feedback functions) that encourage interactivity. Finally, they regularly test the document during its development and before its release to ensure that everything works as it should and that readers will find the content accessible and the navigation straightforward.

➤ Chapter 24 details the tasks specific to on-screen production.

Indexers

Indexers aim to identify all information of potential interest to readers, and to direct them to it efficiently. To do so, they analyse concepts and link those that are related, taking into account both the terminology used in the publication and the types of words and phrases that readers might use to search for the information. A good index not only is of great benefit to users but also lends authority to a publication.

➤ See Chapter 15 for information about indexing for both print-based and screen-based publications.

Printers and replicators

Successful printing of a publication requires great attention to detail, and a thorough knowledge of the qualities of different paper stocks and inks, the different processes involved, and the capabilities of the various items of equipment. Printers can therefore provide valuable advice when a publication is being planned, as well as during the period when the document is being prepared for reproduction. Their expertise can have a significant impact on the quality of the final product.

Replicators produce disks (including CD-ROMs) and videos. Many of them also print the paper accompaniments, such as labels, booklets and wrap-arounds, and package the materials for delivery.

➤ Chapter 25 describes printing processes in detail; Chapter 24 discusses replication.

MANAGING THE TEAM

The publication management role

It requires considerable planning and organisation to assemble and coordinate the professionals needed for a publishing project. This task of publication management can be carried out by a member of the publishing client's organisation, by a separate publication management contractor, or—as an additional responsibility—by a suitable member of the publishing team (such as a senior editor). It is vital that the responsibility for publication management is clearly allocated at the outset.

The publication manager is ultimately responsible for delivering the product specified in the publication plan. Among the tasks involved are the following:

- Prepare or review the publication plan (as described in Chapter 1), to confirm the publishing client's requirements and resolve any outstanding matters.
- Confirm the budget for the project and the procedures to be followed in authorising expenditure.
- Identify the skills required and determine whether these are available in-house or need to be contracted.
- Select each team member, using appropriate procurement processes if contractors are to be involved.

Who will manage the publication process? If a publication's goals in terms of quality, timing and budget are to be met, effective management skills and a close understanding of the work involved in the different facets of the project are essential. Early allocation of the management responsibility is important.

- Develop a detailed project schedule.
- Coordinate the work, monitor progress, and prepare regular progress reports.
- Apply effective quality control procedures throughout.
- Negotiate changes and variations where justified.
- Where warranted, arrange for comprehensive testing before release.
- Evaluate the publication after its release.

Flexibility and integration

The nature of publishing is changing rapidly in response to developments in desktop publishing software, print production technology and electronic publishing. Keeping abreast of these changes is vital in order to assemble the most suitable mix of skills and use them wisely.

As in most areas of rapid technological change, there may be some overlapping of skills and occasional gaps in knowledge as training and practice strive to keep up with developments. For example, some of the skills of information architects, editors and designers—often developed in parallel but separate streams—are highly complementary and should be integrated on the job wherever possible. Graphic designers are increasingly called on to be typesetters, and this can mean that different quality control procedures are necessary.

Particularly in the evolving environment of electronic publishing, too much compartmentalisation of roles should be avoided. Until the approach to these tasks becomes more standardised, the important thing is to ensure that the work is performed well rather than to worry about who actually carries out the various tasks. All team inputs should be carefully scheduled and integrated so that the maximum benefit can be gained from the team's range of expertise. Clear definition of the boundaries of each contributor's responsibilities, authority and accountability is also essential.

Information architecture: This is an emerging profession aimed at applying the skills found in information science, writing, editing and design to the way information is presented. In on-screen publishing, information architects specify what is needed in terms of information organisation, functionality, navigation, labelling and searching, as well as mapping how the content is likely to change over time.

Scheduling

Typical work phases involved in developing a publication to be produced in both printed and screen-based formats are shown in the diagram on page 23. This diagram illustrates the close interaction needed between the various publishing disciplines and the reliance on preliminary advice during the planning stage. The recommended approach for scheduling each of the publishing team inputs is discussed in the following paragraphs.

Research and writing

Scheduling the development of content is often difficult, particularly when there is uncertainty about the scope of the research needed or the nature of the information to be presented. If the text is to be generated by a number of authors—say, for an annual report or a technical document—coordination of contributions becomes an important management task. To contain costs, every effort should be made to ensure that the information is complete and has been approved before publishing work starts in earnest.

Typical work phases for producing a publication in printed and screen-based formats

TEAM MEMBER	PUBLICATION PLAN	CONTENT DRAFTING	CLIENT REVIEW AND APPROVAL OF CONTENT	INFORMATION ARCHITECTURE, EDITING AND DESIGN	NAVIGATION AND FORMATTING	AUTHOR AND CLIENT REVIEW AND APPROVAL	PRE-PRODUCTION	PRODUCTION	CLIENT SIGN-OFF. DISTRIBUTION
PUBLICATION MANAGER	Finalise plan	Manage, supervise		Manage, supervise	Manage, supervise		Manage, supervise	Manage, supervise / Sign off	
AUTHOR	Input	Complete draft text		Input	Input		Check	—	
EDITOR	Input	Input		Do substantive and copy edits	Input		Proofread (including index) / Sign off	Check proofs	
GRAPHIC DESIGNER	Input	Input		Design layout and illustrations / Input to screen display	Input to label design / Format in publishing program and check (alternatively, may be done by typesetter)		Prepare files for printing and brief printer	Check proofs	
ELECTRONIC PUBLISHING TEAM	Input	Input		Structure information / Develop access schemes and screen display / Test for usability	Develop navigation and labelling systems / Prepare programmable functions / Translate into mark-up language / Test for usability		Pre-release testing / Prepare files for replication, and brief replicator	Check disks	
INDEXER	Input	—		—	—		Prepare index	—	
PRINTER, REPLICATOR	Input	—		—	—		Arrange prepress work	Print/ replicate	

— No input during this phase   ▬ ▬ ▬ ▬ ▬ Particularly close interaction during this phase

Editing

There is considerable value in early editorial input, particularly for documents with more than one author and for multimedia documents. The editor can help, for example, to formulate a consistent approach to terminology and other language-related matters and to develop a document's overall structure, style and format.

Apart from this initial involvement, however, detailed editorial input is most effective and efficient if this work starts only after the final, full draft is complete and its content has been approved. If a tight schedule requires editing to start before this stage has been reached, the editor will generally need to work for a longer period on the document to achieve the same final standard.

Achievable schedules: Estimates from practitioners experienced in each aspect of the publishing work will provide a sound basis for developing a realistic schedule.

The time required for editing depends on the state of the draft the editor receives, the extent and timing of changes that authors or reviewers might make to the document after editing begins, and the scope of the editing and associated services required. Realistic estimates should be sought from experienced editors before confirming the detailed timetable.

Graphic design, illustration and photography

Intelligent design can help make a publication easier to understand, so close collaboration between writers and designers should be encouraged.

The design team's early involvement will also contribute to project efficiency. While authors are writing, designers can plan the look and feel of the document and produce mock-ups for discussion, illustrators can start picture research and prepare sample illustrations, and photographers can plan their shooting schedule. Much can be achieved while the document is being drafted, enabling the overall production time to be condensed.

On-screen publishing

The work involved in developing the information architecture usually begins in parallel with the structural editing. On-screen design and display work is integrated closely with the work of the rest of the visual design team, while programming and translation into a mark-up language commence towards the end of the editing and design phase. Usability testing is carried out at intervals throughout the creation and production process, becoming more comprehensive during the final production phase.

Depending on the scope of the publication, other inputs may also be needed. Examples are contributions from application designers, systems hardware managers, network services administrators, online security specialists, and customer support services. Again, early consultation with the selected professionals will help in developing a realistic schedule.

Indexing

Although a publication's index is produced towards the end of the production cycle, an indexer can provide an early estimate of how long the task is likely to take. Provision for this can then be made in the production schedule.

Indexers work with final copy, so it is important that the document is approved before indexing commences. For a screen-based publication, or a paper-based publication that is to have only paragraph numbers in the index, the indexing can begin once each part of the document's content is finalised. Indexes containing page references cannot be started until all the pages have been finally formatted and numbered.

Printing and replicating

The planning associated with printing and replicating should start early. Everything—from the details needed for the briefing process through to how the material will be prepared and presented for reproduction—needs attention during the initial planning phase.

The physical process of printing takes time, with many tasks necessarily being done sequentially. Final scheduling must therefore be based on the printer's proposed timetable. Printers are usually adept at rearranging the flow of work through their facilities to accommodate changes in production schedules, but there are limits (and costs) associated with these changes.

Similarly, a realistic amount of time must be allocated for preparing disks and other media. Replicators should be informed of the proposed schedule and packaging requirements as soon as possible, and their advice sought. As the product nears completion, details of the replication requirements should be confirmed and the replicator kept aware of any possible delays to the schedule.

FINDING THE SKILLS

If the skills needed for a publishing project are not available in-house, what is the best way of finding and contracting suitable people? The names of individuals and companies with publishing experience can be found in business telephone directories, on web sites and in the credits sections of publications. In addition, the various professional societies maintain registers, and there are specialist industry directories available. Recommendations from organisations that have undertaken similar work are also useful. Another way of testing the market is to advertise for expressions of interest.

➤ A number of professional associations involved in publishing are listed on p. 33.

To narrow the field, the capacity of candidates to do the work within the proposed time frame should be confirmed and their experience with comparable projects checked. If potential contractors are identified as early as possible, there is a much greater likelihood of obtaining suitable assistance and facilities at reasonable rates.

Any procurement guidelines governing the publishing organisation's contracting activities should be followed. Is tendering always necessary, for example, or is it acceptable simply to select professionals who have a proven track record? An efficient approach used by some organisations that frequently prepare publications is to establish a panel of suitable publishing professionals from whom to seek assistance as each project arises. The membership of these panels should be subject to regular market testing, however, to check that the range of skills available remains in step with evolving industry standards and expectations.

SEEKING QUOTES

If competitive quotes are to be sought, potential suppliers need to be fully informed about the nature of the project and the services sought. This briefing information should be provided in the invitation document and can be supplemented by a briefing meeting.

Briefing candidates: It is always better to provide too much information than too little. Competing candidates should receive the same information, so that equitable assessments can be made.

After the contractors have been chosen, the briefing material should be reviewed so that any details negotiated during the selection process can be incorporated in the contract agreements. Before work starts, a briefing meeting for the entire team will help team members appreciate the scope of the publishing task and encourage interaction and integration of skills.

Project description

All candidates should be given a detailed project description, along with relevant background information about the client organisation, including its objectives, the market it aims to reach, and the image it wishes to project. A comprehensive brief encourages responses that are carefully tailored to suit the project's needs.

Scope of a typical publication brief

Contact information
Full name of organisation preparing the publication
Names of all contacts
Delivery and postal addresses (including delivery address for quotes, if relevant)
Phone and fax numbers
Email and web addresses

Project description
Context and significance
Objectives
Description of physical product
Scope of work and services required
Any existing materials to be incorporated or matched
Any legislative requirements or specific guidelines to be met
Number of printed copies or replicated units (including parts and packaging, if relevant)

Content description
Content overview (including the most important aspects from the client's perspective)
Intended length and structure
Number and type of illustrations and tables

Audience description
Any marketing appraisals and research
Level of readers' assumed knowledge
Aspects likely to be of most interest to readers
Expectations of readers
Manner in which the publication will be used

Work processes
Where the work is to be done (in-house or at contractors' premises)
Whether in-house facilities, equipment and assistance will be available to contractors

Timing
Deadlines (interim and final) and reasons for these
Indicative schedules for separate tasks
Availability of material for commencement of task
Launch dates

Indicative budget

Task-specific briefings

In addition to the general briefing material, further details specific to each of the different publishing tasks will probably be necessary.

Writing brief

Authors need to know the source and location of any relevant background or reference material, and the contact details of people who could be approached for further information. Any available research capacity that might be useful should be identified. Authors should also be made aware of any style or other conventions used by the publishing organisation.

Editing brief

Editors need to know the stage of completion the manuscript will have reached when it is provided for editing, and the scope of the editing input that is envisaged. Like authors, editors must be made aware of any specific style conventions followed by the publishing organisation, and a copy of any in-house style guide should be provided. They should also be advised of the procedure for checking editorial queries, and the review and approval processes that will be followed.

In addition, the approach to editing mark-up should be discussed. Is it to be done on hard copy? If so, who is to key in and proofread the changes, and should the standard proofreading marks be used? If the editing is to be done on screen, software compatibility should be checked.

Any requirement for the editor to be involved in other project activities—such as in a management, supervisory or advisory role, or in checking proofs or metadata, for example—also needs to be considered.

Design brief

As well as information about the readership and the product descriptions in the general briefing, designers need to know how the proposed publication will fit in with other corporate materials, so that the visual identity system can be maintained. Information about how the publication will be distributed and used will help in planning covers, paper stock, binding and packaging. Designers also need to know in what formats and programs the material will be supplied to them, and whether any existing imagery is to be used.

Any requirement to supervise other team inputs or to locate and brief other contractors should also be discussed.

On-screen publishing brief

On-screen publishing contractors need to know the type of electronic product to be produced and the level of interactivity contemplated. For example, is the publication intended to show a process, to stimulate interaction, to train users? Discussion of how readers are most likely to use, search and interact with the content will help contractors assess the task in terms of information design and the access schemes and navigation systems required.

The requirements relating to on-screen design should focus on results rather than prescribing a process. This will allow the selected contractor sufficient freedom to match the document's content with the most suitable design and construction methods. Similarly, the brief for any programming tasks should be results-based, with attention being paid to the types of hardware and software that might be suitable. The desirability of providing the product in various formats to assist users who have disabilities also needs to be discussed.

➤ Chapter 23 discusses legislation relating to non-discriminatory access to public information.

For usability testing, the brief may cover some or all of the following:

- the environments to be tested—for example, browser versions, operating platforms and download speeds for an Internet publication
- areas for task analysis, to gauge how readers will work with the publication to achieve a specified goal
- areas for interface analysis, to gauge how well readers will understand and assimilate messages and instructions
- specifications for reporting the findings of the analysis.

Finally, on-screen publishing contractors need to know what technology, resources and processes the publishing client will use to support the publication or web site.

Indexing brief

In addition to details about the content, readership and estimated length of the publication, an indexing brief should explain any special content or format requirements for the index itself. These might include the indexing of special features such as tables, captions and illustrative matter; the expected length of the index; and instructions for the layout in which the index is to be provided.

Printing and replicating brief

The methods likely to suit the project best, as well as the available technology and equipment, should be canvassed with potential suppliers of printing and replication services. In many cases the designer will be supplying digital copy (either online or on disk) for reproduction, and the process may be controlled entirely by electronic means.

In addition to the overall brief for the project, a specific printing brief might cover:

- a detailed description of the print job, including the proofing requirements, the number of copies and pages, a description of the format (including finished size), the number of colours and whether there are colour bleeds, the printing processes and the paper stocks desired, the binding and embellishment processes needed, any special features of the project, any security or embargo considerations, and the delivery deadline
- a description of the materials to be supplied to the printer, such as disks, files and scans; the formats and programs used; and any transparencies or originals that have been included.

A similar level of detail is required when briefing replicators.

ASSESSING CANDIDATES

Candidates' submissions or tender responses should be in writing and itemised to avoid any misunderstandings. They should be assessed against the criteria listed in the invitation document, which might include:

- the knowledge, skills, equipment and proposed approaches of potential suppliers, judged against the needs of the project
- the quality of potential suppliers' services, preferably confirmed by reference to previous clients or other referees
- the fees or prices quoted.

The overriding consideration should be value for money—remembering that the apparently lowest prices will not necessarily produce this result.

Knowledge, skills, equipment and approach

Talking to potential suppliers about their contributions to other similar tasks will provide insights into their level of experience and ability to meet deadlines. Their proposed approach to the job should indicate their technical knowledge, capabilities and understanding of what is required. An idea of how well they will communicate and relate with other members of the publishing team should also be apparent from these initial discussions.

Some types of publications call for at least some members of the publishing team to have specialist knowledge of the subject area. For example, a scientific report directed at readers in a particular discipline will probably require writers and editors who are sufficiently qualified to know the accepted terminology and spot technical errors or inconsistencies in the content. On the other hand, if a document is directed at a broader readership—even if the topics covered are complex and technical—writers and editors with generalist backgrounds may better understand readers' needs and more readily notice areas where too much knowledge has been assumed or where the level of language could prove confusing.

Familiarity with the publishing conventions associated with the particular type of document may also be important. For example, the editing requirements for a government agency's annual report will almost certainly differ from those for a textbook for lower primary students, a collection of poetry, or a corporate brochure or newsletter. Knowledge of the writing and editing requirements for screen-based material will also be necessary if the document is to be produced for reading on screen.

Editing standards: The range of skills expected of an experienced editor is detailed in *Australian standards for editing practice* (see p. 33).

When choosing a contractor for an on-screen publishing task, not only technical ability but also expertise in information design and knowledge of the ways in which readers assimilate content are important. In addition, publishing clients will need to be assured that the contractor recognises the likely directions in which the industry may develop and the implications of such change. In the rapidly evolving environment of on-screen publishing, the flexibility and longevity of publishing investments must be taken into account.

Candidates for indexing tasks should be able to demonstrate a good understanding of the principles of editorial style. This knowledge is essential if they are to produce an index that is editorially compatible with the publication; otherwise, a great deal of subsequent copy editing will be necessary.

The different capabilities of print houses also have to be considered. Will their range of printing presses allow them to match a job to a press that suits it? The choice of machine depends on factors such as the type and weight of paper required, the size of the job, the speed of the press, the number of colours, the length of the run, and the complexity and exactness of the work.

Quality of services

Samples of prospective contractors' work will generally provide an idea of the quality of services they offer. The portfolios of designers, illustrators and photographers should give a good indication of their creativity and style in responding to a variety of briefs. The quality achieved by on-screen publishing contractors and indexers can be checked by testing some of their sample products for usability. The level of print quality achieved by a print supplier should be apparent from sample publications.

Assessing the quality of editing is not always as straightforward. Some impression of the scope and final quality of publications can be gained by reviewing other documents on which an editor has worked. However, the result might have been affected by time constraints, by decisions that have overridden editorial preferences, or by the quality of the material the editor was given to begin with.

Any review of sample publications should therefore be supplemented by references from previous clients and other publishing industry contacts—not only in the case of editors but for all prospective members of the publishing team. These references should provide further insight into candidates' capabilities and commitment to quality, and perhaps also into other qualities (such as flexibility and tact) that can affect team success.

Fees and prices

Quotes and estimates received from potential suppliers can differ greatly, and the overall value for money each represents should be the main assessment consideration. Hourly, daily, per-page or per-illustration rates are usual for many publishing jobs. Sometimes an upper limit is agreed for the total cost of a job, although estimates (which can be firmed up later) are more likely if the scope of work cannot be accurately assessed at the outset. If the scope and project processes are clearer, a fixed fee may be negotiated, although this will probably include a contingency provision.

Differences between the prices quoted might be a reflection of potential contractors' relative levels of experience and reputation within the industry. Some contractors also have sliding scales for different types of work or for staff with different levels of experience. More experienced practitioners might see complexities in the project that will require extra work—complexities that could be overlooked by contractors with less insight. Different technical solutions or

> Chapter 15 explains how to evaluate indexes, Chapter 25 suggests ways of assessing the quality of a printed work, while Chapter 24 discusses standards for screen-based publications.

Referees: Previous clients can provide useful insights into the quality of candidates' services.

Value for money: The lowest prices do not necessarily result in value for money. Any reworking arising from inexperience or poor-quality work can be expensive and time-consuming. Candidates' abilities to meet all the relevant goals for a project should be taken into account, not only their immediate impact on the budget.

formats might also be offered. Discussions about the details of candidates' proposed scope of work and services will help establish the basis for such differences.

A tight project schedule can be a further cause of price differences. If the work is likely to require substantial overtime or disruption to other contracts, or if subcontracting of some elements of the work is necessary, these additional expenses will usually be reflected in quotes and estimates.

With printers' quotes, differences in prices can also arise from the availability or otherwise of suitable printing presses and associated equipment. For example, many printers need to 'buy in' particular binding or embellishment processes from other suppliers. Their contracts with those suppliers will be priced differently, often depending on the volume of work they send out, and this will affect their quotes.

Printers' quotes can also differ according to whether or not they already hold sufficient stocks of the chosen paper and board. The cost of paper can account for somewhere between 30 and 50 per cent of a print job, so paper choice has a big impact on printers' quotes.

When only a small amount of material is needed for a print job, the client will be charged for the minimum order size, even if this results in wastage or leftovers. This is standard practice in the printing industry, resulting from the ordering requirements of external suppliers. It is also why there are sometimes paper stocks 'out the back' that can be used for small print runs at little cost. Similarly, dies created for previous clients—for example, a die for an A4 folder—are sometimes retained. It is worth asking the printer whether there are opportunities such as these for cost savings.

Options for materials: Printers can order supplies from a variety of sources, so some preferences (such as environmentally friendly paper and inks and products from Australian and New Zealand manufacturers) can be accommodated. A printer's regular suppliers may, however, have financial arrangements that allow the printer to offer better prices if an 'acceptable equivalent' to the materials chosen is also specified.

CONTRACTING THE TEAM MEMBERS

Before work starts, all contractors should receive written confirmation of engagement. Details of the brief and the agreed products, services, timetable, fees and terms of payment should be clearly documented, as should any other agreed conditions.

The basis for pricing variations should be defined, to cover changes that may be initiated or approved by the client during the course of the work. For example, the client may decide to insert a further round of text changes beyond those agreed in the editing contract, or there may be changes to the illustration requirements or print specifications. When this happens, the client will be expected to meet the cost of the unforeseen work and of any materials the contractor has ordered for the project that are no longer needed.

The conditions that will apply if the project is delayed or stopped should also be noted in writing. The client should expect to be charged (as a minimum) for all work completed to that point. If the project recommences, a new schedule will have to be negotiated, and additional costs might be incurred if it is necessary to accelerate the work program.

Acknowledging contributions:
Acknowledgments are appreciated for
the following work:

- research and writing
- editing and proofreading
- graphic design
- illustrations
- photographs
- animation
- screen-based publishing work
- indexing
- typesetting
- printing
- replication.

ACKNOWLEDGMENTS

Consideration should be given to acknowledging the work of the publishing team. As discussed in Chapter 13, acknowledgments can be shown on the reverse of the title page, as part of a preface, or in a separate acknowledgments section. Generally, either the contributor's name or the business name should be cited, although sometimes both are given.

If a number of different illustrators or photographers have contributed to the publication, it is usual either to label each image with a credit or to link each image with the originator in the acknowledgments. Some publications, such as brochures, do not always lend themselves to a formal list of acknowledgments; in these cases, the designer and printer are often acknowledged in fine print near the edge of a page, often on the inside back cover.

Any stipulations by copyright holders relating to acknowledgment of textual material, illustrations and photographs must always be followed.

PART **1** # Further reading and resources

FURTHER READING

Australian Government Information Management Office 2000, *GovernmentOnline*, <http://www.agimo.gov.au >.

——2000, *Guidelines for Commonwealth information published in electronic formats*, 1:1, <http://www.agimo.gov.au>.

——2003, *Guide to minimum web site standards*, rev. edn, <http://www.agimo.gov.au>.

Australian print standards, 1995, AGPS Press, Canberra.

Council of Australian Societies of Editors 2001, *Australian standards for editing practice*. Copies available from the various state and territory societies of editors.

Department of Family and Community Services 1999, *Better information and communication practices*, Office of Disability, Department of Family and Community Services, Canberra.

Human Rights and Equal Opportunity Commission 2002, *World Wide Web access: Disability Discrimination Act advisory notes*, 3.2, < http://www.humanrights.gov.au>

World Wide Web Consortium 2000, *Web content accessibility guidelines*, 1.0, <http://www.w3.org>.

INDUSTRY ORGANISATIONS

The following organisations are among those that may be able to provide advice on standards and general industry practices. Many of them also maintain registers of practitioners:

Australian Graphic Design Association

Australian Institute of Professional Photography

Australian Interactive Multimedia Industry Association

Australian Library and Information Association

Australian Publishers Association

Australian Society for Technical Communication

Australian Society of Indexers

Australian Writers' Guild

Illustrators Association of Australia

Media, Entertainment and Arts Alliance (incorporating the Australian Journalists Association)

Printing Industries Association of Australia

Public Relations Institute of Australia

Societies of editors in each state and in the Australian Capital Territory and the Northern Territory

Writers' centres in some states and the Australian Capital Territory

Writing and editing

Clear communication must be the goal of all organisations and writers who want the information in their publications to be read and understood. The following chapters offer guidance on the many elements that work together to achieve such clarity.

These elements include:

- tailoring the structure of the information to suit the intended readers and the medium in which the publication is presented

- following the precepts of plain English and the conventions of spelling and usage likely to be acceptable to the audience

- using punctuation, capitals and textual emphasis to clarify meaning.

W R I T I N G   A N D   E D I T I N G

3 Structuring documents for readers 36

How readers absorb information

Organising material to suit reading patterns

4 Effective and inclusive language 48

Awareness of your audience

Characteristics of the different registers

Plain English

Inclusive language

5 Grammar 63

Word classes

Frequently asked questions

6 Spelling and word punctuation 78

Standardisation and variants in spelling

Word punctuation: apostrophes and hyphens

7 Sentence punctuation 95

Using the different punctuation marks effectively

Typography of punctuation

8 Capital letters 118

Background to current practice

Capitals in sentences

Capitals for proper nouns and names

9 Textual contrast 136

Headings and other format-related emphasis

Italics

10 Shortened forms 150

Different types of shortened forms and when to use them

Grammar and punctuation of shortened forms

Special sets of shortened forms

The tone or register you use is also important in engaging readers in what you have to say. A standard register will suit most information documents. There are times, however, when an informal register might work better: perhaps in a brochure on community health, for example. At other times, more formal language might be required, such as for certain legal documents.

Consistency is a further aid to clarity. Recommendations on specific styles are given where alternatives exist—to help in achieving the appropriate standards of cohesiveness and quality. These recommendations should be seen as the Commonwealth Government's 'house style' rather than a denial of the validity of some of the other choices for other purposes. Language continues to evolve, as does the acceptance of new coinages. For this reason, the manual's recommendations are often set within a discussion of changing trends and of the likely needs and responses of different audiences.

WRITING AND EDITING

11 Numbers and measurement 162

When to use words or numerals

Punctuation and spacing of numbers

Common numerical expressions

Units of measurement

12 Methods of citation 187

Notes, references and bibliographies

Different citation systems

Specialised sources and electronic material

13 The components of a publication 233

Covers, preliminary pages and endmatter for printed works

Elements of on-screen material

14 Editing and proofreading 252

The value of professional editing help

Substantive and copy editing

Proofreading

Methods of working and responsibilities

15 Indexing 270

Constructing an index

How to evaluate indexes

Further reading and resources

A selection of style guides, dictionaries, other reference works and web sites 285

Chapter **3**

Structuring documents for readers

HOW READERS ABSORB INFORMATION	**37**
Context and patterning	37
Attention spans	37
Clarity of style and layout	38
Illustrations	38
READING PRINTED AND ON-SCREEN DOCUMENTS	**38**
Linear and non-linear structures	38
Screen characteristics	39
'Scannability'	39
ORGANISING MATERIAL TO SUIT READING PATTERNS	**39**
Inductive and deductive patterns	39
Chapter and section structures	40
Paragraphs and sentences	40
Subsidiary material	41
ORGANISING MATERIAL TO SUIT ON-SCREEN USE	**42**
Size of on-screen sections	42
On-screen organisational structures	42
'SIGNPOSTING' INFORMATION	**43**
Visually highlighted material	44
Bridging words and phrases	45
Links to associated material	46
ILLUSTRATIONS AND TABLES	**46**

To communicate information effectively, publications must be focused on readers' interests and needs, rather than being prepared solely from the author's viewpoint. So how should the content of a document be structured to give it the best chance of being read and understood? Although the answers will differ in some respects depending on whether the document is designed for print or for on-screen use, most of the principles apply to both media.

➤ Chapter 1 explains how a focus on the reader is crucial in planning successful publications. It also discusses factors to be considered when assessing readers' needs.

HOW READERS ABSORB INFORMATION

An understanding of how readers absorb information helps writers structure their material to best effect. Factors to consider are the context in which the information is presented, readers' attention spans, the clarity of the written style and layout, and the benefits of illustrations.

Context and patterning

Readers make sense of an item of information on the basis of what precedes and follows it and what they already know, or assume, about the topic. They also expect information to be presented in logical, conventional patterns—for example, in a chronological, hierarchical, thematic or geographical framework. Breaking conventional patterns can hinder understanding.

Similarly, complex information is more readily absorbed if it is linked back to a context in which readers feel more comfortable. Thus, explaining difficult concepts using everyday examples and familiar language helps to clarify meaning for readers.

Attention spans

Writers and editors should bear in mind the way people focus when reading or scanning. The usual pattern is for a reader's interest to be greatest at the beginning, to wane in the middle, and to rise again at the end. This pattern applies particularly to a publication as a whole but also at the more detailed level of chapters, sections and paragraphs.

Shorter words and shorter sentences are generally more easily understood (although see page 41 for a discussion of rhythm and balance in sentence construction). Similarly, when information is divided into categories, comprehension and recall are greater if the number of items in each group is kept relatively low.

Readers' attention spans can be very brief when searching for information they expect to find easily. A document's signposting and navigation systems must lead them to their goals before their attention is diverted or their patience exhausted.

Clarity of style and layout

➤ See Chapter 4 for detailed advice on using language suited to the readership.

The plain English movement has done much to increase awareness of the need for clear, straightforward, precise language. Unnecessary words and phrases, inflated or obscure language, convoluted sentences and a lack of logical links can all create barriers to understanding.

➤ Chapters 17 and 18 provide guidance on design, layout, navigation systems and typography for both printed and on-screen publications.

Clarity of design is another important aspect of effective communication. Logical, consistent heading hierarchies and labelling systems help readers grasp the structure of information. Comprehension is further aided by an intelligent page layout that uses space, colour, contrast, and the design and placement of text blocks to reinforce relationships and improve readability. Suitable choices of typeface, type size, line length and line spacing also make reading easier.

Illustrations

➤ Chapter 21 discusses how to illustrate text effectively.

Many readers understand and remember certain types of information more readily if it is presented visually rather than just being described. Converting statistical or other comparative data into a diagram, chart or table can clarify meaning dramatically. Other types of illustrations, photographs and moving images can also be very effective and will usually attract readers' attention immediately.

READING PRINTED AND ON-SCREEN DOCUMENTS

Linear and non-linear structures

Paper-based documents are essentially 'linear' in structure, enabling readers to start at the beginning and progress through to the end. Even if a reader is interested only in scanning the publication, the contents list offers a quick overview, supplemented by the subsidiary headings that show the broad direction of the discussion. To get to the next level of detail, a reader can scan a few paragraphs at the beginning of chapters or sections, or stop to read particular items that appear interesting or important—either because of their content or because their design attracts attention. Readers seeking specific information can consult the index.

Documents designed to be used on screen can, however, present a non-linear view. For example, a reader might reach an online publication via a hyperlink from somewhere else and could land in the middle of a section of the publication without any clear idea of the wider context of the information displayed on the screen or the extent of information presented elsewhere in the publication. Even when readers start at a list of contents on a publication's opening screen, there will probably be links to other parts of the publication or to other sites that encourage a non-linear reading approach. Most on-screen readers expect such interactivity, since it is a prime advantage of the medium.

Screen characteristics

The physical characteristics of on-screen publications also influence the way readers use them. Most obviously, readers cannot see the full on-screen document at a glance. A contents list gives an overview, but the document's size and scope cannot be grasped as readily as they might be when looking at a document held in the hand. Among other screen characteristics that affect reading behaviour are screen size and shape, scrolling, and the screen's resolution and emitted light.

Eye movement patterns also differ when reading on screen. With paper-based publications, the direction of readers' eye movements is generally from left to right and back again. In contrast, most screen readers concentrate on the central panel, which is where they have come to expect the main information, before looking at panels on the left and right.

➤ Chapter 17 discusses readers' eye movement patterns in more detail.

'Scannability'

Readers of on-screen publications tend to respond to the characteristics of the medium by scanning material rather than launching directly into a lengthy reading experience. To help them to use on-screen publications efficiently, they expect:

- short, independent sections designed with screen viewing in mind
- informative headings, lists of contents and menu schemes
- emphasis in the text's structure, design and layout that will help them scan for information
- fast links to associated material, within the publication and elsewhere
- clearly labelled navigation paths, to keep them in control of their movements within and beyond the publication and to keep them aware of the wider context of the material they are viewing
- suitable use of the medium's interactive potential.

ORGANISING MATERIAL TO SUIT READING PATTERNS

The ways readers absorb information, from both printed and on-screen publications, should be taken into account when structuring information.

Inductive and deductive patterns

Readers make sense of information on the basis of its context, so it follows that a transparently logical progression of ideas will be a feature of all successful information documents. In terms of the overall structure, there are usually two main options:

- *Inductive pattern:* The writer first introduces the general subject, then describes the details (divided into logical categories), and ends with a conclusion, recommendations or general summing-up.
- *Deductive pattern:* The writer announces the main proposition or conclusion at the beginning and then discusses the supporting arguments, options, or range of matters to be considered.

The likely attitudes and interests of the readership will influence the choice of structural pattern, as will the delivery mode. An inductive approach may be most suitable for readers interested in the full range of information the document contains, either because the document is new and pertinent to them or because it presents the material from a point of view they have not considered before. These readers may respond better to being led through the information step by step before being confronted with a conclusion they might otherwise fail to understand or find difficult to accept.

A deductive approach, on the other hand, usually suits on-screen readers and others who want to scan the material, as well as decision-oriented readers suffering from 'information overload'. Many of these people want to know the conclusion before deciding whether to plough through the detail to confirm that the argument is convincing.

Presenting a summary of the main points, conclusions or recommendations at the front of a publication also responds to readers' established pattern of focusing attention on the beginning of a document or section of text. It does, however, lead to some repetition, and this must be handled skilfully to ensure that the repeated information does not become tiresome. If the document is long, there may be a case for producing the summarised material as a separate document. Summaries are strongly recommended for on-screen documents.

Chapter and section structures

Within the overall inductive or deductive framework, the content should be organised into logical categories that suit the material and give readers a clear overview. Some common types of organisational categories are:

- sequential—following a logical progression, such as steps in a process or a chronological or alphabetical arrangement
- hierarchical—arranged, for example, in order of importance or from the broadest topic levels to the details
- topic-based—categorised, say, by type (such as industry, product, service or location), cause and effect, comparisons or themes.

For a long, printed document, one type of category may be appropriate at the chapter level, while other types may be more suitable at the section and subsection levels. Nevertheless, keeping some structural consistency between the corresponding chapters or sections will help readers grasp the logic underlying the discussion.

Paragraphs and sentences

At the more detailed structural level, the flow of logic through a text is expressed through paragraphs and sentences. To clarify this progression and emphasise the salient points, two general principles need to be followed:

- Keep the focus tightly controlled.
- Keep each sentence and paragraph to a suitable length.

Focus

As readers tend to focus on the beginning and end of a paragraph or sentence, material placed there will gain some prominence—particularly for readers who are scanning the information. This placement also supports the logic. If the main idea is put first, followed by associated details, readers will have a clear indication of the direction of the discussion. Ending a paragraph or section either with a concluding statement or with an idea linking to the following text similarly supports the logical flow.

Keeping the writing succinct also helps to bring out the main points. This is especially important for on-screen material, where improvements in readability have been found to occur if superfluous words and phrases are deleted.

Length

If paragraphs are too long, readers can lose their way in the detail. A paragraph of about three to five sentences is generally considered ideal, since readers can readily grasp the content of a text block of this size. Readers also benefit from the visual rests provided by this frequency of paragraphing.

Sometimes shorter paragraphs—perhaps containing only one sentence—are appropriate. A crisp introductory or concluding statement might well be presented as a single-sentence paragraph, both for logical reasons and for emphasis. The content of some types of publications, such as instruction manuals and information leaflets, often lends itself to short paragraphs. In many instances, though, single-sentence paragraphs betray a lack of integration with the surrounding text. Use them with care.

The length of sentences must be considered too. Short sentences can be a great aid to clarity; they also attract readers' attention. However, a string of short sentences can be irritatingly abrupt. On the other hand, a series of long sentences can be difficult to understand, particularly if the topic is complex. With the exception of particular readerships that need simple sentence construction, most readers appreciate the variety and rhythm achieved through a mixture of sentence lengths—provided that clarity and precision remain the goal.

Subsidiary material

Reading patterns should also be matched in the design and placement of subsidiary material in printed documents. Since readers' interest is highest at the outset, it is a pity to waste this by forcing them to leaf through a lot of subsidiary matter before getting to the main material.

A lengthy glossary and list of shortened forms are generally best placed at the back of a long printed document. Readers can find it overwhelming if they are confronted by pages of specialist language they feel they should understand before they even start reading what the writer has to say. If there is any concern that readers may not be aware of the glossary or other explanatory lists at the back of a document, a clearly highlighted note can be placed on a preliminary page, telling them where to find the information.

The placement of subsidiary material in on-screen documents does not present the same problems: all sections will have been divided into logical groups and can be accessed separately by means of hyperlinks. Similarly, links can take readers directly to explanations or associated material. But these links must be considered

➤ See Chapter 13 for further information about the purpose and placement of subsidiary material in a document.

carefully, since readers may lose the sequence of the discussion if they switch too frequently between different sections of a publication.

The level of detail throughout the text should also be consistent. If particular sections seem overly detailed, some of this material might be better transferred to an appendix—or, for a screen document, placed elsewhere and made accessible through hyperlinks.

ORGANISING MATERIAL TO SUIT ON-SCREEN USE

For on-screen publications, authors and editors should work closely with electronic publishing specialists to structure the content in ways that will help readers find and use the material easily.

Size of on-screen sections

When designing material for on-screen use rather than for print, one of the main differences is the need to break the content down into smaller logical units. The size of these sections needs to be carefully considered.

Sections that are too short result in 'over-granulation' of topics, effectively loosening the linear sequence and impeding recall of information from other locations. Sections that are too long can also hamper readers' recall of what has gone before. A balance must be struck, so that there is enough information in each section to enable clear connections to be drawn between topics without the need for excessive scrolling.

A rough guide for the maximum length of an independently viewed section is the equivalent of about five A4 pages. This length represents a reasonable balance between the time spent in scrolling and in the slower functions of page retrieval and link traversal. It is also helpful to have at least one heading visible per window, to keep readers aware of the context of the information at all times.

Screen-based documents: The recommended maximum length of a separately viewed section of information is the equivalent of about five A4 pages. Long documents should either be restructured for on-screen use or transmitted electronically to be read from a print-out.

Long documents originally designed for print production often do not lend themselves readily to such division without considerable reorganisation of the content. If this is not an option, a summary of the document can be prepared for the screen, with a link to the full document for downloading and printing.

On-screen organisational structures

On-screen publications are often organised using the sequential or hierarchical structures found in many printed documents. However, the electronic medium also enables much looser, web-type organisational structures to be used.

Sequential structures

In general, a straightforward sequential arrangement (for example, a chronologically based discussion or a series of process steps) is better suited to relatively small electronic documents. Longer documents usually require more complex structures.

Sequential structure

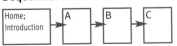

Hierarchical structures

Hierarchical structures can often be used for more detailed material. Most readers are familiar with hierarchical diagrams, such as organisational charts, and can quickly grasp how the topics are likely to be arranged within the publication.

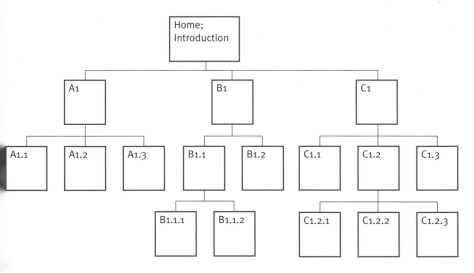

Balanced hierarchical structure

Achieving a good balance between breadth and depth in hierarchical structures is important. (*Breadth* refers to the number of options available at each level of the hierarchy. *Depth* refers to the number of levels in the hierarchy.) If a hierarchy is too deep, readers will become frustrated by having to select and click through a large number of menu pages to reach the information they seek. Further, they may not recognise what they are searching for from the few upper level options offered in the contents, menu or other access scheme, and they may thus search in the wrong area. On the other hand, if a hierarchy is too broad and shallow, the danger is that the options available at the top level will offer readers so many choices that they will find it hard to identify the right one.

Web-like structures

With web-like structures, content is arranged in associative patterns, and there is often an attempt to offer access to everywhere from anywhere within a site or document. Although this type of structure offers readers great flexibility, it can become so complex that it prevents them from forming a mental model of the content. Too many options and navigation paths might simply create confusion, particularly for less experienced on-screen readers.

Web-like structure

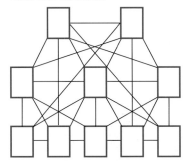

'SIGNPOSTING' INFORMATION

In addition to a clear structure, readers also appreciate having relevant material highlighted, or 'signposted'. Signposting techniques include:

- visually highlighting material on the page or screen

- using effective bridging words and phrases between sections of text to clarify logical relationships
- using cross-references or hyperlinks to provide links to associated material.

Effective signposting contributes greatly to readers' ability to understand the logical progression of the discussion, remember the information presented, and find specific information in the document.

Visually highlighted material

There are many ways of distinguishing material graphically. Headings are among the most important. Others are bulleted, numbered or otherwise indented items; highlighted keywords; text placed in boxes or margins; and captions. Used judiciously, these methods of emphasis are always helpful for readers, but they are particularly important for on-screen readers, who rely heavily on visual cues.

Headings

Headings play several important roles. They:

- map the document's structure
- show readers where to find particular information
- group information into clearly defined and readily comprehensible 'chunks'
- indicate what is to follow.

For maximum effect, headings need to be informative—or, in some contexts, intriguing—and ordered into a logical and clearly distinguishable hierarchy.

➤ For detailed advice on how to create effective headings, see Chapter 9 'Textual contrast' and Chapter 18 'Typography'.

Lists

Bullets offer a very effective way of drawing attention to different elements of a discussion, in both printed and on-screen documents. However, they should be used sparingly and consistently.

First, be sure that the information being highlighted in this way is sufficiently important to warrant the emphasis. If only a few minor items are bulleted within a lengthy section of text, the logical balance of the discussion is likely to be disrupted. Second, avoid overusing bullets, or their value as a tool for emphasis will be lost.

➤ Chapter 9 recommends ways of introducing, setting out, capitalising and punctuating bulleted and numbered lists.

Always preface bulleted series with a lead-in sentence, clause or phrase, and be sure that the text in each item flows logically from this introduction. Ensure, too, that there is more than one bulleted item in each series.

Keywords

Highlighting keywords with bold or coloured type is an approach being used increasingly to improve scannability on screen. Applied carefully, this technique can also be successful in some types of printed material. Again, however, beware of overuse: too much bold type can be difficult to read and can place undue emphasis on specific words within the overall context.

Italics, being less dominant than bold type, can be a useful alternative for emphasising particular words or phrases in some printed documents. However, caution is needed if the document also contains instances of published titles or scientific names, since these are traditionally set in italics and some confusion might therefore arise. Italic type is more difficult to read on screen, so avoid any unnecessary use of italics in on-screen documents.

Underlining should not be used for emphasis. It has become the accepted method for distinguishing electronic links. It also affects readability by covering over the 'descenders' of particular letters (such as g, j, p, q and y).

Text in boxes and margins

The placement of text in boxes and margins offers another way of highlighting information. Because they are usually read independently of the text, boxes should contain information that summarises, expands or otherwise illustrates the main text. If used for short summaries, for example, they can be very helpful to people who are scanning the document to find the major points. In printed documents, summarised information placed in the margin can also be an effective scanning aid.

Captions

Illustrations readily attract readers' attention, so make the most of the associated captions by giving them more than a labelling role. A caption can:

- expand the significance of an illustration, either by linking it to the broader context or by providing subsidiary information that is not discussed elsewhere
- focus greater attention on the illustration by describing particular facets of it in more detail
- reduce the amount of text required in the document by providing information in summary form.

In certain types of documents, captions can even carry the bulk of the information—and in a very digestible form. Given these capabilities, captions deserve careful crafting by writers, editors and designers.

Bridging words and phrases

Another vital signposting method is to preface and otherwise link information, to give readers an idea of what is to come and of how statements relate to each other. A lack of clear links between one paragraph and the next, and between and within sentences, is very common in corporate and government writing and can seriously hamper readers' understanding of the information.

The wide variety of bridging words and phrases that can be used for this purpose underlines the importance of this signposting function. The following examples, which are only a few of the numerous choices available, suggest the valuable role that such simple links can play.

- To indicate supporting detail:

      again   also   another   as well as

      for instance   in addition   in particular   not only … but also

➤ Chapter 9 discusses in detail the various methods of highlighting text and explains the use of italics for, among other things, scientific names and the titles of publications.

➤ Chapter 21 provides advice about the placement of captions.

- To indicate cause and effect or sequence:

  consequently   as a result of   because   first(ly) … second(ly)

  for this reason   given that   in order to   next

  since   this means that   therefore   subsequently

- To indicate comparison or contrast:

  although   despite   however   by contrast

  in comparison with   instead   alternatively   nevertheless

  similarly   while   likewise   on one hand … on the other

Links to associated material

Cross-references and hyperlinks alert readers to the existence of associated material. They also reduce the need to repeat information in different sections of a document, enabling each topic to be dealt with in depth at the most relevant place.

It is important, however, that these links do not cause a disjointed reading experience. Readers must be able to grasp the flow of the discussion without reference to the linked material; otherwise, they can easily lose the thread of the discussion.

Readers should also have a clear idea of the information available at the linked page or site, so that they can choose whether and when to look up this material. Sufficient detail therefore needs to be provided as part of the cross-reference.

ILLUSTRATIONS AND TABLES

Illustrations and tables can be a boon for readers. They can dramatically clarify text, provide visual relief, and serve as quick points of reference. For on-screen documents, there is also the option of using moving images and sound, although it is important that download times and the question of non-discriminatory access are considered. Illustrations should be planned in consultation with the publication designer.

➤ Chapter 19 provides guidance on the layout of tables. Chapter 21 discusses the different functions of illustrations: as description, as clarification, and (using symbolic, textural and atmospheric imagery) as abstract communication. It also provides detailed advice on the selection, placement and reproduction of images and the design of diagrams, graphs and maps. Chapter 23 discusses non-discriminatory access.

To be effective, illustrations and tables should be carefully integrated into the text of a document. Adhering to three basic principles will help achieve this:

- *Balance the presentation of information:* Illustrations and tables should complement, not repeat, the information in the text. They can provide greater detail than the text or alternatively serve as a summary. They can also show examples.
- *Present comparable information in parallel formats:* When information is being presented in a series of tables or illustrations for comparison, the same layout should be used for each element of the series.
- *Explain the relevance:* Some self-explanatory illustrations can stand alone, while others might be used purely for symbolic purposes or as background pattern or texture. Mostly, however, the relevance of each illustration and table needs to be explained in the text or in a caption. Text references should appear before, and as close as possible to, the table or illustration.

EVALUATING A DOCUMENT'S STRUCTURE

- Will the structure appear logical to readers, and will they be able to find their way around the document easily?

- Is the information divided into suitably sized sections? (This is particularly important for on-screen documents.)

- Are the topics that will most interest readers suitably emphasised, through the overall structure, focus within the text, and layout?

- Have reading patterns, particularly the importance of context and focus, been taken into account?

- Is the content easy for readers to scan?

- Has the information been signposted effectively, through clear headings, bridging techniques and cross-referencing?

- Is there an effective balance between short and long sentences, and is the writing clear, succinct and focused?

- Do the design, layout and illustrations support the meaning?

Chapter **4**

Effective and inclusive language

AUDIENCE AWARENESS	**49**
Writing for the audience	49
Primary and secondary audiences	49
Literacy and access	50
USING THE APPROPRIATE REGISTER	**51**
The scale of register	51
Registers and relationships with readers	51
Language differences in formal, standard and informal registers	52
EFFECTIVE COMMUNICATION	**53**
Plain English	53
Motivating the audience	54
Focus	54
INCLUSIVE COMMUNICATION	**55**
Legal requirements	55
Australian cultural diversity	56
References to ethnic groups	56
Inclusive treatment of the sexes	58
References to people with a disability	60
Inclusive treatment of the age range	61

The language of well-written documents helps to communicate information effectively. Language is also the means by which writers create the tone or register of a publication and establish relationships with their readers. For these relationships to be productive, the language the writer uses must take full account of the diversity of knowledge, interests and sensitivities within the audience.

AUDIENCE AWARENESS

Writing for the audience

Depending on the type of document, a writer may be communicating:

- with a single reader—as in a personal letter
- with a particular group identifiable, say, by age, academic discipline or employment—perhaps for a children's book, an article for a specialist journal, or an internal organisational report
- with the Australian public generally (in government brochures on tax or health information, for example)

or

- with the wider world (increasingly via the Internet).

The narrower the readership, the easier it is for writers to gauge the likely responses and to find a suitable way to word the communication. They can summon up everything they know about their readers as they write. When writing for people in the same organisation or area of interest, writers will be aware of common concerns, values and conventions that will influence their language choice and form of expression.

With broader or mixed audiences, it is much less obvious how to pitch the message. This is particularly so when the audience is the public at large, as is the case with much Australian government communication.

Primary and secondary audiences

In some contexts there may be both a primary and a secondary audience to consider. For example, an annual report of a government department is written in the first instance for parliament—the primary audience. But it will also be read by the department's staff, by other government agencies, by potential contractors, by other parties interested in or affected by the department's plans and policies, and by journalists and researchers. This broader, sometimes more remote, group is the secondary audience.

The primary audience for the annual report will be familiar with general government processes and terminology, but these may pose problems for outsiders in the secondary audience. If the document is intended to satisfy all its readers, more things will have to be explained and more details given than would be required for a purely in-house audience. The same applies to other government, business or scholarly reports, which are often replete with terms and acronyms that need no explanation for those close to the organisation or field of study but could be problematic for others.

Sometimes it will be the complexity of the information itself that presents challenges. Environmental reports on development proposals are a case in point. Typically prepared by technical and scientific experts for companies or government bodies, these publications necessarily contain detailed research findings that must be precise enough to meet the requirements of informed assessors as well as being intelligible to the members of the community who are interested in how the proposal could affect them.

Careful consideration of the interests and needs of readers is a vital part of publication planning, affecting the scope and structure of the content as well as the form in which it is produced (as discussed in Chapter 1). Writers need to carry this focus through to the detailed level of language, choosing words and sentence structures that will draw the readers—in both their primary and secondary audiences—along with them.

Literacy and access

Writers should also be aware of the very wide range of reading skills amongst the Australian community. Research published in 1995 indicated that 20 per cent of adult Australians had difficulties in reading and extracting verbatim information from a newspaper article (Wickert and Kevin). This research also found lower reading skills amongst those whose work involved little use of the written word, such as in manual work. Figures from the Australian Bureau of Statistics 1996 Census of Population and Housing showed that around 15 per cent of people who spoke a language other than English at home could not speak English well, while 3 per cent did not speak it at all.

These language constraints have been the concern of government White Papers in 1987 (Lo Bianco) and 1991 (Department of Employment, Education and Training), and of the 1996 *National school English literacy survey*. The problem is being addressed in special programs aimed at improving the levels of literacy among both Australian-born and migrant groups within the community. Writers who aim to communicate with the public at large need to bear these reading difficulties in mind, and keep their language simple.

USING THE APPROPRIATE REGISTER

The language used in communicating on any subject can make or break the relationship with the reader. Readers seeking information have a natural interest in the document that provides it. This interest is fostered when the tone of the document suits the subject matter, and when any responses requested of readers are tactfully phrased. The same kind of care is required in printed and electronic communication as in face-to-face encounters.

The scale of register

Registers are the styles of language we adopt in particular situations. By convention we use a relatively high or 'formal' register in the context of, say, a public or religious ceremony, and one that is casual or 'informal' when chatting with friends over lunch. Between those extremes is what we might call the 'standard register'—the language that might be used, for instance, in meetings and work discussions when making plans with colleagues.

Written registers can also be plotted on a scale from formal to informal. At the high end is the language of documents composed to satisfy the formal requirements of official inquiries or to present the results of academic research. Somewhere in the middle is the standard register of professional magazines and training manuals. At the more informal end of the scale, certain types of brochures and advertisements are sometimes composed in an informal register, and it also appears in various contexts in works of fiction.

Underlying the registers associated with different situations and documents are the different relationships or roles of the participants. The degree of remoteness or closeness between those communicating makes the essential difference between formal and informal registers. The register chosen reflects—and constructs—that relationship, hence its importance in communicating.

Registers and relationships with readers

A formal register is the hallmark of distance between participants. The writer may seem to address the reader from a lofty height—which is useful if the document is intended to enforce action, but not so good if it is intended to establish a collaborative relationship. The formal register is also called on by writers who wish to underscore their respect for someone in authority. Here again the style puts distance between writer and reader.

In contrast, the informal register implies closeness between writer and reader. It assumes mutual familiarity and common knowledge of the situation being talked about, so that things do not have to be explained in full. The informal register is geared to consolidating friendly relations rather than to exchanging extensive information.

For many kinds of government and other information documents, a neutral style of communicating is needed, one that puts neither distance nor undue familiarity into the relationship with readers. This is the role of the standard register, which makes no presumptions about its readers, and informs them fully so that they can act independently on that information. It assumes only that the writer and the readers share an interest in the subject.

Language differences in formal, standard and informal registers

Readers immediately recognise the stylistic differences between the following:

> In discussions yesterday, the Federal Cabinet focused on the formulation of amendments to workers' compensation legislation.

> Cabinet ministers yesterday discussed how to word changes to the laws on workers' compensation.

> Yesterday, Canberra pollies worked on the new workers comp laws.

Those three sentences illustrate respectively the formal, standard and informal registers. They differ in length and in the complexity of their language—the words chosen, and the grammatical constructions used.

Formal register

The first of the illustrative sentences above is heavy with long words: 'formulation', 'amendments', 'compensation', 'legislation'. They turn actions into abstractions and help to set a formal and authoritative tone. This is reinforced by the way the words are being used: in dense phrases (like 'workers' compensation legislation') that are then strung together ('the formulation of amendments to workers' compensation legislation'). Both grammar and vocabulary keep readers at arm's length, require more effort to decipher, and may reduce comprehension of what is being said. Indeed, gobbledygook can often be a by-product of would-be formal style. In most contexts, the need to use the formal register can be questioned—particularly given the widespread acceptance of the principles of 'plain English'.

Standard register

The language of the standard register is illustrated in the second sentence in the set of examples above. Its vocabulary is a mix of the official and the everyday, hence the use of 'changes' and 'laws' as well as 'compensation'. This allows it to be read with little effort by a wide range of readers. Writers in the standard register reduce the density of their language by turning phrases into clauses (thus 'the formulation of amendments' becomes 'how to word changes to'), so that actions come across more clearly for everyone. If something is happening, why not say so?

Informal register

The casual nature of the informal register is achieved at some cost to other aspects of communication. There is less precision—as the third illustrative sentence shows when referring to 'pollies' rather than 'ministers' and to what they were doing (just 'worked on'). Also, while the informal register assumes familiarity between writer and readers, many people who speak English as a second language may not understand colloquial terms such as 'pollies' and 'workers comp'.

In any case, colloquialisms often have limited social and regional currency. Some expressions relating to traditionally male sports and recreations ('behind the eight ball', 'upping the ante') may mystify some women readers, while terms readily understood by teenagers may be unknown to some older readers (the newer meaning of 'rage', for example). Similarly, colloquialisms used in one Australian state or territory may be unfamiliar elsewhere ('refidex', for instance—a word used generically for a street directory in Queensland). The informal register therefore needs to be reserved for very specific audiences and situations.

EFFECTIVE COMMUNICATION

Writers who succeed in communicating will have worked to identify their audience, the diversity within it and the kind of language to use in talking to their readers.

Plain English

Although plain English developed as a general-purpose strategy for improving public communication, its relevance is far-reaching. It can be applied successfully to all types of information documents, and its usefulness in communicating with a broad readership is obvious. Plain English roughly equates to the standard register.

In Australia the plain English movement began in the 1970s, and plain English has been specified in federal legislation since 1983. It highlights a number of methods for achieving clear and accessible communication. Among these are the preference for everyday words rather than lofty vocabulary ('buy' rather than 'purchase'; 'people' rather than 'persons'), and for direct rather than indirect grammatical constructions (such as the active voice instead of the passive). Some of the principal precepts of plain English are listed below.

➤ For a discussion of active and passive constructions, see pp. 54–5.

Some plain English guidelines for language choice

- Use familiar, everyday words that readers will understand.

- Be precise, using enough words to achieve clarity but avoiding unnecessary words that can distract from the main points.

- Vary sentence length, but keep to an average of about twenty-two words.

- Prefer the active voice rather than the passive wherever relevant.

- Engage with the audience by using personal pronouns such as 'we' and 'you', except in formal contexts.

- Use verbs in preference to constructions based on nouns derived from verbs ('explain' rather than 'provide an explanation'; 'apply' rather than 'make an application').

- Break up dense strings of nouns or nouns and modifiers (such as 'the outline development plan land package release conditions').

- Avoid euphemisms, clichés, and overused or 'trendy' words or phrases.

- Prefer simple sentence frameworks, avoiding convoluted constructions such as double negatives ('not unlikely', for example).

Further reading on plain English: Robert Eagleson's *Writing in plain English* provides detailed guidance on plain English practices (see p. 285).

Motivating the audience

Beyond the act of communicating, there is sometimes a need to secure readers' cooperation and willingness to act on suggestions or requests—the severest test of the effectiveness of a document and its language.

Transparency and equality

Language that implies equal status between the writer and readers—that treats the audience as intelligent and responsible—is more likely to engage them. This empathy is best expressed through everyday, direct language that clarifies everything readers need to understand. Unfamiliar, formal language may give the impression that information is being withheld or that the response process could be fraught with difficulty.

A positive approach

Putting requests in a positive framework is also important when seeking readers' cooperation. People are much more likely to respond to positive suggestions for action; negative comments often prompt resistance. The following example reads more like a complaint than a proposal for action:

> Without an information campaign directed to specific groups, misunderstanding of the government's intentions may occur, and diminish the level of acceptance of the program.

The comment is more persuasive if written positively:

> The program is likely to achieve the best results if we focus an information campaign on specific groups, to explain the government's intentions and prevent misunderstanding.

Even when unwelcome news is being presented, readers will generally respond better if it is presented in a considerate manner:

> The director has considered your request sympathetically, but is unable to approve the expenditure as it would set a difficult precedent.

This sentence emphasises sympathetic attention before delivering the unwelcome news. Defusing possible negative reactions and promoting positive cooperation are opposite sides of the same coin—and important in achieving effective writing.

Focus

Keeping the spotlight on the main points is another prerequisite for clear communication.

Conciseness

A concise, direct style will help focus readers' attention where it matters. Language that is brisk and lively delivers its message effectively, without taking unnecessary words to do so. No-one likes a laborious style that takes a paragraph to say what might be expressed in a couple of sentences.

Active and passive constructions

The main focus of a sentence is on its first component—typically its subject—as in the following two examples:

The chairman signed the contract this morning.

The contract was signed this morning by the chairman.

The first example is in the active voice, with the subject ('the chairman') undertaking the action. The second sentence is in the passive, where the subject ('the contract') is being acted upon.

Writers may use either active or passive constructions, depending on what needs to be emphasised. However, the active construction generally encourages the use of stronger verbs that bring the activity to life ('signed') whereas the passive involving a part of the verb *to be* and a past participle—'was signed') is less direct. The ability of the active voice to inject vigour and directness into prose underlies the plain-English preference for this type of construction wherever relevant.

The passive may at times cause ambiguity by submerging responsibility for an action when a more open approach would be clearer and fairer to readers. Compare the following sentences, where the first example leaves open the questions of whether an investigation will be undertaken and who will be responsible for it:

Further investigation will be required to determine the cause of the electrical failure. [passive]

Our maintenance section will investigate the cause of the electrical failure. [active]

Again, there will be times when the passive is the only suitable construction, but remember that misuse of the passive to produce deliberate ambiguity may antagonise readers.

INCLUSIVE COMMUNICATION

Legal requirements

Australia's commitment to inclusiveness is embodied in both federal and state laws. They include the federal *Racial Discrimination Act 1975*, *Sex Discrimination Act 1984*, *Human Rights and Equal Opportunity Commission Act 1986* and *Disability Discrimination Act 1992*, as well as the various state Acts relating to equal opportunity and anti-discrimination. Under this legislation, it is generally unlawful to discriminate on the grounds of race, colour, national or ethnic origin, gender, or physical or mental capabilities.

Linguistic discrimination can take various forms that may marginalise or exclude particular segments of the population—whether unwittingly or not. Stereotypical description of any group of people or a member of an identifiable group is probably the most insidious. There is no place in public documents for uninformed, prejudiced or merely insensitive references of this type. When referring to an individual, that person's sex, religion, nationality, racial group, age or physical or mental characteristics should only be mentioned if this information is pertinent to the discussion. Similarly, any group characteristics should be applied with care.

Writers, editors, designers and other communicators should always bear in mind the diversity within their audiences, and ensure that references to and about particular people or social groups are couched in inclusive terms.

Australian cultural diversity

The historical pattern of colonisation and immigration to Australia has made Anglo-Celtic culture mainstream and the English language dominant. Yet changing patterns of immigration, especially since the late 1940s, have increased the proportion of the Australian population born overseas to almost 25 per cent. At least 50 per cent of the immigrants to Australia in the two decades from 1980 to 2000 came from countries where English is not the national language. Many Indigenous Australians also speak English as a second language.

The cultural and linguistic diversity arising both from immigration and from Australia's Indigenous heritage call for sensitivity on the part of communicators. This goes beyond the need to express public information in plain English (page 53) to ensuring inclusiveness in general, and equity in any references to particular ethnic groups.

References to ethnic groups

Generic expressions

For inclusive reference, particularly in government or other types of information documents, generic terms can be ideal—provided they really represent the population in full. The word *Australian* refers naturally to all communities within Australia, embracing those born here and those who migrated here to take up citizenship.

Indigenous is a similarly useful, short generic reference covering all Aboriginal and Torres Strait Islander peoples. It is a subset of the broader term 'Australian', and is widely acceptable for this purpose. However, the term 'non-Indigenous' should generally be avoided as a way of distinguishing between Australia's original inhabitants and other Australians, as it can be viewed as unnecessarily divisive.

The generic words *migrants* and *immigrants* are probably the most useful in reference to newcomers to Australia, as they make no assumptions about a person's culture or language. However, their use should be phased out once these people have settled and become Australian citizens. Otherwise, these words seem to impose a temporary or marginal status on them within the community.

Terms such as 'ethnics' and 'ethnic Australians' raise some problems of meaning. They should be avoided when they could be seen as implying a 'them and us' distinction, where the suggestion is that migrants are exotic or strange by comparison with people in the mainstream. When used in a straightforward, descriptive way, however—as in 'ethnic and racial groups'—there is no problem.

In generic references to migrants whose mother tongue is not English, the acronym 'LOTE' ('language other than English') is more generally acceptable than 'NESB' ('non-English speaking background'). This is because the latter seems to make using English the reference point for everyone and creates an unnecessary negative for those who do not.

'Indigenous': Always capitalise 'Indigenous' when it refers to the original inhabitants of Australia—as in 'Indigenous Australians' and 'Indigenous communities'. It needs no capitals when used in a general sense to refer to the original inhabitants of other countries. (See p. 57 for more detailed terminology recommended by the Aboriginal and Torres Strait Islander Commission.)

Specific names

Aboriginal and Torres Strait Islander peoples

The most precise and inclusive collective reference for Indigenous Australians preferred by the Aboriginal and Torres Strait Islander Commission (ATSIC) is:

Aboriginal and Torres Strait Islander peoples

This form is recommended as the prime reference in official documents. Other group terms that are also acceptable—but not comprehensive—are:

Aboriginal people(s)

Australian Aboriginals

Torres Strait Islanders

In reference to an individual, ATSIC recommends *Aboriginal* and *Torres Strait Islander* as the nouns to use. These same words are recommended as the adjectives as well.

The words 'Aboriginal' and 'Aborigine' are always capitalised when used in reference to Australian Aboriginal people, but not when they refer to the original inhabitants of other continents. (Note that the term 'native' is best avoided in reference to the indigenous peoples of any country, because of its connotations of primitiveness.)

Rather than broad generic descriptions, many Aboriginal groups prefer to identify themselves in local terms drawn from their own languages. The most widely used local terms, and the areas to which they apply, are as follows:

Koori *or* Koorie:	South-eastern Australia (*Koori* is standard in New South Wales; in Victoria it varies with *Koorie*)
Nunga:	South Australia
Nyoongah *or* Nyungar:	South-west Western Australia (*Nyoongah* is the spelling used by Aboriginal writers from the region; *Nyungar* is the scholarly spelling)
Anangu:	Central Australia
Murri:	Queensland
Yolngu:	Arnhem region, Northern Territory

Within these areas, Aboriginal people identify with particular language groups, such as Warlpiri, Arrernte (Aranda) and Pitjantjatjara, the most widely spoken of the 150 Aboriginal languages still used.

Torres Strait Islanders also have more specific identities, such as the Meriam-speaking people of the eastern Torres Strait Islands.

These regional and linguistic names are used within the Indigenous community, and can also be used by those outside it whenever a specific group is being referred to. However, great care must be taken not to misapply them. 'Koori' is not a synonym for 'Aboriginal', and should not be applied to groups gathered from various parts of Australia.

'Aboriginal(s)' or 'Aborigine(s)'? For government publications, follow the ATSIC preference for 'Aboriginals'. While usage research shows that 'Aborigine(s)' is used in a wide range of publications without disparaging overtones, sensitivity to a group's preferences should be a major consideration when writing about them.

Comprehensive terms: When referring to Indigenous groups from around the country, use the generic term 'Aboriginal and Torres Strait Islander peoples'. (For subsequent comprehensive references, the more succinct 'Indigenous peoples' is generally acceptable.)

Immigrants

Where it is relevant to the discussion, immigrant groups can be named by reference to their (previous) nationality or region of origin—'Americans', 'Spanish', 'Vietnamese', 'Kurds' and 'Welsh', for example. Similarly, neutral terms referring to ethnic identity and religious affiliation such as 'Jews', 'Muslims' and 'Buddhists' are acceptable if these factors are pertinent to the discussion. All such words are capitalised.

Be careful to avoid equating linguistic or ethnic groups with particular religious beliefs. Not all Lebanese people in Australia are Muslims, for instance, and not all Muslims are Arabs.

If comparisons are to be drawn between ethnic groups in Australia, it is more equitable to describe them using similar categories—for example, 'Italo-Australians' and 'Anglo-Australians' rather than 'Italo-Australians' and 'Australians'.

Personal names

References to individuals by name are a further point on which sensitivity is required if documents are to be inclusive and accommodate cultural diversity. Many naming systems in the world differ from that used in English-speaking countries, where given names precede family names.

Some Asian cultures, including the Chinese, Japanese and Vietnamese, present the family name first, as in *Wong Hei* or *Takeshi Noboyuki*—though this is not obvious when the names themselves are unfamiliar. The situation is complicated by the fact that the owners of these names may reverse the order when in an English-speaking context (as *Hei Wong, Noboyuki Takeshi*), anticipating the possible confusion for English-speakers.

Further reading on conventions for non-English names: See p. 286 for bibliographic details of Robert Hyslop's book *Dear you: a guide to forms of address*.

In ascertaining the names of people from other cultures, it is important to use the terms *given name* and *family name*, not 'Christian name', 'first name', 'forename' or 'surname', all of which presume the standard European naming conventions and order of names.

Inclusive treatment of the sexes

Since the 1980s, many areas of sexism in language have been highlighted and addressed, including asymmetry (unequal treatment of men and women), stereotyping of gender roles (the woman as housewife and mother; the man as breadwinner), and gratuitous references to personal characteristics (usually dwelling on a woman's physical appearance). Strategies for tackling the problem have been various, but the most inclusive solution for general purposes is to avoid references to someone's sex, sexuality or marital status except where it is the issue under discussion.

Sex-neutral references to individuals

In English, neutrality is not so easy to attain, because the pronoun system obliges us to choose between masculine and feminine forms (*he, his, him; she, her, her*) in ny singular reference. A selection is necessary even when the subject is generic, s in:

> Every candidate must provide copies of the application to his/her referees.

n the past, the notion of the 'generic masculine' would have dictated the use of is' in that sentence. This usage is now deemed unacceptable and liable to bias eaders towards thinking of a male candidate rather than a female one. The roblem can be avoided by adapting the wording in any one of a number of ways, s suggested below.

Options for avoiding gender-specific pronouns

- Recast the sentence in the plural:

   > Candidates must provide copies of the application to their referees.

- Leave the pronoun out altogether:

   > Every candidate must provide copies of the application to referees.

- Recast the sentence to avoid pronouns:

   > Copies of the application must be provided to referees.

- Repeat the noun:

   > Every candidate must provide copies of the application to the candidate's referees.

- Use the alternative pronouns *his or her* or *his/her* (or *her/his*):

   > Every candidate must provide copies of the application to his or her referees.

   > Every candidate must provide copies of the application to his/her referees.

- Use the gender-free pronoun *you*:

   > You must provide copies of the application to your referees.

- Use the gender-free plural pronoun *they*:

   > They must provide copies of the application to their referees.

➤ Also see p. 76 for the evolving use with some singular subjects of the pronoun *their* (based on notional rather than formal agreement).

Jot all alternatives work equally well for a given sentence, with some options roducing less elegant results than others. In some circumstances, a further lternative—use of the pronoun *s/he*—could be a possibility; however, it works nly for the subject of a verb, not for the object or the possessive form required in he sample sentence. Clearly, there is plenty of choice to suit different contexts.

Occupational titles

Many traditional terms for particular occupations embody the suffix *-man*—for xample, 'businessman', 'policeman', 'salesman' and 'tradesman'. These terms were ccepted in the past when men typically filled those roles, but also because the vord *man* was regarded as a generic term for both sexes. With women now outinely undertaking roles once performed exclusively by men, the use of 'man' in uch titles seems out of step.

Gender-free terms for most working roles are included in *Australian standard classification of occupations* (Australian Bureau of Statistics 1997). A few examples are given below, with those in the right-hand column recommended as replacements for the traditional gender-specific terms on the left:

Gender-specific term	ABS standard term
policeman	police officer
clergyman	minister of religion
fireman	fire-fighter
foreman	supervisor
milkman	milk vendor

The principle of avoiding gender-specific occupational terms means those that specify women should also be set aside. Thus 'actress', 'manageress' and 'waitress' are better replaced by 'actor', 'manager' and 'waiter'. The use of gender-specific modifiers, as in 'woman doctor' or 'male nurse', should only be used where the information is essential to the context.

Compounds that use -*person* have been successfully established in preference to those ending in -*woman* in quite a few cases, such as 'chairperson' (rather than 'chairwoman'), 'spokesperson', 'layperson', 'craftsperson', 'sportsperson' and 'storeperson'. However, usage research shows that very few of these types of compounds—only 'salesperson' and 'tradesperson'—are also used in reference to men in the same roles. These examples apart, the most usable inclusive occupational terms are those that foreground the occupation itself, whether old or new, as in 'doctor', 'drafter', 'artist', 'solicitor', 'programmer' and 'technician'.

Occupational compounds with -*master* are also open to query. In this respect, the recently coined 'web manager' is probably preferable to 'web master', for example.

References to people with a disability

Both generic and specific terms tend to highlight the problems suffered by those with disabilities, as in 'the disabled' or 'the blind'. This form of expression is felt by those concerned to overshadow everything else about them as people, hence their preference for paraphrases that turn things around, such as:

person with a disability

musician with a vision impairment

Lengthy expressions like these may still need abbreviation in subsequent reference (if these are frequent). However, their use as the primary reference helps to foreground the person rather than the disability.

Sight and hearing impairments

The term 'people with a vision impairment' covers a wide range, from those who are partially sighted to those with no useful sight. People belonging to the first group are not 'blind', and with aids to vision will be able to read documents in some visual form. The second group must rely on alternative modes of communication, using aural or tactile channels.

People with a hearing impairment' also embraces a range of people, from those with limited hearing to those with none at all. While they have no problem with print, the inclusion of any aural material—for example in a CD-ROM—may restrict their access.

Among themselves, many deaf people use the Australian sign language (Auslan), and thereby define themselves as members of a language group that is equivalent, say, to Dutch or Yiddish. On this basis, they use the term *Deaf* (with a capital letter) affirmatively as a mark of identity (as in 'the Deaf community'), and would encourage others to do the same.

➤ See Chapter 23 for ways in which publications can be made more accessible for people with different types of disabilities.

Other physical disabilities

Presenting material in both printed and electronic form is usually the most helpful approach to assist people with mobility or manipulation disabilities to gain access to publications.

There are few conventional ways of succinctly referring to problems of manipulation and mobility except as a form of handicap. Again the problem of drawing undue attention to the disability arises with terms such as 'a quadriplegic', although the word itself is relatively neutral. Where there is space to do so, a person's capacity rather than disability can be underscored, as in the following example from news reporting:

> One of the day's most popular [torch] runners was——, a disabled student from St Peter's College, who has become a talented and versatile junior athlete.

Mental disabilities

People with an intellectual disability or brain injury may require help from others in accessing public information, whereas those with a psychiatric disorder may not. Because these types of disabilities are so individual, there are few satisfactory non-technical ways of referring to them. (Note, however, that 'schizophrenia' is a particular type of psychiatric disorder, not a generic term for all psychiatric problems.)

Inclusive treatment of the age range

Australia is an aging society, with a declining birth rate and nearly one in five people aged over sixty. The middle-aged and elderly sections of the population are growing faster than the younger, which has important implications for public communication and the ways in which people of any age are talked about.

References to older and younger people

In the interests of inclusiveness, the language of a publication designed for a broad readership needs to be as timeless and ageless as possible. Both old-fashioned idiom and trendy expressions tend to limit the accessibility of the text to readers across the age range.

References to age should not be used gratuitously, and should always be couched in widely acceptable terms. While the collective term *older people* may be suitable in some contexts, it must be remembered that 'old' is a relative term and needs to be used with care. Perhaps more specific or neutral ways of describing older people can be found in adjectives such as *retired* and *elderly*, the latter being used also in expressions such as 'the elderly' and 'elder care'. The adjective 'senior' is less useful as a generic description because of its use in other contexts (the 'senior partner'; 'senior' to them). But in institutionalised phrases such as 'senior citizens' or 'a seniors card', it presents no problem.

At the youthful end of the age range, the most neutral terms are *young people* and *youth* itself, the latter serving as modifier in terms such as 'youth wages' and 'youth consultation'. Note that while 'youth' is gender-free, it becomes specific to males in the plural. 'Youths' is somewhat negative in its connotations. *Adolescents* and *children* could also be used, where appropriate, for teenagers and pre-teenagers.

Equal opportunity legislation requires that age should not be used to exclude applicants from being considered for a particular position. Job advertisements should therefore focus on the type and extent of qualifications and experience being sought rather than make any assumptions about the age of candidates who might possess such expertise.

CHECKLIST FOR EFFECTIVE AND INCLUSIVE LANGUAGE

- Have the language and sentence structures been designed to accommodate the needs of readers in both your primary and secondary audiences?

- Does the register suit the material and the readership, and have the principles of plain English been followed wherever relevant?

- Is the language suitably inclusive, and have any likely sensitivities amongst the audience been taken into account?

- Have you checked to ensure that there are no gratuitous or stereotypical references in discussions about people?

- If there are any suggestions for action, have these been expressed in positive rather than negative terms?

Chapter 5 Grammar

GRAMMAR AND WRITING	**64**
Order and clarity	64
Style and choice	65
GRAMMATICAL VARIATION	**66**
Transfer	66
Clauses and alternative constructions	67
Agreement	67
About word classes	68
SOME FREQUENTLY ASKED QUESTIONS	**72**
'A' or 'an'	72
'And' or 'but' to start a sentence	72
'Because' and other subordinators to start a sentence	72
'Data'	73
'Fewer' and 'less'	73
'Get' passives	73
'Having said that' (dangling or hanging participles)	74
'Hopefully' as a sentence adverb	74
'However' as a conjunction	74
'It's' and other contractions	75
'That' and 'which'	75
'They', 'them' and 'their' as singular pronouns	75
'To' (the split infinitive)	76
'Were' (the subjunctive)	76
'Whom'	77
'Whose'	77
'With' and other prepositions to end a sentence	77

Grammar is both everything we know about the structure of English and a challenging technical field couched in specialist terminology. Its full scope could certainly not be covered in a brief chapter. The focus here is therefore on achieving clarity in construction, and on understanding the roles played by the basic building blocks of grammar—the various word classes. Responses to some common queries about grammar are also given, founded on extensive usage research into Australian English.

Grammar underpins the meaning of words as soon as we put two or more words together. Sometimes, however—and particularly where clarity is not at issue—grammatical choices may be not so much a matter of right and wrong as about the style best suited to the particular communication, its readers, and the relationship the writer wishes to build with them.

GRAMMAR AND WRITING

Grammar settles the order of words, the associations between them, and the meaning they create. Compare 'The fly flies out' with 'The flies fly out'. Two different meanings (a single fly and a swarm) are constructed by adjusting the order of the same set of words.

In the same way, grammar allows us to connect ideas in longer sentences:

> At the end of the nymphal stage, adult mayflies emerge for a few brief hours of flight, during which time they must mate to secure the next generation.

Despite the various points it has to make, this sentence connects each idea with the next in a meaningful way. The underlying grammar creates a logical sequence to lead readers forward.

Order and clarity

Sentences work cumulatively. The longer they are, the more they demand of the underlying grammar. It must connect elements of the same phrase or clause as well as clarify the boundaries between them, to prevent ambiguity along the way. Yet problems can occur even in a relatively short sentence like the following:

> Enigmatic to his final day, Australia has lost its finest batsman.

We recognise what the reporter was trying to say about the famous Don Bradman; however, the order within the sentence seems to connect the phrase 'enigmatic to his final day' with 'Australia', and thus strains the logic. The intended connection with 'its finest batsman' is impaired by other elements of the sentence coming in between. By altering the order of items in the sentence, clarity is restored:

> Australia has lost its finest batsman, enigmatic to the last.

➤ The problem of unattached phrases at the start of a sentence is further discussed under 'Having said that' p. 74.

Unattached phrases or clauses can also create ambiguity later in a sentence, as in:

> Lipolysis can occur in the milk of cows when chilled too quickly.

In this sentence, the word order separates the final phrase 'when chilled too quickly' from the word 'milk', creating the distracting idea that the cows may get chilled too quickly. Again, with a simple change of order, the grammar of the sentence underscores the point intended:

> Lipolysis can occur in cows' milk when (it is) chilled too quickly.

An extra word or two, as in that revised example, may sometimes help to make the meaning clearer as well.

Writers who want to put two parallel ideas into the same sentence also need to check the order of words to ensure that the phrasing supports rather than hinders the parallelism. In the following sentence, the intended parallel structures (introduced by *neither* and *nor*) are at odds with the sequence of words:

> The committee would consent *neither* to adopting the new policy *nor* reaffirm the old one.

By ensuring that *neither* and *nor* preface the same type of word, the parallelism can be underscored by the grammar to make a more elegant sentence altogether:

> The committee would *neither* consent to the new policy *nor* reaffirm the old one.

These examples demonstrate how care in forming the connections between each element in a sentence enables writers to use the underlying grammar to clarify meaning and communicate effectively.

Style and choice

In addition to providing structure, grammar is a resource for creating alternative styles or registers (as discussed in Chapter 4). The choice between active and passive constructions—both entirely acceptable grammatically—has an impact on the style of a document. Similarly, deciding whether to use *fewer* or *less* with a plural noun such as 'opportunities' is more a matter of style than of grammar—a preference for either the formal or the standard construction (see page 73). The choice of singular or plural after *none* is likewise mostly a matter of style. Compare:

➤ See p. 54 for a discussion of active and passive constructions.

> None of them is prepared to commit any funds to the project.

> None of them are prepared to commit any funds to the project.

The use of the singular 'is' in the first example makes for more formal style than the use of 'are'. The first insists on a strict interpretation of 'none' as 'not one' (and therefore singular) whereas the second takes the whole phrase 'none of them' as plural, referring to several people or groups.

➤ The issue of singular or plural agreement arises with several other kinds of construction: see pp. 67 and 71–3.

There is nothing ungrammatical about the plural with *none*: *The Oxford English dictionary* (1989) shows that it has been the more usual construction for a hundred years. It is probably more common in speech and everyday styles of writing than in formal publications, where writers and editors tend to select constructions that conform to the strictest grammatical canons. In doing so, however, they may distance their writing from more straightforward communication.

Writing does not need to be formal to communicate effectively. Sometimes a formal style may even make a document more difficult for some of its readers to understand. When the aim is to reach a broad public, using everyday expressions and grammatical constructions is a sensible, strategic choice from the range of approaches available in English grammar.

GRAMMATICAL VARIATION

Within the accepted grammatical structures, there are some large areas of variability that help to account for some of the debates about grammatical usage. They include:

- transfer (the movement of words from one word class to another)
- clause structure (alternative constructions of sentences)
- agreement (matching the use of singular and plural forms).

Transfer

Many English words function in more than one grammatical class. The word *hand* is both noun and verb, *after* is a preposition as well as a conjunction, *close* is an adjective, verb and adverb. Dictionaries show these well-established uses but find it hard to keep up with every new grammatical use, especially the tendency to make verbs out of nouns.

English has permitted noun–verb transfers since before Shakespeare's time, and he himself was a master of it, with examples like the 'unchilding, unfathering depths'. There are many examples of nouns of one syllable being moved into new verb roles, as in 'scoping the project', and two-syllable nouns such as *access* and *impact* are now widely used as verbs in institutional discourse—despite reactions from some people outside it. The verbal use is always clear in the grammar of the sentence:

The cuts in interest rates have impacted on many industries.

The use of 'cut' as a noun rather than a verb is likewise perfectly clear in that sentence. Such transfers usually express their meaning economically and clearly, so that even those encountering them for the first time will get the point.

Formal styles are usually bound by a conservative approach to language that resists changing usage. However, an understanding of the ways in which language evolves helps writers and editors to craft publications for a broad readership using familiar, accessible words and constructions. New word transfers should not be overdone, but neither should they be dismissed out of hand when they express an idea neatly.

Clauses and alternative constructions

The kernel of any sentence is its one or more clauses, each embodying a verb. In the previous sentence the two clauses hinge on 'is' (a finite verb with a specific tense), and 'embodying' (a participle, which is non-finite). Non-finite clauses are dependent on the finite ones, and usually house subordinate or supporting detail for something in the finite clause. But writers can always choose whether to make the detail into a finite or non-finite clause, and indeed whether to keep the clauses within the same sentence or to put them into successive ones, as in:

> The kernel of any sentence is its one or more clauses. Each one embodies a verb.

The order of clauses is not fixed grammatically, and should be decided in terms of the intended focus of the discussion. The location of the subordinate clause in the following example depends on whether the writer wants to highlight the process or the outcome:

> The resolution was passed today, although some participants abstained from voting.

> Although some participants abstained from voting, the resolution was passed today.

The option of using *although* (a subordinating conjunction) or *but* (the equivalent coordinating conjunction) is also up to the writer:

> The resolution was passed today, but some participants abstained.

When *but* is used, the two clauses are equally weighted as main clauses, whereas *although* makes the comment about 'some participants' subordinate to the main clause about passing the resolution.

Agreement

Within any clause, the verb must match (or agree with) its subject in terms of singular or plural, as in:

> The office *is* vacant.   The offices *are* vacant.

Similarly, a pronoun should agree with the relevant noun in terms of singular or plural:

> The office gives *its* occupants a view of the park.

> The offices give *their* occupants a view of the park.

This pronoun agreement may also connect with words in a previous clause or sentence, as in:

> The office is vacant. *It* is ideal for us.

The two main kinds of agreement in English are 'formal' and 'notional' agreement. Formal agreement is visible in the matched singular or plural forms of the words in the preceding examples, and is the type of agreement used in most contexts. However, take a sentence such as:

> The police have been alerted.

Here, the plural verb is based on the notion that the word 'police' refers to many officers of the law, even though the word is singular in form. This is notional agreement rather than formal agreement. (continued on p. 71)

ABOUT

Word classes

There are eight major word classes used in modern English grammar. These are discussed in alphabetical order, and examples are given. Some subsidiary terms associated with each class are also explained.

Note that many words do not belong solely to one class, but can be pulled into service in others for the purpose of a particular sentence. (The transfer of words from one word class to another is discussed on page 66.)

Adjective

The role of adjectives is to describe, define or evaluate an adjacent noun:

> a *cool* day
>
> a *French* cheese
>
> an *awful* sound

In a string of two or three adjectives, the order is normally the evaluative first, followed by the descriptive and then the definitive:

> a heavy black steel door
>
> the best Australian minds

(For advice on the use of commas in strings of adjectives, see page 102.)

Comparative adjectives are formed in two different ways, depending mostly on how many syllables they contain:

- One-syllable adjectives take the comparative endings *-er* and *-est*, as in:

> cool … cooler … coolest
>
> large … larger … largest

- Adjectives with three or more syllables are preceded by *more* and *most*:

> descriptive … more descriptive … most descriptive

- Those with two syllables are a mixed bag. Ones ending in *-y* usually take the comparative endings, whereas others take *more* and *most*:

> easy … easier … easiest
>
> grateful … more grateful … most grateful

Less and *least* are the equivalents of *more* and *most* when comparing downwards for all adjectives, no matter how many syllables.

Adverb

Adverbs include a wide range of words that modify not only verbs (as the name suggests) but also adjectives and other adverbs. For example:

> come *quickly*
>
> *most* competent
>
> *very* soon

Two other kinds of adverb can modify a whole sentence:

- attitudinal adverbs, as in

> *Perhaps* it will come today.
>
> *Fortunately* there is still time.

- conjuncts such as *hence*, *however*, *therefore*, *thus*. These connect a sentence with the one before it, as in the following sequence

> The question keeps being raised in parliament. It is *therefore* in the public domain and must be answered.

Adverbs that are based on adjectives end in *-ly* (for example, *quickly*, *fortunately*). Depending on the idiom, certain of these may appear either with or without this suffix:

> It came *close*.
>
> They were *closely* watched.

Conjunction

Conjunctions join smaller parts of sentences together. Some make the two parts equal in status (coordinating them), while others effectively give lower grammatical status to what follows (subordinating it). The parts that are joined may consist of phrases or clauses.

oordinating conjunctions are a small
et that includes *and*, *but*, *or* and *nor*.
ubordinating conjunctions are a larger
roup, indicating such things as:

- time—*as, after, before, since, when,
  while*

- reason and cause—*as, because,
  since, so*

- condition—*if, in case, provided
  (that), unless, whether*

- concession—*although, though,
  whereas.*

While the use of conjunctions at the
tart of sentences is sometimes
ueried, such placement is often
ntirely appropriate (see pages 72–4).

eterminer

eterminers, which form a more
ecently recognised word class (used in
p-to-date grammars and dictionaries),
clude:

- articles such as *the, a, an*

- pronouns such as *my, your, this,
  that, some, any*

- numerals such as *three, four, third,
  fourth.*

hese determiners all work in much the
ame way in noun phrases. For
xample:

the only solution

my best offer

this document

the fourth chapter

eterminers always appear before any
djectives that modify the noun (as in
he first two examples).

Noun

Nouns provide the names for tangible
and visible things such as *tree, sand,
lizard, skiing*, as well as abstract
notions such as *help, information,
sorrow, wish*.

Many nouns represent individual items
that can be counted and made plural—
for example, *tree(s), lizard(s), wish(es)*.
This makes them 'count nouns'.

Other nouns, both concrete and
abstract, are concepts that cannot be
made plural—for example, *skiing, help,
information*. These are called 'mass
nouns'.

Some nouns have both concrete and
more abstract senses and can be used
as either a count or mass noun.
Compare 'Don't count your chickens
before they're hatched' with 'There's
chicken for dinner'.

Plural nouns are usually formed with *-s*
or *-es*. Words borrowed from languages
other than English may have their
plurals formed in the same way or may
retain foreign plurals. Sometimes (as
explained more fully on page 81), both
forms are recognised, as in:

referendum ... referenda *or* referendums

Possessive nouns in the singular are
usually formed with an apostrophe plus
s, as in *lizard's skin*. Plural nouns that
are possessive take the apostrophe
alone: *lizards' skins*. However, the
apostrophe is not needed when the
plural functions as a descriptor rather
than a possessor of what follows, as in
visitors book. (For more on the
descriptive use of plural nouns, see
pages 86–7.)

Preposition

Prepositions indicate relationships with
nouns (in time, space or the abstract
worlds of thought):

after lunch

with the reporter

under no circumstances

Common prepositions such as *by, for,
in, of* and *to* are used to chain phrases
together, as in:

This was agreed *by* the Minister *for*
Immigration *in* recent discussions *of* the
problem.

Some prepositions double as adverbs,
and may then appear at the end of a
sentence. For example:

The new enterprise has gone *under*.

That is where they are *up to*.

(See page 77 for further discussion of
prepositions at the end of sentences.)

Pronoun

Pronouns stand in for nouns and noun
phrases already mentioned (or about to
be mentioned) in a text.

Personal pronouns include *I, you, he,
she, we* and *they*, and the impersonal *it*
is usually added in with them. All
except *you* and *it* have different forms
according to whether they represent
the subject of the sentence or not.
Compare:

I received a letter.

The letter made *me* laugh.

The letter was addressed to *me*.

(Possessive forms such as *my, our, his* and
her are classed as determiners because of
their different grammatical role.)

Demonstrative pronouns such as *this*, *that*, *these* and *those* can substitute for nouns, noun phrases or whole sentences. For example:

> The yellow kiwifruit are imported; *these* are locally grown.

> He says he will endorse the Bill. *That* is what we've been waiting for.

Relative pronouns such as *that*, *who* and *which* represent things, people or situations mentioned earlier in the sentence:

> The swollen river carried a lot of the soil *that* had been loosened by bulldozing upstream.

The relative pronoun *whom*, available when the person is the object of the verb or preposition, is increasingly restricted in its use. (See page 77 for a discussion of changing usage.)

The relative pronoun *whose* is the possessive form. It is used to refer both to people and to things (again, see page 77).

Verb

Verbs express actions or processes (for example, *speak*, *grow*), or states of being (especially with the verbs *have* and *be*).

Verbs change their form or add endings (*-t* or *-ed*) to show the past tense. For example:

> stand … stood teach … taught
>
> drive … drove ring … rang
>
> build … built wait … waited
>
> pass … passed finish … finished

(For a discussion of verbs with alternative past forms, see pages 82–3.)

For many English verbs, the past tense form is used for the past participle as well. For example:

> She *built* the organisation.

> She has *built* the organisation.

These are the regular verbs. Irregular ones use a different form for the past participle, as in:

> He drove to the city.

> He has *driven* to the city.

The past participle is also used in passive constructions, where the action is carried out by someone other than the subject, as in:

> The organisation has been *built*.

> He was *driven* to the city.

All verbs use the ending *-ing* for the so-called present participle, which signifies continuing rather than completed action at the time being spoken of:

> She is *building* the organisation.

> He was *driving* to the city.

The *-ing* participle also serves as an adjective, as in *the driving force*, and is identical with the verbal noun (also called a 'gerund') as in *she likes driving*.

The infinitive is the same for all verbs, and is expressed either with *to* or without it (the 'bare infinitive') depending on the construction:

> They were unable *to agree*.

> They could never *agree*.

Subjunctive forms of verbs are now rather uncommon. The so-called present subjunctive can still be found in mandative sentences (those that express some necessity or requirement):

> The bureau demands that he *pay* the difference.

> It is a requirement that every child *wear* a hat in summer.

The only surviving form of the past subjunctive (*were*) is no longer regularly used in conditional statements (see page 76).

Choices between formal and notional agreement arise with:

    collective nouns and names
    compound subjects
    complex subjects.

Collective nouns and names

A choice between formal and notional agreement needs to be made with collective words for groups, such as:

    clergy   committee   crowd   family   government   orchestra   team

Singular or plural agreement may be used, depending on whether the meaning relates to the group as a whole or to the individuals within it. Compare:

> The family is the basic social unit.

> His family are not inclined to comment.

A similar choice presents itself with the proper names of organisations:

> The Bureau of Meteorology has/have been quick to respond.

> Longman has/have published the book.

When a company name ends in s (and looks like a plural word), it may nevertheless take singular agreement:

> Woolworths is/are advertising its/their new stock.

Singular or plural agreement for organisations' names? While either singular or plural agreement is grammatically correct, the singular is recommended in Commonwealth publications—both for consistency, and to present a cohesive image in references to government bodies and activities.

Compound subjects

When two subjects are coordinated with *and*, the verb following it is often, but not necessarily, plural. Compare:

> Queensland and Victoria *are* competing for the contract.

> Their bread and butter *comes* from government contracts.

The second example shows how things that are regularly combined as a single unit may well take singular agreement.

When the subjects are joined by other linking words known as 'quasi-coordinators'—such as *together with* or *as well as*—the linked element becomes subsidiary to the main subject and should be set apart with commas. The verb should then agree with the main subject:

> The principal, together with the rest of the staff, *is* attending the meeting.

> As well as the horses, the sheepdog *is* to be sold.

Complex subjects

Writers often make use of complex noun phrases in expressing their subject, as in:

> *The outcome of all their discussions* was an innovative policy.

In such cases, the headword of the noun phrase ('outcome') normally decides the pattern of agreement. But when the phrase is an indefinite expression—such as *a lot of, a group of, a number of, a range of*—plural agreement is normal, despite the singular form of the headword:

> A number of people *have* objected to the plan.

For definite expressions of the same kind, however, the singular is usual:

> The number of people objecting *has* been less than expected.

In other expressions of quantity, notional rather than formal agreement can also be used:

> Fifty tonnes [of rice] *is* all that is needed.

SOME FREQUENTLY ASKED QUESTIONS

'A' or 'an'

The choice between these two forms is made on the basis of the first *sound* of the following word. If this is a vowel sound (whether the first letter is a vowel or not), then *an* is the one to use:

> an elephant   an hour   an honour

If the following word starts with a consonant sound, use *a*:

> a helicopter   a hotel   a union

The same applies with initialisms and acronyms:

➤ For a full discussion of initialisms, acronyms and other types of shortened forms, see Chapter 10.

> a GST requirement   a UNESCO committee
>
> an MC   an RAN frigate   an ASIO employee

Some speakers and writers nevertheless give special treatment to words of three or more syllables beginning with *h*, and so are inclined to use 'an hypothesis', 'an historical event'. This is a matter of taste and tradition, but not a grammatical requirement.

'And' or 'but' to start a sentence

Objections are raised from time to time when coordinating conjunctions such as *and* or *but* appear at the start of a sentence. In that position they cannot join anything, but they do connect with the meaning of the previous sentence, and in the case of *but* would contrast with it.

> I'll argue the case. But only if you'll back me up.

➤ See pp. 68–9 for a description of adverbs, conjuncts and conjunctions.

In this position, *but* is in fact working as a conjunct (a connective type of adverb) and forging a logical link with something stated before. Thus *and* and *but* have a conjunct role as well as that of conjunction, and may therefore be used to start sentences.

'Because' and other subordinators to start a sentence

The idea that words like *because, although, since* and *while* cannot be used at the start of a sentence seems to arise out of a mistaken assumption that, because conjunctions join phrases or clauses together, they must have words on either side of them. This does not happen at the start of a sentence, hence this odd prescription. The reality is that a subordinating conjunction goes with the subordinate clause, wherever it is placed:

> We notified the secretary because he is the person responsible.

> Because he is the person responsible, we notified the secretary.

These perfectly grammatical sentences show the subordinating conjunction at two different points in the sentence, prefacing the explanatory clause ('he is the person responsible'). Explanatory and other subordinate clauses (such as those with *if* and *when*) can certainly be used at the front of a sentence, and the conjunction will then be the first word.

'Data'

With *data*, *media* and other classical Greek and Latin loan words whose plurals end in *a*, the question is whether they should be constrained by their classical past as far as grammar is concerned or reflect their English present. In English, *data* is used both as a plural and a singular noun:

> These data come from several sources.

> This data looks promising.

The second example shows that *data* works as a mass noun in English just like *information* (see page 69). Both kinds of construction are well established.

'Fewer' and 'less'

The issue of choosing between *fewer* and *less* with plural nouns is readily resolved in the context of the intended register. In formal writing, *fewer* is used with a plural count noun, and *less* is reserved for the singular mass noun (see page 69):

> fewer positions   less unemployment

This distinction goes back little more than a century, and does not hold for the corresponding word *more*, which is used with both plural count nouns and singular mass nouns ('more retrenchments', 'more unemployment'). Both points help to explain why speakers often use *less* with plural count nouns as well ('less positions', 'less unemployment') and why this use of *less* is at home in more relaxed kinds of writing.

'Get' passives

Widespread objections to the verb *get* probably result from its many different uses in spoken language—as a synonym for words such as 'fetch', 'bring', 'receive', 'gain', 'become' and 'understand'. These more specific words provide a variety of alternatives for use in writing and especially in formal publications.

However, in certain kinds of passive constructions—'get married', 'get divorced', 'get registered'—the use of *get* is the regular English idiom. It implies some active involvement on the part of the subject, and presents a different aspect on the event from the ordinary passive construction 'be married', 'be divorced', 'be registered'.

In such constructions, this subtle and important distinction should be retained. As always, it is the way the word is used that matters, not the word itself.

'Having said that' (dangling or hanging participles)

The objection to dangling participles turns on the occasional ambiguity they can create, as in:

> Rushing to catch the train, her prized new hat blew off.

But is there really a problem in an example like the following?

> I found some of the recommendations unconvincing. Having said that, the report presents many new perspectives.

Here, the word 'said' in the opening phrase of the second sentence might seem to connect with the following noun 'report'. In fact the dangling participle is generated by the need to connect with the preceding sentence. Dangling participles like this are often inconspicuous and harmless, and contribute to the cohesion of the discussion. Only on a perverse reading could dangling participles that are stock connecting phrases (such as *barring accidents*, *assuming that*, and *all things considered*) be taken to connect with the following noun.

'Hopefully' as a sentence adverb

For many people, the typical adverb is one that expresses time, place or manner—such as *yesterday*, *upstairs*, *keenly*—and modifies a particular verb. *Hopefully* can indeed do this, as in:

> They approached the department hopefully.

There, *hopefully* describes the optimism of those making the approach. But it can also be used rather differently, to express the stance of the writer or speaker in relation to a whole sentence, as in:

> Hopefully their comments will be read.

In this case, its role is exactly like that of *regrettably* in:

> Regrettably they didn't speak up.

Both relate to the overall proposition of the sentence and thus operate legitimately as attitudinal adverbs (see page 68).

'However' as a conjunction

Most dictionaries list *however* as an adverb when it is used to mean 'but', 'yet' or 'nevertheless'. In such contexts, careful punctuation is usually needed for clarity:

> However, I will let you know.

> I'm not sure of the outcome; however, I will let you know as soon as this is clear.

There is an increasing trend to use *however* as a conjunction joining two contrasting clauses but with only a comma separating them:

> I'm not sure of the outcome, however I will let you know as soon as this is clear.

This use of *however* is not widely accepted, and should therefore be avoided in standard or formal publications.

'It's' and other contractions

Contracted forms of the verbs *be* and *have* and other auxiliaries (as in *it's clear, it's gone, they'll come, they'd like*) and of *not* (as in *can't, don't*) are commonly associated with speech—which is why they are sometimes said to be 'incorrect' in standard writing. They are not ungrammatical, because they still represent the verb of the clause in compressed or full form. The objections are clearly stylistic, based on the notion that contractions of this kind are too informal for academic and official writing.

However, recent research shows that some of these forms (especially *it's* and *don't*) are appearing more and more in printed material intended for a general audience, such as in newspapers and magazines. They help to tighten the underlying rhythms of the prose. Where a brisk, friendly or interactive style is sought, contractions like these serve a useful purpose, and need only be avoided in the most formal types of documents.

'That' and 'which'

The reason for distinguishing between the use of *that* and *which* in relative clauses is to avoid ambiguity in some contexts. Compare:

> The research findings that were likely to cause embarrassment were never circulated.
>
> The research findings which were likely to cause embarrassment were never circulated.
>
> The research findings, which were likely to cause embarrassment, were never circulated.

The first example makes it clear that the research findings not circulated were the ones likely to cause embarrassment. In the third example, it is plain that none of the recommendations was circulated. The situation described in the middle example is ambiguous: were all of the findings withheld or just the embarrassing ones?

The use of *that* in the first example makes it a defining relative clause: one that provides information that defines or limits the subject. The third example, with *which* and commas surrounding the clause, is a non-defining relative clause: one that adds detail not essential to the main point. (Without this clause, the sentence in this third example would still make its point that the findings were not circulated.)

Where no ambiguity could result, either *that* or *which* could be used:

> The letter *that/which* explains the problem is always preferable to one *that/which* simply thunders about it.

'They', 'them' and 'their' as singular pronouns

The use of the pronouns *they, them* and *their* to refer to an individual has been frowned upon, on the grounds that these pronouns are grammatically plural. Their primary function undoubtedly is to refer back to a plural noun, as in:

> Taxpayers have until next month to submit their returns.

Yet these same pronouns have long been used to refer to indefinite entities that are grammatically singular:

> Everyone must pay their taxes.

Other indefinite pronouns such as *someone*, *anyone* and *none* also tend to be followed by *they*, *them* or *their*. In such instances, the use of these plural pronouns shows notional rather than formal agreement (see pages 67 and 71), and can be safely used as the standard idiom in most contexts. This type of construction has a long history dating back more than four hundred years, but it has acquired a special value recently in the context of seeking inclusive language.

The evolving use of the singular *they*, *them* and *their* makes an interesting comparison with the evolution of the singular use of *you* in place of *thou* and *thee* in early modern English.

'To' (the split infinitive)

Grammarians have long agreed that there is nothing wrong with the concept of splitting an infinitive: 'to boldly go', for example. Earlier objections to this practice turn on the fact that in English the infinitive is usually expressed as two words (*to educate*), whereas in Latin it is embodied in one word (*educare*). In reality the English infinitive can also be expressed as one word (see the 'bare infinitive', page 70). So the idea that the infinitive cannot be split ignores the fact that it has more than one form in English.

There is nothing grammatically objectionable in the following split infinitive, for instance:

> He will need to quickly convert the computing system throughout the entire office.

There may of course be stylistic reasons for not having too many words intervening between *to* and the rest of the infinitive. In the following sentence, 'all our energies' is a clumsy intrusion:

> We ought to with all our energies pursue this goal.

There is no flaw in the grammar of the sentence—although there are certainly more elegant ways of phrasing it.

'Were' (the subjunctive)

The subjunctive *were* is sometimes said to be the only correct form of the verb in conditional or hypothetical constructions, such as:

> If the president were here …

Those using *were* in this way argue that it represents an unlikely or impossible condition, and is therefore different from:

> If the president was here …

But in many situations it is difficult to ascertain just how hypothetical the proposition is, and the conjunction *if* makes it clear that the proposition is conditional. In Australian English the *were* subjunctive is falling into disuse, replaced by *was* for ordinary purposes. This then makes the *were* subjunctive a distinctly formal choice in terms of style.

'Whom'

The pronoun *whom* is the traditional counterpart of the relative pronoun *who*, when it serves as the object of a verb or preposition:

The Cambodian students whom the minister met on Tuesday have come via Hong Kong.

The Cambodian student to whom you spoke is highly regarded.

These are Cambodian visitors, all of whom are well qualified.

The first example shows *whom* used as the object of the verb ('met'), a usage that tends to sound formal these days. Increasingly, the use of *whom* in standard writing is limited to sentences like the second and third, where it follows a preposition.

Where there is no preposition, *whom* can often be deleted to achieve a more relaxed tone:

The Cambodian students the minister met on Tuesday have come via Hong Kong.

'Whose'

As a possessive relative pronoun, *whose* has long been used to refer both to people and to things:

This is the book whose style is so lively.

The lawyer whose style is so lively came to the meeting.

The idea that the relative *whose* can only be used in reference to people probably stems from the fact that the interrogative *whose* can only be used in this way:

Whose style do you enjoy?

'With' and other prepositions to end a sentence

Despite Churchill's famous debunking of the idea that you cannot use a preposition at the end of a sentence (in 'This is the sort of English up with which I will not put'), the idea lives on. This prescription seems to be based on the term 'preposition' itself, which suggests the need to 'pre-pose' such words.

Prepositions are of course normally set in front of nouns (see page 69). But prepositions also function as what we may call 'particles' in association with phrasal verbs, as in *give up, pay off, wait for, write about*. In these contexts, the role of *up, off, for* and *about* is not prepositional, and so there is nothing to prevent them from occurring as the last word in a sentence (with no following noun). For example:

They'll never give up.

The scheme is bound to pay off.

It was the train they had been waiting for.

May I choose another topic to write about?

Chapter **6**

Spelling and word punctuation

SPELLING	**79**
Dictionaries and spelling checkers	80
Placenames	80
Names of organisations	80
Plurals	81
The past tense	82
Variable spellings	83
WORD PUNCTUATION: THE APOSTROPHE	**85**
Possession and common nouns	85
Proper names	86
Possessive phrases and compound titles	87
Nonpossessive and generic phrases	87
Expressions of time	87
Plural forms	87
WORD PUNCTUATION: THE HYPHEN	**88**
Prefixes	88
Suffixes	90
Compound words	90
Hanging hyphens	93
HYPHENATION AT LINE ENDS	**93**
Dividing words	93
Dividing phrases	94

The spelling of words is a large part of their identity. As readers, we recognise words by their familiar forms and by common endings for plurals and past tense. Most of these are standardised and described in large generalist dictionaries. But some aspects of spelling are not systematically dealt with in dictionaries, and they are discussed in the first part of this chapter. The use of apostrophes and hyphens is also covered, since these are other factors that affect word form. This is why they are classed as 'word punctuation' as distinct from 'sentence punctuation'—full stops, commas, question marks and so on—which is the subject of Chapter 7. The use of capital letters, another aspect of word form, is discussed in Chapter 8.

SPELLING

The standard spellings for most English words are less than 400 years old. Manuscripts of Chaucer from the fourteenth century look as if they were written in a foreign language. Documents of that time were in regional dialects, with great variation in spelling, even within documents. In 1582, scholar and teacher Richard Mulcaster produced a list of spellings based on regular principles for almost 9000 English words, and his efforts were followed in the seventeenth century by the publication of other spelling books and pioneering dictionaries. So, by the eighteenth century, English spelling had become standardised for most words. Nowadays, about 98 per cent of words are not subject to variation when used in continuous text.

The fact that most words have a single spelling tends to foster the notion that there is always a 'correct' spelling. Concise and abridged dictionaries support this, since they often omit legitimate variants and say little about inflections (changes in the basic form of a word that show such things as the plural or past tense). Only the comprehensive dictionaries recognise the full range of alternative spellings and take account of inflected and derived forms.

The recommendations put forward in this chapter accord with majority Australian usage, although database research confirms that alternatives are preferred in certain contexts.

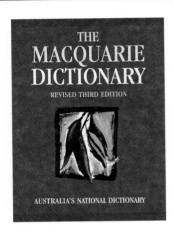

Dictionaries and spelling checkers

If you are in any doubt about the spelling of a word, the first thing to do is to consult a dictionary. This manual recommends that authors and editors of Australian government publications use either *The Australian Oxford dictionary* or *The Macquarie dictionary*, which agree on most aspects of spelling. Choose one of these dictionaries and follow its first preferences consistently—as part of 'house style' or for the specific document.

Although many software packages contain a facility for checking spelling, caution is necessary with these 'spellcheckers' for several reasons:

- They may not be based on an Australian dictionary. Check to see if this is one of the program's options.
- They do not pick up words that, although spelt correctly, are incorrect in the context in which they occur—for example, 'their' and 'there'.
- They do not distinguish between the author's text and any quoted material, the spelling of which should not be changed.

While the *Macquarie* or the *Australian Oxford* dictionaries are recommended as the general references for spelling, neither of them will meet everyone's needs all of the time. Other dictionaries may have particular features—more detailed etymological information, clearer examples, information on word division, or appendixes—that could prove helpful. For scientific or technical writing, specialist dictionaries will also need to be consulted.

The remainder of this section deals with spellings for which the chosen general dictionary may not always provide advice. It includes placenames, the names of organisations, plural forms and past tense constructions. Sets of words with variable spellings are shown on pages 83–5.

Placenames

The postcode listings in Australian telephone directories are a convenient source for the spellings of many placenames in Australia. Authoritative, up-to-date atlases can also be consulted. For more detailed searches for Australian placenames (including the names of geographical features), refer to *Gazetteer of Australia 2000* <http://www.auslig.gov.au>. (Note that Australian placenames do not take apostrophes: see page 86.)

In the case of well-known foreign placenames, the established English forms should be used. For example:

> Beijing   Cracow   Rome   Teheran   Brussels   Florence   Pyongyang   The Hague

Be aware that foreign placenames, including country names, can change over time. Examples of relatively recent changes are 'Bombay' to 'Mumbai' and 'Burma' to 'Myanmar'.

Names of organisations

The full name of an organisation should be spelt as the organisation itself spells it. For example:

World Health Organization *not* World Health Organisation

Department of Defense [US]

...ttention should also be paid to the use of capital letters and apostrophes in the ...ame. For example:

AusAID   Department of Veterans' Affairs

➤ See p. 86 for the omission of the apostrophe in nonpossessive institutional names and plurals.

...urals

...he plural of most English nouns is formed by adding *s* or *es*, as in:

documents   marches   heroes

...the case of nouns ending in a consonant plus *y*, the *y* is replaced by *ies*:

baby ... babies

... small number of nouns have irregular plurals, such as:

child ... children   man ... men

goose ... geese   sheep ... sheep

...ost dictionaries show plural forms only for words that do not form it in the ...gular manner, including words borrowed from other languages (known as 'loan ...ords').

Plurals of shortened forms: See p. 153 for information about the plurals of the various kinds of shortened forms. Note that they do not take an apostrophe when plural. For example:

URLs *not* URL's

...an words

...any English words have been borrowed from Latin, French or other languages ...d offer a choice of plural forms—for example, *chateaus* or *chateaux* and ...ferendums or referenda. For non-specialist writing, the first spelling in either *The* ...ustralian Oxford dictionary or *The Macquarie dictionary* should be adopted and used ...nsistently throughout a document.

...owever, some words of Latin origin tend to retain their original plural form. ...otable are those ending in *us* (the plural of which is usually *i*), such as *gladiolus* ...ladioli), *nucleus* (*nuclei*) and *stimulus* (*stimuli*). Perhaps the retention here may be ...o avoid a perceived clumsiness in the repetition of the *s* in the English plurals ...ladioluses, for instance).

...f the Latin loan words ending in *a* in the singular, the Latin plural (*ae*) is ...eferred only for those words strongly associated with science; examples are *larvae* ...d *vertebrae*. For the words *curriculum*, *memorandum* and *referendum*, the English ...ural is preferred—*curriculums*, *memorandums* and *referendums*.

More than one CV? In Latin, the plural of the term *curriculum vitae* is *curricula vitae*, and this is given priority in both the *Macquarie* and *Australian Oxford* dictionaries, ahead of *curriculum vitaes*.

...ome Latin words are in fact more widely known in their plural form—examples ...e *agenda*, *bacteria*, *data*, *media* and *candelabra*—and are often used as 'collective ...ngulars'. For example:

This data comes from the last census.

The bacteria that causes the infection is becoming resistant to antibiotics.

... some scientific and other disciplines, however, a distinction is frequently still ...awn between singular and plural use for these two examples.

In the case of *media*, the plural form is often, but certainly not always, treated as a collective singular noun in the communication context. For example:

> The media has consistently pointed this out.

but

> The various media are investigating vantage points from which to broadcast the event.

(The singular *medium* has, of course, various meanings unrelated to communication.)

The Macquarie dictionary notes that the trend towards 'collective singular' status is affecting the Greek-based word *criteria* (*criterion* in the singular) but makes no comment in relation to *phenomena* and *phenomenon*.

Most words borrowed from French now take English rather than French plurals. For example:

> bureaus *rather than* bureaux
>
> plateaus *rather than* plateaux

Words of Italian origin take regular English plural forms. For example:

> pergolas   porticos   ghettos

Only in special contexts, such as music, is the Italian plural form likely to be retained as an option; examples are *concerti*, *maestri* and *virtuosi*.

Italicised titles and words

The plurals of publication titles that are conventionally presented in italics are formed by adding the plural *s* in the normal way, but not setting it in italics. If the italicised term itself ends in *s*, no change is necessary. For example:

> The story was covered in three different *Australian Geographic*s.
>
> Several *Canberra Times* were lying on the desk.

If a word is italicised in text because it is not considered as having been absorbed into English yet, then the foreign plural *s* would naturally be in italics as well:

> *auberge … auberges*

Proper names

The plural of any personal or geographical name is formed simply by adding *s* or *e*

> There were three Jameses and two Arthurs at the meeting.
>
> The Murphys always get together on Tuesdays.
>
> There are four Mount Wellingtons in Australia but only one Mount Coot-tha.

The past tense

In English, the past tense inflection (that is, the letter or letters added to the base word, or root) takes several forms, notably *-ed*, *-t* and *-d*, as in *claimed*, *built* and *curdled*. Other verbs undergo internal change to show the past tense; examples are *wrote*, *told* and *trod*. For most verbs, the spelling is fixed, and dictionaries can

...solve any questions. There is, however, a small set of verbs that have alternative *-d* and *-t* endings:

burn ... burned ... burnt

dream ... dreamed ... dreamt

kneel ... kneeled ... knelt

lean ... leaned ... leant

leap ... leaped ... leapt

learn ... learned ... learnt

smell ... smelled ... smelt

spell ... spelled ... spelt

spill ... spilled ... spilt

spoil ... spoiled ... spoilt

...sage research shows that while the *-t* spelling is strongly associated with
...ljectival use of the word, *-ed* is now the majority preference for verbal uses of the
...ast tense and participle, both active and passive. For example:

Bushfires burned out of control.

The entire area had been burned.

The air smelled of burnt gum trees.

...ariable spellings

...s English evolves into an international medium of communication, the
...otivation for international uniformity and consistency is increasing. Yet while
...he process continues, the distinctive British and American spellings remain our
...ference points. Australian usage is positioned somewhere between them.

...Word groups with variable spellings

...able or -eable, as in *liv(e)able* and *us(e)able*
...oth spellings are used in Australia and Britain, whereas *livable* and *usable* are
...tandard in American English. The spelling that drops the *e* before a suffix is more
...egular, and therefore recommended.

...e or e, as in *encyclop(a)edia* and *p(a)ediatrician*
...Where British spelling uses the *ae* digraph, American spelling does without it. In
...ustralia, *encyclopedia* and *medieval* are usually spelt with just *e*, while others (such
...s *anaesthetic*) are usually still *ae*. When the digraph occurs at the beginning of a
...word, as in *aesthetic*, it is always retained. When it occurs at the end of a word to
...ignify a plural form, *-as* is preferred for words in everyday use such as *formulas*.

...ing or -eing, as in *ag(e)ing*
...oth *ageing* and *aging* are used in Britain, whereas *aging* is standard in American
...nglish. The *Macquarie* and *Australian Oxford* dictionaries give priority to *ageing*.
...ome other words with stems ending in *-ge* retain the *e* before *-ing*; examples are

bingeing, *tingeing* and *whingeing*. Others—notably *cringing*, *(in)fringing* and *impinging*—do not. These spellings are the arbitrary products of usage.

-ise or -ize, as in *civilise/civilize* and *dramatise/dramatize*

The *ise* spelling of this suffix has been recommended for Australian government documents since the 1960s. Both spellings are used in Australia and Britain, whereas the *ize* spelling is standard in American English. The *Australian Oxford* and *Macquarie* dictionaries both promote the *ise* spelling, and on that basis it continues to be recommended.

-l or -ll, as in *distil(l)*, *enrol(l)* and *instal(l)*

In British and Australian English the traditional preference is for *distil*, while American English uses *distill*. Amid some variability now in Australia, the recommendations of the *Macquarie* and *Australian Oxford* dictionaries are for *appal*, *dispel*, *enrol*, *enthral*, *expel*, *fulfil* and *instil*, but *forestall* and *install*.

-ll or -l, as in *travel(l)ed* and *model(l)ing*

The alternatives *travelled* and *traveled* symbolise a consistent British–American divergence, the British favouring the *ll* form and the Americans the *l* form. Current Australian practice continues to favour the *ll* form—*cancelled*, *equalled* and *modelling*, for example—and this is generally recommended. Note, however, the recommended spellings of *paralleled* and *paralleling*.

-ment or -ement, as in *judg(e)ment*

While American English has tended to use *judgment*, British and Australian practice has been to maintain both options in *abridg(e)ment*, *acknowledg(e)ment* and *judg(e)ment*. The spellings without *e* are given priority in the *Macquarie* and *Australian Oxford* dictionaries.

-oe or -e, as in *f(o)etus* and *hom(o)eopath*

The *oe* spellings are British, where plain *e* is American. Australian dictionaries prefer the *oe* form for *homoeopath* and *homoeomorphism*—although the simple *e* is preferred for *homeostasis* and *homeothermic*. When it occurs at the beginning of a word, the *oe* spelling persists, as in *oestrogen* and *oestrus*. *Foetus* varies with *fetus* in medical contexts.

-ogue or -og, as in *dialog(ue)* and *prolog(ue)*

The *-gue* spelling is widely used in Australian, British and American English; other examples are *epilogue*, *pedagogue* and *synagogue*. Noteworthy exceptions are *catalog*, which is commonly used by librarians (whereas *catalogue* is in general use), and *analog*, which is used in technical contexts (whereas *analogue* is used in non-technical writing).

-our and -or, as in *colo(u)r* and *hono(u)r*

Although the *-or* form was quite widely used in the nineteenth century in Australia, current Australian usage largely favours the *-our* form, and this is reflected in both the recommended dictionaries. Note, however, that *Labor* is the official spelling for the *Australian Labor Party* and related expressions—such as *Labor voters* and *Labor initiatives*—whereas *Labour Party* is used in both New Zealand and Britain.

or *tt*, as in *benefit(t)ed* and *combat(t)ed*

Spellings with *tt* should be used only if the word's stress falls on the syllable that ends in the *t*—as in *admitted*, *rebutted* and *regretted*. In *budgeted*, *marketed*, *targeted* and *benefited*, the word's stress is not on the syllable ending in *t*, so there is no case for doubling the *t*.

-*yse* or -*yze*, as in *analyse/analyze*

The -*yse* form is more widely used in Australian and British English; the -*yze* form is preferred in American English. The -*ise* form (as in *civilise*) has been recommended for Australian government documents since the 1960s, and the -*yse* form is its natural counterpart. It is the preferred form in both the *Australian Oxford* and *Macquarie* dictionaries and is thus recommended.

WORD PUNCTUATION: THE APOSTROPHE

In English, the apostrophe was originally used to show the omission of a letter or letters—in *think'st*, for example. Since the eighteenth century, it has been used to show when singular common nouns are possessive. In this role the apostrophe separates the stem (or base word) from the possessive inflection (or ending); this is the apostrophe's most straightforward use, the familiar *apostrophe s*. Use of the apostrophe to mark plural possession—most commonly by means of the *s apostrophe*—developed gradually during the nineteenth century. Other issues with the apostrophe are its use with proper names, with joint ownership, in compound titles and generic phrases and in expressions of time.

While the apostrophe is falling out of use in some kinds of phrase, it is also mistakenly overused with plurals—on signs and in some unedited texts.

Possession and common nouns

Singular common nouns

The apostrophe is inserted before the possessive *s* of singular common nouns:

> the government's policies   tomorrow's program

Nouns whose singular ends in *s* are treated in the same way:

> the atlas's size   the lens's range

Plural common nouns

Plural nouns ending in *s* take the *s apostrophe*:

> the governments' budgets   students' answers

In contrast, plural nouns that do not end in *s* take the *apostrophe s*:

> the children's memories   the cattle's feeding pattern

Curiously, perhaps, possessive pronouns do not use the apostrophe *s* at all. Their standard forms are:

> my   your   his   her   its   our   their

and

> mine   yours   his   hers   its   ours   theirs

It's = it is: Note that *it's* with an apostrophe is a contraction for *it is*. It is a mistake to use *it's* for the possessive form of *it*.

Proper names

Personal names

Personal names ending in any letter other than *s* take a simple apostrophe *s*:

Beatrice's sister   Xavier's work   Mr Mahony's house

For personal names ending in *s*, the situation is problematic because of the differing 'rules' that are variously invoked. One such rule involves the sound of the word: if the possessive inflection is pronounced as a separate syllable, it takes an apostrophe *s*; if not, the apostrophe alone should be added. The problem is that different people pronounce such possessives differently. Should it therefore be *Burns'* or *Burns's*? A competing rule has it that names consisting of one syllable always take apostrophe *s* (*Burns's*), whereas those of more than one syllable take only the apostrophe (*Dickens'*). Cutting across these practices is the notion that certain time-honoured names ending in *s* (particularly from biblical and classical sources) take only the apostrophe, whatever their length or pronunciation (*Jesus'*, *Herodotus'*).

Possession and personal names: Use the apostrophe *s* with personal names, even when they themselves end in *s*.

Given this confused situation, the most straightforward course of action is to add apostrophe *s* to any name ending in *s*, however long or short it is and however it is pronounced. Thus:

Burns's poems   Dickens's novels   Herodotus's birthplace

Names of institutions

The apostrophe is disappearing from institutional names containing a plural noun ending in *s* that identifies its function. This has long been the case with titles such as *Securities Commission* and *Libraries Board*, where the plural is inanimate. It is increasingly common for the apostrophe to be dropped from the names of other institutions where the plural word is a human reference—for example, *Geologists Conference*, *Plumbers and Gasfitters Union*. In all such cases, the plural word is not strictly possessive; its relationship with the following word or phrase is associative or descriptive, rather like an adjective. (See page 87 for a discussion of nonpossessive and generic phrases.)

Names of institutions: A possessive apostrophe is not necessary in the names of institutions, professional and industry bodies and other groups. But show the apostrophe when it forms part of the formal name of an organisation.

Placenames

Australian placenames involving possessives are all written without apostrophes:

Kings Cross   Mrs Macquaries Chair   the Devils Marbles   St Marys

St Georges Terrace   Dianas Basin   Flynns Beach   Frenchs Forest

This style, dating back to a 1966 decision by the Geographical Names Board, applies not only to the reproduction of placenames and street or road names in text but also to maps and public signs. The practice is similar in the United States whereas in Britain a name can appear with or without an apostrophe in different parts of the country. There is much to be said for the simplicity of the Australian convention.

Apostrophes in placenames: The names of places, streets and roads in Australia do not take apostrophes, even when they embody possessive constructions.

Possessive phrases and compound titles

A possessive phrase takes the apostrophe on the last word of the phrase:

someone else's books   the editor-in-chief's responsibilities

In the possessive forms of compound titles, the apostrophe *s* is attached to the final word only:

the Leader of the Opposition's stance

the Landscape Architecture Association's membership requirements

Joint ownership or association is shown by placing the apostrophe *s* on the second of the two 'owners':

his mother and father's legacy   Rutherford and Bohr's atom

In contrast, where the ownership is not joint, each name takes an apostrophe:

his mother's and father's voices   Sibelius's and Grieg's works

Nonpossessive and generic phrases

In phrases such as *drivers licence, travellers cheques* and *visitors book*, the plural noun is descriptive rather than possessive. As it describes an association with the following word rather than any direct ownership, no apostrophe is necessary. Some other examples:

After primary school, she went on to the girls grammar school.

The various proofreaders marks are shown in an appendix.

Phrases such as *drivers licence* and *travellers cheques* have become merely generic ways of referring to common items. If used in a non-generic sense, however, an apostrophe is needed:

The young driver's licence was cancelled.

Expressions of time

It was previously conventional to use an apostrophe in expressions of time involving a plural reference, such as:

six weeks' time

three months' wages

The apostrophe is now often left out. Again, the sense of these phrases tends to be more descriptive than possessive.

When the time reference is in the singular, however, the apostrophe should be retained to help mark the noun as singular:

a day's journey   the year's cycle

Plural forms

As a general rule, apostrophes should not be used before the *s* of a plural word—despite the increasingly common mistake seen in examples such as:

fresh apple's and orange's   carol's by candlelight

An exception is for plural references to letters of the alphabet, as in:

Dot the *i*'s and cross the *t*'s.

Mind your *p*'s and *q*'s.

Italics could be used for these examples, although it is still clearer if the apostrophe is retained. Compare:

*i*s and *t*s   *p*s and *q*s

with

i's and *t*'s   *p*'s and *q*'s

➤   See p. 148 for a discussion of the use of italics for distinguishing letters and words being cited in text.

WORD PUNCTUATION: THE HYPHEN

There are few firm rules dealing with uses of the hyphen, and dictionaries are often in disagreement. In general, British dictionaries are more inclined to hyphenate words than their American counterparts; the *Macquarie* and *Australian Oxford* dictionaries lie somewhere between the two. This divergence in practice means that there are no simple rights and wrongs in this aspect of word punctuation.

Some broad principles are offered in this section as a guide; however, the main concern should be to retain consistency in hyphenation throughout a document. A solution is to choose one dictionary and stick to its hyphenation practices, supplementing these where needed with a list of other words showing the preferred house style for hyphenation in each case.

Hyphens can be an important device to avoid ambiguity, but otherwise there is no need to overuse them. The decision about whether or not to use a hyphen must often be based on the context in which the word or words appear.

Prefixes

Hyphens are useful in some sets of words formed with prefixes. They may help to prevent misreading where the vowel ending the prefix is the same as the one at the start of the word attached to it. Hyphens also clarify the meaning of a few formations that might otherwise be confused with established words.

Common prefixes include:

anti-	counter-	extra-	intra-	post-	sub-
auto-	de-	hyper-	mis-	pro-	super-
bi-	dis-	hypo-	neo-	re-	supra-
co-	ex-	inter-	non-	semi-	un-

Doubled-up vowels

When the last letter of a single-syllable prefix is a vowel and the word that follows begins with the same vowel, a hyphen is often inserted to prevent misreading. For example:

de-emphasise *not* deemphasise

pre-eminent *not* preeminent

re-enter *not* reenter

This practice is less crucial if a word is well known, or at least familiar to readers of the particular publication. Thus, as both the *Australian Oxford* and *Macquarie* dictionaries confirm, *cooperate*, *coordinate* and their derivatives are no longer hyphenated.

The combination of two different vowels does not usually require a hyphen—as in *prearrange*, *reallocate* and *triennial*. The only exception is when a hyphen is used to separate the prefix from a single-syllable word beginning with a vowel, to prevent the two parts from being read together as one syllable:

de-ice *not* deice

Two-syllable prefixes ending in a vowel other than *o* and followed by another vowel are often hyphenated, whereas if the base word begins with a consonant the term is most commonly presented as one word:

anti-aircraft *but* antisocial

semi-official *but* semilunar

Two-syllable prefixes ending in *o* are often attached without a hyphen, regardless of whether the letter starting the base word is a vowel or a consonant. For example:

macroeconomics *and* macrobiotic

monoamine *and* monocultural

radioactive *and* radiotherapy

retroactive *and* retrograde

These principles can be extended to new words not yet listed in dictionaries.

Two-syllable prefixes ending in a consonant are rarely followed by a hyphen, even when the base word begins with the same letter as the last one of the prefix. For example:

hyperlink *and* hyperrealism

interactive *and* interrelated

Clarifying meaning

A hyphen is used in new words with prefixes to distinguish them from established words that would otherwise look the same:

re-cover (cover again) *but* recover (retrieve, or regain)

re-creation (creation anew) *but* recreation (leisure-related activity)

re-signed (signed again) *but* resigned (relinquished, or acquiescent)

Hyphens are also used with *co-* ('joint') and *ex-* ('former') in recent formations, whether or not the word attached begins with a vowel:

co-author   co-worker

ex-alderman   ex-president

E-mail or *email*? This was the first of these *e* words to gain widespread currency and is shown in the *Macquarie* and *Australian Oxford* dictionaries as *email*. With the growing number of similar words that use a hyphen, it is possible that *e-mail* will become the preferred form.

The hyphen and the en rule: Note that a hyphen is used in the expression *pre-1914* but an en rule is used in *pre–World War I*. (See p. 109 for further discussion of this principle.)

For the growing set of words prefixed with *e* (for 'electronic'), hyphenation is recommended:

> e-book e-business e-commerce e-shares e-shopping e-zine

The *e* prefix is so small that such words would be in danger of being misread unless the hyphen is there.

Capital letters, numbers, italics and quotation marks

Hyphens are needed if a prefix is followed by a capital letter, a number, or an expression that is in italics or quotation marks. For example:

> pre-Christian era   un-Australian activities
>
> anti-*raskol* measures   pro-'reconciliation' stance

Suffixes

Word-forming suffixes are normally attached directly to the base word, without any hyphen. The commonest suffixes include:

> -able (sizable)   -ate (hyphenate)   -fold (fourfold)   -ful (fruitful)
>
> -ise (patronise)   -ish (greenish)   -ly (costly)   -ment (amendment)
>
> -ness (kindness)   -y (sandy)

A hyphen does, however, precede *-fold* when that suffix is used with a numeral—for example, *300-fold*. When the suffix *-odd* is used with numbers, whether they are presented in words or numerals, a hyphen is always inserted. For example:

> There were 150-odd guests.
>
> Thirty-odd copies of the brochure were lying on the table.

Compound words

A compound consists of two or more words that, together, carry a new meaning. Some formations of this kind start out as two words (separated by a space); then, with increasing use and recognition, they move to hyphenated status and finally merge into one word. Yet hyphens are conventionally retained in some kinds of compounds, especially those where both components consist of more than one syllable.

Compound nouns

Compound nouns constitute the largest group of compound words. Most are readily understood without a hyphen, being either presented simply as two words or merged into one word. But a hyphen is needed in some circumstances.

Verb plus adverb

A compound noun made up of a verb-plus-adverb combination (*shake-out*, *make-up*, *teach-in*) needs to be hyphenated to show that the adverb is linked with the compound rather than with other elements of the sentence. For example:

> The minister gave the go-ahead for the project.

In instances such as this, the hyphen also separates what otherwise might be a distracting sequence of letters.

But the adverb-plus-verb combination is unproblematic and can usually be written as one word:

bypass   downpour   uproar   input

Verb plus noun or noun plus verb

Few compound nouns formed this way actually take hyphens. If the verb has no suffix (such as -ing, -ed or -er), verb-plus-noun and noun-plus-verb combinations are usually joined without a hyphen. For example:

scarecrow   rattlesnake   roadblock

When an inflected verb is the first element, the term is usually presented as two words:

flying saucer   shredded wheat

If an inflected verb comes second and the noun element consists of only one syllable, the expression is typically presented as one word:

bookmaker   stocktaking

But when an inflected verb is preceded by a noun of more than one syllable, the expression is usually presented either with a hyphen or as two words:

cabinet-maker   potato growing

Noun plus noun

Noun-plus-noun compounds vary considerably in terms of hyphenation, even from dictionary to dictionary. But two types are regularly hyphenated: expressions in which each element has equal status, and expressions in which the elements rhyme. For example:

owner-driver   city-state

culture-vulture   hocus-pocus

Noun compounds involving prepositional phrases, such as *editor-in-chief* and *mother-in-law*, are also conventionally hyphenated.

Adjective plus noun

Compound nouns consisting of an adjective followed by a noun are usually written as two words, as in:

black market   red tape   free will

Compound adjectives

When a compound adjective consists of two adjectives, or of a noun plus an adjective, the expression is hyphenated no matter whether it precedes or follows the noun it is describing. For example:

bitter-sweet   accident-prone   red-hot

colour-blind   icy-cold   disease-free

In contrast, compound adjectives that are set phrases consisting of, say, a noun plus a noun or an adjective plus a noun are not usually hyphenated:

> a tax office ruling
>
> the stock exchange report
>
> an equal opportunity employer

If the expression is further modified, a hyphen may be necessary to prevent ambiguity, as in *a retrospective tax-office ruling*.

Compound adjectives involving present or past participles usually take a hyphen:

> a government-owned facility
>
> a heart-rending image

However, a few well-established compounds of this type—for example, *airborne*, *everlasting* and *widespread*—are set as a single word.

Compound adjectives consisting of a participle or an adjective preceded by an adverb ending in *ly* are not hyphenated:

> an elegantly executed manoeuvre
>
> a finely honed argument

But when the adverb in such a compound does *not* end in *ly*, the expression is usually hyphenated:

> a well-known book
>
> a fast-flowing river

If a compound of this kind is modified—by *very*, *exceptionally* or *particularly*, for instance—a hyphen is never used:

> a very well known dancer

Similarly, a hyphen is not used if a compound adjective consists of a comparative or superlative adverb or adjective and a participle. For example:

> a better known dancer
>
> the least appreciated team member
>
> the more advanced students

Very occasionally, however, a hyphen will be needed for clarification. Consider the different meanings of the following:

> The parents lobbied for more experienced staff.
>
> The parents lobbied for more-experienced staff.

Compound adjectives that consist of short adverbial phrases are always hyphenated. For example:

> an up-to-date account   a dusk-to-dawn curfew
>
> a 40-year-old male   surface-to-air missiles

When not to hyphenate adverbial phrases: When these phrases play an adverbial role (rather than acting as adjectival compounds), no hyphen is needed. For example:

The accounts look up to date.

The curfew lasted from dusk to dawn.

Hyphens are also used for compound adjectives involving numbers, whether cardinal or ordinal and whether expressed in words or figures:

a four-part series   a 21-gun salute   a third-storey office

➤ See p.167 for a discussion of the use of hyphens in non-decimal fractions.

Compound adjectives containing capital letters, italics or quotation marks are not usually hyphenated:

a High Court decision

an *in situ* inspection

a 'do or die' attitude

Compound verbs

When compound verbs consist of an adjective plus a noun or a noun plus a verb, they are usually hyphenated:

to cold-shoulder   to gift-wrap

In contrast, when the compound consists of an adverb plus a verb, it is usually presented as one word:

to bypass   to overreact   to undergo

Compound adverbs

The relatively few compound adverbs are usually presented as one word. For example:

barefoot   downstream   overboard

Hanging hyphens

'Hanging' (or 'floating') hyphens are sometimes used to connect two words to a base word or number that they share:

pre- or post-1945

full- and part-time positions

While this form of hyphen can be useful in condensed prose, it is also potentially ambiguous. Fuller wording such as 'full-time and part-time positions' would avoid this problem.

HYPHENATION AT LINE ENDS

The key principle for dividing words and phrases at the ends of lines is to maintain their identity and thus avoid momentary misreading.

Dividing words

In a wide-column format, it is usually possible to avoid dividing words at the ends of lines. But with narrower measures—particularly with justified text, in tables, and in captions to graphs and other illustrative material—artificial breaks are often necessary.

Word-processing packages and computer typesetting programs offer varying degree of sophistication in word division, but there will always be times when authors, editors and others need to make a decision about where to break a word at the end of a line of type. As far as possible, the part of the word before the hyphen at the end of the line should suggest the remainder of the word, to provide a guide to readers.

The following general principles apply:

- Words of one syllable should never be broken—for example, *breach*, *course* and *through*. Some single-syllable words are surprisingly long.
- Words of two syllables are better not broken—although this will sometimes be necessary in narrow columns of text.
- Words of fewer than six letters should not be divided.
- At least three letters should be taken down to the next line.
- The part of the word taken down to the next line should begin with a consonant wherever possible (*fic/tion* not *fict/ion* and *regu/late* not *regul/ate*). However, this rule should be ignored when such a division might mislead—thus, *draw/ings* not *dra/wings* and *solen/oid* not *sole/noid*.
- Compound words can be divided at the boundary between the two components—for example, *data/base* and *over/pass*.
- Words with prefixes or suffixes can usually be divided effectively at the boundary—for example, *neat/ness*, *pre/meditate*.
- Vowel sequences that belong to the same syllable should be kept together—for example, *beauti/ful*, *bor/ough*. Compare *cre/ation* and *co/incidence*, in which the adjacent vowels belong to separate syllables and can conveniently be broken.

Dividing phrases

The following principles apply to numerical phrases, shortened forms, names and dates:

- Figures that form part of an expression of measurement should never be separated from the associated unit (whether a word or shortened form). So expressions such as the following should always be retained on the same line:

    70 kg   200 kilometres $20 million   65 per cent

- Abbreviations or contractions should be kept intact.
- People's initials should not be separated from their family names, and any postnominals are also better kept on the same line. Similarly, short titles (such as *Ms* or *Dr*) should be retained on the same line as the name, although this may not be possible for longer titles (*Professor* or *His Excellency*, for instance).
- Dates expressed entirely in figures should be kept intact. Dates expressed in words and figures—*17 July 2002*, for example—can be broken after the month, but not before it.

Long Internet addresses, or URLs, can be broken at the end of a line after a punctuation mark, provided the full address is contained within angle brackets. Never insert a hyphen at the line break, as it could be read as part of the address details.

Chapter

Sentence punctuation

TERMINATING MARKS	**96**
Full stop	97
Question mark	97
Exclamation mark	98
MARKS USED WITHIN SENTENCES	**99**
Colon	99
Semicolon	101
Comma	101
Dashes	106
Forward slash	109
Ellipsis points	110
BRACKETS	**110**
Parentheses	110
Square brackets	111
Angle brackets	112
QUOTATION MARKS	**112**
Direct speech	112
Quotations	113
Other uses of quotation marks	113
Quotation marks with other punctuation	115
Quotations within quotations	116
TYPOGRAPHY OF PUNCTUATION	**116**
Consistency of font	116
Spacing after punctuation	117

Before 1476, when William Caxton set up his wooden printing press in London, there were no national standards for English spelling and punctuation. Caxton—and later his assistant, Wynkyn de Worde, who took over the press when Caxton died—faced the problem of trying to bring some uniformity to these printed works, despite regional variations in vocabulary and usage. Another century was to pass, however, before uniformity became more widespread. Punctuation as we know it today is the result of changes in both the use and shape of the various marks since that time.

Punctuation marks play a vital role in communication: they make meaning clear by showing readers the relationship between the various components of a written work. Particular clues are used to identify sentences, clauses and phrases, and others are used at the 'micro' scale to clarify words or parts of words. Misplaced punctuation can change the meaning of a word, clause or sentence, or create ambiguity. Insufficient punctuation can do the same and leave readers floundering. On the other hand, too much punctuation can distract and tire readers.

Fashions change. As with words, some punctuation marks can become temporarily overworked and lose their power (at present the dash is a possible candidate); others can temporarily fall out of favour (the semicolon could be a candidate here). Many aspects of punctuation remain the subject of debate, although there seems to be a growing trend to dispense with unnecessary marks.

Minimal punctuation: The trend to minimal punctuation may be a response partly to the minimalist movement in design-related disciplines and partly to the difficulty of clearly distinguishing punctuation marks on screen, given the limitations of current software and screen technology.

In addition to this, writers vary in their sentence-punctuation habits. Some punctuate more heavily than others. In fiction and some non-fiction, 'unorthodox punctuation—the absence of quotation marks, for example—can characterise a particular author, and allowance should be made for this. In government, corporate and other types of information documents, however, it is advisable to avoid any possibility of ambiguity and follow the 'orthodox' uses of sentence-punctuation marks. Not only is careful punctuation an aid to clarity, but it is also a courtesy to readers, many of whom can become irritated by idiosyncratic practices.

➤ Chapter 6 discusses the hyphen and the apostrophe, as use of these marks is classed as word punctuation. Chapter 9 deals with the presentation and punctuation of lists.

TERMINATING MARKS

There are three types of terminating punctuation marks: the full stop, the question mark and the exclamation mark.

Full stop

Also called the full point, point, period or dot, the full stop is primarily recognised as the mark that ends a sentence. It should be followed by one space only, and the first word of any following text usually begins with a capital letter.

Ending a sentence

A full stop marks the end of a sentence that is neither a direct question nor an exclamation. For example:

> Human rights are the basis of a civilised society.

A sentence fragment can also be followed by a full stop. This is especially common with responses to questions:

> Seven hundred pages and not one recommendation.

> What is the deadline for applications? This Friday.

Stylistic variation of this kind should, however, be used sparingly: it can produce an unintended staccato effect.

Other uses of the full stop

The full stop is also used with some shortened forms, as the decimal point in numbers and currency, in numbering subsections and paragraphs in a document (or example, *Section 7.3*), and in expressions of time (*10.30 am*). A further, and relatively new, use for the full stop (or dot) is to separate elements of email and web addresses—for example, *<abc.net.au>*.

➤ See Chapter 10 for information about using the full stop with some types of shortened forms, and Chapter 11 for information about using it with numbers and measurements.

Do not use a full stop after:

- displayed titles of books, periodicals, poems and so on. ('Displayed' titles are those set apart from the text as a title heading, not titles that are being cited as references)

- headings

- page headers (often called 'running heads') and footers

- display lists that comprise short items and follow directly after a heading without any introductory phrase or clause (see page 144)

- captions that are not complete sentences—unless followed by a complete sentence that is also part of the caption, when a full stop is used in both cases

- index entries

- certain types of shortened forms (see pages 152–3)

- symbols for units of measurement (see page 184)

- the three points of ellipsis, even if the end of the sentence has been reached (see page 110).

Question mark

The question mark, or interrogation point, signals a query. It can also be used to express doubt.

➤ For information about the placement of question marks in direct speech, see pp. 115–6.

Questions

Direct questions are always followed by a question mark:

> Did they follow the established procedure?

This is the case even if the question is not phrased in the interrogative form:

> That is the policy?

Tag questions, which are formed by adding an interrogative 'tag' to a statement, also take a question mark:

> The department is obliged to, isn't it?

Similarly, a rhetorical question (a question to which no response is expected) is followed by a question mark, as is an unspoken question:

> What can she have been thinking of?

> How did it come to this? he asked himself grimly.

Doubt

Doubt can also be conveyed by a question mark:

> Giovanni Pierluigi da Palestrina (?1525–1594) was perhaps the greatest composer of music for unaccompanied chorus.

Do not use a question mark after:

- indirect questions

  > Before starting to write, ask yourself who your readers will be.

- polite requests that seek no verbal response

  > Would you please submit your comments by Monday.

- isolated interrogative words in a sentence

  > The electorate will want to know *when* rather than *why*.

Exclamation mark

The exclamation mark, or exclamation point, is used instead of a full stop at the end of a sentence or sentence fragment to provide emphasis. It is used more commonly in informal English than in standard or formal writing.

Emotions

Surprise, disbelief, dismay, indignation and exasperation can all be conveyed by the use of an exclamation mark:

> That can't be the case!

> If only they would listen!

Greetings, wishes and orders

Use an exclamation mark to give emphasis to greetings, wishes and orders:

> Good evening, friends!

> The House will come to order!

➤ For information about using the exclamation mark in quotations and direct speech, see pp. 115–6.

Do not use an exclamation mark:

- too frequently. Its effect is lost if it is overused, and most readers find the repetition irritating

- to draw attention to an error in quoted material. Use instead the italicised word *sic*, which means 'thus', and place it in square brackets: [*sic*]. (However, this insertion should only be used where such editorial interpolation is essential.)

MARKS USED WITHIN SENTENCES

Three types of punctuation marks—the colon, the semicolon and the comma—are used within sentences to bring varying levels of emphasis or to signify degrees of connectedness. Dashes, the forward slash (or solidus) and points of ellipsis also have valuable functions.

Colon

The colon is a marker of relationship and sequence. It can be used after a clause to introduce additional explanatory information, or it can introduce indented material such as dot-point series (see page 142), examples, block quotations and questions. Other useful functions of the colon are to link a title with its subtitle and to introduce formal statements, transcripts and dialogue.

Amplifying, summarising and contrasting

A colon is used to introduce a word, phrase or clause that amplifies, summarises or contrasts with what precedes it:

> We were concerned: the official party had not yet arrived and the ceremony was about to start.

> There is only one word for it: dishonest.

> There were four tickets: not enough for all of us.

Series of items

Sometimes explanatory matter is in the form of a series of items. A colon should be used when these items are in apposition to the introductory clause or are preceded by *the following* or *as follows*:

> Three portfolios were represented: finance, health and defence.

> If we fail to take action there could be serious consequences: increasingly costly losses to agricultural production, with resultant threats to the prosperity of rural communities; further biodiversity loss; and damage to our market advantage as a producer of 'clean, green' goods.

> The map shows the following information: geographic features, population distribution and environmental constraints.

In contrast, when the series of items flows naturally on as part of the sentence—often prefaced by such expressions as *including*, *such as* and *namely*—a colon is not needed:

> A number of species are at risk, including those that reproduce slowly and those at the edge of their optimal range.

Apposition: Words, phrases and clauses are in apposition when they provide explanatory or descriptive information about something already mentioned. They can relate to the subject, the object or another noun phrase in the sentence.

Incomplete lists: Any list introduced by *for example* or *such as* is by definition an incomplete list. Avoid these expressions if you intend to provide a comprehensive list.

The council publishes material dealing with subjects such as aged care, communicable diseases, diabetes, drugs and poisons, and mental health.

We discussed the scope of her review and the Australian painters she had singled out for particular praise, namely Fred Williams, Arthur Boyd and Emily Kame Kngwarreye.

Similarly, when the items in the series form the object of the introductory statement, no colon is needed to introduce them:

The disciplines under review are economics, history and archaeology.

Block quotations

Block quotations (that is, quotations that are set apart from the text) are often introduced by a colon:

The press release began:

In a first for Australian editing, the Council of Australian Societies of Editors has released *Australian standards for editing practice*. These standards aim to confirm the professional nature of editing for publication and emphasise the centrality of the editor's work in the publishing process.

➤ For more on the treatment of block quotations, see p. 113.

Questions

A colon is used to introduce a direct question when the question amplifies or modifies the introductory word or phrase:

The question is this: who will take responsibility?

A capital letter is needed after the colon if two or more complete questions follow:

We ask you: Can you support him? Can you persuade others to vote for him?

However, when the questions are merely sentence fragments, lower-case letters can be used:

What is the basic requirement: fluency in French? a thorough knowledge of the legislative environment? negotiating skills?

Formal statements, speeches, transcripts and dialogue

A colon can be used as a stronger alternative to a comma when introducing formal statements and speeches:

The minister began: 'Your Excellency, ladies and gentlemen …

A comma is sufficient if the introduction is less formal:

The Prime Minister rose and announced, 'Cabinet will make its decision tomorrow'.

It is also common to use a colon after speakers' names in a transcript and in dialogue:

MEMBER FOR WENTWORTH: Thank you, Madam Speaker …

Subtitles and subheadings

A colon is used to introduce the subtitles of books, articles in periodicals, and so on:

The dynamic society: exploring the sources of global change

'Olympic fraud: man in court'

heading with a follow-on subheading is treated in the same way. For example:

> Liberty and property: the case put by Sarah Wills

No capital is necessary after the colon in these contexts.

Semicolon

The break provided by a semicolon is stronger than that provided by a comma but weaker than that created by a full stop. The semicolon can therefore be used to link two clauses that could be treated as separate sentences but that have a closer logical link than such separation would imply. Another important use for the semicolon is in separating a series of phrases or clauses that also contain commas. Although the semicolon is often neglected, it is a very useful punctuation mark and, properly employed, can bring elegance and variety to your writing.

Linked clauses

A semicolon can be used between two parts of a sentence that are closely linked in meaning, provided there is at least a full clause on either side of the semicolon:

> We expect ministerial approval next week; the work can then start immediately.

Alternatively, these statements could be joined by *and* or they could be made into two short sentences. But neither option would produce the same emphasis or rhythm.

Sometimes the second clause is introduced by a connective expression, such as *however, nevertheless, alternatively, that is* or *therefore*, to underscore the connection between two statements. In such instances, be sure to choose a semicolon, not a comma:

> Rain is forecast; however, there are no clouds to be seen.

not

> Rain is forecast, however there are no clouds to be seen.

Internally punctuated run-on lists

If one or more items in a series or list within a sentence contain internal commas, use a semicolon to separate the items:

> The report draws on a number of sources, including current thinking in public health; risk analysis, which has reached great sophistication in analysing investment behaviours; and the results of econometric studies.

> Participants came from Benalla, Victoria; Wellington, New South Wales; and Longford, Tasmania.

> The results were surprising: adult males, 35 per cent; adult females, 52 per cent; and children, 13 per cent.

Comma

A comma marks the smallest break in the continuity of a sentence. Despite this apparently modest role, it can enhance clarity in a number of important ways. General principles associated with the use of commas are discussed in this section, but there are a number of situations where their use becomes a matter of judgment and personal preference.

Some people use commas liberally; others use very few. In either case, the overriding criterion must be whether a comma is needed to ensure that the message is unambiguous and delivered effectively.

Avoiding ambiguity

One of the most important functions of the comma is to eliminate ambiguity:

> He was not run over, mercifully.
>
> For Paul, Thomas would always be a hero.
>
> A short time after, the fire began to lose its fury.

Run-on lists

Commas are used to separate items in a simple series or list within a sentence:

> The details required are name, date of birth, address and telephone number.

Sometimes a comma is needed between the last two items to ensure clarity:

> They should seek the support of landholders, philanthropists, government, and community and industry groups.

Strings of adjectives

As explained on page 68, adjectives have three types of role: evaluative, descriptive and definitive. In a string of adjectives preceding a noun, commas are generally required only between adjectives of the same type. For example:

> The shrub has large, serrated, shiny, heart-shaped leaves. [all descriptive]
>
> Success will depend on hard-working, committed local residents. [two descriptive, the third definitive]
>
> He is a collector of fine old red wines. [evaluative, descriptive, then definitive]

Coordinate clauses

Coordinate clauses are equal in weight (and can thus be read as separate statements) but are linked by conjunctions such as *and*, *but*, *yet*, *or* and *nor*. When the clauses are reasonably long and each has its own subject, a comma is generally used to separate them:

> Australia has one of the world's safest food-supply systems, yet the reported incidence of food-borne illness in this country has increased in recent years.

In contrast, commas are often omitted between two short coordinate clauses, whether they share the subject or not:

> The flight was rough and a number of passengers became ill.
>
> We propose to present papers at international conferences and to have our findings published in journals.

Defining and non-defining clauses and phrases

Defining, or restrictive, clauses and phrases provide information that is integral to defining the subject, rather than being incidental to it. This distinction is particularly important where commas are concerned, as the meaning can be directly affected by whether commas are used or not. Compare, for example:

> All the players who are now back in Kananga strongly deny the charges.

and

> All the players, who are now back in Kananga, strongly deny the charges.

The first example restricts the subject to those players who have returned to Kananga—it is a defining, or restrictive, clause. In the second example, the fact that the players are now back in Kananga is incidental information, so the clause is non-defining and is set apart with commas.

Similarly, phrases that are defining take no surrounding commas, while non-defining phrases do:

> Animals with cloven hoofs can cause serious environmental damage.

> Animals with cloven hoofs, such as goats and sheep, can cause serious environmental damage.

Adjectival clauses and phrases

An introductory adjectival clause or phrase is separated from its subject by a comma:

> Late and flustered, he attracted considerable attention as he bustled into the room.

Adverbial clauses and phrases

An introductory adverbial clause is also usually separated from the main clause by a comma:

> After the proposal had been discussed at length in Cabinet, a press release was issued.

If, however, the introductory phrase or clause is short and there is no possibility of ambiguity, a comma is not necessary:

> If in doubt ask at the post office.

Where the introductory phrase or clause contains numerals and is immediately followed by other numerals, a comma is essential to separate the two sets:

> By 1980, 333 employees had registered.

but

> By 1980 there were 333 employees.

When clauses introduced by *as*, *since* and *while* express time, a comma is generally needed only if momentary ambiguity might result:

> While we were walking in the park the fireworks were exploding over the harbour.

but

> While we were walking in the park, exploding fireworks were illuminating the north side of the harbour.

On the other hand, if clauses introduced by *as*, *since* and *while* express cause or condition, they are followed by a comma:

> Since you have been acting in the position, you might as well put in an application.

Defining and non-defining clauses and phrases: Commas are used to set apart non-defining clauses and phrases but are not used with defining clauses and phrases. See p. 75 for a discussion of the use of *that* and *which* in defining and non-defining clauses and phrases.

An adverbial phrase or nonfinite clause that comes between the subject and its verb is marked off by commas:

> Diligent students, after studying their standard texts, make use of the library.

It might be better, though, to recast a sentence such as this to improve the flow:

> After studying their standard texts, diligent students make use of the library.

Introductory and transitional expressions

Expressions such as *however*, *furthermore*, *for example*, *for instance*, *on the other hand* and *in contrast* are followed by a comma when they introduce a statement and are set apart by commas when they appear elsewhere in the statement:

> For example, single-income families would be adversely affected by such requirements.

> Hugh, on the other hand, knew nothing about it.

A comma or commas need not always be used after or around such words and phrases as *therefore*, *meanwhile* and *no doubt*. Often it is simply a matter of rhythm or emphasis:

> Both sides of the question were therefore discussed.

> No doubt there are two sides to the question.

> There are, no doubt, two sides to the question.

Parenthetic expressions

Using pairs of commas is one way of enclosing parenthetic expressions:

> In the meantime, despite the continuing discussions, disaster was becoming inevitable.

Apposition

Commas can be used to isolate an appositional expression if it is non-defining—that is, if the meaning is still basically intact when the expression is omitted. For example:

> This will exacerbate, not resolve, the problem.

> Dyspepsia, or indigestion, is a frequent problem.

This is also a useful way to introduce a shortened form:

> Post-exposure prophylaxis, or PEP, has been effective in many cases.

Commas are not used with appositional expressions if they are defining—in other words, if they are essential to the meaning of the statement. For example:

> My colleague Neuy Lothi will attend in my place.

In this example, the absence of commas before and after the person's name shows that the writer has more than one colleague. If commas were inserted it would mean that the writer had only one colleague.

Expressions that share an element of a statement

A pair of commas is often needed if expressions share an element of a statement:

> The landholders in the area were concerned about, but could not individually deal with, the growing rabbit population.

Introductory and transitional expressions: Use a comma after expressions such as *however*, *furthermore*, *for example*, *for instance*, *on the other hand* and *in contrast* when they introduce a statement, and set them apart with commas when they appear elsewhere in the sentence.

Parenthetic expressions: These are words, phrases or clauses that are inserted in a sentence but remain grammatically independent of it—that is, they could be removed without affecting the sentence structure (like bracketed text). See pp. 106–7 and 110–11, respectively, for advice on using dashes or round brackets with parenthetic expressions.

➤ See p. 99 for a definition of *apposition* and pp.102–3 for a discussion of non-defining clauses and phrases.

If, however, the elements are short and there is no possibility of misunderstanding, the commas can be omitted:

> Crowds were rushing into and out of the stadium.

Omissions

Commas are often used to show that a word or phrase common to more than one part of a statement has been omitted, particularly where amounts are expressed, whether in words or numerals:

> In 2000 there were seven cases; in 1999, five; and in 1998, four.

> In 2000 there were 142 cases; in 1999, 127; and in 1998, 121.

Titles

Use commas to separate names from titles or affiliations:

> Ms Marika Weinberg, OAM, presented the prizes.

> The letter was addressed to SK Carey, BDS (Hons).

> The President, Ngo Dinh Diem, responded immediately.

In contrast, commas are not used when the title is performing the function of an adjective:

> Prime minister John Curtin proved an able war leader.

➤ For information about titles, affiliations and modes of address, see pp. 126–7 and Appendix A.

What *not* to do with commas

- Don't place a comma between a subject and its verb. This error is especially common when the subject is long:

  > Pensioners whose aids require battery types not normally in stock will have to buy their batteries from commercial outlets.

  not

  > Pensioners whose aids require battery types not normally in stock, will have to buy their batteries from commercial outlets.

- Don't use only one comma when there should be a pair:

  > The conference was held in Strahan, Tasmania, during March.

  not

  > The conference was held in Strahan, Tasmania during March.

- Don't misplace the commas around a parenthetic expression. If the parenthetic element is removed, the sentence must still make sense:

  > We arrived at the gallery mid-morning and, because it had not yet opened, spent the next hour in a nearby bookshop.

  not

  > We arrived at the gallery mid-morning, and because it had not yet opened, spent the next hour in a nearby bookshop.

Dashes

Different types

There are two main types of dashes, or rules: the em rule (—) and the en rule (–). An em rule is roughly the width of a capital M and is commonly known as a dash. The en rule is half the width of an em rule, or about the width of the letter *e*. Variants are the 2-em rule and the spaced en rule, both of which have very specific functions.

The hyphen (-) is also sometimes classed as a dash. It is treated separately in Chapter 6, where word punctuation is discussed.

Typographic style

There is some variation internationally in the way a dash is shown. The predominant practice in British publishing is to use an en rule (rather than an em rule) with space on either side of it. In North American publications it is more common to see an unspaced em rule. Another variant that is seen is the spaced em rule.

The style recommended for the standard dash in Australian government publications is an unspaced em rule; this eliminates any possibility of confusion with the spaced en rule.

The em rule

The em rule, or dash, has three main uses:

* to signify an abrupt change
* to introduce an amplification or explanation
* to set apart parenthetic elements.

Beware of using em rules too frequently. Overuse could indicate that there are too many qualifications and a lack of structural clarity.

Abrupt change

An em rule can be used to signify an abrupt change in the direction of a sentence:

> The main cause of foodborne illness is inadequate cooking—but this is not what we came here to talk about.

Amplification and explanation

An em rule can replace a colon or semicolon when expanding on or explaining a statement. It gives greater emphasis to the information that follows it:

> This is because the effects can occur some time or distance away—for example, vegetation clearing can result in dryland salinity hundreds of kilometres away.

Parenthetic expressions

A pair of em rules can be used to isolate a parenthetic expression within a sentence:

> National policies may change the decision-making environment—water licensing reform is an example—or provide guidance on suitable areas for government investment.

Types of dashes: There are two main types of dashes:

* the em rule (—)
* the en rule (–).

They have a number of valuable uses.

The em rule: spaced or unspaced?
Use an unspaced em rule to avoid confusion with the spaced en rule.

m rules are a good choice if the break is reasonably abrupt or if a word or phrase om the preceding clause is expanded on. Parentheses could be used, but they ould give less emphasis to the bracketed text (see pages 110–11).

umber of em rules in a sentence

Confusion can result if more than one pair of em rules appears in a sentence. Use a ombination of em rules and parentheses instead:

> The current decade (2001–2010) is likely to be characterised by relatively low rates of increase— predicted at 1.5 to 2.2 per cent annually—but the annual rate is likely to rise well above 4.5 per cent in the following decade (2011–2020).

similar combination is required when parenthetic elements that are already set part with em rules contain further parenthetic elements:

> They insisted on knowing everything—everything that her passport must have already revealed (age, place of birth, place of residence, and so on)—and then ignored my presence completely.

The em rule with other punctuation marks: The only punctuation mark that may precede an em rule within a sentence is a closing parenthesis, a question mark or an exclamation mark.

-em rule

he 2-em rule has two main functions:

  to avoid repetition in reference lists and bibliographies

  to mark a sudden break in dialogue or reported speech or to show where letters or words have been omitted.

eference lists and bibliographies

When more than one work by an author or authoring body is listed in a reference st or bibliography, a 2-em rule can be used to avoid repeating the name of the uthor or authoring body:

> Australian Bureau of Statistics 1999a, *Australian demographic statistics, December quarter 1998*, ABS, Canberra.
>
> ——1999b, *Australian social trends*, cat. no. 4102.0, ABS, Canberra.
>
> ——1999c, *Schools, 1998*, cat. no. 4221.0, ABS, Canberra.

➤ See pp. 194–6 and 223 for other examples of using the 2-em rule in a reference list or bibliography.

udden breaks and omissions

 2-em rule can be used to mark an abrupt break in direct or reported speech:

> I distinctly heard him say, 'Go away or I'll ——'.

 this instance a space is used to separate the rule from the preceding word because complete word is missing. If only part of a word is missing, no space is used:

> It was alleged that D—— had been threatened with blackmail.

n rule

 contrast with the em rule, the main function of which is to separate, the en rule a linking device. It is a versatile punctuation mark, having the following main ses in text:

  to show spans of figures, time and distance

  to show an association between words that retain their separate identities

  to link prefixes with what follows in specific circumstances

  to join some types of compound adjectives.

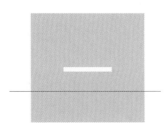

➤ See pp. 141 and 143 for information about using the spaced en rule in lists set apart from the text.

The en rule: spaced or unspaced?
The en rule is a linking device. If there is only one word being linked on either side, use an unspaced en rule; if there is more than one word on one or both sides, use a spaced en rule.

Additionally, an en rule is used for the minus symbol in mathematical settings.

Spans of figures, time and distance

Use an en rule to mean *to* in spans of figures and in expressions of time and distance:

> pages 31–5   75–79 Northbourne Avenue
>
> April–June   2000–01   Sydney–Melbourne trains

The en rule is unspaced in these examples because there is just one word or set of numbers being linked on either side of it. If there is more than one word to be linked on one or both sides, a spaced en rule should be used:

> a Commonwealth – New South Wales agreement
>
> the Alice Springs – Darwin railway project
>
> 52 BC – 108 AD

Association between words

Use an en rule to show an association between words that retain their separate identities:

> a Commonwealth–state agreement   the Asia–Pacific region
>
> cost–benefit ratios   a parent–child relationship

Again, if there is more than one word being linked on one or both sides of the rule, a spaced en rule should be used:

> the United States – Canada trade negotiations

When the en rule is used in this way, the things it links must be parallel in structure—that is, numbers should be linked with numbers, nouns with nouns, adjectives with adjectives, and so on:

> Australian–Japanese research teams   *not*   Australia–Japanese research teams
>
> hand–eye coordination   *not*   hand–visual coordination

Prefixes

When a prefix such as *non-*, *pre-* or *anti-* is attached to a word, a hyphen is often used. If, however, the prefix is attached to more than one word, use an en rule to indicate the more extended link:

➤ See pp. 88–90 for information about using a hyphen to attach a prefix to a word.

> non-refundable goods   *but*   non–English speaking countries
>
> an anti-intellectual proposition   *but*   an anti–harm minimisation stance

Compound adjectives

The situation with compound adjectives is similar to that with prefixes. When a compound adjective precedes the noun it qualifies, it is often hyphenated. If, however, the compound adjective consists of more than one word (or element) on either side of the hyphen, an en rule should replace the hyphen to indicate the broader link:

➤ See pp. 91–93 for information about the hyphenation of compound adjectives.

> an HIV-positive person   *but*   a hepatitis C–positive person

Mathematical settings

Use an en rule, not a hyphen, for a minus sign. It is unspaced when attached to a specific number to indicate a negative value (that is, when it is being used as a mathematical 'adjective'):

−42   *not*   − 42

However, when the minus sign is used as an operative sign (that is, as a mathematical 'verb'), a spaced en rule is used:

10 − 5 [10 minus five]   *not*   10−5

Do not use an en rule:

- as a substitute for *and* with the word *between*

    the period between 1975 and 1999   *not*   the period between 1975–1999

- with the word *from*

    from 1975 to 1999   *not*   from 1975–1999

Forward slash

The forward slash (also known as the solidus, oblique or slash) is used in a number of ways: when showing alternatives; in some shortened forms; in mathematical expressions; as a substitute for *per*, *an* or *a* when units of measurement are abbreviated; and in web addresses. The following are examples:

yes/no

male/female

c/-

(x + y)/(a + b)

60 km/h

http://www.abc.net.au/foreign

Do not use a forward slash:

- with units of measurement that are spelt out

    60 kilometres per hour   *not*   60 kilometres/hour

- to mean *to*

    the 2000–01 financial year   *not*   the 2000/01 financial year

- to show an association between words that retain their separate identities

    a Sydney–Brisbane flight   *not*   a Sydney/Brisbane flight

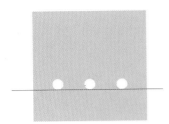

Ellipsis points

Ellipsis points, or suspension points, consist of three full stops (…) and are primarily used to show the omission of a word or words from quoted material:

> 'The new system will simplify current tax arrangements and … will contain measures to compensate low-income individuals and families.'

> 'The new system will simplify current tax arrangements …'

If a paragraph or more is omitted from a block quotation, the ellipsis points can be placed on a line of their own:

> The new direction was emphasised:
>
> > The reform will also restructure Commonwealth–state financial arrangements, since taxes collected under the new system will be treated as state and territory revenue.
> >
> > …
> >
> > Exemptions will be granted to various health, community and charitable services …

When using ellipsis points to show an omission, writers should take great care not to change the meaning of the material they are quoting.

Ellipsis points can also be used to signify indecision and incompleteness, although only some types of writing lend themselves to this:

> But … but … they will soon.

> I felt so isolated. Standing in the yard, watching the other kids play …

With the exception of quotation marks, question marks and exclamation marks, no punctuation mark precedes the first point of ellipsis or follows the last.

How many points? Use only three points, even if the ellipsis points come at the end of a sentence—in other words, don't add a full stop. Word processing and desktop publishing software provides the ellipsis symbol, and a space should be inserted before and after it.

BRACKETS

Brackets are generally used to enclose material that is not essential to the meaning of a sentence—that is, the sentence reads as a grammatical entity if the brackets and the text they enclose are removed.

There are a number of types of brackets: parentheses (or round brackets), square brackets and angle brackets are the most common in the context of this manual. Other types, such as braces (or curly brackets) and slant (or diagonal) brackets, are used in technical contexts such as mathematics and linguistics.

Brackets: Three types of brackets are commonly used in non-technical writing:

- ( ) parentheses
- [ ] square brackets
- < > angle brackets.

Parentheses

The main function of parentheses is to enclose definitions, comments, clarifications, additional information or asides. In some of these cases, commas or em rules can be used to similar effect, although the parentheses tend to reduce the importance of the information inside them:

> Lumholtz's tree-kangaroo (*Dendrolagus lumholtzi*) is nocturnal, spending the day sleeping in the crown of a tree or on a branch.

> The ACCC (Australian Competition and Consumer Commission) has been asked to investigate the matter.

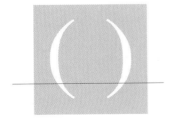

As the economy grows and national income rises, a nation's willingness to meet the needs of its citizens will probably increase (as will its ability to do so).

In 1997–98, 64 per cent ($7.0 billion) of expenditure on welfare services was funded by government, 11 per cent ($1.2 billion) by non-government community service organisations, and 25 per cent ($2.7 billion) by households.

Gertrude Jekyll (1843–1932) was an artist and garden designer.

A further use of parentheses is to enclose cross-references and in-text citations in the author–date style:

The community services workforce consists predominantly of females, the majority of whom work part time (see Table 7.3).

The survey results showed an increase in employment in the sector (Lindsay 1999).

Parentheses within parentheses

One set of parentheses should not be used inside another set. Use a combination of em rules and parentheses instead:

Professor Whimbrel—on his field trips in Western Australia (the Pilbara region) and South Australia—found no evidence of the night parrot, *Geopsittacus occidentalis*, and now believes the species to be extinct.

not

Professor Whimbrel (on his field trips in Western Australia (the Pilbara region) and South Australia) found no evidence of the night parrot …

Punctuation within parentheses

Punctuation within parentheses is determined by the grammatical demands of the enclosed expression:

His theme ('Is town planning necessary?') bored the audience, which consisted mostly of children.

Similarly, a comma follows the closing parenthesis only if a comma would have been used had there been no parentheses:

Loud applause greeted the players (all members of the local dramatic society), who happily took several curtain calls.

A sentence set entirely within parentheses has its concluding punctuation mark within the parentheses:

Simone de Beauvoir was a leading exponent of existentialism. (For a brief discussion of her work see Appendix J.)

Square brackets

Square brackets are primarily used in quoted material to signify editorial interpolations or insertions made by someone other than the author. These interpolations are designed to clarify, to add further information or to point to errors in the original text:

He writes in his biography, 'Although I grew up in Sydney I was born in Wellington [New Zealand], where my father ran a newspaper'.

Parentheses, commas or em rules?
Enclosing parenthetic information in parentheses, as opposed to commas or em rules, tends to reduce the importance of the information.

➤ See Chapter 12 for information about using parentheses in the author–date method of citation.

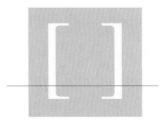

'The High Court [which is in Canberra] is the highest court in the land.'

The child's essay began, 'My family now lives in Canberra but we used to live in Melberne [*sic*], which is much bigger'.

'... *acknowledged* the defects [emphasis added]'.

If parentheses were used in the first two examples, the implication would be that the words inside them formed part of the quotation itself.

Square brackets can also be used to secure clarity in unquoted material.

Jason Ngu and Raoul Nugara had been working on the project for over three years. Nugara worked mostly in the laboratory, although Ngu claimed that he [Ngu] was responsible for the ground-breaking work.

The conventions for using punctuation marks within square brackets are the same as those for parentheses (see page 111).

Angle brackets

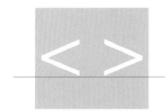

Angle brackets have gained prominence in recent years as a distinctive device for enclosing email and web addresses:

For details of the program, contact Radio National <abc.net.au/rn>.

Email your responses to the director <dwd.hall@mmm.gov.au>, who will be collating the data.

When email or web addresses within running text are enclosed in angle brackets, readers will not be confused by any other adjacent punctuation. An address can also be broken at the end of a line when necessary (although never insert a hyphen). Angle brackets are not necessary, however, if the address is set apart from the text as part of a list or block, where it can be placed on a line of its own.

QUOTATION MARKS

Quotation marks are also called quote marks, quotes or speech marks; they used to be called inverted commas but that term appears to be falling out of favour. Their primary function is to show direct speech and the quoted work of other writers. Other uses are for enclosing the title of a song or an article in a periodical, and for drawing attention to a term that is unusual or recently coined.

The question of whether to use single or double quotes is often debated. In Australia and the United Kingdom both types are widely used; in North America double quotes are the norm.

Single quotation marks are recommended for Australian government publications—in keeping with the trend towards minimal punctuation. Double quotation marks are then used for quotes within quotes.

Direct speech

Direct speech is enclosed in single quotation marks:

'Yes, that is the situation', she replied.

The ambassador declared, 'Not all that we say can have prior approval'.

Media releases—where reported speech often runs from paragraph to paragraph with the occasional 'he said' or similar 'carrier' expression inserted—are treated in the same way:

> The institute's president noted, 'The report deals with a subject of immense complexity in an authoritative but very readable way'.

> 'While drawing out the global aspects of climate change, the report sets the discussion firmly in the context of Australasia and the South Pacific and in this respect provides a valuable reference resource', he said.

In contrast, if several consecutive paragraphs are quoted and there is no intervening carrier expression, quotation marks are used at the beginning of each paragraph but at the end of the last one only.

In plays, transcripts and similar contexts, quotation marks are unnecessary if the direct speech is preceded by the name of the speaker or by such words as *Question* and *Answer* (or their abbreviations):

> LEAR: Nothing?

> CORDELIA: Nothing.

> Q. Did you ever expedite anyone else's application for membership at his request?

> A. At his request? I don't believe so.

Quotations

Use single quotation marks to enclose direct quotations, whether they are sentence fragments, a sentence, or more than one sentence:

> The committee expressed 'grave concern' at the 'discriminatory approach to law enforcement'.

> 'It is complex', he wrote, 'because it combines aesthetic judgments with science and craftsmanship in a kaleidoscope of variables'.

> The glossary defines *aerosol* thus: 'Airborne particle or collection of particles. Erroneously associated with propellant in sprays'.

Quotations that are more than about thirty words long are usually indented from the text margin and set in smaller type. They are called *block quotations* and, because they are differentiated from the text in this way, they do not need quotation marks.

Accurate quotation: Great care must be taken to quote the work of another writer *exactly*.

Other uses of quotation marks

Use quotation marks when referring to the title of an unpublished document, a chapter in a published work, an article in a periodical, an essay, a lecture, a short poem or a song:

> The chapter entitled 'Management, conflict and challenges' discusses the history of national parks as well as contemporary trends in management.

> He delivered his lecture, 'The contribution of the social entrepreneur', clearly and persuasively.

> Have you read Douglas Stewart's poem 'Sun orchids'?

> They quietly sang 'Make me a channel of your peace'.

Quotation marks can also be used in a number of other situations:

- for a technical term on its first mention in a non-technical document

    This 'time-division multiplexing' technique will provide significant benefits.

- for a word or phrase that has been coined or that is being used in a specific sense

    The non-progressive sector will experience a 'cost disease' as wages growth exceeds productivity growth, causing unit costs to rise.

- for ironic emphasis

    The 'policy' was never approved and certainly never implemented.

- for colloquial words, nicknames, slang, or humorous words and phrases in formal writing

    He described the committee's report as a 'blockbuster'.

    They called him 'Mad Dog' Dixon.

The quotation marks are usually unnecessary in any subsequent mentions—although they are a possibility if the subsequent mention is a long way from the first.

An associated use of quotation marks is to enclose matter introduced by such expressions as *entitled*, *marked*, *endorsed*, *the term* and *defined*:

    The papers were marked 'Top Secret'.

    Can anyone in the class define 'karst'?

    The survey used the term 'disability' to mean the presence of one or more of seventeen limitations, restrictions or impairments.

In the first example, the quotation marks could be removed and the words presented in italics or capitals (*Top secret*, TOP SECRET). In the second and third examples, the expressions *karst* and *disability* could be shown in italics without quotation marks (as in this sentence) or perhaps in bold.

➤ See Chapter 9 for information about the uses of italics and bold for textual contrast.

Do not use quotation marks:

- with indirect speech or to enclose familiar expressions

    They said it would be too difficult to implement.

    The swing in Bass was one of many in the landslide that brought the party to power.

- following the expression *so called*

    The so-called policy delivers nothing in reality.

Quotation marks with other punctuation

There is some variation in the practices followed in Australia for the placement of quotation marks in relation to other sentence-punctuation marks. These variations reflect the differences between the North American and British conventions.

➤ See Chapter 12 for information about citing unpublished documents and articles in periodicals.

Within a sentence

In North America it is conventional for closing quotation marks to follow commas but to precede semicolons and colons. In Britain the situation is not quite as simple, although it is more logical. If the quoted material would have contained the punctuation mark in the absence of any interruption, the punctuation mark stays inside the closing quotation mark. On the other hand, if the punctuation mark is part of the carrier sentence, it follows the closing quotation mark.

The following method, which is widely used in Australia and reflects the British practice, is recommended for Australian Government publications:

If the punctuation mark is part of the quotation, keep it as part of the quotation:

'Are you going to apply for the position?' the chairman asked.

'Once it's been given to you,' the tiger said, 'it's always yours'.

If the punctuation mark is not part of the quotation, place it outside the final quotation mark:

Telegraphy has been called 'the Victorian internet'; it was the first practical application of electricity.

'It is new, biotechnology-based knowledge', said the professor, 'that can provide the breakthroughs in agriculture, health and pharmaceuticals'.

Where quoted matter is in parentheses or between em rules, the quotation marks should be placed inside the parentheses or em rules:

His exact words ('We will never surrender') showed his determination.

His exact words—'Never surrender!'—showed his determination.

Quote marks and in-sentence punctuation: If the punctuation mark is part of the quotation, keep it inside the quotation mark. If it is not, place it outside the quotation mark.

Capitalisation: Always capitalise the first word of direct speech—see p. 121.

Ending a sentence

As with quotation marks within a sentence, the North American convention is simply to place a full stop before a closing quotation mark at the end of a sentence. Exclamation marks and question marks are also placed inside the final quotation mark when they are part of the quotation but outside when they are part of the carrier statement.

In Britain, on the other hand, some variation in practices can be seen. One convention often followed is similar to the North American practice, with the terminating punctuation preceding the closing quotation mark if the material quoted forms a full sentence. A different convention is also frequently used, however, where the terminating punctuation is placed before the closing quotation mark only if the quoted material is a full sentence *and* stands completely alone— that is, without any 'he said' or other carrier expression.

It is this latter method, already well established in Australia, that is recommended here: place the terminating punctuation inside the closing quotation mark when there is no carrier expression but outside the closing quotation mark whenever there is a carrier expression:

> 'It's great fun. I love being an advocate.'

but

> She laughed and said, 'It's great fun. I love being an advocate'.

More than one punctuation mark

When two different punctuation marks would logically appear together—one applying to the quotation and the other to the sentence—it is a question of deciding which is the stronger and retaining only that:

> He heard the Speaker call 'Order!'

> A person might ask, 'Why should a prospective employer have access to my medical records?'

but

> Did you hear her say 'Hooray for the digital age'?

Quotations within quotations

For a quotation within a quotation, use double quotation marks inside single ones:

> He praised surrealism for its 'demonstration of freedom' and said that it marked 'an "era" in the history of the human mind'.

TYPOGRAPHY OF PUNCTUATION

Consistency of font

Punctuation marks should be printed in the same font (roman, italic or bold) as the preceding word or expression if they belong to that word or expression. If they relate to the surrounding text as a whole—which is more often the case—they should be printed in the style of the text.

Note the use of italic and roman type for punctuating the following examples:

> Recto: A right-hand page

but

> *Recto:* A right-hand page

> *Freedom! O freedom!*

but

> 'Weltschmerz!—that was the word.'

> She is reading *Whatever happened to compassion?*

but

> What is the meaning of *syntax* ?

Spacing after punctuation

In typewritten (as distinct from typeset) material, it was customary to place two spaces after a colon, semicolon, full stop or other sentence-closing punctuation. Programs for word processing and desktop publishing offer more sophisticated, variable spacing, so this practice of double spacing is now avoided because it can create distracting gaps on a page.

Single space following punctuation: Always use one, not two, spaces after a colon or semicolon, and after a full stop or other sentence-closing punctuation mark.

Chapter 8

Capital letters

CONVENTIONS	**119**
Historical perspective	119
Regional variation	120
Deference and distinction	120
CAPITAL LETTERS IN SYNTAX	**120**
Beginning a sentence	120
In quoted speech	121
In direct address	121
PERSONAL NAMES	**121**
Derivatives of personal names	121
Particles in family names	121
Medial capitals	122
Nicknames and epithets	122
NATIONALITIES AND DISTINCT GROUPS OF PEOPLE	**122**
NAMES OF ORGANISATIONS	**123**
Full and abbreviated names	123
Plurals	123
About using capitals for terms associated with government	124
TITLES AND MODES OF ADDRESS	**126**
Titles	126
Modes of address	127
Deities	127
GEOGRAPHICAL TERMS	**127**
Official geographical names	127

Geographical and political designations	127
Topographical features	127
Local names	128
Buildings, structures and public places	128
Points of the compass	128
TIME INDICATORS AND PERIODS	**129**
The calendar	129
Historical and cultural periods	129
Holidays, religious days and public events	129
SCIENTIFIC NAMES	**130**
Botany and zoology	130
Chemistry and medicine	131
Geology	132
Astronomy	132
Atmospheric phenomena	132
COMMERCIAL TERMS	**132**
Trademarks, proprietary names and brand names	132
Computer and Internet terms	133
PUBLICATIONS	**134**
Titles of books and other publications	134
Elements within a publication	135

entences should always start with a capital letter. Initial capitals should lso be used for proper nouns and for proper names (the names of pecific people, places and organisations). When organisations' names re reduced to a generic element, the capitals can usually be dispensed ith; capitals are retained, however, if the shortened version still carries specific element. Thus, the Attorney-General's Department becomes ttorney-General's' but 'the department'.

ke punctuation, capitalisation is being influenced by minimalist trends. In splay contexts—for example, in the credit lists of television programs—people's ames are sometimes shown without any initial capitals at all. In this chapter we ead a middle path, bearing in mind the expectations of a wide general audience.

ONVENTIONS

istorical perspective

Old English manuscripts, capital letters were associated with the first word in a apter, for which the Latin was *capitula* (which in turn comes from the lettering sed at the top of columns in Roman architecture). The first letter of the word was latively large, 'dropped' over two or more lines, and often illuminated (decorated d coloured) to attract readers' attention.

he term *capital letter* was subsequently applied to the less elaborate but still larged letters used within the line of print to mark the first word of a sentence d for proper nouns and names. These letters were also known as *majuscules* arge letters), while the smaller letters used in the body of the text were called *inuscules*. In early modern printing, the letters were stored in separate boxes (or ises) stacked one above the other, with the *upper case* containing the majuscules d the *lower case* the minuscules.

England in the mid-1500s, John Hart recommended that capitals be used not ıly at the beginning of every sentence and for proper nouns and names, but also r other 'important' common nouns. By the late 1600s, however, some writers ere capitalising *all* nouns, a practice that continued through the following ntury. This provoked a reaction among grammarians, who claimed that the efulness of capitals was being undermined. The modern convention in English at reserves capital letters for the beginning of sentences and for proper nouns d names became increasingly accepted during the nineteenth century.

Recommended capitalisation practice:

- Attorney-General's Department (specific); Attorney-General's (shortened but specific); the department (generic)
- Rottnest Island (specific); the island (generic).

'Capitalisation': The term *capitalisation* and its derivatives are used in this manual to mean using an initial capital letter. The alternative meaning (of using capitals for every letter of a word) is referred to as *full capitalisation*.

Regional variation

All European languages that use the Roman alphabet also use capital letters to begin sentences and for proper nouns and names. Beyond that, however, differences emerge. In French, proper nouns are capitalised but their related adjectives are not—for example, *Italie* but *italien*, *italienne*—whereas in English the adjectival forms are capitalised. In German, all nouns (proper and common) are capitalised—for example, *Essen* is both the city in Rhine–Westphalia and the common word for 'food'.

Capitalisation conventions also vary within the English-speaking world. While there is a trend internationally to reduce the overall number of capitals on a page, it is more marked in the United States than in Britain. Australian practice generally lies somewhere in between.

Deference and distinction

Traditionally, a capital letter has often been attached to a proper name to signify respect for a particular position or organisation or to draw a distinction between two entities with the same generically abbreviated title. For example, employees might refer to their own organisation as 'the Company', 'the Bank' or 'the Department' but to another organisation as 'the company', 'the bank' or 'the department'. The same distinction is sometimes seen in the use of capitals for positions within an organisation's own hierarchy but not for similar positions outside that organisation.

Capitals in legal documents: One of the few remaining widespread uses of capitals to distinguish an otherwise generic word is found in legal documents, where words that have been specifically defined (such as *Schedule* and *Party*) are often capitalised wherever they appear in the text.

With the move to fewer capitals, this practice is rapidly declining. Apart from the apparent inconsistencies that such distinctions can create throughout a document, the practice also gives the impression of an 'us and them' attitude that is inappropriate in material produced for an external audience. Further, the practice does little to aid clarity: if the context does not make the meaning clear, a capital alone will rarely do so.

CAPITAL LETTERS IN SYNTAX

Beginning a sentence

A capital letter should invariably be used at the start of a sentence: readers rely heavily on this cue. This well-established convention is sometimes challenged by proper names that begin with a lower-case letter. For example:

- names deliberately presented in lower case—such as *silverchair*
- business names built on Internet addresses—such as *amazon.com* or *travel.com.au*
- trade names with mid-word capitals designed primarily for display purposes—such as *eBook*.

In these instances, either rearrange the sentence so that the proper name no longer starts it or, if the lower-case first letter is not essential to understanding the name, convert it to a capital at the start of the sentence. The latter approach has traditionally been used for foreign names beginning with a lower-case letter—for example, *de Gaulle*.

In quoted speech

The first word of a piece of quoted speech is capitalised. For example:

> The minister said, 'We don't believe that such compromise is justified'.

When the quotation is interrupted and then resumed, and if no proper noun or name is involved, the first word of the second fragment appears in lower case:

> 'We don't believe', said the minister, 'that such compromise is justified'.

If only a sentence fragment is quoted, and again if no proper noun or name is involved, it also appears in lower case:

> The minister replied that she didn't believe in 'such compromise'.

In direct address

A capital letter is used to mark titles and honorific names used as a form of address:

> 'We think, Professor, there are other options.'

> 'I object, Your Honour.'

> 'Yes, Minister, that is true.'

PERSONAL NAMES

The names of all individuals—real or fictitious—should always be given initial capitals in publications and correspondence. For example:

> Oodgeroo Noonucal   Michael Leunig   Mr Curly

Derivatives of personal names

When a personal name comes to represent a common noun within the language, it sooner or later loses its initial capital:

> braille   furphy   shrapnel

Similarly, personal names that provide the stem for a common word lose their initial capital:

> bowdlerise   boycotted   bloomers

In contrast, derivatives that keep their connection with the individual generally retain their initial capital:

> Machiavellian   Shakespearean   Marxist

Particles in family names

Family names that contain a particle (a preposition or definite article belonging to a foreign language) can raise questions about capitalisation in English. Familiar examples of such particles are *da*, *de*, *della*, *von*, *van*, *le* and *la*. Most, but not all, of

Proper names shown in lower case: Either capitalise these at the start of a sentence or restructure the sentence to avoid the problem. (Restructuring would be necessary for words such as *eBook*, as the adjacent capitals would otherwise look very odd.)

➤ See pp. 124–5 for a discussion of capitalisation of words associated with government. Chapter 7 provides information about the punctuation associated with quoted material.

these particles would be written without an initial capital in the source language. For example:

Leonardo da Vinci   Luca della Robbia   Paul von Hindenburg

but

Jean de La Fontaine   Le Corbusier   Jeanne Du Barry

The particle is often, but not always, omitted when the given name is omitted:

Otto von Bismarck … Bismarck

but

Vincent van Gogh … van Gogh

In English-speaking countries, the foreign particles in personal names are often capitalised as the first stage of anglicisation and may subsequently be absorbed into the main element as one word with a single capital. For example:

Da Costa   *to*   Dacosta   Van Der Meer   *to*   Vandermeer

The capitalisation practice with personal names of this kind is largely a matter of individual preference and family custom, which writers and editors need to ascertain on a case-by-case basis.

Medial capitals

Some personal names have a mid-word, or medial, capital in addition to the initial capital. This is standard for names prefixed with Mc—such as McInerney and McCaughey—but more variable for those prefixed with *Mac* or *Fitz*:

MacDonald   *or*   Macdonald   FitzGerald   *or*   Fitzgerald

The practice of using medial capitals in the names of organisations is a recent and increasingly common trend. For example:

HarperCollins   The ChildCare Property Trust

PricewaterhouseCoopers   The Health eSignatures Authority

Precise citation: Always show a proper name in the style the owner uses.

Nicknames and epithets

Nicknames and epithets are conventionally capitalised:

the Iron Lady   Hagar the Horrible   Alexander the Great

NATIONALITIES AND DISTINCT GROUPS OF PEOPLE

Initial capitals should always be given to names that identify nationalities, races, tribes, clans, the inhabitants of a particular region, the adherents of a particular religion, and the speakers of a particular language:

Turkish   Filipino   Melanesian   Caucasian   Arrernte

Queenslander   Buddhist   Christian   Flemish

➤ Chapter 4 provides advice about referring to Australia's Indigenous peoples.

The names of religions, languages and language groups are also capitalised:

Islam   Sanskrit   Dravidian

In contrast, common words derived from geographical names or regions are often presented without an initial capital:

westernise   venetian blinds   brussels sprouts

If you are unsure about whether to capitalise words of this kind, consult *The Macquarie dictionary* or *The Australian concise Oxford dictionary*.

NAMES OF ORGANISATIONS

Full and abbreviated names

In the full official names of organisations and other bodies such as assemblies and conferences, all words other than articles, prepositions and conjunctions are given initial capitals:

the Department of Finance and Administration

the Academy of the Humanities

When names of this kind are abbreviated to just the generic element for subsequent references, leave them uncapitalised:

the Department of Finance and Administration ... the department

the Academy of the Humanities ... the academy

the University of Western Australia ... the university

the Australian Ballet Company ... the company

the Royal Commission on the Constitution ... the royal commission

the Australian Broadcasting Corporation ... the corporation

Gundagai Shire Council ... the shire council ... the council

the Regional Australia Summit ... the summit

In contrast, when the name of the organisation or body is abbreviated but retains some specific elements, keep the capitals:

the Department of Immigration and Multicultural Affairs ... a matter for Immigration ... the department

the Reserve Bank of Australia ... the Reserve Bank ... the bank

the National Press Club ... the Press Club ...the club

the National Gallery of Australia ... the National Gallery ... the gallery

Plurals

When grouping two or more organisations with the same generic name, the capitals can be dispensed with for the shared generic portion:

the AAA Building Society and the Independent Building Society

but

the AAA and Independent building societies

(continued on p. 126)

ABOUT
Using capitals for terms associated with government

Generally, terms associated with government should be capitalised in the way described elsewhere in this chapter—that is, capitalise the full, official name and the abbreviation of that name when it retains specific elements, but use lower case when the abbreviation is reduced to the generic element. Similarly, when these terms are used generically and are not directly related to a specific name or title, and when they are in the plural or used adjectivally, they should not be capitalised.

Some particular words and applications are described in detail here and a few exceptions explained.

'Government'

The word *government* should be capitalised as part of a formal title or abbreviated specific title, but lower case is generally appropriate elsewhere:

> The Australian Government is responsible for … The government proposes to … This government policy will … The policy will be reviewed by the Australian Government from time to time.

> the Victorian Government … the government

> the Australian and New Zealand governments

> the governments of South Australia and Tasmania

> Sanitation is the responsibility of local government.

> It is the function of government to …

When more than one specific government is being mentioned, a full title may need to be repeated if the context alone is not sufficient to prevent ambiguity.

'Commonwealth'

As a federation, Australia is known as the *Commonwealth of Australia*, and the primary governing body is the *Commonwealth Parliament*. In this context, *Commonwealth* is always capitalised:

> Defence is a Commonwealth responsibility.

> This question was debated at length in the Commonwealth Parliament.

> … under the Commonwealth Government's external affairs powers.

When preparing documents for an international readership, writers and editors should be mindful that the wor *Commonwealth* is much more readily associated with the Commonwealth of Nations (formerly the British Empire). misunderstanding might occur, it is prudent to use the word *Australian* instead of *Commonwealth*. For example:

> the Australian Government

> the Australian Parliament

An uncapitalised *commonwealth* has several meanings, reinforcing the nee for capitalisation in the Australian context.

'Federal'

The adjective *federal* requires a capita only if it forms part of an official title:

> the Federal Court of Australia … the Feder Court … the court

> a federal government initiative

> Defence is a federal responsibility.

The federal government, which is a broad, descriptive term for the Commonwealth (or Australian) Government, does not need to be capitalised.

The states and territories

The same general approach applies to the words *state* and *territory* when these refer to the jurisdictions that make up the Commonwealth of Australia: use capitals for official or abbreviated specific titles but not for generic or plural references. For example:

> The Australian Capital Territory includes Jervis Bay. The territory's total area is more than 2000 square kilometres.

> The South Australian Government initiated the project … The state government will meet regularly to review progress.

> Responsibility has been delegated to the states and territories.

> … under federal–state arrangements.

In many contexts, however, *the Territory* has become the conventional, semi-official term for the Northern Territory. It thus operates as a proper name and has a capital *T*. (See page 127 for other examples of names that have acquired semi-official status.)

'Parliament' and associated terms

As with *government*, *parliament* and associated terms should be capitalised only in full formal titles:

> the Commonwealth Parliament

> the Parliamentary Library

> Parliament House

> The problem was raised in the South Australian Parliament.

Used generically or as an adjective, the word is clear without a capital. For example:

> The debate in parliament continued for hours.

> Federal parliamentary procedures require members to …

> Of the parliamentarians present …

References to the Senate and the House of Representatives—and the equivalent bodies in the states and territories—are always capitalised. For example:

> The proposed revisions will be put to the Senate.

> The Legislative Assembly will vote on the matter tomorrow. The Assembly …

The parliamentary terms *bench*, *front bench*, *back bench*, *front bencher* and *back bencher* do not need initial capitals as they are not part of a formal title.

Particular words needing capitals

Some nouns used in connection with government are capitalised to distinguish them from their generic meaning. These are:

- the Cabinet
- the Treasury
- the Crown
- the House, meaning either parliamentary chamber
- the Budget, but not as an adjective or when plural—*budget provisions*, *the budgetary process*, *successive federal budgets*.

In the legislative context, some other words are always capitalised, whether used in the singular or the plural:

- Act(s)
- Ordinance(s)
- Regulation(s)
- Bill(s).

Similarly, when used alone in a legal context, *the Bar* and *the Bench* take a capital, although this is not necessary for references to *the full bench*.

Government programs and agreements

The names of government programs, treaties, protocols and similar agreements follow the generally recommended capitalisation approach: capitalise full names and abbreviations that remain specific but not abbreviations that consist of the generic element only. For example:

> the National Hepatitis C Action Plan … the Hepatitis C Action Plan … the action plan

> the National Program for the Centenary of Federation … the Centenary of Federation Program … the program

> the Greater Artesian Basin Sustainability Initiative … the Artesian Basin Initiative … the initiative

> the International Convention for the Prevention of Marine Pollution from Ships … the convention

> the Commonwealth–State Housing Agreement … the Housing Agreement … the agreement

> the Treaty of Versailles … the treaties of Versailles and Locarno

Titles

For advice about capitalising titles of specific parliamentary positions such as those of prime minister, treasurer and other ministers, see pages 126–7.

TITLES AND MODES OF ADDRESS

Titles

The official titles of the principals or chief executives of many Australian institutions are capitalised. For example:

> the Governor-General
>
> the Prime Minister of Australia
>
> the Leader of the Opposition
>
> the Chief Justice of the High Court of Australia
>
> the Archbishop of Brisbane
>
> the Chancellor of Murdoch University
>
> the Premier of Victoria
>
> the Minister for Defence
>
> the Secretary to the Department of Industry, Science and Resources
>
> the Attorney-General

When abbreviated to their generic element, however, most of these titles can be presented in lower case without any loss of clarity:

> … according to the Minister for Defence. The minister's view is shared by …

Exceptions are the titles of the current incumbents of the positions of Australian monarch, prime minister and treasurer and of foreign heads of state. All these are capitalised in official publications, even when the titles are truncated or used generically:

> Next week, the Queen will be opening parliament.
>
> the Prime Minister of Australia … the Prime Minister, [name of current incumbent], has announced that … the Prime Minister
>
> The Treasurer will be presenting the Budget on …
>
> the President of the United States of America … President [family name of current incumbent] announced that … the President

In contrast, references to previous incumbents of official positions, and to the offices themselves, are not capitalised:

> When Sir Edmund Barton became prime minister …
>
> She served as vice-chancellor for a decade.
>
> He is supported by the former president.

The Australian prime minister:
References to the current Australian prime minister are always capitalised. References to former Australian prime ministers are not.

Plural references are also presented in lower case:

> the premiers of Queensland and South Australia
>
> the kings of Thailand

The formal titles of members of parliament are capitalised, but generic references can be presented in lower case. For example:

> Senator Olivia Tuckman

the Member for Blantyre, the Hon. Orlando di Stasio, MP

Five senators and three members of the House of Representatives attended the convention.

Thirty places were set aside for members of parliament.

Modes of address

Initial capitals are always used in words that constitute modes of address or honorifics. For example:

Her Majesty the Queen   His Excellency the Governor-General

His Grace the Archbishop of Melbourne   Dame Joan Sutherland

Professor Arthur Delbridge   Ms Strickland

➤ See Appendix A for detailed advice on modes of address and honours.

Deities

The words *God*, *Allah*, *Brahma* and the names of other deities are always capitalised.

In the past, the capital letter assigned to *God* was often extended to the attendant pronouns—*He*, *Him* and *His*; *You* and *Your*; *Thou*, *Thee* and *Thine*—but this is now less common.

GEOGRAPHICAL TERMS

Official geographical names

The official names of countries as well as any commonly used shorter forms are always capitalised, as are the names of states, territories and provinces:

the Grand Duchy of Luxembourg … Luxembourg

the Australian Antarctic Territory

Guangxi Province

Geographical and political designations

Names that designate a group of nations geographically or politically are always capitalised. For example:

South-East Asia   Central America   the Balkans

In contrast, purely descriptive—and unofficial—names for parts of a geographical entity usually do not need to be capitalised:

northern Australia   southern Italy

Sometimes, however, descriptive names of this kind develop semi-official status; they are then usually shown with initial capitals:

Central Australia   Far North Queensland

Topographical features

Names designating particular topographical features—mountains, rivers, valleys, bays, islands, and so on—are always capitalised when cited in full:

the Blue Mountains   the Barossa Valley   Aldgate Creek

When the name is reduced to its generic element, it is usually left uncapitalised:

> the Murray River ... the river   Lord Howe Island ... the island

But when the generic element serves as the conventional abbreviation for a place, it operates like a proper name and remains capitalised. For example:

> the Great Barrier Reef ... the Reef   the Persian Gulf ... the Gulf

When two or more topographical names with the same generic element are combined in the same expression, the pluralised element is presented in lower case:

> the Murray and Darling rivers   the Barossa and Hunter valleys

For clarity, however, an initial capital is retained if the plural element precedes the individual names:

> ... Mounts Alexander and Macedon

Local names

Common names given to parts of a city, state or territory are capitalised. For example:

> the Adelaide Hills   the North Shore   the Western District   the Top End

The names of roads, streets and other thoroughfares are also capitalised:

> George Street   Wickham Terrace   the Monaro Highway

Buildings, structures and public places

The names of buildings, structures and public places are always capitalised when given in full but not when they are abbreviated to their generic element or in plural combinations:

> Adelaide Town Hall ... the town hall
>
> Iron Cove Bridge ... the bridge
>
> the Iron Cove and Gladesville bridges

The names of private properties are capitalised in the same way as other local names; quotation marks are not necessary. For example:

> Victoria River Downs   Glen Stuart

Points of the compass

When abbreviated, the points of the compass are always capitalised (and shown without full stops). When spelt out, they are shown in lower case (and hyphenated when combined):

> W   SE   ENE
>
> west   south-east   east-north-east

TIME INDICATORS AND PERIODS

The calendar

The names of the days and months are always capitalised:

> Thursday   January

The names of seasons are usually left in lower case, as are less commonly used calendar points. For example:

> winter   the summer solstice   a leap year

➤ For more information about the abbreviations used for calendar expressions and time zones, see p. 157.

Historical and cultural periods

The titles of specific periods and events of historical or cultural importance are capitalised; when they are abbreviated to a generic element they are not. For example:

> the Renaissance   the Bronze Age   the Depression
>
> the Second World War ... at the end of the war
>
> The Battle of Long Tan was a significant achievement for the Australian forces. After the battle ...

In contrast, many broad historical and cultural descriptions are frequently shown in lower case:

> the colonial era   impressionist painters   baroque ornamentation

In specialist publications, however, historical or cultural descriptions of this kind are often capitalised—for example, *Impressionist painters, Baroque ornamentation.*)

Numerically described periods are not capitalised:

> the eighteenth century   the nineteen hundreds   the 1900s

The 1990s or the 1990's? Expressions like this do not require an apostrophe.

Holidays, religious days and public events

Capitals are given to the names of all institutional holidays, holy days or periods in religious calendars, and regularly occurring public ceremonies and events:

> Australia Day   Good Friday   Anzac Day
>
> Ramadan   Yom Kippur   Ash Wednesday
>
> the Adelaide Festival   the City-to-Surf   the AFL Grand Final

Note that although *Anzac* is an acronym for 'Australian and New Zealand Army Corps' and thus might be given full capitals, it falls into the category of familiar acronyms that take only an initial capital (see page 153). This usage is enshrined in The Protection of the Word 'Anzac' Regulations, administered by the Minister for Veterans' Affairs.

NL3734(H)/J. Nomarhas

SCIENTIFIC NAMES

Botany and zoology

In botany and zoology, the names of all the taxonomic groupings down to the genus level are capitalised. The species epithet should not be capitalised. For example:

Botany

Division	Angiospermae
Class	Dicotyledonae
Order	Myrtales
Family	Myrtaceae
Genus	*Eucalyptus*
Species	*Eucalyptus marginata*

Zoology

Phylum	Arthropoda
Class	Insecta
Order	Blattodea
Family	Blattidae
Genus	*Blatta*
Species	*Blatta orientalis*

As these lists indicate, the genus and species names are always presented in italics

> There are over 1000 species in the genus *Acacia*. One of the best known is *Acacia baileyana*.

Similarly, subspecies and varietal names are italicised. In botany, there are five taxonomic categories below species level—subspecies, variety, subvariety, form and subform—and as a result it is necessary to give a descriptive term before any subspecific or varietal epithet. This term (for example, 'subsp.' or 'var.') is shown in roman type, is usually abbreviated, and is never capitalised:

> Although originally widespread in the study area, only a few occurrences were found of *Halosarcia indica* subsp. *leiostachya*.

> Fire and disease have caused a decline of the plant *Epacris virgata* var. *autumnalis* in the area surveyed.

A complex area: For more information about the conventions governing the use of scientific names, consult specialist reference works, several of which are listed on pp. 285–7.

In zoology, on the other hand, there is only one taxonomic level, the subspecies, below that of species, and so the abbreviation 'subsp.' before the subspecific name is not used:

> The Tasmanian subspecies of the wedge-tailed eagle, *Aquila audax fleayi*, is classed as vulnerable.

In zoology, a species or subspecies name is never capitalised, even if it is derived from a proper name. In botany, it is formally recommended by the Botanical Code out not obligatory in all cases) that species, subspecies and varietal names derived om proper names be shown in lower case.

When a genus name is repeated, it can be abbreviated to the first letter capitalised and with a full stop) on subsequent mentions. For example:

Epacris stuartii is a small woody shrub; *E. limbata* is somewhat taller.

the discussion involves two or more genera beginning with the same letter—for xample, *Banksia* and *Blechnum*—each genus name can be abbreviated to its first vo letters (*Ba.* and *Bl.*) to avoid confusion.

dding a person's name and date to a species name

technical works, a person's name and date might appear after a species name— *elis catus* Linnaeus, 1758, for example. The name is that of the person who first escribed the species, and the date is the year of publication of the description. Vhen the name and date are enclosed in parentheses, as in *Robshelfordia rcumducta* (Walker, 1869), this parenthetic information alerts the reader to the ct that, in the example, Walker first described this cockroach in 1869 (as *Blatta rcumducta*) but that another author has since allocated it to the genus obshelfordia.

ommon names of plants and animals

eneric names that have become common names, and English derivatives of eneric and other names, are lower-cased and shown in roman type:

camellia   acacia   eucalyptus

streptococcus   staphylococcus   rickettsia

pterodactyl   amoeba   mammal

ommon names are usually capitalised only if they contain proper names:

red-back spider   Norfolk Island pine   Bennett's wallaby

some specialist fields, particularly in ornithology, there is a preference to pitalise common names—for example, *Blue-winged Kookaburra, Wedge-tailed agle, Spotted Nightjar*. However, when lists of common names from different plant d animal groups (including birds) appear together, the dominant convention— at of using lower-case letters—should prevail.

general usage, the names of common breeds of animals generally do not take an itial capital, even if they also refer to a geographical area:

labrador (dog)   siamese (cat)   friesian (cow)

gain, however, in specialist literature these and other less familiar names are metimes capitalised.

hemistry and medicine

hemicals and their compounds are not capitalised:

iodine   carbon monoxide   sodium chloride

Capitals with abbreviations: The word or phrase on which a fully capitalised abbreviation is based (for example, *human immunodeficiency virus*, or *HIV*) is not capitalised unless a proper name is involved—see p. 153.

Unless they contain a proper name, disease and virus names do not take an initial capital either:

> hepatitis B   foot-and-mouth disease
>
> human immunodeficiency virus (HIV)
>
> Down syndrome   German measles

Proprietary names of drugs and other chemicals are capitalised, but the generic names are presented in lower case. For example:

> Celestone V … hydrocortisone
>
> Panadol … paracetamol

Geology

The identifying elements of geological names are capitalised but the generic ones usually are not. For example:

> the Lower Jurassic period   the Mesozoic era

Astronomy

The names of planets, stars, constellations and other astronomical configurations are capitalised:

> the Magellanic Clouds   Ursa Major   the Southern Cross

When astronomical names consist of both an identifying and a generic element, the generic element usually appears in lower case:

> the Crab nebula   Halley's comet

In general, the words *earth*, *sun* and *moon* are capitalised only when they are being referred to in a planetary context:

> The Sun is closer to Venus than to Earth.

but

> The phases of the moon govern the planting cycle.

Atmospheric phenomena

Cyclones and similar phenomena are conventionally given people's names, which are capitalised; the preceding generic element is left in lower case. For example:

> cyclone Tracy   tropical cyclone Aivu   hurricane Andrew

COMMERCIAL TERMS

Trademarks, proprietary names and brand names

Current registered trademarks, proprietary names and brand names should be capitalised. The fact that many of these terms have become household words explains why people who are unaware of a term's origin often fail to use a capital letter. But to print a current trademark, proprietary name or brand name without a capital—and in some contexts (such as in many overseas markets) without the registration or trademark symbol—might be an infringement of its registered status and could lead to litigation.

Trademarks: IP Australia provides a list of registered trademarks on its web site <http://www.ipaustralia.gov.au>.

Larger dictionaries usually show whether a term originated as a trademark or proprietary name but not whether that status has lapsed. Publishers of dictionaries typically adopt a conservative approach and are reluctant to change the capital letter on former trademarks, being keen to avoid litigation themselves. The following trademarks are listed as examples merely to suggest the scope of the problem:

Aqualung	Esky	Pyrex
Aspro	Fibro	Rollerblade
Bean Bag	Frisbee	Sellotape
Band-Aid	Hoover	Technicolor
Biro	Jeep	Thermos
Brylcreem	Kleenex	Vaseline
Caterpillar	Laundromat	Velcro
Cellophane	Masonite	Walkman
Coca-Cola, Coke	Perspex	Windcheater
Doona	Plasticine	Xerox

Brand and model names should also be capitalised. For example:

a Harley Davidson   a Collins Class submarine   a Boeing 767

➤ See p. 147 for further information about presentation of the names of ships, aircraft and other kinds of vehicles.

Computer and Internet terms

The names of items of computer software and hardware (which are usually also proprietary names) and related terms are capitalised and sometimes even fully capitalised. For example:

BASIC   UNIX   IBM PC

Windows NT   Apple Macintosh   AutoCAD

Microsoft Word   QuarkXPress   PostScript

Many dictionaries currently show the following more general words with initial capitals as well:

Internet   the Net   World Wide Web

However, there seems to be a growing tendency to use lower case for these words. For example, lower case appears to be the predominant usage for *web site*, which is also often seen as one word.

PUBLICATIONS

Titles of books and other publications

The titles of books, periodicals, chapters, articles, documents placed on web sites, and so on, begin with a capital letter. The extent of capitalisation after that is a matter of house style or individual preference. This manual recommends minimal capitalisation for all but the titles of legislation, journals, magazines and newspapers, which are conventionally given maximal capitalisation.

Minimal capitalisation for publication titles: This is the style recommended by this manual—except for the titles of legislation and periodicals, which should be given maximal capitalisation.

An example of minimal capitalisation for a cover

Minimal capitalisation

With minimal capitalisation, only the first word of a title and any proper nouns and names (and their derivatives) are capitalised. Titles of published works are placed in italics; titles of unpublished works and of articles or chapters within a published work are set apart by quotation marks. For example:

> *A town like Alice*
>
> *Women's worth: pay equity and job evaluation in Australia*
>
> … in the chapter entitled 'Three Australian engineers'.
>
> … in the article 'On the menu: organic food' in last week's *Bulletin*.

Maximal capitalisation

Maximal capitalisation involves capitalising all words in a title other than articles, prepositions and conjunctions. For example:

> *A Town like Alice*
>
> *Women's Worth: Pay Equity and Job Evaluation in Australia*
>
> … in the chapter entitled 'Three Australian Engineers'.
>
> … in the article 'On the Menu: Organic Food' in last week's *Bulletin*.

Legislation and periodicals

The titles of legislation and of periodicals (journals, magazines and newspapers) are conventionally given maximal capitalisation, and it is recommended that this exception to the minimal capitalisation practice be followed. These titles should therefore be set out as in the following examples:

> *Environment Protection and Biodiversity Conservation Act 1999*
>
> *Business Review Weekly*
>
> the *Courier-Mail*
>
> the *Journal of English Linguistics*

When *The* is shown on a periodical's masthead as part of the title—*The Age*, for example—it can be capitalised when it does not coincide with the ordinary use of the definite article:

> He writes for *The Age*.

but

> … in the *Age* editorial on Monday.

Elements within a publication

It is recommended that references to elements of a publication other than pages be capitalised when mentioned in running text. For example:

This is discussed in Chapter 4.

Population growth between 1995 and 2000 is shown in Figure 3.2.

... (see Table 11)

but

This is discussed on pages 59–63.

Chapter **9** **Textual contrast**

HEADINGS	**137**
Heading hierarchies	137
Effective wording of headings	139
BOXES AND SIDE PANELS	**140**
ITEMISED INDENTED MATERIAL	**141**
Balance	141
Consistent, parallel formats	141
Bullets, numbers and letters	141
Extent of indenting	141
About dot-point series	142
ITALICS	**145**
Books and periodicals	145
Plays and long poems	146
Musical compositions	146
Films, videos, and radio and television programs	146
Works of art	146
Scientific names of animals and plants	147
Legislation and legal cases	147
Ships, aircraft and other vehicles	147
Technical terms and terms being defined	147
Letters, words and phrases cited as such	148
Words used in special senses or with particular emphasis	148
Foreign words and phrases	148
BOLD OR COLOURED TYPE	**149**
UNDERLINING	**149**

Textual contrast—using different page layouts and different fonts and weights—can be very useful for readers. It helps them recognise the structure of a document, the direction of the discussion, and the important points. For readers who are simply scanning the material, it is essential. The contrast also helps to distinguish between various types of information and can even suggest changes in authorial tone.

Two types of textual contrast are discussed in this chapter:

- format-related contrast—in particular, headings, itemised material (including dot-point series), and boxes and side panels for highlighting text
- typographic contrast at word and sentence level—for example, by the use of italics.

It is important to be sparing in the use of textual contrast—too much and the effect is lost.

HEADINGS

Headings are fundamental to textual contrast: they are the signposts for readers. To be effective, they must be carefully graded, distributed and worded.

Heading hierarchies

A clear and logical heading hierarchy shows readers the relative importance of pieces of information. Matters such as balance and differentiation between heading levels need careful consideration when the hierarchy is being developed.

Balance

A well-balanced heading hierarchy provides an effective road map for both paper-based and screen-based documents. Balance is particularly important for the latter, since menu schemes that are too shallow or too deep can impede access and frustrate readers.

Readers find it difficult to remember too many separate items within a single category, so try to break up heading groups into subsets wherever possible. Long documents can benefit from heading hierarchies that result in five or six different levels; any greater subdivision is usually too complicated.

Text preparation and document design: Chapters 17 and 18 concentrate on layout and typography, which are basically about textual contrast as well. However, those two chapters are concerned principally with document design, whereas this chapter is directed more towards the preparation of text. Tables and graphs, which also serve to differentiate text, are dealt with in Chapters 19 and 21 respectively.

Frequency and complexity: The use of headings has increased in publications generally, and hierarchies have become more complex. Care is needed to ensure that headings are used effectively.

➤ Chapter 3 discusses how people absorb information from both paper-based and screen-based documents, how material can be structured to achieve balanced groupings, and the role of headings in aiding comprehension.

➤ See Chapter 18 for detailed advice on the typographical treatment of headings.

Clarity of heading hierarchy: Each successive heading level must be visually (as well as logically) subordinate to those above it in the hierarchy.

Readers also benefit if information is divided into readily absorbable 'chunks' within the heading hierarchy. A useful guide for on-screen material is to keep to maximum of about 200 words between headings (say, somewhere between two and four paragraphs per heading). On most screens, this pattern would enable readers to see at least one heading at any time, thus helping them to remember the wider context of the information. For paper-based documents, a similar frequency of headings is not so crucial, since readers can usually see more text on a printed pa (and particularly on a double-page spread) than they do on a screen. The goal should be to ensure that there is at least one heading (but preferably more) on each open spread of an information document.

Differentiating heading levels

The typographical distinctions between different levels of a heading hierarchy—usually called level 1, level 2, and so on—need to be very clear. Generally, the higher ranked headings present no problem. Readers will have little difficulty recognising, for example, that a level 1 heading (often a chapter heading) represents a broader category than a level 2 heading. The differences in placeme on the page or screen, the headings' relative size and weight, and perhaps differences in colour and font are usually obvious.

Further down the hierarchy, though, the distinctions can sometimes become blurred. For example, if only two of the lower level heading styles appear on a particular page or screen, will it be obvious which heading is subordinate to the other? To avoid confusing readers, make sure that the typography and spacing chosen for each successive heading level combine to make the visual relationship between all levels of the hierarchy absolutely clear.

Numbered headings

Headings in information documents are sometimes numbered for cross-referencin purposes. It is recommended that such numbering be used only if the frequency o internal cross-referencing demands it. The same applies to paragraph numbering

When using numbered headings, it is preferable not to number them below level in the hierarchy. The numbers otherwise become too cumbersome (Section 5.10.3.4, for example), and such detailed cross-referencing is rarely necessary.

Isolated headings

Isolated headings—those not accompanied by another heading of the same hierarchical level—suggest poor document structure and should be avoided. At i simplest, this means that if there is a chapter 1 in a document, there should also a chapter 2. At deeper levels of the hierarchy the same balance remains essentia For example, a level 3 heading numbered 5.4.1 should be followed by a heading the same level numbered 5.4.2. A similar balance is necessary for unnumbered headings.

Linking headings with the text

Ideally, each heading should be separated from the following one by some text. While it is sometimes difficult to avoid having two headings together without intervening text, a string of three such headings is clumsy and does not help to deliver clear messages.

When a heading sits above the text—perhaps even separated from it by a line space—readers may not easily construe the two as a logical unit. Make sure, therefore, that the meaning of the first sentence after the heading is independent, so that readers do not have to refer back to the heading to understand the sentence. Compare, for instance, the improved reading flow of the second of the following examples:

> **Further research**
> The need for this was raised in four of the survey responses.

> **Further research**
> The need for further research was raised in four of the survey responses.

Where the lowest level of a heading hierarchy is run into the text, however, readers will have little difficulty construing the heading and the subsequent text as a logical unit, since they are both on the same line:

> **Further research:** The need for this was raised in four of the survey responses.

Effective wording of headings

If headings are to be worded effectively, three basic principles should be borne in mind:

- Keep headings reasonably brief, without compromising their usefulness.
- Make headings informative or intriguing.
- Keep headings parallel in structure.

Brevity

The optimum length of headings is determined by the content and style of the publication, its readership, and the column width. In general, however, headings that spread to a second line are more difficult to read, harder to recall, and clumsier from a typographic viewpoint.

Informative or intriguing wording

Headings should catch readers' attention, either by providing information or by raising a query. A heading such as 'General' is dull and unenlightening; a more useful alternative might be, say, 'Background to the proposal' or 'The legislative context'.

Phrasing the heading as a question can also be a good tactic for some types of documents, particularly brochures and leaflets, because it provides the opportunity to address readers directly. For example, 'Are you eligible?' is far more likely to gain attention than 'Eligibility requirements'. It is important, however, not to overwork this device: it can become tiresome.

Parallel structure and content

Parallelism is particularly useful in maintaining cohesion through a series of headings. In shorter documents or within a particular section, heading structures might be restricted to all noun phrases, for instance, or they might all be cast as instructions to the reader. Similarly, headings kept to comparable topics will alert readers to material intended for comparison.

Heading specifications: Describe the optimum heading length, as well as the heading frequency and number of hierarchical levels, in the style sheet for a document. This will help achieve consistency in the content and layout of headings during document development.

Compare the two sets of headings that follow: those on the left are balanced and logical in structure and topic, enabling like to be compared with like; those on the right are disorganised and unbalanced.

REGIONAL AID PROGRAMS	*not*	REGIONAL AID PROGRAMS
Papua New Guinea		Papua New Guinea
South Pacific		Aid for the South Pacific
Asia		Asia programs
CROSS-REGIONAL AID PROGRAMS		Cross-regional programs
GLOBAL AID PROGRAMS		GLOBAL PROGRAMS

Similar consideration should be given to the use of headings such as 'Introduction' and 'Conclusion'. Unless used consistently to start and close each chapter or other major division, only one 'Introduction' and one 'Conclusion' are necessary in a document. Readers could well be confused if they find a subsection headed 'Introduction' or 'Conclusion' somewhere in the middle of a publication.

A check of the structure and content of headings within a document should alert the author or editor to any lack of parallelism or similar anomalies.

EVALUATING HEADINGS

- Is the heading hierarchy well balanced and are the 'chunks' of information of a suitable size?

- Is the progression of the information logical?

- Does the weighting given to each topic reflect its relative importance?

- Is the wording of the headings useful for readers?

- Is the visual distinction between each level of the heading hierarchy sufficiently clear?

- Has any heading at a particular hierarchical level been left isolated without at least one other heading at the same level?

- Are the headings parallel in structure and content where appropriate?

- Are any headings too long?

BOXES AND SIDE PANELS

Design contrast: Boxes and panels can be contrasted with the main text by shading, colour, border treatment, or a different but compatible typeface. See Chapter 17 for more information on these layout techniques.

Boxes and side panels (or minor columns) bring contrast to a page or screen and are very useful for highlighting or separating different types of information. As noted in Chapter 3, they are usually read independently of the rest of the text, so they should contain material that can stand alone—material that summarises, extends or illustrates the discussion, for instance. When a heading for this material is necessary, it should be placed inside the box or panel.

As an example, take a policy discussion paper dealing with sustainable resource management in rural Australia. In paper-based form, the document might use oxes for highlighting examples of sustainable practice, and there might also be ide panels for summarised recommendations. On screen, the document might be onfigured with different types of box layouts to separate the examples and ecommendations, while the left panel might contain links to various rganisations involved in sustainable resource management.

TEMISED INDENTED MATERIAL

'or contrast and clarity, itemised material can be set apart from the text by ndenting it and (usually) placing a bullet or similar typographical device at the eginning of each item. This visual signposting helps readers absorb information, articularly when they are scanning material or viewing it on screen.

Balance

temised indented material—often called 'dot points'—is most effective if it is used n a systematic way throughout a document, being reserved for content that is ufficiently important to warrant such emphasis. Beware of overuse: documents vith page after page of dot points fail to convey any sense of a hierarchy of nformation. Also, if there are too many dot points within a single series, readers an easily lose track of the logical connections.

Consistent, parallel formats

There are different types of itemised indented material. At its simplest, a series night comprise only two or three items, each containing only one or two words. Aore often, a series is made up of a set of sentence fragments or full sentences, ometimes even full paragraphs. Regardless of the type, it is important to adhere to he following principles:

- Each series should be presented in parallel format, and each dot point within it should flow logically and grammatically from the introductory, or 'lead-in', material.
- A consistent approach needs to be taken to capitalising and punctuating dot-point series throughout a document.
- There should always be more than one indented item within a series.

Bullets, numbers and letters

Bullets are generally preferable to numbers or letters for itemised indented material, as they are neater and take less space. Numbers or letters should be eserved for cases where it is necessary to show priority or chronology within the eries or where individual items need to be identified for later reference.

Extent of indenting

ndenting should generally be restricted to two levels of subdivision: a bullet is ecommended for the first level of indent and an en rule for the second. Further ubdivision causes too much indentation, spoiling the appearance of a page, wasting pace, and upsetting normal reading patterns. Readers are also likely to lose the hread of the discussion if there are too many stepped divisions.

ABOUT

Dot-point series

In information documents, judicious use of dot-point layouts can be very effective in highlighting the structure and some of the significant aspects of the information. But care is needed to ensure that the flow of the text is retained (through parallel formats) and that a consistent approach is taken to structure, capitalisation and punctuation.

Structure

Each series of dot points should be introduced by a sentence or part of one, to enable the series to be properly integrated into the text flow. The meaning in each of the indented items should follow logically from this lead-in, and the opening of each dot point in the series should be in parallel (that is, have the same grammatical structure).

If all the dot points in a series begin with a sentence fragment, one or more full sentences can be added to any of the items.

Dot points consisting of full sentences can extend to a couple of paragraphs in length; if they are any longer, readers will probably lose the connecting thread.

Capitals

Capitalisation for dot-point series follows normal sentence rules. If all the dot points are full sentences, each should start with a capital letter; if each dot point consists of, or begins with, a sentence fragment, no initial capital is used.

Punctuation

Colon: It is usually necessary to place a colon after the lead-in to clarify the link with the indented information that follows. Although this principle can be relaxed when both the introduction and the dot points consist of full sentences, a colon often remains preferable, particularly if the lead-in words and the first dot point are split between different pages or columns or between different screens.

Avoid using colons within the indented material itself unless the items are full sentences. Otherwise there will be more than one colon within a single sentence structure.

Semicolons and full stops: Different writers and editors take different approaches to punctuating dot points. Some use semicolons at the end of each dot point—except for the last, which takes a full stop. Where all the dot points in a series are short, however, this can create a cluttered appearance.

Other writers and editors use semicolons only for a series that contains one or more dot points with internal punctuation. This reflects general sentence-punctuation principles, but it can appear inconsistent since some dot-point series in a document will take semicolons while others will not.

A third approach—the most minimalist in terms of punctuation—is to use no punctuation at the end of dot points, even the last one.

This manual takes a middle path, one that is designed to secure clarity while also reflecting the trend to less punctuation. The recommended style calls for no punctuation at the end of dot points that are not full sentences—except for the last, which takes a full stop to show that the series is complete. The examples given here, as well as the dot-point series used throughout the manual itself, illustrate this approach. Sufficient clarity is achieved through the use of bullets, en rules, indenting and line spacing to make the intermediate punctuation superfluous.

OME EXAMPLES OF DOT-POINT SERIES IN THE RECOMMENDED FORMAT

Full sentences

ructure:
rallel.

itial capitals:
for normal
ntences.

nctuation:
for normal
ntences;
lon at end
lead-in.

> The committee came to two important conclusions:
>
> • Officers from the department should investigate the feasibility of developing legislated guidelines for future investigations.
>
> • Research should be funded in the three priority areas.

not

ructure:
t parallel.

pitals:
nflicts with
rmal sentence
pitalisation.

> The committee came to two important conclusions:
>
> • That officers from the department should investigate ...
>
> • Research should be funded in the three priority areas.

Two levels of indention

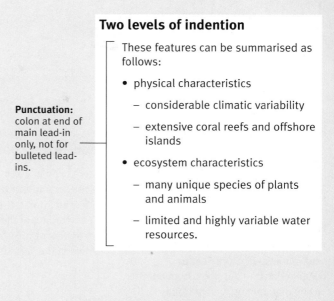

Punctuation:
colon at end of
main lead-in
only, not for
bulleted lead-ins.

> These features can be summarised as follows:
>
> • physical characteristics
>   – considerable climatic variability
>   – extensive coral reefs and offshore islands
> • ecosystem characteristics
>   – many unique species of plants and animals
>   – limited and highly variable water resources.

Sentence fragments

ructure:
rallel.

itial capitals:
ly for lead-in;
lleted items
rt of overall
ntence.

nctuation:
ll stop for last
m (to end
erall
ntence); no
nctuation at
d of interim
ints (spacing
ed instead).

> Assistance is available in several forms:
>
> • monetary assistance
> • equipment or environmental modifications
> • advisory services.

not

ructure:
t parallel.

> Assistance is available in several forms:
>
> • monetary assistance
> • equipment or environmental modifications
> • advisory services can be provided on request.

Sentence fragments, with an extra sentence

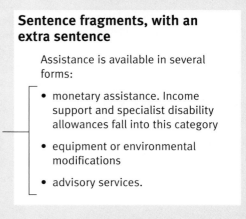

Punctuation:
none after
additional
sentence; full
stop only to
end series.

> Assistance is available in several forms:
>
> • monetary assistance. Income support and specialist disability allowances fall into this category
> • equipment or environmental modifications
> • advisory services.

Spacing

With this limited-punctuation approach to dot points, the amount of line space separating the items becomes important, since the line spacing is often a substitute for end-of-item punctuation. The goal must always be to provide enough space between items to distinguish each one without spreading them too far apart.

For publications where a full-line space is used between paragraphs, a half-line space is usually sufficient to distinguish one dot point from another while maintaining a clear visual connection between them all. Similarly, a half-line space should be used between the lead-in and the first dot point. A full-line space will, however, be necessary between the last line of the series and the new paragraph that follows.

Clarity is also greater if the indents are fairly compact: 5 millimetres is generally recommended for a bullet indent and a further 5 millimetres for the en rule indent. However, these indents could be reduced to 3 and 6 millimetres for a very narrow column width.

'And' in dot points

There is no need to add *and* at the end of the second-last dot point. The indented format, the line spacing, and clear wording of the lead-in material are sufficient to show the relationship between the various items.

'Or' in dot points

A carefully worded lead-in is also usually sufficient to show when dot points are being presented as alternatives. However, if the list consists of more than two items, an *or* could be placed on a separate line before the last item in the list to reinforce the meaning. For example:

Applications must be accompanied by one of the following:

- a valid passport
- proof of address and a current drivers licence

  or

- a tax return for the latest tax year.

Stand-alone lists

Stand-alone lists are often seen in display material, brochures and technical documentation. They contain the type of material that does not lend itself to integration with other text, and so their format need not follow the recommendations for dot-point series.

Generally, stand-alone lists have only a heading without any following lead-in; each item can take an initial capital; and no full stop is required at the end of the list. Indeed, indenting and bullets are usually unnecessary as well. For example:

Furniture and equipment for meeting room

Chairs (25)

Desks (2)

Lectern

Microphone

Overhead projector

Electronic whiteboard

In more discursive writing, greater integration of dot-point series into the text is needed.

ITALICS

There are a number of well-established conventions for the use of italics. They are primarily used for:

the titles of
- books and periodicals
- plays and long poems
- most types of musical composition
- films, videos, and television and radio programs
- works of art
- legislation and legal cases

the names of ships, aircraft and other vehicles

the scientific names of animals and plants (at the genus, species and lower taxonomic levels)

technical terms and terms being defined

letters, words and phrases being cited

words used in special senses or to which a particular tone or emphasis is being applied

foreign words and phrases that are not yet regarded as having been absorbed into English.

Italics are sometimes used as a layout device as well—for lower levels of a heading hierarchy, for example, or to distinguish prefatory material. However, italic type is generally not as legible as roman type, so it should be avoided for lengthy settings, particularly on screen.

Books and periodicals

The titles of books and periodicals are italicised to differentiate them from the surrounding text:

Have you read *The redundancy of courage* by Timothy Mo?

It appeared in an article in *The Australian*.

Nature published the results about a year ago.

A definite or indefinite article that forms the first word of a title can be omitted if its retention would result in an awkward reading. For example:

Timothy Mo's *Redundancy of courage* is frighteningly prescient.

A shortened title can also be used, provided the full title has already appeared in the text and the order of words is not changed:

The *Style manual for authors, editors and printers* is … The *Style manual* recommends …

If, however, only a generic title is used, this is shown in roman type and without an initial capital:

the *Style manual* … the manual

Minimal capitalisation: The following advice on using italics for the titles of publications, music and art assumes a minimal capitalisation approach, as recommended elsewhere in the manual (see p. 134 and Chapter 12).

➤ Chapter 12 provides detailed advice on citing reference material.

Plays and long poems

The titles of plays and long poems are also italicised:

> The theme of Williamson's *Emerald city* is in stark contrast to that of *The club*.

> Have you read *The man from Snowy River*?

Musical compositions

Italics are used for the titles of most musical compositions and of operas and ballets:

> The *Symphonie fantastique* was Berlioz's first major work.

> The enthusiastic audience gave Peter Sculthorpe's opera *Rites of passage* a standing ovation.

> Did you see the Bangarra Dance Company's *Corroboree*?

> *The display* is probably her favourite Robert Helpmann ballet.

In contrast, when a musical work does not have a specific title but is instead identified by its form (and often an opus or catalogue number), it is traditionally shown in roman type. The following presentation is recommended:

> Beethoven's Piano concerto no. 5 in E-flat major, op. 73, is known as the *Emperor concerto*, although Beethoven did not give it this name.

Song titles are also presented in roman type, but in quotation marks and using minimal capitalisation:

> They finished off with a rollicking rendition of 'The road to Gundagai'.

Films, videos, and radio and television programs

The titles of films, videos, and radio and television programs are italicised:

> *The sound of one hand clapping* is set in Tasmania.

> She's a devoted follower of *The epicure's healthy lifestyle* video.

> All those years added up to 5795 episodes of *Blue hills*.

However, the titles of episodes that form part of a radio or television series are conventionally shown in roman type within quotation marks:

> 'The heroin wars' is due to run on *Four corners* next month.

This is the same principle as that applying to articles in journals and to chapters in books.

Works of art

The titles of paintings, sculptures and other physical artworks take italics:

> The National Gallery of Australia bought *A bigger Grand Canyon* in 1999.

> *The thinker* is probably one of Rodin's greatest works.

but

> Rodin's *Thinker* is probably one of his greatest works.

Various conventions: Some publishing houses follow other conventions for citing musical works. The style shown here is recommended for its simplicity and because it is in keeping with the trend towards limited capitalisation.

NAA: A1200-L68827

Scientific names of animals and plants

For animals, the scientific names at the genus, species and subspecies levels are italicised. With botanical names, italics are used for the genus, species, subspecies, variety, subvariety, form and subform levels. For example:

> Heavily grazed areas were characterised by *Cassia nemophila* var. *coriacea*.

➤ See pp. 130–1 for a discussion of botanical and zoological nomenclature.

Legislation and legal cases

The formal titles of Acts and Ordinances and of legal cases are italicised. For example:

> The Western Australian *Young Offenders Act 1994* makes provision for …

> The *Lakes Ordinance 1995* was introduced to …

> The 1954 Privy Council decision in *Hughes and Vale Pty Ltd v. New South Wales* [No. 1] (1954) 93 CLR 1 held that …

The titles of Bills before parliament do not take italics, nor do the informal titles of legislation—thus, the Young Offenders Act and the Lakes Ordinance. In contrast, shortened titles of legal cases remain italicised—thus, *Hughes and Vale*.

➤ See Chapter 12 for further information about citing legislation and legal cases.

Ships, aircraft and other vehicles

The names of specific ships, aircraft and other vehicles are usually italicised, but the names of *types* of vehicles are not:

> Passengers travelling on the *Ghan* had marvellous views of a flooded Central Australia.

> *Solar Challenge* won the race in record time.

> HMAS *Nevertire* was scuttled in 1973.

> A Boeing 737 was used to bring the survivors home.

> They travelled by Jeep for the last part of the journey.

Note that italics are not used for a definite article that is not part of a vehicle's name, nor are they used for the abbreviation 'HMAS'.

Technical terms and terms being defined

When technical terms are being introduced or defined in a document, they are often italicised. For example:

> *Gouache* is a method of painting using an opaque watercolour paint made by grinding pigments in water and then thickening them with a glue-like substance.

> In this instance the term *buffer zone* means an area of land that forms a natural protective barrier.

On subsequent mention there is no need to italicise the term.

Alternatively, single quotation marks can be used to highlight defined terms (see page 114).

Letters, words and phrases cited as such

When a particular letter, word or phrase is being cited, it is often italicised:

> It is spelt with an *e*, not an *a*.

> *Guerrilla* comes from the Spanish word meaning 'little war'.

Again, single quotation marks can be used for the same purpose.

Words used in special senses or with particular emphasis

If a term is used in a sense other than its normal one, it can be italicised to alert readers to this difference. This is often done for words whose meaning has changed. Deliberately misused terms and newly coined ones can be similarly differentiated from the surrounding text. For example:

> Many admirers described Wren's cathedral as *awful* when it was built.

> She said he was under the *affluence of incahol*.

> The *tech wreck* of April 2000 caused a slide into negative territory for much of the sector.

Yet again, quotation marks can be used instead of italics in all these instances.

Italics can also show a change in authorial tone for a word or phrase, usually to indicate irony or added emphasis:

> It was hardly a *biography*, since it dealt almost solely with her writing without relating it to her extraordinary life.

> '*Never* do that!' he cried.

Foreign words and phrases

Foreign words and phrases have traditionally been italicised when they are regarded as not yet fully absorbed into English. How to draw the distinction between words and phrases that have successfully made the transition and those that have not remains a perennial problem, however.

Foreign words and phrases: As a general rule, foreign words and phrases should be used only if there is no precise English equivalent.

With the rapid increase in the number of expressions being borrowed from other languages, dictionaries are tending to italicise borrowed expressions far less frequently than in the past. Nevertheless, dictionaries do differ. Some, such as *The Macquarie dictionary*, do not italicise any 'foreign' words or phrases—on the principle that these borrowings can be regarded as having been absorbed into English if they are sufficiently familiar to warrant a place in the dictionary. Other dictionaries continue to make some distinctions. The best advice is to choose a dictionary and follow its lead: if the term is italicised in the dictionary, use italics; if it is not included in the dictionary, also use italics.

If a term is italicised, it should retain any accents and similar signs appearing above or below letters as well as any capital letters that it would have in its own language.

If the term is in roman type, it might still retain a capital from its source language—for example, the German word 'Zeitgeist' is shown this way in both the *Macquarie* and the *Australian Oxford* dictionaries. Some absorbed terms might also eed to retain accents as an aid to recognition. The French word 'résumé', for example, is shown in roman but with accents in both the *Macquarie* and the *Australian Oxford*, to distinguish it from the English word 'resume'.

OLD OR COLOURED TYPE

old or coloured type is often used in headings and subheadings, but it can also be elpful for contrast at the word and sentence level. It must be remembered, ough, that bold or coloured type is generally the first thing to be noticed on a age or screen and so can be read out of context. Careful thought should therefore e given to precisely what is treated in this way.

some types of documents, bold can be effective for highlighting important aterial such as summaries and lists of recommendations—provided this material reasonably short. Long passages in bold are tiring to read and too visually ominant. Boxes or side panels might prove a less heavy-handed alternative for nger text.

t the word and phrase level, bold or coloured text can also be used to add ontrast. Again, it must be used sensitively, so that the contrast is not seen as owngrading the value of the rest of the information.

NDERLINING

the days of the typewriter, when bold and italic options were not available, nderlining was used for contrast. But there are now two good reasons for not ing it in this way:

It affects legibility by covering the parts of letters that descend below the line.

It has become an established and very useful way of showing hyperlinks.

Italics and accents: Follow your chosen dictionary's recommendations for the use of roman and italic fonts and accents for foreign words and phrases. If the term is not in the dictionary, use italics.

Glossaries and indexes: Bold type (or italics) can be used for the headwords in glossaries and for particular types of page references in indexes.

Underlining: Reserve underlining for showing hyperlinks on screen.

Chapter **10**

Shortened forms

CATEGORIES AND STYLE CONVENTIONS	**151**
About the different categories of shortened forms	152
PARTICULAR SETS OF SHORTENED FORMS	**151**
Grammatical contractions	151
Latin shortened forms	155
Geographical terms	155
Time	157
Organisations	157
Personal names	158
Awards and honours	158
Military ranks and formations	158
Referencing	158
WHEN TO USE SHORTENED FORMS	**159**

Writers use shortened forms of words and phrases to produce more compact expression. If readers are familiar with those that are used, communication can be more efficient. But if the shortened forms might be new to at least some readers, think carefully about whether they really are necessary. A publication's level of formality and the potential number of shortened forms in it should also be taken into account.

CATEGORIES AND STYLE CONVENTIONS

There are three categories of shortened forms: shortened words, shortened phrases and symbols. Abbreviations and contractions are subsets of shortened words, while acronyms and initialisms come under the category of shortened phrases (see pages 152–4). Specific punctuation and capitalisation practices apply to each group.

Other style conventions are also involved. These relate to such matters as plurals and possessives, and to the shortened form's integration into the grammar of a sentence—for example, whether it can be used at the start of a sentence and when to use *a* or *an* before it. Sets of shortened forms that are used in particular contexts are also discussed, including those used for geographical terms, in expressions of time, in business and personal names, and in referencing.

➤ For information about the shortened forms used with numbers and measurements, see Chapter 11. Shortened forms used in referencing are discussed in Chapter 12. For advice on the extensive range of abbreviations, contractions, symbols and signs used in science and mathematics, consult specialist reference works.

PARTICULAR SETS OF SHORTENED FORMS

Grammatical contractions

Grammatical contractions differ from contractions of single words (see page 152) because they involve telescoping two adjacent words and need an apostrophe to indicate the omission of letters. For example:

it's [it is]   don't   can't

you'll   we're   aren't

If there is more than one point at which letters have been omitted, the apostrophe is used for only one of these omission points:

shan't

(continued on p. 155)

ABOUT

The different categories of shortened forms

S H O R T

SHORTENED WORDS

Categories

There are three categories of shortened forms:

- shortened words—divided into abbreviations and contractions

- shortened phrases—divided into acronyms and initialisms

- symbols.

Each requires a different approach in terms of capitalisation and punctuation. Other usage conventions also need to be taken into account.

	Abbreviations consist of the *first letter* of a word, usually some other letters, *but not the last letter*	**Contractions** consist of *the first and last letters* of a word and sometimes other letters in between
PUNCTUATION	Full stop after abbreviation	No full stops
CAPITALISATION	Same as unabbreviated word	Same as uncontracted word
EXAMPLES	para. Mon. Dec. Vic. tel. fig. ch. cont. Co.	Mr Rd Qld Cwlth Pty Ltd dept Bros

E D   F O R M S

	SHORTENED PHRASES		SYMBOLS
onyms strings of initial letters l sometimes other rs) *pronounced as* *rd*	**Initialisms** are strings of initial letters (and sometimes other letters) *not pronounced* *as a word*		**Symbols** are internationally recognised represen- tations of units of measurement, words and concepts
ull stops	No full stops		No full stops
ally all capitals, but er case for some iliar ones (with an initial ital if a proper name)	All capitals		Capitals only if symbol represents a proper name
E IC AN ac tas ba (self-contained underwater breathing apparatus) ar (sound navigation nd ranging)	NSW SBS PC TV CPI (consumer price index) IQ (intelligence quotient)		km W (watt) A$ % & @ ©

Capitalisation of spelt-out forms

Just because an acronym or initialism is presented in capital letters does not mean that the spelt-out form should have initial capitals. Normal capitalisation practices apply. For example, *NSW* becomes *New South Wales* but *an EIS* becomes *an environmental impact statement* and *TB* becomes *tuberculosis*.

Plural forms

Most shortened words and phrases are made plural simply by adding *s*, without a preceding apostrophe. For example:

MPs   *not*   MP's

FAQs   *not*   FAQ's

paras

figs

There are, however, a few abbreviations that double the last letter to show the plural form—for example, 'pp.' for *pages*. These types of plurals are discussed on page 159.

The shortened forms for units of measurement never take a plural *s*, since they are symbols rather than abbreviations or contractions:

6 kg   *not*   6 kgs

Possessive forms

For acronyms and initialisms, the possessive is shown by using an apostrophe in the conventional way:

ANU's policy

the POWs' concert

Interpol's staff

Chapter 6 discusses in detail the use of apostrophes.

Using '*a*' or '*an*' before a shortened form

Let the spoken sound be your guide when deciding whether to use *a* or *an* before a shortened form:

> a UNESCO initiative
>
> an ABC program

Some shortened forms can be pronounced as either an initialism or an acronym. Some people might pronounce 'RAAF', for example, as a single-syllable word, in which case it would be *a RAAF plane* (the usage preferred in the Air Force). Others might pronounce it as 'RdoubleAF', in which case it would be *an RAAF plane*, since the letter *r* is pronounced with a vowel sound.

Starting a sentence

Acronyms and initialisms can be used at the beginning of a sentence:

> TAFE courses cover …
>
> Sonar equipment includes …
>
> CSIRO is …
>
> ABS publications are …

In contrast, it is much better to spell out abbreviated words when they start a sentence:

> Appendix B shows …*not*   App. B shows …

More than one punctuation mark

Only one full stop is shown at the end of a sentence, so in this position an abbreviated word drops its full stop:

> Those attending are from the Natural Gas Co.

With other punctuation marks, the stop is retained. For example:

> Students were asked to analyse the children's characteristics (mannerisms, habits, etc.).
>
> 'Why on earth did you say that, Prof.!' she exclaimed.

Direct speech

When quoting direct speech, retain any shortened forms that the speaker has used:

> 'They will be awarded their PhDs in 2003.'

If the shortened form has not already been explained and readers might not recognise it, the full form should be shown in square brackets:

> 'The BJP [Bharatiya Janata Party] and the Congress have both acknowledged this', he reminded them.

Breaking shortened forms

Do not break a shortened form at the end of a line or separate a numeral from its accompanying symbol.

Some exceptions to general punctuation practice

The word 'number': This word is often shortened to *no.*, which is a contraction of the Italian word *numero*. Unlike other contractions—which do not take stops—a full stop is used in this instance so that confusion with the word *no* will be avoided. The plural, *nos*, is formed like other contractions without a full stop.

Initialisms that can be read as words with other meanings: In fully capitalised headings, some initialisms can be misinterpreted because they consist of the same letters as other common words. For example, *ACT* (for Australian Capital Territory) and *WHO* (for World Health Organization) might be read in a fully capitalised heading as *act* and *who*. To avoid misreading, phrase fully capitalised headings containing such initialisms very carefully or consider using full stops for clarity, as in:

> A.C.T. DEALS WITH TRAFFIC PROBLEMS

not

> ACT DEALS WITH TRAFFIC PROBLEMS

Using an apostrophe to avoid a duplicated letter: There are a few contractions in which a repeated letter might give the impression of a misprint. In these cases an apostrophe is conventionally used to avoid confusion:

> A'asia   *not*   Aasia

Apostrophes are no longer used, however, to indicate missing letters in a contracted word that does not contain adjacent repeated letters:

> Cwlth   *not*   C'wlth

International differences

The style of punctuation recommended here for shortened forms generally reflects British practice. In the United States, full stops are used for most kinds of abbreviations and contractions—Mr. and Ltd., for example.

Grammatical contractions are typical of conversational prose and are increasingly seen in standard writing. Although they are unsuitable for most formal publications, they can help to create a friendly or collaborative tone in publications such as brochures and manuals.

Latin shortened forms

Many Latin shortened forms are used regularly in publications; they are regarded as being thoroughly anglicised and are presented in roman type. The following are among the most familiar:

c. (*circa*, about, approximately)

cf. (*confer*, compare)

e.g. (*exempli gratia*, for example)

et al. (*et alii*, and others)

etc. (*et cetera*, and so forth, and so on)

i.e. (*id est*, that is)

MS (*manuscriptum*, manuscript)

NB (*nota bene*, take careful note)

PPS (*post postscriptum*, second postscript)

PS (*postscriptum*, postscript)

v., vs (*versus*, against)

viz. (*videlicet*, namely)

It is common for *e.g.* and *i.e.* to be used where space is limited—for instance, in tables, illustrations, notes and captions. They can also be used in publications containing many shortened forms—but preferably only with material in parentheses rather than in running text. Elsewhere, it is best to use *for example* and *that is*, particularly in more formal publications.

Similarly, *etc.* should generally be avoided in running text, although in less formal documents it is acceptable with material in parentheses. Be careful, though, that it does not suggest offhandedness or imprecision. Use of *etc.* is redundant in a list preceded by such expressions as *for example* or *such as*, since these expressions already show that the list is incomplete.

Geographical terms

Countries

The names of countries should usually be spelt out in formal publications. For example:

The United Kingdom, the United States and New Zealand agreed …

not

The UK, the US and NZ agreed …

➤ See pp. 214–15 for a discussion of the use of Latin shortened forms in the documentary-note style of citation and p. 227 for those used in citing legal cases.

Punctuation with 'e.g.' and 'i.e.': Although there is a trend to omit the full stops in these two abbreviations, the unstopped forms are not widely accepted; they also contradict the general principle of using full stops for abbreviated words. Retention of the stops in *e.g.* and *i.e.* is therefore recommended. There is no need to follow *e.g.* or *i.e.* with a comma (although a comma is usual after the unabbreviated forms).

In less formal contexts, the shortened forms are becoming increasingly accepted, and even in formal text they may be preferable if repetition of the full names would be tedious and clumsy. They can also be used adjectivally:

> US tariffs have …
>
> In her study of UK foreign policy …

Standard shortened forms for countries' names are also commonly used when space is at a premium—for example, in tables, illustrations, notes, lists and bibliographies.

Australian states and territories

As with countries' names, the names of the Australian states and territories are best spelt out in official publications—except when they are used adjectivally, or when space is limited, or when lengthy repetition would otherwise result. The recommended shortened forms for use in publications are as follows:

> NSW   Vic.   Qld   WA   SA   Tas.   ACT   NT

The order shown here is based on population. Other orders—alphabetical, for example, or based on location or area—might be more suitable in particular contexts.

Although these standard shortened forms are well known to Australian readers, care is needed to ensure that an international readership will not be misled. For example, SA could refer to either South Africa or South Australia, depending on the context. If any misunderstanding might occur, they should be written out in full or explained in a list of shortened forms.

Addresses

Shortened forms are a feature of addresses—for contact details given in publications, on envelopes, in directories and lists, and so on. They are usually presented without full stops:

> 1095 St Kilda Rd   5 Louis Cl   10 Bendemeer Blvd

Other abbreviations and contractions commonly used in addresses are *St* (Street), *Ave* (Avenue), *Cres* (Crescent), *Dr* (Drive), *Esp* (Esplanade), *Gr* (Grove), *Hts* (Heights), *Hwy* (Highway), *Pde* (Parade), *Pl* (Place) and *Tce* (Terrace). Where ambiguity could result—between an abbreviation for *Court* and *Circuit*, for example—it is best to spell them out.

Initialisms used in addresses are punctuated in the standard way. For example:

> PO Box 1   RMB 99

Geographical features

The names of geographical features are often shortened in atlases, maps, tables and illustrations but should be spelt out in general text. Among the more familiar shortened forms are:

> C. (Cape)   L. (Lake)   R. (River)
>
> Mt (Mount)   Mtn (Mountain)   Harb. (Harbour)
>
> I. (Island)   Is (Islands)

Postal standards: To suit Australia Post's mail-sorting equipment, a different style for the shortened forms of the names of Australian states and territories should be used on envelopes and packages. All addresses should show the shortened forms in full capitals and without any punctuation:
NSW   VIC   QLD   WA   SA
TAS   ACT   NT

➤ See Chapter 8 for a discussion of capitalisation practices associated with geographical features and points of the compass.

Compass points

Initialisms are used for points of the compass. They can be used alone or in combination:

    N   E   NW   ESE

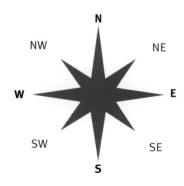

These forms are often used in tables and illustrative material and in the text of specialist works. In general publications the terms should be spelt out and compound forms should be hyphenated. For example:

    The river flowed in a north-westerly direction from …

not

    The river flowed in a NW direction from …

    20 degrees south

not

    20 degrees S   or   20° S

Time

Days and months

The standard abbreviations for the names of days of the week are as follows:

    Sun.   Mon.   Tues.   Wed.   Thurs.   Fri.   Sat.

It is preferable to avoid abbreviating the names of months that have four or fewer letters (May, June and July). The abbreviations for the other months are:

    Jan.   Feb.   Mar.   Apr.   Aug.   Sept.   Oct.   Nov.   Dec.

These abbreviations for the names of days and months should be avoided in general text but can be used if space is limited in tables, illustrations, notes, lists and bibliographies.

When space is limited: In calendars, diaries and other publications where space is limited, minimal forms for the days of the week can be used. They are written without a full stop:
Su   M   Tu   W   Th   F   Sa

➤ Chapter 11 discusses shortened forms for times and dates such as *4 pm, 44 BC, 1600 hours* and *27.12.2001.*

Time zones

Initialisms are used for the shortened names of time zones. The Australian zones are as follows:

    CST (Central Standard Time)   CDT (Central Daylight-saving Time)

    EST (Eastern Standard Time)   EDT (Eastern Daylight-saving Time)

    WST (Western Standard Time)   WDT (Western Daylight-saving Time)

In contexts where these time zones might be confused with those of other parts of the world, or if it is not clear that they are specific to Australia, the letter *A* can be added at the front—for example, *AEST*.

Organisations

Some organisations use shortened forms such as *Pty Ltd, Co.* and *Inc.* as part of their official title; others use the spelt-out forms. Similarly, an ampersand (&) is incorporated in some organisational names in preference to *and*. For example:

> Westel Inc.   Fogg & Co.   Ebiz Pty Ltd
>
> Halloran Brothers   Sydney Dance Company   Kinhill Limited

An organisation's full title, in the form shown on its letterhead (where this can be ascertained), should be used on first mention in a publication. On subsequent mentions, *Inc.*, *Pty Ltd*, and so on, can be omitted.

Personal names

When using initials for people's given names, it was standard practice in the past to follow each initial with a full stop and a space. The trend towards reduced punctuation has, however, overtaken this convention: unpunctuated, unspaced presentation of initials is now the norm in directories and is increasingly common in other types of publications. For example:

> Mary J Nagy   B Bertolucci
>
> WMJ Steinhauser   J-P Sartre

Initials of given names: Use the unpunctuated, unspaced form for the initials of people's given names: *CJ Dennis*.

This practice is recommended for all types of publications.

Awards and honours

As with the initials of given names, it is recommended that postnominals—the shortened forms for academic awards and civil and military honours—be shown without full stops or spaces. For example:

> BA (Bachelor of Arts)   AO (Officer of the Order of Australia)
>
> DipEd (Diploma of Education)   OM (Order of Merit)
>
> PhD (Doctor of Philosophy)   MC (Military Cross)

Commas are used after the person's name and between each postnominal:

> Mr Malcolm Hall, AO, FIEAust

Appendix A provides a comprehensive list of titles and honours.

Military ranks and formations

The armed services use many shortened forms that have become standard in this field. When writing for this specialised audience, follow their preferred methods of presenting military ranks and formations. In more general publications, it is usually appropriate to apply the principles described in this chapter.

Referencing

Common abbreviations

Many abbreviations used in referencing are shortened forms of English words. For example:

> app. (appendix)   ch. (chapter)   ed. (editor)

➤ See p. 191 for a list of shortened forms of English words commonly used in referencing, and pp. 225–6 for examples of the use of shortened forms such as *rr.* and *ss.* when citing legislation.

a limited set of shortened forms, the plural is shown by repeating a lower-case
tter. These take full stops. For example:

ff. (following)   fnn. (footnotes)   ll. (lines)

pp. (pages)   rr. (regulations)   ss. (sections)

here are also some shortened forms that are capitalised and whose plural is shown
repeating a letter. In contrast to the lower-case examples above, these do not
ke full stops—for example, MSS for manuscripts.

hortened journal titles

he titles of journals are often shortened in scientific and other technical works
ee page 205). Use of this kind of shortened form is not recommended for general
aders.

ross-references

save space in technical works, shortened forms can be used in cross-references
esented in parentheses in the text. For example:

… is a good example (see Ch. 7).

This is discussed elsewhere (see pp. 22–7).

ortened forms of this type are best avoided when a cross-reference in text is not
apart by parentheses, and they should not be used to start a sentence. Use the
ll form instead, as in:

Chapter 7 provides an example.

This is discussed on pages 22–7.

dexes

ortened forms of all kinds are used in indexes, which can also contain specific
mbols—for example, the letter g to indicate items appearing in a glossary. All
e shortened forms used should be explained at the front of the index.

HEN TO USE SHORTENED FORMS

any terms are readily understood in their shortened form throughout the
glish-speaking world—those used for personal titles and most country names,
d the common units of measurement and time are examples. These shortened
rms do not need any explanation in a publication; their suitability for inclusion
sts on the type of document and its level of formality.

addition to these widely known forms, most disciplines, industries and
ganisations develop and use specialised shortened forms to save time and space
d to avoid unnecessary repetition. Everyone in the group knows what the
ortened forms mean, and it would be tedious—sometimes even insulting—to
ell them out every time they are used.

ut writers and editors should remember that people outside these circles will
obably not be familiar with the terminology and might find it hard to remember

Precision with page references: Use of the styles *pp. 156 f.* (meaning pages 156 and 157) and *pp. 156 ff.* (meaning pages 156 to, say, 160) is not recommended. Being precise— *pp. 156–7* or *pp. 156–60*—is much more helpful.

➤ See Chapter 15 for a full discussion of indexes.

the shortened forms, even when they are explained on first use. This is certainly likely to be the case if there are many unfamiliar shortened forms in a publication.

When writing for a wide general audience, give careful thought to which, if any, terms really need to be shortened.

SPECIALISED SHORTENED FORMS: DO YOU NEED TO USE THEM?

Who are your readers?

Are most of your readers likely to know the shortened form already? If not, do they need to learn it in order to communicate with people in the particular discipline, industry or organisation or to understand more complex material that occurs later in the document? If the answer to both these questions is 'yes', go ahead and use the shortened form.

Be mindful, however, of whether the shortened form could be misinterpreted by casual readers. A newspaper report about the Meat Industry Authority, for example, would probably be better using *the authority* as opposed to *the MIA*, which someone scanning the article might more readily recognise as the Murrumbidgee Irrigation Area, the Metal Industry Association, or even 'missing in action'.

How long is the term?

Long proper names are often considered prime candidates for abbreviation, but there is usually a readily understandable alternative. If, for example, the proposed shortened form is for the name of a government agency, a company or a committee, a generic reference to the full name used earlier in the document will probably be more useful for non-specialist readers. Thus, consider simply using *the department* instead of *DCITA* in subsequent references to the Department of Communications, Information Technology and the Arts.

How often does the term occur?

If an unfamiliar term is used only two or three times in a document, or only at widely spaced intervals, it is better to avoid shortening it.

If the term is used repeatedly in one particular part of a long document but only very infrequently elsewhere, you might consider shortening it where it is used repeatedly but otherwise spelling it out. Clarity is far more important than arbitrary consistency.

How many shortened forms are candidates for use in the document?

If readers are likely to be confronted by many unfamiliar shortened forms, consider reducing the number—and the strain on readers' memories—by reserving the shortened forms only for terms that appear very frequently in the document.

How should the shortened form be introduced?

Shortened forms that might be unfamiliar to readers should be spelt out the first time they are used. There are three ways of doing this, depending on the context:

- Place the shortened form in parentheses immediately after the first (spelt-out) mention—the *National Disability Advisory Council (NDAC)*. The shortened form can then be used for subsequent mentions. This is the standard style for showing unfamiliar shortened forms.

- Show the shortened form first, followed by the full term in parentheses—*DNA (deoxyribonucleic acid)*. This is the best approach if the shortened form is more readily recognised than the full term but use of the full term is nevertheless warranted.

- Avoid using parenthetic explanations at all by giving the term in full on its first mention and thereafter simply using the abbreviation—thus the *Australian Competition and Consumer Commission* would become the *ACCC* without explanation. This technique works well when the spelt-out term would appear, say, twice in a paragraph or in two consecutive paragraphs, and readers can be expected to make the association readily. It is not a useful approach if the second (shortened) mention is some distance from the first full reference.

Is a list of shortened forms needed?

If a variety of specialised shortened forms likely to be unfamiliar to readers has been used throughout the text, a list of shortened forms is generally necessary. If the list is long, the best place for it in a print-based publication is usually at the back (see page 243), to avoid distracting or overwhelming readers at the outset.

Such a list is generally unnecessary if there are only a few unfamiliar shortened forms, each of which occurs only in a very limited section of text and has been explained when first introduced.

Chapter **11**

Numbers and measurement

CONVENTIONS FOR USING WORDS OR NUMERALS	**163**
About choosing words or numerals for numbers	164
OPENING A SENTENCE	**163**
MEASUREMENTS	**165**
MATHEMATICAL RELATIONSHIPS	**165**
LARGE NUMBERS	**166**
Aiding recognition	166
The terms 'billion', 'trillion' and 'quadrillion'	166
FRACTIONS	**167**
Decimal fractions	167
Non-decimal fractions	167
ORDINAL NUMBERS	**167**
PERCENTAGES	**167**
NUMBERS FOR COMPARISON	**168**
ROMAN NUMERALS	**168**
When to use roman numerals	168
Upper or lower case	169
Spans	169
EXPRESSIONS OF TIME	**169**
Eras	169
Centuries and decades	170
Dates	170
Time of day	172
Time frequency, and the prefix 'bi'	173

TEMPERATURE	**173**
CURRENCY	**174**
Words or numerals	174
Millions of dollars	174
Australian currency	174
Other currencies	175
Former Australian currency	175
About punctuating and spacing numbers	176
THE INTERNATIONAL SYSTEM OF UNITS	**178**
System of quantities	178
SI base units	178
SI derived units	179
Decimal multiples and submultiples	181
Measurement in Australia	182
About using SI units	184
Other units of measurement	185

When using numbers in a publication, there are various decisions to be made about their presentation. First there is the question of whether to show them in words or numerals. Other matters to consider include the use of commas or spaces in numerals comprising four or more digits, how to show numbers at the start of a sentence, and how to deal with fractions.

There are also particular conventions for presenting currency, dates and other time periods. And then there are issues associated with the use of the units and symbols of the International System of Units, as well as the use of the units and abbreviations associated with other measuring methods.

CONVENTIONS FOR USING WORDS OR NUMERALS

Several different conventions could be invoked when deciding whether to present numbers in words or numerals. Some writers and editors vary their approach depending on the type of document and its audience; others apply more arbitrary rules. Some always use numerals where the numbers are followed by units of measurement; others might not. Most of these conventions specify a cut-off point (relating to the size of the number) after which numerals are used, but this point may be set at zero, nine, ten, twenty, one hundred or some other number.

The guidelines set out on page 164 are aimed at achieving an acceptable level of consistency while having regard to the context in which the numbers are used and the style suited to different types of publications. Even so, no set of rules in this area will work equally well in every situation. Writers and editors still need to exercise judgment to ensure that numbers are presented in a clear and natural style in each instance, to avoid distracting or irritating readers.

'Numerals': This word is used throughout this manual to mean numbers expressed in figures.

OPENING A SENTENCE

When opening a sentence, a number should always be expressed in words:

Fifty-seven people attended the rally.

Sixty per cent of hotel employees are casuals.

(continued on p. 165)

ABOUT

Choosing words or numerals for numbers

Two different conventions for the treatment of numbers are recommended, depending on the type of document. However, both approaches require some modification to take particular factors into account.

Type of document

General text: In documents of a general kind—where descriptive or narrative text is predominant and numbers are not a significant focus— use words for numbers up to one hundred:

> The subcommittee will be preparing three separate reports over the next fifteen months.

> In this region, twenty-two different types of plants that are now classed as weeds were identified.

If a general document of this type contains some small, scattered sections of a more statistical nature, numerals may be used for numbers in these isolated sections if this is considered necessary to emphasise numerical precision or to avoid clumsiness. This switch to numerals does not mean that the approach used in the rest of the document must be changed. While consistency is desirable, it may be more important to match the style in different sections to the immediate context.

Statistically oriented text: Use numerals for numbers over nine in documents where numbers occur frequently:

> The hearing was attended by 12 departmental officers and 83 members of the public; in addition, 166 written submissions had been received.

In texts for a scientific or technical audience, use a similar approach to the presentation of numbers, and use SI symbols for all units of measurement.

Other factors

Regardless of the type of document, there are some instances where words are always required for numbers and others where numerals are necessary.

Always use words for numbers that start a sentence. But use numerals for numbers:

- when they are used with a symbol of measurement (including symbols for SI units, for units used in other measurement methods, and for currency and time)

- in mathematical contexts (such as equations and ratios)

- when shown as decimal fractions

- in tables

- in related series of numbers provided for comparison.

These different contexts are described in detail in the subsequent sections of this chapter, as are other instances where choice between words and numerals is involved. Tables are discussed in Chapter 19.

the number is lengthy when expressed in words, it may be better to rearrange
e sentence. For example:

> Six hundred and twenty-one complaints were received.

uld become

> The board received 621 complaints.

milarly, recasting the sentence is often best if other numbers in the same passage
e expressed in numerals; this makes comparisons easier as well as maintaining
nsistency. So:

> Six hundred and twenty-one complaints were received; of these 531 related to under-award pay
> and 90 related to working hours.

uld become

> Of the 621 complaints received, 531 related to under-award pay and 90 related to working hours.

here a number that would open a sentence is accompanied by a symbol (for
ample, a dollar sign) and therefore cannot be expressed in words, the sentence
ould also be rearranged. For example:

> $12 684 was the total collected from one suburb alone.

uld be rewritten as

> In one suburb alone, a total of $12 684 was collected.

➤ See pp. 176–7 for guidelines on the punctuation and spacing of numbers (both in words and numerals).

EASUREMENTS

lways use numerals for numbers that are accompanied by a symbol:

> 8 °C   3 km   45.9 s

/en when the measurement unit is written in full, numerals remain the most
mmon choice for the number:

> 8 degrees Celsius   3 kilometres   45.9 seconds

owever, in general discursive text where precise numbers or measurements play
tle part, words may be appropriate for both the number and measurement:

> He was twenty minutes late.

> The child was ten or eleven years old.

ATHEMATICAL RELATIONSHIPS

umerals should always be used to express precise mathematical relationships,
ch as in equations and ratios:

> $96 + 37 = 133$ *or*   96 plus 37 equals 133

> 5:1

general text, words are an option only where the mathematical relationship is
t intended to be exact:

> Many households—about one in six—are struggling to afford basic necessities.

LARGE NUMBERS

Aiding recognition

Round numbers up to ten million are readily recognisable, whether words or numerals are used:

> two hundred   five thousand   nine million
>
> 200   5000   9 000 000

Larger or more complex numbers expressed solely in either words or numerals can be cumbersome or confusing, so it is often better to use a combination of words and numerals. For example:

> 2.5 million

is generally preferable in running text to

> 2 500 000

or to

> two million, five hundred thousand

An alternative method preferred in much scientific and technical documentation is to use powers of ten:

> 2.5×10^6 [= 2 500 000]

Such notations are more succinct, but they should be used only in publications aimed at readers who can be expected to understand them.

The terms 'billion, 'trillion' and 'quadrillion'

The terms *billion*, *trillion* and *quadrillion* were originally used (as their prefixes suggest) to signify a million multiplied by a factor of two, three and four respectively:

> billion = million x million (10^{12})
>
> trillion = million x million x million (10^{18})
>
> quadrillion = million x million x million x million (10^{24})

This convention has been overtaken internationally by the alternative approach that was instigated by French mathematicians and then adopted by the United States, whereby:

> billion = thousand x million (or 1000 million, or 10^9)
>
> trillion = million x million (10^{12})
>
> quadrillion = thousand x million x million (10^{15})

'Billion': Use this to mean 1000 million.

Australian and international standards (*AS ISO 1000:1998*) now acknowledge this as standard usage, affirming what has long been established in financial writing. However, scientists and statisticians usually avoid *billion*, *trillion* and *quadrillion*, preferring to express critical amounts using powers of ten.

FRACTIONS

There are two types of fractions: decimal and non-decimal.

Decimal fractions

Use decimal fractions whenever it is necessary to convey numerical information fully and accurately:

6.95   3.002   3.002 715

Always use the same number of decimal places for all decimal quantities that are being compared, whether in the text or in a table or illustration:

The levels varied between 6.452 and 7.894 over the period.

not

The levels varied between 6.452 and 7.9 over the period.

When decimal numbers are less than one, a zero should always be placed before the decimal point:

0.25   *not*   .25

Decimal point: Use a full stop on the line as a decimal marker in a numeral. Although the decimal comma is used in some parts of the world, especially Europe, it is not well known in Australia.

Non-decimal fractions

Use hyphens when expressing imprecise non-decimal fractions in words (unless the fraction is preceded by *a* or *an*):

one-third   one and three-quarters   a third   an eighth

When non-decimal fractions are expressed in numerals, use the fraction bar rather than the forward slash to separate the numerator and the denominator:

¾   *not*   3/4

This presentation is preferable because the slash has other functions (see page 109), and in some cases its use with fractions may cause confusion (for example, 1 3/4 for 1¾).

ORDINAL NUMBERS

When using ordinals ('first', 'second', and so on), words are preferable in general text for numbers up to one hundred and for large round numbers:

the third example   the twenty-fifth student   the two-hundredth case

In more numerically dense text or where there are space restrictions (such as in references and captions), use numerals with the relevant suffixes instead:

the 273rd immigrant   2nd edn   a 15th century painting

➤ See pp. 170–1 for a discussion of ordinals in dates.

PERCENTAGES

Percentages can be written in various ways:

15%   15 per cent   fifteen per cent

The symbol % should be used only with numerals, while *per cent* can be used with either words or numerals. In documents where numerals are generally being employed for numbers, it is preferable also to show percentages in numerals with the symbol.

NUMBERS FOR COMPARISON

When a related series of numbers occurs, numerals should always be preferred in statistically oriented text, regardless of the size of the numbers involved:

> The anthology includes 160 poems by 22 women poets, 14 of whom were born in Australia, 4 in New Zealand, 3 in England and 1 in Austria.

However, when two series of numbers are being presented, one series may be expressed in words and the other in numerals for the sake of clarity:

> Of the mothers of the 30 sets of triplets registered during the year, 8 had no previous children, 8 had one child, 7 had two, 4 had three, 1 had four, and 2 had five previous children.

ROMAN NUMERALS

Roman numerals (upper and lower case) and their arabic equivalents are as follows:

Roman and arabic numerals								
I	i	**1**	XI	xi	**11**	XCIX	xcix	**99**
II	ii	**2**	XII	xii	**12**	C	c	**100**
III	iii	**3**	XIX	xix	**19**	CXCII	cxcii	**192**
IV	iv	**4**	XX	xx	**20**	CD	cd	**400**
V	v	**5**	XL	xl	**40**	D	d	**500**
VI	vi	**6**	XLIV	xliv	**44**	DC	dc	**600**
VII	vii	**7**	XLIX	xlix	**49**	M	m	**1000**
VIII	viii	**8**	L	l	**50**	MCML	mcml	**1950**
IX	ix	**9**	LX	lx	**60**	MCMXC	mcmxc	**1990**
X	x	**10**	LXIV	lxiv	**64**	MM	mm	**2000**

When to use roman numerals

Roman numerals are traditionally used for:

- numbering the preliminary pages of books (and sometimes for numbering other elements of documents such as subparagraphs, titles of separate chapters or parts, and appendixes)
- the titles of monarchs and popes.

Using roman numerals for other purposes should generally be avoided, since they are cumbersome and difficult to interpret immediately when more than two numerals are involved (for example, MCMXXVIII).

n addition, they can easily be confused with:

elements of the International System of Units—where 1000 is 'k' (not 'M') and 'M' is the symbol for 'mega' (a million)

some arabic numerals—for example the roman II (two) with the arabic 11 (eleven).

pper or lower case

age and paragraph numbers take lower-case roman numerals, but upper-case man numerals may be used for titles of book elements:

    page viii   subparagraph ii (b)

    Chapter XI   Part V   Appendix III   Plate IV

pper-case numerals are always used for the titles of monarchs and popes:

    Elizabeth II   Louis XIV   Pope Pius XII

rdinal numbers are not identified as such, so roman numerals never take the ffixes *st*, *nd*, *rd* or *th*:

    George V   *not*   George Vth

pans

spans of numbers, no roman numerals are omitted in the second part of the an:

    xxiii–xxix   *not*   xxiii–ix

his differs from the practice for showing spans of arabic numerals, where nnecessary digits are dropped in the second part (for example, *23–9* rather an *23–29*).

➤ See p. 177 for further discussion of spans of numerals.

XPRESSIONS OF TIME

ras

nortened forms such as *BC* (before Christ), *AD* (*anno Domini*, in the year of our ord), *CE* (of the common era) and *BP* (before present) should be presented ithout full stops and with a space separating them from the year. Traditionally, nese era indicators were placed after the year, except for *AD*, which was placed efore it. However, it is now common to place *AD* after the year as well, and this actice is recommended. There should always be a space between the year and ne era indicator. Thus:

    44 BC   1788 AD   50 000 BP

milarly, in references to centuries, the shortened form for the era follows the entury. For example:

    the third century BC   the third century AD   the third century CE

Where to put 'AD': Place the expression *AD* after the year, to match the placement of *BC, CE* and *BP*.

Centuries and decades

The names of centuries can be written either in words or in a mixture of words and numerals:

the eighteenth century   *or*   the 18th century

It is best to avoid abbreviated forms such as '18C' or 'C18', although they might be necessary in contexts where space is limited. Also avoid using roman numerals for centuries, as they are confusing to many readers.

The standard form for representing decades in general text is:

1990s   2000s   2100s

Decades: Do not use an apostrophe when presenting decades in numerals—hence *1990s* not *1990's*. This recommendation is in line with the manual's general advice not to use apostrophes to indicate plurals (see pp. 87, 88 and 153).

In the past, an apostrophe was often placed before the *s*, but there is no grammatical need for it, and the practice is now uncommon.

Expressions such as 'the nineties' are considered colloquial and are not recommended for standard or formal writing.

Dates

Dates as combinations of words and numerals

In correspondence and running text, dates are best presented using numerals for the day and the year but with the name of the month being shown in full:

9 September 1999

This structure is unambiguous, requires no punctuation, and progresses logically from day to month to year. It is typographically preferable to such forms as 'September 10, 2000' or '10th September 2000', because it avoids the potential confusion of adjacent numbers in the first, and requires fewer keystrokes than either. The same structure can also be used when either the day or year is omitted:

Young Endeavour, Australia's sail training flagship, will arrive in Hobart on 18 February.

More than 1700 jobs have been shed since January 1998.

No punctuation is necessary, even when including the name of the day as part of the date:

On Tuesday 1 January 2001 …

Avoid abbreviations when presenting dates in running text:

The Labor Party called an urgent conference on Saturday 22 December.

not

The Labor Party called an urgent conference on Sat. 22 Dec.

Dates in words

Words are preferred where numerals might otherwise start a sentence:

The first of January 2001 was the first day of the new millennium.

Words are sometimes used when ordinals are shown separately without the month, although a numeral with a suffix is also common:

He will leave by train on the twentieth   *or*   ... on the 20th

Dates in numerals

Dates expressed entirely in numerals have the potential to create ambiguity because different countries have different conventions. In Australia and the United Kingdom the conventional sequence is day, month, year; in North America and on many international web sites it is month, day, year; and in Sweden and Germany it is year, month, day.

Because of this, it is best to restrict the numerals-only presentation of dates to situations where space is limited and to local communications. When the numerals-only form is used, either a forward slash or a full stop can be inserted between each group of numerals:

7/12/2001   *or*   7.12.2001

Alternatively, each element of the date can be expressed using two digits:

07/12/01   *or*   07.12.01

This latter form of presentation is commonly used in financial data and on forms, but it should be avoided if it might cause confusion over which century is being referred to.

There is also a variant form of dates that avoids ambiguity by using a lower-case Roman numeral to indicate the month, but it is not much used outside Europe:

7.xii.2001

To facilitate international communication, there is an international standard (ISO 8601:2000) for the writing of calendar dates in all-numeral form. This standard specifies a descending order of year (four digits), month (two digits) and day (two digits). The digits can be shown unspaced, or a hyphen can be used to separate the year, month and day:

20011207   *or*   2001-12-07

The use of this form is becoming more common, especially through the standardisation provided in various computer packages, and should be adopted where there is the potential for ambiguity.

Dates in data systems

'Ordinal dates'—consisting of two or four digits representing the year followed by three digits representing the day of the year—are used to assist the interchange of data among data systems because they avoid the ambiguity inherent in most other all-numeral date forms. The two-digit form for the year is allowed in situations where the century is implied and only the decade and year need be identified; otherwise, four digits are used. The day of the year is shown as a three-digit number, from 001 for 1 January to 365 for 31 December (or 366 in leap years).

Expressing dates: Use the form 7 December 2001 when expressing dates in non-technical documents. All-numeral forms of dates can mislead because international practice varies, so *ISO 8601:2000* should be followed in documents for wide international distribution.

The year and day can be used together or independently; if they are used together in electronic data transfer, the numbers are not separated. Thus:

> 3 December 1997

becomes

> 1997337 [in the four-digit form for the year]

or

> 97337 [in the two-digit form for the year]

If this information has to be read, a hyphen can be inserted between the year and day elements:

> 1997-337 [in the four-digit form]   *or*   97-337 [in the two-digit form]

Time of day

Words or numerals

In documents where very few numbers are used, times of day are often expressed in words, particularly when they involve full, half and quarter hours:

> They arranged to meet at quarter to eleven.
>
> She had to leave at ten o'clock.

Words rather than numerals are also conventional in adjectival phrases such as:

> They catch the eight-thirty bus to work each morning and return by the five-forty.

However, times presented as words often give the impression of approximations, so numerals should be used whenever the exact time is important. For example:

> The bus leaves the city terminal at 8.22 am and arrives here at 2.08 pm.
>
> The night shift begins at 11 pm precisely and ends at 7 am.

The twelve-hour system

With the twelve-hour system of expressing time, the abbreviated forms *am* (*ante meridiem*, before noon) and *pm* (*post meridiem*, after noon) are used to prevent misunderstanding. When the context makes it clear which part of the day is being referred to, the use of *am* or *pm* is unnecessary.

Using 'am' and 'pm': Because they are always preceded by a numeral, *am* and *pm* can be shown without stops as this will not affect clarity. The space between the numeral and the abbreviation should be retained. Thus:

> from 9.15 am to 1 pm

Conventionally, *am* and *pm* are presented in lower case (thus, 9.15 am, 4.35 pm), although in American English they often appear in small capitals, with a colon separating the hours and minutes (9:15 AM, 4:45 PM). The use of full stops between these abbreviated words (*a.m.* and *p.m.*) is declining and, because they are always preceded by a numeral, they can be treated like other symbols associated with numerals, which are unpunctuated.

A full stop should be used to separate the hours from the minutes. Two zeros may be used to indicate even hours but are not essential:

> 9 am   *or*   9.00 am

Under the twelve-hour system, practice differs on the presentation of noon and midnight. Where confusion could be caused by using *12 am* or *12 pm*, it is referable to use the terms *noon* and *midnight*. Thereafter, 12.01 pm refers to the beginning of the afternoon, and 12.01 am to the early morning.

The twenty-four hour system

The twenty-four hour system of expressing time is used where the potential ambiguities of the twelve-hour system must be avoided. Contexts in which this system is conventionally employed include the travel and hospitality industries, some scientific fields and the armed services.

Under the twenty-four hour system, the hours are numbered from midnight (*0000 hours*) to *2359*. Four digits are always used, the first two showing the hours and the last two the minutes. Neither punctuation nor space is inserted. For example:

0045 [= 0.45 am]   0738 [= 7.38 am]   2318 [= 11.18 pm]

Where more precise times that include decimal fractions of seconds are being expressed, colons can be used as the separator (as recommended by ISO 8601:2000). For example:

23:59:17

Time frequency, and the prefix 'bi'

Most prefixes that can be attached to an expression of time to indicate frequency are unambiguous—for example, *tercentenary* and *triennial*. But the prefix 'bi' poses problems, because it means both 'two' and 'twice a … '; so *bimonthly* can mean either 'every two months' or 'twice a month'. It is therefore better to use more specific alternatives in place of this prefix, such as:

twice weekly   fortnightly

twice monthly   every two months

In contrast, *biannual* and *biennial* each have one meaning only: respectively, 'twice a year' and 'every two years'. Nevertheless they are often misunderstood, and so should be used only in contexts where their meaning can be made clear.

TEMPERATURE

In Australia, temperature is generally expressed in degrees Celsius. (The Fahrenheit scale was used until the introduction of the metric system in 1966.) The kelvin is used to express temperature in thermodynamic calculations and kinetic studies.

In documents for a general audience that contain few numbers, references to temperatures included in running text may be expressed in words:

The temperature dropped another eight degrees later in the evening.

Elsewhere, temperature readings in Celsius—either precise or approximate—are always expressed in numerals followed by a space, then the degree symbol (°) followed immediately by the letter 'C'. There is no full stop after the letter 'C' except at the end of the sentence. For temperatures of less than one degree, a zero should always be placed before the decimal point:

15.6 °C   0.5 °C

➤ For further details on these temperature measurement systems, see the tables on pp. 178 and 180.

Temperatures expressed in kelvins are treated like other measurements using SI units (see page 184), and so also take a space between the number and the symbol:

500 K

Because of the potential confusion with its use in expressing negative amounts, the en rule should not be used for spans of temperatures. Instead, the word *to* is recommended, as in:

−8 °C to 4 °C   *not*   −8–4 °C

15 °C to 25 °C   *not*   15–25 °C

En rule: This is the type of dash to use both for spans of numerals and for the minus or negative sign.

CURRENCY

Words or numerals

Amounts of money are usually expressed as numerals combined with symbols:

$150   10c $99.20 $10 234.09

In descriptive and narrative prose, a combination of words and numerals can also be used (although this form is obviously more cumbersome for large and complex amounts):

150 dollars   10 cents   99 dollars and 20 cents

Expressing amounts of money entirely in words is generally reserved for approximations and idiomatic expressions:

This approach is likely to save you thousands of dollars.

Millions of dollars

Millions may be expressed in three ways:

'Million' with decimal fractions: Avoid using 'million' with numbers taken to more than two decimal places. (While *$2.75 million* is clear, *$2.7541 million* would be better expressed in all-numeral form as *$2 754 100*.)

- entirely in numerals

  $1 000 000 $2 700 000 $3 000 000 000

- by the use of the word 'million'

  $1 million $2.7 million $3000 million

- by placing 'm' (unspaced and without a full stop) after the number

  $1m $2.751m $3000m

This latter form is best reserved for contexts where space is at a premium—for example, in tables and graphs. It should only be used in conjunction with the dollar or other monetary symbol; in other contexts, readers may confuse it with the symbol for metre (which is also 'm' but takes a preceding space). The use of 'M' to represent 'million' is uncommon in Australia, and is not recommended.

➤ See also p. 166 for discussion of the words *billion*, *trillion* and *quadrillion*.

Australian currency

Australian currency uses the dollar symbol preceding the number without any intervening space, and a full stop for the decimal point.

$20.75

mounts that are less than a dollar can be shown either with the symbol for cent
'c' with no full stop after it) immediately following the number, or they can be
shown as a decimal fraction of a dollar (always with a zero preceding the decimal
point):

    25c   or $0.25   not $.25

A minimum of two digits must always be shown for cents in a decimal fraction. If
the number of cents is less than ten, a zero must precede it:

    $0.08 [= 8 cents]

not

    $0.8 [which could be read as 80 cents]

Where greater precision is required, more than two digits may be shown after the
decimal point:

    $0.432 $1.0059

Other currencies

The dollar name and symbol are used for the currencies of several countries, and it
is sometimes necessary to distinguish between them. This will be the case in
documents referring to sums of money in both Australian and other dollars, and
for Australian publications designed for an international readership. In such cases
the relevant letter or letters should be placed immediately before the dollar
symbol:

    A$10 000   NZ$5000.00   US$25.90   S$450

Similarly, for non-dollar currencies place the relevant symbol immediately before
the number:

    £375   €850   ¥15 000   Rp650

Alternatively, a three-letter code (specified in the international standard
ISO 4217:1995) is sometimes used when many different currencies are being
referred to:

    AUD10 000 [Australian dollars]

    GBP800 000 [British pounds sterling]

Former Australian currency

Before 14 February 1966, Australian currency was expressed in pounds, shillings
and pence (£ s d). The examples given below illustrate the style used for this
currency:

    £9 8s 7d [no full stops]   £345 11s 3d

    5s 6d   not   5/6   or   £0 5s 6d

To avoid confusion with the pound used as a monetary unit in other countries, the
former Australian pound is distinguished by using the symbol 'A£'.

**A$ or $A?** Use the form A$, which is
the style recommended by the Reserve
Bank of Australia.

The euro: On 1 January 2002 the euro
became the single currency for
Germany, France, Belgium,
Luxembourg, Italy, Austria, Finland,
Holland, Greece, Ireland, Portugal and
Spain. These countries' previous
national currencies (such as the franc
and the Deutschmark) are no longer
legal tender.

ABOUT

Punctuating and spacing numbers

Hyphens

Hyphens are used to connect numbers up to ninety-nine that comprise two words:

twenty-three   fifty-nine   eighty-six

The hyphens are retained when these numbers are part of larger numbers, but the large round numbers themselves do not take hyphens:

one hundred and twenty-four

one thousand   five million

A number expressed in numerals may be joined by a hyphen to other hyphenated words, but hyphenated numbers expressed in words should not (as this can create ambiguity). For example:

a 35-year-old car

or

a thirty-five year old car

not

a thirty-five-year-old car

Commas in numbers shown as words

In large amounts written as words, commas are needed where corresponding spaces would be used between three-digit groups of numerals:

five million, two hundred and fifty thousand, four hundred and twenty-two [5 250 422]

Separating three-digit groups of numerals

In English-speaking countries, commas have traditionally been used to separate groups of three digits within a larger amount—for example, $100,000. However, because a comma is used as the decimal marker in Europe, a thin space is recommended instead of a comma to avoid confusion (as specified in the international standard *ISO 31:1992*).

Recent research shows that the use of commas with numerals is still very common in Australia, and this practice remains a viable alternative in texts not intended for an international or scientific audience. However, the international specification of a thin space as the separator for numerals should be followed in Australian government publications and in any other publication to be distributed internationally.

Four-digit numerals

A space is unnecessary in numerals containing only four digits, since these are sufficiently short to be readily comprehensible. For example:

$6400   3712   0.3214

not

$6 400   3 712   0.321 4

This treatment of four-digit numerals will sometimes need to be varied in tables, to maintain consistent spacing with other large numbers: see the following section on tabular settings.

Tabular settings

In tables or other layouts where the vertical alignment of digits is important for the purpose of comparison or computation, use a thin space for internal divisions of larger numerals. For example:

10 141

1 721

253

69

However, no internal spacing is necessary if the table contains only numbers of no more than four digits:

1721

253

69

(See Chapter 19 for a detailed discussion of table layout.)

Spans of numerals

Use an en rule, not a hyphen, to link spans of numerals, and limit the number of digits in the second part of the span to those essential for clarity. For example:

9–12, 40–1, 45–50, 402–5, 421–39, 440–553

In the following instances, however, it is necessary to maintain more digits in the second part of the span to avoid ambiguity:

* spans ending with numerals from eleven to nineteen

11–12   *not*   11–2

115–17   *not*   115–7

spans of years

1998–99   *not*   1998–9

1998–2001   *not*   1998–01

BC periods

56–55 BC   *not*   56–5 BC

street addresses

135–139 Davey St   *not*   135–9 Davey St

The full span is also traditionally shown for the dates of a person's birth and death. For example:

Sir Henry Parkes (1815–1896)   *not*   … (1815–96).

An en rule should not be used in spans following the words *from* or *between*:

Available in sizes 6–10

not

Available in sizes from 6–10

Open 6–8 pm

not

Open between 6–8 pm

Adjacent sets of numerals

When two sets of numerals appear together in text, insert a comma between them to prevent misunderstanding:

By 2005, 75 more employees will be needed.

Often, however, it is better to rearrange the sentence:

By 2005, an additional 75 employees will be needed.

Spacing

Mathematical signs: When used in an operating role, mathematical signs such as those for addition, subtraction and multiplication take a space either side:

15 − 9 = 6   15 x 4 = 60

When a plus or minus sign is used to indicate a positive or negative value, however, the sign is set next to the numeral without a space:

+100   −50 10^{-2}

(Note that an en rule, not a hyphen, is used for the minus sign.)

There is no space before or after a colon used to indicate a ratio:

1:50 000

Symbols of measurement: A space is required between a numeral and a symbol of measurement (apart from the symbols for degree, minute and second of plane angular measure, see page 183):

500 kg   20 mm

but

45° [degree of plane angle]

Other symbols: There is no space separating a currency symbol from the sum following it or between a percentage sign and the preceding numeral:

A$250   25%

THE INTERNATIONAL SYSTEM OF UNITS

In accordance with the *Weights and Measures (National Standards) Amendment Ac*
1984, most units of measurement used in Australia are those of the International
System of Units (*Système International d'Unités*), which is symbolised in all
languages as 'SI'.

The SI is a practical system of units that constitutes the modern form of the metr
system. SI units are divided into two classes:

* base units
* derived units.

Together, the base and derived units form what is called a 'coherent set of units'.
'Coherent' is used here in the specialist sense to describe a system in which the
units are mutually related by rules of multiplication and division with no
numerical factor other than one. A most important practical implication of a
coherent system is that there is only one unit for each physical quantity that we
measure.

Detailed reference: See *The*
International System of Units, 1998, 7th
edition, and *Supplement 2000: addenda*
and corrigenda to the 7th edition,
published by the Bureau International
des Poids et Mesures (BIPM), for a full
description of the SI and the units
included within it.

System of quantities

The system of quantities used with the SI units is set out by the International
Organization for Standardization (ISO) in *ISO 31:1992*, Parts 0 to 13. ISO has
adopted a system of physical quantities based on the seven base quantities
corresponding to the seven base units of the SI, namely length, mass, time, electr
current, thermodynamic temperature, amount of substance, and luminous
intensity. Other quantities, called 'derived quantities', are defined in terms of the
seven base quantities; the relationships between derived quantities and base
quantities are expressed by a system of equations. It is this system of quantities an
equations that is properly used with the SI units. The effect of the system is that
units are the same everywhere in the world.

'ISO': This is not intended to be an
initialism for the name of the
organisation, but is an independent
word (derived from Greek, meaning
'equal') that occurs as a prefix in terms
such as 'isometric'.

SI base units

Table 11.1 shows the seven base units from which all the other SI units are
derived.

Table 11.1 **SI base units**

Base quantity	Name	Symbol
length	metre	m
mass	kilogram	kg
time	second	s
electric current	ampere	A
thermodynamic temperature	kelvin	K
amount of substance	mole	mol
luminous intensity	candela	cd

Capitals in tables: The general
practice recommended in Chapter 19
of using an initial capital for each text
item in a table has not been followed
in Tables 11.1 to 11.8. The reason for
this exception is to avoid giving the
mistaken impression that these unit
names should be capitalised in text.

SI derived units

SI derived units are expressed in terms of base units by means of the mathematical symbols of multiplication and division.

Some of these SI derived units are named according to their relationship to the unit on which they are based (see Table 11.2). Others have special names (see Table 11.3).

Where units are formed by the multiplication of other units, this can be shown:

- with unit symbols—by using either a raised dot with a space either side or simply a space

    A·s   or   A s

- with unit names—by using a space

    ampere second

Tables 11.3 and 11.4 employ the spaced, raised dot with unit symbols, and the space with unit names, reflecting the practice set out in *The International System of Units*, 1998, 7th edition, and *Supplement 2000: addenda and corrigenda to the 7th edition*, published by the Bureau International des Poids et Mesures.

Table 11.2 Examples of SI derived units expressed in terms of base units

Derived quantity	Name	Symbol
Area	square metre	m^2
Volume	cubic metre	m^3
Speed, velocity	metre per second	m/s
Acceleration	metre per second squared	m/s^2
Wavenumber	reciprocal metre	m^{-1}
Density, mass density	kilogram per cubic metre	kg/m^3
Specific volume	cubic metre per kilogram	m^3/kg
Current density	ampere per square metre	A/m^2
Magnetic field strength	ampere per metre	A/m
Concentration (of amount of substance)	mole per cubic metre	mol/m^3
Luminance	candela per square metre	cd/m^2
Refractive index	(the number) one	$1^{(a)}$

The symbol '1' is generally omitted in combination with a numerical value.

Table 11.3 **SI derived units with special names and symbols**

Derived quantity	Name	Symbol	Expressed in terms of other SI units	Expressed in terms of SI base units
plane angle	radian[a]	rad		$m \cdot m^{-1} = 1$[b]
solid angle	steradian[a]	sr[c]		$m^2 \cdot m^{-2} = 1$[b]
frequency	hertz	Hz		s^{-1}
force	newton	N		$m \cdot kg \cdot s^{-2}$
pressure, stress	pascal	Pa	N/m^2	$m^{-1} \cdot kg \cdot s^{-2}$
energy, work, quantity of heat	joule	J	$N \cdot m$	$m^2 \cdot kg \cdot s^{-2}$
power, radiant flux	watt	W	J/s	$m^2 \cdot kg \cdot s^{-3}$
electric charge, quantity of electricity	coulomb	C		$s \cdot A$
electric potential difference, electromotive force	volt	V	W/A	$m^2 \cdot kg \cdot s^{-3} \cdot A^{-1}$
capacitance	farad	F	C/V	$m^{-2} \cdot kg^{-1} \cdot s^4 \cdot A^2$
electric resistance	ohm	Ω	V/A	$m^2 \cdot kg \cdot s^{-3} \cdot A^{-2}$
electric conductance	siemens	S	A/V	$m^{-2} \cdot kg^{-1} \cdot s^3 \cdot A^2$
magnetic flux	weber	Wb	$V \cdot s$	$m^2 \cdot kg \cdot s^{-2} \cdot A^{-1}$
magnetic flux density	tesla	T	Wb/m^2	$kg \cdot s^{-2} \cdot A^{-1}$
inductance	henry	H	Wb/A	$m^2 \cdot kg \cdot s^{-2} \cdot A^{-2}$
Celsius temperature	degree Celsius[d]	°C		K
luminous flux	lumen	lm	$cd \cdot sr$[c]	$m^2 \cdot m^{-2} \cdot cd = cd$
illuminance	lux	lx	lm/m^2	$m^2 \cdot m^{-4} \cdot cd = m^{-2} \cdot cd$
activity (referred to a radionuclide)	becquerel	Bq		s^{-1}
absorbed dose, specific energy (imparted), kerma	gray	Gy	J/kg	$m^2 \cdot s^{-2}$
dose equivalent, ambient dose equivalent, directional dose equivalent, personal dose equivalent, organ equivalent dose	sievert	Sv	J/kg	$m^2 \cdot s^{-2}$
catalytic activity	katal	kat		$s^{-1} \cdot mol$

(a) The radian and steradian may be used with advantage in expressions for derived units to distinguish between quantities of different nature but the same dimension. Some examples of their use in forming derived units are given in Table 11.4.

(b) In practice, the symbols 'rad' and 'sr' are used where appropriate, but the derived unit '1' is generally omitted in combination with a numerical value.

(c) In photometry, the name 'steradian' and the symbol 'sr' are usually retained in expressions for units.

(d) This unit may be used in combination with SI prefixes—for example, millidegree Celsius, m°C.

These special names and symbols may themselves be used to express other derived units. Table 11.4 shows some examples.

Table 11.4 Examples of SI derived units whose names and symbols include SI derived units with special names and symbols

Derived quantity	Name	Symbol	Expressed in terms of SI base units
dynamic viscosity	pascal second	Pa · s	$m^{-1} \cdot kg \cdot s^{-1}$
moment of force	newton metre	N · m	$m^2 \cdot kg \cdot s^{-2}$
surface tension	newton per metre	N/m	$kg \cdot s^{-2}$
angular velocity	radian per second	rad/s	$m \cdot m^{-1} \cdot s^{-1} = s^{-1}$
angular acceleration	radian per second squared	rad/s^2	$m \cdot m^{-1} \cdot s^{-2} = s^{-2}$
heat flux density, irradiance	watt per square metre	W/m^2	$kg \cdot s^{-3}$
heat capacity, entropy	joule per kelvin	J/K	$m^2 \cdot kg \cdot s^{-2} \cdot K^{-1}$
specific heat capacity, specific entropy	joule per kilogram kelvin	J/(kg · K)	$m^2 \cdot s^{-2} \cdot K^{-1}$
specific energy	joule per kilogram	J/kg	$m^2 \cdot s^{-2}$
thermal conductivity	watt per metre kelvin	W/(m · K)	$m \cdot kg \cdot s^{-3} \cdot K^{-1}$
energy density	joule per cubic metre	J/m^3	$m^{-1} \cdot kg \cdot s^{-2}$
electric field strength	volt per metre	V/m	$m \cdot kg \cdot s^{-3} \cdot A^{-1}$
electric charge density	coulomb per cubic metre	C/m^3	$m^{-3} \cdot s \cdot A$
electric flux density	coulomb per square metre	C/m^2	$m^{-2} \cdot s \cdot A$
permittivity	farad per metre	F/m	$m^{-3} \cdot kg^{-1} \cdot s^4 \cdot A^2$
permeability	henry per metre	H/m	$m \cdot kg \cdot s^{-2} \cdot A^{-2}$
molar energy	joule per mole	J/mol	$m^2 \cdot kg \cdot s^{-2} \cdot mol^{-1}$
molar entropy, molar heat capacity	joule per mole kelvin	J/(mol · K)	$m^2 \cdot kg \cdot s^{-2} \cdot K^{-1} \cdot mol^{-1}$
exposure (x and γ rays)	coulomb per kilogram	C/kg	$kg^{-1} \cdot s \cdot A$
absorbed dose rate	gray per second	Gy/s	$m^2 \cdot s^{-3}$
radiant intensity	watt per steradian	W/sr	$m^4 \cdot m^{-2} \cdot kg \cdot s^{-3} = m^2 \cdot kg \cdot s^{-3}$
radiance	watt per square metre steradian	W/(m^2 · sr)	$m^2 \cdot m^{-2} \cdot kg \cdot s^{-3} = kg \cdot s^{-3}$
catalytic (activity) concentration	katal per cubic metre	kat/m^3	$m^{-3} \cdot s^{-1} \cdot mol$

Decimal multiples and submultiples

A series of prefixes is used to form the decimal multiples and submultiples of SI units. Each prefix has a standard value, regardless of the unit to which it is attached. Thus a kilometre is 10^3 metres, a megajoule is 10^6 joules, and a nanosecond is 10^{-9} seconds. These prefixes are listed in Table 11.5.

Table 11.5 **Prefixes for SI units**

Prefix	Symbol	Factor	Extended form
yotta	Y	10^{24}	1 000 000 000 000 000 000 000 000
zetta	Z	10^{21}	1 000 000 000 000 000 000 000
exa	E	10^{18}	1 000 000 000 000 000 000
peta	P	10^{15}	1 000 000 000 000 000
tera	T	10^{12}	1 000 000 000 000
giga	G	10^{9}	1 000 000 000
mega	M	10^{6}	1 000 000
kilo	k	10^{3}	1 000
hecto	h	10^{2}	100
deca[a]	da	10^{1}	10
deci	d	10^{-1}	0.1
centi	c	10^{-2}	0.01
milli	m	10^{-3}	0.001
micro	µ	10^{-6}	0.000 001
nano	n	10^{-9}	0.000 000 001
pico	p	10^{-12}	0.000 000 000 001
femto	f	10^{-15}	0.000 000 000 000 001
atto	a	10^{-18}	0.000 000 000 000 000 001
zepto	z	10^{-21}	0.000 000 000 000 000 000 001
yocto	y	10^{-24}	0.000 000 000 000 000 000 000 001

(a) Sometimes spelt 'deka'.

Prefixes followed by vowels:
Generally, where the unit name begins with a vowel, both the final vowel of the prefix and the vowel of the unit name are written and pronounced. The only exceptions to this rule are *megohm* (not 'megaohm') and *kilohm* (not 'kiloohm').

Measurement in Australia

The *National Measurement Act 1960* governs the use of measurements in Australia. Within this Act are:

- the National Measurement Regulations (1999), which prescribe the Australian legal units of measurement of any physical quantity and the SI prefixes that may be used
- the National Measurement Guidelines (1999), which prescribe the way in which units of measurement and prefixes may be combined to produce an Australian legal unit of measurement.

Although SI units are always preferred, there are some non-SI units that are still accepted for use with the SI. Table 11.6 shows those non-SI units that have been adopted as legal units of measurement in Australia and that may be used generally. However, they are not all legally accepted in every nation, so care should be taken when using them.

ble 11.6 Non-SI Australian legal units of measurement

uantity	Name	Symbol
und power	decibel[a]	dB
und pressure	decibel[a]	dB
und intensity	decibel[a]	dB
ea	hectare	ha
ergy	electronvolt	eV
nematic viscosity	stokes[b]	St
ngth	nautical mile	n mile[c]
ass	tonne	t
ass	metric carat	CM or ct[c]
ine angle	degree	°
ine angle	minute	′
ine angle	second	″
ne interval	day	d
ne interval	hour	h
ne interval	minute	min
ocity	knot	kn[c]
cosity	poise[b]	P
ume	litre	L or l

Not accepted for use with the International System.

These are centimetre-gram-second (CGS) units, the use of which is not encouraged within the International System.

These symbols are legally accepted in Australia, but not internationally.

ertain units of measurement outside the SI system have special functions in articular industries or disciplines, including in mining, where gold continues to be easured in troy ounces (abbreviated to 'oz tr'), and in aviation, where 'foot' ontracted to 'ft') remains the standard measurement for altitude.

he National Measurement Regulations prescribe the non-SI units that are dditional Australian legal units of measurement and the purposes for which they ay be used. Table 11.7 lists these units together with some examples of their escribed purposes. However, Schedule 2 of the National Measurement egulations should be consulted to ascertain the specific purposes for which they ay legally be used in Australia.

(continued on p. 185)

ABOUT

Using SI units

SI units can be expressed by either their name or their symbol. In non-technical works, the names of units should generally be used. In other publications, the type of content and the likely knowledge and expectations of readers will need to be considered. A consistent approach should be followed throughout a publication to avoid a haphazard mixture of unit names and unit symbols.

Consistency

Only one unit name or symbol should be included in a statement of measurement. For example:

1.234 m   *or*   1234 mm

not

1 m 234 mm   *or*   1 m 23 cm 4 mm

The unit chosen should be the one that makes the statement least cumbersome and easiest to grasp. For example:

47.32 m   *not*   0.047 32 km

500 kPa   *or*   0.5 MPa   *but not*   500 000 Pa

Only one unit for the physical quantities should be used when measurements are being compared, and in tables, lists and illustrations. Thus, in a table where quantities are expressed in metres, any millimetre value should be expressed as a (decimal) fraction of a metre.

Unit names and symbols should not be mixed in the same context. If a symbol is used for one unit, symbols should be used for all units. For example:

km/h   *not*   km/hour

Capitalisation

Except for the word *Celsius* in 'degree Celsius', units and their prefixes are not capitalised when shown in words (unless commencing a sentence). For example:

20 megatonnes   *not*   20 Megatonnes

21 litres   *not*   21 Litres

Most of the symbols are also presented in lower-case letters. The exceptions are:

- the symbol for litre (L), which is capitalised to make it clearer typographically, and is well established in this form in Australian style. (However, the lower case 'l' is still listed as an option within the international and Australian standards)

- symbols for units named after people—for example, Pa for *pascal* and N for *newton*. Note that the unit name is spelt out in lower case but the first letter of the symbol is capitalised

- the symbols for the first seven prefixes shown in Table 11.5—Y (yotta), Z (zetta), E (exa), P (peta), T (tera), G (giga) and M (mega).

Plurals

Unit symbols never take a plural *s* (since they are internationally recognised symbols, not abbreviations of the unit names). Thus:

2 kg   *not*   2 kgs

In contrast, the names of units do take a plural *s* when associated with numbers greater than one. Thus:

1 kilogram   *but*   25 kilograms

1 metre   *but*   1.5 metres

1 degree Celsius   *but*   15 degrees Celsius

However, *hertz*, *lux* and *siemens* remain unchanged in the plural:

10 kilohertz   3 lux   1.5 siemens

Punctuation and spacing

When the SI symbols are used, they do not take full stops (unless ending a sentence). For example:

20 L   *not*   20 L.

15 km   *not*   15 km.

Both the names and symbols for SI units should be separated from the associated numerical value by a space. For example:

22 m   *not*   22m

27 volts   *not*   27volts

−15 °C   *not*   −15°C

However, the symbols for degree (°), minute (′) and second (″) of plane angle do not take a space:

180°   125′   15″

Using 'per'

The word *per* should be used only with the spelt-out names of units of measurement, while the forward slash denoting *per* should be used only with symbols:

75 kilometres per hour   *or*   75 km/h

not

75 kilometres/hour   *or*   75 km per hour

Per should not be abbreviated to 'p'. For example:

Mt/a   *not*   Mtpa

km/h   *not*   kmph   or   kph

Table 11.7 Some additional non-SI Australian legal units of measurement and the purposes for which they may be used

Quantity	Name	Symbol	Examples of purposes
Length	inch	in	automotive tyres or rims, precision pipes, precision fittings, defence equipment, aviation equipment, equipment used in the computer or electronics industries
Length	foot	ft	altitude in aviation, submarine depth
Mass	troy ounce	oz tr	the mass of precious metals
Power	horsepower	hp	engine ratings in the aviation industry or defence equipment
Pressure	millibar	mb or mbar	air pressure in the aviation industry
Pressure	millimetre of mercury	mm Hg	blood pressure
Velocity	foot per minute	ft/min	vehicular vertical speed
Work and energy	kilocalorie	kcal	food energy values

Other units of measurement

Bits and bytes

In information technology, two of the basic ways of measuring are *bits* and *bytes*—used, for example, to measure computer memory storage and the transfer of data between computers:

Bit: This refers to, and is a contraction of, the words 'binary digit'.

Byte: This word has had no fixed definition, but IBM's definition of it as a multiple of 8 bits has generally been accepted as a de facto standard.

Technically speaking, a bit is a unit and a byte is a multiple of a bit (8 times), in the same way that a kilometre is a multiple of a metre (1000 times). Worldwide, it is most common to use 'B' for byte, and either 'b' or 'bit' for binary digit.

The standard SI prefixes and their symbols are often used to form expressions such as kilobit (kb), megabyte (MB) and gigabyte (GB). Because information and computer technology operate on numbers with a base of two, not of ten, these are not strictly accurate measurements—a kilobit should equal 1000 bits (10^3 bits), but is used to denote the amount 1024 bits (2^{10} bits). The relative inaccuracies increase for prefixes denoting higher powers, but these errors are often not important in texts of a non-technical nature. Where accuracy is important, the International Electrotechnical Commission (IEC), recognising that the SI prefix 'kilo' means 1000 and not 1024, has approved a specific set of prefixes as an international standard (see Table 11.8).

Table 11.8 **International Electrotechnical Commission prefixes**

Prefix	Symbol	Factor	Extended form
exbi	Ei	$(2^{10})^6$	1 152 921 504 606 846 976
pebi	Pi	$(2^{10})^5$	1 125 899 906 842 624
tebi	Ti	$(2^{10})^4$	1 099 511 627 776
gibi	Gi	$(2^{10})^3$	1 073 741 824
mebi	Mi	$(2^{10})^2$	1 048 576
kibi	Ki	$(2^{10})^1$	1 024

Note: The IEC prefixes are all multiples. IEC has made no allowance for submultiples.

Imperial measurements

Imperial measurements (such as 'inches', 'miles', 'pounds' and 'pints') should be avoided, except in the following contexts:

- in quotations from historical documents (when SI equivalents can be provided in square brackets if relevant)
- when writing for readers in countries (particularly the United States of America) where imperial measures, or elements of them, still apply. In such instances, SI units can be followed by the relevant imperial units in parentheses if necessary.

For conversions from imperial to SI units, see Appendix B.

Chapter *12* Methods of citation

THE AUTHOR–DATE SYSTEM	**188**
About the author–date, documentary-note and Vancouver systems	190
In-text citations	189
The reference list	189
The citation details: authorship and year	189
The citation details: document information	199
THE DOCUMENTARY-NOTE SYSTEM	**208**
In-text note identifiers	209
First citations	210
Second and subsequent citations	213
THE VANCOUVER SYSTEM	**215**
In-text note identifiers	215
The reference list	216
BIBLIOGRAPHIES	**218**
A bibliography in the author–date style	219
A bibliography in the documentary-note style	219
A bibliography in the Vancouver style	219
An annotated bibliography	219
About government publications	**220**
Organising bibliographies	224

SPECIALISED SOURCES	**224**
Legislation	224
Legal authorities	226
Plays and poetry	228
The Bible	228
The classics	228
Films, videos, and television and radio programs	229
About citing electronic material	**230**
Duplicated material	232
Databases	232

Most authors of non-fiction works use information that originally appeared in other works to expand on or substantiate their statements. Any sources used—and they can range from books and journals to web sites and emails—should be acknowledged, as a matter of courtesy, to secure the author's credibility, to inform readers, and often for reasons connected with copyright. These acknowledgments are called 'citations' or 'references'.

Every citation must be meticulously prepared, to satisfy the objectives of clarity, accuracy and consistency. The method of presentation will be determined to a large extent by the nature of the work and the method of citation chosen.

One very commonly used method of citation, and the method recommended in this manual, is the author–date system (sometimes also called the 'name–year system' or the 'Harvard system'). In the case of print-based publications, brief citations giving the author's name and year of publication are inserted in the text; these are followed at the end of the chapter (or other similar division) or work by an alphabetical list of all the sources used, with all the details that will enable readers to locate any sources that interest them. In the case of electronic material, in-text references can be linked to a full reference list, set of notes or bibliography.

The second method described in this chapter is the documentary-note system (sometimes referred to as the 'humanities style'). It entails a full acknowledgment of sources within footnotes or endnotes, with a note identifier in the text that directs readers to the relevant source citation.

For some scientific (particularly medical) works, a variation of the documentary-note system—the Vancouver system—is commonly used. (This system is also known by other names such as the 'citation–sequence system', the 'citation–order system' and the 'sequential–numeric system'.)

THE AUTHOR–DATE SYSTEM

There are many variants of the author–date system, differing in minor style features such as punctuation, capitalisation, abbreviations and the use of italics. The following interpretation is recommended in the interest of simplicity.

Shared purpose: No matter what method of citation is used, it is important to meet readers' needs by carefully describing the path to your source. Successful referencing calls for:

- clarity
- accuracy
- comprehensiveness
- consistency.

In-text citations

In-text citations should be presented in a consistent style throughout a document.

Wherever possible, parenthetical citations of both author and date (perhaps with a page reference or other similar detail) should be placed at the end of a sentence, before the concluding punctuation: this is least disruptive to a reader. If, however, the citation refers to only part of a sentence, it should be placed at the end of the clause or phrase to which it relates.

When the name of the author is part of the sentence and only the date (and perhaps a page reference or other similar detail) is in parentheses, the citation is best placed immediately after the author's name.

The reference list

A reference list contains details of all authorities—other than personal communications, dictionaries, and newspaper articles and encyclopedia entries for which no author is evident—cited in the text. The purpose of the list is to help people find the works if they want to read further.

Agreement between the in-text citation and the reference list is vital. And particular care with cross-referencing is needed if authorities' names are abbreviated in the in-text citation.

The reference list—generally headed simply 'References'—is usually placed at the end of a work. In multi-author works, loose-leaf publications and works that might be read piecemeal, however, it is often preferable to compile a separate reference list for each chapter or other division and to place these at the end of those chapters or divisions.

➤ See Chapter 13 for information about where to put a reference list in a publication.

The reference list is most often presented in alphabetical order according to the authors' and authoring bodies' names. Letter-by-letter, as opposed to word-by-word, alphabetical order is recommended. If, however, an extensive work deals with a number of distinct themes, or if its sources fall into a number of broad categories—for example, published books and journals, manuscripts, theses, legislation and legal authorities—it may be useful to list the sources alphabetically according to theme or category.

Alphabetical order: Use letter-by-letter, as opposed to word-by-word, alphabetical order in reference lists. For information about organising a reference list other than in strict alphabetical order, see 'Organising bibliographies', p. 224.

If an author includes sources that are not cited in the document but are relevant to the subject, the list is properly called a bibliography. The same method of presentation is used for both a reference list and a bibliography in the author–date system.

The citation details: authorship and year

The family name of the author or authors (or the name of the authoring body) and the year of the cited work's publication or creation are usually all that is required in the text.

(continued on p. 192)

ABOUT

The author–date, documentary-note and Vancouver systems

The author–date system

The author–date system is widely accepted in the physical, natural and social sciences and has gained much popularity in the humanities in recent years. Among its advantages are its relative ease of use and its accessibility: the reader can make an immediate association between an idea or fact and its authority and time of publication. Virtually the only drawback is the occasional need to cite multiple sources at a single reference point in the text, which might cause some disruption to the flow of ideas. Careful drafting, however, can usually avoid this problem.

When authors make an in-text reference to an authority, they identify it instantly by providing, in parentheses, the authority's name and the year of publication; sometimes it is also necessary to provide page or volume numbers, or both. Armed with this information, readers can then go to the alphabetical list of works cited—the list of references—or the bibliography for full publication details.

The documentary-note system

The main distinction between the documentary-note system and the author–date system is that, with the former, all the reader sees in the text is a superscript numeral or symbol, rather than the author's name and publication date. The reader then goes to the foot of the page, to the end of the chapter (or other division) or the end of the work, or to a linked listing to learn the details of the source cited.

There are a number of contexts in which the documentary-note system might be chosen in preference to the author–date system. These include situations where there are too few references in the text to justify a consolidated reference list, or where in-text citations of author and date are likely to become intrusive (perhaps because there are many citations of authoring bodies with long names). With the documentary-note system, only one superscript numeral or symbol appears at any one point in the text, although the footnote or endnote to which it refers may contain more than one cited source as well as further explanatory text or comments.

The Vancouver system

The Vancouver system is used in some scientific (particularly medical) literature. It is similar to the documentary-note system in its use of numerals to label a reference citation point in the text.

There are, however, three points of difference with the documentary-note system. First, each superscript citation numeral refers to a single reference source (and thus several superscript numerals can appear together at one point in the text). Second, the citation numerals are not linked to footnotes but to the sources listed in numerical order in a consolidated reference list at the end of the document. And third, the reference list is usually restricted to bibliographic references and does not include explanatory notes.

Examples of in-text citations

Author–date

This approach (Hodkinson 1995; Starr 1991 suggests that ...

Documentary-note

This assumption has been convincingly refuted.[1]

Vancouver

This assumption has been convincingly refuted.[1,2]

Reference lists, notes and bibliographies: the three systems compared

As interpreted in this chapter, reference lists (for the author–date system), notes (for the documentary-note and Vancouver systems) and bibliographies (in all three styles) share two characteristics:

- With the exception of the titles of periodicals (journals, magazines and newspapers), minimal capitalisation is used.

- No full stops, and no spaces, are used with people's initials.

e author–date and documentary-
te systems share several features:

Book and periodical titles are
italicised.

Single quotation marks are used for
the titles of chapters and other
similar divisions in books and for the
titles of articles in periodicals.

The elements of a citation are
separated by commas.

e only difference lies in the
acement of authors' initials in the
ference list and the notes (but not
e bibliography), and the placement of
e date of publication:

In a reference list using the
author–date system, the authors'
initials *follow* the family name—
because the list is presented in
alphabetical order—and are
immediately followed by the date of
publication.

In notes using the documentary-note
system, authors' initials *precede* the
family name—because the list is
presented in numerical order—and
the date of publication comes at or
near the end of the citation.

tes using the Vancouver system
are with the author–date system the
nvention of placing authors' initials
ter the family name (although in the
ncouver style no comma is used to
parate the two). They share with the
cumentary-note system the
nvention of placing the publication
te at or near the end of the citation.
e Vancouver system differs entirely,
wever, in its punctuation practices.

Examples of entries in a reference list or notes

A book

Author–date

Merry, G 1997, *Food poisoning prevention*, 2nd edn, Macmillan Education Australia, Melbourne.

Documentary-note

1. G Merry, *Food poisoning prevention*, 2nd edn, Macmillan Education Australia, Melbourne, 1997.

Vancouver

1. Merry G. Food poisoning prevention. 2nd edn. Melbourne: Macmillan Education Australia, 1997.

An article in a journal

Author–date

Marchelier, PM & Hughes, RG 1997, 'New problems with foodborne diseases', *Medical Journal of Australia*, vol. 275, pp. 771–5.

Documentary-note

1. PM Marchelier & RG Hughes, 'New problems with foodborne diseases', *Medical Journal of Australia*, vol. 275, 1997, pp. 771–5.

Vancouver

1. Marchelier PM, Hughes RG. New problems with foodborne diseases. *Med J Aust* 1997;275:771–5.

Shortened forms commonly used in citations

The following shortened forms are often used in citations in all three systems:

art.	article
app.	appendix
c.	circa (about, approximately)
cf.	compare (from Latin *confer*)
ch.	chapter
col., cols	column(s)
div.	division
ed., eds	editor(s)
edn	edition
et al.	and others (from Latin *et alii*)
fig., figs	figure(s)
fn., fnn.	footnote(s)
ill., ills	illustrator(s)
l., ll.	line(s)
MS, MSS	manuscript(s)
n., nn.	note(s)
n.d.	no date
n.p.	no place
p., pp.	page(s)
para., paras	paragraph(s)
pl.	plate
pt, pts	part(s)
rev.	revised
ser.	series
suppl.	supplement
vol., vols	volume(s)

In the reference list the same information is provided but, in the case of authors, their initials—with no full stops and no spaces—are placed after their family name, separated from it by a comma.

As a general rule, use only authors' initials in the reference list, regardless of the manner of presentation on the title page of the source. Sometimes, however, it is useful to spell out an author's given name if readers are more likely to recognise the person that way. Degrees and affiliations are not included; honorifics can be included as an aid to recognition but are irrelevant to the alphabetical order:

> Adams, Phillip
>
> Gowers, Sir Ernest
>
> Gowers, General Maurice
>
> Herbst, DD

One author or authoring body

The family name of the author (or the title of the authoring body) and the year of the document's publication or creation—with no punctuation between the two items—are inserted in the text in one of two ways:

> The theory was first propounded in 1993 (Hamilton 1994).

or

> The theory was first propounded by Hamilton (1994).

> The initiative was proposed in 1996 (Tourism Taskforce 1996).

or

> The Tourism Taskforce (1996) proposed the initiative.

In the reference list, these two examples would be presented thus:

> Hamilton, CL 1994,
>
> Tourism Taskforce 1996,

An authoring body with a long name

Sometimes the names of authoring bodies are long. If this is the case and the body is being referred to frequently, it is sensible to use an abbreviation. For example:

> The National Health and Medical Research Council prepared the guidelines in 1998 and 1999 (NHMRC 1999).

Care is needed, however: the abbreviation should then be used for all in-text citations of that body and the reference list should provide a cross-reference:

> NHMRC—*see* National Health and Medical Research Council.

The bibliographic information for the reference should be provided where the name of the organisation is spelt out.

Two or more works cited at one point in the text

two or more works by different authors or authoring bodies are cited at one point in the text, use a semicolon to separate them:

(Larsen 2000; Malinowski 1999)

some citation systems, authors' names are presented in the text in chronological der (by date of publication); in others they are presented alphabetically. An phabetical presentation is recommended by this manual.

Two or more works cited at one point: Present the authors' names in alphabetical order, rather than in chronological order according to the year of publication.

Two or three authors or authoring bodies

hen citing a work by two or three authors or authoring bodies, cite the names in e order in which they appear on the title page and present the parenthetical ference thus:

(Australian Bureau of Statistics & Australian Institute of Health and Welfare 1997)

(Malinowski, Miller & Gupta 1995)

hen the authors' names are incorporated in the text, use 'and' instead of the persand. For example:

Malinowski, Miller and Gupta (1995) disagreed with …

sing these examples, the reference list entries will appear thus:

Australian Bureau of Statistics & Australian Institute of Health and Welfare 1997,

Malinowski, W, Miller, TB & Gupta, K 1995,

'And' or '&'? Use an ampersand (&) for an in-text citation for joint authors when enclosed in parentheses; use *and* when the authors' names are incorporated in the text.

More than three authors or authoring bodies

hen a work has more than three authors or authoring bodies, the in-text ation should show only the name of the first-listed author or body, followed by e expression 'et al.' (meaning 'and others'). For example, a work by Malinowski, rsen, Ngu and Fairweather is cited thus:

(Malinowski et al. 1999)

Malinowski et al. (1999) have found …

e names of *all* the authors or authoring bodies should, however, be provided in e reference list:

Malinowski, W, Larsen, AA, Ngu, B & Fairweather, S 1999,

there is subsequently a textual reference to a work published in the same year by, , Malinowski, Larsen, Ngu and Barlen—or even Malinowski, Miller, Gupta and res—the names of enough authors to show the difference should be given in the -text citation. For example:

(Malinowski, Larsen, Ngu & Barlen 1999)

(Malinowski, Larsen, Ngu & Fairweather 1999)

(Malinowski, Miller et al. 1999)

Citing page numbers or other elements of a work

If a work being referred to is long and page numbers might be useful to the reader, include them in the in-text citation, separated from the year by a comma. The abbreviations *p.* and *pp.* are used. For example:

The initiative was proposed in 1996 (Tourism Taskforce 1996, p. 245).

Hamilton (1994, pp. 145–7) was the first to propound the theory.

The Public Land Use Commission reported … (1996, pp. 27–45; 1997, p. 118).

Page numbers are essential in the text if you are directly quoting someone else's words. They are not usually needed in the reference list, but, if they are, they should appear as the final item of the citation, separated from the preceding one by a comma.

If a volume, section, equation or other element of a work needs to be specified, use the abbreviations *vol.*, *vols*, *sec.*, *secs*, *eq.* and *eqs* in the in-text citation for brevity's sake. For example:

(Public Land Use Commission 1996, vol. 2)

(Hamilton 1994, secs 2, 7)

(Larsen 2000, eqs 2–6)

These details do not usually need to be given in the reference list.

When both volume and page references are necessary, present them thus:

(Public Land Use Commission 1996, vol. 2, p. 23)

(Public Land Use Commission 1996, vol. 2, p. 23; vol. 3, pp. 57–69)

Public Land Use Commission (1996, vol. 2, p. 23)

Public Land Use Commission (1996, vol. 2, p. 23; vol. 3, pp. 57–69)

Note the use of the semicolon in the second and fourth examples.

More than one work by the same author or authoring body

Published in different years

When referring to more than one work by the same author or authoring body, arrange the citation in chronological order by date of publication, starting with the earliest date. For example:

(Public Land Use Commission 1996, 1997)

The Public Land Use Commission (1996, 1997) reported on …

(Public Land Use Commission 1996, p. 237; 1997, p. 159)

A semicolon is used to separate a page reference from a date following it, as in the third example.

The reference list entries should be listed similarly, starting with the earliest publication date. The name of the author or authoring body can be repeated, but it is preferable to use a 2-em rule (without a following space) instead:

Public Land Use Commission 1996,

——1997,

ublished in the same year

ultiple works prepared by the same author and published in the same year are stinguished one from the other by attaching a lower-case letter of the alphabet to e publication date. The order of the listing is established on the basis of the tter-by-letter alphabetical order of the titles, disregarding any initial articles (*a*, or *the*). For example, two 1997 works by the Australian Council of Social rvice—*The emergency relief handbook* and *People in financial crisis*—would be cited 1997*a* and 1997*b* respectively.

the works are cited at the same place in the text, they will appear like this, with micolons as necessary:

The Australian Council of Social Service … (ACOSS 1997a, 1997b).

(ACOSS 1997a, p. 31; 1997b, p. 72)

(ACOSS 1997a, 1997b; Malinowski 1999)

(ACOSS 1997a, p. 31; 1997b, p. 72; Malinowski 1999, pp. 89–99)

he identifying letters are retained in the reference list:

ACOSS—*see* Australian Council of Social Service.

Australian Council of Social Service 1997a,

——1997b,

Malinowski, W 1999,

general, it is unnecessary to note the month of publication, although an author ght opt to do so if the precise timing is important. In this case, the month is aced at the end of the citation, before any page reference. For example:

National Natural Resource Management Taskforce 1999a, *Managing natural resources in rural Australia for a sustainable future*, discussion paper, Agriculture, Fisheries and Forestry—Australia, Canberra, March, pp. 19–41.

uthors with the same family name

works written by authors with the same family name are cited, include the thors' initials in the in-text citation. For example:

The theory was first propounded in 1993 (Hamilton, CL 1994), but since then many of its elements have been hotly debated (see, for example, Hamilton, M 1996, pp. 157–93).

CL Hamilton (1994) first propounded the theory in 1993, but since then many of its elements have been hotly debated; notable among the critics is M Hamilton (1996).

edited, compiled, revised or translated work

-text citations of works in which the role of an editor, compiler, reviser or inslator is paramount are presented as follows (using the abbreviations *ed.*, *eds*, mp., *comps*, *rev.* and *trans.* as appropriate):

Chronological order: Arrange two or more works by the same author, group of authors or authoring body according to their publication dates, starting with the earliest. Use a 2-em rule to avoid repeating the names.

➤ See Chapter 15 for a discussion of the differences between the two systems of alphabetical arrangement— letter by letter and word by word.

(ed. Singh 1998)

… edited by Singh (1998)

(trans. Holfstadter 1999)

… translated by Holfstadter (1999)

In the reference list, these examples would appear thus:

Holfstadter, H (trans.) 1999,

Singh, K (ed.) 1998,

If, however, the author's role remains of primary importance, cite the work using the author's name and acknowledge the editor, compiler, reviser or translator in the reference list, after the work's title or the edition or volume information (see pages 201–2). For example:

Proust, M 1970, *Jean Santeuil*, trans. G Hopkins,

Different types of reference list entries beginning with the same name

In the reference list, a single-author entry precedes a multi-author entry beginning with the same name. A 2-em rule can be used to replace that part of the entry that is repeated. For example:

Neyland, MG 1999,

——& Duncan, F 1998,

Works edited, compiled, revised or translated by someone who has also written or co-authored other works cited in the reference list should appear in the list after the authored works. For example:

Neyland, MG 1999,

——& Duncan, F 1998,

Neyland, MG (ed.) 1990,

——& Duncan, F (comps) 1994,

A work other than a first edition

If a work cited is other than a first edition, give the publication date of the edition being used. For example, in the text:

(Strunk & White 1979)   *or*   Strunk and White (1979)

In the reference list, the edition number is placed after the title of the work:

Strunk, W Jr & White, EB 1979, *The elements of style*, 3rd edn,

Unknown or uncertain dates

Works for which no publication date can be reliably established should be cited using the expression *n.d.* (no date). For example, in the text:

(Al Mahdi n.d.)   *or*   Al Mahdi (n.d.)

and in the reference list

Al Mahdi, S n.d.,

A person or body with various roles:
If a person or body is cited as author, co-author, and editor, compiler, reviser or translator, use the following order:

- single-author entry
- multiple-author entry beginning with the same name
- works edited, compiled, revised or translated by that person or body.

Use a 2-em rule to replace a name that is repeated.

If, however, the publication date can be established with some degree of accuracy, use the abbreviation 'c.' (short for *circa*—about) before the date. For example, in the text:

(Al Mahdi c. 1943)   *or*   Al Mahdi (c. 1943)

and in the reference list

Al Mahdi, S c. 1943,

If the publication date is dubious, use a question mark after the date. For example, in the text:

(Al Mahdi 1943?)   *or*   Al Mahdi (1943?)

and in the reference list

Al Mahdi, S 1943?,

A work for which a publisher has been secured but that is not yet in the process of publication should be cited in the text as:

(Weinberg forthcoming)   *or*   Weinberg (forthcoming)

and in the reference list as

Weinberg, MM forthcoming,

A work that is in the process of publication but for which the publication date is uncertain should be cited thus in the text:

(Weinberg in press)   *or*   Weinberg (in press)

and in the reference list

Weinberg, MM in press,

No ascertainable author or authoring body

Works that do not bear the name of an author or authoring body are cited by title in both the text and the reference list. (In the reference list, any article—*a*, *an* or *the*—beginning the title is disregarded when determining the alphabetical order.) For example, in the text:

This was apparently not the case before about 1995 (*The entrepreneur's guide to the law* 1999).

In *The entrepreneur's guide to the law* (1999) it is claimed that this was not the case before about 1995.

and in the reference list

Dewey, DS 2001,

The entrepreneur's guide to the law 1999,

Epstein, J 2000,

Newspaper articles often provide no details of authorship. When this is the case, the in-text citation should provide the name of the newspaper, the date of its publication—day, month and year—and the page reference (see page 206 for examples).

No author or authoring body? If the name of an author or authoring body is not shown, cite the work by its title and date. The expressions *Anonymous* and *Anon.* should be avoided.

Pseudonymous works

In the text, pseudonymous works should be cited using the pseudonym. For example:

> (Saki 1915)
>
> Eliot (1866)

In the reference list, readers can be informed that a pseudonym has been used if that might be useful. This can be done in several ways:

> Saki (HH Munro) 1915,
>
> Eliot, George (pseud. of Mary A Evans) 1866,
>
> Sand, George (pseud.) 1856,

Use of a short title

Describing the authorship of some kinds of documents can seem to pose problems because of the complexity and length of the authorship details or because the document is better known by a short title bearing the name of, say, a commissioner, chairperson or reviewing body. The short title can be used for the in-text citation. For example:

> The Feachem report (1995) recommended ...
>
> Ralph (1999) recommended ...

The reference list must, however, contain a clear cross-reference to the formal authorship, where the document information should be presented:

> Feachem report—*see* Department of Human Services and Health (1995).
>
> Ralph, JT 1999—*see* Review of Business Taxation.

➤ See pp. 220–3 for a detailed discussion of dealing with documents produced by and for government agencies.

Further, a document commissioned by an institution, corporation or other similar body and which bears on its title page both the name of the author and the commissioning body should generally be listed under the name of the commissioning body. The author can be acknowledged after the title in the document information (see page 221).

Parts of a publication contributed by someone other than the author

When citing a preface, introduction or foreword contributed by someone other than the author of the publication, provide both names. For example:

> Maurois (in Proust 1970) claimed ...
>
> (Maurois, in Proust 1970)

In the reference list provide the details of the publication to which the contribution was made:

> Proust M 1970, *Jean Santeuil*, trans. G Hopkins, Simon & Schuster, New York. Preface by André Maurois.

Citations from secondary sources

For in-text citations of the work of one author as cited in another author's work, provide both authors' names. For example:

Ngu (cited in Larsen 1991) reported ...

(Ngu, cited in Larsen 1991)

n the reference list provide the details of the author who has done the citing:

Larsen, S 1991,

details of the work of the author being cited—in this example, Ngu—can also be provided if this might be useful or of interest to readers.

ersonal communications

information is gained through 'personal communication'—a face-to-face onversation or interview, a telephone call, a facsimile or a letter, for example— that fact is usually documented in the text. It is important, however, to obtain the ermission of the person being referred to.

he information (including the day, month and year) can be provided in running ext or parenthetically. For example:

When interviewed on 24 April 1999, Ms S Savieri confirmed ...

Ms S Savieri confirmed this by facsimile on 24 April 1999.

It has been confirmed that an outbreak occurred in Shepparton (S Savieri 1999, pers. comm., 24 April).

Details needed for personal communications: Full details of the date of a personal communication— day, month and year—should be provided in the text. No entry is needed in the reference list.

ote that the initials *precede* the family name in the parenthetical citation.

etails of a personal communication do not need to be included in a reference list.

you need to acknowledge the organisation a person represents, provide the etails thus:

Ms S Savieri (Australian Institute of Criminology) confirmed this by facsimile on 24 April 1999.

It has been confirmed that an outbreak occurred in Shepparton (S Savieri [Australian Institute of Criminology] 1999, pers. comm., 24 April).

ncyclopedias and dictionaries

the author of an entry in an encyclopedia is named, the principles already escribed can be applied. If no author is evident or if it is a dictionary being cited, rovide the necessary information in the text. For example:

The Macquarie dictionary (1997) defines it as ...

(*The Cambridge encyclopedia of the English language* 1995)

here is then no need for an entry in the reference list.

he citation details: document information

he document information is presented immediately after the details of authorship d the year of publication or creation. The formats for references for books, eriodicals (journals, magazines and newspapers), media releases, published roceedings and unpublished material are described in the following pages.

Books

For books, the document information is presented in the following order:

- title of publication
- as applicable
  - title of series
  - description of work
  - edition
  - editor, compiler, reviser or translator
  - volume number or number of volumes
- publisher
- place of publication
- page number or numbers, if applicable.

Commas are used to separate each item. For example:

> Topp, L & Dillon, P 1996, *Looking to the future: a second generation of drug research*, monograph no. 29, National Drug and Alcohol Research Centre, University of New South Wales, Sydney, pp. 29–45.

Title of book

The title of a book is always italicised; it follows the year of publication, separated from it by a comma. Minimal capitalisation is recommended. For example:

> Comfort, A 1997, *A good age*,

> Intellectual Property and Competition Review Committee 2000, *Parallel importation: interim report*,

Book titles: Use italics and minimal capitalisation. Take care to cite a title exactly as it appears on the title page of the source.

The title cited should be the one that appears on the title page, rather than the one on the spine or cover, where it may have been changed slightly for design purposes.

Within titles, roman type or single quotation marks are usually used to distinguish other titles; the names of ships, aircraft and other vehicles; and other expressions that are conventionally italicised. For example:

> Birtwhistle, BB 1976, *The annotated* Jane Eyre,

or

> Birtwhistle, BB 1976, *The annotated 'Jane Eyre'*,

Whatever style is chosen, it should be used consistently.

When a foreign-language title is cited, the capitalisation conventions of the language concerned should be followed. A translation can be given in parentheses immediately after the original title. For example:

> Jung, CG 1964, *Der Mensch und seine Symbole* (Man and his symbols),

➤ See Chapter 9 for information about expressions that are conventionally italicised.

If only a translated title is given, the original language should be acknowledged. For example:

> Sand, George (pseud.) 1856, *The story of my life* (in French),

tle of series

a work forms part of a series, the name of the series is placed, in roman type and ithout quotation marks, after the title of the work and separated from it by a omma. For example:

> Wilson, C 1984, *England's apprenticeship 1603–1763*, Social and economic history of England,

the series is not a first edition, that information should be inserted after the ries title (followed by the name of the editor, if applicable). For example:

> Wilson, C 1984, *England's apprenticeship 1603–1763*, Social and economic history of England, 2nd edn, ed. Asa Briggs,

escription of work

or some works, it is useful to provide a description, such as a catalogue or other ries number or details of the organisation for whom the work was prepared. Place is information, in roman type, after the title, separated from it by a comma. For cample:

> Australian Bureau of Statistics 1999, *Disability, ageing and carers: summary of findings*, cat. no. 4430.0,

> Dabrowski, W 1999, *Caring for country*, report to the Aboriginal and Torres Strait Islander Commission,

> Topp, L & Dillon, P 1996, *Looking to the future: a second generation of drug research*, monograph no. 29,

Descriptive information: Any description of a work follows the title. It is separated from the title by a comma and presented in roman type, with minimal capitalisation and no quotation marks.

lition

ny edition other than a first edition is noted after the title of the work and fore any volume information. For example:

> Thompson, J & O'Reilly, T 2000, *Mammals of Australia*, 3rd edn, vol. 2,

the revision, reprint or expansion of an edition is important, note this fact:

> Gowers, Sir Ernest 1983, *The complete plain words*, 2nd edn, rev. Sir Bruce Fraser,

'here a work is reprinted in a different form, the original date of publication is nerally placed in parentheses after the publication date of the reprint:

> *Roget's thesaurus of English words and phrases* 1987 (1852),

simple reprint does not warrant specific mention.

litor, compiler, reviser or translator

a work has been edited, compiled, revised or translated but the author's role mains of primary importance, list the work under the author's name and knowledge the role of the editor, compiler, reviser or translator after the title (or ries or descriptive information). The abbreviations *ed.*, *eds*, *trans.*, *rev.*, *comp.* id *comps* are used. For example:

> Blundell, R 2000, *Forest trees of south-western Tasmania*, ed. JB Kirkpatrick,

'hen the role of an editor, compiler, reviser or translator is acknowledged in this ay, the initials precede the surname. There is no need to invert the order because

Where do the initials go? If the role of an editor, compiler, reviser or translator is acknowledged after the title of a work, place the initials before the family name. The family name goes first only if the person's name begins the citation—to preserve the alphabetical order.

the person's name (unlike the author's) is irrelevant when arranging the reference list alphabetically.

In contrast, if the role of an editor (or compiler, reviser or translator) is of primary importance, list the work under the editor's name. For example:

> Kaunda, S (ed.) 1999,
>
> Neyland, MG & Duncan, F (comps) 1994,

In this instance the initials follow the family name, in the same way as an author's do, because the reference list is arranged alphabetically.

If a work cited forms a chapter or other similar division of a book to which a number of authors have contributed, it can be listed thus:

> Bryant, SL 1989, 'Growth, development and breeding patterns of the long-nosed potoroo', in G Grigg, P Jarman & I Hume (eds), *Kangaroos, wallabies and rat kangaroos,*

Note that the titles of chapters and other similar divisions of a book are presented in roman type, within quotation marks, and that minimal capitalisation is used.

Volume number or number of volumes

If only one volume of a multi-volume work is to be listed, insert the volume number (and its title if it has one) after the title of the complete work (or after details of the edition or editor, compiler, reviser or translator). For example:

> Public Land Use Commission 1996, *Tasmania–Commonwealth Regional Forest Agreement: environment and heritage report*, vol. 1, *Background report,*

This information precedes any description of the work—a series title or number, for example.

If two or more volumes of a multi-volume work are to be listed, present the information thus:

> Public Land Use Commission 1996, *Tasmania–Commonwealth Regional Forest Agreement: environment and heritage report*, vols 2 & 3,

If a multi-volume work is to be listed in its entirety, the number of volumes is inserted after the title. For example:

> Public Land Use Commission 1996, *Tasmania–Commonwealth Regional Forest Agreement: environment and heritage report*, 4 vols,

Publisher

The publisher's name is placed after the title of the work, or after the volume, edition, series or other descriptive information. For example:

> Begon, M, Harper, JL & Townsend, CR 1988, *Ecology: individuals, populations and communities*, Blackwell Scientific Publications,
>
> Topp, L & Dillon, P 1996, *Looking to the future: a second generation of drug research*, monograph no. 29, National Drug and Alcohol Research Centre,
>
> Australian Bureau of Statistics 1999, *Australian social trends*, cat. no. 4102.0, ABS,

lthough the publisher's name should normally be cited in full, there are two
:casions when it might be abbreviated: if it appears often or if an authoring body
ith a long name is also the publisher. In both cases, the abbreviation should be
ed consistently and should be explained in a list of shortened forms.

he names of foreign publishing houses should not be anglicised or translated.

a book has been co-published, provide both publishers' names and locations. For
:ample:

> Egerton, MC 1996, *The Australian film industry: an overview*, Dominion Press, Adelaide, & Cinnamon
> Publishing, St Lucia, Qld.

a book has been published by one organisation in association with another, use
e following form:

> Bligh, B 1980, *Cherish the earth*, David Ell Press, Sydney, in assoc. with the National Trust of
> Australia (NSW), Sydney.

ace of publication

he place of publication is the site of the publisher's main editorial offices. If two
˙ more places are listed on the title page or its reverse, cite only the first-listed
ace. This information follows the publisher's name in the citation:

> Comfort, A 1997, *A good age*, Mitchell Beazley, London.

> Madden, R & Hogan, T 1997, *The definition of disability in Australia: moving towards national
> consistency*, Australian Institute of Health and Welfare, Canberra.

a publisher's name makes the place of publication obvious—Melbourne
niversity Press, for example—there is no need to include the place in the
tation.

he place of publication may need explanation if there is another place of the
me name or if the place is little known. Here the nature of the intended
adership and whether or not there is any possibility of confusion must be taken
to account. For example, Cambridge, Mass., cannot be confused with
ambridge, UK, and St Lucia, Qld, will be more useful than simply St Lucia.

no place of publication appears on the title page or its reverse, the expression
p. (no place) can be used. Any other information that might help an interested
ader locate a copy of the book can be added after the citation. For example:

> Raymond, R & Watson-Munro, C 1990, *The energy crisis of 1985*, Castle Books, n.p. Distributed in
> Australia by Horwitz-Grahame, Sydney.

ige number or numbers

ccasionally it is necessary to cite page numbers in the list of references. If this is
e case, present the numbers as the final item of the citation, thus:

> Comfort, A 1997, *A good age*, Mitchell Beazley, London, pp. 31–59.

Foreign places of publication: Use the anglicised spelling of foreign places of publication: Rome, not Roma; Warsaw, not Warszawa; Algiers, not Alger.

➤ For information about the presentation of spans of numbers, see p. 177.

Periodicals

The document information for articles in periodicals—journals, magazines and newspapers—generally consists of the following elements in the following order:

- title of article
- title of periodical
- title of series, if applicable
- issue details
- page reference.

As with books, commas are used to separate each item of the citation. Minimal capitalisation is recommended for the titles of articles; maximal capitalisation is conventionally used for periodicals' titles. For example:

Brent, BB 2000, 'Taking the next step', *Quarterly Review*, vol. 199, no. 9, pp. 33–9.

Cowley, T 2001, 'One people, one destiny', *Australian Geographic*, vol. 61, January–March, pp. 48–67.

Michaelis, PL 1999, 'Farming trends in perspective', *Bingara Observer*, 22 December, p. 21.

Journals

Journals are usually intended for a scholarly readership, and more information about volume number and any other issue identifiers is necessary than is the case for popular magazines.

Title of article: Single quotation marks are used for the title of an article in a journal. For example:

Doll, R 1997, 'One for the heart',

Within article titles, italics or double quotation marks can be used for other titles; for the names of ships, aircraft and other vehicles; and for other expressions that are conventionally italicised. For example:

Mercer, BB 2000, 'Fantasy and *King Lear*',

Nakajima, S 2001, 'Aboard the *Lusitania* to Djibouti',

or

Mercer, BB 2000, 'Fantasy and "King Lear"',

Nakajima, S 2001, 'Aboard the "Lusitania" to Djibouti',

Whichever style is chosen, it should be used consistently.

When citing an article written in a foreign language, a translation can be given in parentheses after the title. For example:

Lalumière, P 1995, 'Note sur une expérience de financement privé des investissements publiques' (Note on an experiment involving private financing of public investments),

Title of journal: Italics are used for a journal title, which is separated from the title of the article being cited by a comma. As noted, maximal capitalisation is the convention for journal titles. For example:

Doll, R 1997, 'One for the heart', *British Medical Journal*,

Capitalisation and periodicals: Unlike the titles of books, the titles of periodicals are conventionally given maximal capitalisation. The titles of articles in periodicals are given minimal capitalisation and enclosed in single quotation marks.

n reference lists in medical and other scientific works, the titles of journals are ften abbreviated. If this is done—and it is recommended only when the titles are ited very frequently and only for the appropriate readership—the abbreviations sed should be those published in the most recent bibliographic index in the elevant subject field (such as the *Index medicus* or the *Chemical Abstracts Service ource index*, known as *CASSI*). Examples of abbreviated journal titles are *Med J ust* for the *Medical Journal of Australia*, *JAMA* for the *Journal of the American Medical Association* and *BMJ* for the *British Medical Journal*. The abbreviated ournal titles should be shown without full stops (an exception to the general rinciples for punctuating shortened forms recommended in Chapter 10).

he title of a foreign-language journal should be cited in the original language, rithout a translation: this will enable interested readers to locate it. Follow the apitalisation of the original when this can be ascertained. For example:

> Lalumière, P 1995, 'Note sur une expérience de financement privé des investissements publiques' (Note on an experiment involving private financing of public investments), *Revue de science financière*,

r

> Lalumière, P 1995, 'Note on an experiment involving private financing of public investments' (in French), *Revue de science financière*,

itle of series: If a journal forms part of a series, the series title should be placed fter the journal title, separated from it by a comma. The series title is presented in oman type, without quotation marks, and using minimal capitalisation. For xample:

> Pilli, L 1999, 'The life of George Bernard Shaw', *Bibliographical Essays*, British history series,

sue details and page reference: The volume number, issue number or other lentifier, and page reference follow the journal title (or the series title); all items re separated by commas. For example:

> Doll, R 1997, 'One for the heart', *British Medical Journal,* vol. 315, pp. 20–7.

each issue of a journal or periodical is paginated separately rather than onsecutively, the issue number or other identifier must be provided. If the issue as both number and identifier (such as a month or quarter), choose one and use consistently. For example:

> Gershuny, J 1996, 'Time use, technology and the future of work', *Journal of the Market Research Society,* vol. 28, no. 4, pp. 335–9.

> Dewhirst, C 1996, 'Hot air over the Himalayas', *World Geographic,* vol. 1, October–December, pp. 51–61.

ometimes a journal will bear only an issue number or other identifier and no olume number. In this case, the issue number or identifier should be placed nmediately after the title of the journal, separated from it by a comma.

Jsually journal citations do not include the place of publication. If, however, two r more different journals have the same title or a similar one—for example, two eriodicals entitled *World Geographic*, one published in Australia and one in the Jnited States, and another entitled *World Geographer*, published in the United

Abbreviating journal titles: In the author–date style, abbreviation of journal titles is recommended only when the titles are cited very frequently and only for the appropriate audience.

Kingdom—show (in parentheses) the place of publication, as set out in the publisher's imprint. For example:

> Bell, J 1996, 'Flying high in the Andes', *World Geographic* (Sydney), vol. 79, no. 4, pp. 19–25.
>
> Cronin, AP 1993, 'The Scottish coastline: waves at work', *World Geographer* (London), vol. 17, autumn, pp. 11–21.
>
> Dewhirst, C 1996, 'Hot air over the Himalayas', *World Geographic* (Washington DC), vol. 1, October–December, p. 54.

Similarly, in the case of little-known journals, it may be useful to provide information about the publisher. This is done in the same way as for books. For example:

> Wood, C 1998, 'Cocaine's chaos', *Connexions*, August–September, Centre for Education and Information on Drugs and Alcohol, Sydney, pp. 11–13.

Magazines

For magazines, the procedure for citing the article title and magazine title is the same as that for journals. The volume and issue or other information is replaced by the date—the day and month, the month, the quarter or other similar identifier. Page numbers follow the date (or other identifier), separated from it by a comma. For example:

> Light, D 2000, 'A tax of the jitters', *Bulletin*, 18 January, pp. 50–1.

If the article runs over to a page towards the end of the magazine, it is helpful to provide both sets of page numbers. For example:

> Treloar, B 1999, 'Grains of sense', *Australian Gourmet Traveller*, November, pp. 29–30, 64.

Newspapers

If the authorship of a newspaper article is evident, follow the procedure described for magazines. For example:

> Towers, K 2000, 'Doctor not at fault: coroner', *Australian*, 18 January, p. 3.

If the authorship is not obvious, provide all the details in the in-text citation. For example:

> (*Sydney Morning Herald* 24 January 2000, p. 12)
>
> … in the *Sydney Morning Herald* (24 January 2000, p. 12).
>
> (*Financial Review* 18 January 2000, editorial)

No authorship details for a newspaper article? If a newspaper article has no author credited, provide all the necessary details in the text; no entry is then required for the reference list.

In this case there is no need for an entry in the reference list.

If a work contains frequent references to newspaper material, it may be best to abbreviate the newspaper titles: *SMH*, for example, could replace *Sydney Morning Herald*. The abbreviation, like the full title, is italicised.

Reviews in periodicals

For citing reviews of books, films, television programs, and theatrical and musical performances, the following document information is usually required after the me of the reviewer and the year of publication:

the title of the review

a description of what is being reviewed and its author

the periodical in which the review appeared

the day and month

the relevant page number or numbers.

esent the information thus:

> Riemer, A 2000, 'Australian gothic revisited', review of *Prelude to Christopher* by Eleanor Dark, *Sydney Morning Herald*, 22 January, p. 12s.

te the page number '12s' in the example just given: the *s* indicates a special, dependently numbered section of the newspaper.

edia releases

general, media releases can be treated as follows:

> Watersmith, C 2000, *BHP enters new era*, media release, BHP Limited, Melbourne, 1 March.

> Smith, A (Minister for Justice and Customs) 1999, *Coastwatch initiative bears fruit*, media release, Parliament House, Canberra, 21 July.

blished proceedings

pers presented at conferences, seminars and meetings are often collected and blished as 'proceedings'. They are cited thus:

> Bourassa, S 1999, 'Effects of child care on young children', *Proceedings of the third annual meeting of the International Society for Child Psychology*, International Society for Child Psychology, Atlanta, Georgia, pp. 44–6.

published material

hen citing unpublished material—a thesis, a manuscript, or an unpublished per or abstract presented at a conference or meeting—present the title of the cument in roman type and in quotation marks. The other details will vary cording to the nature of the document, and their presentation is a matter largely the author or editor. As with all referencing, the primary considerations are rity, consistency, logical order, and providing all the information needed to able the document to be found efficiently.

hen citing a thesis, acknowledge the university under whose auspices the study s undertaken. For example:

> Herbert, KA 1995, 'Parallel knowledge: farmers and scientists and land classification', BAppSc thesis, University of Canberra.

te that the place of publication is not stated here, as the Canberra location can inferred.

eat unpublished papers and abstracts presented at conferences, seminars and etings as follows:

Bowden, FJ & Fairley, CK 1996, 'Endemic STDs in the Northern Territory: estimations of effective rates of partner change', paper presented to the scientific meeting of the Royal Australian College of Physicians, Darwin, 24–25 June.

Corey, L 1997, 'The clinical implications of interactions between HIV and HSV', abstract presented at the 5th annual meeting of the International Herpes Management Forum, Cannes, France, 12–15 August.

If it is difficult to provide details about the location of a manuscript, be systematic

Adams, DE 1917, 'My journey to Khartoum', in possession of MA Adams, Adelaide.

Ecclestone, A 1934, 'A year in the wilderness', in possession of the Mitchell Library, Sydney.

Hudson, DE 1909–18, 'Diary', Hudson Papers, Fisher Library, University of Sydney.

Thompson, BE 1987, 'Recollections of the Raj', in possession of the author, Melbourne.

Some manuscript collections have a file number or other identifier that can be included with the citation, before the details of the collection's location. In general, however, the author, date, title and location are sufficient.

THE DOCUMENTARY-NOTE SYSTEM

Simplicity has been a key criterion in recommending the following interpretation of the documentary-note system. As with all referencing systems, a number of other interpretations exist, but the differences between them and the one presented here are very minor, concerning mainly punctuation and capitalisation.

Notes used for non-citation purposes

Notes can also be used for non-citation purposes—to add information that is explanatory, relevant but not crucial to the argument, or simply of interest.

Note identifiers

Notes are most commonly identified by superscript arabic numerals. Symbols— asterisk (*), dagger (†), double dagger (‡), section mark (§), parallel mark (||), and number, or hash, sign (#)—are generally used only when the number of notes is limited. They are conventionally used in the order shown. If more than six notes are to appear, the symbols are doubled; that is, a double asterisk (**) comes after the hash sign, then ††, and so on. If there are to be more than twelve notes, the symbols can be trebled, although it is better to use superscript numerals instead.

Symbols are preferred in mathematical works, to avoid any possibility of confusion between superscript note identifiers and indices. In tabular material, lower-case letters of the alphabet can be used to prevent confusion with the figures being presented; if, however, the table consists of words, use superscript numerals.

Notes to tables and illustrations are placed at the base of the table or illustration, not at the bottom of the page or at the end of the chapter or elsewhere. They are numbered independently of any footnotes or endnotes. Where a table runs to more than one page, the notes can be placed either at the base of the page on which they appear or at the end of the table, whichever will be more convenient for readers.

Footnotes or endnotes?

For paper-based works, the decision about whether to use footnotes or endnotes is a matter of judgment, depending on the size of the document, the number of notes, and what is deemed to be the more convenient form for the intended readership. Multiple and lengthy footnotes can sometimes cause problems because each note should appear on the same page as its identifier (although a portion of the final one can run over to the next page). They also make a page 'bottom heavy' in appearance and may suggest a poorly developed argument.

In an on-screen environment, footnotes are largely irrelevant, particularly when documents are created in a mark-up language. A more interactive form of noting—such as pop-up or drop-down boxes—is preferred.

In-text note identifiers

In general, the use of superscript arabic numerals (as opposed to superscript symbols) is recommended for both footnotes and endnotes used for citation purposes. It is also recommended that a superscript numeral be placed *before* all punctuation marks save the end-of-sentence ones and, wherever possible, immediately after a direct quotation. This minimises disruption.

In works with few citations, footnotes might be used; where citations are more frequent, however, endnotes are usually preferred. Endnotes may be placed at the end of a chapter or other similar division, or at the end of a book or article. They should be headed simply 'Notes'. When notes appear at the end of a book, some authors and publishers prefer to arrange them by chapter, with the chapter numbers and titles appearing as subheadings.

Notes placed at the end of chapters (or other similar divisions) are preferable for multi-author works, loose-leaf publications, and works that might be read piecemeal.

Number notes consecutively, beginning with '1', and avoid using more than one number at a particular location. When using footnotes, it is wise not to number notes beginning with '1' on each page: number them consecutively through the chapter or article. This makes for simpler cross-referencing; for example, rather than being obliged to write 'see note 2 on p. 17', it is simpler to say 'see note 25'.

If more than one source is referred to at a single location, use only one note identifier: the entry in the notes will show all the sources. Similarly, a number of references in a single paragraph can be combined into one note if the references are logically related. Care is needed, though, to ensure that there is no potential for confusion.

Avoid using note identifiers in headings. A note referring to an entire section, chapter or other component of a document should be unnumbered or unmarked and be placed before the numbered (or marked) notes at the base of the page, at the end of the chapter or article, or at the end of the book or document.

Personal communications—face-to-face conversations or interviews, telephone calls, letters and facsimiles, for example—can be referred to using a note identifier.

Superscript placement: Place superscript note identifiers:

- at the end of a sentence or clause, rather than immediately after the words to which they relate
- *before* all punctuation marks save the end-of-sentence ones
- wherever possible, immediately after direct quotations.

Avoid using superscript note identifiers in headings.

Superscript numbering: In the documentary-note system, only one superscript numeral is used at a reference point, even if more than one source is being referred to there. The single note that it identifies will include details of all the sources.

The details are then provided in the notes. These sources are generally not listed in a bibliography.

First citations

The first citation of a particular source in the footnotes or endnotes provides the same information as that required for the author–date system but in a slightly different order:

- Authors' initials precede the family name (as there is no need for alphabetical ordering).
- The year of publication is placed at or near the end of the citation.

The method of punctuation—using commas to separate each item of the citation—remains the same, and minimal capitalisation is again recommended for all but the titles of periodicals. The conventions described for the use of italics and quotation marks also apply.

First citations: For the first citation of a source, provide the same information as that required for the author–date system. There are only two differences in the sequence:

- An author's initials *precede* the family name.
- The year of publication is placed at or near the end of the citation.

Books

For books, provide the following information in the following order (see pages 200–3 for details):

- details of authorship—initials first
- title of book
- if applicable
  - title of series
  - description of work
  - edition
  - editor, translator, reviser or compiler
  - volume number or number of volumes
- publisher
- place of publication
- year of publication
- page numbers, if applicable.

The following are examples of first citations of books:

1. A Comfort, *A good age*, Mitchell Beazley, London, 1997.

2. Australian Bureau of Statistics & Australian Institute of Health and Welfare, *The health and welfare of Australia's Aboriginal and Torres Strait Islander peoples*, ABS cat. no. 4704.0, AIHW cat. no. IHW2, Australian Government Publishing Service, Canberra, 1997, pp. 59–70.

3. JC Grant, MD Laffan, RB Hill & WA Neilsen, *Forest soils of Tasmania: a handbook for identification and management*, Forestry Tasmania, Hobart, 1995.

4. C Wilson, *England's apprenticeship 1603–1763*, Social and economic history of England, 2nd edn, ed. Asa Briggs, Longman, London, 1984.

5. Australian Bureau of Statistics, *Disability, ageing and carers: summary of findings*, cat. no. 4430.0, ABS, Canberra, 1999.

6. L Topp & P Dillon, *Looking to the future: a second generation of drug research*, monograph no. 29, National Drug and Alcohol Research Centre, University of New South Wales, Sydney, 1996, pp. 29–45.

7. JD Butler & DF Walbert (eds), *Abortion, medicine and the law*, Facts on File Publications, New York, 1986.

8. *Roget's thesaurus of English words and phrases*, ed. & rev. B Kirkpatrick, Penguin, London, 1987 (1852).

9. L Urdang, *Dictionary of differences*, rev. edn, Bloomsbury, London, 1992.

10. DJ Jones, *The Australian dictionary of acronyms and abbreviations*, 4th edn, ALIA Press, Canberra, 1995.

11. Sir Ernest Gowers, *The complete plain words*, 2nd edn, rev. Sir Bruce Fraser, Penguin, Harmondsworth, UK, 1983.

12. Resource Assessment Commission, *Kakadu Conservation Zone inquiry: final report*, 2 vols, Australian Government Publishing Service, Canberra, 1991.

13. Public Land Use Commission, *Tasmania–Commonwealth Regional Forest Agreement: environment and heritage report*, vol. 1, *Background report*, PLUC, Hobart, 1996.

14. M Begon, JL Harper & CR Townsend, *Ecology: individuals, populations and communities*, Blackwell Scientific, London, 1988.

15. SL Bryant, 'Growth, development and breeding patterns of the long-nosed potoroo', in G Grigg, P Jarman & I Hume (eds), *Kangaroos, wallabies and rat kangaroos*, Surrey Beatty & Sons, Sydney, 1989, pp. 97–119.

16. MM Weinberg, *No day at the beach*, Pluto Publications, Adelaide, in press.

17. J Halligan, I Mackintosh & H Watson, *The Australian public service: the view from the top*, Coopers and Lybrand, Canberra, & Centre for Research in Public Sector Management, University of Canberra, 1996.

18. R Raymond & C Watson-Munro, *The energy crisis of 1985*, Castle Books, n.p., 1990. Distributed in Australia by Horwitz-Grahame, Sydney.

19. Department of Foreign Affairs and Trade, *Annual report 1998–99*, DFAT, Canberra, 1999.

Periodicals

First citations of material in periodicals—journals, magazines and newspapers—generally require the following information in the following order (see pages 204–6 for details):

authorship details—initials first

title of article

title of periodical

if applicable

– title of series

– volume number

– issue number or other identifier

date of publication

page number or numbers.

Publishing details: These are not usually provided for periodicals. They can, however, be useful for little-known periodicals or to distinguish between periodicals with the same or similar titles—see pp. 205–6.

Journals

The following are examples of first citations of material in journals:

1. J Gershuny, 'Time use, technology and the future of work', *Journal of the Market Research Society*, vol. 28, no. 4, 1986, pp. 335–54.

2. PG Ney, T Fung & AR Wickett, 'The worst combinations of child abuse and neglect', *Child Abuse and Neglect*, vol. 18, no. 9, 1994, pp. 705–14.

3. A Tomison, 'Child abuse and other family violence: findings from a case tracking study', *Family Matters*, no. 41, winter, 1995, pp. 33–8.

4. D MacKenzie & C Chamberlain, 'How many homeless youth?', *Youth Studies Australia*, summer, 1992, pp. 14–22.

5. C Wood, 'Cocaine's chaos', *Connexions*, August–September, Centre for Education and Information on Drugs and Alcohol, Sydney, 1998, pp. 11–13.

Magazines

For magazines, the procedure for citing authorship details, article title and magazine title in the documentary-note style is the same as that for journals. The year of publication—this time with the day and month, just the month, or the season—comes after the magazine title, with page numbers following the date. For example:

1. D Light, 'A tax of the jitters', *Bulletin*, 18 January 2000, pp. 50–1.

2. B Treloar, 'Grains of sense', *Australian Gourmet Traveller*, November 1999, pp. 29–30, 64.

The second example also shows how to refer to an article whose text begins in one part of a magazine and continues at a later place (with other articles or advertisements in between).

Newspapers

If a newspaper article has an obvious author, follow the procedure described for magazines. For example:

1. K Towers, 'Doctor not at fault: coroner', *Australian*, 18 January 2000, p. 3.

If the article has no obvious author, provide all the details in the text. For example:

(*Sydney Morning Herald*, 24 January 2001, p. 7)

It was alleged in the *Sydney Morning Herald* (24 January 2001, p. 7) that …

Articles that are interrupted by pages containing other material: In such instances, show both sets of page numbers, separated by a comma.

If a magazine or newspaper article is interrupted by pages containing other material, provide both sets of page numbers.

Reviews in periodicals

With the exception of the placement of initials and the date, reviews of books, films, television programs and theatrical and musical performances are treated in the manner described for the author–date system (see pages 206–7). For example:

1. A Riemer, 'Australian gothic revisited', review of *Prelude to Christopher* by Eleanor Dark, *Sydney Morning Herald*, 22 January 2000, p. 12s.

Note the page number '12s' in the example just given: the s indicates a special, independently numbered section of the newspaper.

Encyclopedias and dictionaries

If the author of an entry in an encyclopedia is named, the principles described for newspapers should be applied (leaving out the day and month details). If no author is evident or if it is a dictionary being cited, provide the necessary information in the text.

Media releases

With the exception of the placement of initials and the year of publication, media releases are treated in the manner described for the author–date system (see page 207). For example:

1. C Watersmith, *BHP enters new era*, media release, BHP Limited, Melbourne, 1 March 2000.

2. A Smith (Minister for Justice and Customs), *Coastwatch initiative bears fruit*, media release, Parliament House, Canberra, 21 July 1999.

Published proceedings

Papers presented at conferences, seminars, and so on, and subsequently published as 'proceedings' are treated as follows:

1. QL Choo, G Kuo & R Ralston, 'Vaccination of chimpanzees against infection by the hepatitis C virus', *Proceedings of the National Academy of Sciences USA*, vol. 91, 1994, pp. 1294–8.

Unpublished material

With the exception of placement of initials and the year of publication, unpublished material is treated in the manner described for the author–date system (see page 207). For example:

1. KA Herbert, 'Parallel knowledge: farmers and scientists and land classification', BAppSc thesis, University of Canberra, 1995.

2. FJ Bowden & CK Fairley, 'Endemic STDs in the Northern Territory: estimations of effective rates of partner change', paper presented to the scientific meeting of the Royal Australian College of Physicians, Darwin, 24–25 June 1996.

3. DE Adams, 'My journey to Khartoum', in possession of MA Adams, Adelaide, 1917.

Personal communications

If details of a personal communication are to be provided in the notes—as opposed to a citation in the text itself—provide the person's name, a description of the type of communication, and the full date:

1. S Savieri, interview with the author, 24 April 1999.

2. V Ngu, facsimile, 12 January 2001.

It is important to obtain the permission of the person in question.

Second and subsequent citations

If an author refers to the same source a number of times, a number of different superscript identifiers will be used in the text to refer to that source. Instead of repeating all the details of the first citation in the footnotes or endnotes, a shortened form of the citation can be used on subsequent occasions. This shortened form must contain sufficient detail to provide the reader with an unambiguous indication of the place where the fact, opinion or quoted words are to be found:

1. R Hyslop, *Aye, aye, Minister: Australian naval administration 1939–59*, AGPS Press, Canberra, 1990, p. 89.

2. …

3. …

4. Hyslop, p. 25.

If, however, two or more works by the same author are referred to in the text, it i[s] necessary to differentiate further:

1. R Hyslop, *Aye, aye, Minister: Australian naval administration 1939–59*, AGPS Press, Canberra, 1990, p. 89.

2. R Hyslop, *Australian mandarins: perceptions of the role of departmental secretaries*, AGPS Pres[s] Canberra, 1993, p. 45.

3. Hyslop, *Aye, aye, Minister*, p. 25.

Similarly, recurrent references to articles in periodicals can be abbreviated:

1. G Holst, 'Awake to the lute', *Hemisphere*, vol. 21, no. 4, 1976, pp. 26–38.

2. …

3. Holst, *Hemisphere*, p. 28.

Using 'ibid.', 'op. cit.', 'loc. cit.' and 'id.'

If a readership is familiar with the convention, second and subsequent references can be introduced by anglicised abbreviations of Latin terms, the most common being 'ibid.' (*ibidem*—in the same place), 'op. cit.' (*opere citato*—in the work cited[)] 'loc. cit.' (*loco citato*—in the place cited) and 'id.' (*idem*—the same). The abbreviations are presented in roman type and always start with a lower-case lett[er] even when they appear at the beginning of a note.

An 'ibid.' signifies a reference to the same work cited immediately before it. It ca[n] refer to the same page or to a different one. For example:

1. Australian Institute of Health and Welfare, *Australia's welfare: services and assistance*, AIHW, Canberra, 1999, pp. 128–41.

2. ibid.

3. ibid., p. 160.

An 'op. cit.' refers the reader back to a previously cited work but to a different page:

1. Australian Institute of Health and Welfare, *Australia's welfare: services and assistance*, AIHW, Canberra, 1999, p. 128.

2. Australian Bureau of Statistics, *Causes of death*, cat. no. 3303.0, ABS, Canberra, 1995.

Common anglicised abbreviations of Latin terms: Use the terms 'ibid.', 'op. cit.', 'loc. cit.' and 'id.' only if you are confident that your readers will be familiar with them. Present them in roman type and *without* any initial capitals.

3. Australian Institute of Health and Welfare, op. cit., p. 171.

'loc. cit.' refers the reader back to the same page of a work already cited:

1. Australian Institute of Health and Welfare, *Australia's welfare: services and assistance*, AIHW, Canberra, 1999, p. 128.

2. Australian Bureau of Statistics, *Causes of death*, cat. no. 3303.0, ABS, Canberra, 1995.

3. Australian Institute of Health and Welfare, loc. cit.

'id.' signifies that the work in the second note is by the same author as the work in the first note:

1. R Hyslop, *Aye, aye, Minister: Australian naval administration 1939–59*, AGPS Press, Canberra, 1990, p. 89.

2. id., *Australian mandarins: perceptions of the role of departmental secretaries*, AGPS Press, Canberra, 1993, p. 45.

Other anglicised abbreviations

The following are other, less common, abbreviations used in the documentary-note style:

et. seq.	and following (from Latin *et sequentes*)
f., ff.	following
inf.	below (from Latin *infra*)
q.v.	which see (from Latin *quod vide*)
sup.	above (from Latin *supra*)

These abbreviations—and the word *passim* ('here and there', 'throughout')—are used far less often than in the past and should generally be reserved for formal, scholarly works.

THE VANCOUVER SYSTEM

The following interpretation of the Vancouver system is recommended. Variants do exist, and writers and editors are often required to adapt the system to correspond with the style set by a particular organisation or publisher.

In-text note identifiers

In the text a superscript arabic numeral is allocated to each source when it is referred to *for the first time*. This numeral becomes the unique identifier of that source; if the source is referred to again, the identifying numeral is repeated. The identifiers should be placed *before* all punctuation marks save the sentence-ending ones and, whenever possible, immediately after a direct quotation. This minimises disruption for the reader.

More than one identifier can be used at a single reference point to indicate multiple sources: commas (also set as superscript characters) are used to separate the identifiers and there is no space between the comma and the number following it. For example:

> Zinc deficiency leads to a slower rate of wound healing and decreases wound strength and collagen synthesis: it also diminishes taste acuity.[1,5]

Sources for tables and figures are numbered in keeping with the sequence established at the first textual mention of the source.

The reference list

The method of presenting a citation in the Vancouver system differs markedly from the methods used in the author–date and documentary-note systems as interpreted in this manual. The main features of a Vancouver reference list are as follows:

- Quotation marks are not used for the titles of journal articles.
- Neither book titles nor journal titles are italicised—in fact, italics are not used at all in the reference list.
- Journal titles are usually abbreviated. The abbreviations used should be those listed in the most recent bibliographic index in the relevant subject field—for example, the *Index medicus* or *CASSI* (the *Chemical Abstracts Service source index*).
- All authors are listed when there are six or fewer; when there are more than six the expression 'et al.' ('and others') is added.
- Authors' initials follow their family names, with no intervening punctuation and no space between the initials.
- The principal elements of the citation are separated by full stops. (There are also other differences in punctuation, spacing, and the treatment of volume and page numbers.)

Books

For books, the following information is provided in the following order:

- authorship details
- title of book
- if applicable
  - title of series
  - description of work
  - volume number or number of volumes
  - edition
  - editor, compiler, reviser or translator
- place of publication
- publisher
- year
- page number or numbers, if applicable.

The following examples illustrate the general principles:

> 1. Comfort A. A good age. London: Mitchell Beazley, 1997.

2. National Health and Medical Research Council. Dietary guidelines for older Australians. Canberra: NHMRC, 1999.

3. WHO Study Group. Epidemiology and prevention of cardiovascular diseases in elderly people. WHO technical series 853. Geneva: WHO, 1995.

4. Ringsven MK, Bond D. Gerontology and leadership skills for nurses. 2nd edn. Albany, New York: Delmar Publishers, 1996.

5. DeVines J, ed. Food safety and toxicity. Boca Raton: CRC Press, 1997.

6. Mann JI, Truswell AS, eds. Essentials of human nutrition. Oxford: Oxford University Press, 1998.

7. Truswell AS. Alcohol. In: Mann JI, Truswell AS, eds. Essentials of human nutrition. Oxford: Oxford University Press, 1998;91–103.

8. Shrapnel B. Fats: lessons from antiquity. In: University of Sydney Nutrition Research Foundation publication 5. Sydney: University of Sydney Nutrition Research Foundation, 1998;21–6.

9. Merry G. Food poisoning prevention. 2nd edn. Melbourne: Macmillan Education Australia, 1997.

10. Australian Bureau of Statistics. Causes of death. Cat. no. 3303.0. Canberra: ABS, 1995.

Journal articles

For journals, the following information is provided in the following order:
* authorship details
* title of article
* abbreviated journal title
* year
* volume number
* issue number or other descriptor
* page numbers.

The following examples illustrate the general principles. Note the use of the semicolon to separate the publication date from the volume number and of the colon to separate the volume (or issue) number from the page numbers. Note, too, that no spaces are inserted.

1. Horwath CC. Socio-economic status and dietary habits in the elderly: results from a large random survey. J Hum Nutr Diet 1989;2:173–83.

2. Shekelle RB, Stamler J. Fish and coronary heart disease: the epidemiologic evidence. Nutr Metab Cardiovasc Dis 1993;4:46–51.

3. Albert CM, Hennekens CH, O'Donnell CJ, Ajani UA, Carey VJ, Willett WC et al. Fish consumption and risk of sudden cardiac death. JAMA 1998;279:23–8.

4. Alspach G. Chemosensory impairments in the elderly: nothing to sniff at. Critical Care Nurse 1998;18(2):16–18.

5. Nicklason F, Inderjeeth CA, Parmeswaran V, Greenaway T, Jones G, Dunbabin D et al. The prevalence of vitamin D deficiency in a group of elderly patients hospitalised in southern Tasmania. Aust J Ageing 1996;15(3)(suppl.):S22.

6. Dayton S, Pearce LM, Hashimoto S, Dixon WJ, Tomiyasu U. A controlled clinical trial of a diet high in unsaturated fat in preventing complications of atherosclerosis. Circulation 1969;(suppl. to vols 39 & 40)(July):1–63.

7. WHO–ISH Statement Committee. Prevention of hypertension and associated cardiovascular disease: a 1995 statement. Clin Exp Hypertens 1996;18(3&4):581–93.

8. Medical Research Council. The rice diet in the treatment of hypertension. Lancet 1950;2:509–1

In the case of journal articles for which no author is evident, begin the citation with the title of the article:

1. Top 10 drugs by cost to government—1997. Aust Prescriber 1998;21:106.

It is important to cite the title of a foreign-language journal in that language—to aid retrieval. The title of the article can be shown as it appears or its English translation can be added in square brackets.

Conference proceedings and papers

For conference proceedings and papers presented at conferences, seminars, and so on, follow the principles described for books but include the place and date of the conference:

1. Stuckey SJ, Darnton-Hill I, Ash S, Brand JC, Hain DL. Dietary patterns of the elderly in Sydney. In Proceedings of the 10th Congress of the Nutritionists Society of Australia, Melbourne, 15–19 March 1997. Sydney: Paragon Press, 1997;31–9.

2. WHO Regional Office for the Western Pacific. Report of the working group on public health aspects of marine fish food poisoning, Suva, Fiji, 23–25 February 1981. Manila: WHO, 1981.

Theses

Treat a thesis as you would a book but note the fact that the work is a thesis after the title:

1. Cairns RB. Infrared spectroscopic studies of solid oxygen. PhD thesis. Berkeley, California: University of California, 1965.

BIBLIOGRAPHIES

The term *bibliography* is used in a variety of ways. Most commonly, it means a list containing the sources used in developing a publication and any other sources the author considers might be of use or interest to readers. It can also be used to mean a list of the sources an author cites in a particular work—although such a list would more accurately be called a reference list. In addition, some people use it to refer to a list of sources relating to the subject of the publication but not actually cited by the author—again, however, a more accurate term for this would be a 'further reading' list.

A select bibliography? The term *select bibliography* should generally be avoided: almost all bibliographies are 'select' by nature because it is virtually impossible to list *all* works dealing with a particular subject, which is what *bibliography* originally meant.

This manual supports the most common interpretation of the word *bibliography*.

A bibliography is usually placed at the end of a work, before the index if there is one. It can, however, be useful to place one at the end of each chapter in a multi-author work, loose-leaf publication or work that might be read piecemeal.

bibliography in the author–date style

When the author–date system of citation is used, a consolidated list of references is prepared and placed at the end of the chapter, book or article. If an author wishes to include in this list sources not directly cited in the work, the consolidated list is correctly called a 'bibliography'. The same method of presentation is used in both cases.

bibliography in the documentary-note style

If sources are acknowledged in footnotes or endnotes, an author may not see the need for a consolidated list at the end of the work. If, however, a decision is made to provide a bibliography, with one exception the principles described for citing sources in the documentary-note style apply.

The exception concerns the placement of an author's initials. In a bibliography the author's family name (or the family name of the first-cited author if there is more than one) is placed first—because the bibliography is presented in alphabetical order, not by number. For example, in the notes the entries will appear thus:

1. M Coper, *Encounters with the Australian Constitution*, CCH Australia, Sydney, 1993.

2. Advisory Committee on Trade and National Economic Management, *Report to the Constitutional Commission*, Australian Government Publishing Service, Canberra, 1987.

3. N Wright & B Darby, *The Constitution: shaping the nation*, Legal Press, Perth, 1997.

and in the bibliography

Advisory Committee on Trade and National Economic Management, *Report to the Constitutional Commission*, Australian Government Publishing Service, Canberra, 1987.

Coper, M, *Encounters with the Australian Constitution*, CCH Australia, Sydney, 1993.

Wright, N & B Darby, *The Constitution: shaping the nation*, Legal Press, Perth, 1997.

bibliography in the Vancouver style

A bibliography in the Vancouver style is presented in the same way as the citations given in the reference list.

an annotated bibliography

An author who wants to give readers more information than is necessary to locate each source might produce an *annotated bibliography*. For each entry in the bibliography the author writes a brief description—the source's content, its relevance to the author's own work, its possible value for a reader, or any other information the author considers useful. For example:

Crystal, D 1995, *The Cambridge encyclopedia of the English language*, Cambridge University Press, Cambridge, UK. A comprehensive general reference dealing with the history, structure and worldwide use of English. See, in particular, Chapter 7.

(continued on p. 224)

ABOUT
Government publications

Citation of government publications generally follows the principles described for books, although it can sometimes present difficulties. For example, some publications have no obvious author, some have both a sponsoring agency and a specific author, some are the work of a branch or division of an agency, some are the work of a committee established within an agency, and some are the work of a consultant commissioned to carry out a particular task. Yet others are the result of a commission of inquiry, royal commission, or similar initiative.

In addition, there are parliamentary publications—Parliamentary Papers, Hansard, the *Journals of the Senate*, and the House of Representatives *Votes and Proceedings*—and Commonwealth records.

The discussion that follows is based on the author–date system. The advice applies equally to the documentary-note and Vancouver systems, although the presentation style will differ in the ways described for those systems.

Documents produced by government agencies

If a document produced by a government agency has no obvious author, cite the sponsoring agency as the author:

> Australian Sports Drug Agency 2000, *Testing for EPO*, Australian Sports Drug Agency, Canberra.

If the names of both a sponsoring agency and a specific author appear on the title page, cite the agency as author and acknowledge the individual after the title. For example:

> Department of Veterans' Affairs 2000, *Payments to Vietnam veterans: a summary*, report prepared by S Baslum, Department of Veterans' Affairs, Canberra.

A document prepared by a branch or other division of a government agency, and published by that agency, should usually be listed under the agency's name, with the branch or other division acknowledged after the publication's title. This is because, unlike a committee or similar body established for a specific task, the branch or other division is an integral part of the agency. For example:

> Department of Conservation 2000, *Hydrogen-powered cars: progress to date*, Sustainable Energy Branch, Department of Conservation, Darwin.

If the agency is not the publisher, a different approach is needed. The agency can still be cited as the author, the branch or other division can be acknowledged in parentheses immediately after the agency's name, and the publisher is cited in the usual way. For example:

> Department of Administrative Services (Awards and National Symbols Branch) 1995, *Australian flags*, Australian Government Publishing Service, Canberra.

The in-text citation need refer only to the agency, not the branch or other division:

> (Department of Administrative Services 1995)

or

> Department of Administrative Services (1995)

The jurisdiction: Generally, the jurisdiction is not given; that is, there is no mention of whether the agency in question is a Commonwealth one or a state or territory one. The place of publication usually makes the jurisdiction clear. If, however, there is any possibility of confusion, insert the jurisdiction as part of the details of publication. For example:

> Department of Health and Aged Care 2001, *Rubella incidence in a defined population*, Commonwealth Department of Health and Aged Care, Hobart.

Abbreviating an agency's name: If the name of an authoring agency is long and is cited frequently in the text, it may be necessary to abbreviate the name in the in-text citation. If this is so provide a cross-reference in the list of references or bibliography. For example:

> NHMRC—*see* National Health and Medical Research Council.

Present the publication details where the name is spelt out.

Documents produced for a government agency

A document prepared by a committee or similar body established within a government agency to perform a specific task can be cited in the following way:

> Health Promotion Committee 2000, *The funding of anti-smoking campaigns*, Department of Health, Brisbane.

> Financial Resources Taskforce 2000, *Payments to the states and territories: 2001–02 to 2005–06*, Department of Finance and Administration, Canberra.

A consultant's report: Sometimes a consultant is commissioned to report to government. If the names of both the consultant and the government agency appear on the title page, the report should usually be listed under the name of the agency, with the author acknowledged after the title. For example:

Department of Health and Aged Care 1999, *Hepatitis C: a review of Australia's response*, report prepared by D Lowe & R Cotton, DHAC, Canberra.

When only the name of the consultant appears on the title page, list the document under the consultant's name. For example:

Dabrowski, W 1999, *Caring for country*, report to the Aboriginal and Torres Strait Islander Commission, Canberra.

A publication known by a short title: Sometimes a publication produced by a body commissioned to carry out an inquiry of some kind is better known by a short title—the name of, say, the chairperson or the person responsible for the investigation. In these cases, the short title can be used in the text; in the list of references, the short title should be cross-referred to the formal title of the investigating body, where the full publication details should appear. For example:

Feachem report—*see* Department of Human Services and Health (1995).

Department of Human Services and Health 1995, *Valuing the past ... investing in the future: evaluation of the National HIV/AIDS Strategy 1993–94 to 1995–96*, (Professor RGA Feachem, evaluator), AIDS/Communicable Diseases Branch, DHSH, Canberra.

The same applies to the reports of commissions of inquiry, royal commissions, and so on, and to publications that are better known by their titles than by the names of the authoring bodies:

Bringing them home—*see* National Inquiry into the Separation of Aboriginal and Torres Strait Islander Children from their Families.

Commission of Inquiry into the Activities of Gaming Houses 2000, *Report*, (CBE Oates, chairperson), 3 vols, Department of Sport and Recreation, Adelaide.

National Inquiry into the Separation of Aboriginal and Torres Strait Islander Children from their Families 1997, *Bringing them home*, (Sir Ronald Wilson, president), Human Rights and Equal Opportunity Commission, Sydney.

Oates, CBE 2000—*see* Commission of Inquiry into the Activities of Gaming Houses.

Changes to names or other details

A difficulty that sometimes arises in the citation of government publications is when the name of an agency changes. In these instances, the agency's name should be cited exactly as it appears on the title page of the source document.

In the case of commissions of inquiry, committees of review and similar bodies, there may be a change of commissioner or chairperson during the period of the inquiry or review. This example offers a solution for the citation:

Commission of Inquiry into Financial Transactions on the Internet 2000, *Report*, (commissioners: RL Foote, April 1998 – May 1999; NOE Legge, June 1999 – March 2000), Department of Finance and Administration, Canberra.

Parliamentary publications

The term *parliamentary publications* is used here to refer to publications of the Commonwealth Parliament: Parliamentary Papers, Hansard, the *Journals of the Senate*, and the House of Representatives *Votes and Proceedings*.

The Commonwealth Parliamentary Papers Series: This is made up of documents tabled in the Commonwealth Parliament that either

the House of Representatives or the Senate has ordered to be printed. Among such documents are the following:

- annual reports of government agencies
- the reports of commissions of inquiry, committees of review and similar bodies
- the reports of standing and select committees of parliament
- budget papers
- white papers, which are documents outlining government policy in relation to matters of national importance.

Not all documents tabled in parliament are ordered to be printed. Those that are not are listed either in the *Journals of the Senate* or in the House of Representatives *Votes and Proceedings*. Documents that are ordered to be printed are numbered (starting with '1' for each session of parliament) and are identified by a label attached to the outside back cover. They are published in two formats:

- the 'pamphlet' edition, which is the original tabled document that now carries the ISSN, Parliamentary Paper number and other identification details
- the 'bound volumes' edition, which is produced when all the tabled documents for a parliamentary sitting are gathered together and bound into hardcover books to form a set of volumes. Cite Parliamentary Papers in the following manner:

Australia, Parliament 2000a, *Department of Finance and Administration annual report 1999–2000*, Parl. Paper 32, Canberra.

Australia, Parliament 2000b, *Parliamentary spending: report of the Public Accounts Committee*, (L Bent, chairperson), Parl. Paper 142, Canberra.

Senate Standing Committee on Finance and Government Operations 2000, *The pricing of telephony*, SSCFGO, Canberra.

House of Representatives Standing Committee on Expenditure 2000, *Deregulation of the market for milk*, HRSCE, Canberra.

In the case of the last two examples, if the abbreviated citations 'SSCFGO' and 'HRSCE' have been used in the text, provide a cross-reference in the reference list, thus:

SSCFGO—*see* Senate Standing Committee on Finance and Government Operations.

Many titles published as Parliamentary Papers are first published—generally by the authoring body—in what is popularly known as a 'plain-cover', or departmental, edition. The following method of citation should be used for plain-cover editions:

Department of Finance and Administration 2000, *Annual report 1999–2000*, Department of Finance and Administration, Canberra.

Public Accounts Committee 2000, *Parliamentary spending*, (L Bent, chairperson), Public Accounts Committee, Canberra.

Senate Community Affairs References Committee 2000, *Report on housing assistance*, SCARC, Canberra.

Hansard: References to Hansard (Parliamentary Debates), a verbatim record of what was said in parliament, are presented thus:

Australia, Senate 2000, *Debates*, vol. S25, p. 65.

Australia, House of Representatives 2000, *Debates*, vol. HR103, pp. 2–9.

The Journals of the Senate *and the* Votes and Proceedings *of the House of Representatives:* These are the official records of proceedings in each House. References to them are presented as follows:

Australia, Senate 2000–01, *Journals*, no. 123, p. 718.

Australia, House of Representatives 2000–01, *Votes and Proceedings,* vol. 1, p. 631.

Commonwealth records

The method of citing Commonwealth records differs from that applying to other types of documents. The 'author' for an archival record is the agency responsible for the record's care, and the record is usually part of a series and often unpublished. The National Archives of Australia recommends that a citation of records held in its custody contain as much as possible of the following information:

- the full title of the custodian of the record—for Commonwealth records this is the National Archives of Australia
- the name of the originator of the record—a government agency or, in the case of personal archives, a person
- the series number, title and date range
- the item number, title and date range.

Two main systems are used for keeping Commonwealth records: the CRS System and the Accession System.

The CRS System: The Commonwealth Record Series, or CRS, System is the main system used to identify, locate, document and make available records originated by the Commonwealth itself, by Commonwealth government agencies or by individuals who have

been closely associated with the government. Each of these classes of originators is coded—CO (Commonwealth organisation), CA (Commonwealth agency) and CP (Commonwealth person)—and identification numbers are attached to the codes.

Full citations are presented thus:

National Archives of Australia: Department of External Territories [I]; CA A518, Correspondence files, multiple number series, 1928–56; CK822/1, Immigration policy—New Guinea—return of Chinese evacuees to the Territory, 1949.

National Archives of Australia: Joseph Benedict Chifley, CP M1458, General correspondence from special organisations and persons, 1946–49.

An abbreviated citation can be used for second and subsequent mentions:

NAA: CA A518; CK822/1.

NAA: CP M1458.

The Accession System: An accession is a consignment of records transferred by an agency to the National Archives of Australia. The Accession System is used for documenting these consignments. Full and abbreviated citations are presented thus:

National Archives of Australia: Bureau of Meteorology, Regional Office, Queensland; BP 360/1 Flood warning files, F series, 1908–63.

National Archives of Australia: BP 360/1.

Further advice about citation of Commonwealth records can be obtained from the National Archives of Australia.

Government publications: some examples in the author–date style

The following examples of the citation of government publications are provided as a guide. Note that if the authoring body is also the publisher it is often convenient to use the abbreviated form of the body's name in the publisher's details: the abbreviation is sufficiently close to the spelt-out form to avoid any confusion. The abbreviated form should, however, be explained in a list of shortened forms—see Chapter 13 for information about the placement of such a list.

Agriculture, Fisheries and Forestry—Australia 1999, *Mariculture in the Huon Valley area of Tasmania: recent developments*, AFFA, Canberra.

Australian Bureau of Criminal Intelligence 2000, *Australian illicit drug report 1999–2000*, ABCI, Canberra.

Australian Bureau of Statistics 1999a, *Disability, ageing and carers: summary of findings*, cat. no. 4430.0, ABS, Canberra.

——1999b, *The labour force, Australia*, cat. no. 6203.0, ABS, Canberra.

——& Australian Institute of Health and Welfare 1997, *The health and welfare of Australia's Aboriginal and Torres Strait Islander peoples*, ABS cat. no. 4704.0, AIHW cat. no. IHW2, Australian Government Publishing Service, Canberra.

Australian Institute of Health and Welfare 1999a, *Australia's welfare: services and assistance*, AIHW, Canberra.

——1999b, *Corporate plan 1999 to 2002*, AIHW, Canberra.

Australian National Council on AIDS and Related Diseases 1999, *Proving partnership: review of the National HIV/AIDS Strategy 1996–97 to 1998–99*, ANCARD, Sydney.

Commission of Inquiry into Poverty 1975a, *Law and poverty in Australia*, second main report, (Prof. R Sackville, commissioner), Australian Government Publishing Service, Canberra.

——1975b, *Legal aid in Australia*, Law and poverty series, research report, Australian Government Publishing Service, Canberra.

——1975c, *Poverty in Australia*, first main report, (Prof. RF Henderson, chairman), Australian Government Publishing Service, Canberra.

Commonwealth of Australia Gazette 1993, no. PS24, Canberra, 24 June.

Dabrowski, W 1999, *Caring for country*, report to the Aboriginal and Torres Strait Islander Commission, Canberra.

Department of Defence 2000, *Defence review 2000: our future defence force*, public discussion paper prepared for the Commonwealth Government, Department of Defence, Canberra.

Department of Health and Aged Care 1999, *Hepatitis C: a review of Australia's response*, report prepared by D Lowe & R Cotton, DHAC, Canberra.

Department of Primary Industries and Energy 1997, *National sustainable energy statement*, DPIE, Canberra.

Department of Veterans' Affairs in press, *New arrangements for war service pensions*, DVA, Canberra.

Environment Australia 1997, *Kakadu National Park tour operators handbook*, Biodiversity Group, Environment Australia, Canberra.

Henderson, RF 1975—*see* Commission of Inquiry into Poverty (1975c).

Henschke, C 1998, *Wine production in the Barossa Valley*, report to the Department of Agriculture, Adelaide.

Independent Review of Economic Regulation of Domestic Aviation 1986, *Report*, (TE May, chairman), 2 vols, Australian Government Publishing Service, Canberra.

Intellectual Property and Competition Review Committee 2000, *Parallel importation: interim report*, Attorney-General's Department, Canberra.

Inter-State Commission 1985, *An investigation of the Tasmanian Freight Equalisation Scheme*, vol. 2, *The shipment of wheat to Tasmania*, Australian Government Publishing Service, Canberra.

National Natural Resource Management Taskforce 1999, *Managing natural resources in rural Australia for a sustainable future*, discussion paper, Agriculture, Fisheries and Forestry—Australia, Canberra.

Ralph, JT 1999—*see* Review of Business Taxation.

Resource Assessment Commission 1991a, *Forest and timber inquiry: draft report*, vol. 1, Australian Government Publishing Service, Canberra.

——1991b, *Kakadu Conservation Zone inquiry: final report*, 2 vols, Australian Government Publishing Service, Canberra.

——1992, *Annual report 1991–92*, Australian Government Publishing Service, Canberra.

Review of Business Taxation 1999, *A tax system redesigned: more certain, equitable and durable*, (JT Ralph, chairperson), Department of the Treasury, Canberra.

Steering Committee for the Review of Commonwealth/State Services Provision 1999, *Report on government services 1999*, 2 vols, Productivity Commission, Melbourne.

Wilkins, RL 1996, *Australia at the ready!*, Australian War Memorial & Department of Defence, Canberra.

Organising bibliographies

Most bibliographies are organised according to the principle that the sources are most accessible to the reader if they are listed together in alphabetical order. This is particularly common when most entries are books.

If, however, a bibliography contains a number of different types of sources—book journal articles, theses, legislation, and unpublished works, for example—the author may decide to divide it into sections, according to the type of source.

Further, sometimes an author is dealing with a variety of subjects and will decide to organise the bibliography according to subject.

Another variation is to list sources according to where they can be found. For example, the bibliography for a history that uses a great deal of archival material might be divided into sections relating to the various archives in which the material is held.

SPECIALISED SOURCES

A variety of specialised sources is dealt with in this section, ranging from legislation and legal authorities to television and radio programs and databases.

Legislation

The titles of pieces of legislation—Acts, Ordinances, and Regulations and other forms of delegated legislation (such as rules and bylaws)—should be cited exactly. Neither spelling nor capitalisation should be altered to suit the referencing style of the publications in which they are cited.

Legislation is included in a list of references only if it is important to an understanding of the work. If this is so, it is usually best to set the list apart from the main body of the reference list and present it alphabetically under the subheading 'Legislation'.

Acts and Ordinances

Most Acts and Ordinances have a short formal title that can be used for citation purposes. First references to an Act or Ordinance should always cite this short formal title, in italics, exactly and in full. In subsequent references this title can be shown in roman type and with the date omitted. For example:

> the *Environment Protection (Impact of Proposals) Act 1974* … the Environment Protection (Impact of Proposals) Act …

> the *Casino Control Ordinance 1988* … the Casino Control Ordinance

Note that no comma precedes the year in the formal citation.

If an article (*a, an* or *the*) begins the title of an Act, the article should not be omitted

> The Commonwealth's *A New Tax System (Wine Equalisation Tax) Act 1999* makes provision for …

Italics for Acts and Ordinances? Use italics for formal citations of Acts and Ordinances from all Australian jurisdictions. Do not place a comma between the title and the year.

In the past, the use of italics and punctuation varied according to the particular jurisdiction in Australia. To simplify matters, however, it is now recommended that all elements of the formal titles of Acts and Ordinances be shown in italics.

here are two ways of clarifying the jurisdiction. The first is to make it obvious in he text:

> Victoria's *Equal Opportunity Act 1995* prohibits …

> In Victoria the *Equal Opportunity Act 1995* prohibits …

> The Christmas Island *Casino Control Ordinance 1988* makes provision for …

his method is preferable for works in which legislation is referred to fairly frequently.

he second way of clarifying the jurisdiction is to place that information—bbreviated, in parentheses and in roman type—after the date:

> the *Copyright Act 1968* (Cwlth)

> the *Anti-Discrimination Act 1991* (Qld)

> the *Equal Opportunity Act 1984* (WA)

he titles of Acts of the parliaments of other nations should be presented in man type, with the jurisdiction following in parentheses if it is not obvious from he context. For example:

> The Sale of Foods Act 2000 (UK)

egulations and other forms of delegated legislation

egulations and other forms of delegated legislation (such as rules and bylaws) are resented in roman type. For example:

> the Customs (Prohibited Imports) Regulations

nits of division

he basic units of division are the *section* for Acts and Ordinances and the *gulation* (note lower case) for Regulations. The abbreviations *s.*, *ss.*, *r.* and *rr.* can e used, although they should never appear at the beginning of a sentence.

he following is the recommended style for citing divisions of Acts and rdinances:

> Section 4 of the Commonwealth's *Copyright Act 1968* …

> In ss. 4–7 of the *Copyright Act 1968* (Cwlth) …

> The *Copyright Act 1968*, s. 4, …

> The Copyright Act, ss. 4–7, …

> Section 4 of the *Casino Control Ordinance 1988* …

> In s. 4 of the Casino Control Ordinance …

he recommended style for citing divisions of Regulations is as follows:

> The Commonwealth's Copyright Regulations, r. 18, …

> The Copyright Regulations, rr. 18–19, …

> Regulation 18 of the Copyright Regulations (Cwlth) …

Delegated legislation: Unlike Acts and Ordinances, the formal titles of Regulations and other forms of delegated legislation should be presented in roman type.

Abbreviating 'sections' and 'regulations': Although *ss.* is a contraction, rather than an abbreviation, it still carries a full stop—as *rr.* also does. (This is a convention peculiar to legal documents and is an exception to the general advice on contractions given in Chapter 10.)

> In r. 4 of the Copyright Regulations …
>
> In rr. 18–19 of the Copyright Regulations …

Sections and regulations can be subdivided into subsections and subregulations, paragraphs and subparagraphs:

> the Commonwealth's *Airlines Equipment Amendment Act 1981*, s. 19(1)(a)(ii)
>
> the Public Service Regulations (Cwlth), r. 83(2)(a)(ii)

At the broadest scale, Acts and Regulations are divided into chapters, parts, divisions and subdivisions. It is conventional to give these terms an initial capital when citing them. For example:

> In Part IV of the *Copyright Act 1968* …

Bills

Roman type for Bills: Use roman type for Bills before parliament.

Bills before parliament are presented in roman type because they are, in effect, 'unpublished' at that stage. For example:

> the Regulation of Genetic Material Bill 2000

Legal authorities

The following details are necessary for the full in-text citation of legal authorities
- the name of the case
- reference details
  - the year or volume number, or both
  - the abbreviated name of the report series
  - the page on which the report of the case begins.

Legal authorities are usually included in a list of references only if they are important to an understanding of the work. If this is so, set them apart from the main body of the references and present them alphabetically under the subheading 'Legal authorities'.

The name of the case

Italics and legal authorities: Use italics for the formal title of a case— for example, *The State of New South Wales v. The Commonwealth*. Use roman type for the reference details— for example, (1915) 20 CLR 54.

The name of the case is italicised and the year is placed in parentheses or brackets depending on the report series (see pages 227–8):

> *The State of New South Wales v. The Commonwealth* (1915) 20 CLR 54

When a specific page reference is necessary, the word *at* is conventionally used instead of *p.* (the abbreviation for 'page'). For example:

> *Greutner v. Everard* (1960) 103 CLR 177 at 181

In general, a citation contains only the name of the first-mentioned party on each side; the involvement of other parties is sometimes noted by the term *and others* (or *& ors*) or *and another* (or *& anor*). In most instances it is sufficient to provide only the family name of a person. Corporation names are usually given in full, although abbreviations can be used:

> *Jamieson v. Cooper* (1942) 67 CLR 316

Clark King & Co. Pty Ltd v. Australian Wheat Board (1978) 140 CLR 120

re Smith

re Smith & ors

ex parte Smith & anor

ote that the forms used in the last three examples are appropriate when the etails of the case have been cited in full, with all their reference details, in the eceding text. The expression *re* means 'in the matter of'; *ex parte* means manating from one party [Smith & anor in the example] without notice to e other party'.

the citation of criminal cases, in which the Crown is the prosecutor, (standing for *Rex* or *Regina*) is used (without a full stop) in order to avoid e ambiguity of *King* and *Queen*:

R v. Haddock

however, the Crown is the respondent in a criminal appeal, the order of the tation is reversed, and *The Queen* is given in full:

Haddock v. The Queen

n first mention in the text, an authority should be cited in full. An abbreviated rm or the name by which the case is commonly known can be given in renetheses following the formal citation. After that, the abbreviated or common rm can be used. For example:

The State of New South Wales v. The Commonwealth (1915) 20 CLR 54 (the *Wheat Case*)

eference to an authority sometimes includes the name of the presiding judge or dges: *J* denotes 'Justice'; *JJ* denotes 'Justices'; *CJ* denotes 'Chief Justice' (all ithout full stops). For example:

That was the opinion of Latham CJ and McTiernan J in *Attorney-General (Vic.) v. The Commonwealth* (1946) 71 CLR 237 at 253–6 and 273–4. A somewhat more restricted view was taken by Starke J (at 266), Dixon and Rich JJ (at 271–2), and Williams J (at 281–3).

Italics and abbreviated case titles: Use italics for any abbreviated title a case may be known by. For example, the *Wheat Case*.

eference details

ase citations provide the year, the volume number if there is more than one olume for the year, the abbreviated name of the report series, and the page ference. In general, square brackets are used when there is no volume number id the year is an integral part of the title; the date must be used to identify the rticular volume. The mode of citation is given in most volumes of reports—on e half-title page, at the head of the table of cases, or as part of the running eadline. The following are examples of the modes of citation for reports iblished in Australia:

Australian Company Law Reports	(1974) 1 ACLR 000
Australian Law Journal Reports	(1970) 44 ALJR 000
Australian Law Reports	(1976) 10 ALR 000
Australian Tax Reports	(1970) 2 ATR 000

Commonwealth Arbitration Reports	(1967) 121 CAR 000
Commonwealth Law Reports	(1970) 120 CLR 000
Family Law Reports	(1976) 1 Fam LR 000
Federal Law Reports	(1975) 25 FLR 000
New South Wales Law Reports	[1985] 3 NSWLR 000
Queensland Reports	[1975] Qd R 000
Queensland Weekly Notes	[1970] QWN 000
South Australian State Reports	(1973) 5 SASR 000
State Reports (New South Wales)	(1970) 70 SR (NSW) 000
Tasmanian State Reports	[1970] Tas SR 000
Trade Practices Cases	(1976) 1 TPC 000
Victorian Reports	[1976] VR 000
Western Australian Reports	[1970] WAR 000

A decision at law can appear in more than one report series, so more than one reference might be given. Thus, a case reported in the *Commonwealth Law Repor* and the *Australian Law Journal Reports* might be cited as follows:

In *Commonwealth v. Anderson* (1960) 105 CLR 303; (1960) 34 ALJR 323 …

Plays and poetry

References to plays and poetry are often more precise if given in terms of acts, scenes, lines, verses, and so on. The following forms are recommended:

William Shakespeare, *Romeo and Juliet*, act 3, scene 2, line 74.

or

Judith Wright, *Woman to child*, verse 1, lines 3–5.

Details of sources of this kind are not usually included in a reference list or bibliography.

The Bible

References to the Bible should take the following form:

Psalm 23:6–8

1 Corinthians 13:9; 15:1

Mark 7:11–9:17

Details of biblical sources are not usually included in a reference list or bibliography.

The classics

When referring to the classics, it is necessary to specify only the date of the editi being used, not the date of the creation of the work. The numbering of divisions stanzas or lines, for example) in works of this kind remains the same in all editions, so use division numbers rather than page numbers. It is also customary to acknowledge the translator. For example:

Virgil, *Eclogues*, 'The dispossessed', line 70, trans. EV Rieu, Penguin, Harmondsworth, UK, 1967.

Even in the author–date style the date should be placed at the end of the bibliographic citation, as readers might be confused by the sight of 'Virgil 1967'. The in-text citation should simply give the classical author's name. For example:

As Virgil expressed it, …   *or*   … (Virgil)

Films, videos, and television and radio programs

In the author–date style, in-text references to films, videos, and television and radio programs should contain the title and date of production. For example:

Strictly ballroom (1992)

(*Understanding the GNP* 1982)

The following details should be provided in a reference list:

- title
- date of recording
- format
- publisher
- place of recording.

Any special credits and other information that might be useful can be noted after the citation.

The order in which the information is provided in a reference list varies according to the referencing system being used. The following examples are in the author–date style:

Grumpy meets the orchestra 1992, video recording, Australian Broadcasting Corporation, Sydney. Featuring the Sydney Symphony Orchestra.

Sunday too far away 1975, motion picture, South Australian Film Corporation, Adelaide. Distributed by Rainbow Products Ltd, Sydney, and starring Jack Thompson, Reg Lye and Max Cullen.

What are we going to do with the money? 1997, television program, SBS Television, Sydney, 8 August.

The search for meaning 1998, radio program, ABC Radio, Sydney, 24 March.

The same information is provided in the documentary-note style, the only difference being that the date of recording follows the place of recording:

1. *The search for meaning*, radio program, ABC Radio, Sydney, 24 March 1998.

Films, videos and TV and radio programs: These should be listed by title in a reference list, notes or a bibliography.

(continued on p. 232)

ABOUT

Citing electronic material

When citing electronic material, the principles applying to the citation of paper-based sources are equally relevant: clarity, accuracy, consistency, and a methodical description of the path to the source.

A web site

For a web site, the in-text citation in the author–date style consists of the name of the 'author' (the person or organisation responsible for the site) and the site date (the date of the site's creation or most recent update). A superscript numeral is used for citations in the documentary-note and Vancouver styles.

The following information is required for citing a web site in a reference list, notes or a bibliography:

- author—the person or organisation responsible for the site
- site date—the date the site was created or last revised
- name and place of the sponsor of the source
- date of viewing the source
- URL.

The following are examples in the author–date style:

> Department of Finance and Administration 2001, Department of Finance and Administration, Canberra, viewed 7 August 2001, <http://www.finance.gov.au>.

> International Narcotics Control Board 1999, United Nations, Vienna, viewed 1 October 1999, <http://www.incb.org>.

Web addresses can be given directly in the text, although care is necessary to isolate them from any sentence punctuation if that punctuation could be misconstrued as part of the address. Use angle brackets (<>) to do this unambiguously:

> Details of the program are available from the department's web site <http://www.finance.gov.au>.

> The International Narcotics Control Board's web site <http://www.incb.org> provides details of the program.

A document within a web site

A document within a web site can usefully be considered in the same way as a published document or a book. In the author–date style, the in-text citation consists of the name of the author, editor or compiler and the date on which the document was created or last revised. In the documentary-note and Vancouver systems, a superscript numeral is used in the text.

The following information is required for the reference list, notes or bibliography (with slight differences in sequence depending on the referencing system being used):

- author, editor or compiler
- date of document (the date of creation or the date of the most recent revision)
- title of document
- version number (if applicable)
- description of document (if applicable)
- name of the sponsor of the source
- date of viewing
- URL (either the full location details if these are necessary to find the document or just the main site details).

The following are examples in the author–date style:

> Anderson, J (Minister for Transport and Regional Services) 2000, *CASA approves avgas contamination test*, media release, 23 January, Department of Transport and Regional Services, Canberra, viewed 7 February 2000, <http://www.dotrs.gov.au/media/anders/archive/2000/jan_00/al6_2000.htm>.

> Attorney-General's Department 1998, *Review of the Commonwealth 'Acts Interpretation Act 1901'*, Attorney-General's Department, Canberra, viewed 5 April 2001 <http://www.law.gov.au>.

> International Narcotics Control Board 1999, *International Narcotics Control Board report for 1998*, United Nations, Vienna, viewed 1 October 1999, <http://www.incb.org/e/index.htm>.

In the documentary-note style, the order changes slightly:

> Attorney-General's Department, *Review of the Commonwealth 'Acts Interpretation Act 1901'*, Attorney-General's Department, Canberra, 1998, viewed 5 April 2001, <http://www.law.gov.au>.

s with web sites, the full address of a
ocument within a web site can be
rovided in the text. For example:

Details are available from the Attorney-
General's Department <http://www.law.gov.
au/aghome/legal/pol/cld/aia/part_1.htm>.

general, however, it is sufficient to
ovide only the address of the web
e.

ectronic mail lists, Usenet roups and bulletin boards

the author–date style, in-text
ations for references to electronic
ail lists (list servers or list
ocessors), Usenet groups and
illetin boards consist of the author's
me and the date of posting. A
perscript numeral is used for the
ocumentary-note and Vancouver
stems.

e following information is required
r a citation in the reference list, notes
bibliography:

author's name

author's identifying details—usually
an email address

date of posting

title of posting

description of posting

name of list owner

date of viewing

URL.

e titles of the postings are treated
e articles in a magazine or journal,
d so are in roman, enclosed in
otation marks.

Note the punctuation in the following
example, which is in the author–date
style:

Murphy, L <murphy@rockets.com.au> 2000,
'News for old hacks', list server, 20 January,
National Journalists Association, viewed
7 February, <http://www.nja.net.au/
listserv/>.

In the documentary-note style, the
order is as follows:

Murphy, L <murphy@rockets.com.au>,
'News for old hacks', list server, 20 January
2000, National Journalists Association,
viewed 7 February, <http://www.nja.
net.au/listserv/>.

The title of the posting must come from
the 'subject' line in the message. The
name of the list owner is not on the
message: it is found in the details of
list administration.

CD-ROMs

For an in-text reference in the
author–date style, provide the title (in
italics) and the date of a CD-ROM. For
example:

(*Dr Brain thinking games* 1998)

Dr Brain thinking games (1998)

The bibliographic details are the same
as those required for films, videos, and
television and radio programs (see
page 229). For example, in the
author–date style:

Dr Brain thinking games 1998, CD-ROM,
Knowledge Adventure Inc., Torrance,
California.

In the documentary-note style, the
order is as follows:

Dr Brain thinking games, CD-ROM,
Knowledge Adventure Inc., Torrance,
California, 1998.

Emails

In-text references to emails are dealt
with in the same way as in-text
references to other types of personal
communication (see page 199). For
example:

Ms S Savieri confirmed this by email on
24 April 1999.

In general, it is not necessary to
provide further details, although there
are occasions when this may be helpful
to readers who are keen to pursue the
subject. If this is the case, the email
address can be provided in the
reference list, notes or bibliography:

Savieri, S 1999, email, 24 April,
<ssavieri@rockets.com.au>.

In the documentary-note style, the
order is as follows:

1. S Savieri, email, 24 April 1999,
<ssavieri@rockets.com.au>.

Email addresses should never be cited
without the permission of the owner of
the address.

Duplicated material

Documents and material that have been microfilmed, photocopied or duplicated in some other way are treated in the same manner as books, but with the form of publication being described after the title. The following are examples in the documentary-note style:

1. EWB Huntingdon, *Economies in the Australian beef industry*, microfiche, Australian Livestock Council, Canberra, 1997.

2. C Moss, *The Australian merino: a brief summary of recent developments*, photocopy, Department of Agriculture, Sydney, 1999.

Databases

Databases are identified by their title and producer. The producer is defined as the organisation with financial and administrative responsibility for deciding what will be included in the database. If it is not clear from the title that it is a database, the term *database* should be included.

In a reference list, notes or a bibliography, list the title of the database, the producer, the vendor and the frequency of updating. For example:

AGRIS database, United Nations Food and Agriculture Organization, SilverPlatter (vendor), annual updating.

In a specialised computer publication, other information—such as the time span covered by the database, equipment and software requirements, and corresponding print or microform products—can also be provided.

The components of a publication

BOOKS	**234**
Covers	234
About ordering and paginating book components	**236**
Preliminary pages	238
Text	241
Endmatter	242
Supplementary sections	243
Enclosures	244
Fold-out pages	244
Books divided into volumes	244
Loose-leaf documents	244
BOOKLETS, BROCHURES AND PAMPHLETS	**245**
PERIODICALS	**245**
Periodicals with separate covers	246
Periodicals without separate covers	246
ON-SCREEN MATERIAL	**246**
Material delivered online	247
About Commonwealth Government home pages	**249**
Material delivered via portable media	251

There are no fixed rules about what components a publication should contain or the order in which they should appear. There are, however, well-established conventions for paper-based works and emerging conventions for on-screen material.

In general, the cover and preliminary pages of books and journals provide identifying and copyright details, information about the work's preparation and publisher, a contents list, and sometimes other explanatory material. Booklets, brochures and pamphlets do not need to provide the same level of detail, but their structure and provenance must nevertheless be made clear.

On-screen material should provide similar information, so that readers know precisely what they are reading and where it comes from. Ways of structuring and displaying that information continue to evolve, reflecting the growing understanding of how people assimilate on-screen material.

BOOKS

Books have covers primarily to protect the contents, to identify the work and its author and publisher, and to generate interest and sales.

The text or body of a book is conventionally preceded by the preliminary pages, or 'prelims', and followed by the 'endmatter'. The prelims provide information for libraries, booksellers, researchers and other users; for readers, they offer a list of contents and often other information to clarify the book's purpose and content. In non-fiction works, the endmatter frequently contains appendixes and other material relevant to the text but not easily included in it, a glossary, a reference list or endnotes (and possibly a bibliography), and an index.

➤ The sequence and pagination of the different elements of a book are summarised on pp. 236–7.

Covers

Book covers must be attractive to potential buyers and readers, and sufficiently strong and durable to protect the pages they enclose.

➤ See pp. 304–5 for information about the design of covers.

Softcover books

The front cover of a softcover (paperback or limp-case) book shows the following information:

- title
- subtitle, if any

name of the author, authoring body or editor

edition number, if relevant.

The outside back cover may carry a 'blurb', extracts from reviews, or information about other works by the author. It should also show:

the ISBN (International Standard Book Number) and, if the book is part of a series, the ISSN (International Standard Serial Number)

the publisher's bar code.

The recommended retail price is also often printed on the outside back cover.

The inside front and back covers are usually blank.

Hardcover books

In the past, most hardcover (hardback or casebound) books carried no information or decoration on their front and back covers; the information was placed on the spine or dust jacket. It is becoming increasingly common, however, for dust jackets to be dispensed with—particularly for publications such as textbooks and instruction manuals—and for the cover information and decoration to be printed directly on the binding material.

The inside front and back covers of hardcover books are usually blank. Occasionally, a list of titles in the same series or details of the publisher or authoring agency, or both, appear on the inside front cover.

Depending on the binding style, endpapers can be used for the inside covers. Endpapers usually consist of a textured and coloured heavy paper or they may be printed with a design.

Dust jackets

A dust jacket serves two functions: to advertise the book and to protect it. The title and authorship details appear on the front of the jacket, and the front and back flaps typically carry blurbs about the book and the author. The recommended retail price is often placed at the foot of the front flap. The back of the jacket sometimes carries reviewers' comments or a list of other works on the same or related subjects issued by the publisher. The ISBN (and ISSN if the book is part of a series) should be placed on the back of the jacket, just above the bar code.

Spines

If the spine of a hardcover or softcover book is more than about 5 millimetres wide, it should bear the book's title and the authorship details. The words should run down the spine or, if the spine is wide enough, across it. The name of the publisher or the publisher's logo should appear at the foot of the spine. The same information should appear on the spine of the dust jacket.

It is difficult to place titles and authorship details on narrow spines, and in these cases the author should be consulted about abbreviating the title. For example, a short report entitled *An investigation of a potential extension of intermodal rail services* might have its spine title reduced to *Potential extension of intermodal rail services*. If a book has a subtitle, this could be omitted from a narrow spine.

What is a blurb? A blurb provides promotional information about the author and/or the book. Its purpose is to generate interest and sales.

➤ See pp. 423–5 for information about ISBNs and ISSNs.

Covers of Commonwealth publications: The name of the sponsoring body and its logo or other corporate identifier should be shown on the front cover. Generally, the Commonwealth Coat of Arms should also be used. Chapter 16 discusses placement of the arms and when the arms should *not* be used.

Spine titles: which way?
The title printed on a book's spine should run across or down the spine—not up it.

ABOUT

Ordering and paginating book components

The components commonly found in standard printed publications (such as books and reports) are listed below in the recommended order of appearance. Information about their typography and pagination is also provided.

Not all of the components shown will be needed in every publication: their inclusion depends on the subject matter, the reporting requirements and the publication's degree of formality.

Component	Typography	Pagination	Comments
Half-title page	Compatible with text. No need for special display	i	Page number not printed
Reverse of half-title page	Same typeface as text but smaller font	ii	Page number not printed
Title page	Compatible with book as a whole, including cover. Avoid very large type and avoid more than two typefaces	iii	Page number not printed. Will be page 'i' if there is no half-title and (and reverse half-title) page
Reverse of title page	Same typeface as text but smaller font	iv	Page number not printed. Will be page 'ii' if there is no half-title and (and reverse half-title) page
Letter of transmittal	Often supplied as camera-ready copy. Otherwise, same typeface and font as text	Roman numerals continue	Page number not printed
Foreword	Same typeface and font as text	Roman numerals	Page number shown. Can start either on next page (if there is a letter of transmittal) or on next right-hand page
Contents	Same typeface and font as text. Layout can vary (see p. 240)	Roman numerals	Page number(s) shown. Can start either on next page (after foreword) or on next right-hand page
Lists of illustrations and tables	Same typeface, font and layout as contents	Roman numerals	Page number(s) shown. Can either follow on from contents on same page or start on next page or on next right-hand page
Preface	Same typeface and font as text	Roman numerals	Page number(s) shown. Usually starts on first right-hand page after contents or lists of illustrations and tables
Acknowledgments	Same typeface and font as text	Roman numerals	Page number(s) shown. Can start on next page or on next right-hand page
Summary	Same typeface and font as text. Special design features or paper of different colour may be used as an orientation aid	Roman numerals	Page numbers shown. Starts on right-hand page

It is standard practice for the right-hand pages of books to take odd numbers—pages 1, 3, 5, and so on. All roman numerals used for paginating the preliminary pages are in lower case.

Component	Typography	Pagination	Comments
Introduction	Same typeface and font as text	Roman or arabic numerals	Page number(s) shown. Starts on right-hand page. Choice of roman or arabic numerals depends on relationship with text (see p. 241)
Text	Text typography is discussed in detail in Chapter 18. Design and layout are discussed in Chapter 17	Arabic numerals commencing with 1^1	Page numbers shown. Starts on first right-hand page after introduction. Can be divided into parts, chapters and sections (see pp. 241–2)
Appendixes	Same typeface as text. Smaller font often used	Arabic numerals	Page numbers shown. First appendix usually begins on first right-hand page after text (see p. 242)
List of shortened forms[2]	Same typeface as text. Smaller font often used	Arabic numerals	Page number(s) shown. Usually begins on right-hand page
Glossary[2]	Same typeface as text. Smaller font often used	Arabic numerals	Page number(s) shown. Usually begins on right-hand page
Reference list, endnotes or bibliography	Same typeface as text but smaller font	Arabic numerals	Page number(s) shown. Usually begins on right-hand page
Index	Same typeface as text but smaller font	Arabic numerals	Page number(s) shown. Usually begins on right-hand page
Other components:			
Blank pages preceding divisions such as parts and chapters			Page numbers allocated but not printed
Internal title pages for divisions such as parts			Page numbers allocated but not printed
Landscape pages			Page numbers allocated but not printed
Pages with bled-off illustrations			Page numbers allocated but not printed. (See p. 381 for information about bled-off illustrations.)

Numbered as '1' only if a preceding introduction uses roman, not arabic, numerals.

If they are very short and essential to an understanding of the text, these components can be incorporated in the prelims instead of the endmatter.

Books with spines narrower than about 5 millimetres in width often have their titles printed to run downwards on the back cover, close to the spine fold. This style is commonly seen on government publications.

Preliminary pages

It is conventional to number the preliminary pages of a book with lower-case roman numerals. This practice allows extra material to be added before printing without having to change the page numbering of the main text. For aesthetic reasons, the roman page numbers are not printed on some of the preliminary pages.

Half-title page

A half-title page is sometimes included as the first right-hand, or 'recto', page of a book, its purpose being to protect the title page. The title of the book is printed on the half-title page but any subtitle is not. The title shown there should be exactly the same as the main title shown on the title page. For example, a book entitled *Kakadu: the making of a national park* would simply have *Kakadu* on the half-title page.

Sometimes a half-title page also bears a series title. However, the half-title page should not include the name of the author or the name or logo of the publisher.

Reverse of half-title page

The reverse of the half-title page is often blank, although a list of other works by the same author, details of a series, details of other volumes in a multi-volume work, or a list of contributors can be placed there. An illustration, or frontispiece, is sometimes printed on the reverse of the half-title page when text and illustrations are all printed on the same paper. If the frontispiece is printed separately, it will be 'tipped in'.

Sometimes a title page is designed as an illustrated double-page spread, with the image spilling over onto the reverse of the half-title page.

Title page

A title page should provide the following information:

- title
- subtitle, if any
- name of the author or authoring body
- name of the sponsoring body, if relevant
- publisher's imprint, which consists of the publisher's name and location.

Other information—the name of a compiler, translator, reviser or illustrator, and the publisher's emblem, for example—can also appear.

Reverse of title page

The reverse of the title page (also known as the imprint page, copyright page, verso title or reverse-title page) presents bibliographic information, statements by

Tipping in: This is a process of incorporating a separately printed page into a book by gluing it, along a narrow band of its inner margin, to an adjacent page or to a specially inserted strip known as a 'guard'.

Commonwealth Coat of Arms: The arms should generally be used only once in a publication—on the cover. However, hardcover books may also carry the arms on the title page (see p. 294).

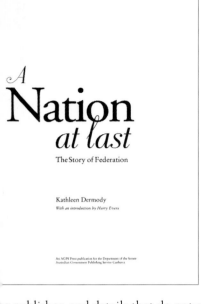

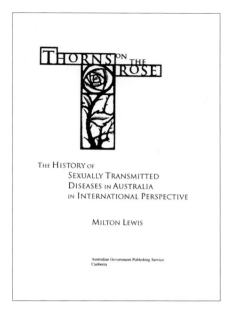

Different types of title pages

...e publisher, and details that do not appear on the title page. Most common ...mong these are the following:

- copyright notice (see page 413)
- publisher's name and address or location
- lists of editions and reprints
- lists of other volumes in a multi-volume work
- library classification information—the ISBN, the ISSN if the book is part of a series, and the CiP (cataloguing-in-publication) data
- name of the editor, designer, photographer, illustrator, indexer and typesetter, as appropriate
- printer's imprint (business name and location).

...formation about the typefaces and paper type used might also be provided. If so, ...is should precede the printer's imprint.

Subsidiary copyright holders: Sometimes contributors such as photographers and illustrators hold copyright in some aspects of a book, even though overall copyright is held by the author or publisher (see Chapter 22 for a discussion of copyright). These people should be acknowledged on the reverse-title page.

...etter of transmittal

...any reports prepared by committees, commissions of inquiry, government ...ganisations, consultants and other bodies contain a letter of transmittal, which is ...covering letter from the head of the reporting body to the responsible minister, ...her authority or client. It is important that the letter be signed and dated with ...e day, month and year of submission.

Secretary's statement: The letter of transmittal in Commonwealth Government annual reports is often called the 'Secretary's statement'.

...oreword

...he foreword is usually written by someone other than the author to support and ...iefly explain the purpose of the work. The writer's name should be placed ...eneath the foreword; a facsimile signature is often placed above the name.

Spelling: Note the spelling of *foreword*—not *forward* or *foreward*.

Examples of contents lists

➤ For information about contents lists for multi-volume publications, see p. 244.

More than one contents list: A contents list that is two or more pages long might be usefully preceded by a summarised version called, say, 'Contents at a glance' or 'Contents in summary'. Alternatively, a short contents list showing only the first level of headings might be included in the prelims, with a more detailed list being provided at the beginning of each part or chapter, or both. The contents pages of this manual demonstrate this alternative approach.

Order of illustration and table lists: The recommended order is generally plates, figures, maps and tables, unless the relative importance of these elements in a particular publication makes a different order more suitable. If there are only a few maps, these can be included in a general list of illustrations.

Contents list

The list (or table) of contents needs only the simple heading 'Contents', rather than 'Table of contents' or 'List of contents'. It sets out the book's main divisions and subdivisions as a broad guide to the reader; it generally does not include minor textual subdivisions, since these can be found through an index. If there is no index, a detailed contents list can be helpful, but it should not extend beyond three heading levels—for example, chapter heading, section heading and subsection heading. Inclusion of any further subdivisions tends to obscure, rather than clarify, a document's structure.

If a contents list consists only of short entries, it may be helpful to use wider side margins than those in the text, to bring the page numbers closer to the entries. Double columns are another possibility, as is unjustified presentation (with the page numbers separated from the entry by a space of 1 or 2 ems).

If a contents list is long, it can be set in a type size smaller than that of the text.

Lists of illustrations and tables

The way in which illustrations (plates, figures and maps) and tables are listed in the prelims—if they are listed at all—depends on their extent. If there are only a few, they can be listed at the end of the contents list, separated from it only by the relevant headings ('Figures' and 'Tables', for example). If they are numerous, each list can start on a separate page; alternatively, the first list can start on the first right-hand page following the contents list and the others can run on from there.

It is not always necessary to provide a list of illustrations or tables: it depends on how helpful the list will be for readers.

Page numbers are assigned to all illustrations printed with the text, even when an illustration covers an entire page and its page number will therefore not be printed on the page.

tipped-in page is not allocated a page number; the expression 'opposite page …' used in the contents list to show its position.

Preface

The preface is usually written by the author. It describes why and how the book was prepared. Acknowledgments can also be included in the preface if they are brief. If a preface is long—say, more than two pages—it is generally better treated as an introduction.

A preface (or introduction) to a new edition should describe the changes made since the previous edition. A similar note should be added to a reprint with corrections if these corrections are deemed important. In both cases, sufficient information should be provided to enable the owner of an earlier version of the book to decide whether to replace it.

Acknowledgments

An author can use the preface to acknowledge help received in the preparation of the work. However, if numerous people helped or many non-bibliographic sources were relied on, a separate acknowledgments section might be more convenient. It could be headed simply 'Acknowledgments'. Alternatively, a lengthy acknowledgments section—as might arise in the report of a committee of inquiry or similar body, for example—can be presented as an appendix.

Summary

Many lengthy information documents contain a summary of findings, which can be called 'Conclusions and recommendations' or simply 'Summary'. The title 'executive summary' is best avoided: it is unnecessarily exclusive.

Introduction

If an introduction is used instead of a preface to discuss why and how a book was prepared, it is treated as part of the prelims and its pages are numbered with lower-case roman numerals. In contrast, if a reading of the introduction is essential to a full understanding of the book, the introduction is treated as the first part of the text and its pages are numbered with arabic numerals.

Terms of reference can be reproduced as part of an introduction, although if they are lengthy they are generally better placed in an appendix.

Text

Chapters are the standard units of division for the text (or 'body copy') of most publications. They are sometimes grouped into parts in longer works.

Parts

Part titles should be brief and pertinent. Unless the part-title page uses a double-page spread (as in this manual), each part should start on a right-hand page. The chapter following the part title can begin either on the reverse of the part-title page or on the next right-hand page (in which case the reverse of the part-title page will be blank).

➤ See p. 138 for a discussion of section numbering.

Numbering parts: There are several options:

- Part One, Part Two
- Part 1, Part 2
- Part A, Part B.

Roman numerals (Part I, Part II) are best avoided, since it is easy to confuse the roman *II* with the arabic *11*.

Reference lists and notes can be placed at the ends of parts or chapters rather than in the endmatter. End-of-chapter placement is often suited to multi-author publications, loose-leaf documents and some types of reference works.

Chapters

The first chapter begins on a right-hand page. Subsequent chapters can start on a right-hand or a left-hand page, depending on factors such as chapter length, the number of chapters, and whether starting all of them on a right-hand page would result in too many blank pages.

Like the title of a part, a chapter title should be a succinct reflection of what the chapter contains.

Endmatter

In non-fiction publications, the endmatter commonly contains appendixes, a list of shortened forms, a glossary, a reference list or endnotes (and possibly a bibliography), and an index. Occasionally there might also be enclosures consisting of separately printed material or disks. In works of fiction there may be no endmatter, or it may simply contain information about the author, or advertisements for other books either by the same author or in the same genre and published by the same organisation.

Each element of the endmatter generally starts on a new page. The typography of the endmatter text and titles should match that of the rest of the publication, although it may be in a smaller point size.

Appendixes

Appendixes usually contain material that relates directly to the text but is too detailed or technical to be placed comfortably there. They might also contain extensive tabular material or graphs.

If there are several appendixes, an appendix title page is useful to divide this material from the main text of the publication. It can simply show the title 'Appendixes' or it can list the titles of each appendix as well. If the appendixes are long, a separate title page for each of them might be preferable. In either case, the title page should be a right-hand page, with the appendix starting on the reverse on the next right-hand page.

Title pages are allocated page numbers but the numbers are not printed.

Title pages for appendixes are also helpful if any of the appendixes consist of externally sourced material that retains its formatting. For example, guidelines issued on an organisation's letterhead and governing some aspect of a reporting task might need to be included as an appendix. Although the page numbering of the differently formatted material will be out of sequence with that of the rest of the publication, the use of appendix title pages will bring uniformity to the appendix titles and their title numbering. The number of pages in the differently formatted material should still be accounted for in the overall pagination of the publication.

Numbering chapters: Chapter titles should be numbered consecutively throughout a book; the numbering should not begin afresh after a part title. Hence, Part 2 should begin with a chapter numbered, say, Chapter 5, not another Chapter 1.

Paginating the endmatter: Page numbering for the endmatter usually continues on from the text.

Numbering appendixes: To differentiate appendixes from the text, it is preferable to use a separate numbering system for them. For example, if chapters are numbered with arabic numerals (Chapter 1, Chapter 2), appendixes could be numbered alphabetically (Appendix A, Appendix B). This distinction makes cross-references clearer.

List of shortened forms

An alphabetical list explaining specialist or unfamiliar shortened forms used in a publication is generally placed after the appendixes and before any glossary. It should be headed simply 'Shortened forms' or 'Abbreviations', as relevant. It should not be incorporated in a glossary.

If a list of shortened forms is brief—say, less than a page—and crucial to readers' understanding of the text, it can be placed in the preliminary pages. Longer lists should be placed in the endmatter, because readers can find them overwhelming at the beginning of a publication.

➤ Chapter 10 provides advice on when a list of shortened forms is necessary.

Lists of shortened forms are often presented in two columns.

Glossary

A glossary explains technical and unfamiliar words—but not shortened forms—used in a publication. It usually begins on a right-hand page, and the entries are arranged in alphabetical order. Two columns can be used, a narrow left-hand one containing the word to be defined and a broad right-hand one containing the definition. Alternatively, the word to be defined can be presented in italics, bold or small capitals; the explanation can then be run on or begin on a new line.

Is a glossary necessary? In-text explanations or footnotes may suffice if only a limited number of terms need explanation and they have been used only in discrete sections of a document.

Reference lists, endnotes and bibliographies

If both a reference list and a bibliography are to be included (or endnotes and a bibliography), the bibliography is placed second and should start on a new page.

It is standard practice to present reference lists, endnotes and bibliographies in smaller type than that used for the text.

Index

As with reference lists, it is standard practice to present indexes in smaller type than that used for the text. Indexes are presented in a multi-column format.

Supplementary sections

Supplementary sections usually contain material that is related to the main text but can be read independently of it. They can be printed on paper of a different colour—an approach often used for the financial statements in annual reports, for example.

If a supplementary section is short (no more than sixteen pages), it can be inserted at the centre of a saddle-stitched book or at a convenient place in a sewn or perfect-bound book. Because material of this kind is interruptive, the section is not paginated. However, the expression 'between pages … and …' should be used at the end of the contents list to note a supplementary section's presence.

➤ See pp. 485–90 for information about book-binding methods such as saddle-stitching and perfect binding.

If a supplementary section runs to more than sixteen pages, it should be placed at the end of the main text and before the endmatter. Because there is then no interruption to the main text, the page numbers usually run on. An exception is when the inserted material is a reprint of a complete document, in which case it retains its original page numbers. However, the number of pages in the insertion should still be accounted for in the overall pagination of the publication.

Enclosures

Sometimes a publication also contains enclosures: free-standing material that has generally been reproduced separately or published elsewhere. This material—which may consist, for example, of brochures, maps or disks—is usually incorporated after the index or placed in a pocket on the inside of the back cover.

Enclosures are not an integral part of a publication, so any numbering system used for them will be separate. Their presence should, however, be noted in the contents list by a phrase such as 'following pages …', 'at back of book' or 'in pocket'.

Fold-out pages

Fold-out pages—which are used when material such as maps and diagrams will not fit within the regular page size—do not bear page numbers, nor are they counted in the pagination. In the contents list, the expression 'facing page …' should be used to indicate their presence.

Any fold-outs tipped in at the back of a book or placed in a pocket at the back should be treated in the same way as enclosures.

Books divided into volumes

If there is sufficient material to warrant it, a book can be divided into two or more volumes, either at a suitable point in the text or at the break between the main text and the appendixes.

When the break between two volumes occurs within the main body of the text, the page numbering continues directly into the next volume. For example, in a two-volume work the first volume might end at page 422; the (post-prelims) text of the second volume should then begin on page 423. In both volumes, however, the prelims are numbered separately, using lower case roman numerals starting with 'i' (although the numbers of the first few preliminary pages will not actually be printed in the final version—see page 236). References should be to page numbers; reference to volume numbers is not necessary because the page numbering runs from volume to volume. The contents list of each volume should contain a summary listing of the contents of the other volume. An index can appear at the end of each volume or at the end of the final volume only.

If, however, the material in separate volumes differs in its nature—for example, if a second volume consists only of appendixes and other endmatter—the volumes can be paginated separately, with the post-prelims section beginning on page 1 in both volumes. The prelims, the contents lists and the index (or indexes) are treated in the same way as those for sequentially numbered volumes, but references should be to both volume and page numbers.

Loose-leaf documents

In loose-leaf documents, the main divisions (chapters or sections) are often paginated independently, using the chapter or section number plus the page number—for example, 4-1, 4-2, 4-3.

BOOKLETS, BROCHURES AND PAMPHLETS

Booklets, brochures and pamphlets generally require much less preliminary information and often have no endmatter. What is important is that enough information is provided to allow the document's authorship, date and place of publication to be readily identified. Sometimes there will also be a blurb or a listing of other titles in the series.

When these types of publications have separate covers (that is, covers made of a paper type differing from that used for the text), page-numbering practices are the same as those described for books. If there are few or no prelims, the first right-hand page of the publication will be page 1. If there are prelims, the title page must always be a right-hand page but other elements can appear as left-hand or right-hand pages. The prelims can be numbered using lower-case roman numerals.

For self-covered booklets, brochures and pamphlets (those with covers of the same paper type as that used for the text), the outside front cover is page 1, although this page number is not shown. Fold-out brochures and pamphlets often have no page numbers at all.

Page numbering: As with books, odd numbers go on the right-hand pages of booklets, brochures and pamphlets.

PERIODICALS

Periodicals (journals, magazines and newspapers) have a different arrangement for their components from that found in books, but clarity and logical order remain the primary considerations.

Although each issue of a periodical is part of a series that might eventually be bound into volumes, it is also complete in itself. As a consequence, it must provide the following details:

- title
- volume and part, where relevant
- date of issue
- name of the sponsoring body
- name of the publisher or distributor, or both
- ISSN and bar code.

Where this information is placed depends on whether the covers of the periodical are intended to be removed for consolidated binding. If the covers are to be removed, none of the essential publishing and identification details should be placed on any of the four sides of the cover (unless this information is replicated in the prelims).

Apart from the identifying information at the front and back, a periodical usually contains a contents list and a series of articles. The periodical's editor will have determined the arrangement of the articles. An editorial often precedes the articles, and there may also be a page or more of letters to the editor. Advertisements might be distributed through the publication or gathered together at the back.

In the case of journals, sometimes each article starts on a fresh page, sometimes not. An abstract might appear at the beginning of each article, beneath the title and authorship details. Footnotes might be used, or there could be endnotes or a list of references following each article. There might also be an index at the back of the journal.

As with books, the right-hand pages of a periodical take odd numbers.

Periodicals with separate covers

Periodicals with separate covers (that is, periodicals with covers that might be removed for consolidated binding) should carry on their outside front cover the periodical's title, the date of issue, the ISSN and the name of the sponsoring body.

A periodical divided into volumes: If a periodical is divided into volumes, a separate title page and contents list, and often an index, should be prepared for each volume. The text pages should be numbered continuously from one issue to the next, throughout the volume. Each new volume will begin at page 1.

With the exception of the ISSN, these details should be repeated on the first page. In addition, the first page should show the volume number and part number of the series (if they exist) and the name of the publisher or distributor, or both. Information about copyright and any restrictions on circulation should also be provided. The first page might also contain a contents list, and the final page (or pages) might contain an index.

Periodicals without separate covers

Periodicals without separate covers are usually in magazine or newspaper format. When they are bound into volumes, no pages are discarded and the necessary publication details for each issue—title, date, sponsoring body, and volume and part number (if any)—appear on the cover page. Supplementary information such as the name of the printer, publisher, distributor or agent, the editorial address and subscription rates can be placed elsewhere, often on page 2 (where the contents list commonly appears) or on the back page.

Issues of a periodical without separate covers are usually paginated separately. Such periodicals are often stapled or simply folded together. They should therefore have on every page a header or footer that gives the title, date and page number, so that any pages that come adrift can readily be identified.

ON-SCREEN MATERIAL

As with paper-based publications, the broad principles governing the arrangement of on-screen material—whether it is delivered online or via portable media such as CD-ROMs and DVDs—are contextual clarity and a logical, efficient path to the information. There are, however, several important differences between paper-based and on-screen publications, and these provide much of the impetus for the evolving conventions relating to the components of on-screen material. The main differences are as follows:

- On-screen reading patterns differ from those used for paper-based reading (see pages 38–9 and 310–12).
- Unlike paper-based publications, which offer clues such as numbered chapters and pages and which have a visible beginning and end, on-screen material provides readers with fewer immediately visible clues about the context of the

information they are seeing and how it relates to the remainder of the site or document.

Most electronic 'pages' extend beyond the bottom of the screen area on many types of monitors, so there is usually part of the page that cannot be seen.

or both online material and material delivered using portable media, the esentation and order of the information may be the same as, similar to, or quite fferent from that in a printed equivalent. Or there may be no printed equivalent. any case, the nature of the content plays a crucial part in how the information designed and displayed.

etadata is a very important component of on-screen material: it uses accepted assification standards to describe the content of a publication in a structured and nsistent way. This information, which search engines use, can be provided for es as a whole, for publications within a site, or for individual pages of a blication.

Metadata standards: The Australian Government Locator Service, or AGLS, is the metadata system used for Commonwealth publications (see pp. 427–8 for details).

aterial delivered online

ur broad categories of sites for online material have emerged to date:

 dynamic sites that draw content from structured repositories such as databases and support highly specific information recovery

 sites containing static documents

 sites concerned with presenting an organisation's image, listing its functions, and offering services to users—services that might also include access to static documents

 portals, or gateways, that serve as entry points to online resources held and managed by specific organisations.

Portals: FedInfo is an example of a portal. It is owned and managed by the Commonwealth Government and leads to agency-specific information.

contrast with paper-based publications, which usually have a linear sequence om the front cover to the title page and other preliminary material, through the xt and on to the endmatter), online material generally has multiple layers, pending on the type of information being presented. The structure is a matter r the creator of the site, but should always be aimed at ensuring easy access to e information.

The need for contextual information: With most material delivered online, any page on any site is accessible at any time to anyone. This indiscriminate access imposes a greater need to repeat basic contextual information than is the case with paper-based publications.

try and exit sequences of a web site

 the past it was common to preface online material with an entry sequence (a lash screen or entry tunnel) through which the reader moved to the home page d on to the content of the site. However, entry sequences were found to be npopular with users, especially for sites designed to deliver information as rapidly possible to a wide range of users, including those with low bandwidth. Many atures formerly associated with the entry sequence—such as news, advertising d the opportunity to register as a member of a group—now appear on home ges.

xit sequences can be useful for obtaining feedback, and they remain common for commerce sites where, for example, a series of steps is necessary to conduct a nancial transaction. For other kinds of sites, exit sequences are optional.

Home page of a web site

The home page of a web site gives a general overview of the site, displaying the breadth of information available on the site and identifying the site's provenance. It provides links to elsewhere in the site and in this respect equates to the content list in a print-based publication.

Navigation aids such as the following might be available:

- clickable lists
- site maps
- a search facility
- buttons such as *Next* and *Top*.

Among other features may be pictures, a help facility, a brief statement about the authoring or sponsoring body's core business, news items, information about particular products and services, contact details, a privacy statement, a disclaimer and advertisements.

However, the essential elements that should always be included on every home page are:

- the title of the site
- the name of the site owner—including a corporate identifier such as a logo where relevant
- the copyright information and other details that customarily appear on the reverse title page of a book—date of publication or revision, sponsor, and so on. (Alternatively, these can be placed on a page directly linked to the home page.)

Home page address format: A home page is usually referred to in the format <http://www.site name.domain name.country extension>. The elements of these addresses are described on p. 429.

Content of a web site

A selection from the content options displayed on a home page will lead to one of three types of content:

- a single, static page or file of content
- a static document consisting of many files or pages
- a dynamic document consisting of one or many pages generated in response to a particular request.

A static page or file of content

A single static page or file of content usually displays the following elements:

- title of the content
- details of the content, shown as text or images
- options for accessing content on other parts of the site
- navigation aids, consistent with those available on the home page.

If the information content of the page or file differs significantly from that on the home page—because of subject specialisation, for example—specifically applied metadata should be created to aid discovery by search engines.

(continued on p. 2

ABOUT
Commonwealth Government home pages

STANDARD ELEMENTS

The home page of every Commonwealth web site should have site-specific explanatory material and overviews or lists of the site's contents. Links to the home pages of other relevant government web sites can also be provided.

In addition, the following standard features should be included—but check the web site of the National Office for the Information Economy (see page 287) for evolving requirements:

- the Commonwealth Coat of Arms—prominently placed (see Chapter 16)
- the organisation's name, logo or other corporate identifier
- the title of the site
- search and help facilities
- contact details and a hyperlinked email address

- a link to FedInfo (the Commonwealth Government's entry point)
- the date of the site's creation or latest revision.

Note that while the Commonwealth Coat of Arms should appear only on the home page, not on every web page, an agency's logo or other corporate identifier should appear on every page and document within its web site.

In addition, the following information should be included on the home page or on a page (or pages) directly linked to the home page:

- copyright statement
- ISBN or ISSN, or both
- disclaimer or governance policy, or both
- privacy statement.

Broad navigation aids that help explain the contents and facilitate movement around the site should be supplemented by local navigation aids once the reader reaches the document's contents (see Chapter 17).

(*For more details:* Privacy requirements are discussed in Chapter 22, metadata and accessibility standards are explained in Chapter 23, and a summary checklist for electronic publishing is provided in Chapter 24, together with advice about on-screen production.)

Home page of Department of Finance and Administration

Static documents consisting of many files or pages

The static content of a site can consist of many files or of one file containing many pages. In either case, the content should be arranged in a logical order so that a reader can move easily from the general to the specific and vice versa.

Static documents within a site need to meet publishing standards similar to those applying to paper-based publications. Where applicable, therefore, they should provide the information that would be contained in the following components of book:

- title page
- reverse title page
- foreword
- contents
- lists of illustrations and tables
- preface
- introduction
- text
- appendixes
- list of shortened forms
- glossary
- reference list or endnotes and possibly a bibliography
- index.

➤ Chapters 16 to 21 and Chapter 24 describe how information provided in static documents within a site is designed and prepared for production. Indexing for on-screen documents is discussed in Chapter 15.

➤ See pp. 305–9 for details of the navigation features and labels necessary to enable readers to stay in control of their movements within a site.

Since any page of a static document can be viewed independently, without visiting the home page, some components of a publication should also appear consistently across a whole site and across all the pages of a document within the site. Among these components—called the 'persistent navigation'—are the name or logo of the site's owner, the title of the document, and contact details.

If part of the content has unique characteristics by virtue of its subject, scope or extent, it may be appropriate to develop it into a subsite, with access and navigation schemes that are separate from those of the home page and other areas of the site. Possible examples are a subsite for a long document such as an annual report or a subsite for a particular section or unit of a large organisation.

Dynamic documents

A growing number of web sites use database-to-web interfaces to provide information that is adjusted in response to a specific query. Two common examples are the results generated by search engines in response to an inquiry, and the response to a user selecting a combination of options on an interactive form provided within a web site.

Results pages of this kind are usually displayed on the screen after being filtered through the site's template. They are generally not linear in structure and they may cover more than a single page, so page navigation devices additional to the standard templated content are usually necessary.

Material delivered via portable media

Electronic material can be made available by means of portable media such as CD-ROMs, diskettes, DVDs and videos, rather than (or in addition to) being presented online. Portable media offer advantages in some circumstances, such as:

- when the volume of information is great
- when the material's interactivity demands files of a greater size than would be suited to web-based delivery.

➤ Chapters 16 to 21 provide advice on design and illustration for portable media. Chapter 24 discusses replication.

These products combine some of the portability of books with some of the interactivity of online material. Like books, they follow a linear path, having a beginning, middle and end. They also have packaging that is similar: a cover showing the title of the publication, information about the originator and publisher, the date of creation or revision, and a copyright notice.

CD-ROMs and DVDs can also come with printed instructions for use, depending on the extent of interactivity they offer. A tutorial, for example, might be highly interactive, whereas other products might simply contain static information, although the opportunities for illustration are vastly expanded in comparison with paper-based publications.

The minimum details for the paper packaging of a CD-ROM, diskette, DVD or video are as follows:

- title
- subtitle, if any
- creator
- sponsoring body, if relevant
- publisher
- place of publication
- date of creation
- copyright notice
- ISBN or ISSN
- bar code
- version and system information.

If a CD-ROM, diskette, DVD or video is issued without paper parts, the label of the disk or video container itself should carry, as a minimum, details of the author, date, version, copyright, and ISBN or ISSN. The opening screen of the disk should also display this information.

Chapter **14** # Editing and proofreading

THE CONTRIBUTION EDITORS MAKE	**253**
SCOPE OF SERVICES	**254**
Categories of tasks	254
Comprehensive editing	254
The editing brief and timetable	254
SUBSTANTIVE EDITING	**256**
Scope of tasks	256
Author collaboration and review	256
About substantive editing: indicative scope of tasks	257
COPY EDITING	**256**
Scope of tasks	256
House style	258
About copy editing: indicative scope of tasks	259
PROOFREADING	**260**
Scope of tasks	260
About proofreading: indicative scope of tasks	261
Allocation of the proofreading work	262
APPROACH TO THE WORK	**262**
Preliminary preparation	262
Managing changes during editing	263
Editorial style sheets	264
Marking up the document	266

TEAM LIAISON AND RESPONSIBILITIES	**267**
The author–editor relationship	267
Responsibility for factual accuracy	267
Copyright and other legal and compliance matters	267
Editorial input to information architecture	268
Editorial input to design	268
Liaison at proofreading stage	269
Liaison with the indexer	269
SEEKING PERFECTION	**269**

he roles of editors vary, depending on their experience and where ey work. Editors nevertheless share a common purpose: to prepare ablications that match the expectations of authors, readers and ablishers, and that meet the budget and timetable for each project.

ome large commercial publishers employ different specialist staff to commission ad assess manuscripts from external authors, to manage the editing and oduction processes, and to do the editing and proofreading work. In smaller ablishing houses, these editorial tasks are often combined. In government and rporate publishing, editors usually work with in-house authors to prepare the formation specified by their agency or company for internal or public release. ese various publishing enterprises also rely to a greater or lesser extent on the rvices of freelance editors.

HE CONTRIBUTION EDITORS MAKE

litors bring to this variety of roles demonstrable knowledge of the language and yle issues and the editing and production processes involved in transforming a ocument into a publication suited to its purpose, readership and mode of delivery. be fully effective, editors must also be flexible and work closely with the other embers of the publishing team to achieve the goals agreed for each publication.

'hen working on a document, editors consider it carefully from three different rspectives: that of the author, of the readers, and of the client or publisher. The arpose of editing is to:

help the author—by ensuring that the structure, expression and design reflect the intentions for the publication, and by correcting errors or inconsistencies in spelling, vocabulary, grammar, punctuation, style and layout that could otherwise distract attention from the author's meaning or diminish the document's credibility

help readers understand the publication—by reviewing the document from the audience's perspective in terms of its emphasis, the level of its language and assumed knowledge and its overall clarity, as well as the suitability of its design, navigation tools and production format to the way in which readers are likely to use it

help the client or publishing organisation—by preparing the document for publication to time and budget requirements and by checking it at each stage of the production process to verify that it will meet the standards specified for it.

Australian standards for editing practice: This publication details the wide range of knowledge and skills editors can contribute to a publishing project (see p. 285).

SCOPE OF SERVICES

Categories of tasks

Editing work can be broadly categorised into the following three levels of input, which are relevant at different stages of the publication process.

- *Substantive (or structural) editing:* This overview involves assessing the document as a whole to see whether its content, structure, language and presentation need refining to meet the publication's purpose and readers' expectations. If this is the case, the editor works closely with the author, the publisher and other team members to achieve the agreed changes.
- *Copy editing:* This phase concentrates more closely on achieving accuracy and consistency in language (vocabulary, grammar, spelling and punctuation), style and layout.
- *Proofreading:* This work involves final checking to ensure that the document is ready to be published.

A comprehensive editing service requires all three levels of input.

➤ For details of the type of work frequently required during substantive editing, copy editing and proofreading, see pp. 257, 259 and 261 respectively.

Comprehensive editing

A comprehensive editing service—involving substantive editing, copy editing and proofreading—should result in a high-quality publication that fulfils the expectations of its author, readers and publisher. A comprehensive edit is appropriate, for example, for most government documents being prepared for public distribution. If more than one author is involved, editing assistance of this kind is usually essential.

However, not all documents require a comprehensive edit to reach a standard suitable for publishing. Manuscripts accepted by book publishers from established academic authors, for instance, often need only a copy edit and proofread prior to publication.

The editing brief and timetable

The envisaged scope of editing tasks should be agreed in principle at the outset, when the production timetable and budget are being developed (see pages 11, 23 and 27). However, until the final version of the document is available for the editor to examine, it is usually not possible to predict the precise amount of editing effort that will be needed. It is therefore a good idea to retain some flexibility in the editing brief and schedule until then.

The ability to assess just how much editing a document needs once it has reached this final stage is one of the hallmarks of a good editor. Experience and an understanding of the intended readership's expectations are important factors in making these judgments. So, too, is the desire to avoid any unnecessary editing, since this can antagonise authors and waste money and time.

The three stages of a comprehensive edit are usually performed sequentially, with each stage resulting in a round of editing queries for the author and the client or publisher. Once the queries are resolved, the editor incorporates the proposed

nanges and reviews their context before moving on to the next level of edit or
ne proofreading. If extensive additions or changes are made following any stage,
rther editing and proofreading may be necessary to ensure that the structure and
ow of the discussion remain logical and that no inconsistencies or style problems
ave been introduced with the changes.

he final editing schedule needs to allow sufficient time for all these editing and
necking tasks to be done properly. Provision for additional time for client reviews
ight also be needed. For example, government documents being prepared for
iblic distribution are often reviewed by progressively senior levels of management
efore being approved for printing.

ocess of comprehensive editing for a document produced for both print and screen

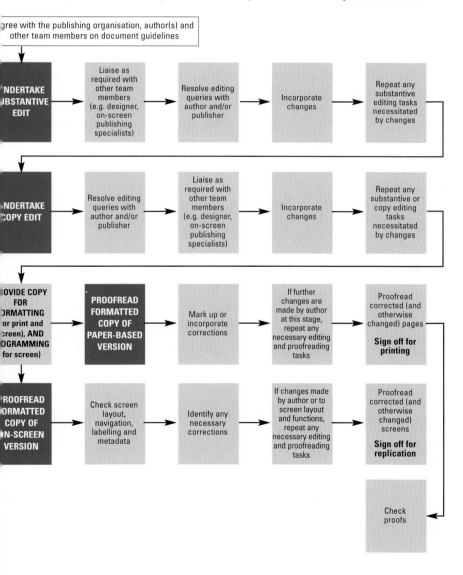

A sufficiently experienced editor can perform all the stages of a comprehensive edit, although in large publishing houses each stage is often allocated to different staff members. When more than one editor is involved in the work, continuity of editorial supervision is usually essential to maintain consistency and efficiency throughout the various stages.

SUBSTANTIVE EDITING

Scope of tasks

Substantive editing concentrates on the content, structure, language and style of a document. Some restructuring and rewording might also be done in the interests of accessibility, clarity, a cohesive style and tone, and a tighter reader focus. Contribution to, or assessment of, concepts for the proposed design, illustration, delivery format and usability criteria is also generally part of a substantive editing brief. Page 257 lists the range of tasks an editor may be called on to undertake as part of a substantive edit.

Clearly, some documents lend themselves more readily than others to the full range of substantive editing tasks. In many multi-author government or corporate publications, for example, the editor may need to impose a uniform style. In other contexts, editing for clarity, reader focus and a cohesive structure may take precedence over questions of style.

Author collaboration and review

Any significant rewording or restructuring calls for the greatest care on the editor part and for continuing close consultation with the author and publisher. A clear distinction should be drawn between rewording and rewriting. Rewording involve rearranging or tightening up what is already written. Depending on the brief, this work may be the editor's responsibility, particularly in the case of multi-author works. Rewriting involves more extensive rework—including adding material or substantially condensing the manuscript—and is essentially an authorial task.

An editor should be alert to every nuance of meaning in a sentence before attempting any alterations. If the meaning is unclear, the author should be asked to explain it or to rephrase the passage. Under no circumstances should an editor resort to guesswork. At the substantive editing stage, it is particularly important for the editor to seek the author's close scrutiny of any suggested rewording that could conceivably lead to a change in meaning.

➤ The process of checking editing queries with the author is discussed on p. 267.

COPY EDITING

Scope of tasks

The purpose of copy editing is to remove mistakes, inconsistencies or other infelicities of expression that could irritate or confuse readers—or embarrass the author. At the copy editing stage, the editor therefore concentrates on the details of language, spelling and punctuation; on achieving consistency of style and

(continued on p. 2)

ABOUT
Substantive editing

INDICATIVE SCOPE OF TASKS

Substantive editing can involve a wide range of tasks. The list that follows is indicative only, since each document presents its particular problems. Different editors and publishing houses are also likely to have differing views on the precise scope of substantive editing.

Structural review

Assess the document's conceptual integrity and whether there is any need for additional material or reader aids— for example, an abstract or a summary, illustrations, hyperlinks, cross-references, a glossary and an index.

Consider whether any alterations are needed to the form of the document, or whether the content might need to be rearranged, expanded or abridged in any way to achieve the most logical structure and an effective focus on readers' interests and needs.

Identify any material that might be better presented in another form—for example, as a table or illustration, or vice versa.

Determine, on the basis of the assessment so far, whether any major rewriting and restructuring are needed to suit the content, readership and delivery mode, and agree with the author or publisher (or both) on who will do this work.

Check that headings and other labelling and navigation aids are sufficient to help readers find information quickly and intuitively.

Provide design and illustration briefs in consultation with the author or publisher (or both), or assess the practicality of the design and illustration specifications already provided.

For on-screen publications, provide editorial input to the information architecture, design and navigation work.

Language and style editing

Ensure that the tone, level of language, and terminology are suited to the readership.

Check that there is a logical flow and suitable weighting of discussion.

Ensure that all information and arguments are presented clearly and unambiguously.

Condense unnecessarily wordy writing, delete any inappropriate repetition and irrelevant material, and resolve any inconsistencies.

Where relevant, establish a consistent style and tone in multi-author works— for example, for certain types of government and corporate publications.

Clarity of presentation and usability

Check that the presentation is effective and user-friendly.

Ensure that the heading hierarchy is clear, logical and consistently applied; that headings are parallel in structure; and that these and other labels, navigation aids and metadata are helpful and accurately reflect the contents.

Ensure that comparative material is presented in parallel design layouts and that information is consistent between the text, illustrations and tables.

Check the appropriateness, placement and clarity of tables and illustrations; ensure that they have suitable legends and captions where required; and check that they will reproduce or download well.

Ensure that referencing suited to the type of document is included and, for electronic documents, that any links to other web sites are appropriate.

Check that any necessary explanations of terms and shortened forms are given in the text or endmatter (or both).

Prepare the cover blurb and running heads if required.

Legal requirements

Check that permissions for reproducing copyright material have been obtained.

Query material that could present problems in terms of legal or regulatory compliance.

Note: The content and structure of these lists of editing and proofreading tasks (see also pp. 259 and 261) owe much to earlier work done by subcommittees of editing societies involved in developing the Canberra Society of Editors' *Commissioning checklist* and the Council of Australian Societies of Editors' *Australian standards for editing practice*.

layout; and on checking references, illustrations, tables, headings, sequences, links and preliminary matter and endmatter. The scope of work usually involved at the copy editing stage is shown on page 259.

If the document has not previously been through a substantive edit, the editor should remain alert for anything that might need to be reviewed by the author or publisher. Perhaps the language is occasionally unclear or varies in tone or focus. Or the structure may be muddled, causing unnecessary repetition. However, unless the editing brief is expanded as a result, the editor should not be expected at the copy editing stage to launch into the extensive editing necessary to remedy these problems.

The final copy editing review involves checking that everything that should be included is in place. To assist with this and to provide a checklist for the other members of the publishing team, the editor of a printed publication might prepare an 'order of book'. This lists all the preliminary pages with their intended page numbering, indicates what the body of the document comprises, and shows the arrangement of the endmatter.

➤ See Chapter 13 for advice on the placement and standard content of preliminary pages and endmatter in both printed and on-screen publications.

For an on-screen publication, a similar checklist can be prepared showing the various components of the publication, including the opening and closing sequences and the metadata. At this stage the editor might also help with usability testing, to check that links work as expected and that no errors are encountered when downloading or opening files.

For illustrated works, the editor generally also prepares or checks the illustration guide. This includes:

- the title (and figure number, if any) of each illustration
- the caption (or a brief description)
- the page number or location in the on-screen document to which the illustration relates
- information on whether the image is a thumbnail (an illustration placeholder in an on-screen document to allow quicker downloads) or a full electronic file, or whether it involves separately prepared artwork.

The illustration guide can also include information about any permissions that are necessary, with provision to tick these off as they are received.

House style

Many publishing organisations have a 'house style' that has been developed to suit the kind of material they publish. These style guidelines generally cover such matters as spelling variants, capitalisation and hyphenation, the use of shortened forms, the treatment of numbers, the method of citation, file-naming conventions, metadata standards, the placement and design of hypertext, and a policy on electronic links.

When copy editing a document by an individual author, an experienced editor will follow the house style intelligently rather than impose it rigidly. This is because each publication—even in the same subject area—has different characteristics and

(continued on p. 2

ABOUT
Copy editing

INDICATIVE SCOPE OF TASKS

Compared with substantive editing, copy editing involves a narrower range of tasks, focusing primarily on style and consistency.

Language

Correct errors of grammar, spelling and punctuation.

Ensure that the meaning is clear; refer to the author or substantive editor if significant rewording appears necessary.

Consistency

Language consistency: Ensure that there is a consistent and appropriate approach to terminology, spelling, capitalisation, hyphenation, shortened forms, and the expression of numbers and quantitative information (or follow a house style covering these elements if required).

Visual consistency: Follow the design specifications for typography, the heading hierarchy, menus and labels, page and screen layouts, tables, illustrations and captions (or establish consistency in these elements if no house style or design specifications are provided).

References

Spot check the accuracy of cross-references and links to other parts of the document (for example, to illustrations and tables) and to external sites; return the document to the author for amendment if necessary.

Ensure that lists of contents, illustrations and tables match headings (and page numbers for printed documents).

Ensure that textual and bibliographic references are complete and consistent in style.

Check that all sources have been acknowledged and that any copyright holders' stipulations have been followed.

Document completeness

For a printed publication, check the copy for the spine, covers, running heads and publisher's blurb.

Ensure that all preliminary matter has been properly prepared and contains all the necessary information, including copyright and library classification data.

Check the body of the document for completeness—for example, summary, text, tables, illustrations, labels, captions, footnotes and endnotes.

Ensure that the endmatter has been finalised—for example, appendixes, a list of shortened forms, a glossary, and references or a bibliography.

For an on-screen publication, check the entry and exit sequences for completeness.

Confirm that the placement of all material is correct, and check the page numbering or other numerical and alphabetical sequences.

Check the index (for content, order, capitalisation, punctuation and layout) once it is available, and spot check page references for accuracy.

Functionality

For an on-screen publication, assist with the testing of elements such as links, form fields and pop-up boxes, as well as the downloading and opening of files.

Check metadata for accuracy, coverage and terminology.

Discretion in applying house style: If an author's style is reasonable and consistent, even if it doesn't conform precisely to the house style, it may be wiser and more efficient not to interfere. But check this approach with the publisher.

➤ The development and application of document-specific style sheets are discussed on pp. 264–5.

Don't confuse proofreading with copy editing: Proofreading is essentially a quality control process, not a substitute for copy editing. The proofreading stage is not the time for inserting another round of author's or editor's changes.

may need slightly different treatment. Authors also expect to be able to express themselves in an individual manner where this is warranted by the context or type of document.

House style becomes more critical for multi-author works and for publications that are part of a series or representative of an organisation. In these circumstances, issues of identity and consistency can be very important in achieving a cohesive or suitably representational style, as well as for efficiency in production.

Even when there is a house style, a supplementary editorial style sheet will be needed for each document. This document-specific guide is essential for ensuring consistency in the editorial choices made at the very detailed level applicable to each new topic and writer.

PROOFREADING

Proof is a generic term for the various forms in which type and graphic material are returned from the typesetter, formatter or printer for checking, before a document is signed off for reproduction. *Proofreading* is the term for these final checking and correction procedures, which are vital for both printed and on-screen documents.

Scope of tasks

The principal aims of proofreading are to verify that there are no discrepancies between the previously approved master copy and the formatted proof, that the document is complete and that the standard of presentation is suitable for publication. The range of verification checks usually carried out at the proofreading stage is listed on page 261.

The proofreader compares the approved version of a document with the first proof, checking each word, punctuation mark and graphic element. Each component of the document is also checked to ensure that everything has been included and is in the correct position. Each page is then further scrutinised to verify that the layout and type specifications have been accurately followed, and that the line breaks, page and screen lengths, and table and illustration placements are suitable.

As a back-up check, a careful proofreader will also be alert for typographical, spelling, linking, sequencing or other errors that may have escaped detection during the copy editing stage or that may have crept in with final amendments. In the case of on-screen documents, the proofreader might also be involved in a final check that everything functions as it should and that suitable metadata has been attached.

Proofreading work involves several passes over the proof, since each element (such as headings, sequences, links and type specifications) is best checked separately. If there are corrections to be made, a second proof will be provided for proofreading. This second proof is read against the first proof (not against the original copy) to ensure that all corrections have been made and that no further errors have been introduced. This can be done most efficiently by placing the two sets of proofs side by side and then checking every correction separately—not only each corrected line but also the lines above and below the correction, to ensure that these have

(continued on p. 2

ABOUT
Proofreading

INDICATIVE SCOPE OF TASKS

Proofreading is basically a quality control exercise, not a substitute for copy editing. The list that follows assumes that a separate proofreader has been employed for the job. Often, however, the editor's scope of work includes proofreading.

Verification of copy

Check against the previous copy for discrepancies.

Check that all amendments have been accurately inserted by the formatter or typesetter.

Integrity check

Check that the document is complete, including (as appropriate):

preliminary matter or entry sequence—cover, dust-jacket material, spine copy, preliminary and home pages, copyright and publication information, and contact details

the body of the document—abstract or summary, text, tables, illustrative material, labels and captions, footnotes and endnotes

endmatter or exit sequence— appendixes, list of shortened forms, glossary, references or bibliography, index and feedback provisions

links and metadata.

Spelling and punctuation errors

If any apparent spelling, typographical or punctuation errors are detected, query these with the editor.

Conformity with specifications

Check conformity with the editing style sheet, including:

- spelling
- hyphenation
- capitalisation
- shortened forms
- numbers, dates, percentages, symbols and equations.

Check conformity with the design specifications, including:

- heading hierarchies, running heads and footers, buttons and roll-overs, and labels
- font
- alignment and spacing
- page or screen layout.

Sequences, cross-references and links

Check the lists of contents, illustrations and tables against the text.

Check all sequences, including the numbering of pages, headings, illustrations, tables and plates.

Proofread the index.

Spot-check the cross-references. If mistakes are found, refer these to the editor for consultation with the author.

Spot-check the functionality of electronic links and the page display. If problems are found, refer these to the editor for consultation with the relevant on-screen publishing expert.

Layout

Check the suitability of page and screen breaks and of word breaks at the ends of lines and pages.

Check for any rivers of white space through the text.

Check that tables, illustrations, captions and labels have been appropriately placed.

Queries

Mark up any queries for the editor to review.

Mark-up

Mark up changes for the typesetter or formatter, using conventional proofreading marks.

not been affected by the change. The top and bottom lines of any page or screen that contains a correction should also be compared between the two proofs, in ca a correction has resulted in a flow-on to subsequent pages or screens. If so, these need to be checked again too.

Finally, it is a wise precaution for the proofreader to read the full proof of the document once again. The purpose is to ensure that no errors or inadvertent changes have been caused anywhere in the document during the re-keying of corrections.

Allocation of the proofreading work

Some publishing houses employ skilled proofreaders to do this final verification work. A fresh view of the document is often helpful at this stage, as the author a editor may have become so familiar with the work that they fail to notice some remaining errors or inconsistencies. On the other hand, there can be benefits in having the editor who worked on the document throughout its development continue with the proofreading, as some types of inconsistencies and other problems may be apparent only to someone with an intimate knowledge of the document.

For some publications it may also be prudent to employ a copyholder: someone who reads from the approved master copy while the proofreader checks that ther are no unauthorised divergences in the proof. Particularly for on-screen documen and for printed documents containing a great deal of tabular matter (such as mathematical or scientific texts or large annual reports), this method of checking different versions is usually the most accurate. Indeed, a copyholder check might also be necessary at earlier stages in the development of these types of documents

APPROACH TO THE WORK

Preliminary preparation

The editor needs to be thoroughly briefed on the project before starting work, an should also read the project file, noting any points that could influence the editir approach.

The editor's next task is to read the document carefully. Generally, no editing should be attempted during this initial reading, but any items that warrant later consideration should be flagged. Anything missing from the document—such as preliminary matter, illustrations or references—should also be noted, so that arrangements can be made to follow these up. In addition, extracting a list of headings will provide the editor with a useful tool for assessing the document's overall structure.

Good editors always keep reference books close to hand (such as dictionaries, grammar and usage books and guides for on-screen publication) and consult them whenever they are uncertain about any of these aspects. They should also consult any other references that have a specific bearing on the document in question (such as statutory guidelines, previous works in the same series, or particular production or access standards).

➤ For a description of the various types of printer's proofs, see pp. 465–8.

➤ Some points to be raised in an editorial briefing are suggested on p. 27.

➤ A number of useful reference works for editors are listed on pp. 285–7.

Managing changes during editing

Methods of working

If the editor is to work on hard copy, this will need to be done on a double-spaced draft of the document; if the editor is to work on screen, an electronic copy should be supplied. In the latter case, software compatibility between the author, editor and publisher should be checked. Responsibility for typing the changes should be agreed beforehand; some editors prefer to type their own changes, while others find it more efficient to use an experienced word processor operator.

Clear trail of changes

During the editing process, the editor will have to check many aspects of the document with the author and the publisher. These queries should either be prepared as a separate list or be marked clearly on the edited copy. The editor must have a system for ensuring that the queries are progressively resolved, so that none are overlooked.

The author has the right to review all the changes proposed by the editor at each stage of editing. A record should therefore be kept of all changes, either electronically (using version control software) or on a copy marked up by hand. As work progresses through successive editing and review stages, revised drafts are usually produced, and these must be clearly identified. The aim should be to develop an auditable trail through the various drafts, showing what changes have been made, who made them and when, and who approved the changes. The editor should also note on each copy when the changes have been incorporated in the next version.

Master copies

Particular care needs to be taken when more than one author or reviewer is working on a document. Editing the wrong version of a draft or incorporating amendments made to superseded drafts can be a frustrating, time-consuming and expensive exercise.

To avoid this problem, the publication manager should save a master copy at each stage and ensure that all the agreed changes from all contributors have been incorporated before issuing the revised master copy. Once the editor starts working on the latest version, other contributors should make no further alterations until they receive the next master copy containing the editor's latest round of changes.

Avoid parallel changes: The editor should not work on a draft at the same time as any authors or reviewers.

Electronic editing checks

Before finalising a document that has been provided in electronic form, editors usually run it through a spelling and grammar checking program. This is a useful back-up, but it should never be seen as a substitute for careful editing and proofreading.

Computer grammar checkers are not sufficiently sophisticated to pick up many of the common flaws in grammar. Readability indexes provide only a very rough (and sometimes misleading) guide to the relevance of a document's written style for particular audiences. And while spellcheckers can be helpful in finding some typographical and spelling mistakes, they will not highlight instances where an entirely wrong (but properly spelt) word has been keyed in.

Late changes

Every effort should be made to finalise changes before a document proceeds to the proofreading stage. As proofreading is a quality control process rather than another editing phase, it is not the time to be considering any significant authorial or editorial amendments.

Alterations at proof stage are likely to be time-consuming and costly, particularly for printed publications. They might require changes to page layouts already completed, not only on the pages where the alterations are made but also on subsequent pages if repagination is needed. In addition, they might necessitate a review of all cross-referencing, links and related sequences throughout a document (such as in textual cross-references, headings and titles, lists of contents and illustrations, and the index).

Rushed insertions at proofreading stage are a common cause of embarrassing flaws in otherwise carefully prepared and edited documents. Even if sufficient time is allowed for substantive or copy editing reviews of the new material, inconsistencies in the overall logic or structure can be introduced that only another edit of the full document might reveal.

The pitfalls of late changes: Rushed insertions at the proofreading stage can be expensive, time-consuming and the cause of embarrassing mistakes.

➤ Chapter 1 discusses the development of preliminary document guidelines and style sheets spanning the writing, editing, design and on-screen publishing tasks.

Editorial style sheets

A detailed, publication-specific style sheet needs to be prepared by the editor and kept up to date as work progresses. It should be developed in harmony with the document guidelines and other style sheets prepared by the designer and on-screen publishing specialists.

If the document is to conform to a specific house style, the editor's style sheet should reflect the approach described in the house style guide. If style inconsistencies are apparent in the draft document, it is often best to choose the options likely to involve the least editorial intervention while still presenting an acceptable, cohesive style throughout the document.

The editorial style sheet is best divided into two parts: general style decisions, and an alphabetical list of words. By noting on this sheet each editorial decision relating to unusual or alternative spellings, capitalisation, hyphenation, shortened forms and general terminology, the editor can maintain consistency in such matters throughout even the longest or most complex document. It also helps to ensure accuracy in citing the proper names of people, places, programs and organisations, as well as references to source material.

If the draft document has been provided in electronic form, an editor can use a search facility to locate instances of a particular stylistic anomaly and change it to conform to the style established. Global replacements can have unintended results however, so it is usually wise to make the changes instance by instance.

An editorial style sheet provides benefits for other members of the publication team as well. It is a crucial reference if more than one author or editor is working

n the document and if a separate proofreader is employed. It is also helpful for
am members working on the design, on-screen publishing, and formatting or
pesetting aspects. Finally, it provides an invaluable reminder on all matters of
yle for any future work—for example, if the publication is to be part of a series or
work on the document is interrupted for some reason.

mple editorial style sheet (first page)

Style sheet: DFAT report

General:

- Lists: no 'and' at end of penultimate points; no semicolons
- Tables: initial capital for each item in each column; column headings ranged left
- Capitals: no initial capital for 'government', 'parliament', 'minister', 'department', etc. when used generically or when not part of specific title
- Punctuation: single 'smart' quotes; no full stops or spaces with initials
- Date spans: condensed form when in same decade (1997–99 not 1997–1999; but 1990–2000)

A

Abu Dhabi

Accelerated Demining Program

anti-personnel

Asia-Pacific Economic Cooperation group (APEC, no 'the')

ASEAN Regional Form (ARF)

Asian Development Fund Act 1987

Australia–China Council

Australian Safeguards and Non-Proliferation Office (cap. P)

B

Bandar Seri Begawan

Better aid for a better future

Biological Weapons Convention

Biosafety Protocol

Bougainville People's Congress

Bridge Standards Project

business-to-business

C

Cairns Group

central Vietnam

Commonwealth Law Ministers' Meeting

consular corps

Consular Travel Advisory Notices Scheme (but 'travel advisory notices')

consulates-general

Cook Islands (no 'the')

countermeasures

counter-terrorism

D

Dhaka

Director General IAEA (no hyphen)

E

East Asia regional strategy

Economic and Social Council (ECOSOC)

F

financial management information system

Fissile Material Cut-off Treaty

fitouts

foot-and-mouth disease

forums

G

Guangxi Zhuang Autonomous Region

Guangzhou

H

Ha Tinh

heads of mission

honorary consuls

I

Incentive Fund; the fund

Inner Mongolia Grassland Conservation Project area

inter-agency

interdepartmental

International Maritime Organization (UN)

International Institute for the Unification of Private Law (UNIDROIT)

Marking up the document

When to use standard proofreading symbols

Many corporate and government documents are prepared on screen, with changes from authors, reviewers and editors being inserted directly into the electronic copy. In contrast, some publishing houses prefer to have all editorial and subsequent author's amendments made on hard copy. In both cases, however, once the manuscript has been typeset or formatted, further changes usually have to be made on hard copy. For on-screen documents this may well be essential, since by this stage the content is likely to have been converted to a mark-up language (such as HTML).

When an author or editor is marking up a manuscript by hand, it is important that the changes are shown clearly. Once the copy editing or proofreading stage has been reached, the conventional proofreading symbols should be used to show the nature of each correction—as long as the people responsible for reviewing the copy and for keying in the corrections are familiar with these symbols.

Standard proofreading symbols: Appendix C shows the most commonly used proofreading symbols and how to use them. These marks have evolved over many years, and are widely recognised in the publishing industry as an unambiguous way of indicating required corrections.

Placement of proofreading marks

Although the same proofreading symbols are used at both the copy editing and proofreading stages, the placement of the correction on the page differs. At the copy editing stage—when the document is still in double-spaced format—the changes are usually shown within the text column, and the symbol indicating the change is placed in the margin to draw attention to the amendment. If there is insufficient space for a longer correction, it should either be written in the margin or be prepared on a separate sheet and keyed to its position in the text.

Once the proofreading stage has been reached, the document will be in its final page layout and there will be insufficient space between text lines for corrections to be inserted clearly. At this stage, both the corrections and the relevant symbols should be shown in the margin, beside the line of text to be amended; the only marks in the text column should be those showing where the changes are to be inserted.

Other notations that are not intended to be inserted in the text can also be written in the margin. These should be in pencil and circled. They may include notes to the typesetter or formatter showing the grading of headings, the location of illustrations and tables, any special characters that need to be inserted, and other details (such as superscript and subscript characters) that might need to be particularly checked after typesetting or formatting. Remaining queries for the author or other team members can be shown in the same way, labelled clearly to show for whom they are intended.

Colour-coding corrections

If charges are to be allocated for amendments at proof stage, a colour-coding system is needed for marking corrections. The corrections should be made on the proof in ink—traditionally blue or black for author's or editor's corrections and re for typesetting errors. If necessary, a third colour can be used to distinguish between the author's and the editor's corrections.

TEAM LIAISON AND RESPONSIBILITIES

The author–editor relationship

Establishing a good working relationship with the author at the outset should be one of the editor's prime goals. The author will appreciate being told of the schedule for the editing work, and will need to understand the review processes in which he or she will be involved. The editor's queries to the author should be phrased clearly and tactfully. The copyright holder (generally the author) naturally has the final say on all questions of content.

Editors should remember that writing any major work is usually an exhausting task and that the document they are given for editing may well be viewed by the author as the finished product—or very close to it. When editorial changes are suggested that, in the editor's view, would materially improve the document, the author will expect cogent reasons for these suggestions. Often the reasons will be based on the editor's view of how readers might respond to the text, since one of the editor's goals is to help the author gain the widest possible readership and acceptance for the work.

Responsibility for factual accuracy

The author is always responsible for the accuracy of the facts given in a document and should double-check them if there is any doubt.

Editors should nevertheless be alert for potential factual discrepancies. For instance, if a new project is reported as having started in 2001 but is elsewhere referred to as a 'year 2000 initiative', a query to the author would be warranted to determine whether the distinction is correct. Statements that appear doubtful on the basis of the editor's general knowledge should also be queried, as should any information (such as timetables, contact details and web addresses) that might change during the production period.

Editors should also do some spot checks on simple calculations (such as total lines in tables) to see whether the accuracy of tabular material might be of concern. Further, any material that appears to be out of date should be queried, and the author should be asked whether it is possible to obtain more recent facts or figures. If quoted material has been included in the text and if reference works have been cited, the editor might need to check these too (depending on their availability and the type of publishing project).

Otherwise, unless it is specified in the brief, an editor is not expected to spend time checking a document for factual accuracy.

Checking the facts: The author is responsible for factual accuracy, but the editor should help by querying apparent discrepancies.

Copyright and other legal and compliance matters

The author is responsible for ensuring that copyright has not been infringed in the document. It is up to the author to obtain clearances for the use of any copyright material, although some publishing houses have staff who help with this.

Because the publisher as well as the author can be held liable for a copyright breach, the editor is expected to know enough about copyright to be able to point

Copyright coverage: Copyright covers not only the text of a work but also the design and artwork, and the format in which the work is produced. Copyright also needs to be considered when planning links to external web sites. See Chapter 22 for details.

➤ Chapters 22 and 23 provide information about various legal and compliance issues.

➤ Chapter 3 discusses structuring of screen-based documents, while Chapter 24 deals with production and testing of on-screen material.

➤ Chapters 17 and 18 discuss typography and design for both printed and on-screen publications.

➤ Chapter 2 discusses some aspects to consider when briefing a designer, illustrator or photographer.

out potential problems that may become apparent during the editing process. The editor should also highlight any material that has not been properly acknowledged and seek clarification from the author.

In addition, the editor should remain alert for material that may cause other legal problems. Editors should therefore have some knowledge of the law relating to libel, obscenity, contempt, privacy and trade practices. The author and publisher should be informed if, in the editor's opinion, there is a likelihood of legal problems arising, so that expert advice can be sought as soon as possible.

Editors of government publications should also be aware of the relevant compliance standards. Among these are requirements relating to social justice and access.

Editorial input to information architecture

As discussed in Chapter 2, information architecture covers the work involved in organising information and devising the access schemes, navigation tools and signposting aids for documents designed for on-screen use. The editor and information architect should work closely together to ensure a logical progression of information and intuitive access routes to the document's content. The editor can also act as 'the reader's advocate' in usability testing, and make sure that the links are suitably labelled and placed and that they take readers to where they say they will.

Editorial input to design

It is vital that editors understand the effect a document's design has on the ability of readers to find and absorb information. Readability, legibility, eye movement and balance all come into play, as do the different effects when text is printed on paper or displayed on screen.

Preparation of design and illustration briefs may be part of an editor's responsibility for a project. If not, it is still a good idea for the editor to be involved in the design briefing and in the subsequent assessment of the proposed design's practicality. This assessment should be based on a sample of representative pages provided by the designer.

Before developing the overall design, the designer will find it helpful to have the editor's advice on details of the document that might need to be taken into account. These could include the depth of the heading hierarchy (as well as examples of the longest and shortest headings), unusual aspects of tables and illustrations, the need for any text highlighting, and requirements for various on-screen devices. If the document is to be released in both print and on-screen formats, the editor needs to be fully aware of the intended design relationships between the two versions, since these can have implications for the document's structure.

The editor and designer should therefore liaise throughout the project. There may be times, for example, when the designer is able to suggest a typographical or layout solution for a problem the editor is facing. Designers are also expert at developing concepts for illustrations that can help explain complex information or that can substitute for lengthy descriptions. The editor and designer should work closely at proof-checking stage too, when both need to review the proofs from their different perspectives.

Liaison at proofreading stage

If a separate proofreader is employed, the editor should provide a detailed style sheet and background briefing, noting any specific problems that might need to be checked or particular editing approaches that have been adopted. At proof stage, changes are likely to be costly and time-consuming, and may prejudice the printing schedule. For these reasons, and to avoid the possibility of unnecessary rework, the proofreader might be asked to consult the editor about any inconsistencies or apparent editing errors before changing them on the proof.

While the proofreading is being done, the author will be reviewing a copy of the proof in order to sign it off for publication. Once these checks are complete, the editor reviews the proofreading mark-up, adds to this copy any final corrections from the author, and checks that all outstanding queries have been resolved. The editor then arranges for these amalgamated corrections to be inserted, and checks successive proofs as required.

Liaison with the indexer

The editor should provide the indexer with editorial guidelines and advice about readers' probable searching patterns and topics of particular interest. Once the index has been completed, the editor needs to proofread it and check sample page references for accuracy and completeness.

SEEKING PERFECTION

Editing and proofreading are all about quality assurance and adding value to a publication. A substantive edit aims to refine a document's structure, language, focus and presentation. A copy edit aims to remedy any language flaws and bring consistency to a document. Proofreading guards against production errors. In concert with the wider publication team, the editor's overall goal is to help produce a publication that will be admirably suited to its purpose, readership and delivery mode.

While striving for the 'perfect' result through these successive phases of work, every editor and publication manager must nevertheless realise that perfection is rarely, if ever, achievable. Budgets and schedules impose constraints on the time that would be allocated to the work in an ideal world. Human fallibility means that the occasional flaw might not be picked up, no matter how painstaking and concentrated the effort. However, if the final copy is compared with the initial draft and the interim marked-up copies, the editor's contribution to a publication's clarity and acceptability will be obvious.

➤ Necessary interaction points between team members during the various phases of a project are illustrated on p. 23.

➤ See Chapter 15 for information about the work involved in indexing, and ways of evaluating indexes.

Chapter **15** Indexing

CHARACTERISTICS OF AN INDEX	**271**
DIFFERENT TYPES OF INDEXES	**271**
OTHER INFORMATION RETRIEVAL DEVICES	**272**
NUMBER OF INDEXES	**272**
INDEX CONSTRUCTION	**273**
About publication-style indexes	274
When does indexing begin?	273
What format should the document be in?	273
How indexers approach the task	276
REFINING HEADINGS	**277**
Arrangement	277
Capitalisation and style	279
Indexing language and language control	279
REFINING LOCATION REFERENCES	**281**
Scattered references	282
Non-textual material	282
Punctuation	282
DOUBLE-INDEXING	**283**
ASSESSING PUBLICATION-STYLE INDEXES	**283**

Indexes are information retrieval devices. They identify all information of potential interest to readers and direct them to it efficiently. A good index increases the value of any work intended to be consulted for information and testifies to the professionalism of its production.

The value of indexing to retrieve information has long been recognised: library catalogues from the Mesopotamian era have been found. But despite this long tradition and the well-established conventions for index preparation, the quality of an index is dependent on the indexer's proficiency.

➤ See Chapter 2 for information about contracting and working with indexers.

The hallmark of good indexing is good analysis. A successful index anticipates readers' needs by linking concepts that are related so that readers are led to the information they are seeking, regardless of the word or phrase they use as their entry point.

CHARACTERISTICS OF AN INDEX

Successful indexes share the following characteristics:

- They identify all significant concepts, consistent with the level of indexing required by readers.
- Each concept is described aptly.
- Complex concepts are thoroughly analysed and dissected.
- The arrangement is logical.
- Related concepts are suitably linked.

Indexers link related concepts by pointing to those that are the same (*doctors* and *medical practitioners*, for example), those that are similar (*doctors* and *nurses*), and those that qualify one another (*doctors*, *general practitioners* and *specialists*). Concordances, such as lists of keywords produced by a computer, cannot do this.

Analytical skills: Because indexers are experts in analysis, they can also provide valuable help in developing the structure of a web site or publication.

DIFFERENT TYPES OF INDEXES

Library catalogues, web site indexes and other databases are usually large and continually growing—their content is potentially unlimited. They identify major themes covered by their content, but not every subject. They are cooperatively produced and are based on a controlled set of terms for searchable subject headings.

Indexes to large, stand-alone works such as journals, encyclopedias and similar reference material are also extensive but have a more limited scope. They identify major themes but might not include all the minor subjects discussed in every article or entry. They are generally produced cooperatively as well. In the case of indexes for journals and other serial publications, for example, different people or teams may be involved in indexing different issues or volumes over a considerable period. Indexes of this kind are therefore also based on a controlled set of terms for headings.

A third type of index is the publication-style index (also known as a 'back-of-book' index), which deals with a single work rather than a corpus. (This single work can be print-based or screen-based, or both.) Publication-style indexes are more detailed than the other types of indexes, since they identify all significant minor concepts discussed in the content as well as the major ones. The main features of a publication-style index are described on pages 274–5.

Chapter focus: Although this chapter deals mainly with publication-style indexes, the intellectual analysis and judgments required of indexers are similar, regardless of the type of index or the medium for which it is produced.

For paper-based documents, a publication-style index is often limited in size by the cost of printing. Electronic indexes are not so constrained, and the medium can be exploited to produce highly specific indexes. A publication-style index is usually created by a single indexer, and the language used for headings derives from the work itself, not from any predetermined listing.

OTHER INFORMATION RETRIEVAL DEVICES

Publications contain other devices to help readers locate information.

- *Contents lists and site maps:* These provide an overview of a publication's structure.
- *Compliance indexes in governmental annual reports:* In accordance with parliamentary guidelines, these indexes identify sections of the report dealing with access and accountability. They do not reference other material.
- *Internal cross-references and hyperlinks:* These direct readers to related material of immediate interest. Unless it is 'bookmarked' by a reader, however, linked information will not be readily accessible for later reference.
- *Keywords:* Electronic keyword searching is most successful with specific search requests. The size of the content, the complexity of readers' information needs and the skills of readers in devising search formulas influence the likelihood of success in a search. When confronted with a series of 'hits' of little or no relevance, most searchers give up.

➤ Chapter 24 discusses the use of search engines for automatic indexing.

Each of these devices has a different purpose and is not intended to provide access to the total content of a publication—which is the role of an index.

NUMBER OF INDEXES

Simple publications such as alphabetically arranged directories usually do not need an index, since the arrangement of the material allows readers to find information easily. As the detail and complexity of the content increase, however, it becomes more difficult to find specific material; indexes then become necessary aids for readers.

ome publications commonly have more than one index. Law reports, for
 xample, usually have separate indexes to cases, legislation and subjects. Similarly,
 and-alone bibliographies often have separate author, title and subject indexes or
 ave a combined author–title index but a separate subject index.

 here are, however, disadvantages in having two or more indexes. First, readers
 ay not realise that more than one index exists. Second, the treatment of similar
 pics is necessarily split between the indexes.

 hese problems are overcome in a combined index, in which more references can
  found at a single heading or sequence of headings. Thus, in a stand-alone
 bliography, references to works written by an author will appear under the same
 eading as references to works about the author:

> White, Patrick
>> biographies
>> *Eye of the storm*

 addition, books and articles about the author's works will appear with the
 ferences to the works themselves:

> *Tree of man*
>> reviews

Indexing government publications: A single index containing references to subjects, names and titles is recommended for the majority of Commonwealth publications.

IDEX CONSTRUCTION

hen does indexing begin?

 dexing should never start before a document's content has been signed off by the
 levant authority. With the content finalised, indexing can begin as the page
 yout of each part of the document is completed. For paper-based documents, this
 eans finalising page numbers, paragraph numbers or other internal numbering
 stems used to locate references.

 he indexer must be notified if any amendments are made after indexing has
 gun. These amendments should be minor only, because the addition of new
 aterial or major rearrangement of the text might necessitate re-indexing, even if
  e text has been tagged electronically.

Re-indexing: Extra work caused by content changes made after the delivery of copy for indexing is usually charged as an additional cost.

hat format should the document be in?

 dexers use computer software to help them compile indexes. Specialist indexing
 ftware is available for indexing both electronic and paper-based copy; some
 dexing functions are also available with various types of word processing and
 ge layout software. The format in which the material should be delivered to the
 dexer depends on the software the indexer will be using and whether the
 ocument is to be produced as a screen-based or paper-based publication.

 a screen-based index is required, the indexer needs electronic copy. Similarly,
 ectronic copy is necessary for a paper-based index if it is to be prepared using an
 dexing facility embedded in word processing or page layout software. On the
 her hand, copy for paper-based indexes prepared using specialist indexing
 ftware should be provided on paper or as a PDF file.

Indexing software: Indexers use various computer software products to help them in their task. This software does not do the indexing for them.

(continued on p. 276)

ABOUT
Publication-style indexes

Each indexing element is called an 'entry'. Each entry is made up of a main heading—which may be followed by one or more levels of subheading, forming 'sub-entries'—and references. For electronic indexes, location references are not needed: readers simply click on the relevant heading to reach the content. Keyword searching within an electronic index is another access tool.

Headings

Headings describe the indexed information.

Entry headings: These begin on the left margin of the column.

Subheadings: These define aspects of the major concept. Subheadings are indented from the column's left margin (although in electronic indexes they can be accessed via a link, to reduce scrolling).

Sub-subheadings: These have a double indention from the column's left margin—2 ems, for example, if subheadings are indented 1 em. In paper-based indexes, however, this type of heading is best avoided by recasting it as a main heading or by running it on after a subheading. Otherwise, the amount of space created on the left of the entry, and the shorter lines, can hamper readability. In electronic indexes, the number of subheading levels can be greater, since

a subheading need not be exposed until the reader clicks on the heading immediately above it in the hierarchy.

Turnover lines: In paper-based indexes, turnover lines are indented to enable readers to distinguish between them and any following sub-entry. Entry heading turnover lines have a double indention from the column margin to distinguish them from subheadings.

Subheading turnover lines also usually have a double indention from the column margin but will need a triple indention (for example, 3 ems) if the index contains indented sub-subheadings.

Alphabetical arrangement: Headings can be arranged in either word-by-word or letter-by-letter alphabetical order. This manual recommends word-by-word order (see page 277). If a heading begins with a numeral, it should generally be ordered as if the number had been spelt out.

Word-by-word arrangement orders each word in a compound heading separately, including hyphenated nouns and adjective–noun combinations. The space or hyphen separating the words is given precedence over alphabetic characters falling in a corresponding position in single-word headings:

New England

New South Wales [the space takes alphabetical precedence over

Newcastle

Letter-by-letter arrangement ignores spaces:

Newcastle [c precedes e]

New England

New South Wales

A paper-based index entry presented in three different ways

Entry headings

Example A

sex of population, 9–11
   employment ——— **Subheadings**
     manufacturing, 66
     primary industries, 44
     services, 52 ——— **Sub-subheadings**

Example B

sex of population, employment and
   manufacturing, 66 ——— **Turnover lines**
   primary industries, 44
   services, 52

Example C

sex of population, 9–11
   employment: manufacturing, 66; primary industries, 44; services, 52

eferences

ere are two types of references:
ation references and cross-
ferences.

cation references: In paper-based
dexes, location references lead
aders directly to the indexed item in
e content. (In electronic indexes,
aders click on the relevant heading to
ach the content.)

ge references lead readers to the
ge containing the indexed
ormation.

ragraph references might be used in
dexes to manuals and reports
ntaining numbered paragraphs. If
ey are used, this feature should be
plained at the front of the index.

ction and subsection references
ght be used when indexing material
ntaining numbered sections and
bsections—legislation, for example.
is approach, too, should be
plained at the front of the index.

ded references might be set, say, in
lic or bold type and could be used to
stinguish illustration or table
ferences from text references, with
e code being explained at the front of
e index.

Cross-references: These lead readers to
other index headings where location
references appear. When more than
one heading is referred to, they are
separated by a semicolon.

'See' references are used in paper-
based indexes for economy. They lead
from one term to a synonymous term
where the location references appear.
Double-indexing (see page 283) should
be used instead in electronic indexes,
where the index's size is generally not
important.

'See also' references are used in both
paper-based and electronic indexes to
lead from one indexed term to a related
or more specific term under which more
information is indexed. They can
appear as the last element of the
subheading structure, regardless of
alphabetical order (as demonstrated in
the index to this manual), or they can
immediately follow the main heading.

Typography of paper-based indexes

The font for paper-based indexes is
conventionally two point sizes smaller
than that of the main text. The index
can be set in two, three or four
columns, depending on the format of
the publication. The total width of the
columns plus the space between them
should equal the full column width of
the main text, so that the margins
remain constant throughout.

The words *see* and *see also* are always
shown in italics.

Examples of cross-references

ATO, *see* Australian Taxation Office ——— ***See* references**
Australian Taxation Office, 54, 99–101, 152
   information technology, 19, 40–1
   staff, 127, 150
…
taxation, 3, 18, 90–108, 152
   rates, 60–3
   rulings, 106, 148, 159–61
   see also Australian Taxation Office ——— ***See also* references**

Regardless of the format, the document to be provided for indexing should be checked to ensure that it is complete—and, in the case of paper copy, to ensure that all pages are in order and numbered correctly. A wise indexer will repeat this procedure on receipt of a document.

The indexer will return the completed index in electronic form. Most publishers of paper-based material also require a hard-copy print-out.

How indexers approach the task

Creators of publication-style indexes read all of the content at least once, in order to identify major themes and minor topics. In the course of compiling the index, they will also re-read sections of the work many times to refine the index headings and to check whether the references need amendment as further references to the same or related points are found.

Subject analysis

In analysing the content, indexers look for themes and topics as well as the names of people, places, organisations and things. For example, a section about AusAID might also be discussing Australia's international aid program. If so, the index should contain an entry for 'international aid' as well as for the organisation itself, together with double-indexing or cross-referencing of related terms. For example:

> aid program
>
> AusAID
>
> Australian Agency for International Development
>
> foreign aid
>
> international aid
>
> overseas aid

Significance

Selecting the fullest textual reference: The first sentence in the following example gives the most information; the second is discarded because it adds nothing more:

> Australia is a federation created in 1901.
>
> Australia is a federation.

Indexers seek to provide references to all *significant* information in the content, not to every item. They choose the fullest possible reference in the text—the one that gives the most information about the subject—then attach any other references that add further detail. References that do not add detail to those already established are discarded.

For this reason, summaries in reports are not indexed: more detailed information is found in the main text. Similarly, information about financial and staffing resources that may appear at the beginning of each section of an annual report is not indexed if it then appears in a consolidated (indexed) table in an appendix to the report.

'Passing references' in text are those that merely mention people, things or subjects without adding information. If something is cited as an example, it will be considered a passing reference if there are no other references to it in the work—and even if there are, the example is unlikely to be the fullest reference. Passing references are not significant, so they are not indexed.

DEFINING HEADINGS

Headings should be chosen to suit the ways in which readers are likely to search for material. To help readers who may not be familiar with a specialised subject, for example, indexers will sometimes use a readily recognisable term that is not actually used in the text—such as a popular variant of a technical term. In these instances, either the variant is cross-referenced in the index to the entry for the technical alternative (where the location references are given) or the location references are repeated in both places.

In addition, the more specific an index is, the more easily readers will find what they are looking for. Indexers make headings specific by breaking down entries into sub-entries. When producing a publication-style index for a paper-based document, however, indexers often need to achieve a compromise between specificity and the size limits imposed by publishing costs. Even so, an entry consisting of a heading followed by a large number of location references is not considered good indexing practice.

Good index headings: Headings that use terms familiar to readers and that define concepts specifically are good index headings.

Arrangement

Headings are usually arranged in alphabetical order. Other logical arrangements can be used at the subheading level in publication-style indexes—recurring themes in works of history or biographical information in chronological order, for instance.

Library catalogues: Non-alphabetical arrangements can be used at the main entry level in library catalogues—for example, classification numbers such as in the Dewey Decimal Classification scheme.

Word-by-word arrangement

Within the overall alphabetical sequence, word-by-word (as opposed to letter-by-letter) arrangement is recommended because it is more commonly used in Australia—for example, in the white pages of telephone books. It is also the way most computer programs sort automatically. Specialist indexing software allows for either method of ordering.

When indexing programs embedded in word processing or page layout software are being used, the automatic ordering system needs to be overridden and changed. This is because the programs order word elements in the following sequence: punctuation marks and most symbols, numerals, then letters. If indexes are generated in this way, headings beginning with a quotation mark will appear before those beginning with a numeral, which in turn will appear before those beginning with a letter.

In word-by-word arrangements, the alphabetical sequence takes precedence, punctuation marks are ignored in the ordering, and numerals are treated as if they were written as words.

Articles, conjunctions and prepositions

When articles, conjunctions and prepositions appear in headings, they are generally treated as words (or letters) in determining the ordering. There are some circumstances where they should not be included, however, and others where alternative ordering conventions are usually followed.

As a general rule, initial articles introducing names and titles are ignored in indexing. 'The Big Company' will thus appear in the index as either 'Big Company, The' or just 'Big Company'. However, indexing standards recommend retaining the article in geographical names such as 'The Hague'. Specialist indexing software allows indexers to 'hide' words from the automatic sorter, so th 'The Hague' can appear at *h*, not *t*, without inversion.

> Haberfield
>
> The Hague
>
> Harare

To achieve the same result when using the indexing functions of word processing or page layout software (which does not have the 'hiding' facility), the heading must be inverted to 'Hague, The'.

Other circumstances in which the article should be included are:

- when it is necessary to avoid ambiguity—as in 'The Lodge' (meaning the prim minister's residence in Canberra)
- when the article is an integral part of an official acronym or initialism—such a the government program known as *ANTS* (short for 'A New Tax System') and its associated legislation, *A New Tax System (Goods and Services) Tax Act 1999*

Initial articles and prepositions in foreign names are used to determine alphabetical order if the indexer thinks readers will look for the phrase under that word. For example, an index to a restaurant guide may place 'La Dolce Vita' under *l* as well a under *d*. But geographic names whose 'foreignness' is no longer recognised should be listed under their first letter: the Sydney suburb of La Perouse, for instance, would be included only under *l*.

Family names containing initial articles and prepositions are shown under the most commonly used form:

> De Heer, Rolf
>
> De La Fosse, A
>
> de la Mare, Walter
>
> La Fontaine, Jean de

The index should also list alternative forms, however, if there is any doubt.

Prepositions are added in subheadings to avoid ambiguity:

> books
>
>> by children
>>
>> for children
>>
>> about spending
>>
>> spending on

Whether these initial prepositions in subheadings should be considered in determining the alphabetical arrangement of subheadings is a matter of debate among indexers. In the example just given, the primary arrangement is determine the keyword. However, some indexers consider this practice an unnecessary complication, on the basis that the preposition is sufficiently important in its contribution to the phrase's meaning to determine the arrangement:

books

  about spending

  by children

  for children

  spending on

Capitalisation and style

Although the first word of a heading is given an initial capital in library catalogues and in some indexing packages embedded in word processing and page layout software, this is not recommended for publication-style indexes. The first word should be capitalised only if it is a proper noun or name or if it is treated that way by the author in the text.

Publication-style indexes should also reflect other style aspects of the publication, from unusual spellings to the way in which spans of figures are expressed.

Author's style: A publication-style index should reflect all aspects of an author's style—from capitalisation and spelling to the terminology used.

Indexing language and language control

The ability to chose precise terms that clearly and succinctly describe the concept being indexed is one of the characteristics of a good indexer. The way headings are chosen, however, depends on the type of index.

Language control is essential to ensure indexing consistency in publishing projects such as:

journals, annual reports and other publications of a continuing nature

large files such as encyclopedias, databases or library catalogues

web sites

major works involving a team of indexers.

Indexers engaged in projects of this kind use a thesaurus to determine the form of headings and to create cross-references. The thesaurus can be developed specifically for the project or it can derive from an external authority. It must nevertheless be dynamic and able to accommodate additions and modifications as language changes; otherwise, it will cease to be in a language familiar to readers. Thesauruses of government terminology must also be kept current as policies and programs (and acronyms and initialisms) change.

Publication-style indexes, on the other hand, should reflect the language of the document. Terms used as headings should therefore be in the author's words as far as possible. This approach does not, however, preclude indexers from using additional terms if they consider readers might first look there for information, even if these terms are not mentioned in the publication's content.

In indexes to multi-author works such as reports and conference proceedings where variations in terminology can occur between authors, the indexer can do one of two things:

- Use all the variant terms as index headings and list all references under each—an approach called 'double-indexing' (see page 283).
- Choose one term (generally the one that has been used most often) as the preferred term and make cross-references to it from the others.

Synonymous and homonymous terms

Synonymous terms have the same meaning—for example, 'labour force' and 'workforce'. They are connected in an index by a *see* reference or by double-indexing.

Homonymous terms sound the same and—of more concern in indexing—may be spelt the same way, but they have different meanings. Indexers usually distinguish between these terms by adding a modifying word or phrase after the main part of the heading. Modifiers might be more precise subject terms—for instance, to distinguish between an award given to honour someone and other types of awards such as an industrial award. Or they might consist of biographical or other details to differentiate between people and places with the same name. For example:

> awards (honours)
>
> awards (industrial)

> Blanchard, Mary (1900–1984)
>
> Blanchard, Mary (1978–)

> Wellington, New South Wales
>
> Wellington, New Zealand

Web-based indexes and other indexes intended for overseas distribution should include references to or from different words used in different countries for the same item—from 'trailers' to 'caravans', for example. They should also include references from foreign spellings; even minor variations should be referenced to permit keyword searching.

Honorifics and titles

It is recommended that honorifics and titles—such as 'Senator', 'the Hon.', 'Dr' or 'Sir'—preceding a person's given name or first initial be placed immediately after the family name (on which the alphabetical sequence is based). This positioning makes the entry clearer in cases where postnominals are also attached to the name.

> Thomas, Professor AAJ, AO

not

> Thomas, AAJ, Professor, AO

Shortened forms in names

For ease of reference, names spelt differently but pronounced the same way should be placed together—a practice followed in telephone books. For example, family names beginning with *Mac*, *Mc* and *M'* should all be arranged as if spelt *Mac*:

macadamia nuts

MacArthur, AB

M'Cay, Henry

McFarlane, Hon. Justice Adrian [the honorific is ignored in ordering, so *Adrian* precedes *David*]

MacFarlane, David

machines

MacIntosh, Catherine

milarly, names beginning with *Saint* and *St* should be placed as if both were spelt *int*:

St Lucia

Saint-Saëns, Camille

ther a cross-reference can be made connecting the *Mc*, *M'* and *St* names to *Mac* d *Saint* respectively, or, if there are many such references (as in a telephone ook), an explanatory note can be inserted.

EFINING LOCATION REFERENCES

is good indexing practice to limit the number of location references following a ading: the longer the string of references, the longer the reader will take to find t whether the information is relevant. For example:

Department of Foreign Affairs and Trade, 4, 6

  finance, 128–9, 152

  information technology, 142–4, 188–90

  staff, 9, 42–4, 64–6

preferable to

Department of Foreign Affairs and Trade, 4, 6, 9, 42–4, 64–6, 128–9, 142–4, 152, 188–90

nce the size of indexes in electronic publications is not constrained by printing osts, the indexes can be much more specific. More subheadings and entry levels n be used, with subsidiary levels being progressively revealed as a reader clicks rough the hierarchy:

Department of Foreign Affairs and Trade

  financial management

    auditing

  information technology

    outsourcing

  staff

    numbers

    consultation

    training

Scattered references

Sometimes many references to a main subject occur one after another in the text but are nevertheless not continuous. Although they might be identified separately and treated as subheadings in an electronic index, in a paper-based index it usually saves space and is more user-friendly to show them as if they were a continuous reference:

184–95

rather than

184, 185, 187, 188, 189, 190, 192, 193, 194, 195

Placing the Latin terms *passim* ('in various places') or *et seq.* (*et sequentes*, 'and following') or the English shortened forms *f.* or *ff.* ('following') after the span is not recommended.

Non-textual material

It is sometimes useful to highlight different types of material being indexed, such as images, maps, and sound or video excerpts. References to this material can be given a code ('m' following a reference to a map, for example) or be shown in italics or bold. The system should be explained at the front of a paper-based index along the following lines:

References in *italics* indicate maps; those in **bold** indicate statistical tables.

...

export markets

East Asia, 5, 8, 12, *15–16*, **110–11**

In electronic publications, the more direct method of naming the format as part of a sub-entry is preferred:

export markets

East Asia

maps

statistical tables

Punctuation

In paper-based indexes, commas are used to separate references from each other. It is recommended that commas also be used to separate a heading from the first reference, so that there will be no confusion when figures appear in both heading and reference. For example:

F-111, 12

not

F-111 12

Cybercrime Bill 2001, 1, 19, 20

ot

Cybercrime Bill 2001 1, 19, 20

electronic indexes (where there are no page numbers), punctuation is often
unnecessary if headings are clearly set out.

DOUBLE-INDEXING

double-index is to index the same concept under more than one heading. It
fers more efficient information retrieval because readers will find all location
ferences to a subject at whatever term they use to enter the index. For this
ason, double-indexing should be used instead of cross-referencing in electronic
dexes. It should also be preferred in paper-based indexes when it takes less space
an cross-referencing. For example:

SBS, 80

…

Special Broadcasting Service Corporation, 80

more economical and allows for more efficient information retrieval than

SBS, *see* Special Broadcasting Service Corporation

…

Special Broadcasting Service Corporation, 80

milarly:

gold, 11

…

minerals, 5

gold, 11

more economical and efficient than making a *see also* reference from 'minerals'.
e also referencing should, however, be preferred in more complex entries to save
ace.

ASSESSING PUBLICATION-STYLE INDEXES

dexes should be assessed by sampling. To do this, you can select words used in
e document's headings, as well as important concepts and keywords in the text,
d then see if they are indexed. From the index, follow entries back to the
•ntent and compare how other important concepts on the same page or screen
e indexed. Many other aspects of an index can also be checked by sampling: see
e following checklist.

EVALUATING INDEXES

Comprehensiveness and consistency

- Is the index complete?
- Does it display a consistent level of indexing?

Headings

- Are subject headings used, as well as headings for names and things?
- Are subheadings (and sub-subheadings) used instead of long strings of undifferentiated references?
- Is the arrangement alphabetical or ordered under some other logical and easily understood method and has it been consistently applied?
- Does the language used in the index reflect the language of the text?
- Are commonly used terms included, even if they have not been used by the author?

References

- Is cross-referencing or double-indexing used to link entries and to make access easier?
- Are location references accurate?
- Are *see* references used only from terms without location references?
- Are *see also* references used only from terms with location references?
- Do *see* and *see also* references all lead to terms with location references?
- Are double-indexed references identical?

Presentation

- Is the language succinct and unambiguous?
- Are there any spelling errors?
- Are there any typographical errors?
- Is the layout correct (punctuation, spacing, fonts and capitalisation)?
- Are any unusual indexing features explained at the front of the index?

Electronic access

- Is the index structured in a user-friendly way?
- Do the links work properly?

Further reading and resources

STYLE GUIDES, DICTIONARIES, STANDARDS AND OTHER REFERENCE WORKS

Australian Bureau of Statistics 1997, *Australian standard classification of occupations*, ABS, Canberra.

Australian Broadcasting Corporation 1989, *Thoughts that burn, words that burn*, ABC.

The Australian concise Oxford dictionary 1997, 3rd edn, B. Moore, Oxford University Press, Melbourne.

Australian Council for Educational Research 1996, *National school English literacy survey*, Department of Employment, Education and Training, Canberra.

The Australian Oxford dictionary 1999, Oxford University Press, Melbourne.

The Australian national dictionary: a dictionary of Australianisms on historical principles 1988, ed. WS Ramson, Oxford University Press, Melbourne.

Bryson, B 1997, *Troublesome words*, 2nd edn, Penguin Books, Harmondsworth, England.

Butcher, J 1992, *Copy-editing: the Cambridge handbook for editors, authors and publishers*, 3rd edn, Cambridge University Press, Cambridge.

Carey, GV 1986, *Mind the stop: a brief guide to punctuation with a note on proof correction*, Penguin Books, Harmondsworth, England.

The Chicago manual of style 1993, 14th edn, Chicago University Press, Chicago.

Collins dictionary 1998, 4th edn (Australian), HarperCollins, Sydney.

Collins pocket dictionary of English usage 1992, ed. G Hardie, HarperCollins, Glasgow.

Comprehensive grammar of the English language 1985, Longman, Harlow, UK.

Council of Australian Societies of Editors 2001, *Australian standards for editing practice*, Council of Australian Societies of Editors. Copies available from the various state and territory editing societies.

Corson, D 1985, *The lexical bar*, Pergamon, Oxford.

Crystal, D 1995, *The Cambridge encyclopedia of the English language*, Cambridge University Press, Cambridge.

Department of Employment, Education and Training 1991, *Australia's language: the Australian language and literacy policy*, Australian Government Publishing Service, Canberra.

Department of Family and Community Services 1999, *Better information and communication practices*, Department of Family and Community Services, Canberra.

——1999, *Inclusive consultation: a practical guide to involving people with disabilities*, Office of Disability, Department of Family and Community Services, Canberra.

Department of Social Security 1990, *Naming systems of ethnic groups*, Department of Social Security, n.p.

Eagleson, R 1990, *Writing in plain English*, AGPS Press, Canberra.

The Economist style guide: a concise guide for all your business communications 1996, John Wiley & Sons, New York.

The encyclopaedia of Aboriginal Australia 1994, ed. D Horton, Aboriginal Studies Press (for the Australian Institute of Aboriginal and Torres Strait Islander Studies), Canberra.

Flann, E & Hill, B 1994, *The Australian editing handbook*, AGPS Press, Canberra.

Golvan C 1989, *Words and law: a practical guide for all those whose business is writing*, Penguin, Ringwood, Victoria.

Gowers, Sir Ernest 1987, *The complete plain words*, 3rd edn, rev. S Greenbaum & J Whitcut, Penguin Books, Harmondsworth, England.

Hale, C (ed.) 1996, *Wired style*, HardWired, San Francisco.

Hart's rules for compositors and readers at the University Press, Oxford 1983, 39th edn rev., Oxford University Press, Oxford.

Huddleston, R 1988, *English grammar: an outline*, Cambridge University Press, Cambridge.

Hudson, N 1997, *Modern Australian usage*, 2nd edn, Oxford University Press, Melbourne.

Hughes, B (ed.) 1993, *Working words*, Viking Penguin, Ringwood, Victoria.

Hyslop, R 1991, *Dear you: a guide to forms of address*, AGPS Press, Canberra.

International Organization for Standardization 1992, *General principles concerning quantities, units and symbols (ISO 31:1992)*, International Organization for Standardization, Geneva.

——1995, *Codes for the representation of currencies and funds (ISO 4217:1995)*, International Organization for Standardization, Geneva.

——2000, *Data elements and interchange formats— information interchange—representation of dates and times (ISO 8601:2000)*, International Organization for Standardization, Geneva.

Knight, GN 1979, *Indexing, the art of: a guide to the indexing of books and periodicals*, Allen & Unwin, London.

Lo Bianco, J 1987, *National policy on language*, Australian Government Publishing Service, Canberra.

Longman grammar of spoken and written English 1999, Longman, Harlow, UK.

The Macquarie dictionary 1997, 3rd edn, Macquarie Library Pty Ltd, Macquarie University, Sydney.

The Macquarie world atlas 1994, Macquarie Library Pty Ltd, Macquarie University, Sydney.

McArthur, T (ed.) 1992, *The Oxford companion to the English language*, Oxford University Press, Oxford.

Murray-Smith S 1989, *Right words*, 2nd edn, Viking, Ringwood, Victoria.

The new Fowler's modern English usage 1998, rev. 3rd edn ed. RW Burchfield, Oxford University Press, Oxford.

Orchard AE & Thompson HS 1999, *Flora of Australia*, vol. 1, 2nd edn, ABRS/CSIRO, Australia.

The Oxford dictionary for scientific writers and editors 199? eds A Isaacs, J Daintith & E Martin, Clarendon Press, Oxford.

The Oxford English dictionary 1989, 2nd edn, Clarendon Press, Oxford.

The Oxford guide to the English language 1984, Oxford University Press, Oxford.

Pauwels, A 1991, *Non-discriminatory language*, AGPS Press, Canberra.

Peters, P 1995, *The Cambridge Australian English style guide*, Cambridge University Press, Cambridge.

Poole, ME 1976, *Social class and language utilisation at the tertiary level*, University of Queensland Press, Brisbane.

Purchase, S (ed.) 1997, *Australian writers' dictionary*, Oxford University Press, Melbourne.

Purchase, S (comp.) 1998, *The little book of style*, AusInfo, Canberra.

Roget's thesaurus of English words and phrases 1982, Longman, London.

Scientific style and format: the CBE manual for authors, editors, and publishers 1994, 6th edn, eds Style Manual Committee of the Council of Biology Editors, Cambridge University Press, Cambridge.

Siegal, AM & Connolly, WG 1999, *The New York Times manual of style and usage*, Times Books, New York.

andards Australia 1998, *The International System of nits (SI) and its application (AS ISO 1000:1998)*, andards Australia, Sydney.

andards Australia and Standards New Zealand 1999, *formation and documentation: guidelines for the content, ganization and presentation of indexes (AS/NZS 9:1999)*, Standards Australia (Sydney) and Standards ew Zealand (Wellington).

ern, G, Bolitho, R & Lutton, R 1993, *The guide to ustralian usage and punctuation*, Collins Dove, North ackburn, Victoria.

runk, W Jr & White, EB 2000, *The elements of style*, h edn, Allyn & Bacon, Needham Heights, Mass.

yle Council proceedings 1986, *Style in Australia*, . PH Peters, Dictionary Research Centre, Macquarie niversity, Sydney.

—1987–8, *Frontiers of style*, ed. PH Peters 1990, ctionary Research Centre, Macquarie University, dney.

—1990–1, *Australian style into the nineties*, . PH Peters 1992, Dictionary Research Centre, acquarie University, Sydney.

—1992, *Style on the move*, ed. PH Peters 1993, ctionary Research Centre, Macquarie University, dney.

—1994, *The national language*, ed. PH Peters 1994, ctionary Research Centre, Macquarie University, dney.

—1995, *Australian style in a pluralist Australia*, . PH Peters 1995, Dictionary Research Centre, acquarie University, Sydney.

—1996, 1997 and 1998, *Style in context—language at ge*, ed. PH Peters 2000, Dictionary Research Centre, acquarie University, Sydney.

e Times atlas of the world 1992, Times Books, London.

dd, L 1995, *A guide to punctuation*, Cassell, London.

alsh, B 1989, *Communicating in writing*, 2nd edn, GPS Press, Canberra.

Walton DW & Dyne GR (eds) 1987, *Fauna of Australia*, vol. 1A, Australian Government Publishing Service, Canberra.

Webster's third new international dictionary 1961, 3rd edn, Merriam-Webster, Springfield, Mass.

Wellisch, HH 1991, *Indexing from A to Z*, HW Wilson Company, Bronx, New York.

Wickert, R & Kevin, M 1995, *No single measure: a survey of Australian adult literacy*, Commonwealth Department of Employment, Education and Training, Canberra.

WEB SITES

Australian Government Information Management Office 2000, *Guidelines for Commonwealth information published in electronic formats, 1:1*, <http://www.agimo.gov.au>.

——2005, *Australian Government Web Guide*, <http://www.agimo.gov.au>

Committee for Geographic Names in Australasia 2005, *Gazetteer of Australia 2005 release*, available through Geoscience Australia, <http://www.ga.gov.au>.

FedInfo, the web site for Australian Government employees, http://www.fedinfo.gov.au

Getty Research Institute, *Getty thesaurus of geographic names*, <http://www.getty.edu/research>.

International System of Units 1998, 7th edn, and *Supplement 2000: addenda and corrigenda to the 7th edition*, available from Bureau International des Poids et Mesures (BIPM), <http://www.bipm.fr>.

IP Australia, for database of trade names, <http://www.ipaustralia.gov.au>.

Modern Language Association 1998, *MLA style: documenting sources from the World Wide Web*, <http://www.mla.org>.

Peck, F 1996, *Hypergrammar*, University of Ottawa, <http://aix1.uottawa.ca>.

PART 3

Designing and illustrating

Good design is integral to effective communication.

But first you must attract potential readers. And they might be hard to attract, because there are so many messages and media competing for their attention. They might also lack the motivation to read what you have to say; most people approach work-related and leisure reading differently, for example. Then there may be times when the information you want to impart is not what your readers most want to know.

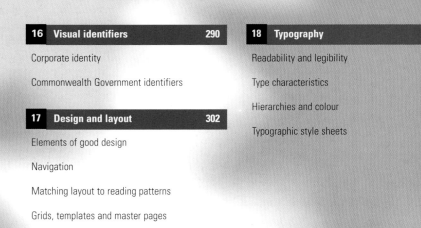

DESIGNING AND ILLUSTRATIN

16 Visual identifiers — 290

Corporate identity

Commonwealth Government identifiers

17 Design and layout — 302

Elements of good design

Navigation

Matching layout to reading patterns

Grids, templates and master pages

18 Typography — 32

Readability and legibility

Type characteristics

Hierarchies and colour

Typographic style sheets

In all these situations, good design will help to:

- attract attention to the publication and distinguish it from competing publications

- entice readers to find out more

- retain readers' attention by making their reading experience more interesting and enjoyable

- deliver the information in a memorable way.

Good design also communicates the professionalism of an organisation, enhancing its image in the marketplace.

Once the intended readership is interested in the publication and motivated to continue reading, good design will clarify the information, improving readability and aiding comprehension. The ability to create that fine balance between text, layout and illustrative imagery is the skill the publication designer brings to both printed and on-screen documents.

ESIGNING AND ILLUSTRATING

Tables	346

ayout and placement

ypography of tables

Forms	359

orms research

sability and testing

21 Illustrating	374

Selecting imagery

Techniques and reproduction

Colour systems

Photographs

Graphs, charts, diagrams and maps

Moving images and sound

Further reading and resources

Some recommended reference works and web sites, and suggested sources for images and sound   404

Chapter *16*

Visual identifiers

CORPORATE IDENTITY	**291**
Logos, symbols and emblems	291
Corporate typography	292
Organisational sub-entities	292
Corporate colours	292
A corporate identity manual	293
Changing an identity	293
COMMONWEALTH IDENTIFIERS	**293**
The Commonwealth Coat of Arms	293
The Australian national flag	298
The Australian Aboriginal flag	299
The Torres Strait Islander flag	300
Royal identifiers	300
The Australian national and heraldic colours	300
Commonwealth agency identification	301
NATIONAL, STATE AND TERRITORY EMBLEMS	**301**

n organisation asserts its uniqueness by systematically using well-
hosen identifiers such as logos, symbols and emblems, supported by
omplementary typefaces, colour palettes and styling, and careful
production. In this way an organisation can communicate its 'brand'
most subliminally.

he Commonwealth of Australia uses a number of identifiers to establish its
nage, both within Australia and abroad. Consistent application of these
entifiers enhances the image of the nation and the government.

CORPORATE IDENTITY

n organisation's image is an amalgam of the impressions gained through the
nge of customer and staff encounters with the organisation. From the way
lephones are answered to the decoration of the front office, from the 'Positions
cant' advertisement to the interview technique, from the style of its documents
the way its staff treat colleagues and customers—an organisation has an image,
hether it manages it or not.

orporate identity is the visual manifestation of an organisation's corporate image.
includes corporate identifiers and colours, stationery and forms, documents,
vertising, signage and web sites.

gos, symbols and emblems

he main identifier—which might be a logo, a symbol or an emblem, or even a
mbination of these—becomes the focus of an organisation's corporate identity.
gos incorporate letterforms with the name in full or in a shortened form.
mbols are mostly non-representational and abstract. Emblems are usually
presentational or pictorial.

his main identifier often sits within a geometrically constructed shape: a square,
ctangle, circle, oval, triangle or other hard-edged shape. Such a shape usually
akes alignment within layouts easier and simplifies the identifier's use with other
nblems, symbols or logos.

n identifier should make a simple statement rather than try to represent all areas
an organisation's endeavour. It can be unwise to be too specific with symbols
d emblems, because an organisation might move into different areas over time.

CORPORATE IDENTITY

Stationery

- Letterheads and continuation sheets
- Memos and minute papers
- Business cards
- Envelopes and labels
- Invoices, purchase orders and cheques
- Compliments slips
- Name tags
- Certificates and forms

Publications

- Annual reports
- Manuals and reports
- Policy and discussion papers
- Media releases
- Tender documentation
- Newsletters and journals
- Web sites and intranets
- CD-ROMs, cassettes, videos and DVDs
- Brochures and information kits

Advertising

- Classified and print advertising
- Posters and flyers
- Internet, radio, television and film advertising

Australia Post logo

Emblem

Symbol with logo

The Australian Taxation Office's tag line
'Taxes—Building a better Australia'

Well-managed use of corporate colour: Australia Post's red was established through red mailboxes, moved across into its vehicle livery, and on into its corporate identity.

If the identifier is broader, it will not have to be changed each time the organisation alters course. It has been said that it takes fifteen years for an identifier to stand alone—to be recognised widely without assistance from typography.

Corporate typography

Corporate typefaces

The font selected for the name of an organisation is regarded as the corporate typeface. This typeface is often used for naming purposes only, in order to maintain its uniqueness among the organisation's myriad font requirements. Sometimes a subtle typographic detail—such as a ligature or swash (see page 326)—is incorporated in the corporate typeface to lend some individuality.

A second type family is then chosen as a workhorse. It becomes the text face for the organisation's newsletters, internal and external reports, advertisements, stationery and correspondence.

This standardisation imparts a degree of corporate consistency across a large organisation, even if each operational unit has its own identifier.

Tag lines

Sometimes a tag line, or 'strap line', is added to a corporate identifier. It can be a motto or a positioning statement that further explains an organisation's purpose.

Typographically, the tag line will complement the identifier; it is usually in either a different typeface or a variant of the corporate typeface. This typographic separation allows the wording of tag lines to be altered to reflect changes in the organisation's direction without affecting the visual identity.

Organisational sub-entities

Large organisations often distinguish their sub-entities (such as divisions or other operational units) with separate identifiers. A level of awareness of the relationship with the parent body can nevertheless be maintained, if desired, by using the same corporate colour palette and variants of the corporate typeface.

Corporate colours

Colour can distinguish an organisation from its competitors. Colours also have subliminal meanings that can make a statement about an organisation's strength attitude. A well-managed corporate colour or colour palette can become almost a important in terms of speed of recognition as the corporate identifier itself.

Each entity within an organisation might be given a different colour for coding purposes. Each colour then becomes a part of the corporate colour palette for the parent organisation.

A corporate colour palette might also be used in a publication program to identif different types of documents. Policy statements, research reports and general information could add three colours to the palette and help staff and regular readers to recognise the type of document. In addition, documents can be colour-coded to indicate their level of urgency, stage of production, or specific audience

corporate identity manual

corporate identity manual defines the level of professional presentation an ganisation expects to achieve on a daily basis. To maintain consistency and courage considered use of the organisation's corporate identifiers through time, e manual sets out the rules governing application of the identifiers to particular ems. It contains specifications for colours and paper stocks, as well as templates d style sheets for each type of corporate document. All artwork for the corporate entifiers and the corporate fonts should also be included in digital form.

ne manual should be available to all in the organisation, with each unit or team ving direct access to a copy of it. A pamphlet circulated to staff explaining the ain standards and details of the corporate identity can be useful in extending derstanding of what is involved. The manual should also be provided to outside ppliers as needed: for example, to graphic designers who may be applying the entity to commissioned projects.

Publication options: A corporate identity manual does not have to be formally published to be effective. It can be a collection of all the corporate identity materials in a ring binder with pockets for disks and samples. Or it might be available only as an electronic document on the organisation's intranet.

anging an identity

nanging an identity may be necessary if important changes to an organisation's le need to be communicated. Such a change must be carefully considered, cause familiarity and an intuitive understanding of the identity may be building nong the organisation's various audiences. Even a name change does not have to ean the end of the old identity; the new name might simply be accommodated using the existing corporate typeface. A corporate identity is an investment at should not be lightly discarded.

metimes staff will suggest changing the corporate identity. They have a far eater awareness of their organisation's corporate identity than external audiences d so might tire of seeing the same colours and designs each day. But identity ange is an extreme measure if it only addresses a staff motivation problem thout taking account of the organisation's other 'publics'—its suppliers, stomers and the wider community.

OMMONWEALTH IDENTIFIERS

ne primary identifier of the Commonwealth as the source of a publication is the mmonwealth Coat of Arms. This identifier is not in the public domain, and so ay only be used officially or with permission. Other national symbols such as the tional flag and the national colours are in the public domain.

her forms of identification are used for different reasons: royal insignia for regal d vice-regal identification; corporate identifiers for particular operational groups thin the Commonwealth; and even stereotypical, non-official images that dily identify Australia in foreign marketplaces.

e Commonwealth Coat of Arms

story and description

ne first official Commonwealth Coat of Arms was granted to the Commonwealth Australia in 1908. However, by Royal Warrant dated 19 September 1912, King

The crest

Authorisation: The Awards and National Symbols Branch, Department of the Prime Minister and Cabinet, is responsible for ensuring that national symbols are protected from debasement, are given due respect and dignity, and are used in accordance with approved procedures and protocol. Inquiries about using national symbols should be directed to that office.

➤ See also p. 298 for information about using the arms with, or as part of, the identifiers of Commonwealth agencies.

George V granted a new design, which is the current Commonwealth Coat of Arms.

The six quarters in the shield represent the badges of the six states as they were in 1912. New South Wales is represented by a cross containing four eight-pointed stars and a lion; Victoria by the constellation of the Southern Cross and a crown; Queensland by a Maltese cross surmounted by a crown; South Australia by a piping shrike (or white-backed magpie); Western Australia by a black swan; and Tasmania by a lion. The star in the crest has seven points, one for each of the states and the seventh representing the Australian territories. It is known as the 'Commonwealth Star' or the 'Federation Star'.

The arms are sometimes incorrectly referred to as the 'crest'. In the language of heraldry, a crest is 'a device above the shield and helmet of a coat of arms'. In the Commonwealth Coat of Arms, the crest is the wreath and the seven-pointed Commonwealth Star.

Using the Commonwealth Coat of Arms

The Commonwealth Coat of Arms is used to identify Commonwealth authority and property. Use of the arms by private citizens or organisations is rarely permitted, since it is contrary to the essential meaning of the arms, may constitute a debasement of the arms, and may give rise to indiscriminate use. The Commonwealth Coat of Arms should never be used where it could wrongly imply a formal guarantee, sponsorship or endorsement by the Commonwealth.

The arms may be used by the following Commonwealth entities:

- the parliament and its departments
- portfolio departments
- statutory and non-statutory authorities
- courts and tribunals.

The arms may not be used by Commonwealth-owned or Commonwealth-controlled trading authorities for the purpose of competing in the marketplace.

Reproducing the Commonwealth Coat of Arms

Placement

The Commonwealth Coat of Arms should have no wording or illustration above or preceding it, but it need not be centred. It should be placed so that other material does not detract from its dignity.

Generally, the Commonwealth Coat of Arms should appear only once in a publication. For paperbacks, it should be displayed on the cover rather than on the title page; for hardcover books, it may appear on the case and dust jacket as well as on the title page. For web sites, it should appear on the home page.

Colour

The arms may be reproduced either in full colour or in a single colour. Full-colour reproductions must match as closely as possible the original colours in the 1912 loured version; different colours are not permitted. Computer reproduction must capable of at least 256 colours.

single-colour reproduction, it is recommended that the Commonwealth Coat of ·ms be reproduced in dark colours befitting its dignity. The colours considered ost appropriate are black, dark red, dark blue and dark green against a light ckground. When using reverse versions, it is recommended that the arms appear white, silver or gold against a dark background.

ne heraldically correct, official versions of the arms have been approved for ₁gle-colour reproduction (see pages 296–7). They may be used as captioned. iefly, the conventional versions are appropriate in formal printing, while the ⁻lised versions have much wider application and are more suitable for printing in ₁all sizes, for use in signage and for viewing on screen.

·ing

ₙe Commonwealth Coat of Arms should always be depicted in its correct ɔportions. It is not to be distorted or redrawn. For the stylised versions, the nimum size is 20 millimetres wide, measured by the length of the rest for the ₁u and kangaroo. The conventional and colour versions benefit from larger ɔroduction.

ₙe full-colour version is available in a range of sizes for screen-based publishing. ₙe minimum size is 100 pixels wide.

ₑe of the arms with other emblems

hen documents are co-authored with state or territory governments, the author sponsoring body can decide whether any arms will appear at all. When the arms appear together, visual equality between them should be maintained. The ɔmmonwealth Coat of Arms should appear on the left, with the state arms on ₑ right in the order shown in the Royal Warrant of 1912: New South Wales, ₓtoria, Queensland, South Australia, Western Australia, Tasmania. Territory ₙs then follow: the Northern Territory and the Australian Capital Territory ith the latter using the arms of the City of Canberra).

hen the Commonwealth Coat of Arms appears with the arms of other nations, ₓual equality between the arms should be maintained. The Commonwealth Coat ·Arms should be given positional precedence on the left; the arms of other ₓtions should appear to the right, in alphabetical order of their names in English.

hen used with an image of the flag, the Commonwealth Coat of Arms should be ₓually superior to the flag, being placed above or to the left of it. When the arms ₑ placed above the flag, the rest for the emu and the kangaroo (stylised versions ₒ. 2 or no. 2R) should be the same width as the flag. The word *Australia* and the ₐnches of wattle may be deleted and an appropriate space inserted.

➤ The colours of the Commonwealth Coat of Arms are shown in the colour section.

THE COMMONWEALTH COAT OF ARMS

Approved versions for single-colour reproduction

Digitised versions of the nine single-colour versions are available at various resolutions for different reproduction methods; contact the Awards and National Symbols Branch, Department of the Prime Minister and Cabinet.

Conventional version no. 1 (outline)
This design is suitable for printing on smooth-surfaced papers. On screen or when reversed, foil-stamped or embossed, it should not be used in sizes less than 50 millimetres wide.

Conventional version no. 2 (shaded)
This design may be used for printed work but is not suitable for reversing, foil-stamping, embossing or on-screen reproduction.

Conventional version no. 3 (solid)
This design is appropriate when a solid conventional design is required with more embellishment than appears in version no. 3A.

Conventional version no. 3A (solid)
This is the standard design for documents published in the Parliamentary Papers Series. It should not be used in sizes less than 20 millimetres wide. It is recommended for general use and is suitable for all processes and for reversing.

Stylised version no. 1 (outline)

This stylised version is for general use but should not be used in sizes less than 20 millimetres wide; nor should it be used on screen or for foil-stamping, embossing or reversing.

Stylised version no. 2 (solid)

This version is recommended for general use but should not be used in sizes less than 20 millimetres wide. It is suitable for all processes except reversing. For reversing, stylised version no. 2R should be used.

Stylised version no. 2R

This design is a thickened version of stylised version no. 2. It is suitable for reversing.

Stylised version no. 3 (solid shield, open supporters)

This version is recommended for general use but should not be used in sizes less than 20 millimetres wide. It is suitable for all processes except reversing. For reversing, stylised version no. 3R should be used.

Stylised version no. 3R

This design is a thickened version of stylised version no. 3. It is suitable for reversing.

The arms used above the flag

Two methods of using the arms to the left of the flag

Incorporation of the arms: Unless use of the Commonwealth Coat of Arms is specified in legislation, Commonwealth agencies wishing to use the arms as part of an identifier should seek advice from the Department of the Prime Minister and Cabinet.

Use of the Commonwealth arms with identifiers of Commonwealth agencies is encouraged, in order to demonstrate the link between the identifier representing the agency and the arms representing the Commonwealth. The arms should always be placed above or to the left of the agency's identifier, to reflect the relative significance of each.

If, however, the Commonwealth Coat of Arms is already incorporated in an agency's emblem or other identifier, the arms should *not* be shown separately. In these situations, the width of the arms, within the identifier, must never be less than 20 millimetres. This needs to be particularly remembered if, for reproduction purposes, a reduction in the identifier's size is being contemplated.

When the Commonwealth arms and the national flag appear together, agency identifiers are not permitted.

The Australian national flag

History and description

The design of Australia's national flag is the result of a competition announced to coincide with Federation in 1901. The selected flag was flown later in 1901 but was not formally gazetted as the 'Commonwealth blue ensign' until 1903. It was officially declared the Australian national flag in the Commonwealth's *Flags Act 1953*.

The national flag is made up of two squares beside each other. The top half of the left square shows the Union Jack of the United Kingdom. The right square contains a representation of the Southern Cross, or Crux Australis; each of its four outer stars has seven points and the small inner star has only five points. The original flag's six-pointed star beneath the Union Jack was changed in 1908 to the seven-pointed Commonwealth Star, to match the star on the crest of the original Commonwealth Coat of Arms.

Reproducing the national flag

The national flag should always be used in a dignified manner and reproduced accurately. All its symbolic parts should be clearly identifiable, even when it is depicted as being flown. It should not be defaced by cropping, by superimposing

The Australian flag's construction template

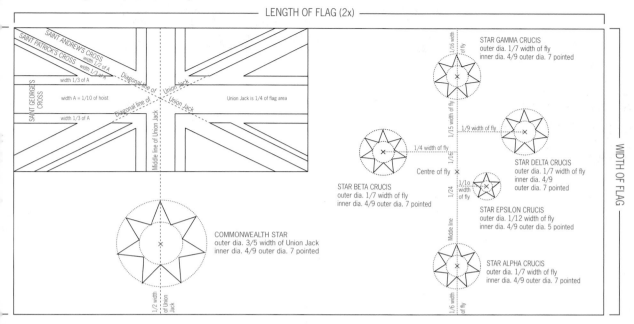

xt or illustrations onto it, or by covering it with other objects. When it is used
1 Commonwealth documents, it should be no less than 20 millimetres wide.

. printing, the colours of the Australian flag are Pantone® 185 (red) and
1ntone® 280 (blue). In process colours, they are specified as 100M.100Y (red)
1d 100C.80M (blue). In hexadecimal colour for on-screen use, FF0000 (red) and
)008B (dark blue) are recommended. In Web 216 colour description, these are
-0000 (red) and 000099 (dark blue).

➤ For a description of the different colour systems referred to here, see pp. 387–90.

he flag may be reproduced in a single colour—provided that colour is either
ack or one of the flag's two colours. However, flag blue is preferred for single-
)lour reproduction.

here is no need to obtain permission to reproduce images of the national flag,
'en for commercial use.

➤ The colour section shows a coloured reproduction of the national flag.

he Australian Aboriginal flag

istory and description

he Australian Aboriginal flag was first flown in 1971 on National Aborigines'
ay. It was proclaimed an official flag of Australia with effect from 14 July 1995.
s design is assigned by copyright to Mr Harold Thomas of the Northern Territory.
he flag may be reproduced with the permission of Mr Thomas, in accordance
ith the provisions of the Commonwealth's *Copyright Act 1968*.

he flag is divided horizontally into even halves, black at the top and red at the
)ttom, and there is a yellow circle in the centre. The black symbolises the
boriginal people; the red represents the earth and the colour of ochre used in

Copyright owner of the Australian Aboriginal flag

Mr Harold Thomas
PO Box 41807
Casuarina NT 0810

Aboriginal ceremonies; the yellow circle represents the sun, the constant renewer of life.

Reproducing the Australian Aboriginal flag

In printing, the recommended colours for the Australian Aboriginal flag are Pantone® 1795 (red), Pantone® 123 (yellow) and black. For printing in process colours, 100M.100Y.30K (red), 100Y (yellow) and 100M.100K (black) are recommended. In hexadecimal and Web 216 colour description, CC0000 (red), FFFF00 (yellow) and 000000 (black) are recommended.

➤ The Australian Aboriginal flag is illustrated in the colour section.

The Torres Strait Islander flag

History and description

The Torres Strait Islander flag was adopted in 1992 during the Torres Strait Islander Cultural Festival. It was proclaimed an official flag of Australia with effect from 14 July 1995. The design was inspired by the late Bernard Namok of Thursday Island and stands for the unity and identity of all Torres Strait Islanders.

The flag has three even-sized horizontal panels, the top and bottom ones being green and the middle one blue. Thin black lines divide the panels. In the centre the blue panel is a representation of a *dhari*, or dancer's headdress, in white; it surrounds a white, five-pointed star. The black symbolises the people, the green represents the land, and the blue the sea. The dhari is a symbol for all Torres Strait Islanders. The star, which is an important symbol for a seafaring people, also represents the five island groups in Torres Strait. White represents peace.

This flag is in the public domain, so permission is not required to reproduce images of it.

Reproducing the Torres Strait Islander flag

For printing, the recommended colours for the Torres Strait Islander flag are Pantone® 3288 (green), Pantone® 301 (blue), and black. For printing in process colours, 100C.80Y.40K (green), 100C.70M (blue) and 100C.100K (black) are recommended. In hexadecimal and Web 216 colour description, 009966 (green), 000099 (blue), 000000 (black) and FFFFFF (white) are recommended.

➤ See the colour section for an illustration of the Torres Strait Islander flag.

Royal identifiers

The regal and vice-regal identifiers in use in Australia include royal arms, seals, crowns and flags. They are used by:

- the Queen in the United Kingdom
- the Queen when visiting Australia
- representatives of the Queen in Australia (the Governor-General and each of the state governors).

Permission: To apply for permission to use royal identifiers and for information about the protocols for their use, contact the Official Secretary to the Governor-General, Government House, Canberra.

The Australian national and heraldic colours

Green and gold

The Governor-General proclaimed Australia's national colours as green and gold in the *Commonwealth of Australia Gazette*, no. S142, of 19 April 1984.

When Commonwealth agencies adopt green and gold, they should use Pantone®
116 (yellow) and Pantone® 348 (green), as gazetted. In process colour, 100Y
(yellow) and 100C.100Y (green) are recommended. In hexadecimal colour for on-
screen use, FFFF00 (yellow) and 006400 (dark green) are recommended; in Web
216 colour description, these are FFFF00 (yellow) and 006600 (dark green).

The national colours may be reproduced without permission.

Blue and gold

Australia's heraldic colours are 'azure' and 'or' (blue and gold), as described for the
wreath below the Commonwealth Star in the Royal Warrant of 1912. The blue is
a deep blue similar to the blue of the national flag; the gold (actually drawn in
yellow) represents the metal. An example of the use of these heraldic colours is
found in the ribbon used for the Order of Australia and several other Australian
honours.

Since the proclamation of green and gold as Australia's national colours, the
heraldic colours have been superseded for most official uses.

➤ See the colour section for examples of the national colours.

Commonwealth agency identification

Each Commonwealth agency is responsible for the design of its identifier, which
must clearly reflect the agency's status as an entity of the Commonwealth
government. Because the Commonwealth Coat of Arms is the primary identifier
of a Commonwealth agency, the agency's own logo is often typographic and
produced with variants that work both with and without the arms as an element.

NATIONAL, STATE AND TERRITORY EMBLEMS

Table 16.1 shows the floral, animal and bird emblems of Australia and its various
states and territories.

Non-official identifiers: A number of images readily identify Australia internationally. The three most potent have been found to be the kangaroo, Uluru and the Sydney Opera House. The map of Australia is also well recognised, as are images of the Great Barrier Reef, Sydney Harbour Bridge and traditional Aboriginal art. So too are the animals, birds and plants featured in the list of emblems, as well as the lyrebird, various parrots and cockatoos, the frill-necked lizard and the shark.

Table 16.1 National, state and territory emblems

	Floral emblem	Animal emblem	Bird emblem
Australia[1]	Golden wattle	Kangaroo[2]	Emu[2]
New South Wales[1]	Waratah	Platypus	Laughing kookaburra
Victoria	Common pink heath	Leadbeater's possum	Helmeted honeyeater
Western Australia[1]	Red and green kangaroo paw	Numbat	Black swan
Queensland	Cooktown orchid	Koala	Brolga
South Australia[1]	Sturt's desert pea	Hairy-nosed wombat	Piping shrike[2]
Tasmania	Tasmanian blue gum	Thylacine[2]	—
Northern Territory	Sturt's desert rose	Red kangaroo	Wedge-tailed eagle
Australian Capital Territory	Royal bluebell	—	Gang-gang cockatoo

No emblem.

Other official emblems are the opal, proclaimed Australia's national gemstone in 1993; the eastern blue groper, proclaimed the fish emblem of New South Wales in 1998; the gogo fish, proclaimed Western Australia's fossil emblem in 1995; and the leafy sea-dragon, proclaimed South Australia's fish emblem in 2000.

Not officially proclaimed.

Chapter **17** # Design and layout

GOOD DESIGN	**303**
Attraction	303
Separation	304
Appropriate communication	304
Format choice	304
COVERS	**304**
NAVIGATION	**305**
Aids for context and movement	305
Where am I?	306
Where do I go next?	307
Types of site navigation systems	307
About navigation devices	308
LAYOUT	**307**
Eye movement	310
How a print layout is read	310
How a screen layout is read	311
Simplicity	312
GRIDS, TEMPLATES AND MASTER PAGES	**312**
Grids in print	312
Grids on screen	313
About design dynamics	314
Creating a grid	316
BALANCE	**318**
Weight distribution	318
Grouping and proximity	318
Centred layouts	319
White space	319
Foreground–background interaction	320

ood design attracts attention, presents information in a manner
ited to the content and the intended readers, and helps to maintain
aders' interest. Understanding reading patterns and the physiological
sponses associated with reading enables a designer to predict how
formation is likely to be gathered from a publication, and to design
e presentation and layout accordingly. Aesthetic pleasure in the
terplay of images and text is part of the attraction, but it is not the
ly reason for seeking good design.

'hen deciding how to lay out a document, designers determine which visual
ements are cues and signposts, which are content, and which could be attractors.
en they determine for each of these elements the size and position that will best
nvey the messages the author wants to send.

OOD DESIGN

traction

lours, images and faces all attract attention quickly. Content attracts too. So, if
e content of a publication can be conveyed succinctly in a title or text block,
xt can also attract. It just has to be the 'right' text, dressed in the 'right' way.

teresting subject matter alone is often not enough. It can be made more
pealing by graphic techniques such as:

 presenting an odd juxtaposition of two or more objects, colours or images
 providing an unusual view or an odd detail
 enlarging something that is normally small
 reducing something that is normally large.

mething unexpected, secret or previously undiscovered attracts. Something
triguing or incomplete attracts. Even something 'unattractive' can attract!

mmunication—particularly at the attraction level—should also be fast, because
tential readers are scanning their visual environment for material of interest.
ey are sifting and making choices without necessarily being aware of how
ickly they make their selections. The need for speed sometimes translates into a
ll for visual simplicity, brevity and clarity.

esign need not be complex to be attractive.

Separation

If the combination of attractors and information is to break through readers' scanning processes, visual differentiation must be built in. A design must be interesting enough to catch and keep readers' attention despite the distraction of competing communications. This is called *separation*—where a design separates itself from competition.

Differentiation is usually achieved by choosing the opposite of the visual language used in similar material. If the reports of many organisations feature a navy blue background, for example, consider using silver. If comparable web sites are full colour, use a limited palette and monochrome pictures. If photographs are a common element, use an illustrative or typographic approach.

Differentiation helps create separation, which in turn helps readers locate and then choose a publication.

Appropriate communication

Design styles need to suit both the publishing organisation and its audience. To gain an understanding of the visual awareness of a particular audience, imagine a group of representative audience members. What types of books and magazines are they likely to read, what films and television programs might they watch, and what sites might they surf on the net? Think of the information, media and materials they would necessarily encounter in their working lives and what they would choose for recreation. Then think about where a potential publication will fit within this visual context.

➤ See Chapter 16 'Visual identifiers' for a discussion of corporate image.

Format choice

A publication's size and shape are determined by its readers' actual or anticipated needs, by production methods, and by marketing (and sometimes distribution) considerations. Print formats usually derive from paper sizes and can also be influenced by machine sizes and established methods of manufacture. Screen formats derive from browser windows and the monitor configuration that viewers are most likely to have.

COVERS

Much of the design of covers, splash screens and home pages is simply aimed at attracting attention. A cover is not the place for telling the full story: it is the place for establishing interest in the publication and its relevance to the reader. A cover can:

- create expectations about the publication's content
- use visual shorthand to indicate the genre or style of the document
- create impressions of the source—the author or the publisher, or both
- encourage potential readers to buy or to continue perusing the publication.

Often a cover will use colour, typography, imagery and minimal text to identify the publication and its source. In addition to showing the title, subtitle and the name of the author or sponsoring organisation, a cover has a marketing objective. To

elp establish the document's credibility, a brief statement about the content or
ance of the publication might therefore be included, and possibly a brief
ography of the author or something about the authoring body.

nagery that illustrates the subject matter is sometimes used for a cover. However,
over imagery is usually treated in a more impressionistic way: to attract while
lowing readers to interpret the context, and to hint at the publication's coverage
ther than defining it. Attitude can also be reflected in design through typo-
aphic, colour and styling choices.

ok covers are often reproduced in printed catalogues and on the Internet at very
all sizes. If a title cannot be read in these small reproductions, an opportunity to
ert readers to the publication's existence is lost. It is also likely to be overlooked
a 'visually busy' bookshop—although this is not such a concern for web sites,
ice they are viewed at close range.

may be necessary to include other information on covers for various reasons (for
ample, the logos of contributing organisations, sponsors or co-producers, as well
contact details). In printed publications, this information is often relegated to
ne back cover; for on-screen documents it might be placed at the bottom of a
ome page, where it is accessible by scrolling. The back covers of books also need
ir codes for pricing and in-store identification.

AVIGATION

ids for context and movement

o produce a suitable design for a publication, it is necessary to have a good grasp
the underlying structure and hierarchy of the information to be presented and of
ow readers might search for and progress through this information. For electronic
ocuments, readers rely on the navigation system, assisted by the document's
raphical user interface', to find the information they are interested in and to
ove about within the document.

ooks have familiar 'interfaces' (covers, preliminary pages, chapters, endmatter,
ctures and captions) and equally familiar 'navigation systems' (contents lists,
napter numbers and page numbers), 'hyperlinks' (cross-references and footnotes)
d search facilities (indexes). Among the electronic interfaces are splash screens,
ome pages, content pages and subsites. Navigation systems can consist of frames,
enus, hyperlinks, site maps and clickable image maps, and search engines provide
dexing functions.

he graphical user interface of a screen-based document usually incorporates a
ombination of visual shorthand (banners, buttons and icons) and consistent
acement and ordering of elements that need to be found easily.

he most effective structures and navigation paths for a particular document
ten become apparent after the likely needs of the audience are considered.
or example, readers who are interested in particular topics but are not sure how
ese might be labelled—or whether, in fact, the publication contains this
formation—will be helped by contextual access tools such as contents lists,

Commonwealth publications:
These should identify their source on
the cover, title page or home page.
Chapter 16 provides details about
Commonwealth identifiers.

Graphical user interface: Often
abbreviated to *GUI*, or simply *the
interface*, this term refers to the
window layout and the graphical display
tools, such as icons, menus and
buttons, that enable users to
manipulate material on screen.

indexes, site maps and other representations of content structure. Most readers also prefer on-screen material that has been structured to make scanning and browsing easier. Like good design, effective navigation systems are not really noticed by readers. However, if readers encounter navigation problems (usually because the navigation structure does not meet their expectations), they often abandon their search.

➤ Chapter 3 deals with ways of structuring documents for on-screen use. Chapter 24 describes different types of access schemes for on-screen searching.

Where am I?

On-screen readers rely on a document's navigation system to orient themselves. On every page there should be some sort of identifier—perhaps a logo in the top left-hand corner—that identifies the site and leads directly to the site's home page. Navigation tools that show the location of the page visible on screen in terms of its place within the overall document also keep readers aware of the wider context of the information they are viewing.

These features, called *persistent navigation*, are the equivalent of running headers or footers and page numbering in a printed publication. (In print, running headers or footers usually feature the book title or part title on the left-hand page and the chapter title on the right.)

On-screen navigation systems

Navigation tools include browser software tools and site-specific tools such as buttons, menus and hyperlinks.

As a site develops, clickable 'breadcrumb' bars can be used on each page to show where the current page fits in relation to the site.

Where do I go next?

Readers develop expectations about the content of an on-screen publication. If terminology suited to them is provided in the menu structures, it will help them understand the document's structure and range of topics. They will then have a fairly good idea of where to go next, including to other, currently invisible, places.

Readers may decide where to go next by:

- using the browser's navigation bar to return to a previously viewed page
- noting where they have already been (through the changed colour of links that indicate pages already visited) so that they can avoid unnecessary repetition
- using other navigation devices to move forward and backward through sequential pages or to jump to another subject location in the text, another menu or an external site.

Types of site navigation systems

Obviously, not all readers will look for the same information; nor will they all use the same searching technique. Documents prepared for on-screen delivery therefore often need a mixture of navigation systems to accommodate a variety of approaches.

Site navigation systems can take one of three forms:

- global systems—which are consistent and uniform in display and function throughout a site (as in navigation bars)
- local systems—which perform specific navigational tasks at the document or subsite level (such as a publication-style index)
- ad hoc systems—which use embedded links (such as hypertext) or associated text (such as *see also* links).

An on-screen document can incorporate navigation features of a printed counterpart—for example, a contents list that is then hyperlinked for on-screen use. However, simply relocating a paper-based navigation system to an on-screen document is unlikely to produce optimum results for on-screen users. It is usually best to amend the document's structure and generate a new navigation system to suit the medium.

LAYOUT

Layout is the placement of elements in a given space or format. The way the elements are arranged affects the order in which they are read and how readers recognise and place the information in context.

Books, newsletters, brochures and flyers place elements in traditionally prescribed positions that aid comprehension of the information and its structure and logical flow. On-screen documents use element placement for the same purpose. (Placement of the various components of printed and on-screen publications is discussed in Chapter 13.)

THE ELEMENTS OF A LAYOUT

Illustrative material

- Images
- Diagrams and charts
- Tables
- Moving images and sound

Identifiers

- Logos, emblems and symbols
- Icons
- Other navigation devices

Textual material

- Headings and labels
- Body text
- Captions
- Links

Navigation devices

Various devices are available to help readers find their way around screen-based publications. They should be chosen to complement the site and the publication.

Frames

Frames divide a web page window into two or more independently scrollable units called *panes*. Often the navigation elements (such as navigation bars and menus) are held in thin vertical or horizontal panes around the sides of the window, with the content of the document being displayed in the larger pane.

Frames can help readers by keeping the navigation details visible while the content pane changes. However, for the purposes of bookmarking, printing and URL locating, and because of differences between browser displays, frames can currently cause considerable difficulties for readers and access problems for visually impaired readers.

Menus

Menus are hyperlinked lists of options, enabling the user to select a particular tool or to move to a particular section within a document. If a contents list is constructed as a menu, it can be made accessible either from a framed navigation pane (where it would be continuously displayed) or from a separate static page. A menu can include short explanatory phrases if necessary, as well as drop-down lists for further subdivision of topics.

Visually, a menu can be arranged as a list, in a hub-and-spoke format, as a three-dimensional representation, or in any other useful arrangement that groups topics and shows their relationships.

Hyperlinks

Readers traverse from one on-screen location to another by using hyperlinks. They are reminded of links already traversed when labels are displayed in a different or dimmed colour.

Hypertext

Hypertext shows that a word or phrase contains a link that can be activated. Hypertext should be sufficiently self-explanatory to give readers a good idea of what they will find at the linked site.

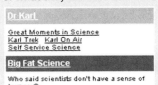

Navigation bars

Navigation bars located at the top and bottom of a web page are generally preferable to bars at the sides of the screen, since the former configuration maximises the screen area available for content. Navigation bars can contain document-specific navigation—*Next page*, *Forward*, *Previous page* or *Back*—or broader devices such as *Search* and *Home*, or a range of content items. Whatever is displayed in the navigation bar should be displayed consistently throughout the site.

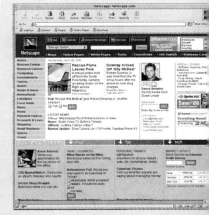

te maps

te maps visually represent the
ntent's structure and relationships
 a manner similar to a flow chart) by
ing colour-coding, visual grouping of
ntent, connecting lines, pointers and
cess paths. They can also deliver
ditional information by briefly
scribing subsites, documents or
her types of content.

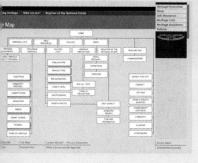

aders should be able to decide
ickly where they are—perhaps a *You
 here* indicator will help—and move
 areas of interest by clicking on the
e map labels, which are hyperlinked
 the content.

Image maps

Image maps contain hyperlinked visual
elements and can be used instead of
lists in contexts where visual cues will
be interpreted more easily than text.
For example, a botanical document
might use an enlarged image of the
parts of a flower to direct readers to
information about those parts. Image
title tags can be used to provide
additional information about where the
links will lead.

An image map showing the clickable
graphic and an overlay showing the
boundaries of the hyperlinked areas

Labels

As signposts to further information,
labels are often shown in a box. The
wording of labels needs to trigger the
correct expectations in readers.
Successful labelling systems therefore
mirror the thinking and language of the
intended readers rather than of the
publication's author.

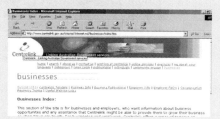

Roll-overs

A roll-over is a 'live' label that is
activated as a reader's cursor moves
across it. In its original presentation on
screen, it is in its 'static state'; once
activated, the revised presentation is
called its 'active state'. The change can
be as simple as a colour change; or it
might be a text change such as a
glossary definition or a foreign
language equivalent (sometimes shown
in a pop-up box); or it might trigger an
animation sequence in another part of
the screen. As the cursor moves off the
live area, the label reverts to its static
state.

Eye movement

An understanding of eye movement through a spatial arrangement allows a designer to create effective layouts that will help readers retrieve the information in sequence. Images and illustrative materials are generally skimmed first, then perhaps captions, then signpost headings and labels, and finally the text. (For on-screen publications, different download times can affect this order.) Within this overall sequence, colour, relative size and positioning are the main determinants of attraction.

➤ Colour and imagery options are discussed in Chapter 21 'Illustrating'.

Because people have physiological responses to colour, colour differentiation can guide readers through a layout. Eyes are attracted to bright colours first, then to darker and muted colours. Bright colours are said to 'advance' towards us, while darker and muted colours 'recede'. So the reading sequence of colour is from brightest element to least bright.

We also tend to be attracted to larger, and thus easier to read, elements before graduating to the smaller elements. As a result, the positioning of larger elements has a big influence on how a layout is read.

In terms of placement, the reading sequence varies according to the nature of the medium and the reading patterns associated with print and screen.

How a single-page layout is read

How a print layout is read

It is often assumed that readers start at the top left-hand corner of a print layout and exit at the bottom right, a progression referred to as *reading flow*. But in many layouts this progression is interrupted because of the complications of the various levels of attraction posed by colour, size and placement. Although the general direction being followed is based on reading flow, readers' attention is drawn to different elements and their eyes jump from one interest point to another.

In publication design there is also a theory that suggests that readers enter a double-page spread at the top right-hand corner as they open the page. Their eyes then sweep over the layout in a parabolic curve, moving across to the top left to recommence reading and finally exiting at the bottom right.

Western readers are taught to read by starting at the top left-hand corner of the text and working their way across and down (going from left to right and back again) until they reach the bottom right corner. This is called *reading gravity*, and it largely determines eye flow in print layouts.

How a double-page layout is read

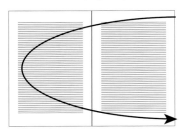

When readers' eyes alight on something, they consequently have a tendency to continue to the right when moving to something else. For this reason, captions are usually designed to be at the bottom or to the right of photographs, rather than above them or to the left.

Given all these considerations, persuading a reader to start viewing a print layout on the left—or attracting them back to the left if there is a dominant image at the centre or on the right—is a significant design task.

aving read a line of type or writing, the eye returns to the beginning of that line
. order to drop down to the following line. This is called the *reading rhythm*. Any
ariation from this causes an interruption that can limit readers' comprehension.

. the case of printed text, comprehension tests show that layouts and typography
.at conform to these physiological responses and natural reading habits are largely
.cceptable to readers. Those that do not conform run the risk of communicating
.effectively.

ow a screen layout is read

.eople who are new to screen reading usually start out reading from left to right, as
.ey have traditionally read print. But they quickly change to a centre–left–right
.an pattern, spending roughly the same amount of time looking at each of these
.reen parts while they determine the likelihood of each area containing a link or
.her information they are looking for.

.eaders may not always look for content in the area towards the bottom of the
.ndow (the 'grey area' in the illustration), just above the browser's status line;
.ey assume that they will already have found the most important information
.rough the centre–left–right scanning pattern. If they do want to inspect
.formation that falls into the grey area, they usually scroll to bring that content
.gher up on the screen, rather than concentrate their attention at the bottom of
.e screen.

.xperienced on-screen readers have come to assume that links and information
.aced in a left-hand column will be content-related items, while any links that
.ight be placed in a right-hand panel will be functional ones (such as *Print this
.ge*, *Search* or *Subscribe*). This assumption may have developed because the right
.nel is nearer the scroll bar, which is the basic functional tool of the on-screen
.vironment.

.ost importantly, it is the central area—the place where content is most likely to
. found—that attracts a reader's attention first on screen. In contrast with the
.ading rhythm associated with print, on-screen readers prefer to scan text, at least
.itially, rather than to read it word for word.

.es will generally still be attracted to pictures before text on a screen. Pictures
.ually come at a suitable text break near a reference to them, and text wrapping is
.ten used to encourage readers to keep reading around the picture and down to
.e remaining text. Bisecting text with a picture is less of a problem on screen
.an in print because readers will scroll to see the text below the picture. In
.inted publications, however, where readers have a wider view, they may be
.nfused about where to look for the continuing text. Will it be below the picture
. at the top of the next column?

.vo particular complications arise for screen-based layouts: moving images and the
.ndow or frame that can hide the full layout from view. Moving images are more
.ely to attract than anything else on the screen, which is why readers should be
.ven the ability to stop the images moving or should even have to click to start
.em. Otherwise, they will be continually distracted by the movement. Blinking

How a screen layout is read

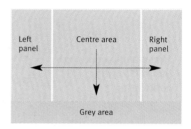

buttons are discouraged for this reason: they are unnecessary (and often annoying) distractions.

Being unable to see a full page within the screen without scrolling is not in itself a major design problem. Indeed, it can resolve some of the complexities caused by attractors in a page layout that draw attention back to themselves—as can happen particularly in double-page spreads. On screen, these attractors are progressively hidden from view as they are scrolled off the screen. As elements move in and out of view, the interplay between them will be less apparent than in a print layout.

Simplicity

Layout is the technique of placing all the pieces. Although the pieces can be complex and multi-layered, good layouts in any medium are often simple.

There is also an element of the invisible in a layout: it is the underlying structure that guides the placement, creating alignments and consistency for regularly occurring elements. Building strength through hidden geometric structures in a layout takes practice and a well-designed grid or set of master pages.

These two pages show the grid for this publication

GRIDS, TEMPLATES AND MASTER PAGES

When designing publications, it is useful to organise the page dimensions into a grid—also known as a *template* or *master pages* and, in web site design, as a *table* and sometimes a *frame*.

Grids give a level of control and consistency to a layout, making it easier to arrange elements in the page area and thus increasing the speed of production. They also bring a cohesive look to the total publication. The use of recurring graphic elements and well-developed typographic style sheets reinforces visual unity.

Grids in print

In a book we always see a double-page spread, so the master page grid for this spread is considered as one unit, rather than as two individual pages. The grid shows the position of all the elements that will be featured in the publication, no matter how infrequently they might appear. The page elements are arranged to conform to divisions of the grid, producing a balanced relationship not only with individual pages but also throughout the work.

Grids do not have to remain identical from page to page. They can be varied to prevent a magazine or long document from becoming monotonous. Part titles and chapter-opening pages in books, and news briefs and regular columns in newsletters, can have master page grids that differ from those applied to the body text or to feature article pages. It is nevertheless important to preserve a relationship between the different grids—for example, by maintaining consistent margins, even though column widths might vary within them. Consistent positioning of elements such as running headers and page numbers also helps to maintain the relationship.

he grid is often divided both vertically and horizontally. A multi-column grid creases the layout possibilities. An odd number of columns also increases layout tential, because there is the option of placing text and images across two or ore columns.

production, the master page grid is applied to each page of the document. Then e text, illustrations and other page elements are brought in. Text blocks are ked so that the words automatically flow from column to column, page to page.

rids on screen

ith a grid for a screen-based publication, the amount of content visible on reen at any time should be maximised by ensuring that the navigation elements nerally take up less than 20 per cent of the window area. (Home pages and other vigation pages will, of course, exceed this ratio.)

he way of maximising the amount of usable screen area is to design layouts that apt to readers' screen sizes. Instead of using fixed pixel sizes, layouts can be ecified as a percentage of screen area. Reconfiguring in this way allows formation to be presented in an appropriate form and reduces the time readers end scrolling.

rtical scrolling is faster than new-page retrieval or link traversal. Horizontal rolling is also possible, but it is usually best not to require readers to scroll both rizontally and vertically within a single document.

A grid sheet and its application

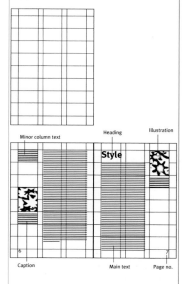

Minor column text   Heading   Illustration

Style

Caption   Main text   Page no.

Grids on screen
When a window is re-sized or a site is viewed on a different-sized screen, a proportional screen design allows the content to reflow into the available screen area.

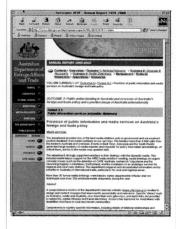

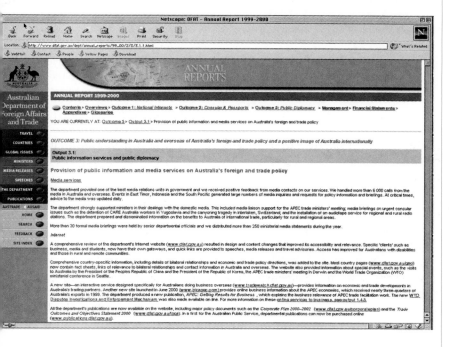

ABOUT

Design dynamics

It helps to have an understanding of the dynamics of design and the language that describes them in order to use them effectively—to attract interest in the first place, to support the content, and to sustain interest throughout a publication.

Contrast

Contrast is arguably the most powerful tool for creating great designs. Images, typefaces, colours and textures can all be contrasted, or used in any combination.

Scale

Scale describes the size relationships between elements on a page. At its simplest, it is the contrast of big with small. Extreme scale relationships— very big with very small—create dynamic, attractive layouts.

Colour and tone

Within a layout, colour and tone should interact playfully. Dark versus light, multicoloured versus monochromatic, intense versus subtle—these are the contrasts of colour and tone that are possible. If you squint at a layout, you can see the pattern of tonal and colourful patches.

Direction

Direction is implied by a line. Readers' eyes will follow a line to the next element so long as the line's direction reflects the standard pattern of reading flow, which is to the right or down rather than to the left or up.

Implied shape

Shape is implied in two ways: elements can be arranged either to fit a shape or to surround a shape (creating a shape in negative). Any elements that are grouped create a group 'area', or shape.

Texture

Texture is created by repetition in a random sequence. More than this, it can suggest a tactile quality in two dimensions.

Implied lines

Implied lines are created by grouping elements along an invisible line (often a grid line). They can simplify and strengthen a layout.

Repetition

Repetition is used to emphasise or to decorate. Anything can be repeated: image or type.

Surface texture

Surface texture can add richness to a layout by lending interesting detail while still maintaining the colour or tonal relationships.

Shape

Images, colours and textures can be cropped into particular shapes, and areas of type can be placed in particular shapes. The geometrically 'pure' shapes of the square, the circle and the equilateral triangle are the strongest shapes in a layout.

Pattern

Repetition in a predictable sequence creates pattern.

Creating a grid

When creating a grid, the margins are generally decided first. Then the remaining space is divided into the desired number of columns or page divisions, with the gutter or space between those columns or cells being defined. The column widths should be designed to accommodate an easily readable text width.

➤ See pp. 331–2 for a discussion of optimum line length for readability.

The placement of 'page furniture'—icons, page numbers, running headers and other regular design features such as content menus—should then be determined. A consistent graphic identity can be maintained throughout a publication by repeating standard logos, buttons, arrows and icons. For a web site, this will minimise frustration with download times because, once downloaded, an image is stored in the cache of the reader's computer.

Maintaining a consistent corporate identity by repeating elements

Margins

In book-publishing terminology, margins are distinguished as the *head* and *foot* (or *tail*) margins but are more widely known as the 'top' and 'bottom' margins. The *back* and *foredge* margins are more readily recognised as the 'inner' and 'outer' margins.

Well-proportioned margins contribute to the pleasant appearance of the double-page spread when a book is opened. Many formulas have been developed for producing balanced page margins, but formulas can be restrictive. There are two main aims when constructing margins: to provide a comfortable or interesting relationship between the margins and the page elements, and between the margins themselves; and to ensure that the margins are practical.

In a book, the type area is usually towards the centre of the book and closer to the top of the page (to account for 'optical centre'—see page 319). The margins conventionally increase in size in the order of inner, top, outer and bottom. However, various binding processes require wider inner margins:

- If the work is to be paperback bound, increase the inner margin by 2 millimetres.

ok margins

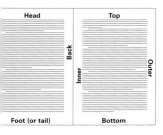

Two-column grid: backing

Two-column grid: non-backing

If the work is to be side-stapled, increase the inner margin by 5 millimetres.
If the work is to be produced for insertion in loose-leaf binders, increase the inner margin by 6 millimetres.

argins are usually arranged so that the type areas on the front and reverse of the ge back up exactly. Unless opaque paper stock is specified, non-backing pages nes that do not have matching side margins) can give rise to distracting show-rough of type and images.

argins in screen-based products are less critical because viewers can resize their ndows and thus upset any balance that has initially been created. The aim ould be to avoid cramping the text while maximising the screen area available r the content.

odular design

variation on grid typography, modular design uses a grid with a number of rizontal subdivisions, or modules. These subdivisions may or may not be spaced ually through the column guides. All the elements for the pages are designed to the modules or groupings of modules. It is then just a matter of piecing together e jigsaw puzzle to make everything fit on the page. A modular approach is often ed for newsletters and magazines, as well as for large works such as encyclo-dias, to streamline the production of multi-image, complex page layouts.

modular grid and its application

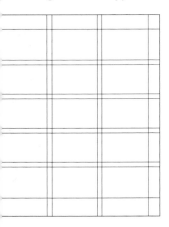
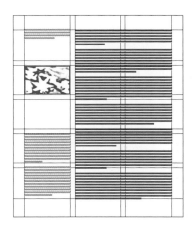
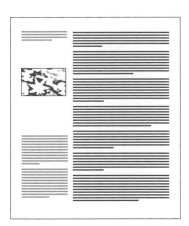

Having some identifiable cross-rules can strengthen any layout by allowing for horizontal alignment of elements. Even if a modular design is not being used, ther will probably be a useful horizontal subdivision that can be applied within a grid. could be a chapter-opening drop, where text starts at a particular depth following the title. Or it could be to do with photograph placement or the positioning of other recurring elements.

BALANCE

Once all the layout elements are finalised, their arrangement within the frame or space becomes the task: how to arrange all the elements within the given area in balanced and visually satisfying manner that supports the relative significance of each piece of information.

Weight distribution

Balance is concerned with comparative 'weight' distribution. In layout terms, one heavy (or dominant) element might balance three lighter elements. Different groupings and placements need to be tried in order to find the most comfortable and workable balance.

The interplay between all the variables of attraction can make it difficult to achieve a good balance. Often something that takes up a large area of the layout i considered a 'heavy' element, while something that takes a small area may be only 'light'. But if that small element is in the most dominant colour—say, bright red— it can counterbalance a large monochrome area. Similarly, a small, animated imag in a web site has greater weight within a design than a large image map, because o the dominance of moving images over static forms.

Grouping and proximity

When they place elements of a design side by side, designers intend readers to interpret this as a cue that the items are related or have been juxtaposed for a reason. In this way, images can be combined to tell an interesting story without any words, demonstrating the potency of this communication technique. Howeve design that uses both words and images is often more powerful and memorable.

Proximity also has a more organisational purpose within a layout. If dealing with many single elements, a reader's eyes will be jumping from piece to piece. It simplifies a layout and makes a stronger statement if there are some groupings to minimise those jumps. Effectively, the reader then jumps from group to group and moves on, the layout having contributed to a more efficient reading experience.

Groupings are also easier to balance. Each group itself becomes an element of the overall composition. So layout becomes simpler, requiring manipulation only of the groups and the space around them, rather than of each individual piece of information.

hysical centre

Optical centre

STYLE

STYLE

entred layouts

entred, or symmetrical, layouts are always balanced: every element is placed enly about the invisible vertical centre line. This approach distributes space ually on either side of the elements and, as a consequence of its absolute lance, is seen as stable and traditional. The disadvantage is that in some ntexts it may be considered too predictable and safe, and not dynamic enough.

ost centred layouts are concerned only with the vertical centre line, but metimes it is desirable to use the horizontal centre line as well. Because of an tical illusion, the horizontal centre line is above the physical centre of a space. nis is why most print layouts have larger margins at the bottom than at the top.

hite space

npty, or 'white', space is desirable in a layout for several reasons. It can give tonal riation to the page and enable elements to be grouped in interesting ways, thout cramming. It also provides a rest space for readers who might be finding e pace of the publication tiring.

nese days, space is rarely completely empty, nor is it always white. It might be ven a background of any colour, even black. In some cases it can be an area of w detail in a photograph or just an area of pale background image with no reground content. Perhaps it is better thought of as a 'quiet area'.

ace often provides balance in a layout. It can even assume weight. When a full-lour photograph is placed in a large area of space with minimal text, the space ll help bring attention back to the text.

hile the use of space as a layout tool affects the cost of printed publications, it ses no additional cost for screen-based publications that are not designed to be wnloaded and printed. However, unlike space in print layouts, space in on-reen layouts is not particularly beneficial. From the perspective of readers, the ore space on the screen, the less successful their scanning and information thering will be. On-screen readers tend to spend much of their time skimming; o much space slows them down and reduces their productivity.

Layout showing implied foreground and background relationship

Style
manual

➤ See pp. 380–1 for a discussion on the selection of backgrounds for illustrations.

This difference in the usefulness of space may also be a consequence of viewing on-screen information through a window, which prevents readers from using their peripheral vision to construct an idea of oncoming material—as they do when reading a printed publication. On-screen readers must therefore constantly reconstruct the document structure in their heads as they navigate or scroll. Excessive space can make this difficult and time-consuming.

Foreground–background interaction

Balance is much more complex in most two-dimensional designs because the design plays with our perception of three-dimensional space. Objects that are small seem further away than larger objects. Colours 'advance' and 'recede', so light text placed on a dark background appears to float in front of the darker colour.

Elements can be positioned on top of other elements, bringing them forward and, by implication, sending the overlapped object back. This is called *layering*. Image collages made in this way are less difficult to read than layered text, or even layered text-and-image. If text readability is accommodated, layered text can be attractive, but it nearly always causes some confusion of the message. Backgrounds should support the foreground, not overpower or interrupt the communication of the message.

EVALUATING DESIGN

Attraction and separation

- Will the cover or initial design distinguish the publication from its competition and attract the desired readership?

- Is the overall design sufficiently interesting to retain readers' attention long enough for the information to be delivered?

- Is the design suitable for the type of information?

- Does it appropriately:
  - identify its source?
  - represent the sponsoring organisation?
  - enhance that organisation's corporate image?

Navigation

- Are there enough contextual aids to orient readers properly?

- Have all the navigation aids been used consistently?

- Does the labelling use terms that will be familiar to readers or that they will be able to interpret readily?

- Will readers be able to develop accurate expectations of the information to be found at linked pages?

- Do the navigation elements leave sufficient page area for content?

Layout

- Does the publication look like a cohesive whole?

- Has the grid provided alignment, consistency and balance?

- Does the layout support the hierarchy of information?

- Will the design promote readability and, in the case of on-screen documents, scannability?

- Is there enough variety, particularly in a long document?

- Are the design features well integrated or are some too intrusive?

- Do the graphic imagery and typography provide enough tonal variations?

- In a print publication, is there enough space to enhance readability and interest, and provide sufficient quiet areas?

- In an on-screen publication, does the allocation of space encourage easy reading while not unduly extending the time spent scrolling?

- Is there a logical flow of images and text?

- Are the graphics logically grouped?

- Are any of the graphics likely to interrupt or distract readers unnecessarily from the text?

Chapter *18* **Typography**

TYPE SELECTION	**323**
Considering the reader	323
Considering reproduction	324
READABILITY AND LEGIBILITY	**324**
Systems of measurement	325
About type	326
Specifying type	331
Line length	331
Leading	332
Text formatting options	334
Variable text depth	337
Text distractions	337
HEADING HIERARCHY	**338**
Signposting	338
Heading and text compatibility	339
Heading stylings	339
TYPE IN COLOUR	**341**
Background–foreground interaction	341
Importance	343
Strobing and flaring	343
Colour changes within text	343
ANIMATED TEXT	**343**
USING TYPOGRAPHIC STYLE SHEETS IN PRINT	**344**

Typography is the art and technique of using type. Typographical style is the way that typefaces, type sizes and spacing are used to improve the look and readability of published material. Although the relative importance of each text component of a document largely determines its typographical treatment, the success of the overall style depends on something more. Typography clarifies messages through the visual cues contained within the chosen typefaces, through the typefaces' interactions with each other and the images and colours chosen to go with them, and through the placement of all these elements on the page or screen.

Type on screen is often in colour on a coloured background, and it can move too. Colour typography in motion needs to be considered just as carefully as the selection of black type for a white page.

TYPE SELECTION

Type is meant to be read—and text type is meant to be read comfortably, without effort or strain. It should also be able to be read quickly, to accommodate readers who are busy.

The appearance of text, headings and paragraphs affects the way readers approach and understand the content. Poor typography has an adverse effect on how we read; good typography has a beneficial effect.

Considering the reader

The choice of type size and, to some extent, typeface depends on the age and reading competence of the readership, the conditions under which the words will be read, and the format of the publication. The type in a child's picture book, for example, will be larger than that in a novel for adults.

Typefaces also have emotional associations. Some look friendlier than others, usually by having more curved shapes within their letterforms; some look futuristic, featuring geometrically constructed letterforms; some look harsh, containing exaggerated triangular shapes and sharp points.

Because text typefaces are used in relatively small sizes, selection of a suitable typeface is important. But more important is the range of the typeface's variants,

A friendly typeface

Life. Be in it.™

and perhaps also the selection of other typefaces that will help to visually define the hierarchy of information.

Considering reproduction

A typeface should be judged not only on an alphabet specimen but also on the way it will appear in a publication. The main points to look for in a setting are the typeface's overall tone, or 'typecolour', and how easily headings can be found within it; the way the letters fit together; and the effect of its design mannerisms on how easy it is to read.

It is important to choose a typeface from the readers' perspective. Its appearance should be checked on screen if it is to be used for a screen-based publication and on a print-out if it is to be published in a printed format.

Examining a sample setting of a few pages containing all the likely variables (headings, captions, text, footnotes, and so on) is the best way of ascertaining whether the typefaces and type sizes are satisfactory and complementary and whether the design decisions will work. The chosen type might appear distorted on screen, or it may not reproduce clearly on the paper stock selected. A range of options should be evaluated until the best typographic solution for the project is found.

Sample output: Always check a sample setting on the medium, or media, chosen for the publication to determine how the final typography will look.

An important distinction:
- *Readability*—the ease and comfort with which material can be read.
- *Legibility*—the clarity of the lettershapes when reproduced.

READABILITY AND LEGIBILITY

Readability and legibility are both fundamental to good typography. Briefly, readability relates to the ease and comfort with which the material can be read and legibility relates to the clarity of the lettershapes when reproduced.

Readability is the more important of the two, since it concerns not only the type (of which legibility is one characteristic) but also how the type is used. A number of typographic factors affect readability:

- whether the typeface reproduces clearly
- the legibility of the letterforms
- the spacing used to separate letters and words—which affects the speed of word recognition
- the length of lines and the spacing between them—which affects readers' ability to recognise both individual words and the line sequence
- whether full capitals are used—in extended text they are harder to read than lower-case letters
- whether there is sufficient contrast for the text to be readable against its background.

Readability measures for print are often not relevant to screen. This is partly because readers have to navigate through the publication while also taking in its information structure and content. It is also because many of the techniques available for formatting type in print are not as readily available or as easily used on screen:

- In web sites, for example, different typefaces and sizes, line lengths and spacing controls are not available to the extent that they are in print.

Readers determine many aspects of on-screen typography by the way they set up their browsers. The limitations of their software and hardware are also important.

Defaults and reader preferences often determine the actual look of the material.

The resolution of screen displays renders subtle font characteristics invisible. When combined with the effects of the distance between the screen and the reader, the viewing angle, and the reflection and flickering of the screen, this produces an average reading speed that is around 25 per cent slower than reading from paper.

To compensate, a good screen layout increases on-screen reading speed by using typography that:

avoids cursive or finely decorated typefaces, preferring typefaces that display a uniform thickness of strokes in their letterforms

uses a larger text size than for print

clearly distinguishes navigational elements from text content

uses typefaces that are common to cross-platform systems

displays content in a way that is easily scanned.

➤ See Chapter 3 for ways of organising material to suit on-screen use.

Systems of measurement

Page and formatting measurements

For computer production, page and formatting measurements are mostly described in millimetres rather than in the traditional print measures of picas and points. Metric paper sizes support this single method of measurement. Most computer design applications will work in millimetres, picas or inches.

Horizontal measurements—including text or column width (known as the 'measure'), page margins, and even tabs and indents—are usually expressed in millimetres. So, too, are vertical measurements covering page depth and heading and paragraph spacing.

Screen measurements

Screen measurements are expressed in pixels (short for 'picture elements'), which are the smallest element of a monitor's screen. Pixels work in a grid arrangement that can be expressed as pixels per linear inch (ppi). On a monitor, the 'resolution' is the number of pixels available to represent graphic detail. The resolution influences the viewing size of text and graphics: the higher the resolution, the smaller will be the text and images.

Type sizes

Sizes of type and leading are expressed in points. In Australia the Anglo-American point system is used, as distinct from the Didot point system used in France and elsewhere in continental Europe. One Anglo-American point is approximately of an inch, or 0.35 millimetres. There are 12 points to a pica, making a pica about 4.2 millimetres.

(continued on p. 330)

Measurement systems

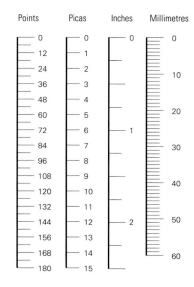

Points	Picas	Inches	Millimetres
0	0	0	0
12	1		
24	2		10
36	3		
48	4		
60	5		20
72	6	1	
84	7		30
96	8		
108	9		
120	10		40
132	11		
144	12	2	50
156	13		
168	14		60
180	15		

Use millimetres: Measurement in millimetres is recommended for all page and column dimensions.

325

ABOUT
Type

It helps to have an understanding of the language that describes typography, as well as of the applicability of type to paper and screen, in order to use type effectively.

The terminology and uses of type have developed from the experience accumulated over hundreds of years of printing on paper. Not all the refinements of paper-based typography are available or applicable to screen-based typography, but there are nevertheless various ways in which the visual display of type on screen can be optimised. (These are discussed later in this chapter and in Chapter 24.)

Type terminology

A typeface: Identifying features distinguish one typeface from other typefaces, just as different features make each human face unique.

A font: Also called a 'fount', a font consists of the capital letters, lower-case letters, numerals, symbols and punctuation marks that make up the full set of characters of a typeface. There is a variety of fonts within each typeface; for example, bold and italics are each separate fonts of a typeface.

Expert sets: These extend a font to include true small capitals, ligatured and swash characters, old-style numbers, true fractions, some text decorations, and other optional forms. Words created with expert sets can be created as graphical images for on-screen display.

A font and its expert set

Lower-case letters

Capital letters

abcdefghijklmnopqrstuvwxyz

ABCDEFGHIJKLMNOPQRSTUVWXYZ

ABCDEFGHIJKLMNOPQRSTUVWXYZ

! ? " " ' ' ' "; : , . / () & - – —

Punctuation and diacritical marks

1234567890

1234567890

Small capitals are slightly thicker and wider, to match the weight of the lower-case and capital letters surrounding them. They are often 'faked' by scaling or reducing normal capitals.

Lining numbers are all the same height and the same width, to maintain alignment in tables.

Old-style numbers are supplied for use in continuous text because they have different sizes that sit well with lower-case letters. They blend into a paragraph format better than lining numbers, which tend to stand out.

¼ ½ ¾ ⅛ ⅜ ⅝ ⅞ ⅓ ⅔ [+ √ π = ≠ ± ≤≥ ∞] @ $ ¢ £ ¥ % # * {} < > © ™ ®

Symbols, mathematical signs and currency icons

ff fi fl ffi ffl Œ œ

Ligatures connect two letterforms into one revised symbol.

R K Q y f

Swash characters developed from calligraphic forms and are mostly capital letters with extended strokes (*R*, *K* and *Q*) and selected lower-case letters (notably *y* and *f*).

abelling type characteristics

ypography has its own language for scribing the characteristics of type. knowledge of some of the most mmon terms makes for better mmunication between the members a publishing team.

eight: This describes the height of the ver-case letter *x*. The x-height helps ermine the necessary line spacing for a t.

ading: Pronounced 'ledding', this scribes line spacing. It is measured from baseline of one line of type to the seline of the next.

Kerning: The spacing between letters is modified by kerning—adding more space or taking some away in very fine increments— to optically rectify uneven spacing caused by a particular character set. Most fonts contain kerning pairs but at larger sizes their limitations become apparent, so detailed kerning is usually confined to display text.

Tracking: In a text selection, tracking is used to place the same amount of space between each letter and word. It is mostly used to track wide, or 'loose', but it can also be used to track 'tight'.

T R A C K   W I D E

TRACK TIGHT

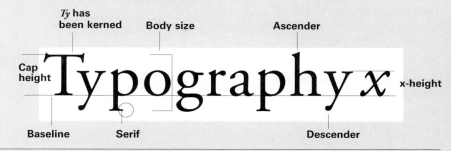

Ty has been kerned   Body size   Ascender

Cap height

Typography *x*

x-height

Baseline   Serif   Descender

---

pe families

e families consist of a set of riants of the original typeface that tch some of the typeface's physical aracteristics. They are extremely eful for bringing emphasis and tinction to various elements of the t while maintaining a cohesive look the typography.

dium, regular or roman: These three ms are used to describe the main edium-weight) font design in various type hilies. The term *roman* is also used to scribe type that is upright as opposed to ics. Medium fonts are designed to be the imum weight for the tone of a text block prolonged reading. There are some iations of medium fonts, called 'demi' or ok', that are slightly darker.

lics: Being based on cursive letterforms, ics slant to the right. Some italic efaces are simply 'obliqued', or leaning, sions of the roman font. Italics are the ne typecolour as their roman interparts—hence medium italics and d italics. They are difficult to read on een. Chapter 9 discusses the ventional uses of italics.

ld, extrabold and black fonts: avier fonts are created by thickening the okes of the letterforms. Bold text is

A sans serif family

Frutiger Ultra Black

Frutiger Black

Frutiger Black Italic

Frutiger Bold

Frutiger Bold Italic

Frutiger Roman

Frutiger Italic

Frutiger Light

Frutiger Light Italic

usually noticed first in a layout so it should be used carefully. The heavier fonts are not recommended for prolonged reading.

Light, extralight, fine and hairline fonts: Lighter fonts are based on the medium font with a thinner stroke. They are not recommended for prolonged reading because both paper reflection and on-screen rendering compromise their readability at anything other than large sizes.

Expanded and extended fonts: These are fonts where the shape of the letterforms has been stretched horizontally and redrawn (not distorted). They are not recommended for prolonged reading.

A hybrid family

Stone Serif Bold

Stone Serif Bold Italic

Stone Serif Semi Bold

Stone Serif Semi Bold Italic

Stone Serif

Stone Serif Italic

Stone Sans Bold

Stone Sans Bold Italic

Stone Sans Semi Bold

Stone Sans Semi Bold Italic

Stone Sans

Stone Sans Italic

Stone Informal

Narrow, condensed and compressed fonts: In these fonts, the shape of the letterforms has been stretched vertically and redrawn (not distorted). Although not usually recommended for prolonged reading, they do accommodate more characters in a narrow column width to make the column easier to read.

327

Classification of typefaces

There are four distinct groups of typefaces: serif typefaces, sans serif typefaces, scripts and display typefaces.

Serif typefaces: These usually have different thicknesses of line and small extensions (serifs) attached to the main strokes of the letterforms.

Bracketed serifs smoothly join the serif to the main stroke of the letterform.

Times Roman

Modern serifs are usually thin, with little attempt at smoothly joining the serif to the stroke.

Bodoni

Slab serifs are much the same thickness as the rest of the typeface and are chunky.

Rockwell

Sans serif typefaces: *Sans* means 'without' in French, so sans serif typefaces have no serifs on the strokes of the letterforms.

Gill Sans

Scripts: Letterforms that have evolved from hand-drawn styles are called 'scripts'. They are mostly used for titling and display purposes and are not recommended for prolonged reading.

Connecting scripts

Regency Script

Non-connecting scripts

Reporter two

Casual scripts

Brush script

Blackletter, Gothic and *Fraktur* are used to describe the style current in Germany in 1450, when Gutenberg was preparing the first movable type.

Old English

Display typefaces: Typefaces that do not fit into the other categories or are used as featured type are called 'display typefaces'. They are used most often in headings and titles and as graphical images for on-screen displays.

PLAYBILL

Picture fonts produce a picture, instead of a letter, with each keystroke.

Symbol fonts, or 'pi' fonts (after the mathematical term), contain mathematical symbols; shapes such as circles, squares, triangles and stars; and other 'dingbats' such as asterisks and arrows.

▲ ■ ◆ ★ ✳ → ⇨

Decorative initials are usually highly ornate capital letters, often contained within borders and on florid backgrounds. In some contexts, raised or dropped initials in text can add distinction to a page. However, because of their visual dominance, care is needed to ensure that a series of decorative initials does not spell out an unintended word.

Ornament fonts feature cherubs, acorns, leaves, flowers and calligraphic swirls in all manner of styles. They are sometimes referred to as 'fleurons' or 'printers' flowers'.

Border fonts are designed to create decorative borders, in a continuous pattern or spaced apart. Usually, a set of border pieces is combined to create corners with connecting middle pieces.

Vector font description: A mathematical description of the curves that create the outline of a letterform or picture, vector font description is used in printer fonts because it enlarges smoothly without affecting output resolution.

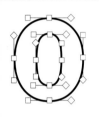

Raster, or bitmapped, font description: A low-resolution, pixelised description of a letterform that is then scaled to the required size, raster font description has the correct width and height but its shape is an approximation only. It is used in most screen fonts because it has a small file, which downloads quickly and takes up little memory when stored.

Anti-aliassing: A pixelised description of a shape that incorporates pixels of different tones to reflect the true shape more accurately, anti-aliassing is used on screen to provide a better approximation of shapes drawn with pixels.

PostScript: A proprietary system of digital page description, PostScript is a device- and resolution-independent standard that allows material to be output at the required resolution by the selected output device—provided it has a PostScript interpreter. Once a file is saved as PostScript, it cannot be changed.

TrueType: A proprietary system of font description, TrueType was developed for use primarily in the PC environment. Its single font description is used for both screen display and printer output and is not dependent on a PostScript interpreter, so it will work in most office printers.

OCR: Standing for 'optical character recognition', OCR describes devices that scan text and convert it into a usable computer text file. Previously dependent on machine-readable fonts, it now has much broader application.

The term *point*: It is standard industry practice to use the shortened form *pt* when referring to type sizes and leading.

x-height comparison

X 24 pt Goudy

X 24 pt Avant garde

x 24 pt Regency script

➤ Cascading style sheets are discussed on pp. 450–1.

Increments between type sizes are usually expressed in whole points—9 pt, 10 pt, and so on. Increments in tenths and hundredths of a point are possible for very fine detailing.

The sizes of different fonts can appear different because of the fonts' design.

The choice of type size depends on the purpose of the text, the readership, and the font's characteristics:

- Type in 6 to 8 pt is normally confined to captions and footnotes.
- For continuous reading, type is usually between 9 and 12 pt, but this varies according to the age of potential readers.
- For primary school readers, text is often set in 14 pt or larger for easier comprehension.
- For older readers and people with visual impairments, text set in the range of 14 to 20 pt is more legible.
- On screen, type is usually set in 12 pt or larger. This is one of the reasons why 12 pt type is the default setting in most software.

Type sizes on screen might also be based on percentages of a 'base font size' specified in a cascading style sheet. The base font size for normal text is determined by the preferences readers set for their screen display. If other text elements are specified in relation to that size, the same heading relationships with the main text can be maintained.

Type spaces

For paper-based publications, type also has a set of fixed spaces used for letters, words and indents. The largest space unit is called an 'em': it is usually the same measurement as the type size (roughly the width of a capital M). A 12 pt typeface would therefore have a 12 pt em space and a 10 pt typeface would have a 10 pt em space. Narrower fixed spaces are as follows:

- An en space, which is half the width of an em, is about as wide as the letter *e* and is used as the width for numerals.
- A thick space is a third of an em.
- A thin space is a quarter of an em, or about the width of the letter *i* or a comma, so it is sometimes referred to as a 'punctuation space'.

It is desirable to set type so that the word spacing matches the thin space. The thin space is also used in telephone numbers and instead of commas in numbers consisting of five or more digits.

'Hard spaces', or 'non-breaking spaces', are used between parts of an expression that should not be split over a line break—for example, telephone numbers and in expressions such as *Mrs EB Bloch* and *3.5 metres*.

For on-screen documents, there is at present no equivalent to the em or en space, although there are ways of creating a non-breaking space when necessary.

ecifying type

pe should be specified by both its point size and the line spacing. This cification is expressed as a fraction—for example, '¹⁰⁄₁₂ pt' or '10 on 12 pt'—and lowed by the typeface and font name.

➤ See 'Leading', on pp. 332 and 334, for more discussion of line spacing.

rif typefaces

rifs have been an integral part of European letterforms since ancient Roman es. Serif typefaces are still the predominant choice for prolonged reading cause most readability tests confirm that most people prefer them. However, eir subtle characteristics do not work as well in their pixelised version on screen.

a serif typeface is used for a screen-based publication, a larger point size should chosen than would be used for a comparable printed publication. It is commended that the point size for running text on screen be no less than 12 pt.

ns serif typefaces

cause of their clarity and the consequently easier recognition of their forms, sans if typefaces are used in works for children who are learning to read. They are o used extensively for signage, being very legible against confusing or moving ckgrounds. And in forms, listings, classified advertisements and telephone ectories they are valued for their legibility at smaller sizes.

e clarity factor certainly makes sans serif typefaces a good choice for type on een. Some say they are less suitable for continuous reading; however, if due ention is paid to leading, many people find sans serif text as easy to read as serif t.

pitals and lower case

e readability of lower-case letters is greater than that of capitals. This is because e ascenders and descenders in the lower-case letterforms give a distinctive ysical shape to each word. We read by recognising word shapes, which is why we metimes misread words set in fonts that have idiosyncratic letterforms ecifically, non-conventional character widths). Word shape is fundamental to ding speed. Indeed, an experienced reader usually recognises a word from just e top half of its lower-case letters, without having to see each entire lettershape.

terestingly, although capital letters are less readable than lower-case letters, the ibility of capitals is greater because each letter has a more distinct shape. This kes capitals a good choice for logos. In contrast, the rectangular word shape at capitals create is their undoing in continuous text: a reader must slow down d look at the lettershapes within each word to decipher the text. This is why it inadvisable to use capitals for anything longer than a heading.

Improving reading speed: For continuous reading, use lower-case letterforms. Don't use full capitals for anything longer than a heading.

ne length

ere is a relationship between the size of the text type and the column width (or easure).

timum line length

'comfortable' reading rhythm is where the reader's eye travels from the start of a e to the end and then moves without disruption to the start of the next line.

This can be achieved by line lengths based on the following:

- one-and-a-half to three alphabet lengths of the chosen font and size
- forty to eighty characters per line
- six to twelve words per line
- sixty characters of the chosen font and size.

Trial settings—where a piece of text is set to a particular measure then tested on readers—can be used to determine the 'comprehension success rate'.

As a general rule, the smaller the type size, the narrower the column width, or measure, should be. Thus, in magazines, newspapers and other large-format publications the type area is broken into two or more columns. On screen—because of the larger type size required and the scrolling difficulties that extended text set in multiple columns creates—single-column text should be used.

Wide measures

Long lines are tiring to read in large blocks; they are also difficult to read without missing a line occasionally or reading the same line twice (called 'doubling'). If a wide measure is really necessary, the way to prevent these problems is to be generous with the amount of space between the lines.

Word spacing

In normal text composition, a word space occupies about the width of the letter i. There is no need to increase the amount of spacing after a punctuation mark or at the end of a sentence. A normal word space between a full stop and the following capital (both of which are strong cues) is sufficient to alert the reader to the new sentence.

Leading

Leading (pronounced 'ledding') describes line spacing. The term comes from the thin strips of metal (lead) that were inserted between lines of movable type in the early days of printing, to separate the lines and prevent the ascenders of one line from touching the descenders of the line above. This interline spacing was defined in variable widths of lead, so a line could be '1 point leaded', '2 points leaded', and so on.

Leading is now measured from baseline to baseline, and the term describes the body size plus the line spacing. It is therefore nearly always larger than the body size.

Improving readability

Readability can be improved by well-considered line spacing—particularly when lines are long. As line lengths approach the maximum end of the optimum range more leading should be specified to enable the reader's eye to travel to the next line without hesitation. Types with large x-heights and correspondingly short ascenders and descenders also need additional leading.

Because leading is usually variable in web sites—unless they are created with cascading style sheets—control should be exercised by defining cell widths. Although tests have shown that people resent scrolling interminably, they will soon give up reading if line lengths are too long.

Recommended measures:

- A maximum line length of eleven to twelve words.
- Narrower measures for smaller type sizes.
- Single-column text for on-screen documents.

Single space after a full stop:
Traditionally, only one space is used after a full stop in typesetting for publication. The convention that called for two spaces after a full stop was a response to mechanical typewriters and is unsuited to the proportional spacing formats offered by word processors and computer typesetting.

Specimen settings and typecolour comparison

10/10 pt Times Roman

10/10 pt Times Roman is called 'set solid' because there is no additional leading, or space, between the lines. Notice the even tone, or typecolour, maintained through flush-left setting.

10/12 pt Times Roman* and *Times Italic*

10/12 pt Times Roman is '2 point leaded' and this is the ratio that is the basis for computer default leading. *Notice how italics make little difference to the typecolour.*

10/12 pt Times Bold and *Times Bold Italic*

10/12 pt Times Bold creates a paragraph of darker typecolour. *Notice how italics make little difference to the typecolour.* Darker paragraphs tend to attract greater attention.

10/10 pt Helvetica

10/10 pt Helvetica is called 'set solid' because there is no additional leading between the lines. Notice the even typecolour maintained through flush-left setting.

10/12 pt Helvetica*

10/12 pt Helvetica is '2 point leaded' and this is the ratio that is the basis for computer default leading—but it was based on the appropriate standard for serif typefaces.

10/13 pt Helvetica

10/13 pt Helvetica is '3 point leaded', which provides a ratio that is better for sans serif typefaces and other fonts with a large x-height than the computer default leading.

10/13 pt Helvetica Italic

10/13 pt Helvetica Italic creates the same typecolour as Helvetica, and so does not draw attention. The form is an obliqued version of the roman, not a true italic form.

10/13 pt Helvetica Bold and *Helvetica Bold Italic*

10/13 pt Helvetica Bold creates a paragraph of darker typecolour. *Notice how italics make little difference to the typecolour.* Darker paragraphs tend to attract greater attention.

10/13 pt Helvetica Black

10/13 pt Helvetica Black creates a paragraph of yet darker typecolour. Dark paragraphs like this tend to attract the greatest attention.

Default leading

Using default leading

Default leading in most page layout programs adds 20 per cent to the body size of the type; 10 pt Times Roman is thus set on 12 pt leading. This default is sufficient for most serif fonts, but fonts with a larger x-height (which most sans serif fonts have) need more leading. The recommended setting for sans serif and other fonts with a large x-height is 30 per cent on the body size; 10 pt Helvetica, for example, is better set on 13 pt leading.

Text formatting options

Text formatting involves decisions about how text is paragraphed and presented within those paragraphs. The aim should be to make the text look inviting to readers and to provide a tonal arrangement against which headings and other elements of the information hierarchy can be clearly discerned.

Unjustified setting

Flush left, ragged right

To achieve even word spacing in typesetting, type is best set unjustified—that is, flush left (also called 'ranged left' or 'ragged right'). Unjustified lines can be set in one of two ways:

- with no word breaks at the ends of lines and therefore no hyphens—this results in wide variation in line length
- with words at the ends of lines being selectively broken and hyphenated— hyphenation can be forced in each instance or a 'rag zone' can be used.

The optical width of flush-left setting is roughly halfway between the shortest and longest lines. This has a particular benefit for multi-column works, where unjustified columns provide greater visual separation between the columns, assisting readers' delineation of the columns.

A rag zone

A 'rag zone' is created using hyphenation programs. A point about 10 millimetres from the end of the line is selected: if a word starts before that point but will not fit on the line, the hyphenation program will hyphenate it; if a word starts after that point but will not fit on the line, the word will be sent to the next line. In this way, the 'rag', or unevenness, of the text block is controlled by occasional hyphenation.

Flush right, ragged left

Type can be set flush right ('ranged right' or 'ragged left') if desired, but this format is unsuited to prolonged reading. It is thought that the readability problem is caused by the lack of a regular point for the eye to return to, which disrupts reading rhythm. If a flush-right format is used, each piece of information should be short and self-contained.

Justified setting

Justified text (or 'ranged left–right' text) creates a text block where both sides are even because each line is set to the same length. This is achieved by redistributing through the line any space that is left over because the next word cannot be accommodated or hyphenated. The space is usually evenly distributed between words but in extreme cases can be distributed between the letters as well.

Justified text often creates an uneven tone to a text block: some lines appear darker and some lighter because of the uneven distribution of spacing in the different lines of a paragraph. Nevertheless—having an eye to selective forced hyphenation—an even, justified text is achievable with most page layout software when the text is spread over a wide measure. Narrow measures, however, result in fewer words per line, and fewer opportunities for inserting spaces between words if justification is required. This is another reason for using an unjustified setting for narrow columns.

Recommended setting

In terms of readability, there is little difference between unjustified text and carefully formatted justified text. In fact, most readers will not notice until asked, and then their preference is usually for justified text because it looks 'neater'.

In spite of this, unjustified text is generally recommended because there is no completely satisfactory typesetting program for desktop production that automatically produces justified text with even word spacing. Preparation of satisfactorily justified text requires a considerable amount of design and editorial intervention.

Centred text

Centred text is not suited to prolonged reading. As with text set flush right, if readers are to readily grasp what is being communicated, line breaks must always be carefully considered and each piece of information or phrase kept self-contained.

Centred text works best when the measure on which it is centred is defined in some way. For example, the fine rules between columns in newsletters define a measure that could be used to centre the headings within. Similarly, a square-cut photograph could define the measure for a centred caption.

Free-form text

For display text and titles, free-form text can quite often be effective. It allows a designer to interpret the rhythm and meaning of the text, creating an interplay of lines akin to that achieved in poetry setting.

Paragraphing

The two main paragraphing options are the indented paragraph and the blocked and spaced paragraph. For text that is further subdivided, there are other, progressively indented and tabbed paragraph stylings.

Text formats

Justified setting

Flush left (note the actual text block width and the optical text width)

Flush left with a rag zone

Flush right

Centred

Free-form

Recommended formatting:
Flush-left unjustified text formatting is recommended for most circumstances.

Indenting

Using an indent for the first line of each paragraph, as opposed to inter-paragraph spacing, provides visual separation without too much interruption to the tonal block of the text. This is the format preferred for most types of printed publications.

Paragraph indention is now largely standardised to the 5 millimetre indent, but it can vary with the text measure. A short measure might have an indent of 3 millimetres (anything smaller is not enough); an indent for a longer measure might extend up to 10 millimetres. Very wide indentions are neither economical nor conducive to comfortable reading and can look particularly awkward when used with short paragraphs. They can, however, be used for effect in brochures, advertising and display typography.

When headings are used with this paragraphing format, the first line of text following the heading should not be indented. In addition, the first line of a marginal note, footnote or caption should not be indented. This blocking of first paragraphs provides a square corner, which looks 'cleaner' than an indent would in this position.

Blocking and spacing

The alternative is to use blocked paragraphs—meaning no indention for first lines but extra spacing between paragraphs for visual separation. The amount of space should not exceed one line and is usually equal to half a line. For example, if text is leaded to 12 pt, an additional 6 pt space would be inserted between paragraphs.

Blocked paragraphs are preferred in screen-based layouts because they segment the text more clearly into easily scanned 'chunks'. This preference should, however, be balanced against the requirement for readers to scroll further as a result of the overall increase in length.

Hanging indents

Subsections and lists are sometimes displayed using hanging indents. These indentions are usually introduced by a bullet, en rule, numeral or letter followed by a tab. Any turnover lines are indented to align with the beginning of the first word of each item.

➤ See Chapter 9 for a detailed discussion of ways of punctuating indented material.

The extent of indention following bullets and en rules is usually the same as the paragraph indent. For indented material preceded by letters or numerals, the extent of indention depends on the width of the widest numeral in the list—for example, (*viii*).

Long passages of indented material spoil the appearance of a page, especially when two or more degrees of indention are used. Indentions in the often complex subdivisions of contents lists can be avoided by using typeface variations to signal different levels of importance.

Line, paragraph and page breaks

Consecutive lines ending with a hyphen look clumsy and should be avoided when possible by means of respacing or word substitution. There should never be more than two hyphens in a row, even in narrow columns.

paragraphs should not be split by an illustration or table since this affects readability. The illustration or table should be placed at the end of a paragraph (as close as possible to the reference to it in the text) or, if the format is suitable, the text can be wrapped around the illustration or table.

Pages should not end with a divided word. Nor should they end with a heading, the first line of a new paragraph, or the first line of an indented list. It is always better to let the page fall short and to start the next page with the heading, new paragraph or list.

The interior pages of a web site should end with navigation tools that enable readers to progress to the next level of information without scrolling back to the top of the screen. The bottom of the page is also the recommended position for the copyright line, which can be hyperlinked to a full copyright notice.

New pages

Chapters and appendixes usually start on a new page. In web sites, new interior pages occur more regularly than in printed publications—to avoid an unrealistic scrolling depth—so subsections of chapters also often start on a new page.

➤ See Chapter 3 for advice about structuring material for on-screen use.

Variable text depth

Book text has traditionally been aligned along consistent bottom margins. This constant page depth was achieved by altering the spacing—mostly around the occasional headings, but sometimes line by line. However, the resultant uneven spacing around headings of a similar level could lead to confusion about a heading's position in the hierarchy.

The use of headings has increased in recent years and heading hierarchies have become more complex, so it has become more important for headings to be consistently spaced to aid recognition of their level. Some adjustment to the bottom page margin is therefore necessary in printed works. Provided that the bottom margin is no more than two or three lines shorter or one line longer (and the additional line does not visually cramp the page number or footer), the adjustment usually goes unnoticed. Even in multi-column formats, there is little need to force the columns to an equal depth, particularly if doing so highlights a consequent distortion of spacing through the columns.

Variable page depths: In printed works it may be necessary to vary page depths by a few lines to keep the correct spacing around headings.

Because of the scrolling facility, the pages of an on-screen publication can be of any depth. Once the depth gets beyond about six screens, however, most readers will not persist. There will also be readers who decide not to scroll at all from the top of the page—unless they are captivated by something in this opening screen and want to find out more.

Text distractions

Widows and orphans

In formatting for print, if a paragraph is split after its first line at the bottom of a page or column, the single line left there on its own is called an 'orphan'. When the last line of a paragraph starts a new page, it is said to be a 'widow'. Orphans and widows disrupt the flow and thus create readability problems.

The solution is to ensure that the last paragraph on a page either retains at least two lines on that page or is moved entirely to the top of the following page. This means that a paragraph of only two or three lines must never be broken between pages.

A watch should also be kept to ensure that no headings are left alone at the bottom of a page, separated from the text that they describe.

Rivers

More often found in justified text (with its variable word spaces), 'rivers' are made up of a series of white spaces that have by chance aligned vertically or obliquely, creating visually irritating white stripes in the grey typecolour of a text block. The argument against rivers is that they subliminally lead readers' eyes down the text and away from the content. Changing to unjustified text, altering words, forcing hyphenation or widening the measure are all potential solutions.

HEADING HIERARCHY

Signposting

The goal of headings and labels is to tell readers about the scope and structure of the information in a publication and to trigger the correct expectation about the ensuing text. As with all signposts of this kind, clarity and speed of comprehension are essential. In text documents, headings are coded by shape, positioning, type selection, size, weight, spacing and colour to demonstrate their relative importance in the hierarchy of information.

➤ Chapter 9 provides editorial advice about heading structures.

Headings that are dark stand out against the typecolour of the text block, so they have a greater role in a hierarchy. They are also the most obvious for readers who are scanning for signposts. As the headings' tone gets closer to the tone of the text block, they become less obvious, although they will still be relied on for comprehensive reading. The relative importance of these lower level headings can be conveyed using a combination of italics, full capitals and varied spacing.

Because lower-case letterforms are more rapidly comprehended, headings in full capitals are best used only when extra distinction is needed in a complex heading hierarchy. In a simpler hierarchy, variations in type selection, size and weight are usually sufficient.

The secret of communicating a heading hierarchy lies in the logical exploitation of contrasts. Different type sizes are chosen to show contrast between important and less important headings. Contrast can be further accentuated by the use of space to isolate or link elements and so reinforce logical groupings.

Heading and text compatibility

Using one type family

Font selection is made easy with families of typefaces, which offer numerous possibilities for heading and text variation.

Sans serif typefaces usually have a larger group of family members. Most serif typefaces have only the 'nuclear family' of four members: medium, medium italic, bold and bold italic. Some families even have both serif and sans serif fonts; examples are Stone and Thesis.

Using two type families

It seems that the most successful typography uses two type families: a quiet, rather anonymous one for text and a louder, more assertive one for headings. The best way to select two typefaces that will go together is to contrast their differences in at least two of the following ways:

classification—serif against sans serif

decoration—plain against fancy

weight or typecolour—light against bold

size—large against small

direction—italics against roman

capitalisation—capitals against lower case

spacing—wide against narrow

shape—expanded against normal or condensed.

These contrasts should then be accentuated for headings, to help readers grasp the hierarchy easily.

Using multiple type families

If use of more than two type families is contemplated, the type classification system becomes useful. It is said that only one typeface from each classification should be used in a design—that is, one serif, one sans serif, one script and one display face. Variants of each face can still be used, of course, although it is inadvisable to mix script fonts with italics because of their often conflicting angles.

Heading stylings

The headings for chapters, parts, preliminary matter and endmatter in books are usually consistent in style, as are the headings for interior pages of on-screen publications. They should be placed at the same distance from the top of the page and in the same relationship to any other consistently appearing 'page furniture' such as spot illustrations, numbering and navigation elements. Use of full capitals or lower case will depend on the copy; long headings are best set in lower case with minimal capitalisation.

Within the text, headings subdivide the chapters or interior site pages into sequences of information. These headings are often related to the titling styles, although they are smaller and less dominant. They are often in a colour that contrasts with the main text, and they might also have rules and boxes around them or typeface variation within them.

A text hierarchy using only one type family

① **HEADING HIERARCHY**

② **Signposting**
The goal of headings and labels is to indicate the scope and structure of information within a publication.

② **Heading and text compatibility**

③ *Using one type family*
Font selection is made easy with families of typefaces.

Minimal capitalisation: Chapter 8 recommends that the trend towards minimal capitalisation be followed; this is also reflected in Chapter 13's recommendations for dealing with the titles of publications in references. Minimal capitalisation in headings maintains this consistency.

Subordinate headings on screen: In an electronic publication, clickable menu options can be devised from subordinate headings contained in the text. If these options are carefully devised, readers will be able to avoid unnecessary scrolling to locate information.

The size of most text headings is close to that of the text type, if not the same. Within the same font and size of type, a number of options are available for these headings. The main ones—from most to least important—are:

- bold full capitals or bold small capitals
- medium full capitals or medium small capitals
- bold lower case
- italic lower case.

Bold lower-case and italic lower-case headings that are 'run on'—that is, where the text continues on the same line as the heading—have less importance than headings on separate lines. Italic capitals are rarely used because their place in a hierarchy is difficult to distinguish.

Spacing headings

Text headings of the same degree of importance should be spaced consistently. The more space above a text heading, the more important it will appear in the hierarchy. There should always be less space below a text heading than above it.

When paragraphs are blocked and spaced, the space above a heading should not be less than the space between the paragraphs, and the space below should not be less than the leading of the paragraph. More space should appear above run-on headings and headings placed in a side margin than between normal paragraphs, although it need not be greater than a full line space.

Heading length

Content recall is greater with single-line headings. Further, if headings appear within a box or rules, runover lines can cause the boxes or rules to impose too much on the layout.

It is therefore a good idea for the publication team to agree on a maximum heading length aimed at avoiding runover lines wherever practicable. This limit can then be incorporated in the design and editing guidelines.

Line breaks in headings

When headings take up more than one line, there are two primary considerations: ease of reading and balanced line lengths. To make reading easier, the subject or 'attractor' words should be at the beginning of heading lines or be featured typographically. The resulting shape of the text block then needs to be taken into account. For example, a long heading:

CLASSIFIED ACCOUNT OF STINGINGS BY JELLYFISH IN AUSTRALIAN AND SURROUNDING WATERS

is better set in two lines, with the top line preferably slightly longer than the second line, as

CLASSIFIED ACCOUNT OF STINGINGS BY JELLYFISH IN
AUSTRALIAN AND SURROUNDING WATERS

or in three lines, preferably in a one-sided pyramid shape, as

CLASSIFIED ACCOUNT OF
STINGINGS BY JELLYFISH IN
AUSTRALIAN AND SURROUNDING WATERS

a side column, a long heading may need to be spread across even more lines. ut narrow multi-line headings limit readability, so they should be edited to a orter length wherever possible.

equency of headings

nce a heading hierarchy has been established, it is advisable to define the desired equency of the headings. In this way, the look of the publication is partially ntrolled by the placement of the various text stylings.

may be decided that a heading should occur roughly every 250 words, to bdivide the text into comprehensible chunks for busy readers. The 'chunking' so helps readers who are skimming to find particular items of information.

oxed headings

ne most dominant heading that can be created is a boxed heading with reversed pe—where the type is made negative, usually to white. The white type is then ntrasted with a solid colour, often black, which is strongest because it uses the aximum available contrast.

cause the solid box is so strong, the reversed text needs to have the dimension at least a bold sans serif font, if not an extrabold. Serifs and scripts can lose finition in such contexts and appear to close up.

cond and subsequent levels of boxed headings can be made with tinted boxes ntaining black headings. The darker the tint, the more important the heading. owever, good contrast between the box and the text in it must be maintained for adability.

ith boxed headings, the box should be considered a part of the layout and ould work within the established grid lines. Further, the spacing around a boxed ading should visually link the box to the text that follows it; that is, the space ove should be greater than the space below. Usually at least one line space is quired above the box and a half-line space below.

Boxed heading hierarchy

> **Reversed bold on black**

> **Bold on tint**

> **White on tint**

➤ For information about grids, see pp. 312–18.

YPE IN COLOUR

areful consideration should be given to the use of coloured type. First, it can eate optical illusions; for example, jarring can result from using two colours of ual tone. Second, people have varying responses to colour, and colour blindness ects a significant proportion of the population (particularly males). Then there e the difficulties of controlling the environment in which the colour is viewed as ll as the reproduction processes. Because of these complexities, it is often eferable to reserve colour for use in graphics, backgrounds and images.

ackground–foreground interaction

eping sufficient contrast between background and foreground is the first thing consider when choosing type colours that will sustain readability and legibility. hether in print or on screen, low contrast can be irritating and fatiguing for unger readers; it can make reading impossible for older people and difficult for people who are colour-blind. When text will also be viewed on mono-colour or greyscale monitors, this contrast is essential.

In print and on screen, black text on a white background has the highest legibility and offers readers the opportunity for greatest comprehension. White text on a black background—called 'negative text' on screen and 'a reverse' in print—has been found to be almost as readable on screen as black on white, but in print it is difficult to read for anything longer than a heading.

In the layout of on-screen publications, other colours can also be used without affecting legibility and comprehension. However, in nearly every combination, darker text on a lighter background has been found to be more readable than the reverse.

Although there is no single colour combination that is always best, most on-screen readers have a distinct preference for any colour combination that contains black (either as a background or as a text colour). White on blue (FFFFFF on 0000FF) and red on yellow (FF0000 on FFFF00) rank fairly highly. Green on yellow (00FF00 on FFFF00) and white on magenta (FFFFFF on FF00FF) rank fairly poorly. The two least readable combinations are red on green (FF0000 on 00FF00) and magenta on blue (FF00FF on 0000FF).

➤ See Chapter 21 for further discussion of colour reproduction.

In print, deep tones are needed against light or pastel paper colours. So the preferred colours for printed text are black, burgundy, bottle green, navy blue, charcoal, chocolate brown and deep purple. When using them in four-colour process, solid (or 100 per cent) cyan or magenta should be specified in the colour description: this will give the type a sharp edge and thus greater clarity.

Background detail

Dramatic colour changes in the background of text should be avoided, particularly with photographic backgrounds. Contrasting text can, however, be positioned over a 'dead area' of a photograph—black text in a flat blue sky, say, or white text in dark shadow areas.

Care is also needed when placing behind text any patterned and textured images that have wide tonal changes. Type is so fine and so dependent on character recognition for comprehension that anything distracting in the background discourages reading. As a result, some background textures intended for a printed publication might need to be manipulated to remove highlights and to blur detail. For on-screen documents, any obvious patterns and textures will serve only to further decrease readability and should be avoided.

Background separation

Sometimes, altering the text itself can separate it from a background. A bold weight can be clearer over a detailed background. Another separation technique is the use of haloes, shadows, or even a fine outline around each letter. This is still not an optimum solution, though, because the haloes, shadows and outlines can become a distraction in themselves.

Background detail and type

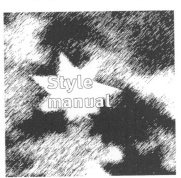

Importance

Colour is an attractor, so a heading level featuring colour will be seen as more important than one without. Used incorrectly within a block of text, however, colour can cause a significant drop in comprehension and readability.

On paper, lengthy stretches of coloured text on a white background have been found to cause a big reduction in the number of readers who continue reading to the end. This has mostly been studied only with mid-tones and pure hues, rather than dark tones, which have long been used for single-colour print jobs. But it does imply that care is warranted when considering coloured text for anything beyond limited use.

Strobing and flaring

On-screen colours that are too similar in tone, and patterns that clash with the pattern of pixels, can 'flare' around their edges or 'strobe', making them difficult to read. This is particularly so if the type is also moving. Altering the tonality of one colour will often create the differentiation needed. If it is a strobing pattern, the pattern should be removed, reproduced at a larger scale, or tonally manipulated to produce less contrast.

Colour changes within text

It is becoming increasingly common for readers to interpret a colour change in a short piece of on-screen text as a hyperlink. The link can be to another site; to another part of the same site; to explanatory material such as a footnote, statistics or a definition; or to an image.

It is a service to readers if browsers' default settings are used for link colours. Readers can then recognise a link or visited links instantly and do not need to learn a separate colour code.

In print, colour change is sometimes used within a paragraph to attract readers' attention to the highlighted words. Readers usually assume that the coloured text can be read like a summary, a signpost or a pull-quote. Colour changes might also be used to distinguish examples from descriptive text. However, coloured type within text blocks can be distracting, so thought should to be given to readers' possible responses.

ANIMATED TEXT

Avoid text that moves too quickly or blinks or zooms: readability tests have found that static text is most successful. If any text is animated, it needs to move fairly slowly to match reading speed, and it should move from *right to left* for languages that read from left to right. It should also be timed to stay on screen for long enough to allow people with different reading abilities to finish it.

A part of the style sheet for this manual

All type flush left

1 Chapter head

36 pt Meta Plus Bold u/lc

2 Main head (PMS 1675)

14 pt Meta Plus Bold SMALL CAPS
6 mm space above

3 Subheading (PMS 1675)

10.5/14 pt Meta Plus Bold u/lc,
2.5 mm space above

4 Sub-subheading (PMS 1675)

10/12.5 pt Meta Plus Medium
Italic u/lc, 4 mm space above

Intro para

11/13 pt Goudy bold u/lc

Body text

10/12 pt Goudy u/lc
2.117 mm space above

Text 1st para

10/12 pt Goudy u/lc
0.5 mm space above

USING TYPOGRAPHIC STYLE SHEETS IN PRINT

Typographic style sheets record all the typographic detail for a publication. Careful use of them ensures consistency in the information hierarchy and layout and speeds up the production process. With desktop publishing and layout programs—if the 'based on' facility in most style sheet applications is understood—a style sheet can be generated to enable font and size changes to be made with very few keystrokes and without entering each style again.

The full text requirements for each level of information should be specified in a style sheet. These will include:

- typeface and weight—bold, italics, and so on
- capitalisation—caps, small caps, lower case
- point size and leading
- tracking—wide, normal or tight letter spacing
- standardised space above or below the type
- formatting—justification, centring, flush left or right
- measure (text width)
- hyphenation preferences—none, rag zone or full
- any indents and tabs
- any rules or background boxes attached to text elements
- colour specifications for text, rules and boxes.

Text paragraphs are the most important type specification in a publication, so all subsequent levels should be in response to the normal text description. Captions, tables, quoted material, running headers, references and footnotes are often one or two point sizes smaller than the text. However, all text should be comfortably readable.

The lower level headings are usually the same point size as the text but with different weight and spacing attributes. As headings become more important, they need to be progressively larger and have more space around them, contrasting the weight, formatting, capitalisation, typefaces and colour.

EVALUATING TYPOGRAPHY

Readability

Are words clearly identifiable?

Is the line spacing suited to the line length?

Is the text size (including in tables and figures) suitable for the readership?

Have the paragraphing choices grouped the text sufficiently?

Have text distractions such as widows, orphans and rivers been eliminated?

Is there sufficient contrast between text and background?

The information hierarchy

Is the tonal arrangement of the text and its interaction with the headings appropriate?

Will readers recognise the difference between each heading level?

Are headings visually linked to the text that follows them?

The typographic style sheet

Is the hierarchy coded correctly?

Is capitalisation consistent?

Are type colours correct and consistent?

Is the spacing around paragraphs and headings consistent?

Chapter *19*

Tables

READABILITY OF TABLES	**347**
Clarity and brevity	347
About tables	348
Clustering	351
Alignment	353
Table width	354
Table placement	356
TYPOGRAPHY OF TABLES	**357**
Type sizes	357
Emphasis	357
Text tables	357

A table is a systematic, typographical arrangement of information in columns and rows. It shows relationships between the items of information in a clear and compact format. Tables are most commonly used to present statistical and financial data that are too complex for description in the text. Tables consisting only of words can, however, be useful for showing comparative information.

Tables should be set out as simply as possible. The material to be presented might be complex, but careful consideration usually reveals what information is best placed in the columns and what is best placed in the rows. The order of priority required by readers and the nature of the information are important determinants of the form of presentation and what needs to be highlighted.

To clarify the relationships between comparative data presented in a series of tables, the same table structure, orientation and measurement units should be used so far as possible.

READABILITY OF TABLES

Data presented in tables must meet specific requirements for completeness and accuracy. When tables are being assembled, however, readers' ability to interpret the data in meaningful ways must always be borne in mind.

In the case of screen-based publications, it should be noted that the devices visually impaired readers use to interpret electronic material find tabled content difficult to assimilate and follow. An optional file containing a text description of the table is usually preferable in these circumstances. Further, it is recommended that use of tables in on-screen publications be restricted to content that actually *requires* tabulation; use of tables as a layout aid for positioning text on screen should be avoided.

➤ See Chapter 23 for recommendations relating to equitable access to publications.

Clarity and brevity

Table titles and internal headings should be brief and clear. Readers skim for indicators of the content in tables, and this makes several factors important:

Titles are best kept to one line.

For accurate visual clustering of the data, row items and headings in the stub should, as far as possible, each take only one line.

Column headings should be brief because the readability of narrow, multi-line column headings is low.

ABOUT
Tables

Table terminology

Table titles: These often consist of a table number, a brief description of the content, and a date or time span.

Column headings: The data in each column are defined by the column's heading. Sometimes the column headings appear in a hierarchical arrangement, being grouped, or 'clustered', for clarity.

Cluster column headings group two or more columns.

Column heading titles describe individual columns or groups of

Table 6.7 **Labour force status, relationship in household, June 2000**

	Employed		Unemployed						
	Full-time	Total	Looking for full-time work	Total	Labour force	Not in labour force	Civilian population aged 15 and over	Un-employment rate	Partici-pation rate
	'000	'000	'000	'000	'000	'000	'000	%	%
MALES									
Family member	3 570.5	4 093.0	201.8	249.9	4 342.9	1 485.4	5 828.3	5.8	74.5
Husband									
With dependants	1 743.6	1 844.1	73.7	78.8	1 922.9	138.8	2 061.7	4.1	93.3
Without dependants	1 159.4	1 302.8	38.0	45.4	1 348.2	903.5	2 251.8	3.4	59.9
Total husband	*2 903.0*	*3 146.9*	*111.7*	*124.2*	*3 271.1*	*1 042.3*	*4 313.5*	*3.8*	*75.8*
Lone parent									
With dependants	39.8	48.4	4.3	5.8	54.2	21.2	75.5	10.7	71.8
Without dependants	25.8	27.7	1.3	1.6	29.2	21.8	51.1	5.4	57.3
Total lone parent	*65.6*	*76.1*	*5.6*	*7.4*	*83.4*	*43.1*	*126.6*	*8.8*	*65.9*
Dependent student[a]	5.3	168.0	7.5	36.7	204.7	251.4	456.1	17.9	44.9
Non-dependent child[b]	525.3	616.8	69.1	72.9	689.8	92.0	781.7	10.6	88.2
Other family person	71.2	85.1	7.9	8.8	93.9	56.6	150.4	9.4	62.4
Non-family member	709.5	806.1	72.5	77.4	883.5	372.7	1 256.2	8.8	70.3
Lone person	380.1	428.7	30.4	33.9	411.3	80.0	491.3	8.2	83.7
Not living alone	329.4	377.4	30.4	33.9	411.3	80.0	491.3	8.2	83.7
Total males	**4 433.3**	**5 084.5**	**293.2**	**348.3**	**5 432.8**	**2 061.0**	**7 493.8**	**6.4**	**72.5**
FEMALES									
Family member	1 702.7	3 245.9	110.2	205.7	3 451.5	2 500.5	5 952.1	6.0	58.0
Wife									
With dependants	520.1	1 ,217.9	30.4	65.0	1 282.9	707.5	1 990.4	5.1	64.5
Without dependants	702.8	1 086.7	23.7	33.5	1 120.2	1 096.9	2 217.2	3.0	50.5
Total wife	*1 222.9*	*2 304.6*	*54.1*	*98.6*	*2 403.1*	*1 804.4*	*4 207.6*	*4.1*	*57.1*
Lone parent									
With dependants	109.2	232.1	20.9	35.1	267.2	205.3	472.5	13.1	56.5
Without dependants	36.0	53.6	5.5	5.9	59.5	104.6	164.1	9.9	36.3
Total lone parent	*145.2*	*285.7*	*26.4*	*41.0*	*326.7*	*309.9*	*636.6*	*12.5*	*51.3*
Total all persons	**6 655.6**	**9 055.9**	**445.7**	**608.6**	**9 664.5**	**5 543.0**	**15 207.5**	**6.3**	**63.3**

a Excludes persons aged 20 to 24 attending school. Also excludes sons or daughters aged 15 to 24 who are classified as husbands, wives or lone parents.
b Aged 15 and over.
Note: Figures are for civilians who were residents of households where family status was determined.
      A section of this sample table has been deleted for display purposes, so the columns do not add up.

Source: Australian Bureau of Statistics (2000).

Labels (left margin): Table title · Cluster column headings · Column headings · The stub · Row headings · Subtotals · Keyed notes · Spanner headings · Totals · Keyed notes · Sources

lumns; they should be phrased in a
nsistent and logical way.

nits define the unit of measurement
pplying to each column.

he stub: This is the left-hand column;
defines the data in each row of the
ble.

roup row headings are major
eadings within the stub that have two
 more row headings within them.

ow headings group row items in the
ub into logical sets.

ow items define each of the data
ws.

panner headings: Dividing a table
thin the data area, spanner headings
e often centred on the width of the
ble. A fine rule or row of dots above
n be used to separate a spanner
eading from previous data and link it
 the data that follow.

ubtotals: Usually presented in italic
pe, subtotals are sectioned by
acing above and below them.

tals: Terms such as *All items* or
ustralia (in the case of tallying data
r states and territories) are often
ed instead of *Total*. Totals are usually
esented in bold type and offset from
e table by a line space above them. It
unnecessary to have a fine horizontal
le above the total line. Totals can also
 shown in a column on the far right
 a table.

ble notes: These present information
at is of interest or explains
terpretations or assumptions used in
oducing the table.

eneral notes can be used for
formation that applies to the entire
ble. They are usually headed simply
ote:' or 'Notes:'. This presentation is
ually preferable to using a
perscript number, letter or symbol at
e end of a table's title. If numbers are
unded in a table, a general note can
 used to explain this.

Keyed notes refer to specific data in the table. They are identified by the relevant superscript numeral, letter or symbol. Empty cells can have an em rule, a symbol such as '..' or the abbreviation 'n.a.' (for *not available*) placed in them: the keyed note should explain why the cells are empty. If an em rule is not used and the cell contains no symbol, a general note can be used to explain the absence of data.

Sources document the location of the original data. They are usually headed simply 'Source:' or 'Sources:'.

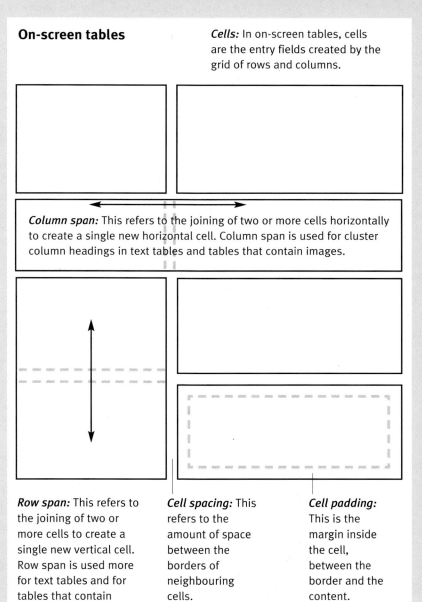

On-screen tables

Cells: In on-screen tables, cells are the entry fields created by the grid of rows and columns.

Column span: This refers to the joining of two or more cells horizontally to create a single new horizontal cell. Column span is used for cluster column headings in text tables and tables that contain images.

Row span: This refers to the joining of two or more cells to create a single new vertical cell. Row span is used more for text tables and for tables that contain images.

Cell spacing: This refers to the amount of space between the borders of neighbouring cells.

Cell padding: This is the margin inside the cell, between the border and the content.

Table titles

Table titles should define the what, the how, the where and the when for their content. Thus they often contain the following:

- a table number, if appropriate
- a title
- a subtitle, if necessary
- a data qualifier, to identify the nature of the data
- a date or time span.

If a table continues over more than one page, continuation indicators are needed after the table title at the head of subsequent pages, as well as at the foot of any page to be continued. It is a good idea to abbreviate the table title on the subsequent pages—just use, say, 'Table 9 (continued)'—otherwise readers might think that the second or subsequent page of a table is the beginning, particularly if they have just flicked to it. Another useful device to avoid this impression is to leave off a bottom rule until the end of the last page of the table.

Table titles should be kept as short as practicable: content recall is higher with single-line headings. Readers tend to skim the first line of titles when seeking specific information and can easily miss important information in second or subsequent title lines. Nevertheless, the information in the title must be sufficient to enable readers to make the correct assumptions about the content. For example, the titles of some types of statistical tables should describe whether the data are original, seasonally adjusted or trend estimates. Further, the titles of tables presented in a series for comparative purposes should be worded in a parallel fashion.

Short titles: Single-line table titles are recommended.

Tables are often numbered because it is a convenient method of linking them to their text reference—and they should always be referred to in the text. References to 'the table above' or 'the table below' can give rise to author correction costs if a table is relocated after pagination for print and the reference has to be changed.

Column headings

Column headings are more easily understood if there are no more than two hierarchical levels. Measurement units such as symbols for currency are additional to this.

Sometimes it is difficult to find a suitable column heading for the stub. A heading should, however, be used whenever possible, since columns without headings look odd. Other columns must always have a heading.

Column headings in on-screen tables should be readable for the total view of the table. If scrolling is necessary, column or stub headings can be lost, making the table incomprehensible.

If the same unit of measurement applies throughout a table, the unit is sometimes incorporated in the table's title, usually in parentheses and at the end. In most cases, it should not be included in any combined list of table titles in the contents section of the publication.

When there are different units of measurement for some or all of the columns, it is usual to place the units at the top of each column in the table. They can appear with the column headings or at the top of the data area of the table. The best position often depends on whether there are spanner headings in the table and whether the units of measurement for the columns change after those headings. If they do, the units should immediately follow the spanner heading, rather than feature with the column headings.

Sub headings and row items

The length and hierarchy of material in the stub often need considerable attention. If a row heading or item runs to a second line, it can:

- create awkward clustering by putting a line of blank space above a row of numbers, thereby drawing unwarranted attention either to that line or to the line above
- confuse the indent levels of the row heading hierarchy, because often a turnover line is also indented.

Spanner headings are perceived to be the most important headings in the hierarchy of the stub because they split the table and divide the stub. Different fonts such as small capitals, bold or italics should be used to show the hierarchy of stub headings. Try to avoid using bullets: they have too great a weight in tables.

> ➤ Heading hierarchies are discussed in Chapter 18.

If further distinction is required, subsidiary items should be indented by no less than an en space. When it is desirable to reduce the length of a table to fit on one printed page, it might be necessary to reduce the line spacing between items in the stub. If this means there is a risk of the distinction between items becoming insufficiently clear, the second and succeeding lines of each stub item can be indented to provide the necessary differentiation. Items in other columns should never be indented.

Data

Data for comparison should be presented in columns. Quarterly or monthly data are best grouped in calendar, rather than financial, years. This is to avoid the possibility of, say, March in the financial year span 2001–02 being misinterpreted by a skimming reader to mean March 2001.

In statistical tables, the order of time is shown from earliest to latest, either across the page or down it. In tables for financial reporting, however, current figures are often placed first, followed by figures from previous financial periods.

Clustering

Information can be grouped vertically and horizontally, each group being delineated by one or more of the following layout techniques:

- the distribution of space around data
- the use of rules and cell borders
- colour and type differentiation.

Spacing

Clustering is usually achieved by inserting extra space between logical sections; this is why it is important to try to avoid turnover lines in the stub that create unintended breaks between the data rows. In a densely set table, the insertion of horizontal bands of white space at logical or regular intervals will make the table much easier to read and comprehend. Even a half-line space will often improve a table's readability without adversely affecting its depth.

Rules and cell borders

Spacing is the most effective means of achieving clustering, but fine horizontal rules or fine dotted rules between groups of data are also useful in some contexts. They can, however, make a table appear more complex than necessary, so they should be used sparingly. Vertical rules should be avoided because they interrupt the necessarily horizontal readability of the rows of data.

Avoid vertical rules: They interrupt readers' eye flow across table rows.

A fine horizontal rule is often needed to separate column headings from the body of the table; it is referred to as an 'inner rule'. A heavier rule placed at the top and bottom of the table (an 'outer rule') helps to define the table's boundaries. The outer rules should not be too heavy; otherwise, the table's connection with its title and notes will be weakened.

A table can have more inner rules in its body if it contains spanner headings and specific sections that these rules can usefully divide. However, a better effect is often achieved by substituting white space.

In on-screen tables, with appropriate cell spacing defined, cell borders and table frames should be set to zero, making cell padding redundant.

Entries separated by white space

78.8	922.9	138.8	261.7	4.1
45.4	348.2	903.5	251.8	3.4
124.2	271.1	42.3	313.5	3.8
5.8	54.2	21.2	75.5	10.7
1.6	29.2	21.8	51.1	5.4
7.4	83.4	43.1	26.6	8.8
72.9	889.8	92.0	781.7	10.6
8.8	93.9	56.6	150.4	9.4
77.4	883.5	372.7	256.2	8.8

An on-screen table with cell borders, padding and frames removed

Before

After

Fine rules separating entries

249.9	4 342.9	1 485.4	5 828.3
78.8	1 922.9	138.8	2 061.7
45.4	1 348.2	903.5	2 251.8
124.2	3 271.1	1 042.3	4 313.5
5.8	54.2	21.2	75.5
1.6	29.2	21.8	51.1
7.4	83.4	43.1	126.6
72.9	689.8	92.0	781.7
45.4	1 348.2	903.5	2 251.8
8.8	93.9	56.6	150.4

Colour and type differentiation

When necessary, rows and columns can also be differentiated by colour or type attributes. Colour can be used as either:

- background colour for a row or column
- the typecolour of a row or column—contrasting bold and light type, or type of particular hue.

➤ See also 'Typography of tables' on pp. 357–8.

olour variation might be used to link like information scattered through a table. or example, average Australian data could be highlighted for ease of comparison ith data for individual states and territories. Colour must not be used 1discriminately, though: it can cause confusion as readers search to find a onnection that is not there.

nother method of improving readability is to place regular bands of a tinted cond colour over, say, every second line in a table. (This approach can also affirm the colour palette of a publication.) When this is done, the column eading block can be coloured too, allowing the rules to be removed and the eadings perhaps to be reversed out of a solid colour. Sometimes the total row will e in a different colour or tone, often one related to the colour of the column eading.

lignment

he positioning of text and data in tables is crucial for accurate visual clustering nd reading of the data.

eft alignment of text and headings

eft alignment, particularly for text across short measures such as table cells or olumns, has been shown to increase readability. It enables readers' eyes to travel ack to the starting point of the line they have just read and then drop to the ontinuation on the next line. Centring and flush-right formatting options should e avoided in all-text tables.

cells or columns are aligned left, the column headings should also align left. In rinted documents with very narrow columns, the column headings can be set ertically (reading upwards), although a 45° angle is preferable for readability.

a table contains rules showing coverage under cluster column headings, the eading may be better centred over the rule. However, when there are many olumns and only a short cluster heading, left alignment means the cluster heading ppears directly over the first column heading, so the reader does not need to earch along the rule for it.

he symbols for the measurement units defining the columns—for example, $, %, o., kg/a—should generally be placed on a separate line and should align with the olumn headings. Symbols for units associated with stub items and headings are est shown in parentheses at the end of those entries.

lignment of data entries

lignment of data entries depends on the style of the entry. It should be:

  flush left—for the stub and any columns containing text

  flush right—for whole numbers

  on the decimal point—for numbers with decimal fractions and for dollar–cent
  amounts.

hin spaces should generally be used to separate groups of three numerals in both hole numbers and decimal fractions. However, if no whole number in the table

Tints of a second colour to aid readability

Forest type	Total area '000 ha	Conserved area '000 ha	Amount conserved %
Acacia	12 298	276	2.24
Melaleuca	4 093	424	10.35
Rainforest	3 583	812	22.66
Casuarina	1 052	39	3.71
Mangrove	1 045	231	22.11
Callitris	867	69	7.96
Other	8 435	770	9.13
Eucalypt	124 463	14 961	12.02
Total	**155 835**	**17 580**	**11.28**

Column headings at a 45° angle

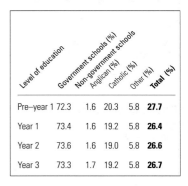

Level of education	Government schools (%)	Non-government schools Anglican (%)	Catholic (%)	Other (%)	Total (%)
Pre–year 1	72.3	1.6	20.3	5.8	**27.7**
Year 1	73.4	1.6	19.2	5.8	**26.4**
Year 2	73.6	1.6	19.0	5.8	**26.6**
Year 3	73.3	1.7	19.2	5.8	**26.7**

➤ See Chapter 11 for a discussion of the use of spaces or commas in numbers.

exceeds four digits—that is, there is nothing above 9999—the numbers can all be shown without a space, to provide greater consistency and save space.

If no rows of data in the body of a table exceed one line—as is the case with most statistical and financial tables—each row should align with the last (or only) line of the corresponding item in the stub. If the stub item contains runover lines and the rows of data also contain runover lines—as is the case for many text tables—the first line of data or text should align with the first line of the stub item.

Rows of dots, or dot leaders, are best not used in tables: they clutter the presentation and can be distracting. They will be unnecessary if a table has been well designed.

Table width

Tables narrower than the page grid

A well-designed table has enough space between the columns for visual separation yet maintains the horizontal readability of the row. This often means that a table does not spread across the publication's full text width because the table is set to its 'natural' measure. The natural measure is usually determined by the width of the column headings and totals, with a narrow, but sufficient, standardised space between them. If tables are unnaturally stretched to match the full text width, the columns can become too widely spaced, making it difficult to read across a row.

As much space as possible should be allowed for columns that contain text. The aim should be to avoid the uneven word spacing and bad word breaks that result from narrow column settings.

In unjustified text, if a table is not as wide as the page grid or column width, it should be set flush left. In justified text, such tables can be centred on the text measure if the text headings are centred.

A table title should not extend much beyond the width of the table itself. Long titles of narrow tables may therefore need to extend to a second line.

Title line breaks and flush-left positioning for a narrow table

Comparison of areas of selected countries

Nation	Area '000 km²
Seven largest countries	
Russia	17 075
Canada	9 976
China	9 596
United States of America	9 629
Brazil	8 511
Australia	7 692
India	3 287
Selected other countries	
France	547
Germany	357
Japan	377
New Zealand	269
United Kingdom	244

ables wider than the page grid

ables set to their natural measure can be as wide as necessary in on-screen ublications: readers can extend the window or scroll to see the full table. It is, owever, advisable to repeat the stub headings and items on the right-hand side of ιe table if scrolling is necessary. If the on-screen layout will be adversely affected ⱴ a disproportionately wide table, it might be better to provide a hyperlink to the ble on a separate page.

ι print, it is acceptable for very wide tables to be displayed in landscape format, ading from the bottom of the page to the top. These tables can then occupy veral pages, with the column headings repeated on the left-hand pages only.

nother print option for a very wide table is to extend it across a double-page read, although great care must be taken to allow sufficient space between the ⱷlumns at the spine. The printer and binder must also ensure that the alignment ross the two pages is maintained. There are two options for improving adability across such long rows:

repeating the headings and items in the stub on the left of the continuation page

or

adding a 'line number' column on the extreme left and right sides of the table if there is enough space.

		Employed		Unemployed		Labour force	Not in labour force	Civilian population aged 15 and over	Un-employment rate	Partici-pation rate	
		Full time	Total	Looking for full-time work	Total						
		'000	'000	'000	'000	'000	'000	'000	%	%	
1	Family member	3 570.5	4 093.0	201.8	249.9	4 342.9	1 485.4	5 828.3	5.8	74.5	1
2	Husband										2
3	With dependants	1 743.6	1 844.1	73.7	78.8	1 922.9	138.8	2 061.7	4.1	93.3	3
4	Without dependants	1 159.4	1 302.8	38.0	45.4	1 348.2	903.5	2 251.8	3.4	59.9	4
5	*Total husband*	*2 903.0*	*3 146.9*	*111.7*	*124.2*	*3 271.1*	*1 042.3*	*4 313.5*	*3.8*	*75.8*	5
6	Lone parent										6
7	With dependants	39.8	48.4	4.3	5.8	54.2	21.2	75.5	10.7	71.8	7
8	Without dependants	25.8	27.7	1.3	1.6	29.2	21.8	51.1	5.4	57.3	8
9	*Total lone parent*	*65.6*	*76.1*	*5.6*	*7.4*	*83.4*	*43.1*	*126.6*	*8.8*	*65.9*	9
10	Dependent student	5.3	168.0	7.5	36.7	204.7	251.4	456.1	17.9	44.9	10
11	Non-dependent child	525.3	616.8	69.1	72.9	689.8	92.0	781.7	10.6	88.2	11
12	Other family person	71.2	85.1	7.9	8.8	93.9	56.6	150.4	9.4	62.4	12
13	Non-family member	709.5	806.1	72.5	77.4	883.5	372.7	1 256.2	8.8	70.3	13
14	Lone person	380.1	428.7	30.4	33.9	411.3	80.0	491.3	8.2	83.7	14
15	Not living alone	329.4	377.4	30.4	33.9	411.3	80.0	491.3	8.2	83.7	15
16	**Total males**	**4 433.3**	**5 084.5**	**293.2**	**348.3**	**5 432.8**	**2 061.0**	**7 493.8**	**6.4**	**72.5**	16

Source: *Labour Force, Australia* (ABS 6203.0)

Line number columns on the left and right of a table split across two pages

ther of these approaches will also help readers if the pages turn out to be ⱪcorrectly aligned when the book is bound. To ensure that all tables of this kind ⱶmain on facing pages, page proofs should be checked if any late changes that ⱷuld affect pagination have been made earlier in the document.

ⱷr printed publications, solutions such as these—or even rearrangement of the ⱶble—are much less time-consuming and costly than printing a wide table on a ⱶparate sheet to be folded and tipped in.

A complicated table reset

Before

Year	Grade (full time)												Total					
	Professor		Associate professor/ reader		Senior lecturer		Lecturer		Senior tutor and demonstrator		Tutor and demonstrator		Full time		Part time		Total	
	No.	Proportion	No.	Proportion	No.	Proportion	No.	Proportion	No.	Proportion	No.	Proportion	No.	Proportion	No.	Proportion	No.	Proportion
		%		%		%		%		%		%		%		%		%
1964	463	8.2	409	7.3	1 392	24.8	1 455	26.0	238	4.2	766	13.7	4 723	84.2	883	15.8	5 606	100.0
1969	773	9.6	634	7.8	1 895	23.5	2 090	25.9	503	6.2	1 079	13.4	6 974	86.4	1 101	13.6	8 075	100.0
1974	939	9.1	963	9.3	2 457	23.7	2 592	25.0	702	6.8	1 492	14.4	9 145	88.3	1 212	11.7	10 357	100.0

After

| Grade (full time) | 1964 | | 1969 | | 1974 | |
	Number	Proportion %	Number	Proportion %	Number	Proportion %
Professor	463	8.2	773	9.6	939	9.1
Associate professor/reader	409	7.3	634	7.8	963	9.3
Senior lecturer	1 392	24.8	1 895	23.5	2 457	23.7
Lecturer	1 455	26.0	2 090	25.9	2 592	25.0
Senior tutor and demonstrator	238	4.2	503	13.4	702	6.8
Tutor and demonstrator	766	13.7	1 079	13.4	1 492	14.4
Total full time	4 723	84.2	6 974	86.4	9 145	88.3
Total part time	883	15.8	1 101	13.6	1 212	11.7
Total	**5 606**	**100.0**	**8 075**	**100.0**	**10 357**	**100.0**

Table placement

A table for on-screen publication can be placed immediately after the paragraph containing the text reference to it.

In print, table placement is more complex:

- A table should be placed as close as possible after the paragraph in which the text reference to it occurs.
- A table should not be inserted into the middle of a paragraph. This will interrupt the flow of the text.
- A table that is less than a page long should not be split between pages. It should start at the top of the following page.
- Provided the context of the discussion supports such placement, it is preferable to place a table at the top or bottom of a page, rather than in the middle.

A space must always be inserted above and below a table placed between paragraphs. Sufficient space must also be inserted between tables when one follows another, to avoid confusing readers. In pages containing nothing but tables, it is best to keep the space between the tables uniform and let the page fall to its natural depth. The table titles on pages of this kind should align at the top.

➤ See Chapter 12 for a discussion of footnotes and endnotes.

Table notes should be placed immediately below the table to which they refer. To avoid the possibility of confusion with text footnotes or endnotes, a different key system should be used; for example, if a publication uses symbols such as asterisks and daggers for footnotes, an alphabet key (a, b, c) is wiser for the table notes.

ith printed publications, depending on the type of publication and the number
tables it contains, tables can be relegated to an appendix or a statistical section
parate from the main text. On screen, a set of tables might be available via
perlinks from their text references. In both cases, the interpretation of the tables
d conclusions based on their content will still be discussed in the main text of
e publication. This discussion can be supplemented by graphs showing trends
vealed by the analysis; the graphs would have as their source a reference to the
rresponding table.

➤ Chapter 21 discusses graphs.

YPOGRAPHY OF TABLES

pe sizes

he typographical treatment of tables should be consistent throughout a work.
Although tables are usually shown in smaller type than that of the text they
company, the decision on their type size should take into account the resulting
vel of legibility—particularly in the case of on-screen tables, where smaller type
es might be illegible.

ble titles should be presented in the same style and size throughout; generally,
e titles should be larger than the type used for the body of the table. The style of
e titles may differ from the styles used for other headings; alternatively, they can
atch the figure titles or even one of the lower level text headings.

olumn headings should generally be in type of the same size as that used for the
dy of the table, although the size of the headings can be reduced if they are
tensive or congested. Italic or bold fonts are often used for column headings.

there are only a few table notes, they can be presented in type of the same size as
at used in the table. If the notes are extensive, they can be set smaller, provided
re is taken to maintain readability. To avoid having to read small type across
de measures, notes can be set in two or more columns. Notes for on-screen
les might be displayed as roll-overs or pop-up text.

mphasis

pographical emphasis within a table usually involves highlighting either a full
w or a full column. Normally, emphasis will be placed on subtotals by using italic
pe and on totals by using bold type.

nphasis might, however, be determined on the basis of comparative data the
le is designed to show. In a state government publication, for example, it could
appropriate to highlight the state data in bold type for ease of location and to
ow Australian averages in italic type for comparison.

xt tables

he type in text tables should be set with even word spacing, flush left and
justified. The first letter of each item in each column should be capitalised. This
proach to capitalisation should also be followed in tables that are a mixture of
xt and figures.

Text tables benefit by not having vertical rules. In a table with many columns, more information will fit across the measure if space and alignment, rather than rules, are used to structure the table.

Text table

Factors threatening biodiversity in Australia

Threat	Description
What has happened to habitats?	Cropping, forestry, mining, grazing, and human settlements have dramatically changed vegetation cover, with 60% of birds and 80% of mammals listed as threatened having declined as a result of habitat loss.
What pests and weeds have been introduced?	Introduced species in Australia include 25 mammals, 37 birds, 8 marine fish, 21 freshwater fish and 3000 weeds. They threaten ecosystems by altering resource levels, community composition, disturbance regimes and the physical environment. See the section 'Marine pollution' for exotic marine species.
Have fire regimes changed?	Before European settlement, fire was used by Aborigines for many reasons including regeneration of food plants. Fires varied in location, season and frequency. Current fire regimes have contributed to the dramatic loss of small to medium sized mammal species from semi-arid/arid environments of Australia's interior.
Have hydrological regimes changed?	Large water storage facilities and small farm dams reduce annual streamflow, having a marked effect on aquatic ecosystems. Physical barriers such as weirs prevent fish from migrating, while alteration of natural river channels removes important aquatic habitats.

EVALUATING TABLES

- Does the layout enable easy comparisons to be made between the data?

- Is material properly grouped?

- Has emphasis been provided where it is due?

- Is the type easy to read?

- Are table titles, column headings, stub headings and row items clear and unambiguous?

- Are all column headings and data rows properly aligned?

- Do numbers tally?

- Are abbreviations and other shortened forms used consistently?

- Are tables placed in the most suitable position following their in-text reference?

ABOUT
National identifiers

THE COMMONWEALTH COAT OF ARMS

Approved versions for colour reproduction

The 1912 Arms

Colour transparency catalogue no. crs a6378/1 can be bought from the National Archives of Australia.

Screen version of the 1912 Arms

A pixelated, digitised version for web sites and other on-screen documents is available from the Awards and National Symbols Branch, Department of the Prime Minister and Cabinet.

FLAGS

The national flag

	100C 80M
	100Y 100M

NAA A1500/1:K7116

The Australian Aboriginal flag

© Harold Thomas. Reproduced with permission.

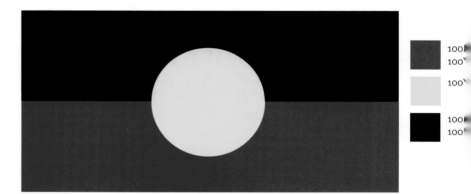

	100Ⅰ 100Ⅴ
	100Ⅴ
	100Ⅰ 100Ⅰ

The Torres Strait Islander flag

	100C 70M
	100C 80Y.40K
	100C 100K

THE NATIONAL COLOURS

100C
100Y

100Y

NAA: A155/1 K7171

Green and gold

Australian cricket teams and many other national sporting groups have traditionally worn green and gold. These are now Australia's official national colours.

100C
80M

100Y

The heraldic colours

The ribbon of the Order of Australia and of several other Australian honours uses the heraldic blue and gold that appear in the crest of the arms.

ABOUT

Colour reproduction

The effect of full colour is achieved in print by using the four-colour process, or 'CMYK'. The colour spectrum is approximated by combining varying amounts of cyan, magenta, yellow and black.

PRINCIPLES OF THE FOUR-COLOUR PROCESS

The process colours are not necessarily printed in the order shown.

Cyan prints

Magenta prints

Yellow prints

Black prints

NAA: A1500/1-K4936

Sample colour bar similar to ones used by printers to check colour balance

COLOUR BALANCE

Under-colour removal

This process involves adjusting the ink levels for cyan, magenta and yellow in the black areas to lessen the drying time on a high-speed print run.

NAA: A1500/1-K7584

CONVENTIONAL HALFTONE SCREENING

This is a four-colour reproduction and a magnified section showing how the colours are combined using different screen angles and a variable dot size. The screen angles create a rosette.

NAA A1500/1-K7584

STOCHASTIC SCREENING

The magnified section of this four-colour reproduction shows how the colours are combined using random pixel distribution.

DUOTONES

A high-contrast black
plate (top left) and a low-
contrast yellow plate
(bottom left) combine to
make a duotone (right).

A standard black halftone
(top left) and a 20 per
cent screen of yellow
(bottom left) combine to
create a flat-tint, or 'fake',
duotone (right).

Chapter **20** # Forms

DOING THE RESEARCH	**361**
Preliminary queries	361
Respondents	361
Processors	361
Investigative stage	362
DESIGNING THE TEXT AND LAYOUT OF A FORM	**363**
Questions	363
About forms	364
Responses	366
Navigating within a form	369
Typography of forms	370
TESTING AND REFINING A FORM	**372**
Pilot testing	372
Post-release testing	373

Successful forms share four characteristics: they are based on careful research; they are well designed; their questions have been devised thoughtfully and are clearly expressed; and they have been thoroughly tested before release.

Careful research means paying attention to all the factors associated with gathering the information and then processing it. The writing task is to structure and phrase the questions so that respondents will be able to understand them readily and answer them accurately. Effective design uses text, typography, colour and layout to make a form easy to fill in and process. For thorough testing, a representative sample of the people who will eventually fill out the form should 'road-test' it, so that any faults in the text and layout can be rectified before the form is distributed.

For most organisations, forms are an important tool for gathering basic information about existing and potential customers, clients, staff and others with an interest in the organisation's activity. The information they gather is used to create the databases that will influence decisions about further communication, new research, information interpretation and planning. The databases must therefore be up to date and valid.

➤ See Chapters 3 and 4 for guidance on structuring and writing documents for their readership and Chapter 16 for a discussion of visual identifiers for organisations.

Well-written, well-designed forms also do much for an organisation's identity. Beyond just a neat application of corporate logos, typefaces and colours, they imply respect and concern for the organisation's constituency.

A successful form using the standard question-and-answer format can be seen as a conversation between the respondent and the organisation seeking the information. As with most conversations, there is a two-way sharing of information, with moments of clarification and enlargement in addition to the question-and-answer sequence.

Many forms are not prepared carefully enough to achieve proper communication. Sometimes the need for a form and the form's precise function have not been clearly established; sometimes the content has not been devised and arranged in such a way as to be clearly understood by the intended respondents. People will probably resent filling in forms like this and will often ignore or override the form instructions. In the end, they might completely lose patience with the form—and

ith the organisation that produced it. With proper research, planning, design and
sting, however, most of these negatives can be avoided, and the information-
thering and conversational experience can be of mutual benefit.

OING THE RESEARCH

reliminary queries

he initial research for a form is done in response either to a perceived need for a
rm or to a request to revise an existing form. Having identified why the form is
eded and precisely what information is sought and why, it is worth considering
e following questions, at the very least:

Who will fill in the form?

Who will process it?

How and where will it be stored?

How regularly will it be accessed?

he answers to these questions will help determine the size of the form, its
ructure and focus, its layout and typography, the most suitable delivery method,
e number of duplicates required and, for printed forms, the kind of paper to use.

espondents

he person filling in the form must be able to do so with as little fuss as possible.
he questions should be set out in an order that is perceived to be logical; they
ould be restricted to those that will elicit only essential information; and they
ould be so phrased that the respondent is left in no doubt about what is being
ked and why. Clear language is essential. Precise, brief questions will not only
roduce more accurate responses but also leave more space for answers.

he form's compilers should take account of potential respondents' particular
aracteristics. The time that may be needed to fill out the form should also
e assessed, as should the likelihood of respondents being able and willing to
ll it out.

form must also comply with any legislation relating to the collection and use of
ata and data confidentiality.

➤ See Chapter 22 for a discussion of the legal obligations associated with collection and use of data and data confidentiality.

rocessors

he form must be able to be processed easily by people and machines. Among the
ctors to take into account here are dispatch, receipt, data capture and
formation gathering.

possible, material for action by a particular person in an organisation should be
ouped together on the form—so long as this does not adversely affect the form's
gic and respondents' capacity to complete the filling-out task. The form should
ave adequate space for any entries, attachments, endorsements or comments that
e part of a response, and it should clearly delineate the space set aside for
epartmental or office use.

In printed forms that will be filed or indexed, the information to be indexed should appear close to the head or side of the form, so that administrative staff can find it easily. In addition, provision should be made in the form's layout for any future binding or filing requirements. These factors must also be considered for screen-based forms that will be printed out for handling and storage.

If a form is to be handled frequently by several people, more than one copy might be required. Copies are usually printed on different-coloured paper and made into multi-part sets for the various users. If the form is on screen, there might be linked versions, which will need to comply with confidentiality and privacy legislation, perhaps by having separate access codes and information filters.

Investigative stage

A form's usefulness should be tested not only while it is being developed but also periodically thereafter. The post-development assessment will take account of any difficulties that have been encountered by respondents and those processing the form. It will also suggest whether the form could be more effectively presented and handled, reducing error rates on the part of both respondents and processors.

The best procedure for evaluating forms will probably be a combination of:

- error analysis
- group discussions and interviews
- observational study.

Error analysis

The purpose of error analysis is to identify the most obvious errors that respondents make. It is therefore the first consideration when redesigning an existing form or releasing a new one. Examination of a number of completed form will show whether the spacing and arrangement have been properly designed and whether the questions are being interpreted in the way the organisation intended. Errors or misinterpretations by respondents tend to fall into five categories:

- A question or section of the form is missed or not completed.
- Additional, unsolicited information is provided.
- The information provided is incorrect.
- Questions are misinterpreted.
- Data are incorrectly transcribed from another source.

Group discussions, interviews and observational study will suggest possible reasons for these errors.

Group discussions and interviews

Although focus groups have been found to have little predictive value, group discussions and interviews can provide a guide to the kind of language that is mos likely to be understood and used by respondents. This can help the compilers of a form to develop a conversational tone for the intended audience.

Interviews with people who have filled out a form often yield information only about what they remember about filling it in, not about what actually occurred. S observation is also needed.

➤ See Chapter 26 for more detail about evaluation, monitoring and testing.

Observational study

When watching people filling in a form, observers look for signs of difficulty or confusion: these are the symptoms of inadequate structuring, writing and form design, and they could well translate into errors in the information collected.

One important finding from observational research has been that a large number of errors in forms can be attributed to respondents not reading instructions, headings, clarifications and explanations. Various approaches can help to overcome this problem:

- The quantity and length of instructions can be minimised.
- The form can be designed to provide only answer spaces but be accompanied by a separate booklet containing the questions and explanations that will help respondents fill out the form correctly.
- Instructions can be linked to the answers. For example:

No—go to question 11

Yes—go to question 12

DESIGNING THE TEXT AND LAYOUT OF A FORM

Questions

The way questions are asked influences how well a form works. When formulating questions, it is important to take into account the following factors:

- the data sought and how much detail is necessary
- the language appropriate for the audience
- the sequencing and grouping of questions
- the amount of space needed for each response
- the processing system that will be used.

Open-ended questions

When form-fillers can answer in their own words, the questioning is called 'open-ended' because it allows for many possible responses. This is more demanding for respondents and processors, since the answers have to be written or typed and might not be readily decipherable or understandable. Open-ended questions therefore need individual processing.

Answer boxes or text entry fields must allow sufficient space for most of the possible responses. To elicit appropriate responses, some examples or instructions might be needed. This can include an explanation of what the respondent should do if a non-response, 'not applicable' or zero answer applies.

Closed questions

Closed questioning gives respondents specific choices. There are three types of closed-question structures—those requiring:

- 'yes/no' answers
- limited-choice answers
- multiple-choice answers.

(continued on p. 366)

ABOUT Forms

It is useful to be familiar with the different elements of forms and the language used to describe them.

Scales or spans: These are usually based on five degrees of variation

Strongly agree ☐   Agree ☐   Undecided ☐   Disagree ☐   Strongly disagree ☐

Line numbering: This can help with cross-referencing in complex forms.

1 Your customer number

2 Are you an Australian resident?

3 Your sex   Male ☐   Female ☐

Printed forms

Response fields: White boxes against a tinted background are often used for response fields. This quickly identifies the place where a response from the form-filler is required.

Office-use fields: A different colour or tone is often used to distinguish office-use fields from the white areas that respondents should fill in.

Tick boxes: Despite their name, 'tick' boxes often need to be crossed, numbered in order of preference, or marked with a horizontal bar.

Instructions: Directions for the correct use of a form are given in the instructions section.

Step numbering: This can clarify the sequence of the requested information.

Arrows and connectors: These can be used to direct respondents to their next task.

Step numbering   Instructions   Office-use field

Application Form
Please print neatly in BLOCK LETTERS with a black or blue ball point pen only.
Print ☒ in appropriate boxes.

Office use only

1 About you

Your customer number   See the **Privacy** note on page 8.

Are you an Australian resident?   Yes ☐   No ☐

Your sex   Male ☐   Female ☐

Your name
Print your full name.   Title—for example, Mr, Mrs, Ms, Miss

Family name

Has any part of your name changed since completing your last form?   Given names

No ☐   Yes ☐ ──▶ Previous name

Your **postal address**
Print the address where you want your mail sent.

Town or suburb

State   Postcode   Country *if not Australia*

Your **home address**
If it is different from your postal address, print the address where you live.

Town or suburb

State   Postcode   Country *if not Australia*

Your date of birth   Day   Month   Year   Please provide your date of birth to avoid delays in processing.

Your daytime telephone number
If we need to ask you about your answers, it is quicker by telephone.   Area code   Telephone number

Tick boxes   Arrows and connectors   Response fields

364

n-screen forms

eb browsers translate standard form ements into defaults, so designers ve limited control over the pearance of forms for web delivery. addition, some recipients will have ecified preference settings in their mputers that can further change the ok of a form—for example, by anging type sizes.

xt entry fields: These offer the most eful way of gathering information:

<input type=text>

What is your name?

[   ]

axlength specifies the number of aracters that can be keyed in. For ample:

<maxlength=16>

uld enable payment using a credit rd with a 16-character identifier:

Your credit card number

[   ]

xt area need not be related to the pected size of the answer. These lds can be designed to accommodate nger responses by allowing scrolling the right or down, or both, to extend e text area:

ow did you get to work this morning?

Describe your journey in
100 words or less

Check boxes: These are used for multiple-choice questions where more than one answer is possible. For example:

Where have you lived?

☑ Victoria
☑ New South Wales
☐ Queensland

Radio buttons: These limit the selection of answers to one. Once selected, no other options are available:

Where do you live?

◯ Victoria
◯ New South Wales
◉ Queensland

Pull-down menus: These have options in a list and will highlight and often display the selected item:

How did you get to work this morning?

Car
Walking
Bike

Scrolling menus: A scroll bar on the right of a menu displays only a small number of possible responses:

Where do you live now?

Victoria
New South Wales
Tasmania
Queensland

Buttons: Created by browser default stylings, buttons are clickable areas:

Custom buttons are created using default browser styling on custom text:

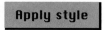

Image buttons are graphics created in an original style; they are used instead of defaults:

Passwords: Protection is given to passwords by replacing the actual characters with asterisks or bullets to disguise the information that has been entered. They provide low-level security:

What is your password?

****

Respondents need indicate only the answer that is most appropriate. Closed questions are thus easier to respond to and easier (and cheaper) to process. A disadvantage is that more effort is needed to develop them: form-fillers rarely have the opportunity to compensate for a poorly framed closed question.

Filter questions

Filter questions ask respondents to make a choice. This then leads them to different parts of the form containing the questions that pertain to their particular circumstances.

Using filter questions can be an efficient approach from both the respondents' and the processing officers' viewpoints. They relieve respondents of the need to read sections of the form that are irrelevant to them, and they reduce the number of errors made as a result of misinterpretation.

With filter questions, the 'no' response should be placed first because the subsequent instruction will usually take the respondent to a question much further down the form. The order of the 'no/yes' answers should be consistent throughout the form.

Responses

When responding, people are likely to:

- keep going through questions as long as there seems to be an order to them or until they come to a difficult or apparently irrelevant question
- mostly avoid reading instructions
- need clear instructions or graphic indicators if they are to jump questions
- miss instructions or explanations that they might have seen had they not jumped to a new question
- choose not to answer something they fail to understand or think is not applicable to them
- seek guidance on the interpretation of a question from the previous and the following questions, assuming those questions will provide context
- scan the topic content to determine a question's relevance.

The most complete answers come from open-ended questioning where comfortable room is provided for the majority of answers to be handwritten or where there are virtually unlimited text entry fields. These are not necessarily the most usable answers, however, because there is little control over their scope. As a result, forms often include a variety of other question-and-answer styles as well.

'Yes/no' answers

There are several ways of asking for 'yes/no' answers. The form might:

- follow each option with a tick box or check box
- ask respondents to circle what is applicable
- include an 'undecided' option.

It has been found that these methods are less confusing than preceding each option with a tick box or asking respondents to delete what is not applicable.

Limited-choice and multiple-choice answers

Limited-choice and multiple-choice answers can be ordered or unordered.

Unordered answers are those where there is no gradation of answers. When a form is to contain unordered answers, an effort should be made to control bias in the pattern of answers. Possible approaches are to start with fairly specific questions and progress to more general ones; to list the most common alternative last; or to list choices randomly. Alternatives should be phrased similarly and be kept to a similar length.

In on-screen forms, radio buttons can be used for limited-choice answers, while check boxes can be used for multiple-choice answers.

Tick boxes and check boxes

Because of the different ways respondents notate tick boxes in print, forms with such boxes usually ask for the boxes to be:

- ticked
- crossed
- marked with a horizontal bar
- coloured in

  or

- numbered to show a preference or order.

Once selected, check boxes on screen will display the programmed cross or tick.

For logic and readability, tick boxes and check boxes should follow a question. They should be placed close to the question, rather than on the extreme right of the screen or page, where it might be difficult to align them with the question.

Dotted lines ('dot leaders') linking questions with answers are never used on a printed form that also contains lines to be filled in. This is to avoid confusing respondents, who might think they are expected to write a response along the leaders.

Small, usually numerical, codes might also be devised for each tick box in a form. These can enable faster processing of the data and are often used in complex surveys.

Scales or spans

Numbers or tick boxes for scaled questions should be evenly tabbed and aligned throughout a form. The definition of the scale should be repeated at the top of each page or screen, or at each question if the boxes are scattered between other types of responses.

Accommodating handwriting

When paper is being chosen for a printed form, the suitability of its surface for handwriting should be considered, as well as the paper's durability and archival quality. When any surface treatments (such as varnishes on printed forms) are being specified, the writing implements respondents are likely to use should also

Application form

Please print neatly in BLOCK LETTERS with a black or blue ballpoint pen only.

Print in appropriate boxes.

JOHN SMITH

(a sample is shown above)

be taken into account. If a form is to be filled in by hand at the originating organisation's offices, the right type of pen or pencil can be supplied.

Response fields should provide sufficient space for form-fillers to enter their responses by hand. Capital letters should be specified because their shape is more readily distinguishable in processing. Additional space may be needed for respondent groups such as younger schoolchildren.

Techniques for standardising handwriting in forms—such as 'combs' or character dividers (where small nicks are placed every 5 millimetres along the line to separate letters) or individual boxes for each letter or numeral—are less successful than simply providing a blank white space for the response.

Spacing for handwritten responses on forms

For handwritten answers to standard information requests on forms, allow 5 millimetres per character and at least 7 millimetres between lines. The following space provisions can be taken as a guide for specific response fields:

- *given names*—40 millimetres each, allowing 8 characters each
- *family name*—50 millimetres, allowing 10 characters
- *address*—140 millimetres, allowing 28 characters
- *business address*—210 millimetres, allowing 42 characters
- *postcode*—20 millimetres, for 4 characters
- *phone and fax numbers*—50 millimetres each, for 10 characters
- *email address*—100 millimetres each, allowing 20 characters
- *URLs*—80 millimetres each, allowing 16 characters
- *credit card numbers*—80 millimetres, for 16 characters
- *expiry date*—20 millimetres, for 4 characters
- *dates*—30 millimetres, for 6 characters, usually specified as 'DD/MM/YY' or 'day/month/year'.

Signature blocks

A signature should be allocated a space 70 millimetres wide and 20 millimetres deep.

Other space requirements

Does the form have to be endorsed or stamped once the respondent has filled it in? If so, is there enough room for the endorsement or stamp?

If there are standard attachments, such as passport-size photographs or address labels, has enough room been left to accommodate them?

Colour-coding response areas

The 'active' area for responses is often white; it may be boxed with a fine border or outline. The surrounding question and instruction area is shaded or colour-tinted to distinguish it from the response area. In that way, respondents can see the extent of their task in filling in the form and can gauge the relative size of the answers expected.

Colour or tonal variation and a clear title should distinguish any area to be used by processing officers for annotation or recording further data.

Navigating within a form

Navigation techniques for forms try to simplify respondents' tasks by clearly identifying the steps involved in responding and by minimising the time needed to respond accurately. To do this, a form will often make use of the following navigation aids:

- clearly defined response areas
- clear subdivision of the content, using section headings
- a clear typographic hierarchy
- information zones for instructions
- numbering
- arrows or connectors.

Subdividing and structuring

When designing a form, it can be difficult to group sets of information while also maintaining logical connections and accommodating processing needs. Often, the first subdivision will separate personal information about the respondent from the opinions or information being sought. If an organisation has numerous forms, it is worth systematising the placement and formats for this standardised information; this will make retrieval, and responding, easier.

Alignment

A system of specific areas or zones created for the various information groupings can simplify respondents' understanding of a form. For example, these areas could delineate:

- information zones that precede a question or are contained in a column to the left of the questions. These can be used for instructions on how to approach the form or individual questions, including any directions or examples
- question zones in the centre
- answer zones that follow the question, either below or to the right of it.

Instructions

There are two main types of instructions used on forms:

- what to do with the form and where to get help with answering it
- how to answer the questions.

Even when they are placed at the start of a form, instructions are often ignored. In spite of this, it is worth remembering that short sentences are generally more readily understood than long ones, and that each sentence should be restricted to a single piece of information.

Instructions should be placed as close as possible to the place where they are to be applied. This often means repeating the same instruction each time it is needed, particularly if it deals with how to answer questions. But instructions should also be easily distinguishable from the questions. Instructions at the end of a form might include a checklist of items from the form, a list of any attachments that are required, and details of what to do next.

There may need to be a diagram showing the form's internal coding, acting as a key to the methods used in the form to provide different types of advice. This technique has been used to explain large forms such as referendum and other voting materials, census booklets and tax returns.

Section headings

Section headings can operate like a summary to make a form look a little easier to fill in. They must be carefully considered in their context, so that they offer a clear overview of the scope or topics covered by the form.

A section heading often prompts respondents to skip over a section if it appears not to apply to their situation, so it can be useful when filter questions or instructions direct the respondent elsewhere. If there are specific forms for different respondents, these summary headings can also help with choosing the correct form.

Numbering

The four standard types of numbering used in forms are fairly self-explanatory:

- question numbering
- step-by-step numbering or section numbering to simplify the process of filling in the form in the correct sequence
- line numbering in complex forms—bold line numbers are often used to highlight specific entries for use later in the form
- answer numbering or coding for ease of processing—this is done particularly with coded tick boxes and check boxes.

Arrows, connectors and links

Arrows and other graphic devices can be used to direct respondents' attention to particular places on a form. Smaller arrows might be used to indicate that not every respondent needs to answer a supplementary question. With filter questions, connecting lines and arrows can be used like a flow chart; on screen, a hyperlink to the next question in the sequence can be used.

Typography of forms

Sans serif typefaces have three particular characteristics that make them ideal for forms: their clarity; their legibility at small sizes; and the variety of weights they offer for use in a hierarchy. They are also easier to read on screen.

Line numbering in tax forms

Answer coding from a consumer survey

9 What type of music do you regularly listen to?

Classical	1	☐
Country	2	☐
Folk	3	☐
Jazz	4	☐
Pop/Rock	5	☐
Other	6	☐

Your name

Print your full name.

▶ **Has any part of your name changed since completing your last tax return?**

NO ☐   YES ☐ → Previous family name

Title—for example, Mr, Mrs, Ms, Miss

Family name

Given names

Previous family name

Your postal address

Print the address where you want your mail sent.

Town or suburb

State ☐   Postcode ☐

▶ **Has this address changed since completing your last tax return?**

NO ☐   YES ☐ → Previous postcode ☐

Graduated arrows

Smaller arrows can be used for supplementary questions

Given name and family name: where to put them?

Possible

Given name
Family name

Also possible

Given name

Family name

Preferred

Given name

Family name

Confusing rules

JACK
Given name
HARRISON
Family name
3/61 AVOCA ST
Address
ALBURY

Given name
          JACK
Family name
          HARRISON
Address
          3/61 AVOCA ST

          ALBURY

acement of type

rms sometimes have instructions in very small type inside response boxes. This is t recommended: it limits the space available for the response. The instructions e better placed outside the box at an easily readable size. With careful alignment, e question and its corresponding response field will still be clear.

rms that have ruled lines and type inside a response field (such as a name and dress section) often confuse respondents, who can be unaware until they reach e bottom of the section that all their responses have been written on the wrong e. The type might be aligned so close to the top edge of the response field that e edge is mistaken for the line on which the information should be written, ther than writing below the type. This confusion can be avoided by tinting the ea outside a response field and by placing the request to the left of the line on ich the answer is to be given.

tablishing a clear hierarchy

addition to the usual hierarchy of headings and the zoning of like information a form's layout, designers of forms often subdivide the content into three logical visions:

instructions

questions

answers.

these, the questions are considered the most important for respondents and are erefore often shown in bold sans serif type. Answer options and scale descriptors usually in the medium weight of the chosen sans serif typeface.

is also often necessary to make a strong visual distinction between instructions d other text. To achieve this typographically, the instructions can be in a second lour and even in a serif typeface.

TESTING AND REFINING A FORM

To develop successful forms, three cycles of testing and refinement are needed. Rarely are all faults identified in the first round of testing, and removing one fault may introduce a new one. So, after two rounds of modification, the third test should confirm that the form's performance is acceptable. Complex forms often require more cycles of testing and refinement.

Pilot testing

Used extensively in developing survey forms, pilot testing involves conducting a small-scale survey, using a proposed design, in order to apply the results to modify and improve the form. The extra expense involved is usually more than offset by superior response and more accurate data collection.

There are three main types of pilot testing, each conducted at different stages of form development:

- concept testing
- question testing
- form testing.

Concept testing

Concept testing very early in the process is designed to determine what information respondents are likely to be able to provide and the range of answers they might give. Typically, open-ended questions are used to elicit all possible responses to a topic. From these results can come a better structured questionnaire with more focused questions and provision for the more common responses.

Groups representative of potential respondents can be involved in discussions to identify possible problems with the concept or topic. The discussions might lead suggestions about who best to approach for the information that is being sought, the best means of collecting that information, and the possible responses.

Question testing

After it has been determined that the information is available, and the matter of who is going to supply it, and how, has been settled, a more formal set of questions can be developed. This set of questions (sometimes referred to as a 'schedule of questions' or a 'question protocol') covers everything to be asked, the order in which the questions will appear, and the language and phrasing to be used.

At this point, the form need not be formatted, although it will have spaces for answers. The questions are thus tested without graphics or layout. A small group test respondents can now be asked to complete the form.

All the means available for evaluating forms can then be used. The results might indicate that changes are needed. Once any changes to the questions have been made, the testing should be done again. Several versions of the form might need be tested before one proves satisfactory.

After a final version of the questions has been settled on, it is important not to change any of the questions while the actual form to be used is being constructed

rm testing

draft version of the agreed and formatted form might be tested in a small-scale n. Most word processing software can generate a good approximation of the rm's final appearance, so a draft can be sufficient for this level of testing.

his test will enable not only the form itself to be tested but all the aspects of the llection procedure as well: distribution, collection, processing and storage. The sults may reveal problem areas other than the questions and the appearance of e form. If so, these will have to be resolved before the form is ultimately eased.

st-release testing

ter the various cycles of testing and refinement have resulted in a form that actions well, the production, distribution, collection and processing cycle begins. is now that the conversation between the individual respondents and the iginating organisation begins in earnest.

nce released, the form should be reviewed at regular intervals. Contact formation should be checked for currency and an overall evaluation should be nducted to ensure that the form still meets the organisation's needs. In this way, orm can continually develop and evolve—with performance analysis, content riation as required, and a cycle of testing and refinement at each iteration.

EVALUATING A FORM'S DESIGN

Is the form easy to use?

Is the information grouped appropriately or logically—for both the person who fills in the form and the person who processes the form?

Is it easy to find where to insert information?

Can each direction be followed without missing essential instructions or information?

Is the language concise and unambiguous?

Do the chosen questioning styles elicit enough usable information?

Do the colours or tones clearly delineate the response areas and the areas set aside for office use?

Do the response areas adequately cater for the handwriting and answer lengths of the majority of respondents?

Do the graphics support navigation but not detract from the purpose of information gathering?

Is it easy to extract the required information from the completed form?

Is confidentiality protected?

Most importantly, has the form been adequately tested?

Chapter 21

Illustrating

ILLUSTRATION OPPORTUNITIES	**375**
Tell—and show	375
Prompt words for illustrations	376
IMAGE SELECTION	**378**
Consistency	378
Background selection	380
PLACEMENT OF ILLUSTRATIONS	**381**
Integration and sequence	381
Standard image formats and sizes	381
Multi-image pages	382
Cut-in illustrations	382
ILLUSTRATION TECHNIQUES AND REPRODUCTION	**382**
Line drawing and reproduction	383
Halftone illustration	383
Halftone reproduction	384
About halftone screens	**385**
COLOUR SYSTEMS	**387**
Gamut	387
On-screen colour	388
Process colour	388
Pantone colour	390
SCALING, CROPPING AND MASKING	**390**
Scaling	390
Cropping and masking	391
PHOTOGRAPHS	**392**
Black-and-white prints	392

Transparencies	392
Digital image files	392
Image manipulation	393
GRAPHS AND CHARTS	**393**
Interpretation of data	393
Line graphs	395
Bar charts, dot graphs and column graphs	396
Pie charts	396
Scattergrams	396
Hi-lo graphs	397
Drawing graphs	397
Illustrated graphs	397
DIAGRAMS	**397**
Flow charts and other process charts	397
Assembly diagrams	398
Storyboards	398
Comic strips	399
MAPS	**399**
Map labelling	399
Statistical mapping	400
MOVING IMAGES	**401**
SOUND	**402**
IMAGE AND SOUND LIBRARIES	**402**
IMAGE COMPRESSION	**402**

...ustrating text involves much more than including illustrations ...epared by an artist to depict something described in the text. ...aphs, diagrams, photographs, sound bites, video clips and animation ...n all help to clarify information and give readers a greater ...preciation of the content of a publication. This chapter deals with ...ustration' in its broadest sense: the use of imagery to depict an idea.

...esigners often prepare most of the illustrative material, and they ...ually brief and commission specialist illustrators as required. In this ...ay, a document is unified visually, which is as important as achieving ...e unified voice that is usually a prerequisite for the text.

...ustrating also entails particular responsibilities. In most contexts—and ...rticularly in the case of government publications—designers should be culturally ...clusive, conceptualising and choosing images that offer suitable representation ...ross gender, race, sexuality and age. They should also be sensitive to different ...ltural beliefs, practices and taboos. It is very easy to fall into using clichéd ...agery.

...signers, illustrators, authors and editors preparing illustrations for publication ...o need at least a basic understanding of the reproduction processes involved, to ...sure that the work is prepared correctly. The different colour systems used for ...nt and screen dictate the ultimate success of all illustrations.

...LUSTRATION OPPORTUNITIES

...n illustration helps to attract readers to the text; it can also communicate ...formation that is difficult to describe succinctly in words. To help create the best ...x of text and illustration, authors should try to visualise how their text might ...t only incorporate imagery but also resonate with it.

...ll—and show

...its most basic, imagery can be used to show an object, place or person. This is ...e technique used in most documentaries, encyclopedias and advertising.

...t readers also respond—almost intuitively—to more complex imagery. Even ...lings, emotions and concepts such as atmosphere or mood can be illustrated ...th colour and texture. Metaphors that use descriptive imagery can create an ...expected connection to a more abstract concept.

Moving and still imagery
- Drawings
- Paintings
- Assemblage, montage and collage
- Comics, cartoons and caricature
- Animation
- Staged and studio photography
- Photos for texture and atmosphere
- Documentary and historical photos

Charts, diagrams and graphs
- Flow charts
- Organisation charts
- Sequence, process and assembly diagrams
- Exploded diagrams
- Bar and column graphs
- Pie charts
- Line graphs
- Scatter diagrams

Maps
- Location maps
- Statistical maps

Sound
- Voice
- Dialogue
- Music
- Sound effects

Prompt words for illustrations

In any document there are terms and phrases that hide an illustration concept. I[f] you learn to 'read' these prompts for illustration, the range of illustrative options will become apparent.

Prompt words and illustration possibilities

'Rule Britannia'
sound
British Coat of Arms
pic

Original areas
map/pic

Westminster
pic

Queens and
kings from
Victoria to
Elizabeth
pic/clips

COMMONWEALTH OF AUSTRALIA
CONSTITUTION ACT

An Act to constitute the Commonwealth of Australia.

[9th July 1900]

WHEREAS the people of New South Wales, Victoria, South Australia, Queensland and Tasmania, humbly relying on the blessing of Almighty God, have agreed to unite in one indissoluble Federal Commonwealth under the Crown of the United Kingdom of Great Britain and Ireland, and under the Constitution hereby established.

And whereas it is expedient to provide for the admission into the Commonwealth of other Australasian Colonies and other possessions of the Queen:

Be it therefore enacted by the Queen's most Excellent Majesty, by and with the advice and consent of the Lords Spiritual and Temporal, and Commons, in the present Parliament assembled, and by the authority of the same, as follows:—

1. This Act may be cited as the Commonwealth of Australia Constitution Act.

2. The provisions of this Act referring to the Queen shall extend to Her Majesty's heirs and successors in the sovereignty of the United Kingdom.

3. It shall be lawful for the Queen, with the advice of the Privy Council, to declare by proclamation that, on and after a day therein appointed, not being later than one year after the passing of this Act, the people of New South Wales, Victoria, South Australia, Queensland and Tasmania, and also, if Her Majesty is satisfied that the people of Western Australia have agreed thereto, of Western Australia, shall be united in a Federal Commonwealth under the name of the Commonwealth of Australia. But the Queen may, at any time after the proclamation, appoint a Governor-General for the Commonwealth.

Short title

Act to extend to the Queen's successors.

Proclamation of Commonwealth

Original coats of arms **pic**

Queen Victoria **pic** 'God save the Queen' **sound**

WA Coat of Arms and map **pic**

Proclamation from Archives **pic**

Descriptive imagery

To identify the people, places and objects that could be illustrated in a publicatio[n] look for the nouns, particularly the proper nouns. The result will be illustration a[t] basic identification.

This is only the first step, though. References to the familiar are less important than references to the new or unfamiliar, so it is often advisable to choose lesser

own or unexpected images from the range of options. Such a selection adds
traction value as well as visual information. But be sure that readers are likely to
receptive to the images: there can be a 'comfort zone' in representations of the
miliar, particularly when a document contains challenging concepts.

ustration can communicate much by implication. For example, when a
otographer is being commissioned to produce portraits for an organisation chart,
ought should be given to the subjects' facial expression, pose and mode of dress,
well as the lighting and background, since all these factors influence readers'
rceptions. This is illustration as description.

hen the text tells a story, contains speech or dialogue, or expresses personal
inion or even argument, it can be thought of as a script with film and sound
tions. The situation that has been described in the text can then be re-created,
ged or constructed, or an original source might be found. It could also be
imated. Storytelling is one of the best ways of engaging people. Prompt words
d phrases such as *Imagine ...* or *For example ...* often start a story.

agrammatic imagery

ferences to numbers, sums of money and percentages often occur in text. These
ggest the opportunity for a graph or table, which might be available from a
urce such as the Australian Bureau of Statistics or be created from original data.

metimes text describes a sequence or process; sometimes it discusses connections
interactions; or perhaps it explains the way something works. In these
uations, a diagram or chart often helps readers to understand the concepts. This
illustration as clarification.

mbolic, textural and atmospheric imagery

ferences to nations, states, corporations, organisations and even families offer a
ealth of possibilities for symbolic imagery. Flags and heraldic emblems, maps,
gos and corporate identifiers can be used for simple identification or can be
corporated in diagrams to show alliances, developments and connections.

ferences to nature and culture suggest textural imagery. Nature offers many
portunities, from the microscopic to the telescopic. Equally, images from
fferent human cultures can be intriguing, exotic and appealing. The diversity of
tural and cultural forms can be used descriptively, atmospherically or
etaphorically. References to culture and descriptions of mood might prompt the
e of colour, texture, sound, music and non-specific or non-descriptive imagery to
nvey an atmosphere.

int of view can also be suggested. This is why designers ask authors and clients
describe what sort of impression they would like readers to gain from a
rticular publication. Words such as *conservative, festive, strong, celebratory, caring,*
ung, soft and *innovative* are all atmospheric descriptors. They can be translated
to graphic interpretations that visually code the presentation.

is is illustration as abstract communication. For it to be successful, however,
ere must be a clear understanding of how the intended audience will decode the

layer of symbolic or abstract information. The decoding is more important than the encoding: the potential for confusion or misinterpretation must be avoided.

Metaphoric imagery

Visual metaphors encode information to be read in a particular way and can be very useful when complex new information is to be presented. They are widely used as a navigation technique in web and multimedia documents. For example, familiar visual metaphors—shopping trolleys, cash registers and service counters– can help potential buyers feel comfortable on the Internet.

IMAGE SELECTION

Once it has been decided where the opportunities for illustration lie in a document, the next task is image selection.

If the budget and schedule allow it, there is the option of generating original material. Using the work of one illustrator, photographer or cinematographer generally brings a valuable cohesiveness to the final look of a publication.

The suitability of an image for enlargement or reduction should also be considered. In the final selection, look for images that have a consistent point of view, colour palette, attitude or even aesthetic. The illustrations used throughout a publication should look like a set, even if they have been brought together from different sources.

It is always a good idea to locate too much illustrative material, rather than to have to use everything that has been found regardless of its quality and suitability. It is usually better to leave out an illustration altogether than to use a poor-quality one.

Consistency

Consistency in illustration throughout a publication can be achieved in a variety of ways, among them the following:

- applying a consistent visual 'attitude' to the selection, use and cropping of images
- maintaining consistent colour palettes within sets of images and across the different types of imagery used
- standardising the labelling and titling to complement the heading hierarchy devised for the text
- using consistent thicknesses for all line rules in the publication.

Visual attitude

An underlying theme or attitude can be conveyed by using bright colour and unexpected angles or viewpoints to suggest a dynamic, fresh organisation. Or the image selection could imply mystery, usually through the use of shadowy, blurry images with indistinct lighting. Insipid, muddled colours with uneven lighting and uninspired documentary photography would be a poor choice, probably suggesting only dullness. Readers absorb the underlying attitude subliminally, so it is worth the effort to convey, at the very least, an image of professionalism and competence.

olour-correction can be used to maintain a consistent set of colours within the
nages, so that the colours are similar in intensity and, if possible, in hue and
nality. If filters are applied, the differing grains and surface textures of
notographs and other types of illustrations obtained from a variety of sources can
so be standardised to some extent.

milarly, consistent border styles for cropped photographs can bring consistency.
his may be as simple as using drop shadows or feathered edges.

olour palette

he colours used for photographs, backgrounds, headings, tables and graphs should
e complementary. The colour palette for a publication is often chosen during the
itial design stages and reflected in featured text, but it usually needs to be
tended to accommodate the available images.

extreme cases, an image can be unusable because it differs too much in colour
aracter and would draw unnecessary attention to itself. If image manipulation
es not help, it is best to leave the image out or to try to locate an alternative.

nsistent labelling and titling

pe that is associated with images usually has one of three roles:

  It is a headline.
  It captions the image, explaining the context and content and reinforcing the
  message of the text.
  It labels parts of the image.

 link these typed elements with their images, appropriate colour, proximity and
acing are essential.

r visually impaired readers, it is important to have textual labels describing all
ages. On-screen images should always contain the 'alt text' attribute, even if no
sible captioning is required.

les

he titles of illustrations are usually quite brief. They do not need to be limited to
bject categories—in contrast with signpost headings in the text, which should
e—because readers' interest has already been attracted by the picture. Titles are
ten in larger type than both captions and labels and should be designed to
mplement the heading hierarchy of the text, not to compete with it.

ptioning

eaders quickly become accustomed to captions and assume that they will be
aced consistently through a publication. Generally, it is unwise to place detailed
ptions above or to the left of an image, since these positions go against reading
avity and many readers will resist this interruption to their reading pattern.

belling

bels are used to identify and clarify detail in graphs and diagrams. They can be
aced close to the elements they describe (as is the case with city names on maps)
 they can be placed outside the image area and connected to the element by

Image borders

Square-cut

NAA A1500/1 K9337

Drop shadow

Vignette

Feathered

➤ See Chapter 17 for a discussion of reading patterns.

means of an arrow or a rule. Sometimes it is necessary to provide a key explaining the type weights, line styles, icons, and colour and shading codes used in an illustration.

Consistent line thicknesses

Consistency can also be achieved through the line thicknesses used in a document. Choose two basic thicknesses—one fine and one of medium weight—for different purposes and use these wherever line work is required in the publication.

Background selection

Colours, patterns and textures

When deciding on a background colour, look at the images that are to appear on it. Usually it is possible to find a colour within them that will enhance each image and define its border. When this colour is used, the images will be better integrated and will look as though they belong against the background. If a patterned or textured background is chosen, it should not distract from the foreground content.

Suitable backgrounds are likely to have two basic characteristics:

- a simplified colour set that complements the foreground images
- not too much variation in tonality, particularly if type is to be overprinted on them.

Backgrounds for web sites often use a repeated element to fill the screen area. In this case it is important to ensure that the desired pattern does in fact appear. It is sometimes necessary to edit the colours at the edges of the original piece so that they will blend more effectively when 'tiled'.

Ghosted images

A ghosted image

Before

A photographic image that is chosen for a background can be 'ghosted' to reduce its tonal range. The deep tones will become light or medium and all the other tones will be recalculated too. Ghosted images are often enlarged to create a background on which the original image and some text are placed.

After

Borders

Images can be given borders to distinguish them from the background or to define their edges, particularly where sky fades away. The border might be simply a fine black hairline, or it might be heavy and decorated in order to create a particular mood or atmosphere. Whatever style is chosen, it must suit the subject matter and the message.

Sometimes a thick band of colour might be chosen as a border, to establish a corporate colour presence within a publication. Care is needed, however, to ensure that the border colour is not too bright, pure or dominant; otherwise, the image may appear 'washed out'.

Colours have associations, and the colour chosen for borders can therefore provide a subtle commentary. But care is needed: in a straightforward portrait with a

ngle-colour frame, an unfortunate colour choice could suggest to readers that the
bject is effeminate, revolutionary, intellectually lightweight, unhealthy—or even
ead!

PLACEMENT OF ILLUSTRATIONS

general, illustrations should be placed close to, and preferably after, the section
text to which they most relate. In some circumstances, however, such as with
olour sections in a book, production limitations can make that proximity
ipractical.

cause the eye is usually attracted to images first, the preferred position for an
ustration is at the top of a page, to conform with reading gravity. This placement
ll not be suitable, though, if it results in the illustration appearing in a section of
e text to which it is not relevant.

Integration and sequence

eally, illustrations are distributed throughout a publication. This might mean
ansferring some illustrations out of heavily illustrated sections to other sections,
here they can be used to illustrate secondary references. Visual 'pace' is generated
some variety in the frequency of illustrations, but an overall impression of
lance is necessary to maintain readers' interest. If it is difficult to create a
asonably regular spread of illustrations, visual pace can be maintained through
atured type treatments.

eaders also often 'read' a picture sequence before reading the text. Thought
ould therefore be given to ensuring that the order of the illustrations conveys
e story effectively and will not lead readers to make incorrect visual connections
assumptions.

A landscape format

illustrations occupy most of a page in a book, it is best to omit textual matter if
more than five lines of text can be accommodated. A page that is taken up
tirely by an illustration need not carry a running header or a page number.

an illustration is moved from the insertion point originally chosen, it is
iportant to check that any text reference to it is amended.

Standard image formats and sizes

ages within a horizontal shape are said to be in a 'landscape' format. Images
thin a vertical shape are said to be in a 'portrait' format. These descriptions of
rmat orientation should not be confused with the content of the image.

A portrait format

ages are usually designed to fit modules in a grid, as described on the master
ges of a document. Because photograph dimensions are usually in the ratio 3:4,
is quite common to create vertical and horizontal standards for illustrations in
at ratio for the grid. The following are among the possibilities:

one-column portrait and landscape formats

two-column portrait and landscape formats

a full-page image—taking up the complete text area but not spreading into
the margin

➤ See Chapter 17 for a discussion of grids and master pages.

Landscape illustrations and captions

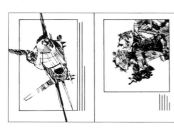

Cut-in illustrations

Square-cut

Contoured image with a text runaround

- a full-page image that 'bleeds'—covering the entire text area and some or all of the margins.

Standardising image sizes is a useful production shortcut. It allows for multiple images to be scanned at the same time, since they will all have the same reduction or enlargement ratio.

In a printed document, an illustration that has to be placed sideways on a page should be oriented so that its left side is towards the foot of the standard page. The title, caption and all labels will have the same orientation as the picture, although the page number will remain in the same position as all other page numbers in the publication.

Multi-image pages

When two or more images are to appear on a page, the decision is whether to group them or to separate them. Often a group, or cluster, creates interesting interplay between the images. However, readers might seek to connect the images conceptually, so a cluster should be used only if the connection is intended.

Clustering can also create multi-dimensional effects. If an image overlaps another image, the top one is seen to be forward. A cluster that layers numerous images can thus create foreground, mid-ground and background effects.

Cut-in illustrations

Any illustration that appears inside the normal text area but not across the full measure is said to be 'cut in'. The cut-in illustration can be:

- square-cut—that is, having a square or rectangular frame
- a free-form shape—where the sides are made of straight lines but at different angles

  or

- contoured—where a shape may have its background removed, like a profile of a face.

Most software for page layout has an automatic text-wrapping facility.

The size of the space between a cut-in illustration and the surrounding text (the 'runaround') should be consistent, at somewhere between 3 and 5 millimetres. Because of the options for resizing the window of a web document, it is preferable that pictures with runaround text in web sites appear on the left, allowing the text to re-wrap down the right if the window or type preferences are altered.

ILLUSTRATION TECHNIQUES AND REPRODUCTION

Line reproduction is capable of great detail but is dependent on the resolution of scanners and output devices. Tonal reproduction systems take a 'continuous tone' image (which includes a full range of tones, like a photograph) and convert it to a line image (or single tone) through the halftoning process.

ne drawing and reproduction

he most familiar type of line drawing is the traditional pen-and-ink drawing, in hich the outlines and all other details are represented in black ink on good-uality drawing board or paper with a smooth surface.

lthough a pen-and-ink drawing is the simplest type of artwork to reproduce, it n cause difficulties if the artist is not experienced in drawing for reproduction. ll lines should be solid and the ink must remain a true black throughout. (Lines at are not of an even density and that fade away or shade off into grey, as with ad pencil drawings, are best reproduced as a tonal image.) Further, if a line awing is to be reduced from its original size for reproduction, the lines must not too close together or too thin.

raperboard is another medium used for the preparation of line drawings. When raped away, its specially prepared black surface reveals a white substrate that rms the white lines and areas of the picture. In this way it provides the look of a nocut or woodcut.

Cartoons: Sometimes cartoons are used in a publication to lighten heavy text. Careful thought should, however, be given to the publication's context and how readers are likely to respond: what is funny to one person is not necessarily funny to someone else. In addition, the cartoonist should be thoroughly briefed.

ne drawing techniques

n and ink	Hand stipple	Line and mechanical tint	Scraperboard

COURTESY BARBARA VAN DER LINDEN

COURTESY BEV TUNKS

COURTESY BARBARA VAN DER LINDEN

COURTESY CATE ADAMS

oviding the basic rules are observed—uniformly solid black lines and stipples or tterns that are neither too thin nor too close together—original line drawings esented on clean paper or illustration board can be reproduced successfully in ack or single colour. Simple line drawings are best drawn oversize, at 150 per nt or even 200 per cent.

alftone illustration

alftone and colour illustrations can be created with computer illustration ckages, which produce the illustrations as digital files ready for various types of tput. They can also be created by hand and scanned directly or converted to a ansparency for scanning as a photograph. When an illustration is converted to a ansparency, a colour bar should be photographed with it to enable accurate olour-correction of the eventual scan.

igital illustration

ften a rough sketch is scanned as the basis for creating a digital illustration. Colours, xtures, filters and effects are then added to create the final illustration file.

Line drawing styles on an Australian banknote

Many different drawing, painting and photo-manipulation programs are available. Their application is limited only by the imagination and skill of the designer or illustrator—and the amount of computer memory available. The mouse, joystick, light-pen and graphics tablet, as well as the computer itself, are merely extensions of traditional illustration tools such as pencils, paints and brushes, and there are a number of specialist illustrators trained solely in the generation of digital images.

Clip art

Existing artwork in many different subject classifications is available for instant illustration. It is provided in many formats: CD-ROM, digital files from the web, duplicate slides or transparencies, or by subscription. Clip art is, however, not recommended for Australian government publications for the following reasons:

- It can be of low or inconsistent quality.
- Many clip art images are already in circulation.
- It is often not of Australian origin.
- Where clip art images feature people, there is little guarantee of legally satisfactory model release.

Clip art: These images are not recommended for government publications.

Halftone reproduction

Continuous-tone material such as a photograph is reproduced by the halftone process, in which the continuous tone is broken down into a series of solid dots separated by white space in printing or into a series of pixels on screen. The finer the halftone image resolution—that is, the greater the number of dots or pixels per inch—the more accurate will be the representation of the original continuous tone.

Computer-controlled scanning and 'screening' processes allow for a wide range of screen densities. In printing, the dot that is created varies in size according to the depth of tone it is trying to represent in the photograph. Black is solid with a barely discernible dot; dark grey has a black area with small white dots that become larger to produce mid-grey; light grey has a white area with black dots that become smaller as the grey gets lighter; and white has the finest dot available, called a 'highlight dot'.

A computer's ability to achieve a variable dot size is determined by the resolution capacity of the output device used. Bromide and film output are capable of high resolution and can therefore render variably sized dots with accuracy. Other line and tone screens generate different types of graphic halftone effects.

Stochastic screening

Instead of a regular pattern of variably sized dots, stochastic screening uses a random placement of same-sized pixels ('picture elements'), the pixel frequency increasing as the image gets darker and decreasing as it gets lighter. Output devices reproduce pixels, so type and images are made up of a fine mesh of squares. As the resolution capacity of the output device increases, the human eye's ability to perceive the squares is reduced; thus, at low resolution the patterns are clearly visible but at high resolution they become too fine to distinguish.

ABOUT
Halftone screens

In halftoning, continuous tone is represented in print by a regular pattern of variably sized dots or a random scattering of pixels. On screen, a regular pattern of same-sized pixels at different light intensities creates a similar illusion.

NAA: A1500/1-K47S2

An enlarged section of a halftone print

An enlarged section of a halftone in print using stochastic screening

An enlarged section of a halftone on screen

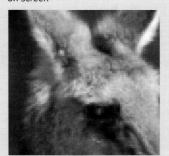

Print and on screen

Quality of resolution

lpi

100 lpi

150 lpi

NAA: A1500/1-K20S2

Image resolution

Variable-dot halftoning

ine screen

A circular screen

A tone dropout that is not screened

Effects screens

Stochastic screening is enabled by computer reproduction processes, and particularly by direct-to-plate printing technology, where the accuracy of the reproduction of very high resolution files can give the perception of continuous tone.

Resolution

Dots per inch

Dots per inch (or dpi) is the measure used to describe the resolution of a printer or output device. The resolution of currently available plain black office printers is usually either 300 or 600 dpi; colour printers often have a resolution of 600 dpi or greater; and an imagesetter can generate film or plates to a resolution of 1200 to 2400 dpi or greater. These dots reproduced by computer are, of course, pixels—squares, not circles.

Pixels per inch

Pixels per inch (or ppi) is the measure used to describe a computer screen's resolution, which is dependent on the manufacturer's specifications for the monitor. If it has 72 ppi resolution—the standard used for web site creation—there are 72 'picture elements' per inch. They are little square boxes that display different intensities of colour on a colour monitor, different intensities of white light on a black-and-white monitor, and varying amounts of black on a liquid crystal display.

Resolution for screen illustrations: The resolution for images created solely for screen-based reading does not need to be greater than 72 ppi.

Lines per inch

To distinguish the resolution of printing or output devices from the resolution of halftone images, lines per inch (or lpi) is used for the latter. The final resolution an image is, however, still dependent on the output device. The average laser printer prints images at 60 lpi; an imagesetter can print at 120 lpi for bromide quality; and it is possible to print direct-to-negative film and direct to plate at 300 lpi and beyond.

The average image screen produced by a plain-paper laser printer is very coarse compared with the film and direct-to-plate stipples available to a commercial printer.

The halftone screen density chosen depends on the surface of the paper on which a halftone is ultimately to be printed. Generally, the smoother the surface, the finer the screen that can be printed; and the finer the screen, the more closely the reproduction will simulate the original continuous-tone image.

Moiré

If the original of a photo or other graphic that needs to be reproduced is unavailable, a previously published image can be re-screened—provided copyright permission has been obtained. Although scanning technology and image-manipulation software might be able to enhance the newly recaptured image, technical problems can occur when re-scanning something that has previously been screened. An unwanted visual effect called a 'moiré pattern' can occur when

e halftone screening for the original reproduction clashes with the angles of the
alftone screens for the re-scan. There are several ways of avoiding this:

Alter the angle of the halftone screen.

Try to shoot the original 'dot for dot' (rather than re-screening at all).

Use stochastic screening—its random pixel distribution will not conflict with
the dot screen of the original.

OLOUR SYSTEMS

olour is what we see reflected from any object or surface. It is dependent on
ailable light.

colour terminology, the 'hue' is the distinguishable, pure form of a colour;
is what makes red distinct from purple. Then there are 'tints' and 'tones' of
lour, which describe, respectively, the lightness or darkness of the hue. This is
nown as the 'value' of a colour; it makes red distinct from tomato and burgundy.
ontrast is the value (or 'intensity') difference between two areas. Black text
a white background has high contrast; black text on a grey background has a
wer contrast.

he application of colour affects the way we read. Background and text colours
ed to provide the right contrast for legibility. Whether in print or on screen, low
ntrast can be irritating and tiring for younger readers; for older readers and
ople who are colour-blind, it can make reading impossible. High contrast also
proves clarity and simplifies scanning, faxing and photocopying.

➤ See pp. 341–3 for a discussion of
type in colour.

olour can also be used in a layout to clarify the structure of information. For web
es and HTML documents, it is also tied to navigation success. Retention of
owser-default colours for links is essential; otherwise, readers have to relearn the
eaning of differently applied navigation colours every time they go to a new site.

eproduction of colour is an attempt to capture the full spectrum on a two-
mensional surface, whether that surface is a piece of paper or a monitor's screen.
here are three main colour systems:

on-screen colour

process colour

Pantone colour.

ch has its limitations.

amut

he problem common to the three main colour systems is to do with their
mut—the subset of the visible colour spectrum that it is possible to capture
curately. Each system manages to capture a slightly different set of colours, so it
not possible to match colours between the systems. Designers and other
embers of a publication team should therefore learn to predict the probable
lours that each system will reproduce.

On-screen colour

On-screen colour is produced by a series of lights that emit different intensities of red (R), green (G) and blue (B). This is referred to as 'RGB'.

The amounts of red, green and blue light used to create colours are described in a six-character alphanumeric code called 'hexadecimal colour descriptors'. The first two characters describe the amount of red light, the middle two describe the amount of green light, and the last two describe the amount of blue light. The tag in HTML are written '#RRGGBB'.

Hexadecimal colour descriptors:
Cyan is #00FFFF, magenta is #FF00FF, yellow is #FFFF00 and black is #000000. Indigo is #4B0082.

Sixteen characters describe the gradations of light intensity. The numerals 0 to 9 are followed by the letters A to F. An intensity of 0 means the lights are off; F is when the lights are fully on.

Web 216

Because of the limitations of some computers, the World Wide Web Consortium has adopted the 256-colour, or 8-bit colour, standard for the web. Some of the 256 colours are unavailable because they have specific uses in browsers and computer systems, so a set referred to as 'web-safe' or 'Web 216' is used. Their descriptors can use only the following six hexadecimal values: 00, 33, 66, 99, CC, FF. Indigo, for example, is modified in Web 216 to #330099.

Greyscale display

Some computer products such as notebooks and personal organisers have Internet access but without colour. As a result, it is necessary to check the colours of a web publication for tonal value and contrast to ensure readability in greyscale.

Process colour

Much printed colour is achieved through the four-colour process. The four colours are:

* cyan (C), a sky blue
* magenta (M), a deep pink
* yellow (Y)
* black (K).

➤ The colour section provides illustrations of this discussion.

They are referred to as 'CMYK'.

The four colours are transparent inks that, when laid over the top of each other, produce a reasonable approximation of the spectrum. They were traditionally reproduced in variably sized halftone dots, each colour's screen being angled slightly to allow the other colours to show through, creating a rosette pattern. Stochastic screening—with its random distribution of pixels to blend the colours—obviated the need for screen angles.

Colour separation

Scanners produce colour separations. Flexible materials such as transparencies are attached to a cylinder that rotates at high speed, and an operator adjusts the machine for the correct exposure and colour balance in each of the four basic olours. The material is then electronically scanned and a set of the four parations is produced simultaneously.

atbed scanners work like a photocopier. They are used for original artworks that e inflexible or slightly three-dimensional.

omputer systems accept the information produced by a scanner and the image n then be brought up on a monitor. It is then colour-edited, layered and mbined or manipulated as desired, brought into a page layout with text and her images, and positioned. The images and text are digital, so there is almost finite potential for manipulating them. Colour can be added or subtracted, d the image changed by deletions and additions, before any film is produced. nally, the completed page is output to film or direct to plate. The final image is ored on disk.

or optimum results, colour separation should be done only after the type of paper, e ink type and density readings, and the colour sequence have been confirmed. his offers the best opportunity for matching colour on the press.

➤ Colour proofing is discussed in Chapter 25.

nder-colour removal and greyscale conversion

a conventional four-colour separation, the richness of the blacks and darker eas in an image is achieved by layering each separated colour almost solid in ose areas. When overprinted, the layers of ink are progressively built up on the ge surface. However, on presses that run at very high speeds (mostly web offset esses used for producing colour catalogues and magazines), the ink drying time quired for each layer slows the press, costing more. So the processes of under-lour removal (known as 'UCR') and greyscale conversion (known as 'GSC') are ed to remove the layers of colour under the black plate, thus increasing speed d cost-effectiveness.

uotones

uotones are made from two separate colour plates, usually black and one other lour. They produce an increased illusion of depth and detail and for this reason e often used in reproductions of black-and-white photography. The lighter of the o colours is scanned as a low-contrast plate, producing most of the mid-tones for e photograph and some more accurate tonal rendering in the lighter areas of the iginal photograph. The darker colour is then scanned as a high-contrast plate, arpening the detail and providing the shadow areas when printed over the mid-ne plate.

pia toning is produced with duotones of black and yellow. It can also be oduced with single or duotone Pantone colours and in CMYK without using the an plate.

Fi colour

igh-fidelity' is the generic term used to describe various processes that extend e colour gamut of the CMYK process by adding additional colours, most mmonly orange and green. The costs of separation and printing are rrespondingly higher.

389

Used in poster printing and high-end publishing, HiFi colour impresses with its richness, particularly when stochastic screening is used to dispense with troublesome screen angling.

Pantone® colour

Pantone is the proprietary name of a US ink producer that has created an international colour standard. The Pantone® Matching System (or PMS) mixes a standard set of pigments in different combinations to create over a thousand colours that should appear the same way no matter where in the world they are printed.

Australia's official colours of green and gold: These are Pantone® 348 (green) and Pantone® 116 (yellow).

The Pantone mixing pigments are given recognisable colour names such as 'Yellow', 'Rubine red' and 'Reflex blue'; the mixed colours are identified with a three- or four-digit number.

Tints of Pantone colours are usually specified in multiples of 5 per cent. For example:

30% Pantone® 185 + 75% Pantone® 102

Metallic colours

Over two hundred Pantone metallic colours have been created by adding various silver, bronze and golden inks to the mixing set. The inks contain fine suspended particles of metal that give an authentic metallic sheen. To maximise this sheen, the sheets can be run through a printing press twice.

Fluorescent colours

For the Pantone fluorescent colours, chemicals are added to the ink mix to produce a glowing effect. Like the metallic colours, fluorescent colours are often best reproduced through a repeat printing, the same material being printed a second time directly on top of the first impression.

Pastel colours

Pantone has created over a hundred solid pastel colours. These light tints are achieved by adding an extender to the regular Pantone ink mixes. The extender has the effect of thinning the colour.

SCALING, CROPPING AND MASKING

Scaling

Scaling is the means of calculating the extent of reduction or enlargement needed to bring an original illustration to its reproduction size. The reproduction size is described in terms of the percentage by which the illustration is to be modified— for example, 'reduce to 50 per cent'. Prints to which the same reduction or enlargement factor is applied can be processed together, so it is economical to use as few scaling factors as possible. For scanning purposes, the sets must also be of even density.

...pping an image

Scaling an illustration

...opping and masking

...opping involves selecting only that part of an image that needs to be shown and ...asking the rest of the image to indicate that it is not to be reproduced. In the ...se of extreme cropping, only the required section of the image is scanned, thus ...oiding a large image file that would be mostly masked. (Remember the necessity ... scanning at the resolution required for final image reproduction.)

...bitrary cropping of a print simply to fit a particular space—without ...nsideration of the effect the cropping will have on the composition of the ...age—should be avoided. To prevent this image misuse, some photographers ...clude a contract provision that prohibits cropping of their pictures.

...halftones have been designed to bleed off one or more edges of a page, the ...ustration should extend at least 3 millimetres over the trimmed edges, to allow ... variations in folding and trimming.

➤ Artwork for bleeds is discussed in more detail on pp. 468–9.

391

PHOTOGRAPHS

Photographs for a publication can be obtained from a number of different sources. Variations in their quality and size, as well as in their format (digital files, transparencies, negatives, prints, and so on), can involve the designer in extra work. For example, each print might have to be separately scaled, manipulated or retouched to improve reproduction quality. Photographs commissioned from a professional photographer are usually of sufficiently high and consistent quality for reproduction.

Black-and-white prints

Black-and-white photographs should be printed on good-quality photographic paper, glossy and preferably of uniform size. As a general rule, they should be a little larger than the desired reproduction size. If necessary, the designer can crop each image area using a semi-transparent overlay.

A soft-lead pencil may be used (lightly) if it is necessary to write instructions on the back, or even on the overlay, of a photographic print. Never use an ink pen or a marker on the back of a picture: it could smudge or transfer to the front of another picture in the pile. Similarly, do not use sharp pencils or ballpoint pens: the indentations they cause will damage the surface and could be reproduced in the scanning process. For the same reason, paperclips, pins and staples should not be used.

Transparencies

Transparencies—colour slides and large-format transparencies—are preferred for colour reproduction because they carry the original image from the camera. A colour print is the second generation of an image (the first being its negative) and each additional process in reproduction reduces the quality of the original image.

Transparencies, especially the smaller sizes, should be scaled carefully because inaccuracies will be accentuated as the image is enlarged to the required size. Slides are sometimes removed from their mounts for scanning.

When labelling transparencies, it is wise to show which is the top (as viewed). Generally, the correct viewing side of a colour transparency is the one without the emulsion, which creates the matt surface.

Digital image files

When digital photographic files are supplied for a document that is to be printed, the same image is often supplied in different resolutions. One will be a 'low res.' (low-resolution) file for placement in the draft document; it will be replaced at prepress stage by a 'high res.' (high-resolution) file. For material that will be output on screen, only the standard 72 ppi image resolution is required.

Digital files can be produced by using a digital camera and downloading the file directly to disk or by scanning a transparency or print. It is necessary to know the final output size and device resolution of the printer or monitor in order to calculate the best image resolution.

age manipulation

gital scans allow the colours, tints, tones and components of an original image be altered and manipulated to an almost infinite degree. Within one image it is ssible to change the colour of a person's hair, include a car from somewhere else d add a logo to its side door, and make the sky blue by removing grey clouds. justments of this kind are undetectable in the final, combined image. Further, olying various filters can make the image appear to have been etched in steel or mped in leather; created with watercolour, chalk, oil paint or crayons; or aged, ed, intensified, rippled, distorted, curved or softened.

ultiple images can be blended into one cohesive montage of images—a 'hybrid age'. When laying out the montage, however, it is important to bear in mind w readers will relate the various components. Further, copyright exists in ginal images, even when only a small part of an image is reproduced, so it is portant that each image making up a hybrid image has copyright clearance.

APHS AND CHARTS

aphs and charts are devices for presenting statistical or other information in torial form. Since their primary purpose is not to illustrate but to illuminate, y should be clear, simple and suitably proportioned, with all superfluous space itted. Small graphs conveying simple messages are more effective than large, nplex graphs.

gardless of the style chosen for graphs and charts, they all show data. In lition to simply displaying the data, however, they should:

present the data in a coherent way

help the reader to make meaningful comparisons

reveal trends

use suitable formats, axes and labels to prevent any misinterpretation of the data.

I graphs should be identifiable by a title, which can be at the top or bottom of graph. If there are more than a few graphs in a publication, they can be mbered for easy text reference. And to ensure that a graph is fully nprehensible, both axes should be succinctly labelled; if necessary, further olanation can be provided in a legend or key.

e interior area of a graph should be respected as its 'data region'. Avoid ttering it with extraneous material: this can detract from the graph's readability.

any graphs illustrate growth, change or sequence, and with screen-based cuments there is an opportunity to animate these changes. The time sequence ild be staged, for example.

erpretation of data

is variation

e range of a graph's axes and the unit values into which they are divided should chosen to show the data in a way that is visually effective and contextually

Comparisons of axes in graphs

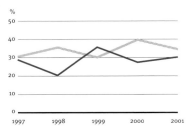

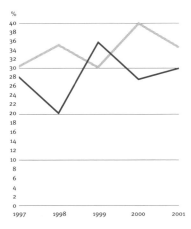

accurate. Two separate graphs can be constructed from identical information, but the results might appear quite different because of the different unit values given to the axes. Which approach is more suitable depends on what the author wants show. Remember, however, that graphs are read visually first, and that changes in axes can cause readers to misinterpret information.

Axis scales

In line and dot graphs and in bar and column charts, the choice of scale and the labelling of axes are vitally important. Logarithmic scales, scales that do not start at zero, highly selective scales, and breaks in a scale can all affect readers' comprehension of the data because the visual representation needs to be modified by reading and assimilating the meaning of the label.

Among the decisions that need to be made about the scales for each axis are the following:

- choosing a range of 'tick marks'—the small nicks or divisions that subdivide th axis and represent the scale—that will cover the range of the data
- choosing scales that will allow the data to fill as much of the data region as possible
- using comparable scales for graphs that are to be compared with each other
- deciding whether to include zero in all magnitude scales
- deciding whether to use a logarithmic scale.

Having decided what approach will provide the best balance in terms of data representation and readability, it is then essential to ensure that the tick marks ar axes are clearly labelled.

Scale breaks are used to show extreme variation in data sets. If they are unavoidable on an axis, corresponding breaks should be shown on the lines that continue to higher figures.

If a graph is wide, fine horizontal rules can be used at regular intervals along the axis to assist reading. If a graph is large, it can also be useful to repeat the axis on the right.

Sometimes it is useful to plot a specific point against which the data items can be compared: a reference line drawn across a graph helps with this. But the line should be positioned carefully so that it does not interfere with the data.

It is unwise to graph different amounts using two different measuring systems—sa numbers of products on the left vertical axis and dollars spent on the right vertic: axis. It is better to use separate graphs to avoid confusing readers.

Comparison of area and volume

Graphs that rely on comparison of area or volume need careful consideration. Readers' perceptions of area and volume are usually poor, and graphs of this kind can be misinterpreted.

For example, if a square has to be shown reduced by half while still retaining its square shape, do not reduce its sides by 50 per cent. The resulting square will be

ly one-quarter of the original square's area. Half its area is a square at
proximately 70.7 per cent of the original size. This can be checked on a
otocopier: to reduce an A4 sheet to A5 (that is, half its size) the machine has to
 set to 71 per cent.

o-dimensional representations of volume are even harder for readers to
mprehend accurately.

ree-dimensional representation

is best to avoid three-dimensional representation in graphs and charts because it
1 mislead. For example, when a three-dimensional bar chart is labelled, the rules
ould align with the back of the bars, not the front, for accurate reading of the
:a.

ree-dimensional pie charts often distort the comparative area of the forward
:es if the side is added to the area of their keyed colour. Readers therefore see
ore of the colour than they should. This effect can be avoided if the side is
aded completely.

e charts, and almost all other statistical charts, become distorted when drawn in
rspective: that which is further away is reduced in size, while the closer elements
:eive undue emphasis.

ie graphs

ie graphs show change in something over time by means of a line connecting
rious points. (The graphs used in hospitals to track changes in a patient's
ndition are an example; in the United States these are called 'fever charts'.)
ie vertical axis on the left of the graph refers to the variable or variables being
:cked, while the horizontal axis at the base shows the time span covered,
vancing from left to right.

ie graphs can be used to show change in two or more categories over time,
ovided the lines remain distinct and do not overlap or come too close to each
1er. Unless they remain well separated, it is unwise to use more than about four
es on a line graph.

hen more than one line is shown, different line styles should be chosen and
:h line should be labelled or identified in a key. The lines can be differentiated
 weight and colour; in the case of single-colour output, different line patterning
les such as solid, broken and dotted can be used. The thickest line will receive
e most attention, although colour also affects the perceived hierarchy of
portance. So allocate the line style according to the importance of the
'ormation; for example, the darkest line is best allocated to a total line when
ere is one.

ode symbols such as squares and triangles on plotted points in line charts are
 necessary and can obscure the data.

 area graphs, which are a subset of line graphs, the area below each line is filled
th colour or shading. Graphs of this type are useful for comparing the difference
tween cumulative sets of figures. However, because the coloured or shaded areas

Illustrating volume
Which square is half the area of the first?

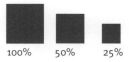

100%   50%   25%

It is clearer if the square is sliced into strips.

100%   50%

Line graph

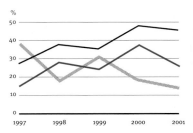

Area graph

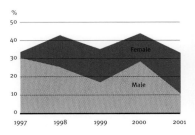

Bar chart

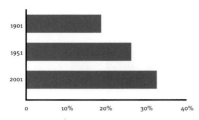

Column graph

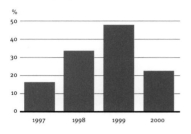

Dot graph

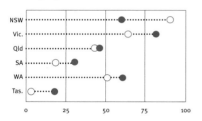

Pie chart

Scattergram

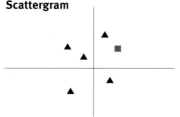

at the front hide the same area attached to the quantities behind them, these graphs are less useful for demonstrating the total size of all but the lowest quantit graphed.

Bar charts, dot graphs and column graphs

Strictly speaking, bar charts and dot graphs are horizontal and column graphs are vertical. Either way, their treatment is much the same. All three show amounts o different but related objects, one axis showing an inventory of objects and the other showing amounts for comparison of the categories.

Bar charts can show two different amounts for each category by moving out to both the left and right from a central labelling point, the amounts furthest from the centre being the largest. In this way, for example, different patterns of use by males and females could be shown for a particular product.

Change over time is usually shown in a column graph. The male–female pattern use in the example just given would thus be shown in side-by-side columns keyed by colour, density or pattern.

Dot graphs use light dotted lines to connect a plotted dot to its label. Readers often find these graphs clearer than bar charts. They are particularly effective wit ranked variables that are presented in order of descending size.

Pie charts

Pie charts always show something that has been divided into its component parts, or 'slices', totalling 100 per cent of the area of a circle. (A circular shape is clearer than an oval.) To create a pie chart, it is therefore necessary to convert all figures to percentages. Avoid dividing the pie into too many slices: unless the are in full colour, thin slices are difficult to key, and too many slices make comparison difficult.

Readers' perceptions of the relative sizes of angles can make pie charts a liability serious comparison is warranted. It has been found that the size of acute angles tends to be underestimated and that of obtuse angles overestimated. If pie charts are chosen for comparing one set of information with another, the following will help readers interpret the data correctly:

- Keep the areas of the pies the same.
- Keep the slices in each pie in the same order, even though their relative sizes will vary.
- Keep the keyed colours and patterns the same.
- Label the pies consistently.

Scattergrams

Scattergrams show frequency distribution by means of points plotted in an area. Areas of greater density of points indicate 'hot spots', from which readers might b able to discern trends. Scattergrams usually need captioning and some text interpretation, but they are very accurate in their depiction of information.

Hi-lo graphs

'Hi-lo' graphs usually graph statistical variation over time. The highest and lowest numbers are given for each time point and the median is usually shown by a dot. Sometimes the medians are connected to form a line.

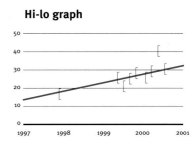

Hi-lo graph

Drawing graphs

Computers can quickly create complex graphs in all the basic types. Specialised graph software simply accepts the values of the x and y axes and creates the graph automatically, complete with shading, colour or patterns.

When patterns are being used for keying parts of a graph, the following should be borne in mind:

The smaller the area, the denser the pattern should be.

The pattern must be carefully oriented. Line patterns should normally be laid at a 45° angle to the sides of a graph. The angle at which the pattern is laid must be identical whenever the pattern is used with the same significance in different parts of the graph. Avoid using patterns that can create optical illusions when juxtaposed.

All patterns must be subordinate to the main features of the graph, so that the basic information or lettering is not obscured.

Illustrated graphs

Occasionally it may be appropriate to substitute illustrative symbols for lines, bars or columns. However, although elaborate illustrated graphs can attract attention, they tend to become ends in themselves, obscuring rather than clarifying information.

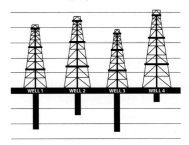

Illustrated graph

DIAGRAMS

Most diagrams show connections between events or optional paths within a sequence or structure. They use:

alignment to indicate simultaneity of events or similar levels of importance

the reading principle of time advancing to the right or down

visual hierarchical systems such as trees and pyramids

straight paths for a process, with distinct start and end points

circles to show repetitive cycles, as in a life-cycle diagram, for example.

Flow charts and other process charts

One of the first tasks in creating a process chart is to identify the discrete points (or nodules) within the process, their sequence, and any optional paths. The detail of the process can then be communicated through a series of arrows, other linking devices and alignments.

The nodules should be given a standardised shape, of consistent size and containing any necessary labelling. In strict flow chart styling, circles represent a completion point, diamonds represent a choice that needs to be made before

**Flow chart with decision point
and optional paths**

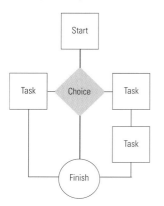

moving to the next event, and squares or rectangles represent options. Direct connections are usually shown with solid lines; broken or dotted lines show optional paths. Numbers can be used to clarify the order of events but are not necessary if the sequence is clear.

Organisation charts

Organisation charts describe both the structure of an organisation and the identit of individuals in it. The stepping and alignment of the components are readily understood in these hierarchical displays. Blocks, connecting lines and corporate colour codings to clarify groupings can also be helpful.

There are three broad types of organisation charts:

- A horizontal hierarchical model shows connected blocks that contain section headings and the names of key staff (and often their position titles).
- A vertical listing shows the hierarchy reading from left to right, instead of from top to bottom, and each column identifies a layer of the organisation. This type of flow chart is ideal for text-only presentation and, by alignment alone, can often communicate a structure without any need for blocks and connecting rules.
- An illustrated horizontal model shows photographs of key staff labelled with their names and sections. It usually includes connecting lines and groupings to show subsets within the organisation.

Critical path diagrams

Critical path planning is depicted in a hybrid form that combines a list of events in a column on the left with the duration of each event graphed on a calendar to the right. In this manner, a production process or project can be defined and its expected duration calculated.

Critical path diagram

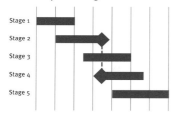

Assembly diagrams

The way something works or is assembled can be presented in diagrammatic form by illustrating each piece and showing links and connections. This is sometimes done by using exploded views, where axonometric projection or perspective shows each element about to join to its adjacent part.

Exploded diagrams can also be animated on screen to show the assembly of their various parts in the correct sequence. Readers should be able to halt the sequence at any point in order to analyse the process and then be able to restart the animation.

Storyboards

Storyboards are created to show transitions on screen. Originating in film and television production, they are now also used for other multimedia production such as interactive CD-ROMs and web sites. Using a combination of text and sketch, they sort out content treatment and visual structure.

The form used in storyboarding is that of a screen-shaped illustration box (usually in the ratios 3:4 for a monitor, 1:2 for a film, and 9:16 for a plasma screen) with a ea of text description below. Using television and film terminology, the text escribes the action on screen, and includes the intended dialogue as well as a escription of any other sound files required and any visual effects.

he storyboard is essentially a planning document. It is also often used as a basis r securing project funding before significant production costs are incurred.

omic strips

he conventions used in comic strips are well established: the comic frame, the quence, the speech and thought balloons, and the text descriptors. The nature of ustration can vary from realistic (even photographic) through highly stylised to tremely simple line drawings. Each style can be effective in describing action or ansition. However, the comic strip form is successful only when it is carefully tuned to the content and the readership. The same applies to cartoons and ricature.

APS

ll topographical description is rarely needed for reference maps that illustrate xt in a publication. These maps need retain only sufficient information for curate reading. There are a variety of approaches:

A broad location map can be supplemented by an inset map (or by maps on following pages) showing part of the main map in greater detail.

Maps can be illustrated by showing landmarks as pictograms or photographs.

Straight-line maps can show the route from A to B by using only a straight line intersected by street names, descriptions of turns, and distance measures.

ap labelling

reference mapping there are numerous conventions associated with identifying e topography of an area and the features of a landscape or cityscape. Colour dings and different line weights are used, as are labelling systems including type d pictograms. The essential parts of most maps, however, are the compass point owing north and a scale to allow readers to estimate distances.

ale bars, keys and legends

ery map should have a simple scale bar at its base. The bar should be roughly tween a fifth and a quarter of the width of the published map, and it should be a eaningful length for the distances represented in the map. Distance is usually pressed in multiples of five, ten or a hundred, with zero being shown on the left the scale bar and the chosen length on the right. Distance intervals should be entified with a nick. A small central nick can subdivide the scale for easy lculation of shorter distances.

explain the particular reference codes used, maps often feature a key or legend x. The source acknowledgment can also appear in this box.

lthough the content of maps is not copyrighted, the representation is. As a sult, if permission to reproduce a map is not given, the map should be redrawn.

Storyboarding terminology

- *Zoom in*—get closer
- *Zoom out*—move away from
- *Pan*—static camera turning to follow action
- *Dolly* or *track*—moving camera following the action
- *FX*—visual or special effects
- *Morphing*—a character or object turning into another character or object by a smooth computer-generated transition
- *SFX*—sound effects
- *Edit*—a cut between two separate pieces of film
- *Cross-fade*—one scene fading out as another fades in
- *Split-screen*—two or more images on screen at once

North compass point

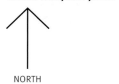

NORTH

Simple scale bar

0   25   50   75   100 km

Some types of maps have an alphanumeric grid system to help readers find particular locations quickly. With these location systems, the horizontal measure is usually divided into letter-coded areas and the vertical measure is number coded—enabling reference to be made to 'F4', for example.

Typography for maps

When maps are being labelled, it is important that the type does not obscure the content of the map. As far as possible, labels should be in the same orientation as the map and, while they may follow some of the mapped features (such as rivers), they should never appear upside down. Some further conventions for applying type to maps should also be observed:

- Use italics to identify natural features.
- Use roman text to identify constructed or artificial features.
- Place labels entirely on land or water, not straddling the two.

Statistical mapping

Statistical maps reveal trends in data across geographic areas. There are three main styles:

- dot density maps
- proportional symbol maps
- shaded distribution maps.

Dot density map

Each of these maps starts with a base reference map with defined research area boundaries. Depending on the type of data to be compared, these boundaries might define neighbourhoods, electorates, suburbs, or any other political, geographic, social or environmental subdivision.

Dot density maps

In dot density maps, dots of equal size appear randomly within the boundary of each area in the study. Each dot represents a fixed unit of data. For example, a dot might represent 10 000 sheep on a map describing livestock distribution. The total number of dots in a particular area represents the total data value for that area, so an area with 40 000 sheep would have four dots.

In this way it is easy to compare distribution over the recorded area. The random positioning of the dots can, however, cause confusion with location markers.

Proportional symbol map

Proportional symbol maps

In proportional symbol maps, a circle or square appears within the boundary of a recorded region. This circle or square is proportional in size to the data value for the region. The disadvantage of this method is that readers find it difficult to gauge comparative area correctly: the size of larger circles is almost always underestimated. Larger circles can also sometimes overlap the data from a neighbouring area.

Shaded distribution maps

Shaded distribution, or choropleth, maps are among the most recognisable mapping styles. In them, shadings are graded in intensity from light to dark to

present gradations in the data. The shadings can represent ratios, percentages or
densities, depending on the nature of the information that is being shown.

One drawback of the style is that it is easy for readers to assume that the data are
uniformly spread across the shaded areas. Further, readers might see large areas of a
shade as being statistically dominant.

Choropleth map

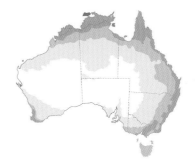

Five shade levels or classes are traditionally chosen to represent:
- an equal count, where each class has an equal number of areas
- equal steps, where each class has an equal data width (0–20 per cent, 20–40 per cent, and so on)
- natural breaks, which are variable class intervals reflecting the data distribution.

The most appropriate method for a particular map depends on what information
readers are most likely to be looking for. The shading convention is to use light
colours for low values and dark colours for high values. It is also important to
choose colours that are clearly distinguishable from each other and that maintain a
good colour balance.

MOVING IMAGES

When moving imagery is incorporated in web sites and CD-ROMs the computer
screen is used to its full advantage. The imagery is mostly accompanied by sound,
but sometimes it is silent.

Access to publications using moving images and sound depends on readers having
the necessary software and hardware. Audience analysis should consider this
crucial factor, as well as readers' likely reactions to the delay in downloading these
files, which are large and therefore slow to download. Exclusive use of sound and
image files—without offering alternative ways of locating the same information—
will also exclude people with particular disabilities.

There are many types of moving imagery to explore:
- documentary footage
- staged or scripted footage
- commissioned footage
- stock footage from moving-image libraries and other sources
- animation of illustrations, graphs, titles or type
- transition animation, where otherwise static material moves on and off in a
  choreographed manner.

Too many techniques used in a screen will compete for attention and can be too
distracting for clear communication. Viewers should always be given the controls
necessary to start and stop the imagery and adjust the volume.

In most cases, original material is shot directly to video or created on screen as a
digital file. Any original film footage is usually converted to video or digital files
for storage.

SOUND

Well-selected sound materials can be used to good effect in screen-based publications. Sometimes a repeating ('looped') sound is used to create an aural background, although this should be considered as carefully as any graphic background. Will it distract from or hinder comprehension of the message or will it be helpful?

As with moving images, users should be able to stop and start the sound and adjust the volume.

There are various ways of incorporating sound:

- voice-over
- recorded dialogue
- sound 'bites' or other documentary sound
- music
- sound effects.

Sounds are often layered, or 'mixed', to create a soundscape. For example, background music might have a layer of sound effects and a narration edited together to create the whole.

Where relevant, alternative sound files of narration can be provided in languages other than English for greater audience 'reach'. Incidentally, the icons most often used to alert people to the availability of different languages are national flags.

IMAGE AND SOUND LIBRARIES

Still and moving images and sound files can be obtained from commercial or government image and sound collections. Radio and television stations, film production companies, illustrators, photographers, photo libraries, other libraries and galleries often have collections that are available for reproduction.

Expect to pay:

- search fees
- usage fees
- reproduction fees for duplication into the media requested
- any copyright, performing rights and clearance fees.

There are numerous rules and practices in the industry. In general, usage fees are based on the size of the audience and the level of reproduction. If a wide audience and distribution are envisaged and the imagery will become the signature imagery for the publication, expect to pay more.

IMAGE COMPRESSION

Image compression is a digital process that removes some of the data from digital image files to make them smaller. After compression, some flexibility in the use of the image is lost; for example, it will not enlarge without obvious pixelisation and it may lose some detail (the loss becoming apparent when the image is enlarged).

PictureAustralia
(a consortium of Australian government image sources)

➤ See p. 405 for a list of government sources for moving and still images and sound.

Nevertheless, compression can be very useful for moving image, animation and sound files.

In traditional film footage, the image on screen changes twenty-four times every second. This is measured as 24 fps (frames per second). Video uses 30 fps. With image compression, however, video can be reduced to only 12 fps by removing almost every second and third frame but retaining the timing. This is why web animations sometimes look jerky. To further reduce the file size, the 'live' area of the screen is usually kept small, and sometimes the image resolution is reduced from 72 pixels per inch.

Compression can further reduce the size of the file by loading the first frame in full and analysing the ensuing frames, changing only the pixels that need to change. This saves reloading each frame in full and can greatly reduce the file size, particularly with static backgrounds and limited editing of the footage.

EVALUATING ILLUSTRATIONS

Appropriateness of illustration selection

- Do the illustrations identify, clarify and reveal what words cannot describe as effectively?
- Do they attract attention and motivate involvement in the content of the publication?
- Does a single vision unite them as a set that ultimately gives the publication a cohesive 'look'?
- Have recurrent colours and complementary colour palettes been used?
- Do the illustrations convey a consistent 'attitude' or point of view?

Illustration placement

- Are the illustrations close to their text reference?
- Is their placement balanced through the publication to provide a good visual 'pace'?
- Does their sequence help readers to identify the flow of the story or discourse?

Technical quality for reproduction

- Has the publication been properly prepared for its reproduction media?
- Is the resolution of the illustrations suited to the format chosen?
- Will colours reproduce clearly and have they been colour-corrected?
- Will colours retain their relative value when reproduced in monochrome?

PART 3 Further reading and resources

FURTHER READING

Bellantoni, J & Woolman, M 1999, *Type in motion: innovations in digital graphics*, Thames & Hudson, London.

Bonnici, P & Proud, L 1998, *Designing with photographs*, RotoVision SA, Crans-Près-Céligny, Switzerland.

Bonnici, P 1999, *Visual language: the hidden medium of communication*, RotoVision SA, Crans-Près-Céligny, Switzerland.

Carter, R 1995, *Working with computer type 1: publications, magazines, newsletters*, RotoVision SA, Crans-Près-Céligny, Switzerland.

——1996, *Working with computer type 2: logotypes, stationery systems, visual identity*, RotoVision SA, Crans-Près-Céligny, Switzerland.

——1997, *Working with computer type 3: color and type*, RotoVision SA, Crans-Près-Céligny, Switzerland.

Department of Administrative Services (Awards and National Symbols Branch) 1995, *Australian flags*, Australian Government Publishing Service, Canberra.

Department of the Prime Minister and Cabinet 2000, *Australian symbols*, Awards and National Symbols Branch, Department of the Prime Minister and Cabinet, Canberra.

Evans, P 1997, *The complete guide to eco-friendly design*, North Light Books, Cincinnati, Ohio.

Flanders, V & Willis, M 1996, *Web pages that suck: learning good design by looking at bad design*, Sybex, Alameda, California.

Fowler, S 1998, *GUI design handbook*, McGraw-Hill, New York.

Gotz, V 1998, *Color and type for the screen*, RotoVision SA, Crans-Près-Céligny, Switzerland.

Hackos, JT & Stevens, DM 1997, *Standards for online communication*, Wiley, New York.

Holmes, N 1991, *Designer's guide to creating charts and diagrams*, Watson-Guptill, New York.

Howard, S 1998, *Corporate image management: a marketing discipline for the 21st century*, Butterworth-Heinemann Asia, Singapore.

Jute, A 1996, *Grids: the structure of graphic design*, RotoVision SA, Crans-Près-Céligny, Switzerland.

Lopuck, L 1996, *Designing multimedia: a visual guide to multimedia and online graphic design*, Peachpit Press, Berkeley, California.

Mandel, T 1997, *Elements of user interface design*, Wiley, New York.

McCanna, L 1997, *Creating great web graphics*, 2nd edn, MIS Press, New York.

McCloud, S 1993, *Understanding comics: the invisible art*, Tundra Publishing, Northampton, Massachusetts.

McKelvey, R 1998, *Hypergraphics*, RotoVision SA, Crans-Près-Céligny, Switzerland.

Meggs, PB 1989, *Type and image: the language of graphic design*, Van Nostrand Reinhold, New York.

Neilsen, J 2000, *Designing web usability*, New Riders, Indianapolis, Indiana.

Nyman, M 1993, *Four colors/one image*, Peachpit Press, Berkeley, California.

Olins, W 1989, *Corporate identity: making business strateg visible through design*, Thames & Hudson, London.

osenfeld, L & Morville, P 1998, *Information architecture r the world wide web*, O'Reilly, Sebastopol, California.

igel, D 1997, *Creating killer web sites: the art of third neration site design*, 2nd edn, Hayden Books, dianapolis, Indiana.

ade, C 1997, *The encyclopedia of illustration techniques*, mon & Schuster, Sydney.

ess, D 1999, 'Designing and evaluating forms in large ganisations', in H Zwaga, T Boersema & H Hoonhout ds), *Visual information for everyday use: design and earch perspectives*, Taylor & Francis, London.

iekermann, E & Ginger, EM 1993, *Stop stealing eep—and find out how type works*, Adobe Press, ountain View, California.

ool, JM, Scanlon, T, Schroeder, W, Snyder, C & Angelo, T 1999, *Web site usability: a designer's guide*, organ Kaufmann, San Franscisco, California.

eidl, P & Emery, G 1997, *Corporate image and identity ategies: designing the corporate future*, Business & ofessional Publishing, Warriewood, New South Wales.

en, J 1997, *Hot wired style: principles for building smart b sites*, Wired Books, San Francisco, California.

heildon, C 1995, *Type and layout: how typography and sign can get your message across—or get in the way*, rathmoor Press, Berkeley, California.

hitbread, D 2001, *The design manual*, University of w South Wales Press, Sydney.

ildbur, P & Burke, M 1998, *Information graphics: ovative solutions in contemporary design*, Thames & dson, London.

illiams, R 1990, *The Mac is not a typewriter*, Peachpit ess, Berkeley, California.

—1996, *Beyond the Mac is not a typewriter*, Peachpit ess, Berkeley, California.

illiams, R & Tollett, J 1998, *The non-designer's web k*, Peachpit Press, Berkeley, California.

WEB SITES

Australian Bureau of Statistics <http://www.abs.gov.au>

Australian Graphic Design Association <http://www.agda.asn.au>

Communication Arts <http://www.commarts.com>

How <http://www.howdesign.com>

Alertbox <http://www.useit.com/alertbox>

Pantone Inc. <http://www.pantone.com>

Print <http://www.printmag.com>

Web techniques <http://www.webtechniques.com>

SOURCES OF IMAGES AND SOUND

The following Australian government bodies are useful sources of photographs, still and moving images, and sound:

AusLIG

AusPic (at Parliament House)

Australian Broadcasting Corporation

Australian Bureau of Statistics

Australian Heritage Commission

CSIRO

Department of Foreign Affairs and Trade

Film Australia

National Archives of Australia

National Gallery of Australia

National Library of Australia

National Museum of Australia

National Portrait Gallery

ScreenSound Australia

Special Broadcasting Service

4

Legal and compliance aspects of publishing

The law and quasi-law (standards, protocols, official endorsements and guidelines) relating to publishing have two effects: they protect and restrict what may be published, and they identify and provide access to published information. Compliance with the law is mandatory; compliance with quasi-law is recommended in the interests of efficient information retrieval.

Copyright law affects most writers, designers and other contributors to a publication. It is therefore a focus of the discussion of legal restrictions on publishing. However, this review also covers other legislation that must be taken into account, such as laws protecting personal information,

22	Restrictions on publishing	408

Copyright legislation

Privacy provisions

Defamation, contempt and offensive material

Disclaimers

23	Identification and access	422

International numbering systems

Metadata

Uniform resource locators

Access for people with a disability

Access for future generations

Documents for parliamentary tabling

Record keeping

personal reputation and community standards. The discussion of legal provisions and defences is for guidance only; legal advice should always be sought whenever such matters arise.

Much of the law and quasi-law aimed at facilitating access to published information concerns suitable identification for published works. Requirements to publish specific information are dealt with only insofar as they affect government—publications to be tabled in parliament, for example. The requirements of the Corporations Law are not considered.

Attention is also drawn to other laws relating to access that potentially affect all publishers. Among these are anti-discrimination provisions, which require the publication of material in formats that will not unreasonably disadvantage people with disabilities, and the legal deposit provisions aimed at preserving publications for future generations.

GAL AND COMPLIANCE ASPECTS OF PUBLISHING

ther reading and resources

slation, standards and guidelines, and
e recommended reference works,
 sites and contacts   435

Restrictions on publishing

COPYRIGHT	**409**
What is protected	409
Who is protected	411
When copyright starts	412
When copyright ends	412
Showing copyright exists	413
Copyright infringement	414
Permission to use copyright material	415
Crown rights	416
Moral rights	417
PERSONAL INFORMATION	**417**
Relevant law	417
Privacy and the Internet	418
DEFAMATION	**418**
CONTEMPT OF COURT	**419**
CONTEMPT OF PARLIAMENT	**419**
OFFENSIVE MATERIAL	**419**
OTHER LAWS RESTRICTING PUBLICATION	**420**
DISCLAIMERS	**420**

The law restricts the publication of some material. Sometimes this is to protect the property or reputation of individuals; sometimes it is to protect community standards. The restrictions can apply within a single Australian state or territory or they can be national, or even international, in their coverage.

Under Australia's federal system of government, the power to make laws is shared between the Commonwealth and the states and territories. Where the Commonwealth has law-making power (as defined in the Commonwealth of Australia Constitution), its laws operate Australia-wide and override any inconsistent state or territory provisions. State and territory laws apply within the state or territory boundary, and laws dealing with the same subject matter may contain different provisions in different states.

The law in Australia is also contained in court decisions, when the courts have interpreted legislative provisions. It is therefore important to seek legal advice on any problems relating to publishing that might have legal implications. (Producers of Commonwealth publications should seek this advice through the Attorney-General's Department or delegated authority. It should be noted, however, that the department cannot advise on publishing practice.)

COPYRIGHT

Copyright is a bundle of rights that are owned by authors and creators of material. The rights are exclusive and allow the copyright owner to prevent unauthorised use of the material by others. Copying material or doing other 'copyright acts' without the copyright owner's knowledge and permission constitutes an infringement of copyright.

Copyright protects the original form in which an idea has been expressed by the creator but not the idea itself. Since copyright is a form of property right, it can be bought and sold in the same way as other property. The law conferring copyright protection in Australia is set out in the Commonwealth's *Copyright Act 1968* and Regulations and case law.

What is protected

The Copyright Act confers on copyright owners certain exclusive rights.

Disclaimer: Information relating to legal matters in this chapter and elsewhere in the manual is provided as a general guide only; it does not purport to be legal advice. The law changes from time to time, and some information may therefore be superseded. Always seek a legal practitioner's advice about any particular legal questions arising from publishing activities.

Copyright approvals: You must obtain the permission of the copyright owner and pay any required licence or royalty fee before including copyright material in a work intended for publication.

➤ In addition to the information provided in this chapter, see pp. 435–6 for some useful reference material about copyright.

Depending on the type of material, these rights include the copyright owner's right to:

- reproduce the work in a material form, including storage on a computer
- publish it—in print, digital or other media
- translate it, digitise it or adapt it in any other way
- communicate it to the public by any means, including traditional broadcasting, electronic transmission or making it available online
- publicly perform it
- commercially rent it (in the case of computer programs and works in sound recordings).

Types of material

The Copyright Act protects 'works', which may be literary, dramatic, musical or artistic in nature. Literary works include most written materials (for example, books, reports, articles, poetry and song lyrics), computer programs, and computer databases of sufficient originality. Length is not important, although single words, slogans and titles are usually not protected. Dramatic works include scripts, screenplays and choreography. Musical works include scores and arrangements. Artistic works include paintings, drawings, engravings and other artworks, logos, maps, plans, photographs, buildings and models.

The Act also protects what it calls 'subject-matter other than works'. This category includes film, sound and video recordings, communications (broadcasts), and the published edition (typesetting, formatting, and so on) of a work.

Originality

The Act protects only 'original' works. A work is considered original if it is the result of its creator's skill and labour. The question of merit or quality is not important. For example, a table containing numbers can be protected by copyright. A compilation of non-original material may also qualify for protection if the compilation is sufficiently distinctive and is the result of skill and labour—a list of web links, for example.

Independence of copyright

Copyright continues to exist independently in a work that forms part of another work. In a book, for example, there may be a separate copyright in the text (a literary work), the illustrations (artistic works), the photographs (artistic works) and the published edition (subject matter other than works). Similarly, for a web page there may be separate copyright in the text (a literary work), graphics (artistic works), moving images (subject matter other than works) and sound (subject matter other than works). In such cases, different people may own each separate copyright.

Ideas and information

Copyright protects the way an idea or a piece of information was originally expressed and recorded but not the idea or information itself. Anyone may write about the Federation of Australia or draw a picture of the Sydney Harbour Bridge; copyright is infringed only if it is a copy of other material.

Copyright covers original material:
- literary, dramatic, musical and artistic works
- subject matter other than works, such as film, sound and video recordings, communications (broadcasts) and published editions.

Originality of compilation: Copying an entry from an address list or table would not infringe copyright. It is the compilation that attracts the copyright, not its components.

➤ See 'Other laws restricting publication', p. 420, for information about Commonwealth legislation that protects certain types of ideas and information.

Who is protected

Geographic coverage

The Copyright Act protects works made or first published in Australia. Copyright owners can also control the right of communicating the material to overseas audiences, since, in respect of the right of communication to the public, the Act defines *the public* to include the public inside and outside Australia.

In addition, the Copyright Act protects works made or first published in a country that has signed an international copyright agreement with Australia. The Copyright (International Protection) Regulations list the countries. These international agreements mean that Australians' works are protected in each of the signatory countries under the law applying in that country. Note, however, that foreign laws may contain provisions that differ from those in Australia's Copyright Act.

Ownership

The owner of copyright is usually the work's creator. If more than one person is involved in a work's creation, ownership depends on how readily distinguishable each contribution is:

- When individual contributions are easily distinguishable, each creator owns the copyright over their contribution—authors of chapters in a book, for example, or contributors to a web site or multimedia production.

  When individual contributions are not easily distinguishable, the work is known as a 'work of joint authorship'. In this case, all contributors share copyright and none may exercise any rights without the permission of the others.

There are, however, exceptions. They relate to works created as part of employment, on commission, or under the direction or control of government.

Works created as part of employment

As a default position, employers, not employees, own the copyright in works created in the course of employment. Independent contractors, as opposed to employees, are not regarded as being under a contract of service and will generally own copyright in their works unless this has been otherwise negotiated.

➤ See 'Crown rights', p. 416, for the special rules applying to material produced under the direction or control of government.

Works created by journalists in the course of employment, however, are jointly owned by the journalist and the proprietor of the publication. Different rules apply to works created before 30 July 1998 from those created from that time onward:

Under current law, journalists own the copyright in their works for the purposes of publication as part of a book and for photocopying (or photocopying photocopies of) hard-copy issues of the work. Proprietors own all other rights.

For works created before 30 July 1998, proprietors own copyright for the purpose of publication in a newspaper, magazine or similar periodical and for broadcasting. Journalists own all other rights.

Commissioned work

Ownership of the copyright in commissioned works varies:

- For a commissioned engraving, painting, film or sound recording, the default position is that copyright is owned by the person or organisation commissioning the work. This position can be varied by agreement.
- For photographs taken before 30 July 1998, copyright is also held by the commissioning person or organisation. However, copyright in photographs taken since that date is owned by the commissioner only if the photograph is for private and domestic purposes. In all other instances, copyright is owned by the photographer. These positions can be varied by agreement.
- Even if the commissioner of a photograph, portrait or engraving owns the copyright, the creator has the right to stop the work from being used for any purpose other than the commissioned purpose.
- For other artistic works, the copyright owner is generally the work's creator.
- Unless otherwise agreed, commissioners of sound recordings and cinematographic films also own copyright in them.

Work undertaken for government

The Commonwealth, state and territory governments own the copyright in materials made or first published under their direction or control or otherwise transferred to them (see page 416).

Transfer of copyright

When an independent contractor or supplier owns copyright, the rights that are usually negotiated allow the copyright material to be reproduced only for a specific or limited range of purposes. Use for any other purpose would be subject to further negotiation and could involve additional payment.

On the death of the copyright owner, copyright becomes part of that person's estate. On the death of a contributor to a work of joint authorship, the copyright is shared between the remaining contributors and becomes part of the estate of the contributor who is the last to die.

When copyright starts

Copyright protection starts when a work is first recorded, written down or made, although there are exceptions for unpublished photographs. Copyright protection is automatic: there is no registration requirement or other formality, and no fees are payable.

When copyright ends

The general rule in Australia applying to the duration of copyright is:

- fifty years after the creator's death

  or

- if the first publication, public performance or communication occurred after the creator's death, fifty years from that date

  or

- if the work is never published, copyright continues indefinitely.

Photographs for private and domestic purposes: Wedding photographers, for example, would not own the copyright on commissioned photographs unless the contract or agreement so provided.

Agreed purposes: Always check the extent of allowable uses in any copyright agreement. For example, it could be that the design for a book cover cannot be reproduced as a promotional poster without specific reproduction permission.

his fifty-year rule also applies to works of joint authorship after the death of the
ntributor who dies last. It applies to government works from the date of first
blication. It does not apply to copyright in a published edition, however:
pyright lasts for only twenty-five years after the date of first publication of the
ition.

ne duration of copyright can vary in overseas countries where the provisions of
cal law protect Australian material.

howing copyright exists

ne Copyright Act does not require the inclusion of a copyright line or copyright
ptice. In Australia, protection exists without them. However, the copyright
ne—the symbol © followed by the copyright owner's name and the year of first
blication or release—must appear in order to ensure protection in some overseas
ountries.

© Jasmine Chaudry 2001

ne phonogram symbol ℗ should also be used on sound recordings to ensure
pyright protection in overseas countries.

copyright notice provides information about acceptable uses of the material and
cludes the copyright owner's contact details for people seeking permission to use
e material in any other way.

bsidiary copyrights existing in a work can also be shown with this information
, if there are too many, in a separate acknowledgments section. In electronic
blications, acknowledgment of copyright in material used should also be
cessible from the screen displaying the material.

Copyright duration: The duration of copyright—generally fifty years in Australia—is calculated from the end of the calendar year in which the relevant event took place.

Placement of copyright information: The copyright line and notice are usually placed on the reverse of the title page of printed publications and on the home page (or a linked page) of electronic documents.

Recommended copyright wording for Commonwealth publications

or paper-based publications:

© Commonwealth of Australia [add year]

This work is copyright. Apart from any use as permitted under the *Copyright Act 1968*, no part may be reproduced by any process without prior written permission from the Commonwealth available through the Department of Finance and Administration. Requests and inquiries concerning reproduction and rights should be addressed to the Manager, Copyright Services, Department of Finance and Administration, GPO Box 1920, Canberra ACT 2601 or by email to <http://www.Cwealthcopyright@finance.gov.au>.

or home pages and electronic documents:

© Commonwealth of Australia [add year of release of home page or electronic document]

This work is copyright. You may download, display, print and reproduce this material in unaltered form only (retaining this notice) for your personal, non-commercial use or use within your organisation. Apart from any use as permitted under the *Copyright Act 1968*, all other rights are reserved. Requests for further authorisation should be directed to the Manager, Copyright Services, Department of Finance and Administration, GPO Box 1920, Canberra ACT 2601 or by email to <http://www.Cwealthcopyright@finance.gov.au>.

Copyright infringement

Copyright is infringed if a person who is not the copyright owner (or someone licensed by the copyright owner) exercises one or more of the owner's exclusive rights without permission. Unauthorised reproduction is the most common type of infringement.

Copyright law prohibits unauthorised reproduction of a 'substantial' part of a work. What constitutes a substantial part is difficult to determine and depends entirely on the circumstances. In general, though, it is the *importance* of what is reproduced, not the amount, that is relevant (see also 'Fair dealing').

Infringement can be indirect. For example, supplying a photocopying machine or computer and knowingly allowing it to be used for infringing copyright would contravene copyright legislation, as would provision of a hyperlink to a site that contained infringing material.

Normally, provision of a hyperlink to another web site will not infringe copyright, although the site proprietor's permission should be sought as a matter of etiquette. Permission is essential, however, if you intend to display another site's content within a frame, giving readers the impression that the content is from your own site or of your own creation. Any permissions applying to copyright material used on the original site may not be applicable under these conditions.

In addition, if the frame of your site remains visible while the material from the other site is displayed, difficulties may arise under consumer protection and trade practices legislation if the impression is given that use of the material has been authorised. It is an offence (both civil and criminal) under the Copyright Act to knowingly remove or alter (without permission of the owner) electronic rights-management information—that is, information attached to, or embodied in, a copy of a work that identifies the work or subject matter and its author or copyright owner, and indicates the conditions of use of the copyright material. It includes numbers or codes that represent such information.

Fair dealing

The Copyright Act contains a number of provisions that allow certain use or reproduction of copyright material without infringement. The most important of these are the 'fair dealing' exceptions, which permit limited reproduction if it is done for:

- research or study
- criticism or review
- reporting of news
  or
- the provision of professional legal advice.

The amount of copying (a 'reasonable portion') allowed under the fair dealing provisions is not specified in the Act and must be determined by the courts. The exception is for research or study, where a reasonable portion is deemed to be

Implied endorsement: Government agencies should consider the question of implied endorsement if links are provided from their web sites to commercial sites without appropriate context.

per cent of a book or 10 per cent of a work in electronic form. The definitions *research* and *study* used in the Act derive from *The Macquarie dictionary*. Current w does not restrict research or study for private purposes only, although how far extends to commercially oriented research has not been tested in the courts.

her exceptions

ther copying permitted under the Copyright Act includes reproduction:

- for the services of the Crown, subject to appropriate remuneration (see page 416)
- by libraries and archives in specified circumstances
- for judicial proceedings or for reports of judicial proceedings
- of computer programs (to make copies for back-up purposes, copies for the normal use and study of the program, and copies to make interoperable products, for security testing and to correct an error)
- for public readings, recital or performance under some circumstances
- as temporary reproductions made as part of the technical process of making or receiving communications
- for the purpose of simulcasting (simultaneous broadcasts in both analog and digital form)
- of one copy of legislation or judgments for a particular purpose.

nder the Act, statutory licences allow certain bodies to reproduce copyright aterial without obtaining the copyright owner's permission for that use, subject payment of a fee to a collecting society. The collecting society then forwards e payment to the copyright owner. These licences exist as a matter of public licy to benefit educational institutions; institutions assisting people with a sability; libraries and archives; and Commonwealth, state and territory vernment agencies. Retransmission licences also provide remuneration to pyright owners for the retransmission of free-to-air broadcasts.

ermission to use copyright material

pyright can be assigned, in total or in part, to someone else. This transfer of ghts may involve a fee, and restrictions and conditions relating to form, time or ography. Any transfer of copyright must be in writing and signed by the pyright owner.

pyright licences

pyright owners can give permission, in the form of a licence, for the use of their aterial, usually with conditions and payment obligations attached. There are two pes of licences:

- Exclusive licences are a guarantee that the rights being licensed will not be licensed to someone else for the period of the licence. They must be in writing and be signed. For government bodies, there may be some cases where policy matters need to be considered when contemplating the granting of exclusive licences.
- Non-exclusive licences do not guarantee exclusive use and more than one may be issued at the same time for the same right. It is recommended that they too be in writing and signed.

The 10 per cent rule: For research or study, the Copyright Act allows one chapter (or 10 per cent) of a book of ten or more pages to be copied or one article from a 'periodical publication' (for example, a journal or magazine). More than one article may be copied, however, if each article deals with the same subject matter.

Copyright collecting societies: These represent copyright owners and collect and distribute royalties on their behalf. A list of these societies is provided on p. 436.

Permission requests

Requests seeking permission to reproduce, display or make available online or to exercise any other exclusive right attaching to copyright material should be in writing and should contain the following information:

- the contact details of the person or organisation making the request
- a citation of the work containing the copyright material, including the author's name, the full title of the work, its year of publication and edition number, and any unique identifiers such as an ISBN, ISSN or URL
- an unambiguous description of the part or parts of the work (such as page numbers, paragraph numbers or URLs) to which the request relates
- the purpose for which permission is sought, the quantity to be used, and the way the material will be used
- the number of copies to be reproduced (for paper-based material) or the address of the web site on which the material is to be included
- the expected publication or release date of the new work that would contain the copyright material.

It may be necessary to apply for many permissions in complex works. Such material should be identified as early as possible in the writing or production schedule, because publication or release of works containing copyright material cannot proceed until all permissions have been granted and any conditions attached to the permissions have been fulfilled.

Crown rights

The Crown is entitled to use any copyright work without liability for infringement so long as the work is used for the services of the Crown. It does not have to obtain the consent of the copyright owner, but is required to notify the owner of the use of the material and to negotiate terms of use (including remuneration). The Commonwealth has an agreement with the Copyright Agency Limited on rates of payment for the photocopying of newspapers, magazines, journals and books under this provision.

The Copyright Act also gives the Crown copyright in its own works, published or unpublished, and in works written by its employees in the course of their employment. Government can, however, enter into an agreement vesting copyright in the author.

Inquiries concerning the administration of Crown copyright should be directed to the Commonwealth Department of Finance and Administration. Requests for permission to use copyright material from Commonwealth publications should also be sent to that department. Requests to use other Commonwealth copyright material, including unpublished materials, should be directed to the responsible government agency. It is important to seek legal advice if problems might arise.

Publication planning: Make time and budget provisions for identifying copyright material, seeking permissions and arranging any necessary payments.

Definition of 'Crown': For the purposes of this discussion, the *Crown* means the executive arm of government, whether Commonwealth, state or territory. Each jurisdiction administers its own copyright.

Legal advice for Commonwealth agencies: Publishing-related matters involving legal policy advice should be directed in the first instance to the Attorney-General's Department. Publishing-related matters requiring legal advice not connected with policy should be directed to a provider of legal services.

oral rights

oral rights were introduced by the Commonwealth's *Copyright Amendment (Moral Rights) Act 2000*, which came into operation on 21 December 2000. The Act now recognises three important rights:

- the right of attribution of authorship—the right of authors to be named as the author in respect of their work
- the right of authors not to have the authorship of their work falsely attributed
- the right of integrity of authorship—the right of authors not to have their work subject to derogatory treatment (that is, a right to object to the material distortion of, mutilation of, material alteration to, or other like treatment of their work that is prejudicial to the author's honour or reputation).

are must be exercised to ensure that any material is properly attributed to the ork's creator, that the attribution is clear and reasonably prominent, and that is in accordance with any manner of attribution the creator has made known, here that is reasonable. Care should also be taken to ensure that no false tribution is made.

he rights of attribution and integrity are subject to a defence of reasonableness— at is, there will be no infringement if it was reasonable in all the circumstances ot to identify the author. Matters to be taken into account include the nature of e work; the purpose for which, and the manner in which, it is used; the context; dustry practice; and whether the work was made in the course of employment.

he legislation makes provision for consent by an author to acts or omissions in spect of a work that would otherwise infringe their moral rights.

oral rights apply to authors of literary, dramatic, musical and artistic works and film-makers (including producers, directors and screenwriters). These rights main with the author even if copyright in the work has been transferred to meone else, and they may be exercised by the author's legal personal presentatives after the author's death. Moral rights generally last as long as the pyright lasts in the work concerned.

lms are treated differently from literary, dramatic, musical and artistic works. or example, the right of integrity of authorship applies only to films made after December 2000; however, this right applies in relation to 'works' made fore 21 December 2000 (although only in respect of attributable acts done after at date). The author's right of integrity continues until the death of the author; respect of works, it lasts as long as the copyright.

ERSONAL INFORMATION

elevant law

he Commonwealth's *Privacy Act 1988* regulates the collection, storage, use and sclosure of personal information as well as entitling individuals to access and rrect information about themselves. Access to and correction of personal formation held by Commonwealth agencies is also regulated by the *Freedom of formation Act 1982*.

Definition of 'use': In the Privacy Act, *use* is defined to include the information in a publication.

➤ Further information on compliance with privacy obligations can be obtained through the Office of the Federal Privacy Commissioner—see p. 435 for contact details.

Commonwealth agencies must comply with the Information Privacy Principles set out in s. 14 of the Privacy Act when collecting and handling personal information. As of 21 December 2001, many private sector organisations must also comply with the National Privacy Principles in Schedule 3 of the Privacy Act. The relevant principles should be considered when including personal information in a publication.

Privacy and the Internet

This legislative environment is also designed to ensure that web site operators collecting personal information online take reasonable steps to ensure that Internet users know who is collecting the information and how it is to be used, stored and disclosed. People can access their personal records and correct them if they are wrong. Organisations are required to safeguard personal information they hold from unauthorised access and disclosure, and so must consider data security and encryption where relevant.

The Federal Privacy Commissioner has issued guidelines in relation to web sites that are used to collect personal information. The content of Commonwealth web sites must comply with these guidelines, which include:

- providing a prominently displayed privacy statement detailing what information is being collected, why, how it is to be used, if it is to be disclosed and to whom, any law that authorises the collection, and any other security or privacy matters

- ensuring that, where an online form is used to collect personal information, a privacy statement appears on the same page as the form or is prominently linked to it

➤ See *Guidelines for federal and ACT government World Wide Websites* <http://www.privacy.gov.au> for details of mandatory requirements for Commonwealth agencies collecting personal information.

- using sufficiently secure means to collect the information, and offering individuals an alternative way of providing personal information to the agency other than via the web site

- complying with Information Privacy Principles 1, 2, 3, 10 and 11 in relation to the publication of personal information on the web.

DEFAMATION

A defamatory statement about a person or corporation is one that is perceived to lower the reputation of that individual or organisation in the eyes of ordinary members of the community. The person making the statement must have communicated the information to someone other than the 'body' referred to. The defamed body need not be named in the statement; it is sufficient that the third person identifies the person or organisation.

The dead cannot be 'defamed'. But a statement made about a dead person could indirectly defame a living associate of the dead person.

Defamation arising from spoken words is called 'slander'. Defamation arising from matter recorded in a permanent form is called 'libel'. In legal effect, there is now little or no difference between slander and libel.

The particulars of defamation law vary between the states and territories, but the following general principles apply:

- It is not a defence to claim that there was no intention to defame or that a reasonable mistake was made.
- Truth is not necessarily a defence.
- Fair comment in the public interest may be a defence.
- The freedom of speech implications of the Commonwealth of Australia Constitution may allow the publication of material about government and political matters.
- Statements made in the course of parliamentary or judicial proceedings, and the printing and publication of papers under the authority of parliament (Hansard, for example), are protected by absolute privilege.
- Publication of material in furtherance of a legal, social or moral duty, and not done with an improper motive or in bad faith, may be protected by qualified privilege.

Parliamentary privilege: This protects Hansard but does not cover reproduction of material from Hansard in another publication.

Qualified privilege: Examples of work in this category might be fair reports of parliamentary and judicial proceedings.

These defences should never be relied on as the basis for publication of defamatory material without legal advice.

CONTEMPT OF COURT

Contempt of court consists of two distinct elements. The first, which is now rarely applied, is the offence of 'scandalising'—that is, intemperately or unreasonably criticising courts or judges. The second, and more important, is known as the 'sub judice' rule. This concerns the publication of words that are likely to interfere seriously with the administration of justice. The rule is commonly invoked by state attorneys-general or the Commonwealth Director of Public Prosecutions to punish the publishers of material that is likely to interfere with the fair trial of a person charged with a criminal offence.

CONTEMPT OF PARLIAMENT

An act that tends to obstruct or interfere with Houses of parliament, their committees or members constitutes contempt of parliament. Each House of the Commonwealth Parliament and some state Houses have the power to judge and punish such acts. Contempts that may be constituted by publication include:

- attempted improper influence of a member or a parliamentary witness
- unauthorised publication of evidence taken by a parliamentary committee in camera or of a confidential document of a committee
- wilful misrepresentation of the proceedings of a House or a committee.

AUSPIC 000909.03

OFFENSIVE MATERIAL

Films, videos and certain other publications must be classified in Australia to restrict the sale and distribution of material that is offensive to the reasonable adult person or that is unsuitable for minors.

Classification of films and videos is the responsibility of the Classification Board and applies Australia-wide. Classification of print publications is dealt with under state and territory legislation. However, under a cooperative scheme between the Commonwealth and the states and territories, publications may also be classified by the Classification Board. (Tasmania and Western Australia do not participate in the cooperative scheme but have similar state-based arrangements; Queensland participates in the scheme but does not recognise 'restricted' categories.)

Offensive Internet content is prohibited. The law allows members of the public to complain about offensive content to the Australian Broadcasting Authority. The authority may decide to direct the host of the content to remove the material from its service if it is hosted in Australia or, if the service is hosted elsewhere, may notify the content to suppliers of approved filters.

'Extreme' material—child pornography and sexual violence, for instance—is refused classification. It is illegal to sell or hire extreme material and it is prohibited on the Internet.

Complaints: Members of the public can complain to the Australian Broadcasting Authority about material on the Internet, postings to newsgroups and other stored information. Ordinary email, chat services and voice transmitted over the Internet are not covered under the 'offensive material' provisions.

OTHER LAWS RESTRICTING PUBLICATION

Copyright law protects the way an idea or a piece of information was originally expressed and recorded but not the idea or information itself. However, the following Commonwealth legislation may protect certain words, expressions, illustrations and ideas:

- the *Trade Marks Act 1995*
- the *Designs Act 1906*
- the *Trade Practices Act 1974*.

In addition to providing protection for confidential information and trade secrets, the Trade Practices Act contains a range of provisions to protect consumers from false and misleading conduct, including in advertising and in making claims and statements.

Where material is offered for sale—in a web site, printed catalogue or order form—consumer rights and legislation should be recognised by including the seller's contact details, itemised costs, and statements about applicable currencies, privacy provisions and refund policies.

DISCLAIMERS

Information producers may wish to try to limit any liability from subsequent use of the information by including a disclaimer. Disclaimers are best placed on the reverse of the title page of a paper-based publication and as a link from the home page or other pages, as appropriate, in a web site. Disclaimers can, for example:

- warn about the general nature of the material or its accuracy or reliability
- urge the reader to seek professional advice
- distance the publisher from views presented in a discussion paper
- state that references or web links to products and services do not constitute endorsement.

isclaimers should be used carefully, particularly with the increasing use of the ternet to distribute information. It is doubtful, for example, that a disclaimer can otect the host of a web site from responsibility for links to other sites that ntain material infringing copyright or from the application of the other laws scussed in this chapter. Nor does the use of disclaimers absolve a government ency of the responsibility for:

- maintaining the accuracy of the information on its web site
- keeping evidence, in the form of records such as change logs and web site snapshots, of what information was displayed on its site and when.

RESTRICTIONS ON PUBLISHING: A CHECKLIST

Copyright and protection of original works

- Has written permission been obtained and have all associated conditions been met for the use of any copyright material?

- Have a copyright line and an appropriate copyright notice been included?

- Have the rights of owners of original works been sufficiently protected in accordance with the *Trade Marks Act 1995*, the *Designs Act 1906* and the *Trade Practices Act 1974*?

Personal information

- Has all personal information been handled in accordance with the provisions of the *Privacy Act 1988*?

- Has any need for access to personal records been considered in accordance with the provisions of the *Freedom of Information Act 1982*?

- Have the Federal Privacy Commissioner's guidelines been followed for web sites and other online activities?

Legal review

- Have any legal problems that could arise been considered in the light of legal opinion? For example, does the publication contain any material that could be construed as defamatory, offensive, false or misleading, or in contempt of court or parliament?

- Has a disclaimer been included if relevant?

Chapter ***23***

Identification and access

INTERNATIONAL NUMBERING	**423**
International Standard Book Numbers	423
International Standard Serial Numbers	424
Bar codes and EANs	425
Agency and publisher numbers	426
LIBRARY-BASED SERVICES	**426**
Cataloguing-in-publication data	426
Electronic serials	427
METADATA	**427**
UNIFORM RESOURCE LOCATORS	**428**
About URLs	429
ACCESS FOR PEOPLE WITH A DISABILITY	**428**
Legislative requirements	428
On-screen technologies	430
Matching production formats to disability	430
ACCESS FOR FUTURE GENERATIONS	**431**
National and state legal deposit schemes	431
Commonwealth library deposit and free issue schemes	431
OTHER COMPLIANCE REQUIREMENTS FOR COMMONWEALTH PUBLICATIONS	**432**
Documents tabled in parliament	432
Electronic publications	433
Record keeping	433

published information is to reach its intended audience, it must be
sy to identify, locate and access. This means using internationally
cognised numbering systems for identifying and cataloguing
iblications. It also means attaching metadata to electronic
iblications so that they can be found by search engines, and
oviding on-screen material in suitable file formats that are clearly
belled. Copies of many types of publications should also be lodged
specified libraries.

addition, as part of the Commonwealth Government's strategies for social
stice, access and equity, every Commonwealth agency should strive to make its
iblications accessible to all Australians, regardless of their language, culture or
cation and regardless of whether they are disabled in any way.

dustry standards and legislation dealing with access to published information
eate the environment in which these goals can be achieved.

TERNATIONAL NUMBERING

ie international numbering system adopted in Australia requires that each
iblication, whether in print or electronic form, be identified by a unique
mber—an ISBN (International Standard Book Number) or an ISSN
iternational Standard Serial Number). In some cases, both numbers are needed
· a publication. The numbers enable any title, in any language, to be identified
ywhere in the world. They make communication between publishers and
oksellers more efficient, and they simplify library cataloguing and lending
stems.

r codes and agency or publisher numbers are also used to assist in identifying
iblications.

ternational Standard Book Numbers

BNs have been used since 1967 to identify 'monographs'—publications that are
mplete in themselves and are not part of a series. Monographs include single-
d multi-volume books and reports, brochures, and any other one-off publications
ch as organisational histories and exhibition catalogues.

Allocation of ISBNs: Thorpe
Bibliographic Services allocates ISBNs
for Australian publications (see p. 437
for contact details).

423

Structure of an ISBN

An ISBN consists of ten digits divided into four groups of various configurations. The groups are separated by spaces or hyphens. For example:

ISBN 0 642 41471 8   *or*   ISBN 0-642-41471-8

ISBN 0 7337 1211 8   *or*   ISBN 0-7337-1211-8

The groups of numbers categorise a publication in the following way:

- The first 'group' (a one-digit or two-digit code) identifies the national language or geographic area of publication. Australian publications are identified by the single digit 0 or 1.
- The second group is the publisher's prefix. The code used to signify a Commonwealth government publication is 642.
- The title number, which uniquely identifies the publication's title, is represented by the third group of numbers.
- The last digit is a 'check' digit—a number between 0 and 10, with 'X' standing for 10. It is the product of an equation involving the first nine digits and is used to verify the ISBN's validity.

Different versions of a publication

ISBNs are unique; once assigned, they cannot be re-used on other publications. New ISBNs should be obtained for different versions of the same publication, be a new edition or the same edition in a different format—hardcover or softcover, paper-based or electronic, Internet or CD-ROM.

Multi-volume sets

A publication forming part of a multi-volume set has two ISBNs, one for the volume identifier and one for the set. The volume identifier is listed first:

ISBN (volume 2) 0 642 41472 6

ISBN (set)   0 642 41475 0

Placement of ISBNs

For a paper-based publication, the ISBN should appear with the publishing data the reverse of the title page and on the dust jacket or back cover above the bar code. For an electronic publication, the ISBN should be placed with the copyright and bibliographic data on the title screen (or a screen directly linked to it) and on any labels and containers for disks.

International Standard Serial Numbers

ISSNs have been used to identify serial publications since 1972. Serial publications are periodical publications that are intended to continue indefinitely—for example, journals, newsletters, magazines, newspapers and annual reports.

Different ISSNs should be allocated to continuing supplements and subseries and to the same title published in different media.

Allocation of ISSNs: The National Library of Australia allocates ISSNs for Australian publications (see p. 437 for contact details).

Structure of an ISSN

An ISSN consists of eight digits divided by a hyphen into two groups of four:

ISSN 1032-2019

Unlike the groups of digits in ISBNs, ISSN groups do not provide categorial information about the serial title. The last digit is a check digit; it is the product of an equation involving the first seven digits and is used to verify the ISSN's validity.

When to change an ISSN

A new ISSN should be allocated after major changes to the wording or order of words in the title of a serial. For example, if an organisation or government agency changes its name, its next annual report should have a new ISSN. However, if it issues a regular newsletter that does not include the organisation's name in its title—say, *Zfiles*—and this title is retained at the name changeover, the *Zfiles* ISSN does not need to change.

An ISSN and an ISBN

When a publication forms part of a series but has a title that differs from the series title (for example, a publication in a technical series), it requires both an ISSN and an ISBN. The ISSN is listed above the ISBN:

ISSN 1030-3170

ISBN 0-642-39957-3

Placement of ISSNs

For paper-based serials, the ISSN should appear on each issue, either on the reverse of the title page, at the top right-hand corner of the front cover, or elsewhere with the publisher's information. For electronic serials, the ISSN should appear on the title screen (or a screen directly linked to it) and on any labels and containers for disks.

Bar codes and EANs

Publications intended for sale should carry a number called an 'EAN-13' and a bar code, which is the machine-readable form of the number. This international product-numbering convention is followed in the retail book trade, and Commonwealth agencies preparing publications for sale should also adhere to it.

Structure of an EAN-13

The thirteen digits of an EAN are divided into three groups: a prefix, a product identifier and a check digit. The product identifier incorporates a publication's ISBN or ISSN. A publication forming part of a series but with a title differing from that of the series should be identified by its ISBN, not its ISSN.

Scope and display of bar codes

The recommended bar code size for Commonwealth publications is × 39 millimetres. The ISBN or ISSN is displayed above the bar code and the EAN-13 below it. Bar codes carrying ISBNs should be reproduced vertically

Little Book of Love
ISBN 0-642-10733-5

9 790642 107335

Bar code and EAN
The letters *EAN* are the initials of the original coding scheme (European Article Number), and the *13* represents the thirteen-digit bar code. Other schemes operate for other bar-coding and packaging requirements.

(picket-fence style); those carrying ISSNs can be reproduced either vertically or horizontally (ladder style).

The bar code colours that are most easily scanned are black bars on a white background or white bars on a dark background. Blue, green and brown also scan successfully. Yellow, orange and red are invisible to scanners and should be used only as background.

Placement of bar codes

A bar code carrying an ISBN should be placed on the back cover of a printed publication. A bar code carrying an ISSN should be placed on the front cover, towards the bottom left-hand corner and at least 5 millimetres from the binding edge and foot. Bar codes for electronic publications such as CD-ROMs should be placed on a visible part of the packaging.

Agency and publisher numbers

Some government agencies and commercial publishers assign in-house numbers to their publications. Australian Bureau of Statistics catalogue numbers, for example, are the standard means of identifying and referring to the bureau's publications. In most cases, however, agency numbers are of value only to the assigning agency. They should therefore be used in addition to ISBNs and ISSNs; they should not replace them.

LIBRARY-BASED SERVICES

Cataloguing-in-publication data

The 'cataloguing-in-publication' (CiP) information is a library catalogue entry for a publication; it is prepared in advance and reproduced in the published work. The National Library of Australia offers this service for material intended for permanent preservation. CiP information is not available for serial publications.

The National Library recommends that CiP entries be reproduced on the reverse of the title page of a paper-based publication and on the title screen (or a screen directly linked to it) in an electronic work. The ISBN usually appears as part of the CiP data.

> **Colour:** Before commencing full production, it is wise to test the colour combination chosen for a bar code to see whether it scans successfully.

> **Generating EANs and bar codes:** A number of software packages can generate EANs and bar codes. Further information is available from EAN Australia (see p. 437 for contact details).

Example of CiP data

> **National Library of Australia Cataloguing-in-Publication data:**
> Style Manual for authors, editors and printers
>   5th ed.
>   Bibliography.
>   Includes index.
>   ISBN 0 644 29770 0
>   ISBN 0 644 29771 9 (pbk.)
>   1. Authorship—Style manuals.
>   2. Printing, Practical—Style manuals.
> 808.02

[C]P entries are listed on the National Library's Kinetica database and become part [of] the national bibliographic record. Queries and applications should be directed [to] the National Library's CiP Unit (see page 437).

[El]ectronic serials

[Au]stralian journals online is a listing of electronic serials maintained by the [N]ational Library of Australia. The aim of the list is to facilitate access to [Au]stralian Internet resources. The library also catalogues selected items, which are [in]cluded on the Kinetica database and become part of the national bibliographic [re]cord. Details about registration are available from the National Library (see [pa]ge 437).

[M]ETADATA

[M]etadata is information about a document's content and physical properties that [In]ternet search engines use to find web material. This coded description is usually [co]ntained in the head section of an electronic document and is not visible to [re]aders unless they choose to look at the mark-up code underlying the document.

[Th]e amount of material being placed on the Internet continues to expand [dr]amatically, and readers can find it increasingly difficult to locate content that [mi]ght be of interest to them. By attaching metadata to electronic documents, [pu]blishers can do much to overcome this problem, and this practice is therefore [str]ongly recommended. Metadata can be provided for web sites, for publications on [a s]ite, and for individual pages of a publication.

[U]se of the Australian Government Locator Service has been endorsed at [mi]nisterial level for all electronic information produced by Australian [go]vernments. AGLS is a metadata standard of nineteen descriptive elements based [on] the internationally recognised Dublin Core metadata set.

[A]GLS metadata

[Th]e AGLS metadata set consists of the following elements:

[S]ignifying ownership and creators

    Creator
    Publisher
    Contributor
    Rights

[S]ignifying content

    Title
    Subject
    Description
    Source
    Language

The Kinetica opening screen
The Kinetica database is used by Australian and overseas libraries for copy cataloguing and for inter-library lending.

Metadata: All electronic documents should contain metadata to help readers find them. Under the Government Online Strategy, all Commonwealth documents are required to adhere to the AGLS metadata standard, which is accessible through the National Archives of Australia's web site (see p. 437).

- Relations
- Coverage
- Function
- Audience
- Mandate

Signifying electronic or physical manifestation

- Date
- Type
- Format
- Identifier
- Availability

For further consistency in describing government functions, the National Archiv has sponsored a thesaurus of plain English terms. Called the *Australian Government's interactive functions thesaurus*, or *AGIFT*, it is recommended for use by all Commonwealth agencies when preparing the 'functions' metadata element of AGLS.

UNIFORM RESOURCE LOCATORS

URLs (uniform resource locators) are the Internet addresses of material available on the World Wide Web.

The Internet Corporation for Assigned Names and Numbers is the international body responsible for managing domain names. National governments manage policy on the top-level names within their own country code. The *Australian government domain guidelines* sets out the principles determining the eligibility of names within the '.gov.au' domain (see Office for Government Online, page 436

ACCESS FOR PEOPLE WITH A DISABILITY

Legislative requirements

It is unlawful in Australia to discriminate unreasonably against people with a disability. Section 23 of the Commonwealth's *Disability Discrimination Act 1992* makes it unlawful, for example, to discriminate in relation to the provision of goods and services (a category that includes publishing). It is also unlawful to discriminate against people on a range of other grounds.

Of particular concern to Commonwealth agencies, s. 29 of the Disability Discrimination Act makes it unlawful to discriminate in relation to the administration of Commonwealth laws and programs. Under the Commonwealth Disability Strategy, all Commonwealth agencies are also required to meet the information needs of people with disabilities. As a consequence, Commonwealth publishers should always consider alternative publication formats that are accessible to members of their audience who have a disability.

➤ Further information about the provisions of the Disability Discrimination Act can be obtained from the Human Rights and Equal Opportunity Commission. The Office of Disability, Department of Family and Community Services, can provide further information about the Commonwealth Disability Strategy. See p. 437 for contact details.

ABOUT
URLs

http://www.fed.gov.au/style.htm

This is a URL

ements of a URL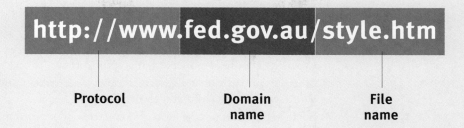

Protocol   Domain name   File name

e protocol

e protocol is the transmission code
at enables computer interaction and
cument retrieval. Other codes can be
ed instead of *http*—for example, *ftp*.
e *www* element is not always
cessary: it depends on how the URL
s been registered.

e domain name

e domain name is made up of the
e name, the generic domain name
d the country code.

e site name: This is chosen by the
e owner (a person or an
ganisation), and registered. In the
ample shown, *fed* is the registered
breviation for the federal
vernment.

The generic domain name: This is an
international classification that shows
the type of organisation. Some of the
best known generic names are:

> gov—government
>
> edu—education
>
> org—affiliated groups (non-profit
> organisations)
>
> com—commercial
>
> asn—associations
>
> net—network infrastructure and providers
>
> conf—short-duration conferences and
> exhibitions

The country code: The country of origin
is identified by this two-letter code. The
code for Australia is *au*. Sometimes the
country code is omitted, most
commonly in the United States.

The file name

The file name is the name of a
document within the site. It can
also incorporate a code showing the
format of the information—*html*, *pdf*,
and so on.

Punctuation

The example shows the punctuation
used to separate the elements of a
URL. Accurate punctuation is essential.
When shown within other text, Internet
addresses are best enclosed in angle
brackets, so that the address and its
punctuation are clearly distinguishable
from the text and its punctuation.

Conventions for file naming

The international convention for file
naming was based on early system
requirements and assumed that a file
would have an individual name of not
more than eight characters and a file
extension of not more than three
characters (that is, *filename.ext*). Under
this convention, the file extension (for
example, *html*) was abbreviated to
three characters (hence *htm*). These
length restrictions have since been
relaxed.

On-screen technologies

On-screen technologies can ease problems of access to information for many people with disabilities by making publications more widely available and in a variety of formats. Text on a screen can be enlarged for reading, for example, and text-to-speech converters can read electronic text from a screen. To enable these and other benefits to be gained, however, publishers must do more than merely place a document on a web site. Difficulties such as the following must be considered:

- Current electronic text readers and braille output devices cannot deal with information or links presented in graphic format.
- Materials provided in audio format are not accessible to deaf people and people with some other hearing impairments.
- Some approaches to text form or colour render access difficult or impossible for people with impaired vision.

W3C checkpoints: The W3C guidelines contain checkpoints that have priority levels assigned to them to reflect their impact on accessibility. At the time of writing, the aim for most Commonwealth web sites was to comply with the Priority 1 Checkpoints.

It is therefore essential to provide an effective, accessible alternative to any feature that does not offer equal access. This can best be achieved by adhering to the *Web content accessibility guidelines* produced by the World Wide Web Consortium (W3C). The Australian Government has adopted these guidelines as the standard for all its web sites, as part of the Government Online Strategy (see National Office for the Information Economy, page 436).

W3C on-screen accessibility guidelines for people with disabilities

Among other things, the World Wide Web Consortium guidelines currently include the following recommendations, which should be followed for all Commonwealth online documents:

- Provide 'alt text' (alternative text) for all images, animations and other active features.
- Provide captioning and transcripts for audio material, and text descriptions for video material.
- Summarise or use the 'longdesc' (long description) attribute for graphs and charts.
- Summarise tables or make them understandable for line-by-line audio reading.
- In hyperlinks, use text that makes sense when read out of context—for example, avoid using *Click here*.
- Use signposting techniques such as consistent headings, lists and other content structures.

➤ See Chapter 24 for more information about preparing electronic documents using features and file formats that improve on-screen accessibility.

Matching production formats to disability

Not all people have access to the Internet and relevant computer technology, so Commonwealth agencies should ensure that documents are also available in accessible hard-copy formats. Table 23.1 shows appropriate formats for a variety of disabilities.

Table 23.1 **Formats appropriate for different disability groups**

Production format	Type of disability				
	Visual	Hearing	Intellectual	Mobility	Manipulatory
Audio cassette	✓			✓	✓
Braille	✓				
Disk	✓			✓	✓
Internet	✓	✓		✓	✓
Large and illustrated print	✓		✓		
Plain English			✓		
Radio	✓			✓	✓
Video including captions		✓	✓	✓	✓

Source: Department of Family and Community Services (1999).

ACCESS FOR FUTURE GENERATIONS

National and state legal deposit schemes

Section 201 of the Commonwealth's *Copyright Act 1968* places an obligation on publishers to lodge copies of their works in certain Australian libraries. The objective is to preserve Australian works for the use of future generations and to ensure that appropriate bibliographic control and identification are provided for these publications. In terms of the Act, *publishers* includes private individuals, groups and societies, as well as commercial and government publishers.

Under this national legal deposit scheme, Australian publishers of *library material* must lodge a copy of the material with the National Library of Australia within a month of publication. Library material includes 'a book, periodical, newspaper, pamphlet, sheet of letter-press, sheet of music, map, plan, chart or table'. It does not include reprints but does include new editions containing additions or alterations to the original work. At the time of writing, it does not include electronic publications, although the National Library welcomes notification about these works (see page 437 for contact details).

State laws also require that material published in the state be deposited with the relevant state library; in New South Wales, Queensland and South Australia this extends to lodgment with certain other libraries too. These requirements operate in addition to s. 201 of the Copyright Act and may differ from it in terms of the type of material to be lodged and the time frame for lodgment. The legal deposit officer at the relevant state library should be contacted for further information.

Commonwealth library deposit and free issue schemes

The Commonwealth library deposit and free issue schemes operate in addition to the legal deposit requirements of the Copyright Act. Their purpose is to create library collections of Commonwealth government publications that are freely available to the public. The library deposit scheme covers the National Library of

Australia, the six state libraries and the State Reference Library of the Northern Territory. The free issue scheme covers publicly funded universities in all states and territories.

The Department of Finance and Administration is responsible for administering both schemes. All Commonwealth agencies should give the required number of copies of each publication they produce to that department, which then distributes them to libraries. This includes non-book materials such as CD-ROMs and disks. Publications subject to embargo should be provided to the department only after they have been tabled in parliament or otherwise released from embargo.

Further information: Contact the Department of Finance and Administration (see p. 437) for further information about the library deposit and free access schemes, including details of the number of copies required for distribution.

OTHER COMPLIANCE REQUIREMENTS FOR COMMONWEALTH PUBLICATIONS

Documents tabled in parliament

The tabling of documents in parliament is a way of keeping parliamentarians informed and ensuring openness and accountability in government. Many Commonwealth Acts require that certain types of information be prepared for publication and then tabled in parliament before public release. The minister responsible for a department is required to table the department's annual report, for instance. A minister can also table other documents if they are deemed to be of interest to the parliament and the community—for example, the reports of royal commissions.

Once a report has been tabled in the Commonwealth Parliament, it may then be incorporated in the Parliamentary Papers Series by order of either House. The purpose of the series is to provide a comprehensive collection of papers about the interests and activities of the parliament and government of the day and to preserve these records for the public, researchers and future generations.

Printing standards

Production requirements: All documents to be tabled in the Commonwealth Parliament must conform with specifications covering:

- paper size (B5 format) and paper quality
- use of the Commonwealth Coat of Arms and titling requirements
- illustrations and inserts
- colours, covers and binding.

All reports to be tabled in the Commonwealth Parliament must conform to the standards detailed in *Commonwealth printing standards for documents tabled in parliament*. The standards cover production matters and the supply of copies for the Parliamentary Papers Series. They also cover special requirements for annual reports, the reports of royal commissions and other bodies of inquiry, and policy information and policy discussion papers.

Annual reports

Commonwealth agencies must produce their annual reports in accordance with requirements described in the following documents prepared by the Department of the Prime Minister and Cabinet:

- *Requirements for departmental annual reports*, approved on behalf of parliament by the Joint Committee on Public Accounts and Audit under the *Public Service Act 1999*
- *Guidelines for presentation of government documents, ministerial statements and government responses to the parliament*.

fficers responsible for preparing annual reports for Commonwealth agencies
ould ensure that they have the latest versions of these documents, which are
ailable on the web site of the Department of the Prime Minister and Cabinet
ee page 435).

mbargoes

 publication to be tabled in parliament is under embargo until after its tabling.
mbargoes can also be placed on some other publications—those to be launched
 a minister, for example. Library deposit and press copies of publications under
nbargo should not be sent until the embargo has been lifted.

ectronic publications

ommonwealth agencies producing CD-ROMs, disks and Internet and intranet
blications must conform to the standards contained in the *Guidelines for
ommonwealth information published in electronic formats* (see Department of
nance and Administration, page 435). These standards cover many aspects of
oduction, and provide advice on best practice relating to access, legal
onsiderations, authenticity and other Commonwealth requirements.

ne parliamentary Joint Committee on Publications and the Human Rights and
jual Opportunity Commission have endorsed these standards.

ecord keeping

nder the *Archives Act 1983*, Commonwealth agencies are legally obliged to retain
d dispose of Commonwealth records properly, including web-based records. The
quirements for recording online activity are detailed in *Archiving web resources:
licy and guidelines for keeping records of web-based activity in the Commonwealth
overnment*, which is available from the National Archives of Australia web site
ee page 437).

IDENTIFICATION AND ACCESS: A CHECKLIST

Numbering and cataloguing

- Has an ISBN or ISSN been included?

- Have an EAN-13 and a bar code been applied if the publication is to be sold?

- Have CiP data been provided for publications that should be included as part of Australia's bibliographic record?

- Has the National Library been advised if the publication is an online journal?

Electronic publishing and metadata

- If it is a Commonwealth publication, does it conform to the *Guidelines for Commonwealth information published in electronic formats*?

- Has metadata been applied if the material is to be published online?

- Does the metadata conform to the AGLS standard?

Access for people with a disability

- Has the publication been provided in a format that will allow reasonable access by people with a disability, in accordance with the Disability Discrimination Act?

- If it is an electronic publication, have the World Wide Web Consortium's accessibility guidelines been followed?

Access for future generations

- Have copies of the publication been lodged under the legal deposit scheme?

- If it is a Commonwealth publication, have copies been lodged under the library deposit and free issue schemes?

Documents tabled in Commonwealth Parliament

- Have the parliament's printing and production requirements been observed?

- If the publication is an annual report, does it comply with the guidelines issued by the Department of the Prime Minister and Cabinet?

Record keeping

- If it is a Commonwealth publication, have the legal requirements for retention or disposal been complied with?

- If it is published on a Commonwealth web site, have the government's archival requirements been met?

PART 4 Further reading and resources

COMMONWEALTH LEGISLATION

Archives Act 1983

Copyright Act 1968

Copyright Amendment (Moral Rights) Act 2000

Designs Act 1906

Disability Discrimination Act 1992

Freedom of Information Act 1982

Privacy Act 1988

Public Service Act 1999

Trade Marks Act 1995

Trade Practices Act 1974

STANDARDS AND GUIDELINES

(Many of the standards and guidelines listed here are available in hard-copy formats. However, the Internet versions are cited for Commonwealth government publications because many are updated frequently.)

Attorney-General's Department 2005, *Commonwealth Copyright Administration*, Attorney-General's Department, Canberra, <http:// www.ag.gov.au>.

Australian Government Information Management Office 2000, *Guidelines for Commonwealth information published in electronic formats*, Australian Government Information Management Office, Canberra, <http://www.agimo.gov.au>.

——2001, *Commonwealth library deposit and free issue schemes*, Australian Government Information Management Office, Canberra, <http://www.agimo.gov.au>.

——2003, *Guide to minimum web site standards*, rev. edn, Australian Government Information Management Office, Canberra, <http://www.agimo.gov.au>.

——2003, *Publication Guidelines*, Australian Government Information Management Office, Canberra, <http://www.agimo.gov.au>.

——2004, *Government domain policies*, Australian Government Information Management Office, Canberra, <http://www.agimo.gov.au>.

——2005, *Australian Government web guide*, Australian Government Information Management Office, Canberra, <http://www.agimo.gov.au>.

Department of Family and Community Services 1999, *Better information and communication practices*, Office of Disability, Department of Family and Community Services, Canberra, <http://www.facs.gov.au>.

Department of Finance and Administration 1997, *Governance arrangements for Commonwealth government business enterprises*, Department of Finance and Administration, Canberra, <http://www.finance.gov.au>.

Department of the Prime Minister and Cabinet 2004, *Guidelines for the presentation of government documents, ministerial statements & other instruments to Parliament*, Department of the Prime Minister and Cabinet, Canberra <http://www.pmc.gov.au>.

——2005, *Requirements for departmental annual reports*, Department of the Prime Minister and Cabinet, Canberra <http://www.pmc.gov.au>.

Human Rights and Equal Opportunity Commission 1999, *Accessibility of electronic commerce and other new service delivery technologies for older Australians and people with a disability*, Human Rights and Equal Opportunity Commission, Sydney, <http://www.humanrights.gov.au>.

——2002, *World Wide Web access: Disability Discrimination Act advisory notes*, 3.2, Human Rights and Equal Opportunity Commission, Sydney, <http://www.humanrights.gov.au>

International Organization for Standardization 1992, *Information and documentation—International Standard Book Numbering (ISBN) (ISO 2108:1992)*, International Organization for Standardization, Geneva.

——1998, *Information and documentation—International Standard Serial Number (ISSN) (ISO 3297:1998)*, International Organization for Standardization, Geneva.

National Archives of Australia March 2001, *Archiving web resources: policy and guidelines for keeping records of web-based activity in the Commonwealth Government*, National Archives of Australia, Canberra, <http://www.naa.gov.au>.

Office of the Privacy Commissioner 2001, *Guidelines for federal and ACT government websites*, Office of the Privacy Commissioner, Sydney, <http://www.privacy.gov.au>.

Parliament of Australia 2002, *Printing standards for documents presented to Parliament*, Parliament of Australia, Canberra, <http://www.aph.gov.au>.

Standards Association of Australia and Standards New Zealand 1997, *Information and documentation—International Standard Book Numbering (ISBN) (AS/NZS 1519:1997)*, Standards Australia and Standards New Zealand, Homebush, New South Wales, & Wellington, New Zealand.

World Wide Web Consortium 2000, *Web content accessibility guidelines, 1.0, W3C recommendations*, World Wide Web Consortium, <http://www.w3.org>.

OTHER REFERENCES

Attorney-General's Department 1998, *Copyright law in Australia: a short guide*, Attorney-General's Department, Canberra, <http://law.gov.au>.

——2000, *Copyright reform: 'Copyright Amendment (Digital Agenda) Act 2000'*, Attorney-General's Department, Canberra, <http://law.gov.au>.

Australian Copyright Council 2001, *Copyright in Australia: an introduction*, information sheet 610, Australian Copyright Council, Sydney, <http://www.copyright.org.au>.

Australian Government Solicitor 1996, *Defamation and the public sector*, legal practice briefing no. 28, Australian Government Solicitor, Canberra, <http://www.ags.gov.au>.

CONTACTS

Copyright collecting societies:

- Australasian Mechanical Copyright Owners' Society Ltd <http://www.amcos.com.au> for recording of musical works and for copying sheet music

- Australasian Performing Right Association Limited <http://www.apra.com.au> for broadcasting and publ performance of musical works

- Copyright Agency Limited <http://www.copyright.com.au> for literary works

- Phonographic Performance Company of Australia Lt <http://ppca.com.au> for broadcasting and public performance of sound recordings, and for public exhibition of music videos

- Screenrights <http://www.screen.org> for films, for sound recordings and audiovisual products, and for educational copying of broadcasts

- National Indigenous Arts Advocacy Association Inc <http://www.niaaa.com.au> for artistic works by Indigenous Australians

Attorney-General's Department
<http://www.ag.gov.au> for administration of Crown copyright

Australian Government Information Management Office
<http://www.agimo.gov.au> for information on library deposit and free issue schemes

Department of the Prime Minister and Cabinet
<http://www.pmc.gov.au> for guidelines for preparing annual reports and other documents for tabling in parliament

EAN Australia <http://www/ean.com.au> for information on bar codes

Human Rights and Equal Opportunity Commission
<http://www.humanrights.gov.au> for information on disability discrimination legislation

National Archives of Australia <http://www.naa.gov.au> for:

Australian Government Locator Service metadata standards

Australian Government's interactive functions thesaurus

National Library of Australia <http://www.nla.gov.au> for:

CiP data

ISSNs

registration of electronic serials

legal deposit scheme

Office of the Privacy Commissioner
<http://www.privacy.gov.au> for information on privacy legislation

Office of Disability, Department of Family and Community Services <http://www.facs.gov.au> for information on the Commonwealth Disability Strategy and publishing issues relating to disability legislation

Thorpe Bibliographic Services <http://www.thorpe.com.au> for ISBNs

Producing and evaluating the product

Monitoring, quality assurance, testing and other refinement activities are essential adjuncts to the development of a publication's content and design. Finally, however, the project reaches the production phase, which sees a technical transformation of the document into reproducible form.

Preparation for uploading to the Internet, replication, printing and binding—all the processes that create a finished product—calls for knowledge of the different types of output equipment and an understating of the form in which the document must be presented for this last phase. Specifications also need to be prepared for the technical specialists who will be handling the replication or reproduction.

| 24 | On-screen production | 440 |

Converting printed documents

Creating material for on-screen use

Testing

Search engines and indexing

Broadcasting and maintenance

Replication

| 25 | Paper-based reproduction | 462 |

Proofs

Prepress

Paper

Traditional printing

Digital printing

Embellishment

Binding

While publishing technology continues to advance rapidly along with
the potential for higher output quality, we are seeing a reduction in the
financial, time and staff resources being allocated to preparing and
producing publications. So it is a major project management task to
maintain a realistic production schedule and to know when to rely on
professional support.

Once the final product has been reproduced and is in your hands or is
ready to be published on the Internet, how do you evaluate it? What
checks should you make and what questions should you ask before
releasing it to the wider world?

The project may be finishing, but your audience is about to see the results
for the first time. How will you gauge their responses once they have read
it, and how will you judge its overall success?

Soon you will be moving on to your next project—while your last is only
just beginning to communicate its message. It's a good idea to revisit it
occasionally, however, to remind yourself of its lessons.

ODUCING AND EVALUATING THE PRODUCT

Monitoring, testing and evaluating 492

onitoring during the project

uality assurance

st-release evaluation

Further reading and resources

Some recommended reference works and
web sites   502

Chapter **24**

On-screen production

STANDARDS FOR ELECTRONIC PUBLISHING	**441**
BROWSERS, READER SOFTWARE AND MONITORS	**442**
Browsers	442
Software readers and lite viewers	443
Monitors	443
TYPES OF ELECTRONIC PUBLICATIONS	**443**
About conversion from print to screen	444
Converting printed publications for viewing on screen	446
Converting documents to enable digital transmission for end-user printing	447
Creating material specifically for on-screen use	448
AMALGAMATED REVIEW	**452**
TESTING ON-SCREEN MATERIAL	**453**
About testing and evaluation plans	454
SEARCH ENGINES AND INDEXING	**455**
Automatic indexing	455
Publication-style indexing	456
GOING LIVE ON THE INTERNET	**456**
Broadcasting	456
Maintenance	456
REPLICATION OF PORTABLE MEDIA	**457**
Quotes and specifications	457
The master disk	457
The CD production process	457
Artwork for printed components	458

**he electronic distribution of information requires careful
nsideration—not only of how the publication is written, structured
d designed, but also of how it is to be transmitted and how it will
n be found, opened, displayed and used by the intended audience.**

e steps involved in any conversion from an existing printed format must be
ught about. The document will have to be supplied with appropriate access and
vigation schemes, be accessible to the widest possible audience and be designed
on-screen reading. If it is to be delivered via the Internet, it will have to be
sposed into a mark-up language or a file format suitable for transmission. The
racteristics of browsers and search engines must be taken into account, as well
andwidth restrictions and screen attributes. Relevant testing must be organised
ore release. If the publication is to be in the form of a disk or tape,
ngements for replication also need to be made.

➤ See Chapter 3 for advice on writing and structuring material for use on screen, and Part 3 for information about the design and navigation of screen-based publications.

ANDARDS FOR ELECTRONIC PUBLISHING

ndardised approaches are essential to achieve workable and efficient publishing
ctices. International and industry standards for on-screen publishing have
eloped (and continue to evolve) covering such aspects as minimum
ormation provision, the preparation of files for transmission, metadata, record
ping and archiving, accessibility, security, privacy and authentication.

e Commonwealth Government has also produced standards for the content,
ign and functionality of its electronic publications. These standards are derived
n the broad, internationally accepted principles for electronic publishing, as
l as reflecting more specific standards such as those developed for disabled
ess and web authoring by the World Wide Web Consortium (commonly known
W3C).

➤ A guide to the minimum standards applying to Commonwealth web sites is provided by the National Office for the Information Economy (see p. 502). For discussion of other Commonwealth-specific requirements, see Chapter 13 (standard publishing components for electronic documents and web sites), Chapter 16 (Commonwealth identifiers), Chapter 22 (privacy), and Chapter 23 (metadata and accessibility).

ny government agencies build on these broader guidelines to develop in-house
dards aimed at establishing consistency in the details relevant to their own
ge of activities. Similarly, in-house guidelines are maintained by many
mmercial and other organisations producing electronic publications.

house guidelines for the development of web content generally need to include
ctions relating to:

he current organisation of the site and provisions for growth

he site's goals

- content policy and coverage
- content structure
- writing and editing styles for on-screen reading
- graphic design and corporate identity
- formats that will suit target audiences, including the treatment of graphics and tables (taking bandwidth into account)
- navigation, labelling and mark-up
- indexing and metadata
- file-naming conventions
- revision controls
- testing and approval processes
- maintenance.

BROWSERS, READER SOFTWARE AND MONITORS

Browsers

Generally, on-screen material is not delivered to the reader using the application software in which it was created; rather, it is accessed through specialised viewing software programs called browsers. Microsoft Internet Explorer and Netscape Navigator are two widely used browser programs, but there are many other web browsers available (including those that use voice to describe the content of web pages for people with visual impairments).

Browser information: Many web sites provide information on different browser types and versions, often giving market penetration statistics as well.

All browsers interpret web pages in slightly different ways. This means that the form in which authors and site creators see their on-screen documents—using their particular browser type and version—may not represent the way the same documents will be displayed on the screens of readers using different browsers or different computing hardware and software.

Common differences between browsers include:
- the screen space available for the content
- margin differences at the edges of screens—where some browsers will not display content
- the extent of screen area used by browser toolbars
- different interpretations of text, alignments of tables and graphics, spacing, line breaks, and other attributes that dictate the way the content looks on screen
- the personalised settings applied by some readers which override the display settings intended by a publication's creator
- their ability to translate scripts and other interactive commands.

Scripts: These are used in web pages to increase the dynamic delivery of textual and graphical information beyond that usually achievable with static mark-up. Scripts provide commands that are executed either by the server delivering the web pages or by the browser interpreting the web pages being delivered by the server.

In order to predict how the design and layout will look for a wide range of readers, the publication must first be tested in a variety of likely environments, using different browsers and browser versions.

●ftware readers and lite viewers

ith 'reader' software, a file can be read and printed out by recipients but its
ntent generally cannot be changed. For example, a file transmitted in Adobe
:robat as a '.pdf' file can be viewed through an Internet browser, or through the
e Acrobat Reader if the file has been downloaded or delivered on a CD-ROM
other portable media.

➤ See pp. 447–8 for discussion of PDF (Portable Document Format) files.

her software programs have companion 'lite viewers'. These enable readers who
not have the full version of the particular program to open and read the file.
>wever, they cannot save or edit it.

●nitors

hen web sites and online publications are being developed, it is important to
:e the resolution of readers' screens into account. Monitors display material
ng pixels, so this is the measurement used for describing screen size. Current
ndard screen sizes are:

640 × 480 pixels (small screens)

800 × 600 pixels (average screens)

1024 × 768 pixels (medium screens)

1280 × 1024 pixels (large screens).

>wever, a browser's frame and toolbar take up some of the space calculated
these screen sizes. Therefore, while the area of a small screen is said to be
) × 480 pixels, it would be more realistic to assume a usable screen area of
) × 310 pixels. The 'lowest common denominator' screen size recommended
Commonwealth web sites is 800 × 600 pixels, but the screen display should
grade gracefully' to 640 × 480 pixels.

'Degrading gracefully': In the context of web page design, 'degrading' refers to how the page will be displayed through older or less popular browsers. To 'degrade gracefully' means that images and text will be displayed in roughly the same way across a variety of browsers and platforms.

though some colour monitors can display more than 16 million differently
loured pixels, the international standard palette for the web has only
6 colours. Web graphics should be designed using this standard palette, since
>st readers would be unable to see many of the colours in an image designed
a monitor of greater capacity.

➤ See Chapter 21 for further discussion of pixels and the web palette.

'PES OF ELECTRONIC PUBLICATIONS

`ormation might be made available electronically for any of the following
nmon reasons:

an existing printed publication needs to be converted for viewing on screen

an existing printed publication needs to be converted for digital transmission
and printing out by readers

a new document needs to be created solely for on-screen use.

different approach is required for each of these different publishing projects.

(continued on p. 446)

ABOUT

Conversion from print to screen

The following steps should be followed when converting existing printed material for on-screen use.

1 Gather the material

Assemble all the components of the publication:

- all preliminary pages, including covers, title and reverse-title pages, introductory material and contents list
- the full text
- all graphic images and any artwork that needs to be scanned
- any appendixes, glossary and other endmatter
- index terms and other metadata.

2 Develop the architecture

Different parts of the printed document can be stored in different files to form the structural basis of the on-screen material. This grouping of files will influence the interactivity and functionality of the completed on-screen publication, from how a search engine will index the material to where dynamic functions are delivered.

3 Develop the access schemes

Access schemes should display content in an order or sequence that reflects both the logic of the content and the approaches likely to be taken by different readers. Tables of contents and indexes are two of the many access schemes that readers of printed publications are familiar with. These can be converted to become access schemes for on-screen publications as well.

Two readily recognisable access schemes used for on-screen documents are the 'exact' and 'ambiguous' types.

Exact access schemes: These provide explicit access to easily categorised material either through:

- alphabetical access—directories, encyclopedias and dictionaries, for example
- chronological access—television a radio guides, diaries and certain types of historical material
- sequential access—instruction manuals

or

- geographical access—atlases and travel guides.

Ambiguous access schemes: In these types of schemes, information is divided into topics. They are termed 'ambiguous' schemes because the w in which an author names and structures a topic may be quite different from the various ways in which readers might search for it. However, when developed carefully from a range of likely perspectives, these types of schemes are often mo

Paper to HTML

Print

Screen

seful than exact schemes, as readers
e frequently uncertain as to precisely
hat it is that they are looking for.

Develop the navigation tools

elevant navigation elements of the
inted document can be recrafted and
tegrated in a navigation bar or
nsole panel.

eaders or footers: These elements
at identify the name, part, chapter or
ction title in a printed publication
ight be effectively transformed
r on-screen documents into, say, a
readcrumb' bar (which progressively
splays the linked structural hierarchy)
a *You are here* pointer.

ge numbers: These usually become
ntextual navigation aids that might
e labelled as:

« previous » « next » « 1 2 3 » *or* « top »

aphic images: These might be
anslated into icons with particular
eanings. For example, a logo might
ecome a 'hot spot' which returns
aders to the home page.

In-text references: These become
navigation aids when they are
hyperlinked.

5 Construct the content

The text and any graphics become the
content of the on-screen material. The
style and structure of the text will usually
have to be adapted to suit the way
readers search, scan and absorb on-
screen information (see Chapter 3). The
typography, page layout, images and
tables must also be reviewed in order to
determine the most suitable way for the
text and graphics to be reproduced for
screen viewing (see Part 3).

The content will then need to be
converted to a file type (such as HTML
or PDF), to enable the document to be
digitally published for on-screen
viewing. While this conversion process
can be achieved automatically, there
are many common conversion
problems that will require attention
(see pp. 446–7).

Finally, the content should be checked
to ensure it complies with electronic
publishing standards.

6 Show relationships between the printed and on-screen formats

Maintaining a visual connection
between a printed publication and the
online version is important. For
example, the title page or cover of the
paper-based document could be the
basis for the opening screen of the
online version. (This opening screen
should also, however, provide access
and navigation aids.)

aper to PDF on screen

brochure

PDF made to fit screen

Converting printed publications for viewing on screen

A publication primarily written and designed for paper-based reading can be converted to work acceptably on screen.

Common choices for static documents are to convert them either to a screen-based PDF file or to a mark-up language such as Hypertext Mark-up Language (HTML). This conversion can be done automatically; however, adjustments will have to be made to ensure that the output conforms to in-house guidelines and on-screen document specifications.

For example, automatic conversion of a long document might result in a single HTML 'page' of the entire document. This will have to be structured logically into separate sections or 'screens' of acceptable length. The recommended maximum length of separate sections for viewing on screen equates to about five A4 printed pages (see page 42).

Other common problems requiring attention relate to particular character conversions, paragraph and table formatting, depiction of the page layout, and residual mark-up code.

Character formatting

Some word-processing keyboard characters (such as quotation marks, ampersands, bullets and em and en rules) do not convert readily. They must therefore be identified and replaced by ASCII characters during the proofreading process following conversion. Small capitals and coloured text do not convert exactly either; they too need to be detected and amended.

Paragraph formatting

Common paragraph formatting techniques such as indenting, tabbing, multiple line returns, borders and shading often do not convert with accuracy. Sometimes it is necessary to explore the base code of the converted file in order to rectify any errors.

ASCII (American Standard Code for Information Interchange): This is a computing standard that uses a string of binary digits to represent the set of letters in the Roman alphabet and other typographic characters.

A page and its HTML file

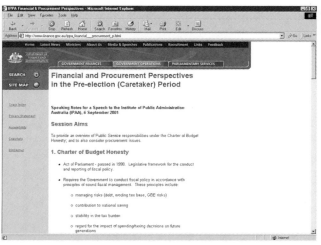

Table formatting

Word processing and professional desktop publishing programs offer a greater range of tabling options than is available in the mark-up languages. Cell, row and text alignment often does not convert, and table borders and shading will require careful review.

Page layout

There are no fixed page lengths for the screen, so headers, footers and page numbers from the printed document are often automatically converted as part of the linear text sequence, appearing mid-sentence in the converted text.

Page-specific cross-references in the original text also need to be adjusted to exploit the creation of hyperlinks.

Multi-column text is often converted as single-column text. In addition, the alignment of text and illustrations may not resemble the original after conversion.

Residual code

Word processing and professional desktop publishing programs often use a lot of formatting code that translates into the mark-up code but is not actually required to enable the document to be displayed on screen. If not filtered before conversion, this extra code will bulk out a file and slow down the loading of the page on the screen.

Residual code and access: When converting a file to rich text format (.rtf) or plain text format (.txt) for use by people who are visually impaired, it is important to remove residual code that may otherwise render the file useless for their purposes. (See Chapter 23 for other factors that should be taken into account to help readers with disabilities to access publications.)

Converting documents to enable digital transmission for end-user printing

Sometimes the task will be to prepare an existing publication for transmission via the Internet—although the document is not intended primarily for viewing on screen, as readers are expected to prefer to print it out and use it in that form.

Original files

The danger of using proprietary file types (such as Microsoft Word for Windows or Lotus Notes) for this activity is that readers must have the right computer operating system and application program (or a lite viewer of the program) to open the downloaded file after they have saved it to their computers from the Internet.

If it is important that the publication be viewed and printed by readers in exactly the same format, layout and fonts as the original, then a PDF is currently the most common approach to use.

Portable Document Format

Adobe Acrobat's Portable Document Format (PDF) files provide an exact visual replica of hard-copy material both for on-screen display and for printing. This is often not achievable through the use of mark-up languages. PDFs can also contain metadata that allows them to be located and searched by Internet search engines.

Any computer file that can be sent to an office laser printer should be easily convertible to PDF. Because PDF files are platform-independent, they will work regardless of the type of computer or operating system that readers may be using.

Accessibility of PDF files: The Adobe web site has an accessibility section <http://access.adobe.com> that contains tools and resources to help PDF creators make their files accessible to people with certain types of disabilities.

Material designed primarily for print and then converted into a PDF file cannot be considered as material designed for on-screen use, since the potential of the electronic medium will not have been properly exploited. However, material designed primarily for on-screen use can also be formatted as PDF files, and in some cases PDFs become a valuable alternative to HTML. PDFs can contain advanced navigation, hyperlinking and searching options, while still maintaining the character of the original document and overcoming many of the conversion difficulties that occur with the mark-up languages.

Creating material specifically for on-screen use

There are now many documents created primarily for use on screen, either as web-based documents or for portable media such as CD-ROMs and DVDs. Often the web-based publications are supplemented with compressed files for downloading and printing, should individual readers prefer to do that. Planning for this type of publication is best started at the commencement of document development; the results are unlikely to be optimised if the material is simply a conversion of a printed document.

Conceptual planning

Documents designed specifically for use on screen allow authors to explore opportunities for introducing elements such as:

- animation, video, sound and other techniques—which can add power and emphasis to many messages
- colour—which can be included readily without the costs associated with reproducing colour in print
- interactive components—which can help readers to understand the message and to respond. These components could include the creation of virtual environments, feedback forms, customised database-to-web information delivery and tailored search results.

Delivery methods must also be selected to suit the content. Material that can be contained in file sizes that do not cause extended waiting times is more suited to Internet delivery. Documents that require large multimedia files with specific plug-ins may be better supplied on CD-ROM. Documents consisting of lengthy text may be best produced as PDFs for downloading and printing out.

The type of content, the effectiveness of its delivery and the ease of its use are the deciding factors in the success of on-screen material. Readers almost never return to an on-screen document that either did not meet their information needs, was difficult to navigate around, or was unacceptably slow to download or use (because its creators had ignored bandwidth or other factors).

Content development

When the components that will make up the on-screen document have been decided, the content can be drafted. Text drafting is generally easier using word processing software; however, the construction of other components such as the images, screen layout or animation will require specific software applications, as will the access and navigation elements.

➤ Chapter 1 discusses the planning for screen-based publications, while Chapter 3 looks at ways of structuring and writing for on-screen reading. See Part 3 for design issues related to page layout, typography, tables, forms and illustrations for screen display.

File structuring

When designing the file structure of an on-screen document, all the text files should be located in a folder identified as containing the text, and all the graphics files should be assembled in a separately labelled folder for graphics. An image from the graphics folder can then be used many times by linking to it from different locations.

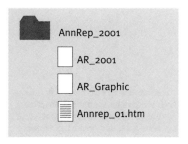

AnnRep_2001

AR_2001

AR_Graphic

Annrep_01.htm

Visual components

The main benefits in using visual components for on-screen material are as follows:

To show growth, movement or transition: The display of a chart might be staged, for example, to show progressive levels of detail; diagrams in a tutorial might be animated; or options of zooming in on an image or showing video documentary footage could be offered.

To provide layers of information: Pop-up boxes are one option when space limitations prevent all the information being displayed at once.

To augment graphic images: Related information could be displayed when an element of an image is selected. For example, a mechanical component in an engineering diagram could display prices and availability in a corresponding table.

To display three-dimensional information: Computer-aided design systems could be used, for instance, to show three-dimensional images from various aspects.

To attract attention: Animation, video or other movement techniques can attract attention to particularly significant elements of a document.

Graphic file formats

There are many types of graphic file formats: for still and moving images, video, sound and virtual reality. The choice depends on the type of image and how it will be used. For example:

GIF (Graphics Interchange Format) is a format that is widely used for electronically published images. A GIF graphic is stored as a sequence of pixels with red, green and blue (RGB) colour values and can be used on various operating systems.

JPEG (Joint Photographic Experts Group) refers to a format developed from a set of standards devised by this group for compressing digitised, still, continuous-tone (photographic) images in greyscale, monochrome or full colour.

Because of factors such as bandwidth and download times, care should be taken to use graphics appropriately. Graphics that are employed merely as decorative items or that do not help readers to understand or locate information are better left out of online publications.

Graphical and other visual displays also need to be described adequately in order not to discriminate against readers who are visually impaired (see pages 430–1).

Mark-up languages

A mark-up language is used to construct web pages and to instruct the browser how to display the pages for the screen. The main mark-up languages used to hold on-screen publication content are derived from the Standard Generalized Mark-up Language (SGML), an information management standard adopted by the International Organization for Standardization. These mark-up languages are Hypertext Mark-up Language (HTML), Dynamic HTML (DHTML), Extensible Markup Language (XML) and other less well-known, subject-specific mark-up languages such as MathML and NewsML.

<i>	Start italics
</i>	End italics
<b>	Start bold
</b>	End bold
<table>	Start table
<tr>	Start table row
<td>	Start table cell
</td></tr></table>	Nested closing tags for cells, rows and the table

XML mark-up tags: This example illustrates how XML tags can describe content:

```
<person_id="p11" sex="m">
  <person_name>
    <given_name>Matthew</given_name>
    <family_name>James</family_name>
  </person_name>
</person>
```

Rapid change: Web mark-up is a constantly changing environment. It is advisable to seek professional advice on trends, issues and standards, or keep up to date with the latest research published online and in print.

Hypertext Mark-up Language

HTML is commonly used for publishing on the World Wide Web. Standards for its use are set by the World Wide Web Consortium.

HTML is a presentation language. Its standardisation of typographic attributes enables browsers to present content in a limited, but mostly predictable, way. It also creates layouts incorporating text, sound, and moving and still images by using a system of embedded 'tags' that are translated by web browsers.

While HTML files can be generated through an automatic conversion by a word processing or desktop publishing program, conversion problems usually litter the file. This means that considerable time must be spent in cleaning up erroneous code (see pages 446–7). The tools used for creating the marked-up text are also used to design the web page, insert graphics, create pop-up windows and apply hyperlinks.

Extensible Markup Language

Unlike HTML, which is a presentation language, XML is used to define the structure of data rather than to describe how the data will be presented. While HTML can be used to format a table, for instance, XML can be used to describe that table's data elements.

Both HTML and XML make use of tags and attributes. HTML specifies how the text between the tags will look in a browser; XML uses the tags to identify the type of data between the tags. For example, '<p>' in an XML file is not a paragraph tag as in HTML; depending on the context, it may mean a price, a parameter, a person, or anything determined by the 'document type definition' (DTD). The DTD identifies the tagged elements, their special purposes and the structure of a document in an XML file. XML is 'extensible' because authors can extend the language definition with their own set of tags.

Using XML, authors and publishers can thus design their own document types, and tailor them to meet an audience's particular needs. With style sheets, XML can enhance browser presentation and performance. Because of its flexibility, it can also make information more accessible and reusable.

Cascading style sheets

A cascading style sheet is used to give greater control over the look of a web page. It incorporates instructions for typefaces and font attributes for headings and text, as well as layout specifications such as alignment, spacing and colours. When a reader accesses the site, this style sheet is sent to the reader's computer.

The style sheet can either be created as a separate document that is linked to all the documents within a site or be imported at the beginning of each text file, allowing different style sheets to be used for different web pages. There are also local style tags available (called 'inline styles') that can be inserted to override the master style sheet as necessary.

The use of a cascading style sheet is important for accessibility. It also supports the use of an aural cascading style sheet, which specifies how a document will sound when rendered as speech. Aural cascading style sheets allow authors and users to specify the volume of spoken content, background sounds, spatial properties of sounds and a host of other properties that aid accessibility.

Hypertext

Hypertext has two main functions:

- as information links—where embedded in-text hyperlinks indicate that other related information is available elsewhere
- as navigation tools—where structural links enable readers to move to other levels of content within a document.

Information hyperlinks

Hyperlinks embedded in the content of a document usually act as pointers to supplementary information. How successful readers will be in using these links generally depends on how well they are able to predict where the link will lead and how relevant the linked information will be to them.

These types of hyperlinks can be links to information (in either text or graphic form) that is located:

- within the same web page
- on another web page but within the same document
- outside the document but within the site
- outside the site.

Hyperlinked text can be programmed to:

- generate an additional browser window containing the new content, with or without standard navigation or toolbars. (A hyperlinked glossary of terms would be suitable for this type of treatment, for example, since readers only need to see the required definition and can then close the new window)
- generate new text to replace the existing hyperlinked text in the same browser window
- cause another part of the window to change its information display while the hyperlinked text remains on screen.

Navigation hyperlinks

Navigation hyperlinks are essential in enabling readers to move around on-screen information. Document navigation can use hyperlinks displayed as:

- text—for example, in menus and labels
- icons—such as arrows for *Up* or *Next*, or an image for *Home*
- image maps containing 'hot spots' that are linked to the information indicated.

'alt' and 'title' attributes

The 'alt' (or 'alternate' text) attribute may be used as part of an image's mark-up tag to provide information about that image. Most browsers will display the 'alt' attribute in the space reserved for the image while the image is loading. This helps readers decide whether to wait for the image to be displayed or to move on.

However, the primary value of 'alt' text is to those people with visual impairments who use specially designed browsers that convert web files to audio output,

Display of information hyperlinks: These can be shown either as a list (for example, a static, dynamic or drop-down list) or as paragraph text identified by colour or underlining (or both). It is advisable to retain default browser link colours when constructing these links, as these colours have become a de facto standard.

The 'alt' attribute
(as an image loads)

```
<a href="http://www.finance.gov.au">
<img src="../images/finance_logo.gif"
alt="Department of Finance and
Administration Logo"> </a>
```

The 'title' attribute

```
<a href="www.naa.gov.au/govserv/agls/"
title="The National Archives of Australia is
the lead Agency for AGLS metadata"> The
AGLS metadata </a> has 19 prescribed ...
```

allowing them to 'hear' web pages rather than to 'view' them. When 'alt' text is attached to an image, these users can understand what the image is about. If an image is being used as a hyperlink (and tagged with the prefix <a href>), the 'alt' attribute will also make this clear.

The 'title' attribute performs a similar function to the 'alt' text in providing reader with preliminary explanations. When attached to a hyperlinked item, it describes the destination of the link. Readers can thus gauge what to expect from a link—whether, for example, it provides navigation or information. Such explanations improve readers' ability to navigate, browse and scan on-screen documents.

AMALGAMATED REVIEW

Advice on preparing electronic publications is spread throughout this manual, to tie in with discussions of corresponding aspects of printed material. This summary checklist is provided as a reminder of the many elements that may need to be checked before final testing takes place and publishing approval is sought.

SUMMARY CHECKLIST FOR ELECTRONIC DOCUMENTS

Identification

- Does the document clearly identify the site or document owner (or sponsor), and the document's title and author?

- Have the standard document identifiers been attached:
  - ISBN or ISSN (or both)?
  - AGLS metadata?
  - copyright statement?

- Are there any other acknowledgments that should be included?

- Has the relationship to (and location of) any printed counterpart been made clear?

- Is the date of publication shown (and has this been changed to the date of last revision where applicable)?

- Have contact details (and any relevant feedback mechanisms) been provided?

Content

- Does the coverage meet applicable in-house policies relating to information provision?

- Has the content been organised as small blocks of related information within a clear hierarchy?

- Has the document been written and edited to facilitate on-screen reading and scanning?

- Have all privacy requirements been met?

- Has a disclaimer or similar statement been included (where relevant)?

esign and navigation

Does it reflect in-house corporate identity requirements?

Has it been designed to suit screen characteristics (such as size, shape and resolution)?

Do all coloured images meet the Web 216 colour standard for the Internet?

Is the content structure clearly displayed?

Does it include the necessary search facilities (including a topical index and/or keyword searching)?

Does it have the relevant persistent navigation elements on every screen, so that it is linked to any larger information structure (such as the host web site)?

Have clear and efficient navigation routes been provided within the document, and is every page suitably linked (that is, no dead-end pages)?

ccess and transmission

Does it meet the W3C guidelines for non-discriminatory access?

Have suitable file formats been chosen?

Have technical aspects such as bandwidth, access speeds, file sizes and browser compatibility been taken into account?

STING ON-SCREEN MATERIAL

ery publication, whether prepared for print or screen, needs to be checked oroughly before release, to ensure that it is clear, complete and free of barrassing errors and that it complies with the required standards.

r on-screen documents, however, there are the additional technical aspects that e critical to success. Will readers be able to find the document on the site or rough a search engine? Will they be able to open it easily (and print it if cessary)? Will the navigation features work correctly? Will the screen display atch expectations?

l these questions, and many more, need to be addressed in a testing and aluation plan. To release a screen-based publication before it has been monstrated to operate successfully is a waste of time and money. It will also lect poorly on the author or sponsoring organisation.

sting and evaluation of the design and display of on-screen material should be dertaken regularly during the development of a publication. This work is best mmenced early in the production process, when changes are easier to make and s expensive.

➤ See Chapter 26 for a general discussion of monitoring, testing and evaluation procedures.

(continued on p. 455)

ABOUT

Testing and evaluation plans

Why test?

Readers' computing environments will differ from the one in which the publication was developed. The publication must therefore be able to work efficiently on various platforms and configurations—for example, with slow modems and older versions of browsers, software and hardware.

The various ways in which readers may try to use or interpret the information also need to be anticipated. It is important not to test just the 'correct' or intended way of navigating or using the on-screen material: as many alternatives as possible should be tested to see if there are opportunities for misinterpretation.

When should testing occur?

Regular functionality and usability testing should be undertaken throughout the development and production cycle. Do not test when there is no desire (for political, commercial or other reasons) to implement any necessary changes. Usability testing is not a validation process: its purpose is to discover and rectify design and display problems.

Where should testing take place?

Testing can be undertaken at the development site, at a site that is representative of the likely audience's environment, in purpose-built usability laboratories or anywhere else that has the appropriate equipment.

What tools are needed?

The tools used in the testing process can be as simple as paper copies of the document with pencils for making notes, or they may be as advanced as eye-tracking and video-monitoring equipment in usability laboratories.

Who should be involved?

People not previously engaged in developing the publication should be involved. The roles to be filled are those of:

- observers or facilitators, who will contribute knowledge about the goals and expectations of the testing process
- participants, who will represent the intended audience
- usability engineers, who will systematically evaluate the on-screen designs for problems related to effectiveness, efficiency and reader satisfaction.

The composition of testing teams usually reflects the resources available and the level of analysis required of the results.

What is tested?

Functionality or performance testing includes checking links, menus, scripts and navigation tools for consistency and accuracy.

Usability testing assesses the effectiveness, efficiency and satisfaction of readers in answering questions and locating information.

How is it tested?

Testing should be systematic, with definable outcomes. Methods for testing include analysis of the screen designs and observation of task-oriented interactions. Testing may be carried out by individual testing, by one-on-one observation, by mediated group discussions, or by a combination of these methods.

What can go wrong?

Results can be affected by bias: in observers, in evaluators and among participants. In addition, there is a risk that participants may not react well to the test or to the material.

What can be discerned from the results?

Problems become apparent through recurrent patterns of mistakes or remarks about difficulties. A number of similar comments would suggest that an issue should be further investigated; single reports of difficulties can be given a lower priority.

is important to define what is going to be tested, and how, before starting. Clear
ecifications at the outset should see most functional and usability errors being
entified early. Defining audience expectations will also help to focus the tests
d observations. For example, if finding a certain level of information in three
ouse clicks is an on-screen standard, then counting mouse clicks should be
corporated in the testing method. Setting goals for testing and evaluation is
itical to determining when sufficient testing of the document or site has been
mpleted.

ie intention of testing must be to find errors, not hope to avoid them. A test
an will outline what is to be tested, how often and when; who will do the
sting; and how the results will be responded to. Every link, button and menu
lection should be tested to be certain it is properly programmed and displays the
rrect content.

ome helpful functionality tests can be automated to save time. Among these are
sts for response and download time, HTML validation, linkrot identification,
d site accessibility rating for readers with disabilities.

the end of the testing program, a full prototype of the document or site should
developed and tested again. This will allow for wider feedback, quality
surance and formal approval procedures to take place before broadcasting live on
e Internet.

Linkrot: This is a colloquial term for a previously active hyperlink that is now invalid—most commonly because the destination URL is no longer operational.

EARCH ENGINES AND INDEXING

arch engines are computer programs that search through large amounts of text
other data. They may operate across the entire World Wide Web, or they may
applied to a single site containing many documents or to a subsite or single
cument.

arch engines work by using a program called a 'spider', 'crawler' or 'robot' to
low links from a top-level URL to pages within a site. When pages are found,
e spider sends keyword information from the text or metadata fields back to its
me site to be indexed or to update previous indexes. When a reader initiates a
arch by entering a query, the query is checked against the search engine's
yword indexes. The best matches are returned as 'hits'.

sability research shows that most readers of on-screen material go straight to the
arch button on entering a site or document. They are focused on a task and want
find the required information quickly. Useful results are produced when the
ht concepts or words have been indexed.

tomatic indexing

dexing by search engines is automatic and comprehensive and reflects the
rrent content. However, the results are literal, usually with inclusive, rather than
clusive, coverage.

yword searching is the most common type of text query and retrieval operation
rformed by search engines. The keywords indexed by search engines are the ones

they have been programmed to treat as significant. Words that are mentioned towards the top of a document or words that are repeated several times throughou are more likely to be deemed important.

One of the problems readers experience with keyword searching is that search engines have difficulty discerning between homonyms (such as *hard* meaning 'difficult' and *hard* meaning 'firm'), which often results in a large and inappropria search response. Other difficulties relate to the inconsistent treatment of word stems, singular and plural words and tenses. Authors should consider which word their readers are likely to use in keyword searches, and provide appropriate terminology.

The design of a site's search query page and its search results page also influences the perceived accessibility of the site. The search query page (or form) should never be more than one click away from anywhere in the site or document. Man sites and documents incorporate the search link in the standard navigation template used for each page.

➤ For a discussion of metadata and the associated requirements for Commonwealth documents, see Chapter 23.

Search engine web sites: Information on the capabilities and idiosyncrasies of major search engines can be found on Internet sites devoted to search engine operations.

Publication-style indexing

Authors or professional indexers can produce publication-style indexes for individu documents. These indexes are based on terms and concepts that it is envisaged readers might want to search for in that particular document—in contrast to the automatic indexing provided by search engines. However, publication-style indexe require frequent maintenance if they are attached to dynamic documents or sites.

➤ For a detailed description of publication-style indexing, see Chapter 15.

GOING LIVE ON THE INTERNET

Facilities provided by an Internet service provider (ISP) are necessary in order to broadcast over the Internet. An Internet address, or URL, for the site or docume will also be necessary.

Broadcasting

The web offers many mechanisms for broadcasting content to a potential audience. Alerting search engines to content is the best way to have a site noticed by web users. Other useful approaches include broadcasting to appropriate list servers, as well as to w managers of related sites who might be interested in creating links to the information, and to any relevant portal sites that might direct readers to the publication.

Commonwealth broadcasting: On establishing a new home page, Commonwealth agencies are required to notify the web manager at <www. fed.gov.au>.

Maintenance

Readers expect online documents always to be up to date. A rigorous maintenan regime is therefore needed to manage all the components of an online resource— which, after all, is one of the public faces of an organisation.

Maintenance means more than keeping the content timely and appropriate. Access schemes should also be kept current and relevant to the material being published; navigation systems should be routinely checked to ensure they remain suited to the often changing requirements of readers; and the design of the site a its documents should be kept fresh but reasonably uniform.

➤ More information on evaluating a publication after release is provided in Chapter 26.

EPLICATION OF PORTABLE MEDIA

the on-screen publication is to be produced in a portable media format, rangements must be made for its replication. Replication companies can be lentified through industry lists or other directories.

uotes and specifications

equests for replication quotes should include the following details:

- the name and contact details of the commissioning organisation and of the project manager
- the type of replication required—such as CD-ROM, diskette, DVD, video or audio tape
- the quantity of replications required—usually 50, 100, 250, 500, 1000, then in multiples of 1000 units
- the estimated total size of the files on the master to be replicated
- the file types on the master
- the required packaging
- specifications (file types and versions) of the artwork for printed parts
- the date on which the master should be available
- the date on which the replicated units are to be returned
- the delivery address for these units
- any other special requirements.

he following items should be supplied to the selected replicator:

- a master disk
- artwork for the printed components
- a specification sheet detailing the work required and any special features needing attention.

he master disk

he master disk should be provided on a CD-R or 'write once' disk. It should be lly tested beforehand because there is no pre-production proofing process prior to he master being replicated.

he master disk must be free from scratches and fingerprints. It should be clearly arked with the title of the work on both the case and the disk itself. Labels should ot be attached to the master disk, so any writing should be done directly onto the on-recordable side of the disk with a soft, felt-tipped pen. It is best to take all the aper parts out of the case in which the disk is being provided to the replicator.

he CD production process

he creation of a CD is a complex process. In brief, a laser beam is used to 'expose' the gital master content in a spiral track on a glass disk that is coated with a photo-resist yer. The exposed glass master is then nickel plated using a nickel sulfamate solution, ilt up to the required thickness for a 'stamper'. The stamper is peeled off the glass aster and further treated to form a stamper 0.285 millimetres thick.

CD-ROM vital statistics:

- Compact disk capacity is 74 minutes or 650 Mb.
- The basic unit of data is a 'sector', which contains 2352 bytes of information.
- CD file systems
  - ISO 9660 is generally used for IBM-compatible computers
  - Macintosh HFS (Hierarchical File System) is designed specifically for Apple Macintosh computers
  - Hybrid ISO 9660.MAC HFS is for multi-platform use.

457

The stamper is loaded into an injection moulder. Molten polycarbonate is injected, forming a clear disk with the data track moulded on one side. The data side of the disk is coated under vacuum with a reflective layer of aluminium, which is then sealed and protected by a liquid polymer resin. The labelling details are screen-printed on top of this protective layer.

Artwork for printed components

Artwork for the label and printed accompaniments (the booklet and tray inlay) should be provided on a separate disk from the digital content master disk. The art disk must be clearly identified as such, along with the title of the work and other contact details. Colour laser proofs of all the artwork should be provided for the replicator's reference.

➤ See p. 251 for a list of the identifying details to be provided on disks and their packaging.

Disk labelling

The disk itself is generally screen-printed using either:

- up to five different spot colours
- halftones and duotones

  or

- four-colour process (which requires a solid white background to be preprinted).

Screen process
Stencil printing

The CD replicator can output artwork files to film in preparation for screen-printing. However, film could be supplied instead (but check the replicator's requirements before film is made).

The minimum recommended type size for titles and other identifying details is 5 point—in positive print with a line width of 0.15 millimetres. However, if the type is to be reversed out, the minimum type size should be 7 point with a 0.25 millimetre line width.

Trapping for screen-printing on the disk requires a minimum overlap of 0.4 millimetres (an overprint stroke or outline of 0.8 millimetres).

Standard industry logos identifying the type of disk (digital audio, data storage, photo CD or digital video) are recommended.

Packaging

CD-ROM cases can vary considerably, depending on the number of disks in each case and on customer requirements. However, the most popular packaging options are:

- jewel cases with clear, white or coloured trays. These may consist of either:
  - a standard case and tray
  - a double, triple or quad case and two black trays
  - a maxi slimline (single) case with no tray

    or

  - a double slimline case
- vinyl pockets with single, double or triple pockets
- cardboard wallets.

(continued on p. 4

Cutaway of a CD

Ink silk-screened

Top coat liquid polymer

Aluminium coating

Moulded polycarbonate

The printable area of a CD

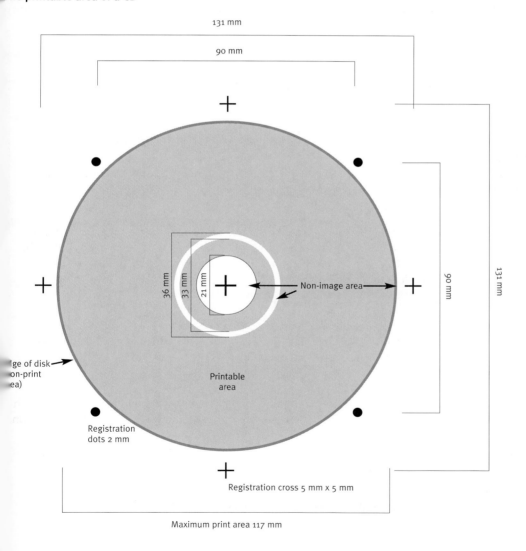

131 mm

90 mm

36 mm

33 mm

21 mm

Non-image area

90 mm

131 mm

Edge of disk (non-print area)

Printable area

Registration dots 2 mm

Registration cross 5 mm x 5 mm

Maximum print area 117 mm

**The standard industry
logos**

Digital audio

Data storage

Digital video disk

**Four-page CD booklet
specifications**

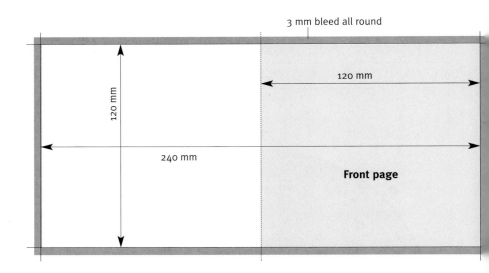

3 mm bleed all round

120 mm

120 mm

240 mm

Front page

CD tray inlay specifications

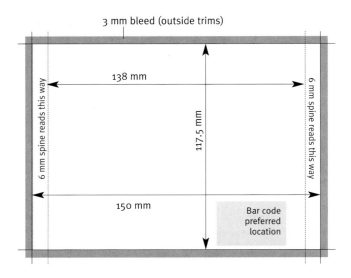

3 mm bleed (outside trims)

6 mm spine reads this way

6 mm spine reads this way

138 mm

117.5 mm

150 mm

Bar code
preferred
location

CD-ROMs in jewel cases are generally packaged into cartons specially made to take 100 units; the filled cartons weigh approximately 10 kilograms. CD-ROMs in vinyl pockets are usually packaged in boxes of 250, weighing about 15 kilograms.

Chapter **25**

Paper-based reproduction

PREPARING TO PRINT	**463**
Production costs	464
Quality control	465
Cost-saving techniques	465
PROOFS	**465**
First-level proof	466
Second-level proof	467
Final proof	467
PREPRESS	**468**
Artwork	468
Trapping	470
Imposition	470
PAPER	**471**
Paper-making	471
Paper coatings	471
Choosing a paper	471
Recycled paper	475
Specifying paper	476
International paper sizes	476
TRADITIONAL PRINTING	**478**
Offset lithography	478
Letterpress	480

DIGITAL PRINTING	**481**
Laser printers	481
Ink-jet printers	481
On-demand printing	482
Just-in-time printing	482
Personalisation	482
EMBELLISHMENT	**482**
Engraving and diestamping	483
Foil stamping	483
Embossing and debossing	483
Diecutting	483
Laminating	484
Varnishing	484
BINDING	**485**
Paper binding	485
Loose-leaf binding	487
About case binding	488

rranging for a document to be printed is a significant project
anagement task. It entails contracting and coordinating a range of
ifferent suppliers, and checking the quality of the services they
rovide for the project. Knowledge of the processes and techniques
wolved enables suitable production decisions to be taken.

rinting—or reproducing text and images on a sheet of paper—has
eveloped to the point where traditional printing presses stand side
y side with computerised output options. Together they provide
nancially viable options that enable the distribution of a
rofessionally presented document on paper to a mass audience
r to an audience of one. Preparation techniques for both are
most exclusively digital.

here are also important environmental factors to consider in the creation of a
inted product. Many of the production processes involve chemicals and by-
oducts that must be managed to reduce their harm to the environment—but
tential impacts can be minimised by making appropriate choices at the outset.

lthough one of the most environmentally friendly choices is to publish
ectronically, there are still good reasons to produce paper-based publications,
cluding:

  the convenience and familiarity for readers that traditional publication formats
  offer

  accessibility, since the audience is not dependent on technology to read the
  publication

  the tactile and other useful physical qualities of printed material.

REPARING TO PRINT

he planning of a print job starts once a printed product has been conceptualised.
he entire process—from how the material will be prepared and presented for
inting, through to the selection and briefing of a printer—must be thought about
refully.

➤ Chapter 2 summarises many of
the aspects that should be considered
when selecting a printer.

most cases, digital copy will be supplied to the printer, either online or on disk,
d complete control of the process may be maintained electronically. The

Internet enables the download of all production-ready files directly. However, there is also the alternative of supplying 'camera-ready copy' (a clean set of separated artwork or film) from which the printing house creates plates for a traditional press.

To know what needs to be supplied, discuss with the printer the methods that best suit the project and their facilities and services. And discuss it early, as changes late in the process can incur significant extra costs.

Production costs

There are two kinds of production costs: fixed costs and variable (or 'run-on') costs.

Fixed costs usually occur only once in the production cycle and do not rise as production increases. They include the costs of:
- writing, editing and indexing
- design, artwork and print preparation
- film and platemaking
- machine 'make-ready' (the preparation of presses, mixing of inks and initial test runs) and 'wash-up' (cleaning of the presses).

Variable costs rise with increases in production and the consumption of more materials. They include the costs of:
- paper and other materials used
- machine running time during the printing and binding processes
- packing and delivery.

Final estimates are then converted to a 'cost per unit'. This is the total of the fixed costs, plus the total variable costs of the chosen print run, divided by that quantity.

The number of copies in an edition therefore influences the unit cost. It will be cheaper per unit to produce 10 000 copies than 1000 copies, because the fixed costs are spread over a greater number of copies. A publisher must balance this factor against expected distribution in order to establish an economically viable print run for a project. The temptation to choose a longer print run just to lower the unit cost must be avoided. Not only are there the higher initial costs to be considered, but there are the storage costs and the environmental problem of disposal that follow from the production of more copies than the potential market requires.

➤ See p. 31 for other factors affecting printers' quotes.

Failure of the publication team to meet any part of the reproduction schedule can result in increased costs and a delay in publication. Most suppliers will have scheduled the project around commitments to other clients. Rescheduling depends on the availability of staff and machine time. While publications can be produced quickly if topicality and the potential market provide sufficient inducement, this is also often at the expense of other scheduled printing work and can incur a cost penalty.

Quality control

Quality control is a vital part of every manufacturing operation. Each stage of the work must be completed efficiently and accurately if the finished product is to be of a high standard. Work must therefore be carefully planned and supervised throughout the production process.

Cost-saving techniques

Preliminary discussions with a printer may elicit ways in which savings can be made. Sometimes, reducing the trimmed size of the publication slightly or arranging to print four-colour process on only one side of the sheet will reduce costs considerably. Small changes to the process may also yield significant savings in fixed costs. In most cases, such changes affect the printer's planning, so the earlier that these possibilities are canvassed, the greater the likelihood of cost-effective printing.

Ganging up

If there are a number of printing jobs that will be printed on the same paper stock with the same colours, there is the opportunity to 'gang them up' on press by printing two or more jobs concurrently.

Ganging up better utilises the capacity of printing presses and enables larger sheets of paper to be used, thus saving on fixed production costs. It is easiest to do this with a series of pamphlets, posters, flyers or information sheets. Even if the different items in the series are to be distributed at different times, it may be worthwhile to have all of them printed at the same time and then stored for progressive release.

A printer will advise how to prepare artwork for ganging up, trimming and folding.

Preprinting

To make a saving in printing costs for corporate colours, it is sometimes a good idea to preprint blank 'shells' for newsletters or other regularly produced publications a few months or even a year in advance. These shells can be stored, and brought out for overprinting with the content for each new issue. Sometimes this may mean that only a one-colour overprint is required for each issue instead of a multicolour job, thus saving on fixed costs for each run. Another advantage of preprinting colour work is that colour matching and accuracy are assured in successive issues.

Pamphlet series, covers and any other regular formats that an organisation uses can also benefit from this approach. Templates should be created for the overprinted material, and the preparation of artwork discussed with a printer.

Longevity: When creating a preprinted shell, ensure that no material has been included that is likely to change during the life of the preprint. In particular, avoid names, phone numbers and dates.

PROOFS

There is a series of proofing stages (summarised in the figure overleaf) that a publication may have to pass through during the prepress and printing processes. Galley and page proofs, revise proofs, dyeline proofs, colour proofs, press proofs and press checks could all be required, depending on the significance and complexity of the job.

Any changes made to the publication content become progressively more expensive and time-consuming with each stage, so every effort should be made to avoid late amendments. Anything beyond minor changes at page-proof stage, for example, may require considerable work in repositioning illustrations and tables and in checking any changed numbering. Changes after film has been made will involve the cost of new film as a minimum. Once the plates have been made, changes become even more prohibitive in terms of cost and time.

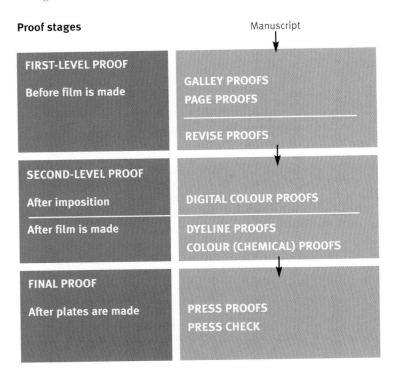

Proof stages

Manuscript

FIRST-LEVEL PROOF Before film is made	GALLEY PROOFS PAGE PROOFS REVISE PROOFS
SECOND-LEVEL PROOF After imposition	DIGITAL COLOUR PROOFS
After film is made	DYELINE PROOFS COLOUR (CHEMICAL) PROOFS
FINAL PROOF After plates are made	PRESS PROOFS PRESS CHECK

First-level proof

Galleys and page proofs

Proofs provided by a typesetter or printer for proofreading are usually generated by a plain-paper laser printer from typesetting or imagesetting equipment and will be in the form of galleys or page proofs.

Galley proofs show the typeset material before it has been divided into separate pages. Galleys are often used for long or densely illustrated documents, to allow amendments to be made without affecting page lengths and the placement of figures and tables.

Page proofs, on the other hand, show the typeset material divided into page lengths. They should be checked for the appropriateness of the layout, image placement and reproduction.

evise proofs

the proofs are found to contain a large number of errors, or if the addition or eletion of significant material is unavoidable, a revise proof may be ordered. If rther minor corrections still need to be made, the typesetter should be asked to neck that these are incorporated correctly. The editor or author can then use the ext stage of proofs to verify that this has been done satisfactorily.

econd-level proof

igital colour proofs

igital colour proofs are available after the document has been arranged in multi-ıge format, but before the prepress, film and platemaking stages. If they are colour ser prints, these proofs will be less expensive than the colour proofs made later ɔm platemaking film but will not give an accurate colour match. If they are pplied as an electronic file or PDF (see pages 447–8), they can be checked on reen for accuracy of content and placement, but, again, they will not give an .curate colour match.

yeline proofs

the document contains illustrations, or if it is to be printed in colours other than ıack, dyeline proofs may be ordered to verify that all elements of the copy, cluding illustrations, are correct and in the right position. Dyeline proofs are epared from the film. They are provided on chemically coated paper and can be pplied in folded sections.

ɔlour proofs

ɔmetimes known as chemical proofs, colour proofs are necessary for four-colour ɔrk. They allow colour to be checked for accuracy, the positions and sizes of ustrations to be verified and, if necessary, a final check to be made on proof ıanges requested earlier. For colour proofreading, the proofs should always be ıecked against the original artwork or photographs and the relevant colour stem. Any corrections, as well as any production imperfections found on the oof, should be clearly marked using a chinagraph pencil.

ɔlour proofs are expensive. Nevertheless, a revise colour proof should be ordered changes are so complex that further detailed checking becomes essential.

ɔlour proofs are also regarded as a 'contract' proof: by signing them off, the client cepts the quality of all components. If there is still uncertainty about quality, the ient can wait for the press proof before signing off.

nal proof

·ess proofs

lso known as a machine proof, a press proof is the initial print of a work taken ther from the printing press assigned to print the whole run or from a special ɔofing press. A press proof is ordered where precise colour matching is critical to .e quality of a job. It should therefore be checked to ensure that the colours atch the originals or those on the latest approved colour proof and that there is proper colour matching across double-page spreads. These proofs may also be required to ensure that any unavoidable last-minute corrections have been made. Press proofs are expensive.

Press check

A press check is the last stage at which checking can be done before the entire publication is printed. It entails standing beside the press with the printer and approving sample printed sheets from each section before printing continues.

PREPRESS

'Prepress' is the name given to that part of the production process that occurs after a page proof is finally approved for publication and signed off. It involves preparing the design file for reproduction, taking into account all the requirements for the selected reproduction process. Prepress specialists therefore consider what will happen to the imagery and type when printed, given the physical properties of the paper and the vagaries of the chosen printing technique. They then adjust the digital files accordingly.

The preparation of images takes the most attention. Prepress techniques ensure that they have been scanned at the appropriate resolution so that pixels will not be visible in the reproduction. Prepress operators will also try to maintain consistent colour levels between different images. On porous papers, halftone dots will look larger because wet ink will seep beyond the edges of the dot into the clear area, effectively deepening the tone of the image. So, in prepress, each dot will have to be correspondingly reduced in size to accommodate the expected 'dot gain' on press, in order to achieve the best reproduction of the image that is possible on that paper stock.

➤ See Chapter 21 for a discussion of colour reproduction techniques.

Prepress often involves replacing the images with high-resolution versions. Until this stage in the process, images will usually have been incorporated in digital files at low resolution, to enable faster on-screen display and laser printer output. The high-resolution images needed for printed reproduction increase the file size of the project beyond the level that most desktop computing systems can accommodate.

➤ Chapter 21 discusses halftone resolution and lpi (lines per inch).

In addition, prepress operators will select the appropriate screen resolution to suit the printing press and paper stocks selected. On a porous stock, for example, a 100 lpi halftone screen may be selected; on a high-quality smooth paper, a 150 lpi screen or higher is likely to be required.

Artwork

Some prepress functions relating to artwork have to be considered by the graphic designer when producing a final page file.

Bleeds

Photographs and areas of colour (or even just type) that run off the edge of a page are said to 'bleed'. Pages that bleed are printed on a larger sheet of paper and immed. Wherever this occurs, a minimum of 3 millimetres of extra image area ust be supplied outside the trim. However, the image must be positioned ccurately within the area that will be seen on the page *after* it has been trimmed. or example, an image in a box that bleeds to the right should be centred on the ea that will appear on the trimmed page, not centred within the wider box.

im marks

or speed and economy in production, publication pages will usually be printed larger sheets, which are then folded and trimmed. To guide the trimming, ort fine lines are provided on each corner of the artwork. These lines start millimetres away from the trim edge and continue away from the page, so that ey will print on the excess sheet and not accidentally appear in the page area. In ost cases they are added automatically by page layout or imposition software.

egistration marks

order for a multicolour file to be printed 'in register' (where each colour is ositioned precisely in the correct relation to the other colours when it is printed), gistration marks are placed outside the page area. These small crosses appear in e same place on each layer of film produced for the page. The printer ensures ey align when they are printed so that the colours will be placed accurately.

lour control bars

ophisticated laser scanning techniques are used to produce process colour parations. To ensure compatibility with similarly advanced colour densitometry spectrophotometry systems, it is advisable to make certain that both the colour parator and the printer are working to the same colour density standards. Ink andards, paper type, proofing systems and colour control bars should all be ordinated.

ith four-colour process colour, a standardised colour bar is added to the printed eets. (See the colour section for an example.) It includes solid ink patches of ch process colour, two-colour overprinted patches of the process colour solids, reen tints of each process colour, and two-colour overprints of the screen tints. press, the printer assesses the performance of the press by comparing the colour r on the printed samples against the approved colour proof. This comparison will ow any discrepancy in ink level and any misregistration, dot gain or blurring. ch problems are monitored continually throughout the print run, with justments being made where necessary.

fects of binding and trimming

thicker books with staples down the spine, the inner or back margins have to be creased progressively from the outer pages so that the outer margins appear latively constant through the trimmed book. The graphic designer should discuss is aspect with a printer, as the imagesetter's imposition program can achieve this riation automatically.

e increased inner margin for binding processes (such as side and ring binding) eds consideration by the graphic designer when creating the document's master ge template.

Area of bleed, and position of trim marks

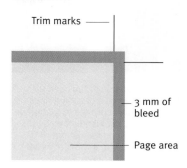

Trim marks

3 mm of bleed

Page area

Registration marks

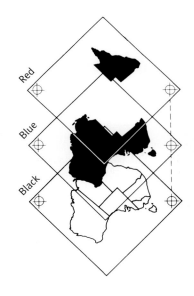

Red

Blue

Black

➤ See discussion of margins in Chapter 17.

Spreading and choking

A simple example of the need for trapping is when a black dot appears in a red square. The red can continue under the black, just deepening the black (left). If the red did not continue under and the black was slightly misregistered, a small crescent-moon shape in white might appear (right).

An eight-page imposition

Front

4	5
8	1

Back

6	3
2	7

	1
2	3
4	5
6	7
8	

A flat plan of an eight-page section, printed in full colour on one side and single colour on the back. The flat plan shows the colour break-up for layout planning. In this example, the full-colour pages are tinted.

Trapping

Where colours appear side by side in a design, slight movement during printing needs to be accommodated (to avoid the colour of the paper showing through). This is achieved through a process called 'trapping'. It involves 'spreading' light colours (or expanding them slightly into the area of dark colour) and 'choking' the dark colours (so that these do not 'spread').

Trapping becomes extremely complex when various colour combinations occur side by side.

Imposition

Publications are normally printed in sections of eight, sixteen, thirty-two or sometimes sixty-four pages. Printing in small sections increases machine time and is less economical.

In order to print a section of thirty-two pages (sixteen pages on each side of a sheet) so that each page will be in the correct sequence and in alignment when printed and folded, an 'imposition' is created. The even-numbered pages appear to the left of the odd-numbered pages.

Prepress operators and printers usually prepare an imposition.

Flat plans

On the occasions where different colours are printed on each side of a sheet, the colours will fall on alternate pairs of facing pages. Imposition showing the designer where the colours will fall is conveyed in a 'flat plan'. Flat plans are used in magazine and book publishing to plan a publication's sequence (based on the positioning of colour throughout the publication) and the placement of advertising.

Wrapping, inserting and tipping-in

Sometimes illustrations or text pages will be printed on a different type of paper from that used for the main text. They must then be produced as four-page units in order to facilitate 'wrapping' (around a section) or 'inserting' (into a section). The method chosen (either wrapping and inserting, or printing on a single paper stock that will achieve a satisfactory compromise for both purposes) will be determined to some extent by a careful comparison of costs and production times.

Wrapping, inserting and tipping-in

Outside wrap

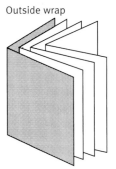

Insert

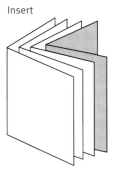

Tip-in

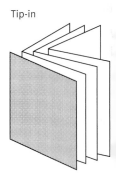

'ip-ins' are used in special circumstances and usually take the form of a single
eet (such as a frontispiece, a fold-out map or an illustration). They are glued
ong the edge of a page's inner margin and, consequently, will not lie flat when
rned.

APER

here are many varieties of papers, all with different characteristics suited to
fferent purposes. These characteristics are determined by the various raw
aterials and processes used during paper-making and the coatings added to the
per afterwards.

aper-making

ost paper is made from cellulose plant fibre obtained from wood, straw and
parto, although hemp, cotton and linen fibres obtained from waste rags and
her sources are also used. In Australia, most fine papers are made from wood. It
'pulped' or broken down into its fibres either by mechanically disintegrating it or
chemical processes. The pulp is subjected to various bleaching, digesting and
fining processes. Fillers such as white clay or titanium dioxide are added to it to
prove the surface and colour of the paper. Size (starch) is also added to stiffen
e paper and reduce absorbency.

aper coatings

lso referred to as 'art papers', coated papers are graded A1, A2 and A3 in
scending order of coating quality. Coated papers produce a sharper print
pression than uncoated papers and give much better resolution of halftones and
e detail. During paper-making, a thin layer of pigment (white clay or calcium
rbonate), combined with various additives, is applied to the paper's surface.
oatings can be gloss (reflective), suede, satin or dull (low or little reflection), or
att (non-reflective).

hoosing a paper

electing the right stock for any piece of printing calls for an awareness of the
aracteristics of paper, an appreciation of printing and binding requirements, and
regard for readers. Although the final choice may be affected by cost and
ailability, the suitability of the stock can be established by considering what is
ing to be printed on it, what treatment it will have to stand up to, how long it
ll have to last, and how and where the publication will be used.

haracteristics of different papers

e following characteristics should be considered when choosing paper:
 the finish on the paper (surface texture, gloss, reflection and whiteness) that
  will be needed to achieve the required quality of reproduction for type, colour
  and images and that will match the desired level of importance or prestige
 its bulk and weight, as this will determine how thick and heavy the publication
  will be

- its opacity, which will determine how much of the next page will be visible through the sheet
- its strength and flexibility for press handling, folding, and the amount of use th publication will be likely to receive
- its archival quality, which will determine the age at which it will have to be discarded
- its printability, or how well it will respond to inks and the physical process of moving through the printing press.

Many different papers are available for books, reports, newsletters and publicity material. The choice depends on the significance of the document as well as on it market, prestige, selling price, distribution, size and complexity.

Finish

The look and feel of paper (its 'finish') influence the way in which it prints.

Gloss

Gloss-coated paper is not suited to publications that are predominantly textual, as light reflected from the shiny surface can be annoying and affect readers' concentration. However, a gloss finish is often preferred to a matt finish for halftone reproduction (especially of four-colour illustrations), in which sharpness, detail and brilliance of colour are essential.

Reflection and whiteness

Surface light reflectance (paper brightness as distinct from light glare) is a characteristic of 'high-white' papers. Whiteness of paper varies considerably, ranging from warm (creamy off-white) to cool (blueish snow-white). Colour printed on the whiter papers is brighter and cleaner, and halftones tend to be mor distinct. However, the crisp contrast of black ink against white paper, while superficially attractive and effective for brief or ephemeral publications, may cause visual discomfort if used in books that demand sustained reading.

The actual shade of white is determined by the kinds of bleaches used and the variety of dyes (such as fluorescent whitening agents) blended into the pulp. High whiteness is subject to some degree of eventual fading because of the effect of ligh on the fluorescent dyes used to produce that brightness.

Textured papers

Paper may be embossed during paper-making by running the sheet between two rollers that impress a pattern into its surface. These patterns are known by the different textures they simulate: linen, felt, leather, and so on.

Papers for special tasks

It is worth considering synthetic or latex-impregnated papers for maps or field books and for other contexts where hard wear or soiling must be expected (for example, in kitchens, factories and mechanical workshops). These stocks are generally superior to fibre papers for such purposes because of their resistance to water and grease, and their toughness. However, synthetic stock is much more expensive than paper. The initial cost should therefore be weighed against the lif

xpectancy of the publication and the resistance properties of the paper under
harsh conditions.

It is most important that advice on the use of synthetic stocks be obtained from
the supplying merchant before specifications are finalised.

Bulk and weight

The bulk of a book is governed by the thickness of the paper stock used and by the
number of pages. The choice of paper also has a considerable effect on the weight
of a book, which in turn can affect the handling and distribution costs.

It is therefore necessary to choose a thin paper to prevent a book such as a
dictionary from bulking too much. Conversely, a thick paper may be specified to
give more bulk to a book with a small number of pages.

A book's ultimate thickness must be considered when format is being decided. A
wrong choice may result in a floppy, outsize book or in one so thick that it must be
split into two or more volumes.

Measuring paper thickness

The thickness of a piece of paper is measured in micrometres (μm)—sometimes
known by the older term 'microns'. Thickness is not proportional to substance.
Owing to their lower density, some bulky papers and boards are in fact lighter than
thinner stock.

The thickness of a book (in millimetres) can be ascertained by using the following
formula (remembering that a leaf is one sheet of paper—accounting for two pages):

$$\frac{\text{Number of leaves} \times \text{thickness of stock}}{1000}$$

To this figure must be added the thickness of covers, fold-outs, and so on.

Grammage

The weight, or mass, of paper is called 'grammage' and is expressed in grams per
square metre (g/m^2 or, more commonly, 'gsm'). Thus a particular paper may be
referred to as being 90 gsm, irrespective of the sheet or reel size in which it is
made.

The most commonly used grammages for publications range from about 70 gsm,
when book weight is a factor, to about 140 gsm for prestigious volumes. Most
publications are printed on papers of from 80 to 110 gsm. Since the weight of a
book affects its distribution costs, it is useful to be able to calculate its final weight
when deciding on the paper to be used. The formula is:

$$\frac{\text{Area of 1 page in mm}^2 \times \text{gsm}}{1\,000\,000} \times \text{number of leaves}$$

To this weight must be added the grammage of the cover (by the same formula)
and any carton or other packaging.

Choosing a lighter weight of paper has an environmental benefit, as lighter papers
use less raw material.

Dummy: If requested, a paper merchant or printer will often make up a 'dummy' (a blank book of the size, paper stock and binding specified).

Opacity

The less opaque a paper is, the more the print and images on the reverse or next page will be visible through the paper. Because showthrough affects readability as well as appearance, the opacity of a proposed text paper is always an important consideration. Showthrough is related to the weight of the paper to some extent, and is also more noticeable with high-white papers than with off-white or tinted papers.

Strength and flexibility

When used in connection with paper, the word 'strength' relates to folding endurance, tear resistance, tensile and burst strengths (its ability to stretch), and stiffness. Not all of these properties can be achieved in one type of paper—for example, a paper able to withstand constant folding and unfolding will also have good tear resistance but low tensile strength.

The folding strengths of rag and wood-free papers are superior to those of other papers. High-density papers also withstand folding and flexing better than low-density ones.

Grain direction

The term 'grain direction' refers to the predominant direction of the fibres in a sheet of paper. Grain direction affects both expansion potential (which is important in register printing) and folding. Book sections need to be folded with the spine parallel to the grain direction.

Archival materials

Sample books: Paper properties are described in manufacturers' and merchants' paper 'swatches' (or sample books).

Work that is meant to last (such as a reference manual) will need a paper that can withstand constant use and will not deteriorate or discolour rapidly with age. For such purposes, it is necessary to choose either archival-quality paper or a plastic-coated or synthetic stock.

The life expectancy of paper depends basically on the nature of the pulp and the acidity (or pH) of the paper. Paper that retains many of the natural elements of wood is highly unstable and deteriorates rapidly unless kept under optimum conditions.

Archival (permanent) papers, which are made from rag pulp or rag and highly refined wood-free pulp, are alkaline. They stand up well to constant handling and are formulated to last for at least 500 years. The average wood-free publication papers approximate a neutral pH and have good life expectancy.

Printability

Papers vary in printability—that is, in the way they accept ink, in the way they handle on the printing press, and in the speed at which they can be run through the press. Printability therefore inevitably affects production times and costs. A 'bargain' paper may, for instance, prove to be more costly overall than a dearer one of better quality because the machine time will be increased as a result of frequent web breaks or sheet-feeding problems.

Cover stocks

Cover stocks range from heavyweight papers to two-sided boards (with a similar quality of finish on both sides), one-sided boards (with a lower quality finish on the back) and specialty boards. Most are available in white, but boards also come in a wide range of colours. Specialty boards vary widely in texture, colour and strength. Metallic-surfaced boards are also available.

The thickness of cover board is quite important. Thickness does not necessarily mean strength. Some one-sided boards are intended for packaging, because their thickness provides insulation and protection. However, these boards are not strong enough to resist the continual folding or flexing to which the covers of softbound publications are subjected.

Matching covers to internal pages: Many specialty cover stocks will have matching text weights.

Availability

Ranges of paper are subject to being discontinued or superseded. A paper should therefore not be specified until the printer or paper merchant has confirmed that it is readily available. If it is not, a decision must be made on whether to wait until it can be obtained or to select another stock.

For major publications, paper requirements (both qualities and quantities) should be established as early as possible so that the printer can buy in or retain sufficient stock for the job. If it is likely that final quantities will not be established until late in the program, an alternative stock should be specified to help avoid production delays that might occur if the first choice becomes unavailable.

Paper costs

Paper is a basic factor in the cost of printing: its initial cost forms roughly 30 to 50 per cent of the total cost of the printed job. If the wrong paper is chosen, however, that cost can increase considerably.

To gain maximum value for money, the dimensions of a publication should be related as closely as possible to those of the full sheet of paper on which it will be printed. This is because the cost of the whole sheet (of the size providing the most efficient cut) is charged, not just the cost of the area used. When sufficient notice of major work is given, printers may be able to have a paper made or sheeted to the most suitable size, but this is not always achievable at short notice.

Imported specialty stocks should only be used in sizes proportionate to the full sheet (with additional attention given to the grain direction required for folding). If not, a considerable amount of offcut may result, and the value of the unused paper is likely to prove surprisingly high.

Commonwealth purchasing guidelines: In the context of achieving 'best value for money', Commonwealth agencies are requested to consider goods of Australian and New Zealand content when evaluating offers from suppliers. Some agencies also prefer to specify recycled and 'environmentally preferred' papers.

Recycled paper

Recycled paper may be composed entirely of recycled fibres or of a blend of recycled and new fibres. Paper made from raw materials, usually wood, is known as 'virgin' fibre paper because it has been made into paper for the first time.

Recycled content could be described as 'post-industrial waste', where paper has been through a manufacturing process and has then been returned to the mill for repulping. It may include residues or by-products from other industries not usually

associated with paper-making, or it may comprise offcuts, remainders, spoiled wor
or 'broke' (spoilage and waste from the paper mill). 'Post-consumer waste' describ
paper that has been collected after use and returned for processing.

Most paper mills and distributors identify recycled papers by the percentage of
recycled fibres they contain and their suitability for particular uses. The archival
properties of recycled papers depend on the types of waste paper used as the fibre
source. If the collected waste paper can be sorted, different grades of papers and
boards can be made.

Specifying paper

Sheet paper is normally packed in 'reams' (500 sheets). The particulars included i
paper-makers' descriptions are as follows:

- kind of paper
- colour
- grammage
- size of sheets
- grain direction
- mass (in kilograms per 1000 sheets).

The mass per 1000 sheets is used for calculating the mass of a consignment for
transport and storage purposes and for pricing when the paper is sold by mass.

Paper in reels is usually sold by grammage, mass, reel width, reel diameter and
internal core diameter. Boards are normally sold and packed in hundreds, and
described by grammage, thickness or mass.

When specifying paper for printing, it is necessary to indicate the kind of paper
(by its generic description or its market name) and the grammage and colour. It i
also helpful to give the name of the maker or supplier. For example, a generic
description might be '100 gsm white A2 matt art', while a specific description
(market name) could be '100 gsm Australian Paper Impress matt art'.

The normal designation when specifying paper for bookwork assumes that the pa
is upright, the depth being the greater dimension. A landscape format, where the
depth is the lesser dimension, is indicated by adding the letter 'L' to the
designation: thus A4L is 210 millimetres deep × 297 millimetres wide. Notice
the depth is given first when quoting the two measurements: a book 250 ×
176 millimetres is deeper than it is wide, and a book 176 × 250 millimetres is wid
than it is deep.

International paper sizes

Commonwealth Government publications, stationery and forms should
generally be printed in sizes recommended by the International Organization
for Standardization (ISO). ISO sizes are described in *Australian Standard
AS 1612:1999*. ISO sizes are stated as 'trimmed' sizes (the size of the finished wor
after trimming).

In each of the three series of ISO sizes—A, B and C—the shape of the basic size and of all normal subdivisions is the same. The sides are always in the proportion 1:√2 (that is, approximately 1:1.414).

In the A series, the basic size is A0 (1189 × 841 millimetres), which occupies an area of 1 square metre. All A sizes derive from this standard and are described by the letter A followed by a number. For example:

- A1 is half of A0
- A2 is half of A1
- A3 is half of A2
- A4 is half of A3.

For sizes larger than A0, the number precedes the letter—for example, 1A is twice the size of A0. (Note also that these sizes are entirely distinct from the A1, A2 and A3 grades for art paper, where the 'A' grading refers to coating quality.)

The B series is based on the size B0 (1414 × 1000 millimetres) and the normal subdivisions provide sizes between the A subdivisions—for example, B5 is midway between A4 and A5. C sizes, based on C0 (917 × 1297 millimetres), fall between the A and B sizes.

The regular subdivisions of A, B and C sizes are shown in Table 25.1.

ISO proportions

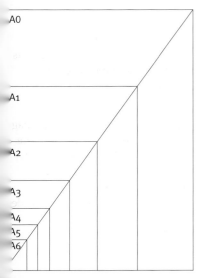

The proportions of the sides are constant in all regular sizes.

Regular subdivisions of ISO sheet size

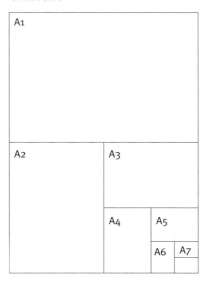

Relationship between A, B and C sizes

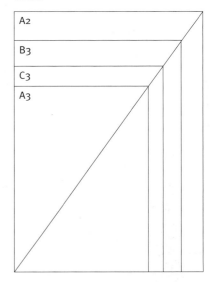

Irregular subdivisions of an A0 sheet

An A0 sheet can be divided economically in various ways to produce irregular sizes which, although not in the proportion 1:√2, are related to the regular subdivisions. An A0 sheet could be divided to produce the sizes ⅓ A4, ⅔ A4 and A4 + ⅓.

A0

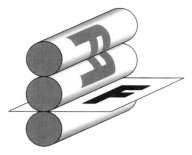

⅓A4	⅓A4	⅔A4	A4+⅓
⅓A4	A4		
⅓A4		⅔A4	
⅓A4			

Offset

Printing from a flat surface

Table 25.1 **ISO trimmed sheet sizes for paper**

A series		B series		C series	
Size	Measurement (mm)	Size	Measurement (mm)	Size	Measurement (mm)
A0	1189 x 841	B0	1414 x 1000	C0	1297 x 917
A1	841 x 594	B1	1000 x 707	C1	917 x 648
A2	594 x 420	B2	707 x 500	C2	648 x 458
A3	420 x 297	B3	500 x 353	C3	458 x 324
A4	297 x 210	B4	353 x 250	C4	324 x 229
A5	210 x 148	B5	250 x 176	C5	229 x 162
A6	148 x 105	B6	176 x 125	C6	162 x 114
A7	105 x 74	B7	125 x 88	C7	114 x 81
A8	74 x 52	B8	88 x 62	C8	81 x 57

Note: For the permissible allowances for trim see *Australian print standards*.

TRADITIONAL PRINTING

Technological developments in traditional printing enable multiple reproductions to be made from a single source at a consistent quality and at ever more amazing speeds. For large print runs for a mass market, traditional printing provides matchless service, offering diverse processes—many of which can be done simultaneously.

Understanding some of the strengths and drawbacks of each process within the two most common types of traditional printing—offset lithography and letterpress—enables appropriate production decisions to be made that maximise the quality, usability and economic viability of a project.

Offset lithography

Offset lithography is a planographic printing process where the image lies on the printing surface, or the 'plane'. Essentially, the image is printed from the flat surface of a lithographic plate (which is wrapped around a cylinder) onto a second rubber-blanketed cylinder, which then offsets the image onto paper carried round a third cylinder, called the 'impression' cylinder.

The printing image on the plate is ink-receptive, and the non-image areas are water-receptive. Plates are produced photographically from images on either positive or negative film that is exposed onto the plate. However, there are also systems in which the image is transferred directly to the plate (called 'CTP' or 'computer-to-plate') from a digital artwork file.

The printing plate is kept damp by the application of water (with added chemical to form 'fountain solution') so that, when it is inked, the grease-based ink adheres to the printing image and not to the damp non-printing area.

Offset lithography has a number of advantages. For example, fine images can be printed on coarse paper, since they are printed from a rubber surface instead of

Alternative methods of copy preparation for printing

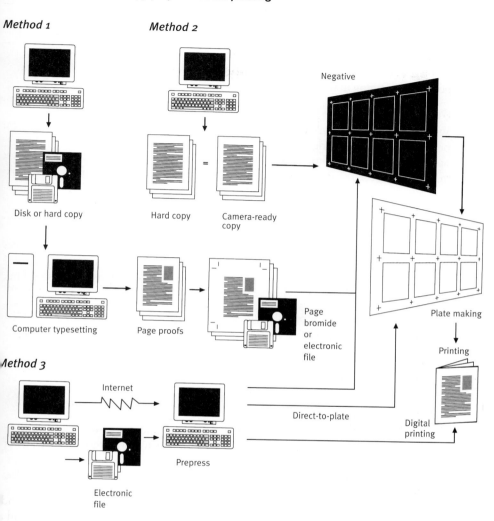

Method 1

Disk or hard copy

Computer typesetting

Page proofs

Page bromide or electronic file

Method 2

Hard copy

Camera-ready copy

Negative

Plate making

Printing

Method 3

Internet

Electronic file

Prepress

Direct-to-plate

Digital printing

irectly from the metal plate. Offset machines can operate at high speed,
roducing 15 000 impressions or more an hour.

Multicolour offset printing

ach colour 'deck' on an offset machine has the three basic cylinders: the plate,
e blanket and the impression cylinders. Multiple decks are used for carrying four-
rocess colours, plus HiFi inks, corporate or particular Pantone colours (perhaps
uorescent or metallic), and even varnishes 'in-line', so that all colour and some
nishes are deposited on the paper in one pass through the machine.

dvanced computerised colour control can pre-program ink settings by evaluating
e ink dispersion for individual plates before the printing starts. This process
ables the correct colour balance to be achieved while the press is running.

➤ See Chapter 21 for a discussion of colour systems.

Different types of offset processes

Sheet-fed offset

As the name implies, sheet-fed printing is where sheets of paper are gripped and pulled through the press. Sheet-fed machines can cater for anything from small jobbing work (such as business cards) up to large-volume multicolour bookwork, posters, packaging and promotional printing.

Web-fed offset

Web-fed offset machines are fed paper from a reel. The paper is pulled through the press continuously during the printing processes, which are followed by finishing operations (such as folding and guillotining) at the end of the machine pass. These machines are used to produce magazines, newspapers, catalogues, directories, books and other good-quality printing in-line. Owing to their high operating cost and faster running speed, they are generally used for long-run work.

Waterless printing

Waterless offset (or 'dry lithography') achieves better quality than the normal 'wet' offset without the use of dampeners. In order to use this process, conventional offset machines need to be converted to accommodate the different plates and ink required.

The plates are etched out of a silicone coating on an aluminium plate, so the ink sits on the aluminium. This is then transferred to the blanket and impression cylinders, as with normal offset lithography. The etching of the silicone enables the process to print a finer dot and therefore gives a greater level of detail to an image.

Reel of paper
Used in web offset printing

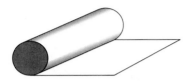

Letterpress

Letterpress, the oldest of the printing processes, is a relief printing process now mostly used for various embellishment tasks. The image is transferred by means of a raised ('relief') printing surface that is inked and brought into contact with the paper under pressure. The printing plate is usually made from photopolymer, which is exposed photographically and then etched to provide the relief printing surface.

The simplest letterpress machine is the sheet-fed platen, in which the entire printing area is brought into contact with the paper at the same time. This kind of machine is used for small jobbing work, such as the printing of letterheads, invitation cards and handbills. In other letterpress machines, the type is still placed on a flat surface, but the paper is fed round a curved impression cylinder that rotates against the printing surface.

Faster speeds than with either of these processes are achieved by rotary machines, in which the printing image is also on a curved plate; the impression cylinder and the printing cylinder both rotate so as to be in constant contact. The paper may be fed to the printing machine mechanically or manually and either as single sheets or from a reel.

Letterpress
Printing from a raised surface

DIGITAL PRINTING

The combination of computing and photocopying technology has brought about the development of digital printing, which has made short-run printing financially viable. The output can range from office copying to highest quality, four-colour output; from envelope labels to personalised books that are almost indistinguishable from a traditionally printed publication. A particular feature of digital printing is its ability to take a digital file with an appropriately prepared database and produce an individualised publication for a specific person.

Laser printers

Laser printers have emerged as an alternative means of reproducing images of comparable quality to those from traditional presses when used with laser imagesetters and computers for printing on quality paper.

Laser printers linked to image processors have been particularly useful in the production of proof copies. Such copies allow proof checking to be carried out before high-resolution output. But short-run printed matter and personalised, variable-data printing can also be produced by this method. Some equipment may be limited in the volume of output, and there may be restrictions on the range of paper sizes that can be used, but publications up to A4 in size are easily accommodated.

The quality of the image is governed by the ability of the equipment to produce raster dots (or pixels) of high density. Currently, the dot resolution from most office laser printers is either 300 or 600 raster dots per inch (dpi), but the resolution of commercial digital colour-printing units can be up to 2400 dpi or greater.

Most sheet-fed office laser printers are of the hot-fusion type, where the image is produced by heat and pressure, and print only in black. As they are directed digitally from desktop computers, the faster and more sophisticated machines are particularly useful for producing up-to-date listings in small quantities (such as inventories, price lists, and so forth) where the database is continually updated.

There are also reel-fed, cold-fusion machines, which are much slower but have the advantage of being able to print on a wider range of materials and in multiple colours. These are particularly useful for printing promotional and business-form products.

Ink-jet printers

Ink-jet printing is used to produce variable images on business-form presses and on booklet bindery lines to personalise publications. In this process, a computer controls a battery of ink-jet guns attached to a printing press or a binding machine. Each gun fires tiny dots of ink at very high speed, creating a matrixed image.

Ink-jet colour copiers use the same principle of projecting minute ink droplets but have a number of batteries for each colour. They were used in the graphic arts industry to supply colour proofs of artwork created on computer for initial

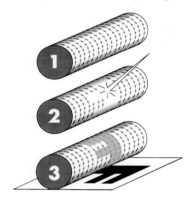

Laser
Laser optics and electronic printing

proofing, but are now used for short-run colour printing and personalised, varia▊
data printing.

On-demand printing

A digital document uploaded to a web site is available to anyone connected to
site via the Internet or intranet to print out as required. This approach suits ma▊
types of information material and documents that are likely to be regularly
updated. It enables users to determine if they need a hard copy and, if so, to pri▊
it out on their own printers. By using a file format such as a PDF, the formatted
layout can be maintained.

➤ See pp. 447–8 for a discussion of
PDF files and the enabling software,
Adobe Acrobat.

Just-in-time printing

In a similar manner to on-demand printing, digital files for just-in-time printin▊
are stored, but in this case they are usually held at outlets such as information
counters, offices, shops or commercial print shops. When a customer requests t▊
content, it is printed and bound on digital printing equipment at the outlet. Jus▊
in-time printing resolves warehousing and updating problems, distribution and
inventory control. It is how legislation—which is frequently updated—is produ▊
for sale, for example.

If a customer requests particular sets of information (say, a combination of chap▊
extracted from different books), it may all be bound into the one document. W▊
the right production software, it is also possible to create indexes and contents
listings for these hybrid publications.

➤ See Chapter 22 for a discussion of
copyright.

Personalisation

Personalisation, or 'variable-data printing', uses a database to tailor a new
document for each audience member. Information about individuals is gathered
and stored on the database and appropriately coded to allow elements to be fed
into a publication file prior to printing. In this way, text and even images can b▊
customised.

The database is gradually built up based on demographics and the responses fro▊
readers to questionnaires and email forms. Subjects that the 'audience of one' i▊
interested in may also be identified and coded. Readers' personal preferences ar▊
choices therefore determine the product they receive.

Although a variable-data printing operation is expensive to establish, once
operational it can be a persuasive form of communication. This technology is
enabled by high-quality digital printing without plates, allowing the digital
information to be changed each time it is sent to the front-end processor of the
digital press.

EMBELLISHMENT

The term *embellishment* describes a variety of finishing processes that can enhar▊
a publication. Because they were prohibitively expensive in the past, these
processes have come to be associated with prestige publications. However, they

ow a realistic financial option when additional protective coating, particular apes or tear-offs, or a generally more exclusive form of presentation is being ught.

ngraving and diestamping

graving from copper or steel dies or plates and diestamping are 'intaglio' inting processes, where the image lies beneath the surface of the plate (in a milar way to an etched image). The level of detail achieved and the slightly dented surface that is created are used to produce high-quality corporate entities, cover designs and exclusive packaging.

oil stamping

oil stamping (or 'foil blocking')—an embellishing operation that uses the inciples of relief printing—involves applying pigmented foil to paper or other aterial under heat and pressure by means of a specially etched die. It is essential make certain that there is complete compatibility between the paper or other nding material and the foil.

oils are made from a thin metallic, plastic or synthetic layer on a polymer carrier eet with a bonding layer. When the heat of the die is transmitted to the paper pressing, the glue melts and transfers the foil to the page.

oils can have glossy, dull or matt finishes, which may be metallic or flat colours. ome foils are opaque, some are translucent or transparent, and some have been epared with hologrammed patterns.

mbossing and debossing

nbossing is a stamping or blocking process that is designed to lift the paper over particular area to create an image. 'Debossing' stamps a depressed image into the per.

he blocks can be raised to one or more levels (with various edge treatments such bevels), or they may be fully sculpted. In most cases, female and male dies are eated, so the paper is stamped from the front and back simultaneously. The dies e heated and stretch the fibres of the paper. Softer papers with cotton or rag ntent are recommended for this process, because their fibres are more flexible d less likely to tear under the pressure of the stamping.

he page that is embossed might be previously printed or even foil stamped. 'Blind nbossing' (or 'blind blocking') is stamping without foil. Since it relies for its fectiveness on the shadows created by the impression, a paper or card with itable properties must be chosen.

There no foil is involved, embossing is an environmentally friendly process to use.

iecutting

or pop-ups and odd-shaped formats (such as circles), a letterpress forme is epared with blades in place that match the cutting pattern supplied as artwork. his will then be stamped at the end of a print-run by a modified letterpress

Intaglio
Printing from an etched surface

➤ See p. 480 for a description of relief printing.

machine, so that the blades cut through the paper. Any further assembly of the diecut paper or board is done by hand.

Diecutting is used for folders, greeting cards, stickers and envelopes—for any paper product that has an irregular shape.

Because this process does nothing but cut and fold the paper, diecutting (including perforation and scoring) is another environmentally friendly embellishment process. The blades and formes can, in many cases, be reused.

Perforation

Perforations in paper products enable specific areas to be separated or torn off easily. They can also be used to assist in binding operations.

Perforations can be stamped like diecuts, using blades that have regular notches in them. The paper remains uncut above each notch.

There are some perforation machines for small jobbing work that can be added to modified letterpress machines. However, they perforate in a straight line only.

Scoring

To create scored lines in paper or board, the knife edges of a die are replaced with dulled-edge metal rules. A scored line assists the folding of the material for binding operations.

Laminating

Lamination is a technique in which clear plastic film is applied to a printed sheet. It can be applied in liquid or sheet form, and gloss, satin and matt finishes are available. Laminates are used to give protection to a product, and gloss laminates often intensify and enhance the colours and the image beneath.

Artwork can be created for 'printing' liquid laminate to particular areas of the paper or board to match the design.

Lamination prevents the paper from being recycled because of the difficulty of removing the plastic from the fibres.

Varnishing

Varnish is applied like ink and is often added during the print run. The solvent-based coating can either be printed over the entire sheet area or be placed in particular areas (using a separate plate made from artwork).

Varnishes are available in matt, satin, semigloss or gloss. Two types of varnish might be applied, for example, to contrast matt and gloss finishes. Sometimes a varnish will be tinted with a small amount of ink to make the artwork created for the varnish easier to see and to provide tonal variation to the page.

BINDING

Binding comprises the series of operations by which printed sections or sheets are fastened together.

The major binding styles are paper binding (for 'paperback' or 'softcover' publications) and case binding (for 'hardcover' or 'hardback' publications). Loose-leaf binding is also regularly used because it suits publications that must open out flat.

The choice of binding depends on the use for which the book is intended, the type of binding equipment available and the cost.

Paper binding

A paperback book is one enclosed in a soft or flexible cover made either from a cover paper or a light board. The pages may be secured to the cover in one of several ways.

Saddle-stitching

In saddle-stitching, the pages are imposed and folded in such a manner as to allow each section of text to be inserted into the next. Staples (or 'wires') are then pushed through the 'saddle' from the cover to the centre of the book.

The thickness of the text block should be no more than 5–6 millimetres, depending on the folding characteristics of the paper chosen; the grain direction should ideally run from top to bottom, as with all books. If a text block is more than 6 millimetres thick, the trimming of the books can be adversely affected and there is likely to be an unsightly gape at the fold.

High-speed equipment enables the sections and cover to be gathered, inserted, stapled and three-way trimmed in one continuous operation.

Side-stitching

In side-stitching, the sections are gathered in sequence and staples are then inserted from the side. Side-stitched books have strength but do not lie flat when open.

Covers are usually creased about 5 millimetres from the spine to provide a hinge. They are then glued to the spine, and—to cover the staples—a short distance round the sides as well.

Perfect binding

High-speed in-line equipment is used for perfect binding. Folded sections of text are gathered into blocks, which are then automatically channelled into the binding machine. They are held tightly in clamps, spine down, and are carried across rotating cutting blades that remove the folds on the spine to expose the edges of the text paper. The book blocks, still clamped, move over rollers where hot-melt glue is applied to the spines. At the next station, the covers are applied to the wet glue. Guillotining then completes the process.

The type of paper used for both text and cover will affect the strength of the binding and its longevity.

A 'dummy' book: It is advisable to produce a dummy book as soon as the number of pages is known. It can be used not only to ensure that the final strength and appearance of the book are satisfactory (very thick books may need to be split into two volumes, for example) but also to help in the preparation of the artwork for the cover and dust jacket. The dummy can also be useful in assessing packaging requirements and distribution costs.

Side-stitching

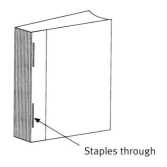

Staples through

**Different binding
methods**

Saddle-stitching

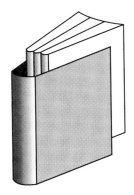

Section sewn

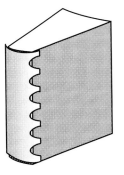

Comb binding

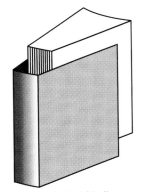

Perfect binding

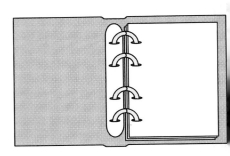

Ring binding

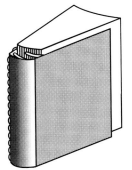

Half-Canadian binding

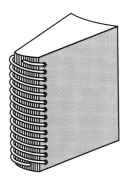

Spiral binding

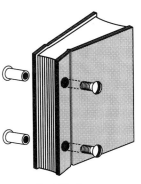

Post binding

Burst binding

In burst binding, the sections of text are pierced along the spine with slot perforations during the folding operation. The sections are then collated and bound by a method similar to that used in perfect binding. The only difference is that the spine of the book is not removed; instead, glue is rolled onto the spine and forced through the perforations so that the book is securely held together. The cover is then applied to the wet glue on the spine.

Section sewing

Section-sewn books are prepared and sewn in the same manner as in the casebound process, but the use of endpapers is optional. Endpapers are usually incorporated when a better quality finish or additional strength is required. Covers may be attached by one of the following methods: gluing to the spine only (no endpapers used); gluing to the spine and drawing-on the front and back covers to the endpapers; or gluing to the spine and pasting the front and back covers onto the first and last pages of text (self-endpapers). Three-way trimming then completes the process.

The covers are usually made of card of about 200 to 260 gsm.

Thread sealing

Thread sealing is a cost-effective alternative to section sewing. It is carried out during the folding process and involves each section being folded and sewn on the spine. The individual sections and their threads are then glued together and the cover drawn on. Although the sections are sewn within themselves, they are not sewn together as in the section-sewing process, and may therefore prove to be slightly less durable. However, thread sealing provides much greater strength than other glued bindings and shares with section sewing the advantage of producing publications that will lie flat when opened.

Loose-leaf binding

In loose-leaf binding, once the text of a book has been gathered, it is trimmed on all edges and the separate leaves are then bound. Individual leaves in loose-leaf publications are more prone to wear and tear along the binding edge than leaves in fully bound publications.

Spiral (or wiro) binding

Spiral (wire or plastic) binding is the most usual and most automated method of loose-leaf binding, but it does not allow amendments (replacements of single leaves of text) to be made. However, spiral-bound books lie perfectly flat when open, which is a considerable advantage when they are used for reference purposes.

Another derivative of spiral binding is 'half-Canadian' binding. This method conceals the wire with a cover, which forms one piece with the spine that wraps around the spiral-bound sheets.

Burst binding

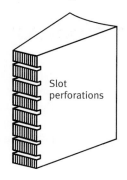

Slot perforations

➤ See 'About case binding',
pp. 488–9.

ABOUT
Case binding

Case binding can give a book the prestige implied by hardcovers and help it withstand heavy or prolonged use. There are a number of stages in case binding.

Folding

Sections (or signatures) of sixteen or thirty-two pages are the most commonly used. However, sections of eight, twenty-four or sixty-four pages are also sometimes used.

Endpapering

After folding, the endpapers are attached to the first and last sections by a narrow strip of glue along the spine. They may be printed or plain.

Gathering and collating

Sections are gathered together in sequence. Collating marks (called 'signature' or 'section' marks) are printed to predetermined positions on the spine of each section. These form a stepped pattern down the spine of the book that makes it possible to check quickly and accurately whether the sequence is correct.

Signature marks printed onto the spine fold

Correctly gathered

Incorrectly gathered

Transposed

Missed section

Case binding

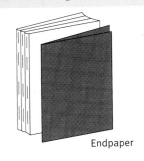

Endpaper

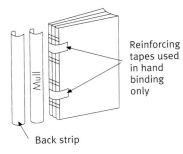

Mull

Reinforcing tapes used in hand binding only

Back strip

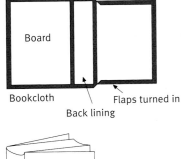

Board

Bookcloth

Back lining

Flaps turned in

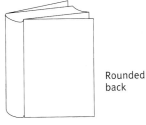

Rounded back

Sewing

The collated sections are sewn together with thread. Section sewing is generally considered to be superior to all other methods in terms of the durability and appearance of the book.

Nipping

The spine of the book can be 'nipped' (put under pressure) to remove air from the sections. This makes the book firmer, in readiness for gluing.

Book-back gluing

To hold sections firmly in place for trimming, a thin layer of glue is applied along the spine. The book is run, spine down, over glue rollers and then over heating elements that ensure adequate drying before trimming.

Trimming

Trimming approximately 3 millimetres of waste paper from the head, foredge and tail of the book separates the individual leaves and gives the book clean, smooth edges. Three-way guillotines are normally used, as they are the most accurate and fast.

In terms of trim dimensions, the case of a bound book should overlap 3 millimetres at the head, tail and foredge. Thus the trimmed page size of a B5 book is 250 x 176 millimetres, the size of the case boards is 256 x 179 millimetres, and the overall size (including the rounded back) is approximately 256 x 185 millimetres. The width will vary according to the extent of the rounding.

Rounding and backing

The book is held firmly in a machine that rounds the back over curved formers. Then, with backing irons, it flares it to form the joint around which

e pages will bend when the book is
pened. The rounded spine minimises
rain on the binding.

square back is generally used with
ooks up to 15 millimetres thick. It is
ot recommended beyond that, as it
aces the binding under strain and
equent use may cause the spine to
eak.

ning

provide adequate reinforcement,
ue is applied to the spine, and a strip
mull (open-mesh material) extending
out 25 millimetres round each side
the book is laid over it. A layer of
ue is then applied to the mull and a
rip of heavy paper is placed over the
tire spine area. The mull has the vital
nction of providing the hinge
tween text and case.

eadbands and tailbands

corative headbands and tailbands
e attached to the heavy paper strip
the spine during lining. They are
ade from a woven fabric and come in
arge range of colours and patterns.

sing-in

e casing-in machine rolls glue onto
e protruding pieces of mull and onto
th the front and back endpapers. The
ok is then guided into its pre-made
se.

ilding-in

e building-in machine applies
essure to the sides of the cover to
sure a firm bond between case and
dpapers. Simultaneously, the joints
tween the sides and the spine are
essed firmly into shape.

Adhesive binding

This method of binding perfect-bound
cased books is often used in Australia.
The books are glued with either cold
glues or a range of hot-melts and are
capable of being rounded and square-
backed.

Case making

Case-making machines position the
front and back boards of the cases
(varying in thickness from about 1800
to 3500 micrometres) in a controlled
position that allows the binding
material to be turned in 16 millimetres
on all sides. A heavy strip of paper is
also fed and glued to the spine area
between the front and back boards.
The case may be preprinted or foil-
blocked.

Quarter binding

Quarter binding is a method of case
binding in which one type of material is
used for the front and back covers and
another for the spine of a book. For
example, cloth or leather may be used
for the spine, and paper for the covers.

Jacketing

The application of the dust jacket can
be done by hand or machine. Accurate
positioning is important, as the jacket
not only provides protection for the
book but is also a major medium for
display. It is usually best to laminate a
dust jacket to give it durability. On
some prestigious books, the jackets
are folded back on the tops and
bottoms. This is called a 'French fold'.

Slipcases

A slipcase is a box that is created as a
separate bound cover that slips snugly
over a casebound book. The spine is
visible, but the covers and pages of the
book are protected on all other sides
by the slipcase. A slipcase could be
created to protect a book, to indicate
its prestige or to hold a set of books.

A slipcase

Case-binding materials

Traditionally, woven bookcloth has
been the most popular material used
for case binding, but heavyweight
embossed papers, nitrocellulose-
coated papers and PVC-coated papers
have also been used. Leather is used
for some prestigious books, but is very
expensive. Since the number of locally
produced fabrics is extremely limited,
most materials have to be imported.
Consequently, early planning is
essential in order to ensure supply.

Comb binding

Comb (plastic) binding is similar to spiral binding except that a clip-in device resembling a comb is used instead of the plastic or wire spiral. This method's advantages and disadvantages are the same as those of the spiral method except that it is possible to replace pages. After reopening the comb, pages can be removed and inserted, and the comb closed again. However, if this is done often, can weaken the binding.

Ring binding

Ring binding is commonly used for price lists, catalogues and other works requirin frequent amendment. The rings can be readily snapped open to allow new or amended pages to be inserted. Ring-bound publications lie flat when open.

Post binding

Post binding allows the removal and replacement of leaves, but books bound in this way do not lie flat when open.

EVALUATING A PRINTED DOCUMENT

Based on *Australian print standards*, this list is provided as an aid for checking the quality of printing and binding.

Printing

- Is the printing clean, sharp and legible?
- Is the printed image square with the edge of the paper?
- Is there any density variation from page to page?
- Do the finished copies reflect all the specifications?
- Has the correct number of copies been received?

Inking

- Is there any smudging of the ink?
- Are there any ink spots or extraneous marks where there should not be?
- Is there any 'set-off' from copy to copy (where ink from one page dirties the adjacent sheet)?
- Is the ink colour correct, and is it consistent within and between copies?

Images

- In multicolour solid printing, is the colour registration as requested and are the colours clear and sharp?
- Have all the image specifications been followed?
- Do any of the images contain mottles, scratches, broken screens, holes, plugging, and so on?

Type

- Is there any broken type?
- Are any of the characters filling in with ink (for example, *e* and *o*)?
- Is there any doubling, ghosting or blurring?
- Is there any showthrough of text or images?

Paper

- Does the paper look and feel like the paper specified?
- Are there any variations of colour or quality within one finished copy or from one copy to another?
- Is there any dirt on the paper?
- Does the paper surface have ruptures, creases or tears?

Trimming and finishing

- Have all finished copies been trimmed to the required size?
- Are all edges clean and even?
- Has the printed material been folded properly and are the folds in the proper position?
- Is any drilling or hole punching complete and clean?

Binding

- If adhesive binding has been used, are the spine edges clear of excess glue?
- Are all pages securely fastened in each finished copy? (The best way to check this is to crack open a book and see if any pages come loose.)
- Are there any faults on the cover?

Packing and delivery

- Are the packages crushed or scuffed?
- Do they have broken seals or exterior damage?

(Either of these may indicate interior damage to the contents.)

Chapter **26**

Monitoring, testing and evaluating

MONITORING DURING THE PROJECT	**493**
Why monitoring is important	493
Monitor against what?	494
How to monitor	494
Managing changes	494
QUALITY ASSURANCE AND TESTING	**494**
What can quality assurance achieve?	494
Final checking	495
Testing electronic publications	495
Approval for publication	495
POST-RELEASE EVALUATION	**496**
Defining success	496
Project records	496
Seeking feedback	497
Weighting the evaluation criteria	498
Results of the evaluation	499
CLOSING THE LOOP: THE COMMUNICATION STRATEGY	**500**
Extending the content	500
Making the publication more accessible	500
CONCLUSION	**500**

The progress of any publishing project must be checked regularly against the requirements established at the outset, in the publication plan. Monitoring points should be included in the schedule in order to verify that the work is proceeding in line with the planned budget and timetable and at the desired level of quality. As part of the final production phase, the document's suitability for release should be confirmed through comprehensive inspection or testing.

> Chapter 1 discusses the content of a publication plan and its provisions for monitoring progress.

After publication, an overall evaluation—both of the publication itself and of its development process—is important. The aim should be to discover how well the publication is meeting the objectives of its creators and sponsors and the expectations of its readership. This evaluation might suggest a need to revise the publication or to develop related projects. Similarly, a review of the publication process will probably offer insights that will help guide the planning and management of future work.

The checking processes described in this chapter are relevant to any publication, large or small, electronic or print, complex or simple. While their extent—and the level of formality with which they are applied—can vary, the chances of success for any publishing project will increase if the processes are applied systematically.

MONITORING DURING THE PROJECT

Why monitoring is important

As a project progresses, it is easy for the work to drift away from the original intent. Some tasks might become more complicated than envisaged and take longer to complete. New ideas might emerge, and promising avenues beckon. The objectives, scope or expected audience might change, necessitating adjustment of the publication plan.

Monitoring provides a regular reminder of the project's targets and concentrates the work effort on meeting them. Its role is not to suppress change or new ideas but to allow balanced judgments to be made about how to handle them. Effective monitoring, and the project management actions that flow from it, focus on reducing unnecessary work, applying resources to greatest effect, and reacting promptly and practically to any changes that are called for.

Monitor against what?

The project's publication plan, which is the guide for all contributors to the project, serves as the primary reference during monitoring. It generally comprises:

- a communications strategy that defines the objectives of the publication and it intended audience
- writing and editing guidelines that define the content and style
- design specifications for the chosen delivery mode or modes
- a management plan that identifies the resources to be used and sets targets for time, quality and cost. It is this management plan, updated to reflect any agree changes, that provides the detailed basis for monitoring throughout the project

➤ For the recommended scope of a management plan, see pp. 13–14.

How to monitor

Monitoring involves systematic, disciplined comparison of actual achievement against specified targets. The management plan should clearly detail monitoring points (or 'milestones') at which progress is checked against the schedule and budget. Quality checks are also done; they generally involve considered judgment as well as reference to the writing and editing guidelines and the design specifications.

The monitoring points in the work program can be set at regular intervals—for example, at weekly or monthly project team meetings—or be timed to coincide with the completion of specific phases or the production of interim drafts. Regula intervals are usually preferable, since this allows for the earliest possible detection of any deviations from targets. The results of monitoring are usually presented in the form of progress reports, which should be kept in the project records.

Team meetings, particularly for larger publication projects, are a useful forum in which any problems or difficulties can be aired and resolved in a collaborative wa If a comparison with the schedule shows that time has been lost in one task, ways can be canvassed of making it up during subsequent work, or arrangements can be made for performing more tasks in parallel. If it becomes clear that one or more targets are in jeopardy, difficult decisions may be called for and a compromise struck between time, cost and quality.

Managing changes

Most projects encounter the need for change, whether it is introduced from outside or initiated within the team. Part of the monitoring effort should be directed at assessing, realistically and promptly, the impact of proposed changes or the schedule, budget and quality targets. All requested changes should be recorde and either formally accepted as variations or rejected.

Variations: The procedures for dealing with variations during a project should be established as part of the initial planning (see pp. 13–14).

QUALITY ASSURANCE AND TESTING

What can quality assurance achieve?

Quality assurance involves a systematic series of actions designed to check that a product is being developed according to the standards of quality defined at the utset. A specialised form of monitoring, it can be used for any project, service facility.

or a large publication project with many contributors, a formal quality assurance stem may help to bring a high level of consistency and increased communication etween all involved. Quality assurance principles can also be applied to smaller rojects, where the process might be as simple as creating and adhering to a set of necks and approvals at various stages before a document is released.

ut use of a quality assurance system does not, in itself, guarantee a high-quality iblication. These formal systems rely on detailed specification of processes, and eriodic inspections to see that these processes are being followed. Although this a valuable practice, it can generate a false sense of security by suggesting that iality can be 'inspected in' after the event. Its success also depends on the ilidity of the processes specified for the particular publication.

uality products result from a quality culture that is embedded in the publishing am from the outset. If all members of the team hold and apply high standards, ien regular quality checks—whether through a formal quality assurance system or irough a series of more subjective overviews—will bring consistency and further improvement to what is already a high-quality base.

➤ Standards are available for reference if formal quality assurance systems are to be used (see p. 502).

inal checking

o matter what form of quality checking is used, it is vital that the final draft of a ocument be subjected to careful scrutiny before it is released, to ensure that it eets all the planned requirements. Because members of the publication team will y now have become very familiar with the document, it is often a good idea to ave an external overview as well. Sufficient time must be allocated in the hedule to allow these final checks to be carried out properly; cutting corners at iis stage can threaten the success of the entire project.

What should be checked? The checklists throughout this manual provide reminders about things to check during a publication's development and final sign-off procedures.

esting electronic publications

lectronic publications should be tested throughout the production process, but a nal comprehensive testing program is essential at the last stage of production efore release. This period is often used as an 'embargo' period, when a publication ın be released to a restricted set of readers who keep the contents confidential ıtil general release is approved.

etting specific goals for testing is critical to determining when sufficient testing as been done. These goals can be incorporated in a test plan that outlines what is ɔ be tested, how often and when it will be tested, who will do the testing, and ɔw the results will be treated.

➤ Chapter 24 details the testing procedures for electronic publications.

pproval for publication

he ideal time to release a publication is after all faults and errors have been iminated. (For an electronic publication, for instance, this means when it works erfectly on all platforms, for all its users, all of the time.) In the real world this me never comes. The time to stop is usually determined by the number and significance of the errors found. Under an iterative quality review and testing program, the error rate will decline progressively to a point where checking can be justifiably ended.

As with most things, the more resources that are committed to the quality assurance and testing process, the more likely it is that the publication will be well received by its intended readership and reflect well on author and publisher. However, the best approach—which in the long run is almost always the most economical—is to 'build in' the quality from the outset rather than trying to 'inspect it in' later.

POST-RELEASE EVALUATION

Defining success

A publishing project should be evaluated after the publication has been in use for a time, in order to enable its overall success to be gauged. Informal assessments often lead to hasty, and not necessarily accurate, conclusions about the strengths and weaknesses of the product. To obtain the full benefits of evaluation, a more rigorous method is usually warranted. A professional approach is to base this evaluation on the effectiveness criteria established in the publication plan, modified to take account of any major changes that have occurred during the project.

➤ See p. 12 for a discussion of effectiveness criteria.

Essentially, the evaluation should aim to determine:
- whether the publication has achieved its defined purpose, from both the client and the users' perspectives
- the overall cost of the project—taking full life-cycle costs into account (see page 12)
- how efficiently the project was conducted and whether the schedule was met.

Project records

Project records are needed for monitoring progress, but they also provide a case history that is essential for evaluation and future planning. The project file or archive should therefore contain:
- the publication plan, in which the intent, scope, desired quality, budget and timetable are established
- records showing the decision path throughout the project, highlighting the changes occurring during project development and their effects on the costs, timing and quality of the production
- records of all variations sought and their acceptance or rejection
- progress reports
- a progressive tally detailing all costs incurred
- any feedback records, analysis and reports.

Successive versions of the draft publication should be kept during the project to show the extent of the changes, who made them and who authorised them. At the

...aluation stage, these can also be a reminder of the extent of work done by the ...blication team.

...eeking feedback

...ow feedback works

...esponses from readers are needed if an evaluation is to be valid and useful. The ...edback can be obtained in several ways. If representative readers are identifiable, ...may be possible to approach them directly for comments. Responses can also be ...ncouraged from a wider audience by including in the publication a request for ...omments (giving contact details) or by inserting a questionnaire or mail-back ...rds. Seminars and consultative meetings might also be relevant in some ...rcumstances.

...ost feedback techniques have some weaknesses that can skew the results. A ...tisfied audience is less likely to provide feedback, so more of the comments can ...e expected to be negative. Responses to interviews and surveys are based on ...eople's recall of their reactions to a publication, which can differ from the ...enefits or difficulties they actually experienced when reading or using it or from ...s ultimate value to them over time. However, short on-screen surveys can be ...uite successful if they ask simple questions that relate to readers' needs (such as ...Vhy are you visiting our site?') rather than seeking opinions.

...o generate the greatest number of representative responses, it is necessary to ask ...e right questions at the right time. If the audience needs time to consider the ...nplications of a publication, for example, it is best not to seek feedback ...mediately after the publication's release.

...ocus groups

...he use of focus groups is an informal technique used for seeking feedback. It ...nerally involves bringing together about six to nine people, usually with a ...oderator, to elicit responses and discuss concerns and ideas. It can be used to test ...esign and content ideas during a publishing project or to evaluate the finished ...oduct.

...ocus groups can, however, deliver misleading results. Members might give what ...ey think is the preferred or socially acceptable answer, for instance. There might ...so be personalities who dominate a group but whose views do not reflect those of ...e majority.

...'here a screen-based publication is being discussed, group members' recollection ...' their success in using it might not reflect their actual experience. They may also ...ot be the best predictors of what they really need in terms of on-screen ...nctionality. Direct observation of a focus group using a screen-based publication ...therefore recommended to supplement the results of focus group evaluations.

...arket research

...arket research may be useful for planning a project and can also help in ...aluating the project's success. When the research is carried out both before and ...ter the launch of an information publication, the results can be compared in order to gauge people's awareness and understanding of the information. If the research is designed to find out whether the information has led to a particular behavioural change, it might take some time for evidence of the impact to become apparent, and the research should be timed to take this into account.

Weighting the evaluation criteria

A necessary tool
Feedback can provide useful indications of whether a project has met or exceeded readers' expectations, while a review against the effectiveness criteria can give an overview from the publishing side. The importance of each assessment criterion will, however, vary from project to project. For some documents (such as those to be tabled in parliament) time is of the essence, and failure to meet the time deadline will be regarded as overall failure, no matter how high the quality of the document might be. In other contexts, some time or cost overrun might be acceptable, particularly if the quality of the product is enhanced as a result. A systematic evaluation technique that reflects the priorities in each case is essential.

To achieve this, the criteria can be weighted to provide an overall picture of how well the project has succeeded. In determining the weightings to use, it is generally necessary to consult a number of people with different interests in the publication (from the client through to representatives from the primary and secondary audiences), as well as to review the records of the planning stage when the objectives for the project were being decided.

An example of weighted assessment
Table 26.1 provides a hypothetical example of a weighted assessment. The subject of this example is a government agency's annual report, produced in both printed and screen-based formats.

The publication is necessarily aimed at several audiences. The primary audience is the parliament, to which the agency is obliged to report annually, at a prescribed time and in a defined format. Other readerships are the agency's customers or clients, its management and other staff, and the general public (which could include researchers, for example). Each audience group is given a different weighting factor to reflect its relative importance in terms of the project's objectives.

The next step is to develop the criteria that will indicate how well each group was served by the publication. In the example, the criteria are as follows:

- *Scope and content:* Did the report meet all of the statutory reporting requirements? Were the various readership groups able to obtain the information they needed?
- *Presentation:* Was the report easy to read and visually appealing? Was it structured to highlight important material? Were readers able to find particular information quickly? Did readers encounter any navigability problems?
- *Cost:* Was the project completed within budget?
- *Time:* Did the report meet the tabling schedule for parliament? Was it available to the other audiences in a timely fashion?

Accessibility: Did the report reach those for whom it was primarily intended? Were the other interested parties able to locate it easily?

Table 26.1 Using weighted criteria to judge an annual report: a hypothetical example

Aspect of publication	Marks per item (max.)	Audience				Final score
		Parliament	Customers and clients	Staff	Public	
Scope and content	20	17	5	12	5	—
Presentation	10	7	5	5	5	—
Cost	5	3	4	3	3	—
Time	10	8	4	9	3	—
Accessibility	5	3	4	4	3	—
Subtotal	50	38	22	33	19	—
Weighting factor	—	0.60	0.20	0.15	0.05	—
Weighted maximum	—	30	10	7.5	2.5	50
Actual score	—	**23**	**4**	**5**	**1**	**33**

— Not applicable.

Each separate audience is then assessed against the criteria. Obviously, some aspects that are very important to one group will be less important to another, and the requirements of the primary audience (in this case, members of parliament) can be expected to rank most highly.

In this way it is possible to compare complex objectives and describe total performance in a way that is readily understood—for example, by a numeric total or a percentage.

Results of the evaluation

The results of the evaluation can be used in various ways:

They will indicate whether any further work is required to meet the project's objectives.

For the production team members, the results will provide feedback about their work that can help them in planning future projects.

They will offer insights that the client organisation might find useful for future projects. For instance, has the project produced any unexpected advantages that could be followed up? What about disadvantages or problems: were they expected and planned for, or have they come as a surprise? On the basis of this experience, could the project definition and supervision procedures currently in use be improved?

Project evaluation thus becomes a learning experience and a planning event for future similar tasks. Observations should be documented (which can be as simple as creating a checklist) in order to provide a useful record for future reference.

Weighting techniques: To assess performance against each criterion, a simple numeric scoring technique can be established, as in Table 26.1. Alternatively, a star rating could be used—one star to represent a low level of performance against a criterion and five stars to represent the highest level.

CLOSING THE LOOP: THE COMMUNICATION STRATEGY

The process of developing a publication began with the communication strategy (see pages 5–12). Now that the publication has been launched and evaluated, it is time to reassess that strategy.

A reassessment might result in one of at least three possible conclusions:
- The publication has met its intended purpose satisfactorily and no further action is needed.
- The publication has reached its intended readers but has not met all their needs. A related possibility is that the publication has met readers' needs at the time of release but is expected to become outdated quickly.
- The publication contains the desired content but has not reached all of the intended audience.

In the case of the last two conclusions, further work may be needed to extend the content or to make the publication more accessible.

Extending the content

If a publication has not satisfied all the needs of its users, consideration should be given to providing additional or more up-to-date information. For a screen-based publication, this difficulty might be resolved by regular revision, provision of links to other sites, and perhaps production of supplementary printed material. In the case of a print-based publication, additional or revised information could be distributed through interim revisions, a new edition or a web site.

Consideration could also be given to producing supplementary newsletters, brochures or journals. If the information needs continual updating and if regular data collection makes this feasible, uploading to the web or information kiosks could be an option, as could providing material for printing on demand.

Making the publication more accessible

If a publication has not been effective in reaching its target audience, its marketing and distribution should be reconsidered. Pricing policies and sales locations might need to be reviewed. Development of an alternative print or electronic product might improve accessibility. Some markets or audiences might need the same message but with examples relevant to their areas. (This could be an opportunity for offprints, where particular chapters or sections of a book are reprinted and bound separately for special distribution.) Advertising might also be necessary to increase awareness of the document.

CONCLUSION

Producing a successful publication is a complex exercise that calls for a mix of skills: project management, writing, editing, design and technical production. This manual tracks the life cycle of a publication project, from its conception (or 'gleam in the eye') to evaluation of the finished publication and planning for the next one.

Quality publications reflect and promote the values of their initiators. This manual provides publishing guidance, but only a publication's sponsors can provide the will, determination and enthusiasm—and the corresponding budget and timetable—that are needed to generate effective and appealing publications.

By producing easy-to-use, high-quality publications, organisations display their own corporate standards of accuracy, consistency and reliability, and their desire to communicate effectively with their many different audiences.

PART 5 Further reading and resources

FURTHER READING

Adams, JR 1977, *Media planning*, 2nd edn, Business Books, London.

Adler, E 1991, *Print that works: the first step-by-step guide that integrates writing, design, and marketing*, Bull Publishing, Palo Alto, California.

Australian print standards 1995, AGPS Press, Canberra.

Campbell, A 1993, *The new designer's handbook*, Little, Brown & Co, London.

Dumas, JS & Redish, JC 1999, *A practical guide to usability testing*, Intellect, Portland, Oregon.

Goldberg, R 1996, *Multimedia producer's bible*, IDG Books Worldwide, Foster City, California.

Greenwald, M & Luttropp, J 1997, *Graphic communications: design through production*, Delmar Publishers, New York.

Krug, S 2000, *Don't make me think: a commonsense approach to web usability*, Macmillan, Indianapolis.

Niederst, J 1999, *Web design in a nutshell*, O'Reilly, Sebastopol, California.

Nielsen, J 2000, *Designing web usability: the practice of simplicity*, New Riders, Indianapolis.

Pipes, A 1997, *Production for graphic designers*, 2nd edn, Laurence King, London.

The printer's enemies n.d., Australian Paper, Melbourne.

Sidles, CJ 1998, *Great production by design: the technical know-how you need to let your design imagination soar*, North Light Books, Cincinnati, Ohio.

Standards Australia International Ltd 1999, *Paper sizes (AS 1612:1999)*, Standards Australia, Sydney.

Standards Australia International Ltd 2000, *Quality management systems: fundamentals and vocabulary (AS/NZS ISO 9000:2000)*, Standards Australia, Sydney.

Standards Australia International Ltd 2000, *Quality management systems: requirements (AS/NZS ISO 9001:2000)*, Standards Australia, Sydney.

WEB SITES

Adobe Systems Incorporated <http://access.adobe.com> (for assistance in making PDFs accessible to people with visual impairments).

Australian Government Information Management Office 2000, *Guidelines for Commonwealth information published in electronic formats*, <http://www.agimo.gov.au>.

——2003, *Guide to minimum web site standards*, rev. edn, <http://www.agimo.gov.au>.

World Wide Web Consortium 2000, *Authoring tool accessibility guidelines, 1.0*, World Wide Web Consortium <http://www.w3.org>.

——2000, *Web content accessibility guidelines, 1.0*, W3C recommendation, World Wide Web Consortium, <http://www.w3.org>.

Appendixes

A Titles, honours and forms of address 504

B Metric conversion table 519

C Standard proofreading marks and how to use them 521

Appendixes

Appendix A — Titles, honours and forms of address

This appendix offers guidance on general practices governing the presentation of the titles, honours and forms of address in common use in Australia. More detailed advice is provided in specialist references.[1]

TITLES AND HONOURS

A title preceding a person's name may be a conventional title (such as Mr or Ms), an honorific title (for example, *Dame* or *Sir*), or a title derived from rank, qualification or status (for example, *Lieutenant Commander*, *Doctor* or *The Honourable*). Honorifics and initialisms indicating a rank, qualification or status that are placed after a person's name are known as postnominals. Examples are *AM* (Member of the Order of Australia) and *FRACP* (Fellow of the Royal Australasian College of Physicians). Like other initialisms (see Chapter 10), postnominals are shown without full stops; commas are used for separating two or more sets of postnominals.

Conventional titles

In English, the conventional titles are Mr, Ms, Mrs and Miss. In the case of the last three, usage has been changing in Australia, and many people now use Ms for all adult females, the notion being that, like Mr, Ms does not disclose marital status. Disagreement about this usage does, however, persist. The best approach is to try to ascertain the preference of the person being addressed. If this is not possible, it is safest to use Ms.

Many other cultures have their own system of titles and, although the use of conventional English titles might be acceptable, it is polite to ask the person in question what they prefer and make an effort to comply.

Australian honours and awards, and their order of precedence

The British honours and awards system was used in Australia until 1975, since when a distinctively Australian system has been progressively introduced. The many Australians who have received British honours or awards are nevertheless entitled to continue to use their titles and postnominals and to wear the relevant decoration on specific occasions. A number of non-Australian awards and titles may also be conferred by the Sovereign on Australian citizens, either at the Sovereign's discretion or upon the recommendation of the Governor-General.

---

1 The following reference works are recommended: Joel, A 1988, *Australian protocol and procedures*, 2nd edn, Angus & Robertson, Sydney; *Debrett's handbook of Australia* 1991, Debrett's Peerage (Australasia) & Collins, Sydney; Hyslop R 1992 *Dear you: a guide to forms of address*, AGPS Press, Canberra; Department of Social Security 1987, *Naming systems of ethnic groups*, Migrant Services Section, Department of Social Security, Canberra; and the most recent edition of *Who's who in Australia*, Information Australia Group, Melbourne.

504

The order of precedence for Australian honours and awards as at 30 June 2000 is shown in Table A.1. This order is amended from time to time, with amendments being published in the *Commonwealth of Australia special gazette* series. Different categories of honours and awards are distinguished in the table as follows:

Uniquely Australian honours and awards (that is, those coming within the Australian System of Honours and Awards) are shown in italicised bold type.

Other current honours and awards are shown in coloured type.

Awards that were relevant in Australia from 1901 to 1991 but are no longer conferred by the Sovereign on Australian citizens are shown in roman type.

Foreign awards that are not conferred in Australia but the wearing of which is approved by the Governor-General are also shown in roman type.

Table A.1 **Order of precedence for honours and awards in Australia**

Title of honour or award	Postnominal initials
Victoria Cross for Australia	*VC*
George Cross	GC
Cross of Valour	*CV*
Knight/Lady of the Garter	KG/LG
Knight/Lady of the Thistle	KT/LT
Knight/Dame Grand Cross of the Order of the Bath	GCB
Order of Merit	OM
Knight/Dame of the Order of Australia	*AK/AD*
Knight/Dame Grand Cross of the Order of St Michael and St George	GCMG
Knight/Dame Grand Cross of the Royal Victorian Order	GCVO
Knight/Dame Grand Cross of the Order of the British Empire	GBE
Companion of the Order of Australia	*AC*
Companion of Honour	CH
Knight/Dame Commander of the Order of the Bath	KCB/DCB
Knight/Dame Commander of the Order of St Michael and St George	KCMG/DCMG
Knight/Dame Commander of the Royal Victorian Order	KCVO/DCVO
Knight/Dame Commander of the Order of the British Empire	KBE/DBE
Knight Bachelor	1
Officer of the Order of Australia	*AO*
Companion of the Order of the Bath	CB
Companion of the Order of St Michael and St George	CMG
Commander of the Royal Victorian Order	CVO
Commander of the Order of the British Empire	CBE
Star of Gallantry	*SG*
Star of Courage	*SC*

(continued)

Table A.1 continued

Title of honour or award	Postnominal initials
Companion of the Distinguished Service Order	DSO
Distinguished Service Cross	*DSC*
Member of the Order of Australia	*AM*
Lieutenant of the Royal Victorian Order	**LVO**
Officer of the Order of the British Empire	OBE
Companion of the Imperial Service Order	ISO
Member of the Royal Victorian Order	**MVO**
Member of the Order of the British Empire	MBE
Conspicuous Service Cross	*CSC*
Nursing Service Cross	*NSC*
Royal Red Cross (1st Class)	RRC
Distinguished Service Cross	DSC
Military Cross	MC
Distinguished Flying Cross	DFC
Air Force Cross	AFC
Royal Red Cross (2nd Class)	ARRC
Medal for Gallantry	*MG*
Bravery Medal	*BM*
Distinguished Service Medal	*DSM*
Public Service Medal	*PSM*
Australian Police Medal	*APM*
Australian Fire Service Medal	*AFSM*
Ambulance Service Medal	**ASM**
Emergency Services Medal	**ESM**
Medal of the Order of Australia	*OAM*
Order of St John	1
Distinguished Conduct Medal	DCM
Conspicuous Gallantry Medal	CGM
George Medal	GM
Conspicuous Service Medal	*CSM*
Australian Antarctic Medal	*AAM*
Queen's Police Medal for Gallantry	QPM
Queen's Fire Service Medal for Gallantry	QFSM
Distinguished Service Medal	DSM
Military Medal	MM

(continue

Table A.1 continued

Title of honour or award	Postnominal initials
Distinguished Flying Medal	DFM
Air Force Medal	AFM
Queen's Gallantry Medal	QGM
Royal Victorian Medal	**RVM**
British Empire Medal	BEM
Queen's Police Medal for Distinguished Service	QPM
Queen's Fire Service Medal for Distinguished Service	QFSM
Commendation for Gallantry	1
Commendation for Brave Conduct	1
Queen's Commendation for Brave Conduct	1
Commendation for Distinguished Service	1
War Medals/**Campaign Medals/Australian Active Service Medal** (in order of date of qualifying service)	1
Australian Service Medal 1945–1975/Australian Service Medal/ *Rhodesia Medal* (in order of date of qualifying service)	1
Police Overseas Service Medal	1
Humanitarian Overseas Service Medal	1
Civilian Service Medal 1939–1945	1
Polar Medal	1
Imperial Service Medal	1
Coronation, Jubilee, Remembrance and Commemorative Medals (in order of date of receipt)	1
Defence Force Service Medal	1
Reserve Force Decoration	**RFD**
Reserve Force Medal	1
Defence Long Service Medal	1
National Medal	1
Australian Cadet Forces Service Medal	1
Champion Shots Medal	1
Long Service Medals	1
Independence and Anniversary Medals (in order of date of receipt)	1
Foreign awards (in order of date of authorisation of their acceptance and wearing)	2

1 No postnominal initials attached.
2 Postnominals as appropriate.
Note: Bold italic type indicates current Australian honours and awards.
       Coloured type indicates other current honours and awards.
       Roman type indicates British awards no longer conferred on Australians (since 1975), and
       foreign awards approved by the Governor-General.

No full stops: Note that no full stops are used in postnominals; a comma separates different sets of postnominals.

➤ See pp. 517–18 for the form in which to show university degrees and membership of professional associations. Forms of address for members of parliament are shown on pp. 512–13.

Presentation of postnominals

The postnominals associated with the honours and awards listed in Table A.1 are shown in their order of precedence: the higher the honour, the nearer it is placed to the person's name. For example:

Dr DJ Silberberg, AC, CBE   Ms Marjorie Trimmer, MBE, OAM

When a person is promoted within an order, the postnominals associated with the lower ranked award or honour are no longer used. Thus, if a Member of the Order of Australia (say, Ms *Margaret Norton*, AM) is promoted to become an Officer of the Order, she becomes Ms *Margaret Norton*, AO (not AO, AM).

Postnominals for honours and awards precede those for Queen's Counsel (QC) or Senior Counsel (SC) and Justice of the Peace (JP). Other postnominals are then given in the following order:

- university degrees and diplomas
- membership of professional associations
- membership of parliament.

Prefixed titles

Prefixed titles of rank and status are placed immediately before a person's name and after any honorific forms of address. Vice-regal, ecclesiastical and armed services titles usually precede all others. Thus:

Her Excellency Dame Nora Yeomans   Cardinal Sir Brian Tobin   General Sir James Butler

Sir and Dame

Provided that no title of higher rank is more appropriate, the following honours for men entitle the holder to the prefixed title *Sir* (in addition to the use of the postnominals):

KG   KT   GCB   AK   GCMG   GCVO   GBE   KCB   KCMG   KCVO   KBE

The award of Knight Bachelor also confers the title *Sir*, but no postnominal initials are attached to the person's name.

Similarly, provided that she holds no higher rank, a woman can use the title *Dame* if she has received one or more of the following honours:

GCB   AD   GCMG   GCVO   GBE   DCB   DCMG   DCVO   DBE

When addressing a person entitled to *Dame* or *Sir*, it is customary to use their preferred given name before their family name:

Dame Sandra Dahl   Sir George Ashcroft

The wife of Sir George Ashcroft is called Lady Ashcroft; it is not customary to use her given name. In contrast, a husband derives no title from being married to a dame; thus Dame Sandra Dahl's husband would simply be called Mr Frederick Dahl.

The Honourable

At the federal level in Australia, the title *The Honourable* is accorded holders of the following offices (although there are qualifying periods in some instances):

- members of the Executive Council
- parliamentary ministers
- President of the Senate
- Speaker of the House of Representatives
- judges of the High Court
- presidential members of the Industrial Relations Commission
- judges of the Federal Court
- judges of the Family Court.

In the Australian states and territories, holders of the following offices are accorded the title *The Honourable* (although, again, there may be qualifying periods):

- members of the Executive Council
- members of the Legislative Council
- Speaker of the Legislative Assembly (except in the Australian Capital Territory)
- Leader of the Opposition (Tasmania)
- judges of the Supreme Court
- Chief Judge of the Family Court (Western Australia)
- President of the Industrial Court (South Australia).

Capitalisation and shortened forms:
The Honourable is usually shortened to *The Hon.* or *the Hon.* except in the most formal contexts. A capital *T* should be used for *The* when it appears at the start of a sentence, address line or list item. Otherwise, use *the Hon.* In a list, for example, it would be:

The Hon. Rohan Thomas

Senator the Hon. Jack Graham

FORMS OF ADDRESS

General correspondence

In correspondence, forms of address are the ways of beginning and ending a letter. They consist of three parts—the salutation, the recipient's name, and the complimentary close.

Named and unnamed recipients

Where the name of the recipient is known, the conventional form is:

Dear Ms Vigano … Yours sincerely

If the name, but not the gender, of the recipient is known, there are two options (although neither is particularly elegant):

Dear C Wall   *or*   Dear Charles Wall

If the name of the recipient is not known or if an impersonal approach is warranted, the usual salutation is:

Dear Sir … Yours faithfully

Dear Madam … Yours faithfully

➤ Pages 510–13 and 515–16 provide information about addressing people accorded the title *The Honourable*.

It is helpful for recipients if writers of correspondence identify themselves precisel
giving their preferred titles and any postnominals. This approach enables
recipients to use the form of address they know will be acceptable when
responding.

Married women

It is no longer customary to address a married woman by using the given name or
initials of her husband in the address line. Also, not every married woman choose
to take her husband's family name. Care is needed to accommodate individual
preferences.

A group of recipients

When writing formally to a group of women, the salutation *Mesdames* is preferabl
to *Dear Mesdames*. (*Dear Madams* is not used in Australia.) Better still, address th
women by name:

Dear Mrs de Bruin, Ms Ferreira and Ms Schmidt

or

Dear Freda de Bruin, Silvia Ferreira and Irena Schmidt

For men, the salutation *Messrs* can be used when addressing brothers (for example
Messrs Gerard and Michel Blanc), but it should not be used for father and son, who
should be addressed as *Mr Gerard and Mr Louis Blanc*. *Messrs* is also acceptable
when addressing a partnership (but only if all the partners are men)—for example
Messrs Golightly and Limburner.

Royalty

Her Majesty's title in Australia is *Elizabeth the Second, by the Grace of God Queen
Australia and Her other Realms and Territories, Head of the Commonwealth*. Letters t
the Queen should be addressed to the Private Secretary to Her Majesty The
Queen.

The title of the Queen's husband is *His Royal Highness Prince Philip, The Duke of
Edinburgh*. Letters to Prince Philip should be addressed to the Private Secretary tc
HRH The Duke of Edinburgh.

The Queen's eldest son is *His Royal Highness The Prince Charles, Prince of Wales*.
Letters to Prince Charles should be addressed to the Private Secretary to HRH
The Prince of Wales.

The capitalised *The* is used only for the formal titles of the Queen and her
immediate family, as in the formulation 'The Prince Andrew'.

Viceroyalty

Governor-General of Australia

It is customary to address the Governor-General of Australia using *His* (or *Her*)
Excellency the Honourable before the person's name (including any prefixed title,
given name, family name and postnominals), then the words *Governor-General of*

the Commonwealth of Australia. However, variations are sometimes required to suit the titles of different incumbents of the office. For example:

> His Excellency the Right Reverend Dr Peter Hollingworth, AC, OBE, Governor-General of the Commonwealth of Australia

Correspondence with the Governor-General should be addressed to the Official Secretary at Government House, Canberra. If the Governor-General is addressed personally, the appropriate salutation and close are:

> Your Excellency … Yours faithfully [formal]

> Dear Governor-General … Yours sincerely [less formal]

The wife of a governor-general is addressed as *Her Excellency* or *Your Excellency*. Similarly, the husband of a governor-general would be addressed as *His Excellency* or *Your Excellency*.

Governor of a state

For a governor of a state, the title *His* (or *Her*) *Excellency* precedes all other ranks and titles. A governor's spouse is not known as *Her* (or *His*) *Excellency*.

Correspondence with a state governor should be addressed to the Official Secretary at Government House in that state. Correspondence with the wife or husband of a state governor should be addressed to the Official Secretary or the Private Secretary.

Lieutenant-governor (of a state)

Normally, a lieutenant-governor of a state is not known as *His* (or *Her*) *Excellency*. In the absence of the governor, however, he or she is addressed as:

> His (or Her) Excellency the Lieutenant-Governor of …

Administrator of the Northern Territory

The Administrator of the Northern Territory is addressed as *His* (or *Her*) *Honour the Administrator*, followed by any prefixed title, given name (or initials), family name and any postnominals. For example:

> His Honour the Administrator Dr DM Forman, AC

If a person bearing the title *The Honourable* is appointed Administrator, the correct title is *His* (or *Her*) *Honour the Honourable* …

Correspondence with the Administrator should begin with *Dear Administrator* and conclude with *Yours faithfully* or, less formally, *My dear Administrator … Yours sincerely.*

Knights and dames

There are various orders of knighthood—the Garter, the Thistle, St Patrick, the Bath, the Star of India, St Michael and St George, the Indian Empire, the Royal Victorian, the British Empire and Knight Bachelor. Knights and dames are distinguished by being addressed as *Sir* or *Dame*, with the relevant postnominals after their names (except for Knight Bachelor, which has no postnominals).

Members of Australian parliaments

The initialism showing that a person is a member of an Australian parliament is always shown last (that is, after any other postnominals to which the person is entitled).

Prime minister

The form of address for the Prime Minister of Australia is *The Hon. [given and family names], MP, Prime Minister of Australia.* For example:

The Hon. John Howard, MP, Prime Minister of Australia

The appropriate form to use in correspondence is:

Dear Prime Minister ... Yours faithfully [formal]

My dear Prime Minister ... Yours sincerely [less formal]

In the past, prime ministers were appointed to the Privy Council and thus received the title *The Right Honourable*, but this is no longer the case.

State premiers

State premiers are addressed in the following way:

The Hon. [given and family names], MLA, Premier of Tasmania

Correspondence with a premier should begin with *Dear Premier* and conclude with *Yours faithfully* or, less formally, *My dear Premier ... Yours sincerely.*

Chief ministers

The form of address for the Chief Minister of the Australian Capital Territory is:

Dr (or Mr, Ms, Mrs and so on) [given and family names], MLA, Chief Minister of the ACT

The Chief Minister for the Northern Territory receives the title *The Honourable* and should be addressed as:

The Hon. [given and family names], MLA, Chief Minister for the Northern Territory

(Note that it is Chief Minister *for* the Northern Territory, not *of.*)

Correspondence with a chief minister should begin with *Dear Chief Minister* and conclude with *Yours faithfully* or, less formally, *My dear Chief Minister ... Yours sincerely.*

Ministers

Ministers in the federal, state and Northern Territory parliaments take the title *The Honourable*. For example:

The Hon. Fred Whyte, MP (or MLA or MHA), Minister for Energy and the Environment

The title *Senator* precedes *the Hon.* if the minister is a member of the Senate:

Senator the Hon. Denise Lyons, Minister for Communications

Ministers of the Australian Capital Territory Parliament are addressed in the following way:

Ms (or Mrs, Miss Mr, Dr, and so on) Jan Melville, MLA, Minister for Urban Services

orrespondence with ministers should be in the following form:

> Dear Minister … Yours faithfully [formal]
>
> My dear Minister … Yours sincerely [less formal]

lembers of the Commonwealth Parliament

lembers of the House of Representatives in Australia's Commonwealth
arliament have no title before their name but use the initials *MP* after their
ame. For example:

> Ms Olivia Gesualdo, MP

hey are addressed as *Ms, Mrs* or *Mr* (or *Dr, Dame, Sir,* and so on, as the case may
e).

he initials *MP* follow any other postnominals showing any honour or award
onferred on the member or any rank or position they might hold. For example:

> Sir Guthrie Featherstone, QC, MP

he initials *MHR,* which are sometimes used, are not officially sanctioned.

lembers of the Senate have the title *Senator* before their name but no initials
esignating parliamentary status after their name. For example:

> Senator Ralph Nelson

he appropriate forms to use in correspondence are as follows:

to a member of the House of Representatives

> Dear Sir (or Madam) … Yours faithfully [formal]
>
> Dear Mr (or Ms, Mrs, Miss, Dr and so on) … Yours sincerely [less formal]

to a senator

> Dear Senator … Yours faithfully [formal]
>
> My dear Senator … Yours sincerely [less formal]

embers of state and territory parliaments

lembers of state and territory parliaments generally use the initials *MLC*
Member of the Legislative Council), *MLA* (Member of the Legislative Assembly)
 MHA (Member of the House of Assembly) after their name. For example:

> Ms Alisha Cohen, MLA

owever, some members prefer the initials *MP* after their name.

orrespondence with a member of a state or territory parliament should begin
ith *Dear Ms* (or *Mr, Mrs, Miss, Dr,* and so on) and conclude with *Yours faithfully*
, less formally, *Yours sincerely.*

cal government

cal government brings with it a variety of titles—for example, *Mayor, President,*
lderman, Councillor—and a variety of associated conventions.

Lord mayors

The lord mayors of Adelaide, Brisbane, Hobart, Melbourne, Perth and Sydney have the title *The Right Honourable* attached to their offices but not to their names. (This means that they are not called, say, 'The Right Honourable Jennifer Walker': the title is attached to the words 'the Lord Mayor'.) The lord mayors of Brisbane, Hobart and Sydney are *aldermen*; the lord mayor of Melbourne is *councillor*; and the lord mayors of Adelaide and Perth are addressed by their conventional title (Mr, Ms, and so on). Thus:

> The Rt Hon. the Lord Mayor of Brisbane, Alderman Rosemary Danvers
>
> The Rt Hon. the Lord Mayor of Melbourne, Councillor Graeme Donald
>
> The Rt Hon. the Lord Mayor of Adelaide, Ms Karen Reid

Note that the title *Alderman* does not change if the lord mayor is a female.

The lord mayors of Darwin, Newcastle and Wollongong are addressed as *The Right Worshipful the Lord Mayor of* ...

Correspondence with a lord mayor should begin with *Dear Lord Mayor* and conclude with *Yours faithfully*.

There is no specific honorific for a lord mayor's spouse. The wife of a lord mayor is addressed as, say, *The Lady Mayoress of Hobart*.

Mayors

The mayor of Geelong is addressed as *The Right Worshipful the Mayor of Geelong*. Mayors of other cities are addressed as *His* (or *Her*) *Worship the Mayor of* ... The wife of a mayor is addressed as, say, *The Mayoress of Dubbo Ms* (or *Dr, Mrs, Miss* and so on) *Cecile Bird*.

Correspondence with a mayor should begin with *Dear Mayor* and conclude with *Yours faithfully*.

Shire presidents, aldermen and councillors

A shire president is addressed as, say, *President Carboni*, an alderman (male or female) as *Alderman McTiernan*, and a councillor as *Councillor Ngu*.

Formal correspondence with these office bearers should begin with *Dear President, Dear Alderman* or *Dear Councillor*, as appropriate, and conclude with *Yours faithfully*. Less formal correspondence can begin with *Dear President Carboni, Dear Alderman McTiernan* or *Dear Councillor Ngu* and conclude with *Yours sincerely*.

Diplomats

Ambassadors (representatives of non-Commonwealth countries), high commissioners (representatives of Commonwealth countries) and nuncios (the representative of the Holy See) have equal status and are called *His* (or *Her*) *Excellency*. For example:

> Her Excellency Ms Paola di Lampedusa, Ambassador of ...
>
> His Excellency Dr Alexander Kennard, High Commissioner for ...

ormal correspondence with an ambassador or high commissioner should begin ith *Your Excellency* and conclude with *Yours faithfully*. Less formally, the salutation an be *Dear Ambassador* (or *High Commissioner*) and the communication can onclude with *Yours sincerely*.

he wife of an ambassador or a high commissioner is entitled to the honorific *Her xcellency* when in the country to which her husband is accredited, although use of is title is now less common than it was in the past. The husband of an nbassador or high commissioner is not entitled to the honorific *His Excellency*.

ther diplomatic staff (such as chargés d'affaires and counsellors) and consular opointees (such as consuls general, vice-consuls and honorary consuls) are ldressed by name and appointment—for example, *Monsieur Michel Petit, Chargé Affaires*.

lergy

or guidance in addressing office holders in different faiths, see *Dear you: a guide to rms of address*.[2] Note that a spiritual title precedes a temporal title.

diciary

the High Court, the Federal Court and the Family Court in the federal dicature and in the supreme courts in the states and territories, judges are usually ldressed simply as *Justice* and bear the title *The Honourable*. For example:

> Justice Daphne May
>
> The Hon. Justice Daphne May

district and county courts, judges are addressed as *Judge* and bear the title *His or Her) Honour*. For example:

> Judge Martin Beatty
>
> His Honour Judge Beatty

presidential member of the Australian Industrial Relations Commission has the me status and rank as a judge of the Federal Court and is thus entitled to the efix *The Honourable*.

dges of the High Court, the Federal Court and the Family Court and presidential embers of the Australian Industrial Relations Commission retain for life the title he Honourable. A judge who has been appointed a member of the Privy Council tains for life the title *The Right Honourable*.

judge who is a knight or dame is customarily addressed as *The Honourable Sir …* *The Honourable Dame …* For example:

> The Hon. Sir William Hector, AC, KBE

n subsequent mention, *Sir William* can be used.

he appropriate opening salutation and complimentary close in correspondence e as follows:

Hyslop R 1992, *Dear you: a guide to forms of address*, AGPS Press, Canberra

- to the Chief Justice of the High Court of Australia

  Dear Sir or Dear Madam ... Yours faithfully [formal]

  Dear Chief Justice ... Yours faithfully [less formal]

- to the Chief Justice of the Federal Court of Australia or the Family Court

  Your Honour ... Yours faithfully [formal]

  Dear Chief Justice ... Yours faithfully [less formal]

- to a justice of the Federal Court or the Family Court

  Your Honour ... Yours faithfully [formal]

  Dear Judge ... Yours faithfully [less formal]

- to the President or Deputy President of the Australian Industrial Relations Commission

  Your Honour ... Yours faithfully [formal]

  Dear Judge ... Yours faithfully [less formal]

- to a commissioner of the Australian Industrial Relations Commission

  Commissioner ... Yours faithfully [formal]

  Dear Commissioner ... Yours faithfully [less formal]

- to a judge of a state or territory supreme court, district court or county court

  Your Honour ... Yours faithfully

Armed services

In formal correspondence, officers in the armed services are addressed by their rank, given name or initials, family name and any postnominals; thus, *Rear Admiral Felix Liou, AO*. In informal correspondence, officers of the rank of army lieutenant, navy sub lieutenant and air force flying officer and below are given conventional titles (*Mr, Ms, Mrs* or *Miss*). Officers of the rank of colonel and above can be addressed by their rank alone, without their name. Non-commissioned officers and other ranks are addressed by their rank and family name, not by their given name—thus, *Private Fotheringham*.

Postnominals for honours and awards are shown immediately after the family name and before abbreviations that indicate service or regiment.

Military ranks consisting of more than one word do not take a hyphen—for example, *Lieutenant Colonel*. A military rank precedes other titles. Chaplains have military rank but they are addressed with their ecclesiastical title only.

Table A.2 shows the order of precedence in Australia's armed services.

Table A.2 **Armed services ranks in Australia: order of precedence**

Army	Navy	Air Force
Field Marshal	Admiral of the Fleet	Marshal of the Air Force
General	Admiral	Air Chief Marshal
Lieutenant General	Vice Admiral	Air Marshal
Major General	Rear Admiral	Air Vice Marshal
Brigadier	Commodore	Air Commodore
Colonel	Captain	Group Captain
Lieutenant Colonel	Commander	Wing Commander
Major	Lieutenant Commander	Squadron Leader
Captain	Lieutenant	Flight Lieutenant
Lieutenant	Sub Lieutenant	Warrant Officer
Second Lieutenant	Midshipman	Flight Sergeant
Warrant Officer 1[1]	Warrant Officer	Sergeant
Warrant Officer 2[2]	Chief Petty Officer	Corporal
Sergeant	Petty Officer	Leading Aircraftman
Corporal[3]	Leading Seaman	Aircraftman
Lance Corporal[4]	Able Seaman	—
Private[5]	—	—

— Not applicable.
[1] Or *Regimental Sergeant Major.*
[2] Or *Sergeant Major.*
[3] *Bombardier* in Artillery.
[4] *Lance Bombardier* in Artillery.
[5] *Gunner* in Artillery; *Sapper* in Engineers; *Signalman* in Signals.

Academics and professionals

Academics

The use of postnominals representing tertiary qualifications is usually restricted to correspondence within the academic community or in cases when the qualifications are cited as a warrant of expertise. For example:

Dr RJ Griffin, FRHistS, FASSA

Note that the title *Doctor* can be abbreviated to *Dr* in this situation, although it is not abbreviated in the form *Dear Doctor.*

Medical practitioners are customarily addressed as *Doctor*, whether or not they hold a doctorate—except for male surgeons who have traditionally been known as *Mr*. In Australia, it has also become common for dental surgeons and veterinarians to take the title *Doctor.*

The address for chancellors, vice chancellors and professors takes the following form:

Professor Xavier Chan, Vice Chancellor, Monash University

Professor S Lander, Department of Aeronautical Engineering, University of Sydney

or

Dr S Lander, Professor of Aeronautical Engineering, University of Sydney

In formal correspondence, the salutation should be *Chancellor* (or *Vice Chancellor* or *Professor*) and the close *Yours faithfully*. Less formally, the salutation can be *Dear Chancellor* (or *Vice Chancellor* or *Professor*).

If the holder of a doctorate is knighted, *Doctor* is no longer used; the correct form of address shows the details of knighthood followed by the details of the doctorate. For example:

Dame Adrienne Garner, DBE, DDS

The situation differs, however, for a chancellor, vice chancellor or professor who is knighted:

Chancellor Sir Eric Newsome

Postnominals indicating master and bachelor degrees are not usually shown in official or academic correspondence.

Professionals

Professionally qualified people addressed in the context of their profession take their prefixed and postnominal professional titles. For example:

Dr Brent Hulot, CPA

or

Dr Brent Hulot, Certified Practising Accountant

Conventions for non-English names

Many naming systems in use throughout the world differ from that followed in English-speaking countries. For example, in some systems the family name is traditionally presented first, although individuals might dispense with this convention when in a predominantly English-speaking environment. It is important to make inquiries about the correct form of address if in doubt.

To avoid the appearance of cultural bias, use *given name* or *personal name* instead of *Christian name. Family name* is also more widely understood than *surname*.

While many Indigenous Australians have adopted English-style given names and family names (and so take the corresponding titles—say, Mr or Ms), some prefer to be addressed by their traditional names, with no conventional title. It is worth taking the time to find out what form of address is most acceptable.

Appendix B

Metric conversion table

When converting measurements in imperial units into SI units, use the conversion factors shown in Table B.1, which are those stipulated in the National Measurement Regulations (1999). Imperial measurements should be converted into SI in most instances (see page 182).

Table B.1 **Conversion from imperial to metric units**

Quantity	Imperial unit	SI unit	Conversion factor—imperial to SI equivalent
length	mile	metre	1 609.344
	chain (ch)	metre	$22 \times 0.914\,4$
	yard (yd)	metre	0.914 4
	link (lk)	metre	$22 \times 0.914\,4 \div 100$
	foot (ft)	metre	$0.914\,4 \div 3$
	inch (in)	metre	$0.914\,4 \div 36$
area	square yard	square metre	$0.914\,4^2$
	square foot	square metre	$0.914\,4^2 \div 9$
	square inch	square metre	$0.914\,4^2 \div 9 \times 144$
	acre (ac)	square metre	$4\,840 \times 0.914\,4^2$
	rood (rd)	square metre	$1\,210 \times 0.914\,4^2$
	perch (p)	square metre	$30.25 \times 0.914\,4^2$
mass	ton (tn)	kilogram	$2\,240 \times 0.453\,592\,37$
	short ton (sh tn)	kilogram	$2\,000 \times 0.453\,592\,37$
	hundredweight (cwt)	kilogram	$112 \times 0.453\,592\,37$
	quarter (qr)	kilogram	$28 \times 0.453\,592\,37$
	stone	kilogram	$14 \times 0.453\,592\,37$
	pound (lb)	kilogram	0.453 592 37
	ounce (oz)	kilogram	$0.453\,592\,37 \div 16$
	dram (dr)	kilogram	$0.453\,592\,37 \div 256$
	grain (gr)	kilogram	$0.453\,592\,37 \div 7\,000$
	slug	kilogram	$32.174 \times 0.453\,592\,37$
	troy ounce (oz tr)	kilogram	$480 \times 0.453\,592\,37 \div 7\,000$
	pennyweight (dwt)	kilogram	$24 \times 0.453\,592\,37 \div 7\,000$
volume	cubic yard (cu yd or yd³)	cubic metre	$0.914\,4^3$
	cubic foot (cu ft or ft³)	cubic metre	$0.914\,4^3 \div 27$
	cubic inch (cu in or in³)	cubic metre	$0.914\,4^3 \div 466\,56$
	gallon (gal)	cubic metre	$4.546\,09 \times 10^{-3}$
	quart (qt)	cubic metre	$4.546\,09 \times 10^{-3} \div 4$

(continued overleaf)

Table B.1 continued

Quantity	Imperial unit	SI unit	Conversion factor—imperial to SI equivalent
	pint (pt)	cubic metre	$4.546\ 09 \times 10^{-3} \div 8$
	gill	cubic metre	$4.546\ 09 \times 10^{-3} \div 32$
	fluid ounce (fl oz)	cubic metre	$4.546\ 09 \times 10^{-3} \div 160$
	fluid drachm (fl dr)	cubic metre	$4.546\ 09 \times 10^{-3} \div 1\ 280$
	minim (min)	cubic metre	$4.546\ 09 \times 10^{-3} \div 76\ 800$
velocity and speed	mile per hour (mile/h or mph)	metre per second	$1\ 609.344 \div 3\ 600$
	mile per hour (mile/h or mph)	kilometre per hour	$1.609\ 344$
	foot per minute (ft/min)	metre per second	$0.304\ 8 \div 60$
work and energy	kilocalorie (kcal)	joule	$4.186\ 8 \times 10^3$
	calorie (cal)	joule	$4.186\ 8$
	British thermal unit (Btu)	joule	$1\ 055.056$
power	horsepower (hp)	watt	745.7
pressure	millimetre of mercury (mm Hg)	pascal	$133.322\ 19$
	millibar (mb or mbar)	pascal	100

Appendix

Standard proofreading marks and how to use them

Standard proofreading marks have evolved over many years and are an unambiguous, widely recognised means of indicating required corrections. Some of the more frequently used marks are illustrated on pages 523–5. The same symbols are used for both copy editing and correcting printers' proofs, but the placement differs (see page 266).

For an example of a marked-up copy and the corrected proof, see pages 526–7.

PLACEMENT OF MARKS

To indicate a correction, marks are required in both the text and the margin.

The corrections in the margin should be adjacent to the line of text where the change is to be made. If there is more than one alteration in a line, show the corrections from left to right in the order in which they are to be made and separate them by a vertical line or slash. To keep the corrections closest to their point of insertion, use the left margin for corrections to be placed in the left-hand side of the text column, and the right margin for those on the right-hand side of the text column.

ADDING MATERIAL

To add material to the text, place a *caret* ($\wedge$) at the relevant spot in the text and write the additional character, word or words in the margin.

To insert something in a 'superior' position in the text (such as an apostrophe, quotation mark or superscript character), use the same caret in the text, but in the margin use a reversed caret ($\curlyvee$) with the relevant symbol or character above it— for example, $\curlyvee^{2}$. To indicate a subscript character, place the caret over the character in the margin—for example, $\underset{\wedge}{x}$.

To insert a full stop, show it within a circle in the margin, so that it can be clearly seen. Semicolons, colons, question marks and exclamation marks, if written clearly, need no further identifying marks. However, to avoid having a question mark mistaken for a query, follow it with the word *set* within a circle.

Deletions

The *delete* mark ($\mathcal{G}$), which is placed in the margin, is used only when something is to be removed from a line. Do not use it if another letter, word, line or paragraph is to be inserted in place of the deleted matter.

In the text, indicate the matter to be deleted by drawing a diagonal line through the letter or a straight line through the word or words. Where a letter is to be deleted from the middle of a word, show the delete mark in the margin within *close up* marks ($\mathcal{G}$).

Anything to be removed should not be obscured by heavy marking, as the person making the corrections needs to be able to distinguish which characters to take out. If a comma or full stop, or even a single letter, will be completely covered by the textual delete mark, then circle it instead, so that it remains visible.

The form of the delete mark written in the margin need not be exactly as shown in the list on page 523. Be careful, however, that any variant you use will not be confused with any handwritten letter or numeral.

Spacing

Use the *close up* mark (⊃) to indicate where there is too much space between letters, words or lines. The same mark is used in both the line and the margin.

Sometimes a word space is misplaced so that the last letter of one word appears at the beginning of the next. When this happens, place the close up mark followed by a *space* mark (#) in the margin; in the line itself use a close up mark and a vertical line in the appropriate position.

Use the space mark in the margin when more space between words is required, and place a vertical line or caret in the text where the space is to be inserted. If word spaces in a single line are unequal, write the *equal space* sign (*eq. #*) in the margin and place a caret in the text where the problem occurs. Note that spacing between words in successive lines will vary in justified setting.

Transposition

When you need to move anything from one position to another, use the mark for *transposing* (*trs*) in the margin. It can refer to letters, words, phrases, lines and paragraphs. The text mark goes alternately below and above the material to be transposed—for example, c⟲a .

Spelling out

If you want to indicate that an abbreviation or numeral should be spelt out, circle it in the text. In the margin either write *spell out* or, if there could be any doubt about the spelling, write the full word.

Remember that this change will make the line longer (unless the change is small enough to be accommodated within the same line of type). If the change means that words run over to the next line, it may also alter the length of the paragraph and possibly the page as well.

Reinstating material

When you want to show that something previously marked for alteration is to remain unchanged, place the word *stet* in the margin and use dots or hyphens under the crossed-out material in the text to show what is to remain. Where a note in the margin also needs to be crossed out, *stet as set* will clarify what you want to let stand.

Common proofreading marks

Instruction	Textual mark	Margin mark[1]
Correction is concluded	None	/
Insert in text the matter indicated in the margin	⅄	*New matter followed by* /
Delete	Strike through characters to be deleted	⑦
Delete and close up	Above and below letters to be taken out	⑨
Leave as printed	Under characters to remain	*stet*
Change to italic	Under characters to be altered	*ital*
Change to even small capitals	Under characters to be altered	*s.c.*
Change to capital letters	Under characters to be altered	*caps*
Use capital letters for initial letters and small capitals for rest of words	Under initial letters and under the rest of words	*c. & s.c.*
Change to bold type	Under characters to be altered	*bold*
Underline word or words	Under words affected	*underline*
Change to lower case	Strike through CHARacters to be altered	*l.c.*
Change to roman type	Encircle characters to be altered	*rom.*
Wrong font. Replace by letter of correct font	Encircle characters to be altered	*w.f.*
Change damaged characters	Encircle character(s) to be altered	*x*
Substitute or insert character(s) under which the mark is placed in 'superior' position	/ through character or ⅄ where required	γ *under character* (e.g. 2)
Substitute or insert character(s) over which the mark is placed in 'inferior' position	/ through character or ⅄ where required	√ *over character* (e.g. x)
Use ligature (e.g. ffi) or diphthong (e.g. œ)	Enclosing letters to be altered	⌢ *Enclosing ligature or* ⌣ *diphthong required*

Words printed in light italics in this column are instructions and not part of the marks.

Instruction	Textual mark	Margin mark[1]
Substitute separate letters for ligature or diphthong	Through ligatured letters or diphthong to be altered	*Write out separate letters followed by* /
Close up (delete space between characters)	lin⌣king characters	⌢⌣
Insert space[2]	⅄	#
Insert space between lines or paragraphs	Between lines to be spaced	#
Reduce space between lines[2]	(Connecting lines to be closed up)	*less # close up*
Make space appear equal between words	Equal | between | words	*eq. #*
Reduce space between words[2]	Between | words	*less #*
Add space between letters[2]	Between tops of letters requiring space	*letter #*
Transpose	Between characters words or	*trs*
Place in centre of line	Indicate position ⌈with⌉	*centre*
Indent one em	⌐	☐ *or* ☐1
Indent two ems	⌐⌐	☐☐ *or* ☐2
Move matter to right	At left or right side of group to be moved	⌐
Move matter to left	At right or left side of group to be moved	⌐
Move matter to position indicated	At limits of required position	*move*
Move to next line or page	⌐	*take over*
Move to previous line or page	⌐	*take back*
Raise lines[2]	Over lines to be moved ↑ Under lines to be moved ⌐	*raise*
Lower lines[2]	Over lines to be moved ⌐ Under lines to be moved ↓	*lower*
Correct the vertical alignment	‖ At left or right of lines to be adjusted	‖
Straighten lines	Through lines to be adjusted	══

1 Words printed in light italics in this column are instructions and not part of the marks.

2 Amount of space may be indicated.

Instruction	Textual mark	Margin mark
Begin a new paragraph	⌐Before the first word of the new paragraph	*n. p.*
No fresh paragraph here	Between⌐ paragraphs	*run on*
Spell out abbreviation or numeral in full	Encircle ⟨words⟩ or ⟨numerals⟩ to be altered	*spell out*
Insert omitted portion of copy	Between the ⟨omitted	*out — see copy*
Substitute or insert comma	/ through character or ∧ where required	*, /*
Substitute or insert semicolon	/ through character or ∧ where required	*; /*
Substitute or insert full stop	/ through character or ∧ where required	*⊙/*
Substitute or insert colon	/ through character or ∧ where required	*⊙/*
Substitute or insert question mark	/ through character or ∧ where required	*? /*
Substitute or insert exclamation mark	/ through character or ∧ where required	*! /*
Insert parentheses	∧ or ∧∧	*(/)/*
Insert brackets	∧ or ∧∧	*[/]/*
Insert hyphen	∧	*/-/*
Insert en rule	∧	*/⁻ᵉⁿ/*
Insert 1-em rule	∧	*/⁻ᵉᵐ/*
Insert 2-em rule	∧	*/⁻²ᵉᵐˢ/*
Insert apostrophe	∧	*ʾ*
Insert single quotation marks	∧	*ʾ ʾ*
Insert double quotation marks	∧	*ʾʾ ʾʾ*
Insert ellipsis	∧	*… /*
Insert forward slash	∧	*Ⓘ*
Refer to appropriate authority anything of doubtful accuracy	Encircle words ⟨etc.,⟩ affected	*Ⓠ*

Marked-up copy

Chinese (Overseas)

l.c./

Forms of address used among chinese living outside China are generally different from those employed in the People's Republic of China. Pronunciation and romanization vary according to the dialect: for example Tan and Chan are the same name in Hokien and Cantonese respectively.

caps/ *s/* *ital/ital/* *k/*

Spelling frequently varies to conform with European orthography: e.g. Chong in Singapore and Hong Kong (British spelling) is rendered Tjong in Indonesia (Dutch spelling).

spell out/ *run on/* *#/* *ital/* *ital/*

Chinese who have lived in Indo-China often adopt a Gallic spelling: for example Qui for Kee. The outdated English romanization system mentioned above is more commonly used by Mandarin speakers outside the People's Republic of China. The following points should be noted

s/ *(:)/* *ital/ital/* *a/ n.p./*

- Normally, English-speaking Chinese men are referred to by non-Chinese as Mr and unmarried women as Miss. Although women in the Peoples Republic of China do not change their family names on marriage, most Chinese women outside that country would accept being addressed by their husband's name preceded by Mrs and indeed would expect to be so addressed.

trs/ *ital/* *ital/* *(/ ital/)/*

- Lim Yew Lee for example, should be addressed orally as 'Mr Lim', not 'Mr Lee'. In correspondence the three names should be used. Among close friends and family members he would usually be addressed on the familiar level as 'Yew Lee'.

take over/

Owing to Western influence, some overseas Chinese place their family names last and signify the change by linking the personal names with a hyphen for example 'Mr Yew-Lee Lim'. Sometimes the personal names are abbreviated to initials for business purposes, for example 'Mr Y.L. Lim'.

bullet/ [/l.c./ l.c./ *less #* *(:)/ trs/(:)/ #/*

When the Malaysian titles Dato or Tun are bestowed on Malaysian Chinese the full Chinese name is used, for example 'Tun Tan Seiw Sin', when first mentioned. Later 'Tun Tan' may be used.

bullet/ [/ e/ ,/ *ital/ital/ (:)/ trs/*

The corrected proof

Chinese (overseas)

Forms of address used among Chinese living outside China are generally different from those employed in the People's Republic of China. Pronunciation and romanisation vary according to the dialect: for example *Tan* and *Chan* are the same name in Hokkien and Cantonese respectively.

Spelling frequently varies to conform with European orthography: for example *Chong* in Singapore and Hong Kong (British spelling) is rendered *Tjong* in Indonesia (Dutch spelling). Chinese who have lived in Indo-China often adopt a Gallic spelling: for example *Qui* for *Kee*. The outdated English romanisation system mentioned above is more commonly used by Mandarin speakers outside the People's Republic of China.

The following points should be noted:

* Normally, English-speaking Chinese men are referred to by non-Chinese as *Mr* and unmarried women as *Miss*. Although women in the People's Republic of China do not change their family names on marriage, most Chinese women outside that country would accept being addressed by their husband's name (preceded by *Mrs*), and indeed would expect to be so addressed.

* 'Lim Yew Lee', for example, should be addressed orally as 'Mr Lim', not 'Mr Lee'. In correspondence the three names should be used. Among close friends and family members he would usually be addressed on the familiar level as 'Yew Lee'.

* Owing to western influence, some overseas Chinese place their family names last and signify the change by linking the personal names with a hyphen: for example 'Mr Yew-Lee Lim'. Sometimes the personal names are abbreviated to initials for business purposes: for example 'Mr Y.L. Lim'.

* When the Malay titles *Dato* or *Tun* are bestowed on Malaysian Chinese, the full Chinese name is used: for example 'Tun Tan Siew Sin', when first mentioned. Later, 'Tun Tan' may be used.

Note: This passage is taken from Hyslop R 1991, *Dear You: a guide to forms of address*, AGPS Press, Canberra.

Index

The index is arranged alphabetically word by word. Punctuation within simple words has been ignored. A bold **s** following a page reference indicates that the reference appears only in the side column; references to items discussed in both columns are not marked in this way.

'a', *see* indefinite articles

-*a*, as singular and plural forms, 81–2

A paper sizes, 477–8

abbreviated organisational names, 123

abbreviated publishers' names, 203

abbreviated titles, 205, 206, 216
  legal authorities, 227–8
  tables, on second page, 350
  see also short titles

abbreviations, 152, 154, 155–61
  dates in running text, avoid, 170
  in documentary-note system of referencing, 214–15
  Hon., 509
  in indexes, 282
  in in-text citations, 191, 194, 195–7, 203
  in legal authorities, 226–7
  legislative units of division, 225
  lists of, 41, 237, 243
  scientific names, 130, 131
  of *per*, 184
  see also acronyms; Latin abbreviations; symbols

-*able* or -*eable*, 83

Aboriginal Australians, 56, 57

Aboriginal flag, 299–300

abrupt changes in sentence direction, 106, 107

abstract nouns, 69

academics, 517–18

access, 16–17, 48–62, 428–32
  'alt' and 'title' attributes, 451–2

access schemes, 444

Accession System, National Archives of Australia, 222

accuracy, responsibility for, 267

acid-free papers, 474

acknowledgments, 32, 236, 239, 241

acronyms, 72, 153, 154
  Anzac, 129

migrants whose mother tongue is not English, 56
  see also initialisms

ACSS, 450–1

action plans, government, 125

active and passive constructions, 54–5, 70, 73–4

Acts, 125, 224–6, 415

AD, 169

address, *see* modes of address; postal addresses

adhesive binding, 489

adjectival clauses, 103

adjective-plus-noun compounds, 91

adjectives and adjectival phrases, 68, 103
  capital letters, 120, 121, 124–5: inclusive use, 56**s**, 57, 58, 61
  compound, 91–2, 108
  determiners precede, 69
  fewer and *less*, 73
  inclusive, 56–8, 60–2
  participles as, 70, 83
  personal titles as, 105
  strings of, 102
  time of day, 172

administrator of Northern Territory, 511

adolescents, 62

adverb-plus-verb and verb-plus-adverb compounds, 90–1

adverbial clauses and phrases, 103–4

adverbs, 68, 72
  compound, 93
  in compound adjectives, 92
  hopefully, 74
  prepositions doubling as, 69

advertising and advertisements, 62, 420
  placement in periodicals, 245: citing articles split by, 206

-*ae*- or -*e*-, 83

-*ae* plural form, 81

age of readers, type selection and, 330

age range, inclusive treatment of, 61–2

agency numbers, 201, 426

agency sponsoring bodies, *see* sponsoring bodies

AGIFT, 428

AGLS metadata, 427–8

agreement, grammatical, 67, 71–2

agreements, governmental, 125

aircraft, 147, 200, 204

aldermen, 514

alignment
  in forms, 369
  in tables, 176, 353–4
  see also placement

alphabetical arrangement, 274
  in-text citations, 193, 195
  indexes, 277–9
  reference lists, 189, 192, 197
  see also letters of alphabet

'alt' attribute, 451–2

alternatives, indicating, 109

although, 67, 69, 72–3

am, 172–3

ambassadors, 514–15

ambiguity, *see* clarity

ambiguous access schemes, 444

amendments, *see* change

American readers and practices, 166, 186, 280, 39*5*
  am and *pm*, 172
  dashes, 106
  dates, 171
  quotation marks and other marks, 112, 115
  shortened forms, 154
  spelling, 83–5

American Standard Code for Information Interchange (ASCII), 446

ampersands, 157–8, 193, 226

mplification and explanation, punctuation indicating, 99, 100, 106, 110–11

n', *see* indefinite articles

hangu Aboriginal group, 57

nd, 109
  in dot points, 144
  in in-text citations, 193
  starting sentences, 72
  subjects coordinated with, 71

anor and *& ors*, 226

gle brackets, 112

nglo-American point system, 325, 330

imal emblems, 301

imals, 130–1

imation, *see* moving images

nnotated bibliographies, 219

nual reports, 432–3, 498–9
  compliance indexes, 272
  ISSNs, 425
  readership, 49–50

swer fields, on forms, 363, 364, 365–9, 371

ti-aliassing, 329

nzac, 129

ostrophes, 81, 85–8
  in shortened forms, 151, 153, 154

pendixes, 237, 241, 242

position, 99, 104

abic numerals, *see* numbers

chival paper, 474

chival record keeping, 433

rchives Act 1983, 433

chives and manuscripts, 208, 222

ea, *see* measurement

ea graphs, 395–6

med services, 158, 516–17

rows and connectors, on forms, 364, 370, 371

t (coated) papers, 471, 472

ticles, grammatical, *see* definite article; indefinite articles

ticles, periodicals, *see* periodical articles

tificial word breaks, 93–4

tistic works, 146, 410, 412, 417, 436
  see also illustrations

s, clauses introduced by, 103

s follows, 99

s well as, 71

scenders, 327, 332

SCII, 446

Asian names, 58

asides, enclosing in text, 110–11

assembly diagrams, 398

associations between words, 108, 109

asterisk (*), 208

astronomical names, 132

at, instead of *p.* (page), 226

atlases, 156

atmospheric imagery, 377–8

atmospheric phenomena, 132

attention spans, 37–8

attitudinal adverbs, 68, 74

attraction of design, 303, 310, 311–12, 318, 343

attribution of authorship, 417

audience, *see* readers and readership

audio, *see* sound

audio-cassette format, 431

aural cascading style sheets, 450–1

Australian Aboriginal flag, 299–300

Australian currency, 174–5

Australian Government publications, *see* government publications

Australian Government Locator Service, 427–8

Australian Government's interactive functions thesaurus, 428

Australian honours and awards, 504–8

Australian images, 301**s**

Australian journals online, 427

Australian measurement system, 182–3

Australian national and heraldic colours, 300–1

Australian national flag, 298–9

Australian Oxford dictionary, 80

Australian spelling, 80, 83–5

Australian states and territories, *see* states and territories

author–date system, 188–208, 224–32
  audio-visual media, 229
  electronic publications, 230–1
  government publications, 220–3

authors and authoring bodies, 20, 23, 29
  briefs, 27
  corrections on proofs, colours for marking, 266
  editors and, 253, 256, 263, 267
  moral rights, 417
  names in books, placement of, 235, 236, 238, 239
  state or territory government co-authored works, 295
  see also copyright; writing

authors and authoring bodies, in citations, 189–99
  documentary-note system, 210
  electronic publications, 230–1
  government publications, 220–3
  Vancouver system, 216–18

automatic indexing, 455–6

availability of paper stock, 475

awards, *see* personal titles

axes of graphs, 393–4

B paper sizes, 477–8

back bench and *back bencher*, 125

back covers, 235, 244

back (inner) margins, 316–17

back of book, *see* endmatter

back-of-book indexing, 270–84

background–foreground interaction, in design, 320, 341–2

background selection, 380–1

backing and rounding, 488–9

balance, 318–20

ballets, *see* dramatic works

Bar, 125

bar charts, 394, 396

bar codes, 425–6, 460

bare infinitive, 70

base font size, 330

baseline, 327

BC, 169

'because', *see* subordinating conjunctions

bench or *Bench*, 125

between, 109, 177

'between pages … and …', 243

bi-, 173

Bible, 228

bibliographic control, 426–7, 431–2
  metadata, 248, 427–8, 447

bibliographies, 190–1, 218–19, 237, 243
  electronic publications in, 230–1
  organising, 224
  2-em rules, 107

billion, 166

Bills, 125, 226

binding, 485–90
  inner margins and, 316–17

bird emblems, 301

bird names, 131

birth dates, 177

bitmapped font description, 329

bits and bytes, 185–6

black and white photographs, *see* photographs

black fonts, 327

    see also bold fonts

blank pages, 237

bleeds, 237, 468–9

'blind', 60

blind embossing (blind blocking), 483

blinking buttons, 311–12

block quotations, 100, 110, 113, 336

blocked paragraphs, 336

blue and gold, 301

blurbs, 235

boards, 475, 487, 488

body size, 327

bold fonts, 114, 149, 327, 333

    run-on headings in, 340

    in tables, 357

book-back gluing, 488

book reviews, citation of, 206–7, 212

booklets, brochures and pamphlets, 245, 431–2

    with CDs, 458, 460

books, 234–44

    citing, 189–203, 210–11, 216–17

    Coat of Arms, 294

    ISBNs, 423–4

    library deposit arrangements, 431–2

    see also copyright; editions; periodicals;
        publication components; publication titles;
        volumes

border fonts, 328

borders, 328, 379, 380–1

    cut-in illustrations, 382

    see also margins

botanical emblems, 301

botanical names, 130–1

bottom margins, 316, 337

boxed headings, 341

boxes, 45, 140–1, 341

BP, 169

bracketed serifs, 328

brackets, 99, 110–12, 154

    see also parentheses

branches within organisations, 220, 221, 292

brand names, 132–3

breadth, in hierarchical structures, 43

bridging words and phrases, *see* conjunctions

briefs, 25–8, 254–5

brightness of paper, 472

British practices, 83–5, 106, 115, 154

broadcasts, 146, 229, 456

    copyright material, 410, 415, 436

    disability groups, appropriate format for, 431

    reviews in periodicals, 206–7, 212

brochures, *see* booklets, brochures and pamphlets

browsers, 442

Budget or *budget*, 125

budgets, 11–12, 13

    production costs, 464, 465: paper, 475

    quotes and estimates, 30–1, 457, 464

building-in, 489

buildings, names of, 128

bulk, of paper, 473

bulleted lists, 141–4, 336

bulletin boards, citation of, 231

burst binding, 487

business addresses, on forms, 368

business names, *see* organisational names

but, 67, 72

buttons, 365, 367

    blinking, 311–12

bytes, 185–6

C (Celsius), 173

c (cent), 175

c. (circa), 197

© (copyright symbol), 413

C paper sizes, 477–8

Cabinet, 125

calendar, 129, 157

camera-ready copy, 464

cap height, 327

capital letters, 114, 118–35, 326, 327

    am and *pm*, 172

    after colons, 100

    compound adjectives containing, 93

    Deaf, 61

    decorative initials, 328

    dot-point series, 142, 143

    ethnic group names, 56**s**, 57, 58

    handwritten responses on forms, 368

    in headings, 154, 338, 339, 340

    Hon., 509

    in index headings, 279

    in organisational names, 81

prefixes before, 90

readability and legibility, 331

roman numerals, 169

shortened forms, 152–3: *see also* acronyms;
    initialisms

song titles, 146

stand-alone lists, 144

table items, first letter of, 357: when not
    followed, 178

capital letters in citations, 190

    foreign titles, 200, 205

    legislation chapters, parts, divisions and
        subdivisions, 226

captions, 45, 379

    full stops in, 97

    when illustrations sideways (landscape), 382

    type size, 330

cardinal numbers, *see* numbers

cars, 147, 200, 204

cartoons, 383**s**

cascading style sheets, 330, 450–1

case binding, 488–9

case making, 489

casebound books, *see* hardcover books

casing-in, 489

casual scripts, 328

catalogue numbers, 146, 201, 426

cataloguing-in-publication (CiP) data, 426–7

CD-ROMS, *see* portable media

CE, 169

cells in on-screen tables, 349, 352

censorship, 419–20

centred layouts, 319, 335

    tables and, 353, 354

cents, 174, 175

centuries, 129, 169–70

chancellors, 518

change management, 13–14, 31, 494

change of corporate identity, 293, 425

changes made after indexing starts, 273

changes made during editing, 263, 264

chapters, 40, 209, 241–2

    authors' copyright, 411

    in citations, 202

    in legislation, 226

    offprints, 500

    references in running text to, 135

    titles, 113

aracter dividers on forms, 368
aracter formatting for digital conversion, 446
arts and graphs, 379, 393–8, 431
  see also maps; tables
eck boxes, 365, 367
ecklists prepared by editors, 258
emical (colour) proofs, 467, 481–2
emicals, 131–2
ief ministers, 512
ildren, 62
inese names, 58
oking and spreading, 470
oreography, *see* dramatic works
oropleth maps, 400–1
hristian name', 58
ronological arrangement in in-text citations, 193, 194
P data, 426–7
rcular screens, 385
ation–sequence (citation–order, Vancouver) system, 190–1, 215–18
ations, 187–232
  editorial tasks, 259
  in tables, 348
J, 227
arifications, enclosing in text, 99, 100, 106, 110–11
arity, 38, 64–5, 102
  editorial tasks, 257
  hyphens used for, 88–90, 92
  passive constructions, 55
  in tables, 347–51
asses, botanical/zoological, 130
assics, references to, 228–9
assification of publications, 419–20
auses, 64–5, 67
  punctuation, 99–104
  relative, 75
  see also words and phrases
ergy, 515
p art, 384
osed questions, 363, 366–7
uster column headings, 348, 349, 353
ustering, 351–3, 382
MYK (four-colour process), 388–90, 469
•-, 89
at of Arms, 293–8
ated papers, 471, 472

co-authored works, *see* multi-author works
coined words or phrases, 114
collating and gathering, 488
collective nouns and names, 71, 82
colloquialisms, 52–3, 114, 122
colons, 99–101, 106, 177
  dot-point series, 142
  quotation marks and, 115
  spacing after, 117
  in time expression, 172, 173
  see also semicolons
colour, 310, 343, 387–90
  in background, 380–1
  bar codes, 426
  Coat of Arms, 294–5
  digital illustration, 383–4
  form response areas, coding using, 369
  halftones, 383–7, 391, 472
  high-white papers, 472
  multicolour offset printing, 479
  prepress, 468–70
  in tables, 379, 352–3
  tone and, 314
  type in, 341–3
  visual attitude, 378–9
colour control bars, 469
colour palettes, 292, 379
colour proofs, 467, 481–2
colour separations, 388–9, 469
colour slides, 392
colours
  corporate, 292, 465
  flags, 299–300
  heraldic, 301
  for marking errors on proofs, 266
  national, 300–1
column graphs, 394, 396
column headings, 348–9, 350–1, 353, 357
column span of cells, 349
column width (measure), 331–2, 354–5
comb binding, 486, 490
combs on forms, 368
comic strips, 399
commas, 101–5
  in citations, 191: as superscripts, 215–16
  direct speech after, 100
  after *e.g.* and *i.e.*, 155
  with *however*, 74–5

  in indexes, 282–3
  in legislation, not used to separate year, 224
  with numbers, 105, 176, 177
  after parentheses, 111
  postnominals and, 158
  quotation marks and, 115
  subjects linked by 'quasi-coordinators', 71
comments, enclosing in text, 99, 100, 106, 110–12
  see also cross-references
commercial terms, 132–3
commissioned works, 377, 412
commissioning bodies, *see* sponsoring bodies
committee reports, 220
common nouns, *see* nouns
Commonwealth, 124
Commonwealth Coat of Arms, 293–8
Commonwealth identifiers, 293–301
Commonwealth Parliamentary Papers Series, 221–2, 432
Commonwealth publications, *see* government publications
Commonwealth records, 222
Commonwealth Star, 294
communication strategy, 5–12, 500
comp., comps, 195–6, 201
compact disks, *see* portable media
company names, *see* organisation names
comparative adjectives, 68, 73, 92
comparisons, 68, 73, 92
  data in tables, 351
  between ethnic groups in Australia, 58
  involving numbers, 168
compass points, 157
compilations, 410
compilers, 238
  in citations, 195–6, 201–2
completeness of document, editorial tasks to ensure, 259
complex subjects, agreement with verbs, 71–2
compliance indexes, annual reports, 272
components of publications, *see* publication components
compound subjects, agreement with verbs, 71
compound words, 90–3, 94, 108
comprehension, 37–8
comprehensive editing, 254–6, 257
compressed fonts, 327
compression of images, 402–3
computer bits and bytes, 185–6

computer databases, 232, 271, 410, 427
  see also Internet
computer publications, *see* electronic publications
computer screens, 386, 388, 443
computer software, *see* software
computer terms, 133
concept testing of forms, 372
conciseness, 54
'Conclusion', 140
concrete nouns, *see* nouns
condensed fonts, 327
conditional statements, 76–7
conference proceedings, 207–8, 213, 218
  indexes, 279–80
conformity, proofreading tasks to ensure, 261
conjunctions, 45, 67, 68–9
  in dot points, 144
  however, 74–5, 101
  starting linked clauses, 101
  starting sentences, 72–3
  see also 'and'
conjuncts, 68–9, 72
connecting scripts, 328
connectors and arrows, on forms, 364, 370, 371
consistency, 259
  in imagery selection, 378–80
consonants, 72, 94
constellations and stars, 132
consultants' reports, citing, 220–1
contempt, 419
content development, 14–15, 22–4, 36–186
  electronic publications, 448–52
  see also authors and authoring bodies; editing
contents lists, 236, 240
contents outline, 14–15
context and patterning, 37
contextual information, 247**s**
contoured cut-in illustrations, 382
'contract' proofs, 467
contractions, 151, 152, 155, 156
  Dr, 517
  with full stops, 154, 225
contractors, 25–31
  copyright and, 411, 412
contrast, 314, 341–2, 387
  textual, 136–49
  see also fonts; headings
contrasting expressions, introducing, 99

conversion of documents, 444–8
coordinate clauses, 102
coordinating conjunctions, 67, 68–9
  'quasi-coordinators', 71
  starting sentences, 72
  see also 'and'
copy
  for editing, 263
  for indexing, 273–4
  for printing, 463–4, 479
copy editing, 256–60
copy verification, proofreading tasks to ensure, 261
copyholders, 262
copyright, 409–17
  acknowledgment stipulations, 32
  Australian Aboriginal flag, 299
  Coat of Arms, 293, 294**s**
  editors' responsibilities, 267–8
  image manipulation, 393
  royal identifiers, 300
Copyright Act 1968, 409–17, 431
Copyright Agency Limited, 416, 436
Copyright Amendment (Moral Rights) Act 2000, 417
copyright collecting societies, 415, 416, 436
Copyright (International Protection) Regulations, 411
copyright licences, 415
copyright (reverse of title) pages, 236, 238–9, 420
corporate colours, 292, 465
corporate identity, 291–3, 316
corporate identity manuals, 293
corporate typefaces, 292
'correct' spelling, 79
correspondence
  dates in, 170
  forms of address, 509–10
  letters of transmittal, 236, 239
  see also postal addresses
costs, *see* budgets
councillors, 514
count nouns, 69
country codes used in URLs, 429
country names, *see* geographical names
court, contempt of, 419
court reports and court cases, 226–8, 415, 419
court judges, 515–16
covers, 234–5, 238, 304–5, 475
  booklets, brochures and pamphlets, 245
  periodicals, 246

creators, *see* authors
credit card numbers, on forms, 368
'crest', 294
criminal cases, citation of, 227
criteria, 82
critical path diagrams, 398
cropping, 391
cross-references, 46
  in indexes, 275, 281, 282, 283
  proofreading tasks, 261
  to publication components/elements, 135
  in reference lists, 221
  shortened forms in, 159
  see also in-text citations
Crown, 125
Crown copyright, 416
CRS System, National Archives of Australia, 222
CSS, 450–1
cultural diversity, 55–62
cultural periods, 129, 169–70
currency, 174–5
curriculum vitae, 81**s**
custom buttons, 365
cut-in illustrations, 382
cyclones, 132

d (pence), 175
dagger (†), 208
dames, 508, 511, 515, 518
dangling participles, 74
dashes, 106–9
  see also hyphens
data, 81
data entries in tables, 351, 353–4
data systems, dates in, 171–2
databases, 232, 271, 410, 427
date of edition, 196
  classical works, 228, 229
date of publication
  author–date system, 189, 192–99, 201, 206
  classical works, 228
  in copyright line, 413
  documentary-note system, 210, 212
  legal authorities, 227
  see also multiple works, citation of
date of recording, 229
date of viewing web site, 230
date of web site creation/last revision, 230

dates, 170–1
  of birth, 177
  on forms, 368
  in legislation, 224
  at line ends, 94
  spans of figures, 108
  after species names, 131
day of publication, 197
days of week, 129, 157
deaf people, 61, 431
death, legal rights and, 412, 413, 417, 418
death dates, 177
debossing, 483
decades, 170
decimal fractions and decimal points, 167, 173, 174–5
decimal multiples and submultiples of SI units, 181–2
decorative initials, 328
deductive patterns of writing, 39–40
defamation, 418–19
default leading, 333, 334
defence force, 158, 516–17
defining clauses and phrases, 75, 102–3, 104
definite article (the), 69, 147
  initial, in publication titles, 134, 145: legislation, 224, 278
  treatment in indexing, 278
definitions in text, enclosing, 110
degrees, academic, 517–18
degrees, temperature, 173–4
deities, 127
delegated legislation, 125, 225–6
demonstrative pronouns, 70
departmental editions, 222
deposit of library materials, 431–2
depth in hierarchical structures, 43
depth of text, 337
descenders, 327, 332
description of project, 26
descriptive imagery, 376–7
descriptors, see adjectives and adjectival phrases
design, 15–17, 24, 288–405, 420
  briefs, 27
  editorial input to, 268–9
designers, 20, 22, 23, 24, 239
determiners, 69
diagrams, 377, 397–9
  see also graphs and charts; maps; tables

dialogue, 100, 113
  see also direct speech
dictionaries, 79, 80
  citation of entries, 199, 213
Didot point system, 325
diecutting, 483–4
diestamping, 483
digital colour proofs, 467
digital conversion, 444–8
digital illustration, 383–4
digital image files, 392
digital printing, 481–2
digital publications, see electronic publications
diplomats, 514–15
direct questions, 98, 100
direct speech, 98, 112–13, 121
  introducing, 100
  shortened forms in, 154
  see also quotations
direction, in design, 314
disability, people with, 60–1, 330, 428–31, 451–2
  'alt' and 'title' attribute, 451–2
Disability Discrimination Act 1992, 428
disclaimers, 420–1
  this manual's, 409
discrimination, see inclusive communication
diseases, 132
disks, see portable media
display titles, 97, 154
display typefaces, 328
distance, expressions of, 108
distance, measurement of, see measurement
distributors' names, 246
diversity, 55–62
  see also disability, people with
divisions and branches within organisations, 220, 221, 292
Doctor, 517
document completeness, editorial tasks to ensure, 259
documentary-note system, 208–15, 219
  electronic publications, 230–1
  films, programs etc., 229
dollars and cents, 174–5
domain names, 428, 429
dot density maps, 400
dot graphs, 394, 396
dot leaders, 354, 367

dot points, 141–4, 336
dots, see full stops
dots per inch, 385, 386
double-indexing, 283
double-page spreads, 310, 355–6
double quotation marks, 112, 116, 204
doubt, expressions of, 98
doubtful dates of publication, 197
dpi, 385, 386
draft documents, see copy
dramatic works, 113, 146, 228
  moral rights, 417
  reviews in periodicals, 206–7, 212
  see also copyright
drawing for reproduction, 383
drawings (works of art), 146, 410, 412, 417
drop shadow borders, 379
drugs, 132
dubious dates of publication, 197
dummies, 485s
duotones, 389
duplicated material, 232
  see also copyright
dust jackets, 235, 294, 489
DVDs, see portable media
dyeline proofs, 467
dynamic web documents, 250

e- (electronic), 90
-e- or -ae-, 83
-e- or -oe-, 84
-eable or -able, 83
EANs, 425–6
earth or Earth, 132
ed., eds, 195, 201
-ed past tense form, 82–3, 84
editing, 14–15, 252–69
  assessing quality of, 30
  briefs, 27, 254–5
  scheduling, 23–4, 254–5
editions, 235
  in citations, 195–6, 201
  ISBNs, 424
  prefaces or introductions for, 241
editorial style sheets, 15, 264–5
editors, 20, 23, 29, 239
  corrections made by, 266
  names, 235: in citations, 195–6, 201–2

educational purposes, reproduction done for, 414–15

effective communication, 53–5

effectiveness, criteria of, 12

effects screens, 385

e.g., 155

-eing or *-ing*, 83–4

elderly, 62

electronic indexing and indexes, 272, 280, 281, 283, 455–6

electronic mail, *see* email

electronic publications, 7, 8–10, 246–51, 440–61
  accessibility, 430–1
  boxes and side panels, 141
  briefs, 27–8
  citation methods, 230–1, 232
  clip art not recommended, 384
  Commonwealth standards, 427–8, 433
  contents outline, 14–15
  copyright material, 410, 413, 414, 415
  copyright wording recommended, 413
  editorial tasks, 258, 259, 261
  forms, 362, 365, 367, 370
  headings, 138, 339**s**
  international numbering, 424, 425
  layout, 311–12, 313, 316, 317: white space, 319–20
  library deposit arrangements, 431, 432
  metadata, 248, 427–8, 447
  record keeping, 433
  notes, 209
  paragraphs in, 336
  scheduling, 23, 24
  storyboards, 398–9
  structuring for readers, 38–9, 40, 41–3
  tables, 349, 350, 352, 355, 356, 357
  testing, 453–5, 495
  text, 343: depth, 337
  typography, 324–5, 330, 342, 343
  see also Internet; navigation; portable media; software; web sites

electronic publishing teams, 20–1, 23, 29

electronic-rights management information, 414

electronic tools, *see* software

elements of publications, *see* publication components

elements of statement, expressions sharing, 104–5

ellipsis points, 110

em rules, 106–7

em spaces, 330

emails, 90**s**
  addresses, 112: on forms, 368
  citation method, 231

email lists, citation of, 231

embargoes, 433

embellishment, 482–4

emblems, 291–2, 301
  publishers, 238
  use of Coat of Arms with other, 295
  see also logos

embossing, 472, 483

-ement or *-ment*, 84

emotions, expressions of, 98

emphasis, 43–6, 136–49
  coloured type, 341–3
  ironic, 114
  see also fonts; headings

employment, 62
  copyright and, 411–12, 416
  occupational titles, 59–60

en rules, 106, 107–9, 177

en spaces, 330

enclosures, 244

encyclop(a)edia, 83

encyclopedias, 272, 317
  citation of entries, 199, 213

end of book, *see* endmatter

end of chapters, endnotes placed at, 209

end of copyright, 412–13

end of lines, 93–4, 330, 336
  see also settings

end of pages, 337–8

end of sentences, 189
  with prepositions, 69, 77
  see also exclamation marks; full stops; question marks

endmatter, 41, 209, 241, 237, 242–3
  see also bibliographies; indexing

endnotes, 209, 237

endorsement, implied, 414**s**

endpapers, 235, 487, 488

English as a second language, 50, 52, 56

English grammar, *see* grammar

English language styles, 51–3, 431

engraving, 483

enlargement of illustrations, 391

entry and exit sequences of web sites, 247

environmental reports, 50

episodes of radio/television series, 146

epithets, 122

eq., eqs, 194

equality of language, 54

equations, in-text citations, 194

-er, 68

eras, 129, 169

error analysis, forms, 362

errors on proofs, marking, 266
  see also proofreading

-es plural forms, 81

-ess, 60

essay titles, 113

-est superlatives, 68

estimates and quotes, 30–1, 457, 464

et al., 193, 216

et seq., 282

etc., 155

ethnic groups, 56–8, 122–3

euro, 175**s**

evaluation, 496–9
  forms, 362–3, 373
  see also testing

event names, 129

ex-, 89

ex parte, 227

exact access schemes, 444

exclamation marks, 98–9, 117
  other punctuation with, 107**s**, 110, 111, 115–16
  superscripts placed after, 209, 215

exclusive copyright licences, 415

'Executive summary', 241

exit sequences of web sites, 247

expanded fonts, 327

expert sets, 326

expiry date, on forms, 368

explanation and amplification, punctuation introducing, 99, 100, 106, 110–11

exploded diagrams, 398

extended fonts, 327

extrabold and extralight fonts, 327

eye movement patterns, 310–11

f., 159, 282

'facing page ...' , 244

facsimile and telephone numbers, 330, 368

factual accuracy, responsibility for, 267
Fahrenheit scale, 173
fair dealing, 414–15
families, botanical and zoological, 130
family names, 58
    authors with same, 195, 196
    on forms, 368, 371
    particles in, 121–2, 278
fax and telephone numbers, 330, 368
feathered borders, 379
federal or *Federal*, 124
    see also 'Commonwealth'
Federation Star, 294
feedback, 497–9
fees and prices, 30–1
feminine and masculine forms, 58–60
    see also modes of address
'fever charts', 395
fewer, 73
ff., 159, 282
field books, 472–3
figures, see illustrations; numbers
file formats, 449
file names, URLs, 429
file structures, 448**s**
film, see moving images
filter questions, 366, 370
final proof, 467–8
finance (currency), 174–5
    see also budgets
financial information, see tables
fine fonts, 327
finish, of paper, 472
finite clauses, 67
first citations, documentary-note system, 210–13
first letters
    column items, in tables, 357
    words, indefinite articles preceding, 72
first lines, 336, 337–8
    see also start of sentences
'first name', 58
first pages, 337
    booklets, brochures and pamphlets, 245
    periodicals, 246
first word
    index headings and subheadings, 277–9
    publication titles, 134, 145: legislation, 224
    see also alphabetical arrangement; start of
        sentences

fixed costs, 464
flags, 298–300
flaring, 343
flat plans, 470
flatbed scanners, 389
flexibility of paper, 474
floating hyphens, 93
floral emblems, 301
flow charts, 397–8
fluorescent colours, 390
flush left, 334, 335, 353, 357
flush right, 334, 335, 353
focus, in writing, 40–1, 54–5
focus groups, 362–3, 497
foil blocking (foil stamping), 483
-*fold*, 90
fold-out brochures and pamphlets, 245
fold-out pages, 244, 355
folding, 488
folding strength of paper, 474
folios, see page numbers
the following, 99
'following pages …', 244
fonts, 236–7, 326, 327, 330
    cascading style sheets, 330, 450–1
    maps, 400
    punctuation marks, 116
    see also bold fonts; italics; typefaces
foot (bottom) margins, 316, 337
footers, see page headers and footers
footnotes, 209, 330
foredge margins, 316
foreground–background interaction, in design, 320,
    341–2
foreign legislation, 225, 411
foreign names, 58, 80, 120
    beginning with lower-case letter, starting
        sentences with, 121
    treatment in indexing, 278
foreign publication titles, citation of, 200, 204, 205,
    229, 218
foreign publishing houses, 203
foreign words and phrases, 148–9
    capital letters, 120
    plural forms, 81–2
    treatment in indexing, 278, 280
    see also Latin abbreviations
'forename', 58

forewords, 236, 239
    citation method, 198
formal agreement, grammatical, 67, 71–2
formal register, 51, 52, 65–6
formal statements and speeches, introducing, 100
format, 325, 334–7
    'published edition', 410, 413
    text tables, 357
formations, military, 158
forms, 359–73
forms of address, see modes of address
forthcoming publications, 197
forward slashes, 109, 171
four-colour process, 388–90, 469
four-digit numerals, 176
fractions, 167
frames, 308
France, 120, 166, 325
    loan words from, 82, 149
free-form cut in illustrations, 382
free-form text, 335
Freedom of Information Act 1982, 417
frequency of time, 173
from, en rules not used in spans following, 177
from … to, 109
front bench and *front bencher*, 125
frontispiece, 238
full stops, 97
    abbreviated journal titles without, 205
    with brackets, 111
    in citations, not used between initials, 190
    in dates, 171
    decimal points, 167, 173, 174–5
    dot-point series, 142–3
    with quotation marks, 115–16
    superscripts placed after, 209, 215
    Vancouver system, 216
    see also exclamation marks; question marks
full stops, and shortened forms, 152–3
    am and *pm*, 172
    contractions, 154, 225
    e.g. and *i.e.*, 155
functionality testing, 259, 494
future generations, access for, 431–2

galley proofs, 466
gamut, 387
ganging up, 465

gathering and collating, 488

gender inclusiveness, 58–60

generic expressions, 87

   ethnic groups, 56

   organisational names, 123–5

   personal titles, 126

   publication titles, 145

   topographical features, 128

'generic masculine', 59

genus names, 130, 131

geographical names, 127–8

   apostrophes not used in, 86

   common words derived from, 123

   connecting two used adjectivally, 108, 109

   plural forms, 82

   shortened forms, 155–7

   spelling, 80

   treatment in indexing, 278

   see also maps; place of publication

geological names, 132

German practices, 120, 171

gerunds, 70

get passive constructions, 73–4

ghosted images, 380

GIF (Graphics Interchange Format), 449

given names, 58

   on forms, 368, 371

global replacements, 264

gloss-coated paper, 472

glossaries, 41, 237, 243

gluing, book-back, 488

gods, 127

gold and blue, 301

gold and green, 300–1

government identifiers, 293–301

government or *Government*, 124

government publications, 220–3, 431–3

   Crown copyright, 416

   see also parliamentary publications; standards

government terminology, 123, 124–7

Governor-General, 510–11

governors of states, 511

grain direction, paper, 474

grammage, 473

grammar, 54–5, 63–77

   different registers, 52–3

   see also punctuation; spelling

grammar checkers, 263

grammatical contractions, 151, 155

graphic design, *see* design

graphic file formats, 449

graphs and charts, 379, 393–8, 431

   see also maps; tables

Greek loan words, 82

green and gold, 300–1

greetings, expressing in writing, 98

greyscale, 388, 389

grids, 312–18

   illustrations and, 381–2

   tables narrower and wider than, 354–6

group row headings, 349

grouping and proximity, in design, 318

GSC, 389

gsm, 473

hairline fonts, 327

half-Canadian binding, 486, 487

half-title pages, 236, 238

   for parts of publication, 237, 241

halftones, 383–7, 391, 472

hand stipple, 383

handicap, *see* disability, people with

handwriting, on forms, 367–8

hanging hyphens, 93

hanging indents, 336

hanging participles, 74

Hansard, 222, 419

hard spaces, 330

hardcover books, 235, 238, 488–9

   placement of Coat of Arms, 294

hardware names, 133

Hart, John, 119

Harvard system, *see* author–date system

hash sign (#), 208

he, 58–9

head margins, 316

headbands, 489

headers, *see* page headers and footers

headings, 137–40, 338–41

   capital letters and, 154, 338, 339, 340

   colours used for, 379

   first line of text following, 336

   on forms, 370

   full stops and, 97, 154

   in indexes, 274, 277–81, 282–3

   note identifiers in, avoid, 209

   pages not to end with, 337

   in tables, 348–9, 350–1, 353, 357

hearing impairments, people with, 61, 431

her, 58–9

Her Excellency, 510–11, 514–15

Her Honour, 525

Her Honour the Administrator, 511

heraldic colours, 301

hexadecimal colour descriptors, 388

hi-lo graphs, 397

hierarchical structures, 43

   see also headings

HiFi colour, 389–90

high commissioners, 514–15

high-white papers, 472

higher education degrees, 517–18

highlighting, *see* emphasis

him and *his*, 58–9

His Excellency, 510–11, 514–15

His Honour, 525

His Honour the Administrator, 511

historical periods, 129, 169–70

HMAS, 147

holidays, 129

home pages, 248, 249

homonyms, 80, 280, 456

the Honourable, 509, 511, 512, 515

honours, *see* personal titles, honours and awards

hopefully, 74

horizontal measurements, typographical, 325

horizontal rules in tables, 352

House of Representatives, 125

   Votes and Proceedings, 221, 222

house style, 258–60

however, 74, 101

hue, 387

humanities style, *see* documentary-note system

humorous words and phrases, 114

hurricanes, 132

hybrid images, 393

hybrid publications, 482

hypertext and hyperlinks, 46, 309, 414, 451–2

Hypertext Mark-up Language (HTML), 388, 446, 45

hyphens, 88–94

   compass points, 157

   consecutive lines ending with, 336

   non-decimal fractions, 167

   with numbers, 90, 93, 176

   pages not to end with, 337

   rag zones, 334, 335

hypothetical statements, 76–7

plural form, 81, 82
 id., 214
 ns, 326
, 214, 215
eas and information, protection of, 410, 420
entity, 10, 290–301, 316, 465
 ., 155
 s plural form, 81
 strated graphs, 397
 stration guides, 258
 stration titles, 379, 382
 see also captions
 strations and artwork, 374–405
 CD-ROM printed components, 458, 460–1
 converting from print to screen, 445
 graphic file formats, 449
 indexing, 282
 notes to, 208: Vancouver system, 216
 paragraphs not split by, 337
 prepress, 468–9
 proofs, 467
 shortened forms used in, 156
 in tables, 349
 see also colour; logos
 strations, lists of, 236, 240–1
 strators, 24, 32, 238, 239
 age and sound libraries, 402
 age buttons, 365
 age compression, 402–3
 age maps, 309
 agery, see illustrations
 ages of Australia, 301s
 migrants, 50, 56, 58
 perial measurements, 186, 519–20
 plied endorsement, 414s
 plied lines, 315
 plied shape, 315
 portance, colour indicating, 343
 position, 470
 print (reverse of title) pages, 236, 238–9, 420
 prints, 238, 239, 246
 press publications, 197
 -text citations, 189, 192–9
 electronic documents, 230, 231
 government publications, 220
 see also cross-references
 -text citations, citing, 198–9
 -text note identifiers, 209–10, 215–16

inclusive communication, 48–62
 see also disability, people with; modes of
  address
incompleteness, see omissions
indecision, indicating in writing, 110
indefinite articles (a, an), 69, 72, 109
 initial, in publication titles, 134, 145: legislation,
  224, 278
 with shortened forms, 72, 154
 treatment in indexing, 278
indefinite pronouns, 65–6, 76
indention
 indexes, 274
 lists, 336, 337
 paragraphs, 336
indexers, 21, 23, 30, 239
 editors and, 269
indexing and indexes, 24, 97, 237, 270–84
 briefs, 28
 by search engines, 455–6
Indigenous Australians, 56, 57
 flags, 299–300
indigenous peoples, 57
indirect questions, 98
indirect speech, 98, 113, 114
inductive patterns of writing, 39–40
infinitive verbs, 70, 76
informal register, 51, 52–3
information and ideas, protection of, 410, 420
information architecture, 22, 23, 268, 444, 448
 see also design
information hyperlinks, 451–2
Information Privacy Principles, 418
information retrieval devices, 272, 280, 455–6
 contents lists, 236, 240
 site maps, 309
 see also cross-references; hypertext; indexing
infringement of copyright, 414–15
-ing or -eing, 83–4
-ing participle, 70
initialisms, 72, 153, 154, 157, 169–70
 MP, 513
 plurals, 159
 in postal addresses, 156
 see also acronyms
initials, 158
 in citations, 191, 192, 195, 199, 201–2:
  documentary-note system, 219
 at line ends, 94

ink-jet printers, 481–2
inline styles, 450
inner margins, 316–17
inner rules, 352
inserting, 243–4, 470
inside back covers, 235, 244
inside front covers, 235
institutional names, see organisational names
instructions, on forms, 369–70, 371
intaglio printing processes, 483
integrity check, 261
integrity of authorship, 417
intellectual disability, people with, 61, 431
intellectual property, 409–17, 420
 see also copyright
intensity of light, 388
International Electrotechnical Commission prefixes,
  185–6
International Organization for Standardization, 178
international paper sizes, 476–8
International Standard Book Numbers (ISBNs),
  423–4, 425–6
International Standard Serial Numbers (ISSNs),
  424–6
International System of Units, 178–82, 184
Internet, 133, 455–6
 accessibility, 430–1
 offensive content, 420
 'web manager'/'web master', 60
 see also electronic publications; emails
Internet addresses, see URLs
Internet or internet, 133
interpolations, see comments
interrogation points, see question marks
interviews, for form testing, 362
intranet publications, 433
introductions, 140, 237, 241
 contributed by someone other than author,
  citing, 198
 to indexes, 282
ironic emphasis, 114
ISBNs, 423–4, 425–6
-ise or -ize, 84
islands, see geographical names
ISO, 178
 paper sizes, 476–8
isolated headings, 138
ISSNs, 424–6
issue numbers of journals, 205

Italian loan words, 82
italics, 145–9, 114, 327, 333
    compound adjectives containing, 93
    elements normally in, in titles, 200, 204
    legal case titles, abbreviated, 227**s**
    letters of alphabet, plural references to, 88
    in maps, 400
    pluralising titles and words in, 82
    prefixes before expressions in, 90
    punctuation marks and, 116
    run-on headings in, 340
    in tables, 357
    Vancouver system, 216
itemised material, *see* lists
-*ize* or -*ise*, 84

J, 227
jacketing, *see* dust jackets
Japanese names, 58
jewel cases, 458, 461
JJ, 227
job advertisements, 62
joint authorship, *see* multi-author works
joint ownership or association, apostrophe
    showing, 87
journalists, works created by, 411
journals, *see* periodicals
Journals of the Senate, 221, 222
JPEG (Joint Photographic Experts Group), 449
judges, 515–16
judicial proceedings, 226–8, 415, 419
jurisdiction, when indication needed, 220, 225
just-in-time printing, 482
justified settings, 335, 338

kelvins (K), 173, 174
kerning, 327
keyed notes, 348, 349
keyword searching, 272, 280, 455–6
Kinetica database, 427
kings and queens, 169, 227, 300, 510
knights, 508, 511, 515, 518
Koori (Koorie) Aboriginal group, 57
Korean names, 58

-*l* or -*ll*, 84
labelling
    CDs, 458

images, 379–80, 382
    maps, 399–400
    navigation devices, 309
    photographs and transparencies, 392
Labor, 84
ladder style, 426
Lady, 508
laminating, 484
landscape format, 381 382, 476
    page numbers not printed, 237
    wide tables, 355
language, 48–62
    see also grammar; words and phrases
language editing, 257, 259
'language other than English', 56
languages and language groups, 55–6, 57, 58, 122
    Deaf people, 61
    see also foreign language words and phrases
large numbers, 166, 176
    of dollars, 174
    International Electrotechnical Commission
        prefixes, 185–6
    SI unit decimal multiples and submultiples,
        181–2
large print, 431
laser printers, 481
last line of paragraphs, 337–8
latex-impregnated papers, 472–3
Latin abbreviations, 155
    am and *pm*, 172–3
    bi-, 173
    in documentary-note system of referencing,
        214–15
    in in-text citations, 197
    in legal authorities, 227
    not recommended in indexes, 282
    sic, 99
Latin plural forms, 81–2
law reports and law cases, 226–8, 415, 419
law-making power, 409, 419
layout, 307–18
    conversion from print to screen, 447
    proofreading tasks, 261
    tables, 351–3
leader dots, 354, 367
leading (line spacing), 144, 331, 332–4
least, 68
lecture titles, 113

left alignment, tables, 353
    see also flush left
legal advice, 409, 414
legal authorities, 226–8, 415, 419
legal deposit, 431
legal documents, 120**s**
legal requirements, 182–3, 409–20
    age, 61
    disability access, 428
    editorial responsibilities, 267–8
    inclusiveness, 55
    record keeping, 433
    see also copyright
legibility, *see* readability and legibility
legislation, 125, 224–6, 415
length, *see* measurement
length of headings, 340–1
length of lines, 331–2, 334
length of on-screen sections, 42
length of paragraphs, 41
length of sentences, 41, 64–5, 101
less, 68, 73
letter-by-letter alphabetical arrangement, 189, 195,
    274
letter spacing, 327
letterpress, 480, 483–4
letters, *see* correspondence; postal addresses
letters of alphabet
    as appendix numbers, 242
    character dividers on forms, 368
    hyphenation (word division) and, 88–9, 94
    identifying works published in same year, 195
    indefinite articles before, 72
    itemised indented material, introducing, 141
    textual references to, 88, 148
    see also alphabetical arrangement
letters of transmittal, 236, 239
libel, 418–19
library-based services, 426–7
library catalogues, 271, 277**s**, 279
library deposit, 431–2
licences, copyright, 415
lieutenant-governors of states, 511
life-cycle costs, 12
ligatures, 326
light fonts, 327
    see also italics
light intensity, 388

limited-choice answers, on forms, 363, 366, 367
line and mechanical tint, 383
line breaks in headings, 340–1
line drawing and reproduction, 383
line ends, 93–4, 330, 336
   see also settings
line graphs, 394, 395–6
line length, 331–2, 334
line numbering, 355, 364, 370
line screens, 385
line spacing (leading), 144, 331, 332–4, 352
line thickness, 380
linear structures, 38, 42
lines, implied, 315
lines per inch, 386
linguistics, *see* language
lining, 489
lining numbers, 326
links, 46, 414, 451–2
   see also conjunctions; cross-references; navigation
lists (series of items), 141–4, 336
   display, 97, 154
   hanging indents, 336
   proofreading tasks, 261
   punctuation, 99–100, 101, 102, 142–3
lists of contents, 236, 240
lists of illustrations and tables, 236, 240–1
lists of references, *see* bibliographies; reference lists
lists of shortened forms, 41, 237, 243
te viewers, 443
teracy, 50
iterary works', 410
/ or -l, 84
an words, *see* foreign words and phrases
c. cit., 214, 215
cal geographical names, 128
cal government officials, addressing, 513–14
cation references in indexes, 275, 281–3
gos, 291–2, 301, 331
   copyright material, 410
   standard, for CD-ROMs, 458, 460
   see also emblems
ng poems, 146
ose-leaf binding, 486, 487, 490
ose-leaf publications, 209, 218, 244, 317
d mayors, 514

'LOTE', 56
lower-case letters, 331
   when questions are sentence fragments, 100
   regulation (unit of division), 225
   superscript note identifiers, 208
   see also capital letters
lpi, 386
-*ly*, 68, 92
lyrics, 410

m or *M* (millions), 174
M', 280–1
Mac, 122, 280–1
Macquarie dictionary, 80
magazine articles, citation of, 206, 212
magazines, *see* periodicals
maintenance of electronic documents, 456
majuscules, 119
males and females, 58–60
   see also modes of address
-*man*, 59–60
management, 4–17, 21–31, 416**s**, 492–501
managers, 21–2, 23
management plans, 13–14, 494
mandative sentences, 70
manipulation disabilities, people with, 61, 431
manipulation of images, 393
manuscripts and archives, 208, 222
   see also copy
maps, 399–401, 410
   library deposit arrangements, 431–2
   paper stock, 472–3
   shortened forms used in, 156
   see also geographical names
margins, 316–17
   long headings in, 341
   text in, 45, 140–1
mark-up languages, 449–52
market research, 497–8
marking up, 266
masculine and feminine forms, 58–60
   see also modes of address
masking, 391
mass, *see* measurement
mass, of paper, 473
mass nouns, 69, 73
-*master*, 60
master copies, 263

master disks, 457
master pages, *see* grids
mathematical relationships, 165
mathematical signs, 109, 177
maximal capitalisation, 134
maxlength, 365
mayors, 514
Mc, 122, 280–1
measure (column width), 331–2, 354–5
measurement, 165, 178–86
   graphs comparing area and volume, 394–5
   metric conversion table, 519–20
   paper, 473, 476–8
   temperature, 173–4
   typographical, 325, 330–1
   units, setting in tables, 350–1, 353
   see also resolution; time indicators and expressions
media, 82
media releases, 113, 207, 213
medial capitals, 122
medical literature, citation system for, 190–1, 215–18, 219
medical terms, 132
medium type, 327
members of parliament, 126–7, 509, 512–13
men and women, 58–60
   see also modes of address
-*ment* or -*ement*, 84
mental disabilities, 61
menus, 308, 365
Mesdames, 510
metadata, 248, 427–8, 447
metallic colours, 390
metaphoric imagery, 378
metric conversion table, 519–20
MHR, 513
microfilmed material, citation of, 232
micrometres (microns), 473
midnight, 172–3
migrants, 50, 56, 58
military, 158, 516–17
millions, *see* large numbers
minimal capitalisation, 134, 146, 190, 339**s**
minimum punctuation, 96**s**
minuscules, 119
ministers, 512–13
ministers of religion, 515

Miss, *Mrs* and *Ms*, 504
minor columns (side panels), 45, 140–1, 341
minus sign, 109
MLA, 513
mobility disabilities, people with, 61, 431
modern serifs, 328
modes of address, 127, 509–18
   see also personal titles, honours and awards
modes of delivery, 7–10
   see also electronic publications
modifiers, grammatical, *see* adjectives; adverbs
modifiers, in indexing, 280
modular design, 317–8
moiré, 386–7
monarchs, 169, 227, 300, 510
money, 174–5
   see also budgets
monitoring projects, 493–5
monitors, 386, 388, 443
monographic material, 423–4
   see also books
montages, 393
month of publication, 195, 197
months of year, 129, 157
moon or *Moon*, 132
moral rights, 417
more and *most*, 68
motivation of audience, 54
motor vehicle names, 147, 200, 204
mottos, 292
   see also logos
mountains, *see* geographical names
moving images, 311–12, 401, 402–3
   animated text, 343
   citations, 229
   copyright, 410, 412, 436
   disability groups, appropriate format for, 431
   exploded diagrams, 398
   moral rights, 417
   offensive material, 419–20
   reviews in periodicals, 206–7, 212
   standard industry logo, 458, 460
   titles, 146
   see also sound
MP, 513
MS, 155, 159
Ms, *Mrs* and *Miss*, 504
multi-author works, 256

bibliographies, placement of, 218
   citation, 193, 196, 209
   copyright, 411, 412, 413
   indexes, 279–80
   state or territory government co-authored works, 295
multicolour offset printing, 479
multi-column formats, 317, 334, 337
   indexes, 275
   side panels/columns, 45, 140–1, 341
multi-image pages, 381, 382
multimedia, *see* moving images; sound
multi-page spreads, 310, 355–6
multi-part sets of forms, 362
multi-volume works, *see* volumes
multiple-choice answers, on forms, 363, 365, 366, 367
multiple indexes, 272–3
multiple publishers, 203
multiple references to single work, 213–15
   legal authorities, 227
   legislation, 224
   Vancouver system, 215
multiple works, citation of
   author–date system, 193, 194–5
   documentary-note system, 209, 214
   Vancouver system, 215–16
Murri Aboriginal group, 57
musical compositions, 146
musical reviews, citations of, 206–7, 212
musical works, 410, 417, 431, 436

name–year system, *see* author–date system
names
   copyright owners, 413
   ethnic groups, 56–8, 122–3
   legal cases, 226–7
   see also geographical names; organisational names; personal names; titles
naming systems, 58
Namok, Bernard, 300
narrow fonts, 327
National Archives of Australia, 222
national colours, 300–1
national flag, 298–9
National Library of Australia, 426–7, 431–2
National Measurement Act 1960, 182
National Measurement Regulations, 182, 183

National Privacy Principles, 418
nationalities and ethnic groups, 56–8, 122–3
'native', 57
natural measure, 354–5
navigation and navigation systems, 17, 305–7, 308–9
   converting from print to screen, 445
   forms, 369–70
   hyperlinks, 46, 309, 414, 451–2
navigation bars, 308
n.d., 196
negative language, 54
negative text, 342
neither, 65
'NESB', 56
Net or *net*, 133
   see also Internet
new editions, *see* editions
new pages, *see* first pages
newsletters, 317, 465
newspaper articles, citation of, 197, 206, 212
newspaper titles, 134, 206
newspapers, 134, 145, 245–6
   journalists, copyright and, 411
nicknames, 114, 122
nipping, 488
no., 154
no author or authoring body, 197, 206
   documentary-note system, 212, 213
   government publications, 220
   Vancouver system, 218
no date, 196
no place of publication, 203
'no/yes' answers on forms, 363, 366–7
non-breaking spaces, 330
non-connecting scripts, 328
non-decimal fractions, 167
non-defining phrases and clauses, 75, 102–3, 104
'non-English speaking background', 56
non-exclusive copyright licences, 415
non-finite clauses, 67
non-linear structures, 38, 43
none, 65–6
noon, 172–3
nor, 65
North America, *see* American readers and practice
note identifiers, 208, 209–10, 215–16
notes, for non-citation purposes, 208–9
   see also table notes

notes system, *see* documentary-note system

notional agreement, grammatical, 67, 71, 72

noun phrases, 71–2, 87, 90–1

noun-plus-noun compounds, 91

noun-plus-verb compounds, 91

noun–verb transfers, 66

nouns, 69, 90–1
  agreement, grammatical, 67, 71–2
  capital letters, 119–20
  instead of pronouns, to avoid gender specificity, 59
  possession, 85–7, 153
  see also adjectives; names; pronouns

n.p., 203

number, shortened form of, 154

number (hash) sign (#), 208

numbers (numerals) and numbering, 69, 163–77, 326
  chapters and appendixes, 242**s**
  compound adjectives involving, 93
  on forms, 368, 370
  headings, 138
  in index headings, treatment of, 277
  itemised indented material, introducing, 141
  at line ends, 94
  lines: in forms, 364, 370; in wide tables, 355
  prefixes before, 90
  punctuation with, 103, 105, 108, 109, 176
  spacing with, 176, 177, 330
  superscript note identifiers, 208, 209–10, 215–16
  tables, 350: notes to, 208, 216
  see also measurement; page numbers; spans of figures

Nunga Aboriginal group, 57

Nyoongah (Nyungar) Aboriginal group, 57

obliques, 109, 171

observational studies, for forms, 363

occupational titles, 59–60

OCR, 329

-odd, 90

-oe- or *-e-*, 84

offensive material, 419–20

office-use fields, forms, 364

official positions, *see* personal titles, honours and awards

offprints, 500

offset lithography, 478–80

-ogue or *-og*, 84

old-style numbers, 326

older and younger people, 61–2, 330

omissions, punctuation indicating, 110, 151, 152, 154
  in bibliographies and reference lists, 107
  words or phrases common to more than one part of statement, 105
  see also shortened forms

on-demand printing, 482

on-screen publications, *see* electronic publications

op. cit., 214–15

opacity of paper, 474

open-ended questions, 363

operas, *see* dramatic works

'opposite page …', 241

optical character recognition, 329

optical vs physical centre, 319

opus numbers, 146

or, in dot points, 144

-or and *-our*, 84

order of book, 258

order of precedence, 504–8

orders, botanical and zoological, 130

orders, emphasising in writing, 98

ordinal dates, 171–2

ordinal numbers, 69, 93, 167, 169–71

Ordinances, 125, 224–5

organisation charts, 398

organisation of documents, *see* publication components; structuring documents

organisational authoring bodies, 220–3

organisational identity, 10, 290–301, 316, 465

organisational names, 120, 122, 123–5
  agreement with verb, 71
  changing: and corporate identity, 293; and ISSN, 425
  in legal cases, 226–7
  personal communication source affiliations, 199
  possessive forms, 86, 87, 153
  shortened forms in, 157–8
  spelling, 80–1
  treatment in indexing, 278
  see also publishers, citation of

organisational sub-entities, 220, 221, 292

originality, copyright and, 410

ornament fonts, 328

ornithological names, 131

orphans, 337–8

-our and *-or*, 84

outer margins, 316

outer rules, 352

output device resolution, *see* resolution

outside back covers, 235

overlapping images, 382

ownership of copyright, 411–12

p. (page), 194

p., not short for *per*, 184

Ⓟ (phonogram symbol), 413

packaging (CD-ROM cases), 426, 458, 460–1

page endings, 337–8

page headers and footers, 97, 445
  persistent navigation, 250

page layout, *see* layout

page measurements, 325

page numbers and numbering, 236–7
  booklets, brochures and pamphlets, 245
  converting from print to screen, 445
  externally sourced material, 242, 243
  illustrations printed with text, 240
  loose-leaf documents, 244
  periodicals, 246
  references in running text to, 135
  tipped-in pages, 241
  volumes, 244

page proofs, 466

page references, 206, 207
  author–date system, 194, 197, 203, 205
  documentary-note system, 214–15
  in indexes, 275, 281–3
  legal cases, 226

paintings, 146, 410, 412, 417, 436

pamphlets, *see* booklets, brochures and pamphlets

panes, 308

Pantone colour, 389, 390

paper, 31, 471–8

paper-based publications, benefits of, 7, 10

paper-based publications, conversion to screen, 444–7

paper binding, 485–7, 488–9

paper-making, 471

paper sizes, 476–8

papercover books, 234–5, 294

paragraphs, 40–1, 335–7
  formatting for digital conversion, 446
  index references to, 275
  in legislation, 226
  numbering, 138

parallel mark (II), 208
parallel structures
  associations between words, 108
  headings, 139–40
  itemised indented material, 141, 143
  in sentences, 65
parentheses, 110–11
  with em rules, 107
  indexes, use in, 280
  in-text citations in, 189, 192–9
  measurement unit symbols associated with table stub items, 353
  name and date after species name, 131
  places of publication distinguishing journals with same title, 206
  shortened forms, introducing, 161
parentheses within parentheses, 111
parenthetic expressions, punctuation separating, 104, 105, 106–7, 110–11
parliament or *Parliament*, 125
  contempt of, 419
  documents tabled in, 432–3
parliamentarians, 126–7, 509, 512–13
Parliamentary Debates (Hansard), 222, 419
Parliamentary Papers Series, 221–2, 432
  Coat of Arms design for, 296
parliamentary privilege, 419
parliamentary publications, 221–3, 419, 432–3
  Acts, 125, 224–6, 415
part title pages, 237, 241
participles, 70, 83
  compound adjectives involving, 92
  dangling or hanging, 74
  -ll- or *-l-*, 84
particles in family names, 121–2, 278
parts (publication component), 241–2
passim, 282
passing references, 276
passive structures, 54–5, 70, 73–4
passwords, 365
past participles, 70, 83, 84, 92
past subjunctive, 76–7
past tense, 70, 82–3
pastel colours, 390
pattern, in design, 315
patterning and context, 37
PDF files, 445, 447–8
p(a)ediatrician, 83

pen-and-ink drawing, 383
pence, 175
people, 55–62, 122–3
  see also modes of address; personal names
'people with a hearing impairment', 61
'people with a vision impairment', 60
per, 184
per cent or *percent*, 168**s**
percentages, 167–8
perfect binding, 485, 486, 489
perfection, 269
perforations, 484
periodical articles, 204–7
  copyright, 411, 415**s**, 420
  documentary-note system, 211–13, 214
  subtitles of, 100
  Vancouver system, 216, 217–18
periodical titles, 134, 145, 204–5
  ISSNs change when changed, 425
periodicals, 245–6
  Australian journals online, 427
  indexes, 272
  ISSNs, 424–6
  library deposit arrangements, 431–2
  modular design, 317
periods, *see* full stops
permanent papers, 474
permission to use copyright material, 415–16
persistent navigation, 250
-person, 60
personal communications, 199, 213
personal information, 417–18
personal names, 58, 121–2
  copyright owners, 413
  on forms, 368, 371
  nicknames, 114, 122
  plural forms, 82
  possessive forms, 86
  separating titles and affiliations from, 105
  after species name, 131
  see also authors and authoring bodies, citation of; initials; personal titles
personal pronouns, 58–9, 69
  capital letters, 127
  possessive, 77, 85
  plurals as singulars, 75–6
personal titles, honours and awards, 126–7, 504–18

  in direct speech, 121
  at line ends, 94
  possessive form, 87
  postnominals, 94, 105, 158, 505–8, 513, 517, 518
  separating from name, 105
  treatment in indexing, 280
personalisation (variable-data printing), 482
pH of paper, 474
photocopied material, 232
  see also copyright
photographers, 24, 32, 239
photographs, 377, 392–3
  bleeds, 468–9
  colours used for, 379
  copyright, 412
  duotones, 389
  ghosted images, 380
  graphic file formats, 449
  halftone reproduction, 384–6
phrasal verbs, 77
phrases, *see* words and phrases
phylum, zoology, 130
physical disabilities, people with, 60–1, 431
physical vs optical centre, 319
pi fonts, 328
picas, 325
picket-fence style, 426
picture fonts, 328
pie charts, 396
pilot testing, forms, 372–3
pixels, 325, 384–6, 443
pixels per inch (ppi), 386
place of publication, 203, 207
  periodicals with similar titles, 205–6
placement
  bar codes, 426, 460
  Coat of Arms, 294
  copyright information, 413
  disclaimers, 420
  illustrations, 337, 381–2
  in-text citations, 189
  in-text note identifiers, 209, 215
  international numbering, 424, 425
  periodical advertising, 245: citing articles split by, 206
  tables, 354, 356–7
  type, on forms, 371

placenames, *see* geographical names
'plain-cover' editions, 222
plain English, 53, 431
planets, 132
planning, 2–33
planographic printing processes, 478–80
plant emblems, 301
plant names, 130–1
plays, *see* dramatic works
plural nouns, 69, 81–2
    apostrophes, 85, 87–8
    organisations with same generic name, 123
    personal titles, 126
    shortened forms, 153, 154
    topographical features with same generic
        element, 128
    youths, 62
plural pronouns, 59, 65–6, 67, 85
    as singulars, 75–6
plural references to letters of alphabet, 88
plural verbs, agreement with subject, 65–6, 67,
    71–2
m, 172–3
PMS (Pantone) colour, 389, 390
poetry, 113, 146, 228, 410
point of view, in illustrations, 377–8
points (punctuation), *see* full stops
points (type sizes), 325, 330, 331
    disk label identifying details, 458
points of compass, 157
points of ellipsis, 110
polite requests, expressing in writing, 98
political and geographical designations, 127
politicians, 126–7, 509, 512–13
pop-up text, 357
popes, numerals in titles of, 167
pornography and violence, 419–20
Portable Document Format (PDF) files, 445, 447–8
portable media, 433, 457–61
    bar codes, 426
    clip art not recommended, 384
    disability groups, appropriate format for, 431
    international numbering, 424
    library deposit arrangements, 432
    replicators, 21, 23
    storyboards, 398–9
    see also moving images; sound
portals, 247**s**

portfolios and samples, assessing, 30
portrait format, 381
positive language, 54
possession, grammatical, 77, 85–7, 153
post binding, 486, 490
post-release evaluation, 496–9
    forms, 373
postal addresses, 156, 177
    on forms, 368, 371
postcode listings, 80
posters, 390
postnominals, 94, 105, 158, 505–8, 513, 517, 518
PostScript, 329
pounds, shillings and pence, 175
pp., 194
ppi, 386
pre-teenagers, 62
precedence, order of, 504–8
prefaces, 236, 241
    contributed by someone other than author,
        citing, 198
prefixed titles, 508–9
prefixes
    en rules with, 108
    hyphens with, 88–90, 94
    International Electrotechnical Commission
        prefixes, 185–6
    SI unit decimal multiples and submultiples,
        181–2
    time frequency expressions, 173
prejudice, *see* inclusive communication
preliminary pages, 236–7, 238–41, 243
    multi-volume works, 244
premiers of states, 512
prepositions, 69
    ending sentences, 77
    treatment in indexing, 278–9
prepress, 468–71
preprinting, 465
present participles, 70
present subjunctives, 70
preservation for future generations, 431–2
press check, 468
press proofs, 467–8
press releases, 113, 207, 213
pre-teenagers, 62
prices and fees, 30–1
primary audiences, 49–50

prime ministers, 512
printability of papers, 474
printed publications, benefits of, 7, 10
printed publications, conversion to screen, 444–7
printers, 21, 23, 31, 481–2
    imprints, 239, 246
printing, 24–5, 478–82
    briefs, 28
    converting documents to enable digital
        transmission for, 447–8
    preprinting, 465
    standards for tabled documents, 432
printing processes, 462–91
Privacy Act 1988, 417–18
private property names, 128
process charts, 397–8
process colour, 388–90, 469
processing requirements for forms, 361–2, 363, 366
production, *see* reproduction
production costs, *see* budgets
production specifications, 15, 17
professional qualifications, 518
professors, 518
programs, government, 125
    see also broadcasting; software
project description, 26
project evaluation, 496–9
    forms, 373
project management, 4–17, 21–31, 416**s**, 492–501
project managers, 21–2, 23
project records, 496–7
pronouns, 67, 69–70
    capital letters, 127
    possessive, 85
    see also personal pronouns
proofreading, 260–2, 264, 269, 521–7
    colour, 467
proofreading symbols, 266, 521–7
proofs, 465–8, 481–2
    colour-coding errors marked on, 266
proper nouns, *see* geographical names;
    organisational names; personal names
property names, 128
proportional symbol maps, 400
proprietary names, 132–3
protocols, government, 125
protocols, URLs, 429
proximity, in design, 318

543

pseudonymous works, 198
psychiatric problems, 61
pt, 330**s**
public domain material, 299, 300, 301
public events, names of, 129
public image (identity), 10, 290–301, 316, 465
public place names, 128
publication briefs, 25–8
publication components, 233–51
    citations, 194, 198
    notes referring to whole, 209
    order of book and illustration guide, 258
    references in running text to, 135
    see also chapters
publication management, 4–17, 21–35, 416**s**, 492–501
publication managers, 21–2, 23
publication plan, 4–17
    monitoring, 493–5
publication standards, *see* standards
publication-style indexing, 270–84
publication subtitles, 234, 238
    punctuation introducing, 100
publication titles, 234, 235, 238
    capital letters, 134
    on CD labels, 458
    displayed, 97, 154
    ISBNs and ISSNs, 423–6
    italics, 145, 191: when not, 191, 216
    legislation, 224–5, 278
    plural forms, 82
    in quotation marks, 113
    series, 201, 205, 238
    within titles, 200, 204
    Vancouver system, 216
    see also headings; table titles
publication titles, citation of, 191
    author–date system, 197, 200
    films, programs etc., 229
'published edition', 410, 413
published proceedings, citation of, 207, 213, 218
publisher numbers, 201, 426
publishers, citation of, 202–3, 206
    government publications, 220
publishers' imprints, 238, 246
publisher's prefix, ISBNs, 424
publishing skills, 19–20, 25, 29–30, 271
publishing standards, *see* standards

publishing team, 18–32
pull-down menus, 365
punctuation, 85–117
    abbreviated journal titles without, 205
    author–date system, 191, 194, 195
    in dates, 170, 171
    documentary-note system, 191
    lists, 99–100, 101, 102, 142–3
    with *however*, 74–5, 101
    in indexes, 277, 282–3
    in organisational names, 81
    proofreading tasks, 261
    with shortened forms, 151–3, 154, 155, 172
    stand-alone lists, 144
    superscripts and, 209, 215
    URLs, 429
    Vancouver system, 215–16
    see also apostrophes; commas; colons; full stops; parenthesis; quotation marks
punctuation marks with other punctuation marks
    brackets, 111
    ellipsis points, 110
    em rules, 107**s**
    full stops following abbreviations, 154, 155
    quotation marks, 115–16
purpose of publication, 6

quadrillion, 166
qualifications, 517–18
qualified privilege, 419
quality, 10, 30
quality control, 494–6
    see also testing
quantity, *see* measurement
quarter binding, 489
'quasi-coordinators', 71
The Queen, 227, 510
    royal identifiers, 300
queens, numerals in titles of, 169
question marks, 97–8, 117
    with other punctuation marks, 107**s**, 110, 111, 115–16
    superscripts placed after, 209, 215
questions, 98
    introducing, 100
    on forms, 363, 366–7, 370, 372
    responses to, 97
quotation marks, 110, 112–16
    compound adjectives containing, 93

elements in titles normally in italics, 200, 204
    episodes of radio/television series, 146
    prefixes before expressions in, 90
    titles in, 191
    titles not in, 216
quotations, 100, 113
    interpolations, 99, 111–12
    note identifiers, 209, 215
    omissions in, 110
    spelling, 80
    see also direct speech
quotations within quotations, 116
quotes and estimates, 30–1, 457, 464

R, 227
r., 225–6
RAAF, 154
radio, *see* broadcasts
radio buttons, 365, 367
rag papers, 474
rag zones, 334, 335
ragged (ranged) left, 334, 335
ragged (ranged) right, 334, 335, 357
ranged left–right text, *see* justified settings
ranks, military, 158
raster dots, *see* pixels
raster font description, 329
ratios, 177
re, in legal authorities, 227
readability and legibility, 36–47, 324–44
    indexes, 274
    tables, 347–58
readability indexes, 263
reader software, 443
readers and readership, 6–7, 49–50
    aids for context and movement, 305–7
    feedback from, 497–9
    foreign, 186, 280
    form respondents, 361, 362–3
    good design and, 303–4
    publications not effective in reaching, 500
    registers and, 51–2
    shortened forms and, 160
    type selection for, 323–4, 330
reading, 310–11
    on-screen, 16
    skills, 50
recommended retail price, 235

record keeping, 433
    project records, 494, 496–7
recto (right-hand) pages, 238, 241, 242
recycled paper, 475–6
reduction of illustrations, 391
reel-fed laser printers, 481
reference lists, 189, 192–208, 237, 243
    electronic publications in, 230–1
    government publications in, 220–3
    when legal authorities included, 226
    when legislation included, 224
    2-em rules, 107
    Vancouver system, 216–18
    see also bibliographies
references, *see* citations; cross-references;
    indexing
references from previous clients, 30
referencing, *see* citations
reflection of paper, 472
registered trademarks, 132–3
registers, 51–3
registration marks, 469
regrettably, 74
regular type, 327
regulation (unit of division), 225
Regulations, 125, 225–6
relative clauses, 75
relative pronouns, 70, 75, 77
release of publications, 495–6
relief printing processes, 480, 483–4
religious beliefs, and linguistic or ethnic groups, 58
religious days, 129
religious groups, 122
religious office holders, 515
repetition, in design, 315
reported speech, 113, 114
reprints, 201
reproduction and replication, 24–5, 382–93,
    440–91
    briefs, 28
    printing standards, 432
    replicators, 21, 23
    see also copyright
requests, expressing in writing, 98
research, for form design, 361–3
research or study, reproduction done for, 414–15
residual code, 447
resolution, 385, 386

digital image files, 392
image compression, 403
monitors, 386, 443
respondents to forms, 361, 362–3
response fields, forms, 363, 364, 365–9, 371
-ress, 60
restrictive clauses and phrases, 75, 102–3, 104
résumé, 149
retail price, recommended, 235
rev., 195, 201
reverse of half-title page, 236, 238
reverse of title page, 236, 238–9, 420
reversing, 342
    CD-ROM printed components, 458
    Coat of Arms design for, 297
    headings, 341
reviews in periodicals, citations of, 206–7, 212
revise proofs, 467
revisers, 238
    in citations, 195–6, 201–2
revisions of publications, 201, 500
    see also editions
rewriting and rewording, 256
RGB, 388
rhetorical questions, 98
right-hand pages, 238, 241, 242
The Right Honourable, 514, 515
The Right Worshipful, 514
ring binding, 486, 490
rivers, *see* geographical names
'rivers' (white spaces), 338
roll-overs, 309, 357
roman numerals, 168–9
    in dates, 171
    page numbers, 236–7, 238
roman type, 327
rotary printing machines, 480
round brackets, *see* parentheses
rounding and backing, 488–9
rows in tables, 348, 349, 351, 352–4, 355
royal identifiers, 300
royalty, 169, 227, 300, 510
rr., 225–6
rules
    on forms, 371
    in graphs, 394
    in tables, 352, 353
run-on headings, 340

run-on lists, 101, 102
runaround, 382
running heads, *see* page headers and footers

s. (section), 225
s (shilling), 175
-s plural form, 81, 82
    company names ending in, 71
-'s possessive form, 85–8, 153
-s' possessive form, 85, 86
saddle-stitching, 485, 486
Saint, 281
sample settings, 324
samples and portfolios, assessing, 30
sans serif typefaces, 327, 328, 331, 341
    leading (line spacing), 334
scale, in design, 314
scale bars, maps, 399
scaled questions, on forms, 367
scales of graphs, 394
scaling, 390, 391, 392
'scandalising', 419
scanners, 426
    colour separation, 388–9, 469
scattered references, indexing, 282
scattergrams, 396
schedules and scheduling, 11, 22–5, 254–5, 464
scientific writing, 81, 130–2, 164, 166
    Vancouver system, 190–1, 215–18, 219
scoring, 484
scraperboard, 383
screen-based publications, *see* electronic
    publications
screen layout, how read, 311–12
screen measurements, *see* pixels
screen-printing, 458
screens and screening, 384–7
scripts, 328, 341, 442**s**
scrolling menus, 365
sculptures, 146
search engines, 455–6
seasons, 129
sec., secs 194
second citations, documentary-note system,
    213–15
secondary audiences, 49–50
secondary sources, citations from, 198–9
Secretary's statement, 239**s**

section headings, on forms, 370
section mark (§), 208
section sewing, 486, 487
sections (printing), 470
sections of Acts, 225, 226
sections of publications, 40
 index references to, 275
 in-text citations, 194
 notes referring to whole, 209
 offprints, 500
 supplementary, 243–4
 see also references, 275, 283
 see references, 275, 283
self-covered booklets, brochures and pamphlets, 245
self-covered periodicals, 246
semicolons, 101
 dot-point series, 142
 in in-text citations, 194, 195
 quotation marks and, 115
 spacing after, 117
seminar proceedings, 207–8, 213, 218
Senate, 125
 Journals, 221, 222
Senators, 512
'senior', 62
sentence direction, abrupt changes in, 106, 107
sentences, 40–1, 64–5, 101
 mandative, 70
 within parentheses, 111
 punctuation, 95–117
 registers, differences between, 52
 see also end of sentences; clauses; start of sentences
separation, 342
 of colours, 388–9, 469
 good design, 304
sepia toning, 389
sequential–numeric (Vancouver) system, 190–1, 215–18, 219
sequential structures, 38, 42
series numbers, periodicals, 246
series of items, *see* lists
series titles, 201, 205, 238
serif typefaces, 327, 328, 331, 341
 leading (line spacing), 334
'set solid', 333

settings (justified or unjustified), 334–5, 338, 357
 table alignment, 354
sexes, inclusive treatment of, 58–60
 see also modes of address
shaded distribution maps, 400–1
shape, in design, 315
she, 58–9
s/he, 59
sheet-fed laser printers, 481
sheet-fed offset, 480
sheet-fed platen, 480
shillings, 175
ships, 147, 200, 204
shire presidents, aldermen and councillors, 514
short poems, 113
short sentences, *see* length of sentences
short titles, 145, 221
 Acts, 224
 legal cases, 227
 on spine, 235
 see also abbreviated titles
shortened forms, 104, 150–61
 Anzac, 129
 countries, 155–6, 175
 indefinite articles preceding, 72, 154
 in indexes, 280, 282
 in in-text citations, 191, 194, 194–7, 203: linking to reference list, 192, 221
 legislative units of division, 225
 lists of, 41, 237, 243
 migrants whose mother tongue is not English, 56
 in names, 280–1
 postnominals, 94, 105, 158, 505–8, 513, 517, 518
 pt, 330**s**
 time expressions, 157, 169–70, 172–3
 see also abbreviations; spelt-out terms; symbols
SI units, 178–82, 184
sic, 99
side column headings, 341
side panels, 45, 140–1, 341
side stitching, 317, 485
sideways illustrations, 382
sight impairment, people with, 60, 330, 431, 451–2
signature blocks, on forms, 368
significance, indexing concept of, 276
signposting information, *see* emphasis
'since', *see* subordinating conjunctions

single quotation marks, *see* quotation marks
singular nouns, *see* plural nouns
singular possessive forms, 85, 153
singular pronouns and plurals, 75–6
Sir, 508, 511, 515, 518
site date, 230
site maps, 309
size of images, 381–2
size of on-screen sections, 42
size of paper, 476–8
size of sentences, *see* length of sentences
size of type, *see* type sizes
sizing of Coat of Arms, 295
skills, 19–20, 25, 29–30, 271
slab serifs, 328
slander, 418–19
slang, 114
slashes, forward, 109, 171
slipcases, 489
small capitals, 172, 326, 340
so-called, 114
softcover books, 234–5, 294
software (computer programs), 16, 80, 263, 397, 382
 copyright material, 410, 415
 global replacements using, 264
 halftone and colour reproduction, 383–7
 for indexing, 273, 277, 278
 names, 133
 readers, 443
solidus, 109, 171
songs, 146, 410
sound, 402–3
 'alt' attribute, 451–2
 aural cascading style sheets, 450–1
 copyright, 410, 412, 413, 436
 disability groups, appropriate format for, 431
 standard industry logo, 458, 460
 see also moving images
sources, *see* citations
space and spacing, 319–20
 am and *pm*, 172
 blocked paragraphs, 336
 cells in on-screen tables, 349
 in citations, not used between initials, 190
 currency expressions, 174
 around cut-in illustrations, 382
 dot-point series, 144

forms, 363, 368
around headings, 340, 341
leading (line spacing), 144, 331, 332–4, 352
numbers, 176, 177, 330
between letters, 327
between personal initials, 158
proofreading marks, 522
after punctuation, 117
SI units and numerals, 184
around tables, 356
in tables, 352, 354
in temperature expressions, 173, 174
2-em rules indicating breaks and omissions, 107
type spaces, 330
Vancouver system, 216
spaced em rules, 106
spaced en rules, 106, 108, 109
spanner headings, 348, 349, 351, 352
spans of figures, 177
in indexes, 282
roman numerals, 169
specialised sources, citation of, 220–32
species names, 130–1
specifications, 15, 17, 457, 476
speech, *see* direct speech
speech marks, *see* quotation marks
spelling, 79–85
legislation titles, 224
proofreading tasks, 261
see also capital letters; punctuation
spelling checkers, 80
spelt-out terms, 522
compass points, 157
currency expressions, 174
measurement units, 184
numbers, 163, 165–8, 176
of shortened forms, 153, 161, 184
time expressions, 169–71, 172–3
spines of books, 235, 238, 488
spiral binding, 486, 487
split infinitives, 76
sponsoring bodies, 198, 238
government publications, 220
web sites, 230, 248
spreading and choking, 470
square brackets, 99, 111–12, 154
square-cut borders, 379, 382
ss., 225

St, 281
stand-alone lists, 144
standard register, 51–2
standards, 14–17
CD logos, 458, 460
colour, 388
dates, 171
disability access, 430–1
electronic publications, 430–1, 441–2: home
pages, 249
international numbering, 423–6
large numbers, 166
metadata, 427–8
paper sizes, 476–8
printing, for tabled documents, 432
see also legal requirements; measurement
stars and planets, 132
start of copyright, 412
start of sentences, 119, 120–1
with conjunctions, 72–3, 103
dates at, 170
after headings, 139
numbers, 163, 165
shortened forms, 154
state and territory governments
states and territories, 125, 156
classification of publications, 420
emblems, 301
government documents co-authored with, 295
governors, lieutenant-governors and
administrators, 511
law-making, 409, 419
legal deposit requirements, 431
parliamentarians, 509, 512
static documents, web sites, 248, 250
statistical texts, 164
see also graphs and charts; tables
statistical mapping, 400–1
step numbering, on forms, 364
stereotyping, *see* inclusive communication
stipples, 383
stochastic screening, 384–6
storyboards, 398–9
strap lines, 292
street addresses, *see* postal addresses
strength of paper, 474
strobing, 343
structural reviews of documents, 257

structure of language, *see* grammar
structures, names of, 128
structuring bibliographies, 224
structuring documents, 36–47, 138, 233–251
stub headings, 348, 349, 350, 351, 352, 355
stub items, 348, 349, 351, 353–4, 355
study or research, reproduction done for, 414–15
style editing, 257
styles of language, 51–3, 65–6, 431
style sheets, 15, 264–5
cascading, 330, 450–1
typographic, 344
sub-entities of organisations, 220, 221, 292
subheadings, 101
in indexes, 274, 278, 281, 282
in electronic publications, 339**s**
in tables, 350
subject indexing, 273, 276
'subject matter other than works', 410
subjects (grammar), 105
agreement with verb, 65–6, 67, 71–2
pronouns, 69
'sub-judice' rule, 419
subjunctive verbs, 70, 76–7
subordinate headings, *see* subheadings
subordinate legislation, 125, 225–6
subordinating conjunctions, 67, 68–9
starting sentences, 72–3, 103
subparagraphs, in legislation, 226
subsections, 336
index references to, 275
in legislation, 226
subsidiary material, 41–2, 237, 241, 242–3
see also bibliographies; indexing
subspecies names, 130–1
substantive editing, 256, 257
sub-subheadings, in indexes, 274
subtitles, *see* publication subtitles
subtotals in tables, 348, 349, 357
sudden changes in sentence direction, 106, 107
suffixes, 81–5
adverbs based on adjectives, 68
comparative adjectives, 68
hyphens, 90, 94
-*ing* participles, 70, 83–4
occupational titles, 59–60
-*ly*, 68, 92
-*'s* possessive form, 85–8, 153

summaries, 236, 241

summarising expressions, introducing, 99

sun or *Sun*, 132

superlative adjectives, 68, 92

superscript note identifiers, 208, 209–10, 215–16

supplementary sections in books, 243–4

surface light reflectance of paper, 472

surface texture, in design, 315

'surname', 58

suspension points, 110

swash characters, 326

Swedish dates, 171

symbol fonts, 328

symbolic imagery, 377–8

symbols, 154, 328

    am and *pm*, 172

    copyright ©, 413

    of corporate identity, 291–2

    currency, 174–5

    degrees (°), 173–4

    measurement units, 165, 178–86: in tables, 350–1, 353

    note identifiers, 208

    per cent (%), 168

    phonogram Ⓟ, 413

    proofreading, 266, 521–7

    spacing between numeral and, 177

synonymous terms, 280

synthetic papers, 472–3

-*t*- or -*tt*-, 85

-*t* past tense, 82–3

table of contents (contents lists), 236, 240

table notes, 348, 349

    numbering, 208, 216

    placement, 356–7

    type sizes, 357

table titles, 348, 350, 354

    pages containing nothing but tables, 356

    type sizes, 357

table width, 354–6

tabled documents, 432–3

tables, 346–58, 410

    alignment, 176, 353–4

    colours in, 352–3, 379

    conversion from print to screen, 447

    library deposit arrangements, 431–2

    paragraphs not split by, 337

proofreading, 262

    shortened forms used in, 156

    see also graphs and charts

tables, lists of, 236, 240–1

tag lines, 292

tag questions, 98

tail (bottom) margins, 316, 337

tailbands, 489

taxonomic groupings, 130–1

technical terms, 114, 147

technical writing, 164

teenagers, 62

telephone numbers, 330, 368

television programs, *see* broadcasts

temperature, 173–4

templates, *see* grids

'10 per cent rule', 415

tense, grammatical, 70

terminating punctuation marks, *see* exclamation marks; full stops; question marks

terms being defined, 114, 147

terms of reference, 241

territories, Australian, 125, 156

    Ordinances, 125, 224–5

    see also states and territories

tertiary qualifications, 517–18

testing, 12, 495–6

    coloured bar codes, 426**s**

    editorial tasks, 259

    electronic publications, 453–5, 495

    forms, 362–3, 372–3

    sample settings, 324

text, 237, 241–2

    alignment, in tables, 353

    converting from print to screen, 445

    forms, 364, 365, 369–70, 371

    when illustrations occupy most of page, 381

    runaround, 382

text depth, 337

text entry fields, forms, 363, 364, 365, 367–8, 371

text formatting, 334–8, 357

text tables, 353, 357–8

text-wrapping, 382

textual contrast, 136–49

    see also fonts; headings

textual cross-references, *see* cross-references; in-text citations

textual imagery, 377–8

texture, in design, 315

textured papers, 472

that and *which*, 75

'the', *see* definite article

theatrical works, *see* dramatic works

their and *them* as singular pronouns, 75–6

thesauruses, 279, 428

theses, 207, 218

they as singular pronoun, 75–6

thick spaces, 330

thickness of cover board, 475

thickness of lines, 380

thickness of paper stock, 473

thin spaces, 176, 330

Thomas, Harold, 299

thread sealing, 487

three-dimensional representation, on graphs and charts, 395

tick boxes, 364, 367

time indicators and expressions, 169–73

    apostrophes in, 87

    capital letters, 129

    clauses introduced by *as*, *since* and *while*, 103

    shortened forms, 157, 169–70

    spans of figures, 108

    see also dates

time frequency, 173

time of day, 172–3

time zones, 157

timetables and timeframes, 11, 13, 22–5, 254–5, 273

tints, 387

tip-ins, 470–1

tipped-in pages, 238, 241, 355, 244

'title' attribute, 452

title pages, 236, 238, 239

    for appendixes, 242

    as citation source, 193, 200

    placement of Coat of Arms, 294

titles

    illustrations, 379, 382: *see also* captions

    legal protection of, 410

    occupational, 59–60

    see also headings; personal titles; publication titles

to, in *from … to*, 109

to (infinitive) verbs, 70, 76

together with, 71

one, 314
  headings, 338
  justified text, 335
  typecolour, 324
ones, 387
  duotones, 389
  halftones, 383–7, 391, 472
op margins, 316
opographical features, *see* geographical names;
  maps
orres Strait Islander flag, 300
orres Strait Islanders, 56, 57
otals in tables, 348, 349, 357
racking, 327
rade names, *see* organisational names
rade Practices Act 1974, 420
ademarks, 132–3, 420
rans., 195, 201
anscripts, 100, 113
  see also direct speech
ansfer, grammatical, 66
ansfer of copyright, 412
ansitional expressions, 104
anslations, 200, 204, 229, 410
anslators, 238
  in citations, 195–6, 201–2
ansparencies, 392
ansparency of language, 54
apping, 458, 470
reasury, 125
eaties, 125
rillion, 166
im marks, 469
immed sizes, 476, 478
imming, 465, 488
rueType, 329
t- or *-t-*, 85
urnover lines, 336
  in indexes, 274
welve-hour system of time, 172–3
wenty-four hour system of time, 173
-em rules, 107
ype area, margins and, 316–17
ype sizes, 323–4, 325, 330
  CD-ROM printed components, 458
  column width and, 332
  contents lists, 240
  headings, 340

tables, 357
type spaces, 330
typecolour, 324
typefaces, 236–7, 323–4, 326–8
  cascading style sheets, 330, 450–1
  corporate, 292
  for forms, 370
  heading and text compatibility, 339
  labels, 380**s**
  publication components, 236–7
  see also fonts
typesetters and typesetting, 239
  proofs, 466–7: marking errors on, 266, 521–7
  'published edition', 410, 413
typography and typographic style, 236–7, 322–45
  cascading style sheets, 330, 450–1
  dashes, 106
  for corporate identity, 292–3
  forms, 370–1
  headings, 138
  indexes, 275
  labels, 380**s**
  maps, 400
  punctuation, 116–17
  tables, 357–8

-*ums* plural form, 81
uncertain dates of publication, 197
under-colour removal (UCR), 389
underlining, 149
uniform resource locators, *see* URLs
unit costs, 464
United Kingdom practices, 83–5, 106, 115, 154
United States, *see* American readers and practices
units of measurement, *see* measurement
university degrees, 517–18
unjustified settings, 334, 335, 357
  table alignment, 354
unpublished material, 197, 207–8, 213, 218
  copyright, duration of, 412
unspaced em rules, 106–7
unspaced en rules, 108–9
updating publications, 500
upper-case letters, *see* capital letters
URLs (web addresses), 428, 429
  angle brackets enclosing, 112
  business names built on, 120
  in citations, 230–1

dividing at line end, 94
  on forms, 368
usability testing, 12, 28, 454
Usenet groups, citation of, 231

value for money, 30**s**
value of colour, 387
Vancouver system, 190–1, 215–18, 219
variable costs, 464
variable-data printing, 482
variable dot halftoning, 385
variable text depth, 337
variations, *see* change
varieties, botanical, 130
varnishing, 484
vector font description, 329
vehicles, 147, 200, 204
verb–noun transfer, 66
verb-plus-adverb compounds, 90–1
verb-plus-noun compounds, 91
verbal nouns, 70
verbs, 70, 76–7
  agreement, grammatical, 65–6, 67, 71–2
  compound, 93
  contractions, 75
  passive, 54–5, 70, 73–4
  with none, 65–6
  see also adverbs; clauses
verification of copy, tasks to ensure, 261
verso title (reverse of title) pages, 236, 238–9, 420
vertical rules in tables, 352
vice chancellors, 518
viceroyalty, 510–11
video, *see* moving images
vignette borders, 379
violence and pornography, 419
viruses, 132
visual attitude of illustrations, 378–9
visual identifiers, 10, 290–301, 316, 465
visually impaired people, 60, 330, 431, 451–2
voice, active and passive, 54–5, 70, 73–4
vol., *vols*, 194
volume, *see* measurement
volumes and volume numbers, 244, 246
  citations, 194, 202, 205
  International Standard Book Numbers (ISBNs),
    424
Votes and Proceedings, 221, 222

vowels, 72, 88–9, 94
vulgar (non-decimal) fractions, 167

waterless printing, 480
web addresses, *see* URLs
web browsers, 442
Web contact accessibility guidelines, 430
web documents, *see* electronic documents
web-fed offset, 480
web-like structures, 43
'web manager' or 'web master', 60
web site or *Web site*, 133
web sites, 133, 247–50
   backgrounds, 380
   citation methods, 230
   copyright material, 410, 411, 413, 414
   copyright wording recommended, 413
   disclaimers, 420–1
   indexes, 271
   interior page endings, 337
   line spacing (leading) and line length, 332
   privacy considerations, 418
   storyboards, 398–9
Web 216, 388
website or *web site*, 133
weight distribution in design, 318
weight of paper, 473
weighted assessments, 498–9
were subjunctive, 76–7
which and *that*, 75
'while', *see* subordinating conjunctions
white space, 319–20, 352
whiteness of paper, 472

whom, 77
whose, 77
wide graphs, 394
widows and orphans, 337–8
width of column (measure), 331–2, 354–5
width of tables, 354–6
wiro (spiral) binding, 486, 487
wishes, expressing in writing, 98
-*woman*, 60
women and men, 58–60
   see also modes of address
wood-free papers, 474
word breaks, 93–4
word-by-word alphabetical arrangement, 274, 277
word-processing documents, formatting for digital conversion, 446–8
word punctuation, 85–93, 154
word spacing, 330, 332
   justified and unjustified settings, 334–5
   text tables, 357
words and phrases, 78–94, 114
   cited as such, 88, 148
   in headings, 139–40
   in index headings, 279–81
   legal protection of single, 410
   ordering, 64–5
   phrasal verbs, 77
   registers, differences between, 52–3
   single, on last line of paragraph, 337–8
   see also clauses; conjunctions; foreign words and phrases; lists; nouns; shortened forms; verbs
work positions, advertising for, 62

workers' titles, 59–60
'works', 410
works of art, 146, 410, 412, 417, 436
works of joint authorship, *see* multi-author works
workshop proceedings, 207–8, 213, 218
World Wide Web, 133
World Wide Web Consortium (W3C), 430, 388
wrapping, 470
writing, 14–15, 22, 36–186
   briefs, 27
   by hand, accommodating on forms, 367–8
   rewriting and rewording, 256
   see also authors and authoring bodies
written registers, 51–3

x-heights, 327, 330**s**, 332
-*x* plural form, 82
XML, 450

-*y*, plural of words ending in, 81
-*y*, usual comparative ending for, 68
years, in dates, 170–2, 177
   see also date of publication
'yes/no' answers, on forms, 363, 366–7
Yolngu Aboriginal group, 57
you, 59
younger and older people, 61–2, 330
youth, 62
-*yse* or -*yze*, 85

zoological emblems, 301
zoological names, 130–1